Bartholomew MacCarthy

The Codex Palatino-Vaticanus, No. 830

Texts, translations and indices

Bartholomew MacCarthy

The Codex Palatino-Vaticanus, No. 830
Texts, translations and indices

ISBN/EAN: 9783337241292

Printed in Europe, USA, Canada, Australia, Japan

Cover: Foto ©Lupo / pixelio.de

More available books at **www.hansebooks.com**

Royal Irish Academy.

TODD LECTURE SERIES.
VOL. III.

THE CODEX PALATINO-VATICANUS,

No. 830.

(TEXTS, TRANSLATIONS AND INDICES.)

BY

B. MAC CARTHY, D.D.,

*Royal Irish Academy's Todd Professor of the Celtic Languages;
Examiner in Celtic, Royal University of Ireland.*

DUBLIN:
PUBLISHED AT THE ACADEMY HOUSE, 19, DAWSON-STREET.

SOLD ALSO BY

HODGES, FIGGIS, & CO., GRAFTON-ST.;

AND BY WILLIAMS & NORGATE.

LONDON: | EDINBURGH:
14, Henrietta-street, Covent Garden. | 20, South Frederick-street.

1892.

PREFATORY NOTE.

THE luni-solar criteria employed in the following pages, and Tables I., III., IV., V., VII., VIII., IX., of Lecture IV. belong to the Old Style, which was superseded in 1582 by the Calendar of Aloysius Lilius, commonly designated the Gregorian.

The numbering, sectional distribution and lettering of the texts are an arbitrary arrangement for the purpose of reference.

After Lecture II. had gone to press, I learned that the metric tracts in the Book of Ballymote were published, without a translation, by Prof. Thurneysen: this transcript I have not read.

YOUGHAL, *October, 1892.*

CONTENTS.

	PAGE
LECTURE I.,	3
NOTES,	31
TEXT,	38
INDEX,	72
LECTURE II.,	93
NOTES,	114
TEXTS (Metric):—	
I.,	120
II.,	128
III.,	132
IV.,	138
V.,	140
TEXT (Historical),	142
INDEX,	214
LECTURE III.,	237
NOTES,	259
TEXTS:—A,	278
B,	286
INDEX,	318
LECTURE IV.,	335
NOTES,	389
TEXTS:—PROSE,	396
VERSE,	408
INDEX,	438

LECTURE I.

THE CODEX PALATINO-VATICANUS,

No. 830.

TODD LECTURE SERIES.—Vol. III.

CORRIGENDA.

Page 13, line 32, *to* "here set forth" *add* "underneath the diagram."
,, 243, *dele* ll. 22-5.
,, 259, line 18, *for* "son of Con," *read* "son of Cu."
,, 266, ,, 35, *after* "Faelan," *insert* "son of Colman."
,, 394, ,, 21, *for* "*DE TEMPORUM RATIONE,*" *read* "*DE DOCTRINA TEMPORUM.*"

THE CODEX PALATINO-VATICANUS, No. 830.

CREATION OF HEAVEN: CREATION, FALL AND PENANCE OF ADAM AND EVE.

(*From* LEBAR BREC.)

DURING the Thirty-years' War, after Maximilian of Bavaria gained the battle of Prague over Ferdinand of Bohemia, the Palatinate was occupied by the Imperial troops. Two years later, Heidelberg, the capital, was captured. The collection of MSS. in the Library was forwarded to Pope Gregory XV. in the year following. By him the donation was deposited in the Vatican. In the Catalogue it is denoted the *Palatine*. In 1816, most of the MSS. were restored by order of Pope Pius VII. Amongst those retained is a thick vellum quarto, bound in boards and covered with red velvet. It bears the number 830. On the inside of the cover is pasted a printed note which reads as follows:—

Sum de bibliotheca quam, Hiedelberga capta, spolium fecit et P. M. Gregorio XV. trophaeum misit Maximilianus, utriusque Bavariae Dux, S. R. I. Archidapifer et Princeps Elector. Anno Christi CIƆ.IƆ.CXXIII [1623].

On the first folio is written: *Iste liber pertinet ad Librariam S. Martini, Moguntiae*, 1479. How it passed from that monastery to Heidelberg, we have no means of determining. The volume contains the well-known Tripartite Chronicle of our countryman, Marianus Scotus. During the time that I worked in the Vatican Library, I took occasion to go carefully more than once through the entire Codex. In setting forth the results, I shall deal first with what is known of the Compiler; next, with the contents and characteristics of the MS.; thirdly, with the entries that throw light upon persons and events of domestic interest; finally, with the text and linguistic value of the native items.

Respecting Marianus, all the known facts connected with his life, save one, have been put on record by himself and in his own handwriting. An instance of being one's own biographer and amanuensis is unique, as far as I am aware, in our native literature. As such, some interest attaches thereto. He was called in Irish *Mael Brigte* (Calvus Brigitae), *devotee of Brigit*, the national patroness. The name Marianus (*devotee of Mary*) was doubtless given on the occasion of his becoming a monk on the Continent. He was born in 1028.* Of his parentage or tribe he has left no mention. That he belonged to the *half of Conn*—to use the term retained by himself—that is, the northern half, can be inferred from the fact that he gives a Catalogue of the Irish kings who sprang from that moiety of Ireland.

In 1052, at the age of twenty-four, he abandoned the world :† most probably entering the monastery of Moville, Co. Down. The establishment was then presided over by Tigernach of Mourne, who died in 1061. Four years later, he became a pilgrim ; went over sea and arrived at Cologne, as he is careful to note, upon Thursday, August 1, 1056.‡ That the expatriation was not of his own seeking can be plainly deduced from an entry in the Chronicle, under date 1043. Recording the death of an incluse in the monastery of Fulda, he says the deceased had been a religious of Inniscaltra (in the Shannon). For having, however, given a drink to some brethren without permission, he was banished by his superior, Corcran (*ob.* A.D. 1040), not alone from the community, but from Ireland. A similar sentence, he adds, was pronounced upon himself by Tigernach, for some slight fault not stated.§

Why he wended his way to Cologne we learn from some of his entries. In 975, Archbishop Eberg donated the abbey of St. Martin in that city to the Irish monks. The obits of four of the superiors are recorded. As will be seen, however, the years of their respective incumbencies as given in the text cannot be reconciled with the marginal dates. The sum of the former erroneously falls short by twenty years of the latter. The error (of transcription) occurs in reference to Elias (so called on the Continent from the partial simi-

---

* Note A. † Note B. ‡ Note C. § Note D.

larity of the name to the native Ailill). This we learn from the Annals of Ulster, which agree with Marianus respecting the year of his obit.* In this community, becoming a monk, he remained for close upon two years.

In connexion herewith, it will not be out of place to describe the salient features of the profession to which the remainder of his career was devoted. Inclusion, in the technical sense, was a phase of monachism which never made its appearance in Ireland. It originated on the Continent, in conjunction with the Benedictine monasteries. Thereby an effort was made to unite the active life of the cenobites with the contemplative existence of the anchorites. Incluses, that is to say, were more restricted than monks and less isolated than hermits. Their existence, it may be concluded, was owing to a desire on the part of the Church authorities to utilize as teachers and spiritual directors men whose lives were solely devoted to study and prayer.

A *Regula Solitariorum*, in sixty-nine chapters, has been preserved.† It was the composition of a monk called Grimlaicus, who dedicated the compilation to his namesake, a priest. The latter, Mabillon conjectures, lived at the papal Court during the pontificate of Formosus (A.D. 891-6). The date, accordingly, falls within the second half of the ninth century. From this Rule it will suffice to mention such portions as are pertinent to the life and literary labours of Marianus.

The abode of the incluse consisted of a cell, an oratory and small garden : the whole surrounded by a high wall. Outside the precincts were cells for disciples who were instructed by the solitary and supplied him with necessaries through an opening. The oratory lay so contiguous to the monastery church, as that the occupant could hear the reading and join the brethren in psalmody through the aperture. Postulants were selected from those most distinguished for piety and learning. Foreigners had to come provided with commendatory letters, signed by the bishop or abbot. The period of probation was two years. The ceremony of inclusion consisted of the selected brother prostrating before the bishop and community and reciting a formula of perseverance. On rising, he was inducted into the cell. The doorway was then built up and sealed by the officiating bishop

---

* Note E.   † It is given in Migne's *Patrologia*, tom. ciii., col. 575-664.

with the episcopal signet. Thenceforward the solitary was not to issue, except by command of lawful superiors, or upon occasion of unavoidable necessity. Of the latter we have an instance in the burning of Paderborn, when an Irish incluse refused to come forth from the cell to save his life.

The work-a-day routine consisted of devotional practices, advising such as came for instruction and teaching the pupils. These duties alternated with manual labour and recreation. Sundays and festivals were devoted exclusively to religious and studious exercises. Daily celebration of Mass was, however, left discretionary. Knowledge of Scripture and the Canons was prescribed, in order to be enabled to counsel persons differing in age, sex and profession. Erudition sufficient to confute Jews and heretics was to be acquired. As such opponents were not likely to come to hear, it follows that the incluse had to draw up written refutations. The library at his disposal must consequently have been of fair amplitude.

Of the furniture of the cell, incidental mention is made in the Chronicle of the *matta*, or mattress. Respecting burial, the Rule is silent. But from Marianus it can be collected that the body was deposited where death took place. He had a grave, which he was not destined to occupy, dug during his first enclosure.

At Eastertide, A.D. 1058, Siegfried, Superior of Fulda, visited the abbey of St. Martin. Whether by invitation or at his own request, Marianus accompanied him on returning, in order to become a recluse. On the Friday before Palm Sunday (April 10), an event had occurred which naturally excited great interest, especially amongst the Irish inmates, in continental monasteries. The episcopal city of Paderborn, in Westphalia, with its two abbeys, was burned to the ground. In one of them an Irishman, named Padernus, had lived an incluse for a number of years. He had foretold the catastrophe and, when his prediction came true, refused to leave the enclosure, losing his life in consequence. Marianus adds that he was regarded as a martyr. Wherefore Siegfried and his companion went northwards out of their way to visit the scene. On the Monday after Low Sunday, the 27th of the same month, Marianus informs us that he prayed on the mattress from which his countryman had passed to his rest.*

---

* Note F.

Within a year, on Midlent Saturday (*i.e.* the Saturday before the fourth Sunday of Lent), March 13, 1059, Marianus was promoted to the priesthood. This took place, he tells us, at Würtzburg, in the church containing the body of St. Kilian, the Irish martyr-apostle of Franconia. Herein we have a circumstance that deserves to be noted. Contrary to the custom that prevailed in Ireland, the community of Fulda had no bishop-monk for the performance of episcopal functions. Otherwise, a candidate for enclosure would not have been sent elsewhere to receive Holy Orders. Being thus ordained, Marianus became a professed incluse, on the Friday after the festival of the Ascension (May 14). The cell had probably been vacant since the death of Animchad, whose name sufficiently denotes his nationality, sixteen years previously.*

A decade having passed and Siegfried having been meanwhile appointed to the see of Mayence, Marianus, by order of the bishop (by whom he was evidently appreciated), with the consent of the new abbot, was conducted to that episcopal city. He arrived there, he does not fail to note, on the Friday before Palm Sunday, April 3 (1069). On Friday, the tenth of the following July, the feast of the Seven Brothers, Martyrs, the oratory of the inclusory of St. Martin was dedicated in honour of the Apostle St. Bartholomew. Immediately after the ceremony, Marianus was enclosed for the second time.† Here he lived thirteen years and died in 1082, at the age of fifty-four.‡

Respecting the contents and characteristics, the MS. consists of 170 folios. Of these, the matter of the first twenty-four (folio 25 is blank) has no necessary connexion with what is contained in the remainder. It was prefixed, partly as being the work of the Compiler§ and partly as being made up of illustrative and cognate material. The chief items are nineteen Solar Cycles of 28 = the Dionysian (so-called) Great Paschal Cycle of 532 (fol. 1–3); three "Emendations" of the Vulgar Era,—one, a rearrangement of the consular series from Lentulus and Messalinus to A.D. 532; another taken from St. Jerome; the third, from the Roman Martyrology, Passions of Popes and Decretal Epistles (fol. 4–13); a list of native kings (fol. 15); a catalogue of Popes from

---

* Note G.   † Note II.   ‡ Note I.

§ It is also in his handwriting. See p. 15, *infra*. The parchment is likewise inferior.

St. Peter to John [XII.], *de regione Violata* (recte : *Viae Latae*), who is said to have succeeded on the fourteenth Indiction (A.D. 956 [It is continued down to Paschal II. (1099-1118) in a different hand.] fol. 16); two Dionysian Great Paschal Cycles,—A.D. 1-532 : 533-1064, with a historical event attached to each year (fol. 18-24). Some of these entries are strangely inaccurate. For instance, Elias, Abbot of Cologne, is said to have died A.D. 1012 (= 990). The true year (Note E (a, b)) was 1042. The slaying of Brian Boru is assigned to 1029 (= 1007). In the Third Book of the Chronicle, we find correctly at A.D. 1036 (= 1014) : *Brian, rex Hiberniae, parasceue Paschae, feria vi., ix. Kal. Maii, manibus et mente ad Deum intentus, occiditur.*

Folio 26 a. Along the upper margin runs the following in rubric:—
In nomine Sanctae Trinitatis, Ressurrectionis Christi inquissitio incipit, quam Marianus Hibernensis, inclusus, congregavit.

In this *Prologue*, Marianus professes to have discovered, " with great labour," partly from authority and partly from reason, why [in assigning Easter to March 28, moon 21] the thirty-fifth year of the (five) Dionysian Cycles (= the Passion year, A.D. 34) is opposed to Scripture and the Church, which, according to Marianus, place the Resurrection on March 27, moon 17.

His proofs will be considered later on.

Folio 27 b. *Finit Prologus. Incipit hinc Mariani Scoti Cronica clara. Incipiunt capitula primi libri.*

The chapters number 22. Three of them are noteworthy. The first is : *De disputatione Dionissi Exigui supra Passionem et Resurrectionem Christi.* This is the well-known *Epistle to Petronius*, which Dionysius prefixed in explanation of his five Paschal Cycles. The third and fourth are:

De inquisitione capitis mundi et primae hebdomadae initii saeculi.

De Pascali ordinatione et de Passione et de Resurrectione Dominica, argumentatae et inquisitae (sic) *a capite mundi.*

These are the longer recension of the *Epistle of Theophilus*, or the spurious *Acts of the Council of Caesarea*, which imposed upon Bede (*De temp. rat., xlvii*), as well as upon Marianus. Owing no doubt to the misleading diction of the headings, the present transcript escaped the notice of the latest editor of the forgery.*

---

* Krusch : *Der 84 jährige Ostercyclus u. seine Quellen*, Leipzig, 1880, pp. 303-310.

Folio 28. *Incipiunt capitula libri secundi, qui est Incarnationis usque in Ascensionem Domini.*

These amount to 83 and are followed by those of the Third Book. The latter divisions, 96 in number, are not carried into effect in the text of the Chronicle.

Folio 31 b. *Primus liber, ab Adam usque ad Christum.*
Folio 71 a. [The Second Book begins here without any title.]
Folio 101 a. *Incipit tertius liber.*
Folio 165 b, at A.D. 1098 (= 1076), the following is found in the hand-writing of Marianus:—[The book is represented as addressing the reader.]

> *Multum ob excerptos legimus barbaricos*
> *Reges iustificandos gestaque turbida egenos:*
> *Collige litteram anteriorem; uoluito summam,—*
> *Existat numeratus author: intra require,—*
> _{.i. librum}
> *Rectus omnes me tulit in nouum ordinem laudis.*

"Collecting" the initial letters of the words in the two opening lines, we get Moelbpızce; in the next two, claupenaıp; in the last line, pomcınol: Moel-bpızce, claupenaıp, pomcınol— *Moel-Brigte, the incluse, collected me.* With this is to be compared the expression, folio 26 a, *Marianus, inclusus, congregavit.*

Of the foregoing, the Third Book has been edited by Waitz, in the *Monumenta Germaniae Historica* of Pertz (*Scriptorum tom. v.*).* It was reprinted in Migne's *Patrologia* (tom. cxlvii.). A notable, in fact a fundamental, characteristic of the Chronicle, as may be seen in the edition of Waitz, is that the reckoning of Marianus differs by 22 from the Vulgar Era. On the left are placed his own; on the right, what he calls the Dionysian years. The method of arriving at this conclusion is explained in the *Inquiry* on folios 26, 27 and at greater length in his Second Book.

First (*Lib. II., cap. xii.*), he follows Bede (*De temp. rat., cap. xlvii.*) in fixing the Resurrection in the 34th year of our Lord, March 27, moon 17. In the first of the Decemnovennal Cycles written by Dionysius, this Easter occurs in the 13th year, namely A.D. 544. It

---

* He has also described the contents of fol. 1–26 and transcribed all the headings.

consequently belongs to the previous 532nd year, which is likewise No. 13 in the Cycle of 19. A.D. 12 should accordingly be A.D. 34.

Bede had already applied the same principle in a different way. Since A.D. 566, according to Dionysius, has the Paschal criteria of A.D. 34, he ironically bids you thank God, if, upon opening the Dionysian Cycles, you find moon 14 on Thursday, March 24 and Easter on March 27, moon 17, assigned to 566.* (The year in question has the 14th of the moon on Sunday, March 21 and Easter, as already observed, on March 28, moon 21). But to point out a defect is easier than to supply the remedy. Bede propounded no solution himself. *Plurimum observatus, nihil lucis infudit.*†

Whether Bede and Marianus were right or wrong, or partly right and partly wrong, respecting the Resurrection, is irrelevant in this place. For, beyond prefixing its years to his cycles and giving rules for finding the cyclic (Golden) number of a given A.D. year, Dionysius had demonstrably nothing to do with determining the Vulgar Era. St. Cyril of Alexandria wrote five Paschal Cycles, from the 153rd to the 247th of Diocletian (A.D. 437-531). Commencing with the 248th, Dionysius wrote five more (A.D. 532-626). For the reasons set forth in his Preface,‡ the continuator substituted the years of the Incarnation for those of Diocletian.

To render his work of any practical utility, St. Cyril must have had a Reckoning showing the ferial incidence and bissextile position of the 153rd of Diocletian. To construct a Cycle irrespective of the two main elements of the Paschal lunisolar computation were to labour

---

* Sicut quingentesimus tricesimus tertius primo, ita quingentesimus sexagesimus sextus tricesimo quarto per universos solis et lunæ concordat discursus. Et ideo circulis beati Dionysii apertis, si quingentesimum sexagesimum sextum ab Incarnatione Domini contingens annum, quartam decimam lunam in eo ix. Calendarum Aprilium, quintâ feriâ, repereris et diem Paschæ Dominicum vi. Calendarum Aprilium, lunâ decimâ septimâ, age Deo gratias, quia quod quaerebas, sicuti ipse promisit, te invenire donavit (*De temp. rat., cap. xlvii.*).

† Anonymous Preface to the Dionysian Cycles, in the works of Bede.

‡ Nos a ccxlviii.vo anno eiusdem tyranni potius quam principis inchoantes, noluimus circulis nostris memoriam impii et persecutoris innectere, sed magis elegimus ab Incarnatione Domini nostri Iesu Christi annorum tempora praenotare: quatenus exordium spei nostrae notius nobis existeret et causa reparationis humanae, id est, Passio Redemtoris nostri, evidentius eluceret (*Epistola ad Petronium*).

THE CODEX PALATINO-VATICANUS, 830. 11

in vain. The futility of an attempt of the kind is proved conclusively by the spurious Anatolius.* A genuine Easter Computus, in fact, presupposes an Era. Now, the requisite solar criteria of the opening year of St. Cyril can be found only by reference to the Vulgar Reckoning. Thereby we get A.D. 437; first after Bissextile; Dominical Letter C. Applying the Alexandrine Epact (9 = Golden number I), the result is Easter upon April 11.

This fundamental principle will carry us farther. Theophilus, the predecessor of St. Cyril, composed a (lost) Paschal Table of 100 years, from the fifth consulship of Gratian. In 457, Victorius of Aquitaine published his discovery, the Great Paschal Cycle (the solar of 28 × the lunar of 19). That the solar basis of these two dissimilar works was the Vulgar Era, is shown, to give but one proof, in a note appended to the Leyden transcript of the Prologue of Theophilus. In the first year, we are told, March 1 was Sunday, moon 9 and Easter was April 12, moon 21: that is, in the 380th from the Incarnation and the 353rd of Victorius.† The sole clue to this is the Common Computation. A.D. 380 is therein Bissextile, with the Dominical letters E D. March 1 thus coincided with Sunday. With respect to the Epact, in the Alexandrine Cycle the year is the same as 437, Golden Number I. The different ferial incidence, however, alters the Paschal recurrence noted above by a day.

With regard to Victorius, the same Computation proves that his Cycle began (proleptically) with A.D. 28, to which year he (erroneously) assigned the Passion. Hence, to equate his numeration with the A.D., we have, as the Leyden computist rightly calculates, to add thereto the 27 Incarnation years which he omitted. In this way we get 353 = A.D. 380. The Epact is 9 (Victorian Golden Number XI = Alexandrine I), which, in connexion with D, gives the Easter of Theophilus.

Now, the Cycle of Victorius was a modification of the lunar portion of the Cycle of 84, the solar criteria of the prototype being preserved

---

* Buchorius: *De Doctrina Temporum*, etc., Antverp. 1633, pp. 439–449. Krusch : *Der 84jährige Ostercyclus*, etc., pp. 316–327.

† An. I, Graciano u. et Theodosio, Kal. Mar. fcr. i., luna nona : dies Pasche ii. Idus Apl., luna xxi: hoc est, anno ab Incarnatione $\overline{XPI}$. ccclxxx.; iuxta cyclum uero Uictorii anno cccliii (Krusch, *ubi sup.*, p. 226).

12   THE CODEX PALATINO-VATICANUS, 830.

in their integrity. The Vulgar Era is thus carried up to A.D. 46, the initial year of the Paschal Cycles and Tables of 84. The five Decemnovennal Cycles of Dionysius, it accordingly follows, contain no data for rectifying error in the Vulgar A.D. Era.

The 22 years in question Marianus next professes (*Lib. II., cap. xviii., xix.*) to find in the regnal years, months and days (as given by Bede) of the Roman Emperors, from the 15th of Tiberius to A.D. 703, the date employed in Bede's Tract *De temporibus* (*cap. xiv.*) to exemplify the rule for finding the Incarnation year. But the uncertain character of such a calculation is strikingly exhibited in the following typical examples, in which Marianus differs from Bede and, what is of more significance, both are at variance with a far higher authority, the *Imperia Caesarum* of the fourth century.

	(*a*) Marianus.*	(*b*) Bede.†	(*c*) Imper. Caes.‡
Caligula,	4 y., 10 m., 8 d.	3 y., 10 m., 8 d.	3 y., 8 m., 12 d.
Claudius,	14 y., 8 m.,§ 28 d.	13 y., 7 m., 28 d.	13 y., 8 m., 27 d.

In addition, the sum of the months and days of (*a*) is, according to Marianus, one year, five months and thirty-six days !‖

The system constructed with such labour is thus seen to be without foundation.

The caligraphy is an uncial minuscule with capitals of the same class. The execution (of which no fair opinion can be formed from the imitations given in the edition of Waitz) is fully equal to that of any coeval MS. which I have examined, either in fac-simile or in the original. In some parts, the writing is done in columns; but in the greater portion it has, most inconveniently, been carried across the page. There are forty lines in each column or page. A compara-

---

* *Lib. II., cap. xviii.*   † Chronicon (*De temp. rat., cap. lxvi.*).

‡ Mommsen: *Ueber den Chronographen vom J.* 354 (*Abhandlungen d. K. S. Ges. d. Wiss. Erster Band*, Leipzig, 1850), p. 646.

§ 7 m., in the Third Book of the *Chronicle*, A.D. 44 [= 22].

‖ Gaius imperavit annis quatuor, mensibus decem, diebus octo. Claudius, annis quatuordecim, mensibus octo, diebus viginti octo. Adde menses decem Gaii: fit annus et menses quinque, dies triginta sex (*Lib. II., cap. xviii.*). The reading of the Third Book of the *Chronicle* makes the total of the Second Book correct.

tively rare feature, in works of the kind, is the insertion of pictures and a diagram explanatory of the text.

Folio 37 a. Nearly one-half of the column is occupied with two illustrations, placed side by side, respectively representing the Fall and the Redemption. In that to the left of the reader, the tree with leaves and fruit stands in the centre. Entwined round the trunk appears the serpent, with a yellow apple in its mouth. On the left (of the spectator), stands a figure superscribed *Adam*. At his feet flows a fountain, with *fons* written overhead. On the right we have Eve, her left hand holding an apple, the right presenting a larger one to Adam. He has his left raised in the act of refusing, whilst the right is placed upon the tree.*

The picture in juxtaposition depicts the Crucifixion. Rather high over the body is a tablet with *Ihs. Nazarenus*. The feet rest upon a board. Neither in them, nor in the hands, do nails appear. On your left is a figure with a nimbus inscribed *S. Maria*. The left hand is placed on the mouth, the other points upward towards the cross. On the opposite side appears a second figure, the nimbus lettered *S. Iohannes*. The right hand rests on the mouth, with the left pointing up to the cross.

Folio 103 a. Here are two representations, the Deposition and Crucifixion, one above the other. In the upper, *Maria* holds the left hand of the body—Joseph has his hands placed around the waist and united in front. Overhead is written *Ioseph deponit corpus*. A third person holds a hammer in the right and with the left applies an instrument to the nail in the right foot, evidently intended to pourtray the act of extraction.

In the lower, stands the Cross bearing the body, having at each side two figures respectively marked overhead *Maria* and *Iohannes*.

Folio 40 b. At the top of the second column, the following representation of the ark is drawn (see next page). The compartments have inscriptions which for convenience are here set forth (see next page).

---

* One of the sculptured niches in the western gable of the eleventh-century church of St. Declan, Ardmore, co. Waterford, has a representation of the Fall, which, as far as it goes, is identical in design with that of the Marianus Codex. In the centre is the Tree of Life, with the serpent coiled round the trunk. At either side stand Adam and Eve.

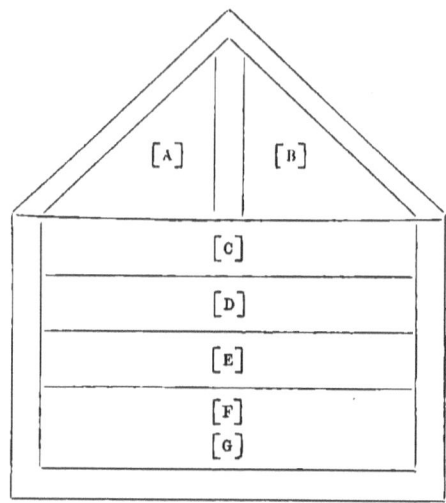

[A] *Hic Noe cum filiis,—typus Christi cum apostolis.*
[B] *Hic erant aves,—typus martyrum.*
[C] *Oves hic,—typus virginum.*
[D] *Hic animalia qui carnem non edunt,—typus coniugum.*
[E] *Hic qui carnem edunt,—typus peccatorum vel ferocium hominum.*
[F] *Hic stercus missus,—typus inferni.*
[G] *Arca super undas,—typus ecclesiae super fluctus huius seculi.*

[Compare the *similitudo Arcae Noe* in the *Dubia et Spuria* of Bede (Migne, *Patrol.* xc., col. 1179), the inscriptions of which are substantially the same as those here given.]

The execution was in all cases the work of the scribe (to be mentioned immediately) and is extremely crude.

The facts relative to the transcription of the Codex are of such interest as to render it matter of regret that more of a similar kind have not been placed upon record. Marianus had passed three years in his second enclosure, when one day a compatriot presented himself at the monastery. He had come through Scotland on his pilgrimage. Being a competent scribe and knowing Latin, he was employed to

THE CODEX PALATINO-VATICANUS, 830. 15

copy the Chronicle.* During the progress of the work, on Thursday, June 28, of the year of his arrival, he paused from his copying to write the following note along the top margin of folio 33 a :—

Iſ oemen dún indiu, a Moel-bṗigte, clúṗenaiṗ, iṗin cluṗail in Maʒancia, iṗin Dapóóen ṗia pól Pecaiṗ, iṗin cec bliadin den dleʒaid, .i. iṗin bliadin iṗṗomaṗbac Diaṗmaic, ṗí Laiʒen : ocuṗ iṗ iṗide cecna bliadain canacṗa a Albain *in perigrinitate mea. Et scripsi hunc librum pro caritate tibi et Scotis omnibus, id est Hibernensibus, quia sum ipse Hibernensis.*—It is pleasant for us to-day, O Moel-Brigte, incluse, in the inclusory in Mayence, on the Thursday before the feast of Peter, in the first year of the [penitential] rule [imposed upon me], that is, in the year in which was killed Diarmait, king of Leinster : and this is the first year I came from Scotland on my pilgrimage. And I have written this book for love for thee and the Scots all, that is, the Irish, because I am myself an Irishman.

Den dleʒaid, the parchment shows at a glance, is a correction made by the writer. Of the original reading, all, except denn, was erased. Then, by prolonging the connecting stroke to the left and joining the down lines at foot, the second n was made into a d. Next, an l was drawn, resting upon the upper right hand angle of the (second) d, and eʒaid (with the e curved) was added on. The lection thus became dendleʒaid = de in dleʒaid.

An entry in the Chronicle enables us to fix with certainty the year in which the foregoing was written : A.D. 1094 [= 1072]. *Diarmait, rex Lagen, viii. Idus Februarii, feriá secundá, occissus.*† Diarmait, King of Leinster, was slain February 6, on Monday. That being leap-year and the Dominical Letters A G, February 6 fell on Monday and June 29, the feast of SS. Peter and Paul, on Friday. The scribe and Marianus were, accordingly, correct in the notation of the year and days of the week.

That his pilgrimage was not voluntary, the foregoing shows. To judge from a splenetic outburst that took place a calendar month later, his temper, in all probability, was the cause of his banishment.

---

* His work extends from folio 26 to folio 150.

† In the Dublin copy of the *Annals of Ulster*, it is stated that he was slain on Tuesday, the seventh of February. Note K.

Fol. 67 a.* Ir obenn dún indiu, a Mél-brigte, cluremair, Dia-Mairt, ii. Kl. Aug., mani bepntair rcoloca manertrech Maurich braplace dampa pop lebeunn in tige coittcenn, *ut cecidi cum tabulis in fundo stercoris. Sed gratias ago, nec mersus sum in stercore Francorum. Sed tamen oro discentes, ut dent illis maledictionem.*—It is pleasant for us to-day, O Mél-Brigte, incluse, Tuesday, the second of the Kalends of August [July 31], if the farm-workers of the monastery of [St.] Martin had not made a trap for me on the platform of the common house, *ut cecidi, etc. Discentes*, doubtless, has reference to the students under the instruction of Marianus.

The unique feature of the Codex consists in this, that another hand (the *secunda manus* of Waitz) went throughout, correcting and supplementing the work of the copyist. What has been done of the kind in the Third Book will be found marked off in the edition of Pertz. My examination has resulted in the discovery that the alterations and additions were effected by the Compiler. It has, likewise, supplied rectifications of some of the published Latin and Irish readings and yielded additional native gleanings.

The items of domestic interest fall, for convenience of treatment, into three divisions,—hagiographic, linguistic and historical. In dealing with these, I shall illustrate them in connexion with cognate material to be found in other authentic sources.

I.—Of Irish Saints, but four are found mentioned with any detail in the Chronicle,—Patrick, Brigit, Columba and Columbanus. Respecting the first named, the following, in the hand-writing of the scribe, is given at the year 394 [= 372].

(1) *Sanctus Patricius nascitur in Britania insula ex patre nomine Calpuirn. Presbyter fuit ipse Calpuirn et filius diaconi nomine Fotid. Mater hautem erat Patricii Conches, soror sancti Martini de Gallia.*

The Notes will show to what extent these statements are borne out by the Confession of St. Patrick, the Patrician Documents in the Book of Armagh† and the Tripartite Life.

---

* Comparison of his two notes shows that the scribe's rate of progress was a folio per day: proving him to have been an expert penman.

† In quoting the *Book of Armagh*, I assume that the contents of the missing (first) folio have been supplied by the *Brussels Codex*. Note L.

On the margin, Marianus added, in five lines:—

(2) *Sucat nomen in babtismate,*
Cothpaege, ⲇⲓⲁⲙⲃⲇⲉ ⲓⲥ ⲡⲟ-
ⲅⲛⲁⲙ ⲇⲟ ⲥⲉⲧⲏⲁⲣⲧⲣⲉⲃ,
[Cothraege, whilst he was a-serving four tribes]
Magonius a Germano.
Patricius, id est, pater civium, a papa Celestino.

With this is to be compared what is given in Tirechan.* It corresponds almost verbally with the Tripartite: Sucaiⲧ ⲁ ⲁⲓⲛⲙ ⲟ ⲧⲩⲣⲧⲓⲃⲓⲃ. Cothⲣⲁⲓⲅⲓ ⲇⲓⲁⲙⲃⲩⲓ ⲓⲥ ⲡⲟⲅⲛⲁⲙ ⲇⲟ ⲥⲉⲧⲏⲡⲩⲣ. *Magonius a Germano. Patricius, id est, pater civium, a papa Celestino.* Sucait [was] his name from [his] parents; Cothraigi, whilst he was a-serving four, etc.

At folio 138, A.D. 410 [= 388], the text has:

(3) *Sanctus Patricius cum duabus sororibus suis, id est, Lupait et Tigris, venditur in Hiberniam. Sanctus quidem Patricius venditur ad regem nomine Miluc, filius nepotis Buain, in aquilone Hiberniae, cuius porcorum pastor erat Patricius. Et Victor angelus loquebatur saepe cum eo. Duae vero sorores venditae sunt in Conallae Muirtemne.*

Six folios farther on (fol. 144, lower margin), additional matter is given by the Compiler, with *hoc ante sex folia debuit scribi* appended.

(4) *Sanctus Patricius, genere Brittus, cum esset xvi. annorum, venditur in Hibernia ad Milco[i]n, regem Dalnaraede. Cui sex annis servivit, et ab angelo Victore semper consolabatur, de lapide quodam cum eo loquens, qui ibi manet.*†

The passage relative to Victor agrees with Tirechan and with Fiac's Hymn.‡ The corresponding portion of the Tripartite is missing.

A.D. 416 [= 394]. In the text we have:

(5) *Cum Sanctum Patricium noluit dominus suus dimittere, nisi pro massa aurea, servavit sanctum[-us] Patricium[-us] precepto Victoris angeli quidam [quemdam] porcorum (quorum custos fuit Patricius et pastor), qui fodit massam auream quam sanctus Patricius [reddit] domino suo pro se.*

---

* Note M. † Note N. ‡ Note O.

On the same folio, in the margin, Marianus gives the substance as follows:

(5 a) *Sanctus Patricius reddit massam auream domino suo pro se. Cum enim dominus eius noluit eum dimittere nisi pro massa aurea, servavit Patricium[-us] precepto Victoris angeli quidam [quemdam] porcorum (quorum erat pastor), qui fodit massam.*

Somewhat similar statements are to be found in the scholia upon Fiac's Hymn in the Franciscan copy of the *Liber Hymnorum*. But they seem to be unhistorical and only prove that those who gave them currency were not acquainted with the *Confession* of St. Patrick. The captive, we are there informed, had no thought of escape until it was suggested by a voice in his sleep. Even then, he was not blind to the obstacles. The ship was some two hundred miles away. The seaport was unknown to him, nor had he any acquaintance there. This shows that he felt there was great risk of re-capture.*

A. D. 424 [= 402]. The text contains:

(6) *Sanctus Patricius, cum esset xxx. annorum, veniens Turoniam tonditur a Sancto Martino tonsurâ monachicâ, quia servilem tonsuram antea hucusque habuit. Deinde trans Alpes ivit, ad occidentalem partem australem Italiae, ad Germanum, episcopum civitatis nomine Al[ti]siodorus, et legit apud eum xxx. annis divinam Scripturam in insula nomine Alanensis.*

The connexion between Martin and Patrick is also stated in the Tripartite Life. Capaill Pacpaic dino co Mapcan 1 Copinip ⁊ pobepp beppad manai͠g paip, ap ba beppad mo͠gad ba[i] paip piam copin—Patrick indeed went to Martin in Tours and [Martin] shaved the tonsure of a monk upon him, for it was the tonsure of a slave that was upon him hitherto.

At A. D. 453 [= 431], the copyist wrote:

(7) *Ad Scotos in Christum credentes ordinatus a papa Celestino Palladius primus episcopus missus est. Sanctus Patricius, genere Brittus, a sancto Celestino papa consecratur et ad archiepiscopatum Hibernensem, ubi signis atque mirabilibus predicans totam insolam Hiberniam convertit ad fidem.*

The opening sentence is taken from the Chronicle of Prosper, with the variant *missus est* for *mittitur*. With regard to the

---

* Note P.

second sentence, Marianus made alterations that are of special significance. To understand them, I reproduce the arrangement of the lines in the MS. :

(7 a) *Sanctus Patricius, genere Brittus, a sancto Celestino papa consecratur et ad archiepiscopatum Hibernensem, ubi signis atque mirabilibus predicans totam insolam Hiberniam convertit ad fidem.*

In the first line, *post ipsum* (referring to Palladius) was placed before *Sanctus*. Then, after *Hibernensem*, in line 2, *mittitur* was written overhead. A line of deletion expunged *sig*. and *per annos lx.a* was added after *ubi*. Finally, in line 3, Marianus prefixed *sig* to *nis*. The reading thus became :—*Post ipsum Sanctus Patricius . . . . mittitur, ubi per annos sexaginta signis . . . convertit ad fidem*,—new evidence in support of sixty years as the duration of the missionary life of St. Patrick in Ireland.

Finally, at A.D. 513 [= 491], the text runs:

(8) *Sanctus Patricius, Hiberniae archiepiscopus, anno cxxii. beatissimo fine obiit. Annorum xvi. venditur; vi. annos in servitute; xl. in Romanis partibus;* *lx. annos in Hibernia predicavit.*

The textual figures in (6) and (7 a) amount to 120, the received age of St. Patrick. They are in agreement with the marginal dating. Similarly, the total under A.D. 491 (8) corresponds with the items there given. No correction was made by Marianus to bring the two sums into harmony. The discrepancy, which is trifling, occurs in determining the period between the liberation of St. Patrick, in his twenty-second year and the commencement of his mission in Ireland. That the time was of lengthened duration is proved by a passage in the *Confessio*, which, so far as I know, has hitherto been overlooked. The cause of his coming hither to preach the Gospel were the voices of those by the wood of Fochlut, which he heard in the house of his parents. According to the Book of Armagh† and as was to be expected, he journeyed to that locality soon (in the second year) after his arrival in Ireland. The visit took place, he himself informs us, very many years—*post plurimos annos*—after he received

---

* Note the expression *Romanae partes*, which includes Britain.   † Note Q.

the invitation.* This demolishes at once the fantastic hypothesis lately propounded, that St. Patrick came as a missionary priest before he arrived as a bishop.† The duration of his labours here assigned is in accord with all reliable authority. The birth and death are, however, dated two years in advance.

With reference to St. Brigit, at folio 148, A.D. 543 [= 521], Marianus inserted in the text: *Sancta Brigitta, Scotta, virgo, in Hibernia obiit.*

On the upper margin of the same folio, he wrote in five lines: [The first quatrain is in *Rannaidhacht Bec*,—heptasyllabic lines, ending in dissyllables; the second, in *Debide* (for which see Lecture II.).]

Ol Pacpaéc :
A bpiзic, a nóeb challec,
A bpeó óip oo na Oépeb,
Cpíca blíaoan зen cpéoem,
bennac 'epenn oap m'épc :

bennac 'epenn in cec oú,
bennac Ulcu ep Conaccu,
bennac Laзniu in cech can,
Acup bicbennac pipu Muman.

Quoth Patrick :
O Brigit, O holy nun,
O flame of gold to the Desies,
Thirty years without faith,
Bless Eriu after myself :

Bless Eriu in every place,
Bless the Ultonians and Connacians,
Bless the Lagenians at every time [always],
And ever bless the men of Munster.

These quatrains are also to be found, according to Mr. Stokes, in a MS. in the Royal Library, Paris.‡ The second couplet of the first is quoted by Ussher§ from what he calls the *Testament of Patrick*, but he has not given a reference to any accessible authority. The author of the Life of St. Brigit given in the Bollandists was ac-

---

* Note R.   † *The Tripartite Life, &c.*, Ed. W. Stokes, p. cxli.
‡ *The Tripartite Life, &c.*, pp. cxxxiv-v.   § *Britan. Eccles. Antiq.*, p. 450.

quainted with a document somewhat similar. He gives the same lines, with the omission of ᵹen ċpeḃem—*without faith. Per triginta annos, beata Brigitta, post mortem meam benedic Hiberniam.* The kernel was, doubtless, that she lived for thirty years after St. Patrick—a fact attested by every authority of repute. As her death took place in, or about, 523 (Marianus being here likewise two years in advance), the theory that places the obit of the national apostle before A.D. 470 has no reliable basis.

Respecting St. Columba, four of the leading facts in his life have been recorded. Of these, the first and second were marginal addenda of the Compiler.

A.D. 545 [= 523]. *Colum Cilli nascitur in Hibernia.*

A.D. 585 [= 563]. *Colum Cille egit cath Culi Dremne.*
[Colum Cille caused* the battle of Cuildrevny.]

A.D. 587 [= 565]. *Colum Cilli de Hibernia predicaturus [enavigavit] in Britania, cum esset xlii. annorum, predicavit vero postea xxxiiii. annis.*

With this is to be connected one native portion of the heading of Chapter 63 (Book III.): *Et in his temporibus* [circa A.D. 595] *fuit*† *Columba Baetinique in Scotia* [Scotland].

Here the intervals are the same as in Adamnan, who states that in the second year after the battle of Cuildrevny (near Drumcliff, co. Sligo), at the age of forty-two, the Saint set out for Iona, where he lived for four-and-thirty years (until his decease). *Hic, anno secundo post Cule Drebinae bellum, aetatis vero suae xlii., de Scotia ad Britaniam pro Christo perigrinari volens, enavigavit* (*Vit. Col., pref. ii.*). *Per annos xxxiv. insulanus miles conversatus* (*ib.*).

To settle the chronology, accordingly, it only requires to determine the time of either the birth, the battle, or the death. As was to be expected, the data relative to the last are the fullest and most reliable. To deal adequately with those given in Adamnan would entail the discussion of questions lying outside the scope of the present Lecture. This becomes the less necessary, as certainty is attainable by methods more direct and equally conclusive. The choice,

---

* Note how the battle is attributed to the instigation of St. Columba. Cf. *Adamnan*, Additional Note, p. 247 *sq.*

† Singular, according to the Irish idiom, whereby the number of the verb is determined by that of the subject next following.

it is conceded, lies between 596 and 597.* St. Baithine above mentioned was first cousin of St. Columba and second abbot of Iona. His Acts relate† that he died on the festival of his predecessor, St. Columba, namely, Tuesday, June 9. These criteria denote 593, 599 (Lit. Dom. D) and 604 (Lit. Dom. E D). As Baithine, there is no doubt, was alive in the first and dead before the last of these years, his obit is thus to be referred to 599.

The question next arises, by how long did St. Columba predecease him. A quatrain in a Brussels MS. (quoted by Dr. Reeves, *Adamnan*, p. 309) professes to give the information.

baɔup cena, pɛ𝄒a a ln,	There were moreover, behold the complement,
Ceıɔpe bliaona, nı hanpıp;	Four years [between them], not untrue;
Oeıoencu baıchın' ı pup,	Later [was] Baithine on this side,
Colum pop ɔup ı papɔup.	Colum [was] first in Paradise.

Taken in connexion with 599, this stanza, as it stands, assigns the death of St. Columba to 595: an impossible date, as can be shown indisputably. According to the Computation followed in Iona, the Easter of 595 fell in March. But we have the Saint's word that in the year wherein he was called to his reward Easter fell within April (In Paschali solemnitate nuper Aprili peracta mense.—Adamnan, *Vit. Col.* iii. 23). This Paschal incidence belongs to 596 and 597. As ꝏı (two) would make the line a syllable short, we have consequently to read ɔeopa (three), which satisfies the scansion and, in addition, agrees with the solar data given above in referring the death of St. Columba to A.D. 596. The conclusion thus derived from independent and undesigned evidence is confirmed by the above quoted figures of Adamnan, which give the Saint an age of seventy-six years.

In each of his three dates Marianus is accordingly three years in arrear.

The year of the decease of St. Columba being thus established, we are enabled to correct, once for all, a calculation connected with

---

* See *Adamnan*, p. 312.

† Note T. Strange, notwithstanding, that the Bollandist editor concluded Baithine died in 601. Note U. Dr. Reeves (*Adamnan*, p. 182) makes no use of the passage, except to show the coincidence of the festivals of Columba and Baithine. O'Clery (*Martyrology of Donegal*, June 9) characteristically states that St. Columba died in 599 and St. Baithine, *four years later*, in 600!

the advent of St. Patrick as missionary. The wonder is how anyone at all conversant with native chronological reckoning could have been betrayed into an error so uncritical and misleading. Gilla Coemain, it is asserted,* places the coming of St. Patrick 162 years before the death of Gregory the Great. But that pope, as everyone is aware, died A.D. 604. Accordingly, St. Patrick's arrival must be fixed at A.D. 442. But, what is the fact? The versifier in question makes Columba and Gregory die in the same year.† Yet, with this before him, a recent editor‡ prints two notes, one under the other, the first giving the death of Columba in 592; the second, that of Gregory in 604. To the last he appends, with approval, the deduction just dealt with. How far Gilla Coemain was justified in synchronizing the death of Gregory and the death of Columba, is beside the question. The fact that he did so is the foundation for any historical conclusion from this part of his poem.

Of St. Columbanus we have but a meagre *résumé* of the principal events in his career. It is in the hand of the scribe:

A.D. 611 [= 589]. *Sanctus pater Columbanus ex Hibernia, insula Scotorum, cum sancto Gallo aliisque probatis discipulis venit in Burgundiam ibique, permittente Theodorico rege, monasterium quod Luxovium dicitur edificavit. Exinde a Brundichilda fugatus Almaniam ingreditur, ubi sanctum Gallum reliquit. Ipse vero in Italiam transiens monasterium quod Bovium dicitur edificavit, ubi multorum pater monachorum extitit.*

To the heading (already mentioned) of Chapter 63, Marianus added: *Tunc sanctus pater Columbanus ex nostra sanctissima insula Hibernia, quae sanctorum nominatur, cum sancto Gallo et aliis probatis discipulis in Burgondiam venit. Et in his temporibus* [&c., as given p. 21, *supra*].

The date here given is that of the advent of the Saint into Burgundy. It is a matter of regret that the year of his death was not given. Owing to a mistake of transcription (*xi. Kal. Dec.* for *ix. Kal. Dec.*), the feast is assigned in some of the later Martyrologies to November 21. But the obit took place on the morning of Sunday, November 23, A.D. 615.§

---

* *St. Patrick*, by Dr. Todd, p. 396.   † Note S.   ‡ *Tripartite Life*, p. 537.
§ See *Irish Ecclesiastical Record*, Series III., vol. 5, p. 771 *sq.*

24 THE CODEX PALATINO-VATICANUS, 830.

II.—The portions of linguistic interest are the following twelve quatrains, in *Debide* metre, upon four independent subjects:

A.—Folio 38, top margin:

Cenn apb Adaim, ecnocc páb,	The head high of Adam, brilliant saying,
A cip glan, gnianba dapab;	[Was formed] from the earth pure, sunny of Garad;
A bpunnecop, nab bpécbpon,	His breast, not a lamentable falsehood,
A cip alaenn Apabion	From the land beauteous of Arabion
(no Apabon, no Abilon).	(or of Aradon, or of Adilon).
A bpu a laban ip lia,	His belly from Laban
A coppa a cip Dagapia* (no dagonia),	His feet from the land of Dagaria (or Gagonia);—
Do bapigne Dia bia beoin,	For him God made them of his good-will–
A h[ḟ]uil bo uipce† inb aeo[i]p;	His blood of the water of the air;
A anim bo cinpiub be,	His soul from the spirit of God,
Donibnacc bo, ba gnim glé,	(God) granted [it] to him, it was a deed conspicuous,
Fep cocnic bpac, buibnib gell,	
Ip lep cec pac, cec popcenn.	[God is] the man who hath power over doom, with troops of vouchers,
	To him belongs every cause [beginning], every end.
Cenn [apb] Abaem.	The head [high] of Adam.

The transcription displays much carelessness and, by consequence, corruption, especially in the vocalismus. Thus we have Abaim, Abaem, alaen; huil [= h[ḟ]uil]. In declension, the dative of a masculine *ia*-stem is made to end in *e* (uipce), instead of *iu*. (Cinpiub, dative of an *a*-stem, is given correctly.) The most glaring instance of the kind, however, is aeop for aeoip, where the omission of the letter destroys the rhyme and sense.

With respect to the composition, the variants of lines 4 and 6 go to prove that Marianus was the author and, furthermore, that he employed some of the proper names from memory. The sense, at least to me, is in part enigmatical. I have found the subject similarly treated in the text appended to this Lecture and in the following from a Tract on the Creation in the Book of Ballymote:‡

[The original is doubtless a mediæval Latin legend.]

---

* Perhaps this is to be read b'Agopia—*of Agoria*. Cf. the Ballymote extract (p. 25) and the L. B. text (e).

† The MS. form is uipq; (i.e. *uis* and the contraction for *que*).

‡ Photographed edition, p. 15 b.

THE CODEX PALATINO-VATICANUS, 830.   25

Is amlaid cna donisni Dia in   It is thus indeed God made man,
duine, ıdon, a c[h]onp do calum: namely, his body of earth: to wit, his
ıdon, a cend a cın Ɉanad; a ucc ⁊   head from the land of Garad; his bosom
a bnuindi a cın Anabıa; a bnu a   and his breast from the land of Arabia;
Lodaın; a c[h]onna a cın Aɉonıa;   his belly from [the land of] Lodain; his
a ḟuıl do uırcı[u] ın ae[ı]n; a anaıl feet from the land of Agoria; his blood
do aeon; a c[h]ean do ceınıd; a   from water of the air; his breath from
aınm do cınned Dé. Is amlaıd   air; his heat from fire; his soul from
sın acac na ııı. duılı ı n-ɉac   the spirit of God. It is thus the four
duine.   elements are in every human being.

B.—Folio 39 b, left margin, about half-way down:

Eua mater humani generis.
Dec bliadna [no]bae Eua   Ten years was Eve [alive]
D'ér Adaem ı n-ımneda,   After Adam in afflictions,
Ac coı den no[ḟ]nı[c]ɉnımı,   A-weeping tears with great diligence,*
Co nonnuc nenɉ rınlıɉı.   Until exhaustion of long illness took her
                                      off.

In the third line, den was at first omitted by oversight and subsequently placed overhead. The fourth line stands thus, without a break, in the MS.:

Cononnucnenɉrınlıɉı.

The quatrain is a transcript. It is to be found in *Lebar Brec* (Lith. ed., p. 90, lower margin):

X. m-bliadna nodoı Eua   Ten years was Eve
D'eır Adaım ḟnı hımneda,   After Adam [exposed] to afflictions,
hıc cuı den [no]ḟnı[c]ɉnıme,   A-weeping tears with [great] diligence,*
Co nunmanb nenc rınlıɉe.   Until exhaustion of long sickness killed
                                      her.

With respect to fidelity in copying, comparison results favourably for the fourteenth-century (L. B.) scribe. Thus we have boı—bae, d'eır—d'ér, Adaım—Adaem (gen), ḟnı[c]ɉnıme—[ḟ]nı[c]ɉnımı (gen. of masc. *u*-stem). On the other hand, rınlıɉı (gen. of masc. or neut. *ia*-stem) of Marianus, not rınlıɉe of L. B., is the true reading. The errors in the transcription of the final words of the second distich arose from overlooking the fact that e and ı assonate with each other.

---

* Literally, *of tears of great diligence.*

C.—Folio 40 a, lower margin:

Cetpop, coic [lege pé] [ṗ]ióic iap
ḟıp,
ȝen uabop, ȝen imánım,
Iṛ e lín in ȝneȝa ȝlaen,
Claenne Eua acuṛ Aḃaım.

Four persons, [and] five [read six] score, in truth,
Without boast, without over-reckoning,
It is the complement of the pure flock
Of the children of Eve and of Adam.

Ḋa macc beac ap ṗıċıc ann,
Oen ben ceċ ḟıp, norḃıȝbann;
Eṛ ṗıċı macc, mop ın lep,
Eṛ ḋa mnae ım ceċ oen ḟep.

Two sons [and] ten over twenty therein,
One wife marries each man [of these];*
And twenty sons, great the amount,
And two wives to† every one man [of these].

Coıca macc, ḋa macc co m-blaeḋ,
(Ḋa mac ap coıcaec co m-blaec)
Ḋa ınȝen ap reċcmoȝaec,
Eḋ ón ṗuc Eua ḋo claen
(Iṛ eḋ) [ṗuc Eua ḋo claen]
Ḋ' Aḋam, cén bae ı colaınn.

Fifty sons, [and] two sons with fame,
(Two sons over fifty with fame)
Two daughters over seventy,
This [number] indeed Eve bore of children
(It is this) [number, etc.]
For Adam, whilst he was in the body.

Sıl, ṛoṛap na macc mın
Ruc ın ṗıȝan ḋo'n ṗopıȝ;
Seċna, ṛoluṛ, ȝpıan ṗa ȝel,
balıṇ‡ ṛoṛap nan n-ınȝen.

Sil [was] the youngest of the sons fair,
[Whom] bore the queen for the great king;
Sechna, light, sun that was bright,
It was she (?) was youngest of the daughters.

These verses I have not succeeded in discovering elsewhere. The variants of the third quatrain and the debased graphic forms may perhaps be taken as proofs that we have here the work of Marianus himself. Against this is scarcely to be placed the fact that the numerals (104) of the opening line do not correspond with the sum of those in the second and third stanzas. The substitution of ṗé (six) for coıc of the text (= 124) would have removed the discrepancy. Three-fourths of the composition present serious corruptions in almost every line.

---

* Literally, one wife of each man *takes them* (respectively).
† Literally, *around*.   ‡ ba hı?

C. forms.	Old-Irish forms.		C. forms.	Old-Irish forms.
l. 1, cetrop,	cetnap.	l. 9, blaeḋ,	blaiḋ.
2, ʒen,	cen.	,, coicaet,	coicait.
3, ʒlaen,	ʒlain.	(9a), blaet,	blait.
4, claenne,	clainne.	10, ḋa,	ḋi.
7, er,	ir.	,, reċtmoʒaet,	reċtmoʒait.
,, fiḋi,	fiḋe.	11, claen,	clain.
8, ḋa,	ḋi.	12, bae,	bai.
,, mnae,	mnai.	15, fa,	ba.

blaeḋ and blaet, ʒlaen and ⁊ḋaim, claen and colainn show that the foregoing list was the result of carelessness or caprice.

Respecting the subject matter, I know of nothing cognate, except what is stated in *Saltair na Rann*—that, namely, Adam had seventy-two sons and an equal number of daughters.

D.—Folio 47 b, lower margin :

ben romanbrat fin ʒaba,	A woman the men of Gabaa killed,
Inʒen fin ḋo tneiḃ Iuḋa,	Daughter of a man of the tribe of Juda,
⁊ fen ḋo tneiḃ Leui loir,	Her husband [was] of the tribe of valiant? Levi,
Ir fair [no]himreḋ* ecoir.	It is upon him was committed injustice.
Coica¹ [*lege* coic] mile, mor² in cat,	Fifty [*read* five] thousand, great the
Serca mile fen n-anmaḋ,³	battalion,
Ḋo h[ṗ]il⁴ Iacoiḃ, er⁵ eol ḋam,	[And] sixty thousand of armed men,
⁊en⁶ [*lege* im] aén⁷ mnae⁸ ḋaroċna-tar.⁹	Of the seed of Jacob, it is known to me, On account of one woman they fell.
Timcell ban acur mac¹⁰ mín¹¹	Besides† the women and sons fair
Trebe beoḋa beniaminn,¹²	Of the spirited tribe of Benjamin,
Ir timcell inḋ air rolaḋ	And besides† the destruction that was
Fon muncer¹³ lobir¹⁴ ʒalaḋ.	inflicted Upon the people of Jabes Galaad.

VARIANTS OF HARLEIAN, 1802.

¹ Coic.   ² man.   ³ n-anmaḋ.   ⁴ fil.   ⁵ ir.   ⁶ imm.   ⁷ oen.   ⁸ nindi.   ⁹ ḋoroċnatar.   ¹⁰ matt.   ¹¹ miin = mín of text.   ¹² beniamin.   ¹³ muintir.   ¹⁴ labir.

---

* The omission of the verbal particle arose from pronouncing himreḋ as a trisyllable ; m and r not coalescing in sound.

† Literally, *around* (governing the genitive).

28 THE CODEX PALATINO-VATICANUS, 830.

Continued on folio 48 a, top margin :

Τριċα τρen [ṗ]ep αρ cec cepc, αcup τρι [*lege* coic] mιle ρeρcαc, Τρuαʒ ιn τ-αbbαρ poḃoρḃαe— α mαρbαḃ ule ιm oen mnαe.	[In all] thirty brave men over an exact hundred, And three [*read* five] thousand [and] sixty [thousand], Pitiful the cause that was for them [=they had]— To be killed, all of them, on account of one woman.

Of some of these quatrains there is evidence to prove that Marianus was not the author. The second and third are found in the *Mael-Brigte Gospels*, a twelfth-century MS. of exquisite caligraphy in the British Museum (Harleian, 1802, folio 11 b, top margin).* They were inserted to illustrate *Rachel plorans filios suos* [Jer. xxxi. 15] of Matt. ii. 18 : concerning which expression the following is also given, with the heading *Ag*[*ustinus*] : *Rachiel plorans—quia tribus Beniamin pene deleta est a toto Israel, quae erat de semine Rachel, propter struprum in uxorem Levitis commissum.*

The reference is Judges xix.-xx. In the second verse, the reading of Marianus makes the total of Jews slain 110,000 ! The Harleian reckoning falls 30 short of the true number. Coic has to be read as a dissyllable to satisfy the scansion. In the final quatrain, coic (five), in place of τρι (three), is requisite to make the text correspond with the original (65,130).

In transcription, the opening stanza, except the fourth line, which requires another syllable, is given accurately. In the portions occurring in both MSS., nine of the fourteen variants (1, 4, 5, 6, 7, 8, 9, 13, 14) establish the superiority of the later copy. Marianus, as was his wont, gave αe for αι in poḃoρḃαe and mnαe of the two closing lines.

In reference to the date of the composition of A, B, C, D, the depraved vocalismus and consonantismus of the Marianus Codex would at first sight lead the pieces to be classed under the so-called Middle-Irish. Here, however, an inference of the kind would be unwarranted. In the first place, B and D, which are demonstrably copies and not originals, exhibit forms that are quite Zeussian in *Lebar Brec* and the *Moel-Brigte Gospels*. Furthermore, instances of pronominal in-

---

* See *Proceedings* R. I. A., vol. v., p. 45 *sq.*

fixation, such as ᴠ[o]-a-ꝑıȝne [a = ea] (A), ꝑo-ꝑ-ꝑuc [ꝑ = eam] (B), ꝑo-ᴠo-ꝑ-ʙae [ꝑ = eis (ᴠo is metrical)] (D), constitute internal evidence of a kind to place the compositions wherein they occur in the category of Old-Irish.

We have, accordingly, to conclude that to determine the date of authorship from the mere linguistic phenomena of mediæval Irish MSS. is uncritical and illusory.

In connexion with A, I append a text from *Lebar Brec*. It gives the names of the "sods" from which the parts of Adam's body were formed, namely, *Malon, Arton, Biblon* and *Agore*. What these signify, I am unable to explain. The main interest of the Tract consists in its relation to *Saltair na Rann*. *Saltair na Rann*, or *Psalter of Verses*, so-called in imitation of the number of Psalms, is made up of one hundred and fifty, mostly short, poems in *Debide* metre, amounting to 1947 quatrains. They deal with Old Testament incidents, except CLXI., CXLII., which treat respectively of John the Baptist and the Incarnation and CXLIII-CL., which are devoted to the life of our Lord. The work, as far as our present knowledge extends, exists in its entirety only in one MS. (of the twelfth century), in the Bodleian Library, Oxford, Rawlinson B 502. From this it has been "edited," that is, printed, with a meagre Index verborum, but without translation, collation or explanatory notes, in the *Anecdota Oxoniensia*.*

To show the radical imperfection of the publication, a note to the Preface informs us, with respect to No. I., that a prose abstract of part of the poem is to be found in the first volume of the *Brehon Laws*, pp. 26-30. Incredible as it seems, no use has been made of that material to clear up any of the many textual difficulties. Nay more, judging from the note and another statement in the Preface, the writer was unaware that what had been done in the *Brehon Laws* in the case of sixty quatrains had been effected for more than eleven hundred in *Lebar Brec*.

As regards the authorship, the title is followed by a statement that the *Psalter* was composed by Oengus Cele De. (He flourished at the close of the eighth century and the opening of the ninth and was the compiler of the well-known native rhymed Calendar (or Martyrology) called by his name.) This attribution may be well

---

* Oxford, 1883.

founded. For the verbal corruptions can be fairly charged to the transcription. No doubt, events and persons of the tenth century are mentioned. In No. XII., namely, it is stated that one thousand years, less eleven, elapsed from the Nativity to the first Cattle Plague (in Ireland). The names of contemporary kings at home and abroad are also given, together with a notice of an incursion of Danes. Mention is also made of Dubdalethe,* successor of St. Patrick (Archbishop of Armagh). But the eleven quatrains in question (XII., ll. 2337-80), as they have no necessary connexion with the context, are, it may be safely concluded, adventitious. Their presence can be naturally accounted for. A tenth-century computist connected to his own time the chronology from Adam to the Nativity contained in the *Psalter* and then added the historical items just named. We can go even farther. The internal evidence, as set forth hereunder, enables us to detect the work of a second interpolator:

Saltair na Rann, XII. (ll. 2293-2344).

a Ll. 2293-6, From Adam to Deluge, ... 2240 years.

1 {b ,, 2297-2300, ,, Deluge ,, Abraham, . . 962 years [944].†}
  {a ,, 2301-4,   ,, Adam   ,, Abraham, . . [3202]‡ 3184.}

2 {b ,, 2305-8,   ,, Abraham ,, Exodus, . . 540 years [524].}
  {a ,, 2309-12, ,, Adam   ,, Exodus, . . [3742] 3708.}

3 {b ,, 2313-16, ,, Exodus ,, David, . . . 500 years [456].}
  {a ,, 2317-20, ,, Adam   ,, David, . . . [4242] 4164.}

4 {b ,, 2321-24, ,, David   ,, Captivity, . . 569 years [585].}
  {a ,, 2325-28, ,, Adam   ,, Captivity, . . [4811] 4749.}

5 {b ,, 2329-32, ,, Captivity ,, Incarnation, . . 566 years [447].}
  {a ,, 2333-36, ,, Adam   ,, Nativity, . . [5377] 5196.}

6 {b ,, 2337-40, ,, Nativity ,, Cattle Plague, . 989 years [988].}
  {c ,, 2341-44, ,, Adam   ,, Cattle Plague, . [6366] 6184.}

The mere juxtaposition, it will scarcely be questioned, establishes that no author could, with serious intent, have composed the *a* quatrains and the *b* quatrains of the foregoing. The reckoning of the

---

* In the preface to the Oxford edition, he is stated to have died A.D. 1061. But this is egregious confusion. Dubdalethe, who, the text says, lived at the same time as Brian Boruma (to take the best known of the rulers mentioned), died A.D. 998—more than half a century before his namesake.

† The bracketted figures in this column are derived from the *a* verses.

‡ The bracketted figures in this column are derived from the *b* verses.

THE CODEX PALATINO-VATICANUS, 830.   31

former is in the total within three years of that of Eusebius (who was known to Oengus);* that of the latter is based upon the computation of the Septuagint. Furthermore, 6 *b* is one year in excess of 6 *c*—5 *a* and equally in arrear of the (correct) date (A.D. 988) derivable from 6 *c*, which agrees with the Annals of Ulster. The *b* verses are thus discovered to be interpolations,—at variance not alone with the original text, but likewise with the quatrain (6 *c*) introduced by the hand that inserted the other historical matter.

The *Lebar Brec* version embodies, with the exceptions pointed out in the textual Notes, the contents of Nos. II., IV., VI., VII., VIII., IX. and XI. of the *Psalter*. The similarity of expression, too close and too frequent to arise from coincidence, to which may perhaps be added the formula *ut dixit* [*poeta*], proves that the prose was a precis of the corresponding poems. If so, the abstract was made from a somewhat shorter recension and a better transcript than those of the Bodleian Codex. This is confirmed, with regard to the form, by the variants of No. X.

The Variants and Notes exhibit the data upon which the deductions regarding the recension and the text have been based.

NOTES.

A.—CHRONICLE OF MARIANUS.

A.D. 1050 [= 1028].   Ego, miser Marianus, in peccatis fui in hoc anno natus.

B.—CHRONICLE OF MARIANUS.

A.D. 1074 [= 1052].   Ego, Marianus, seculum reliqui.

C.—CHRONICLE OF MARIANUS.

A.D. 1078 [= 1056]. Ego, Marianus, peregrinus factus pro regno coeleste, patriam motuavi, et in Colonia, v. feria, Kal. Aug., monachus effectus.

D.—(a) CHRONICLE OF MARIANUS.

A.D. 1065 [= 1043]. Animchadus, Scottus, monachus et inclusus, obiit iii. Kal. Feb. in monasterio Fuldensi. Super cujus sepulchrum visa sunt lumina et psalmodia audita. Super quem ego, Marianus Scotus, decem annis inclusus, super pedes ejus stans cotidie cantavi missas.

Willibelmus, monachus et presbiter conversus clericus et sapiens, districtius[-or]

---

* The (lost) Martyrology of Eusebius was one of the sources of the Calendar of Oengus (Epilogue of the Calendar, l. 140).

et religiosior omnium monachorum Fuldensium, sicut nos vidimus, Animcadum rogavit ut se benediceret. Eadem vere ipsa nocte, sicut mihi incluso super Animcadum confirmavit, somniavit Animcadum in suo sepulchro stantem, nimio fulgore candentem, et extensa sua manu se ab eo benedici. Cumque etiam fossa sepulchri mei iuxta latus ejus in nocte nondum completa permaneret aperta, totam ipsam noctem mellifluo odore scilicet conduxi.

Qui, quia cum licentia senioris sui, nomine Corcram[-n], in insola Kelt[r]a caritatem fratribus fecit, paucis vero remanentibus post alios exeuntes potumque petentibus ipse sine licentia prebuit, et inde etiam tunc sicut primum potum seniori misit. Ideo die crastino non tantum de insola Kelt[r]a, sed de tota Hibernia ipsum senior projecit: quod humiliter complevit. Ita Tigernach Borchech [*lege* -ch] mihi culpabili in aliqua levi culpa pronuntiavit.

(b) ANNALS OF ULSTER.

Ɑ.ꝺ. m.° xl.° Copcnan cleineó, cenn Eoppa ım cpabuꝺ ⁊ ım ecna, ın Chpıpco paupauıc.

A.D. 1040. Corcran, the cleric, head of Europe with respect to piety and to wisdom, reposed in Christ.

E.—(a) CHRONICLE OF MARIANUS.

A.D. 997 [= 975]. Ebergus, archiepiscopus Coloniensis, immolavit Scottis in sempiternum monasterium Sancti Martini in Colonia. Quibus primum abbas preerat Minnborinus Scottus, annis xii.

A.D. 1008 [= 986]. Minnborinus, abbas Scottorum monasterii Sancti Martini in Colonia, obiit xv. Kal. Aug. Kilianus, abbas Scottus, successit annis xvi.

A.D. 1025 [= 1003]. Kilianus, abbas Scottorum Sancti Martini Coloniae, xix. Kal. Jan. obiit.

A.D. 1026 [= 1004]. Helias, Scottus, post eum successit annis xx.

A.D. 1058 [= 1036]. Propter religionem districtam disciplinamque nimiam et propter aliquos Scottos, quos secum habebat Helias, Scottus abbas, qui monasterium Sancti Pantalionis et Sancti Martini in Colonia pariter regebat, Piligrinus, Coloniensis episcopus, invidis viris instigatus, Heliae ait: Nisi usque dum ipse, Piligrinus, de curte regia revertisset, nec Helias neque alius Scotus in monasterio Pantalionis fuisset.

Tunc Helias atque alii Scoti quibus episcopus dixit condixerunt: si Christus in ipsis fuit peregrinis, ne umquam omnino ad Coloniam vivus venisset de curte episcopus Piligrinus. Et ita Dominus complevit; atque Helias duo monasteria regnavit.

A.D. 1064 [= 1042]. Helias, Scottus abbas, obiit iii. Id. Apr.: vir prudens et religiosus, et ideo monasterium Sancti Pantalionis cum suo, id est, Sancti Martini, sibi datum est.

Ipse obtimum missalem monachi etiam Franci sine licentia conscriptum in commune monachorum, in monasterio Sancti Pantalionis, igne consumpsit, ne alius sine licentia conscriberet, aut tale aliquid fecisset.

Cui successit Maiobus, Scotus, virgo, patiens et sapiens, annis xviii.

A.D. 1083 [= 1061]. Maiobus, abbas Scotorum Coloniae, obiit.

[Foillanus post eum successit, Marianus added.]

THE CODEX PALATINO-VATICANUS, 830.

(b) Annals of Ulster.

Ⅽ.ⅅ. m°.xl°.11°. Ailill Mucnoma, cenn manaċ na n-Ꝟoeiḋél ın Colonıa, quıeuıt.

A.D. 1042. Ailill of Mucknoe [Co. Monaghan], head of the Irish monks in Cologne, rested.

F.—Chronicle of Marianus.

A.D. 1080 [= 1058]. Badaebrunna civitas cum duobus monasteriis, id est episcopatus et monachorum, feria vi. ante Palmas, igne consumitur. In monasterio autem monachorum erat Paternus nomine, monachus Scotus, multisque annis inclusus, qui etiam combustionem prenuntiabat, ambiens martyrium pro nullo foris exivit, sed in sua clausola combustus per ignem pertransivit in refrigerium. De cujus etiam sepulchro quaedam bona narrantur.

Ipsis vero statim diebus, feria ii. post octavas Paschae, exiens de Colonia, causâ claudendi, cum abbate Fuldense ad Fuldam, super mattam in clausola ipsius, ubi supra eamdem mattam combustus et passus est, ego oravi.

G.—Chronicle of Marianus.

A.D. 1081 [= 1059]. Ego, Marianus indignus, cum Sigfrido, abbate Fuldensi, iuxta corpus Sancti Kiliani, martiris, Wirziburc ad presbiteratum, sabbato medi[a]e Qua[d]ragesimae, iii. Id. Mart., [promotus]; et feria vi. post Ascensionem Domini, pridie Idus Maii, inclusus in Fulda per x. annos.

H.—Chronicle of Marianus.

A.D. 1091 [= 1069]. Ego, miser Marianus, iusione episcopi Mogontini et abbatis Fuldensis, feria vi. ante Palmas, iii. Non. Apr., post annos x. meae inclusionis solutus, de clausola in Fulda ad Mogontiam conductus.

Dedicatio capellae clausolae monasterii Sancti Martinii in Mogontia, in honore Sancti Bartholomei apostoli, vi. Idus Iul., feria vi., Sanctorum vii. Fratrum in festivitate. In qua clausola eodem die ego, Marianus, pro peccatis meis secundo includor.

I.—Chronicle of Marianus.

Folio 166 b. A.D. 1082. Obiit Marianus, inclusus.

K.—Annals of Ulster.

Ⅽ.ⅅ. m°.lxx° 11°. Ⅾiarmaıc, mac Maıl-na-mbó, ɼı Laıꝟen ⁊ Ꝟall, ꝺo tuıtım ı cat (Cat Oḋḃa) la Conċoḃuɼ hUa Mael-Seċlaınn, la ɼıꝟ Temɼac: ⁊ áɼ Ꝟall ıme (ıꝺon, ı Maıɼt ⁊ ı ɼept lo Feḃɼa).

A.D. 1072. Diarmait, son of Mailna-mbo, king of Leinster and of the Foreigners, fell in battle (the battle of Odhbha) by Conchobur Ua MaelSechlainn, [namely] by the king of Tara and slaughter of the Foreigners [took place] around him (that is, on Tuesday and on the seventh of the Ides of February [Feb. 7]).

THE CODEX PALATINO-VATICANUS, 830.

L.—(a) Confession of St. Patrick.

Ego, Patricius . . . patrem habui Calpornum, diaconum, filium quendam Potiti, filii Odissi presbyteri, qui fuit [de] vico Bannavem Taberniae.—*Book of Armagh*, folio 22 a.

(b) Life of St. Patrick [*Brussels Codex*].

Patricius, qui et Sochet vocabatur, Brito natione, in Britannis natus, Cualfarni[-o] diaconi[-o] ortus, filio, ut ipse ait, Potiti presbyteri, qui fuit [de] vico *Bannavem thabur indecha* . . . matre etiam conceptus Concesso[-a] nomine.—Cod. Brux., *Documenta, etc.*, ed. Hogan, p. 21.

(c) Tripartite Life.

Pacnaic, bino, bo bnecnaib Ailcluabe a bunabup. Calpuipnb ainm a atap; uapalpacapc he. Pócib ainm a penatap; beoċan acacomnaic. Concepp ainm a matap; bi Pnangcaib bí ɔ píup bo Mapcan hí.	Patrick, then, of the Britons of Ailcluade [was] his descent. Calpuirnd [was] the name of his father; an archpriest [was] he. Fotid [was] the name of his grandfather; a deacon he chanced [to be]. Concess [was] the name of his mother; of the Franks [was] she and a sister to [St.] Martin [was] she.

M.—Tirechan.

Inveni quatuor nomina in libro [ad]scripta Patricio apud* Ultanum, episcopum Conchuburnensium : Sanctus Magonus, qui est clarus; Succetus, qui est [deus belli]; Patricius [qui est pater civium]; Cothirthiacus, quia servivit quatuor domibus magorum.—*Book of Armagh*, folio 9 b.

N.—(a) Tirechan.

Et empsit illum unus ex eis [scil. magis], cui nomen erat Miliuc Maccu Boin, magus et servivit illi septem annis omni servitute et duplici labore et porcarium possuit eum in montanis convallibus. Deinde hautem vissitavit illum anguelus Domini in somniis in cacuminibus montis Scirte, iuxta montem Miss.—*Book of Armagh*, folio 9 b.

(b) Muirchu Maccu Machtheni.

De quo monte [*Miss*], multo ante, tempore quo ibi captivus erat [et] servierat, pres[s]o vestigio in petra alterius montis, expedito gradu vidit angelum Victoricum in conspectu eius ascendisse in caelum.—*Ib.*, folio 3 a.

---

* *Apud.*—Literal rendering of Irish la (by).

THE CODEX PALATINO-VATICANUS, 830. 35

O.—Fiacc's Hymn.

Arbeṅc Uiccoṗ ṡṗi ṡniab	Said Victor to the slave [waves:
mil coṅceṗṗeḃ ṗoṅ coṅna;	Of Mil[iuc] that he should go over
Ṗoṅṗuiḃ a ċoiṗṗ ṗoṅṗinḃ leic,	He planted it, his foot, on the flag,
Maṅaiḃ ḃia aeṗ, ni ḃṗoṅna.	It remains after him, it wears not out.

P.—Confession of St. Patrick.

Et ibi scilicet quadam nocte in somno audivi vocem dicentem mihi: *Bene ieiunas, cito ituris ad patriam tuam.* Et iterum, post paululum tempus, audivi responsum dicentem mihi: *Ecce, navis tua parata est.* Et non erat prope [navis]; sed forte habebat ducenta milia passus et ibi numquam fueram, nec ibi notum quemquam de hominibus habebam. Et deinde postmodum conversus sum in fugam et intermissi hominem [quo]cum fueram sex annis. Et veni in virtute Dei qui viam meam ad bonum dirigebat et nihil metuebam donec perveni ad navem illum.—*Book of Armagh*, folio 23 b.

Q.—Book of Armagh.

Foedus pepigerunt per manus Loiguiri, filii Neill, Patricius et filii Amolngid cum exercitu laicorum [et] episcoporum sanctorum et inierunt iter facere ad montem Egli. Et expendit Patricius etiam pretium quindecim animarum hominum, ut in scriptione sua adfirmat,* de argento et auro, ut nullum[-us] malorum hominum inpederet eos in via recta transeuntes totam Hiberniam; quia necessitas poscit illos ut pervenirent Silvam Fochlithi ante caput anni Pascâ secundâ, causâ filiorum clamantium clamore magno, [quorum] voces audivit in utero matrum suorum dicentium: *Veni, Sancte Patrici, salvos nos facere.* Foll. 10 d, 11 a.

R.—Confession of St. Patrick.

Putabam enim ipso momento audire vocem ipsorum qui erant iuxta Silvam Focluti, quae est prope mare occidentale. Et sic exclamaverunt: *Rogamus te, sancte puer, venias et adhuc ambulas[-es] inter nos.* Et valde conpunctus sum corde et valde amplius non potui legere. Et sic expertus sum, Deo gratias, quia post plurimos annos prestitit illis Dominus secundum clamorem illorum.

S.—Gilla Coemain's Chronological Poem.

Cṗiċa ḃliaḃan, cṗi ḃliaḃna,	Thirty years, [and] three years,
Ċóiṗ o ṗen ḃola iaṅma,	It is right from that to go afterwards,
Co ḃaṗ maic Ṗhaeiḃilmċi i n-hl,	To the death of the son of Fedilmidt in I[ona],
Iṗ co eṗcecc Ṡṗiṡoṗii.	And to the decease of Gregory.

—*Book of Leinster*, p. 131, ll. 42-3.

---

* Vos autem experti estis qua[n]tum erogavi illis qui indicabant per omnes regiones quos[-as] ego frequentius visitabam; censeo enim non minimum quam pretium quindecim hominum distribui illis.—*Confession of St. Patrick*.

† That is, to St. Columba.

T.—EXTRACT FROM ACTS OF ST. BAITHINE.

Tertia feria, dum Sanctus Baithinus in ecclesia iuxta altare Dominum oraret, sopor pene mortis super eum illic cecidit. Cum autem fratres circa eum lamentarentur, Diermitius, minister Columbae, ait: *Ecce, fratres, videtis quod inter duas solemnitates seniorum vestrorum magnum intervallum non erit.*

Haec eo dicente, Baithinus, quasi de gravi somno excitatus, ait: *Si inveni gratiam in oculis Dei et si cursum perfectum in conspectu eius consummaverim usque hodie, ego confido in eo quod usque ad natale senioris mei non obiturus ero.* Quod sic, fere post sex dies, factum est (AA. SS. Jun. ii. 238).

U.—EXTRACT FROM EDITORIAL PREFATORY NOTE TO FOREGOING.

Tempus mortis et regiminis ita definit Colganus in Appendice 5 ad vitam Sancti Columbae, cap. 3, sect. 4, ut dicat ipsum quarto post decessoris sui mortem anno obiisse; unum dumtaxat annum ubi invenerit Usserus non indicat ipse: secundum quem ea ratione obiisset Baithenus DXCVII., cum in ipsius sententia S. Columba decesserit anno praecedenti. Ego, qui in commentario praevio ad prolixiora Acta S. Columbae eorum opinionem praetuli qui affirmant Sanctum istum ex hac vita migrasse uno anno serius, et ex communi Hibernorum sententia (quamdiu nulla in contrarium affertur ratio) credere malo quatuor annis Sanctum Baithenum praefuisse: consequenter eum anno DCI. finem vitae pariter et regimini imposuisse existimo (*Praefatiuncula*, ib. 233).

Lebar Brec.

CREATION OF HEAVEN: CREATION, FALL AND PENANCE OF ADAM AND EVE.

Lebar brec.

a. Dorigne¹ dia imorro in rigteċ uaċtaraċ do flog² ampa airċaingel³, hi rilet beiċ cutruma in domain. Atat tri muir and dino hi timċell in rigtige: ibon, múr do gloine⁴ uaine⁴ ⁊ múr do⁵ dergor ⁊ múr do⁵ ċorcair glain. Fil⁶ caċir and ⁊ ri comleċan, co ceṫri primdoirrib ruirri. Ir e met caċ doraír⁷ dib rin, ibon, mile ceimend fri a ċomur. Fil⁶ dino cror⁸ de or in ceċ⁹ dorur dib rin. Hite pempa, roarba¹⁰ ⁊ en dergóir for ceċ croir ⁊ gemiu¹¹ dermair¹¹ do lica logmair ceċa croire. Aingel dino co n-a flog² o rig in rigtig ceċ laei¹² co clairceclaib¹³ ⁊ ceolaib¹⁴ hi timċell ceċ¹⁵ oen ċrori.¹⁶ Fil⁶ and raiċti¹⁷ fo ċomair ceċ doraír⁷ ⁊ ir cutrumma fri talmain co n-a muraib¹⁸ ceċ raiċti dib ⁊ fond argait fuċib. Ocur bruige fo blaċ ⁊ luibib¹⁹ ligdaib¹⁹ ⁊ mur argait gil im ceċ raiċti.¹⁷ Seċt n-airroptaig²⁰ ann iar rin, imon primcaṫraig di ceċ leṫ co forṫaib diairmib ⁊ mur crebuma im ceċ²¹ n-airroptaċ.²² Ocur ir amlaid attat, i n-a freit imon primċaṫraig ⁊ ni faguba ramail do met ceċ airroptaig²³ dib ⁊ riat lan do luibib¹⁹ examlai[b]. Da mur dec dino na n-airroptaċ²² ⁊ na raiċti,¹⁷ cinmotat²⁴ na tri muir filet²⁵ imon primcaṫraig. Ceṫraċa dorur dino hi t-[r]reib in riċid, cenmotat a rigdoirre. Tri doraír⁷ ceċa raiċ[t]i ⁊ tri doraír ceċ¹⁵ airroptaig²⁶ ⁊ ceṫri doraír⁷ uada[ib] immaċ o'n airroptaċ

VARIANTS OF SALTAIR NA RANN.

(The bracketed numeral indicates the number of the Poem.)

a.—(II.) ¹ dorigni. ² fluag. ³ árcaṅgel. ⁴⁻⁴ glain huaine. ⁵ di. ⁶ fail. ⁷ doruir. ⁸ croir. ⁹ caċ. ¹⁰ d doubled. ¹¹⁻¹¹ gemm dermor. ¹² lai. ¹³ clarrċetal. ¹⁴ ceol. ¹⁵ caċa. ¹⁶ ċrore. ¹⁷ raiċti. ¹⁸ muireib. ¹⁹⁻¹⁹ lubaib ligaibib. ²⁰ n-airroptaig. ²¹ caċ. ²² n-airroptaċ. ²³ airroptuig. ²⁴ cenmṫat (the elision is to suit the metre). ²⁵ failet. ²⁶ airroptaiċ.

LEBAR BREC.

a. Moreover, God made for the distinguished host of archangels the upper royal dwelling, which[1] is ten times as large as the world[1]. Now, there are therein three walls around the royal dwelling: namely, a wall of[2] green crystal[2] and a wall of red gold [colour] and a wall of pure purple [colour]. There is a city therein and it[3] is square, with four chief doors thereto[4]. This is the size of each door of those, to wit, a thousand paces [wide] in its measure. There is also a cross of gold on each door of those. They are thick [and] very high and a bird of red gold [is] upon each cross and very large gems of precious stone [are] on[5] every cross[5]. Now, an angel with his host [is placed] by the king of the royal dwelling every day with choirs and melodies around each cross. There is in it a lawn in front of each door and as large as the earth with its walls is each lawn of them and a foundation of silver under them. And a sward in[6] bloom and [with] beauteous herbs and a wall of pure[7] silver around each lawn. Eight[8] porticoes [are] therein also, around the chief city on every side, with numberless supports and a wall of bronze around each portico. And it is thus they are: [namely,] distributed[9] [equally distant] around the chief city. And there hath not been found the like of[10] the [great] size of each portico of them and they [are] full of divers herbs. Twelve also [are] the walls of the porticoes and of the lawns, besides the three walls that are around the chief city. Forty doors likewise [are] in the circuit of the royal abode, besides its regal doors. Three [are] the doors of each lawn and

---

a.—[1-1] Literally, in which are ten equalities of the world.

[2-2] The expression can also signify *of pure green* (lit., *of green purity*).

[3] Lit., she; caṫıɼ (city) being feminine.   [4] Lit., upon her.

[5-5] Lit., of every cross.   [6] Lit., under.   [7] Lit., white.

[8] The reading of *S. R.*; L. B. has *seven* (ϝeċċ).

[9] Lit., in their distribution.   [10] Lit., to.

40 Lebar brec.

[a] imectrac immac fririn cetna atcomarcc. Ocur comla argait cec dorair⁷ do na raictib rin ⁊ comla creduma fri doirrib²⁷ na n-airrortac²⁸. Na rrictmuir rilet o'n mur mor amac²⁹ hi timcell na n-airrortac²², ramailter³⁰ a n-airde o talmain co hercai³¹. Muir na raicti¹⁷ dino, doranta do findruine³² ⁊ ir e tomur a n-airde, idon, o talmain co grein. Tri muir dino rilet imon rrimcatraig, ramailter a n-airde o talmain co firmamint³³. Suidiugud³⁴ na mur imon catraig, idon, trian cec mur dib rec araile beor. Ir e dino in t-airdrig uilecumactac foraiger na forta rin imon rrimcatraig ⁊ im na raictib ⁊ im na herrortacaib.

b. Rorocit¹ dino rloig² ril Adaim d'indraigid cec forraid dib rin. Did dino cec rlog³ roleit dib 'n-a n-errortaib⁴ ⁊ 'n-a raictib⁵ rerrin. Na noim⁶ dino ⁊ na noimuaga⁷, rcertair⁸ iatride rririn rlog amuig⁹ ⁊ bertair documm na morcatrac iat. Ocur ni teit irin catraig rin actmad [redmad, MS.] oen triar do doinib¹⁰ in domain: idon, duine¹¹ co n-dan n-dligtec n-de ⁊ duine og co coimet a firinne ⁊ duine amra, aitriget. Coimrcertair¹² dino na noim¹³ irin noemcatraig: idon, cac dib for¹⁴ a rrimdorur.¹⁵ Na doirre¹⁶ rin imorro, co n-delbaib* ⁊ co lecaib logmaraib ⁊ co comlaḋaib dergoir. Tri hatcomairc cec dorair¹⁷ dib rin ⁊ atcomarc re¹⁸ cec¹⁹ n-oen¹⁹ mur dib orin amac. Aurdrocait dino na n-dorur noem rin, hite taitnemaca do dergor. Airde²⁰ cec ceimen²¹ [ar]aile²² inntib, co riact in rrimdun. Ir cain in rlog³ roroic²³ in conair rin dar lebendaib glainide. Ir mor cet ⁊ ir mor mile do noemaib roroic²³ in conair rin illebendaib glainedaib ⁊ aurdroctib dergoir. Rilet ann raicti blaite²⁴ ⁊ iat bienua

²⁷ doirri. ²⁸ n-irrortac ²⁹ immac. ³⁰ ramlaitir. ³¹ herca. ³² findruim. ³³ rirmimeint. ³⁴ ruidigud.
b.—¹ roroic. ² rluaig. ³ rluag. ⁴ n-airrortac. ⁵ raictib. ⁶ noeb. ⁷ núibhuaga. ⁸ rcerdair. ⁹ immaig. ¹⁰ doeneib. ¹¹ duni. ¹² congerdair. ¹³ naeb. ¹⁴ dar. ¹⁵ -dorur. ¹⁶ doirri. ¹⁷ dorur. ¹⁸ for. ¹⁹⁻¹⁹ cac oen. ²⁰ airdbiu. ²¹ ceim. ²² araile. ²³ roraig. ²⁴ blaci.

* After this word there is a lacuna (= space for three letters) in the Lithograph. Perhaps the word was oir—*of gold.*

three [are] the doors of each portico and four doors from them outwards, [**a**] [that is, one] from [each] external portico out towards the first bulwark (?). And a fastening of silver [is] on[11] each door of those lawns and fastenings of bronze [are] upon the doors of the porticoes. The connecting walls[12] that are from the great wall out around the porticoes, their height equals [that] from earth to moon. Now, the walls[12] of the lawns, they are made of copper and this is the measure of their height, namely, from earth to sun. The three walls[12] also that are around the chief city, their height equals [that] from earth to firmament. The [relative] position[12] of the walls around the city [is this], to wit, a third each wall of them [is] beyond the other. Now, it is the high-king all-powerful that establishes those supports around the chief city and around the lawns and around the porticoes.

b. Now, fare the hosts of the seed of Adam to attain each seat of those. However, each host of them is apart in their own porticoes and lawns. But the saints and the holy virgins, these are separated from the host outside and they are carried unto the great city. And there goeth not into that city except one-third of the people of the world: namely, the person with the righteous gift of God and the pure person that[1] kept his truth[1] and the person of[2] distinguished penance[2]. Moreover, the saints are separated in the chief city: to wit, each of them over a chief door. Those doors also, [they are adorned] with figures and with precious stones and with fastenings of pure[3] gold. Three bulwarks(?) to each door of those, and a bulwark(?) to each wall of them from that outwards. Now, the passages of those holy doors, they are delightful [and made] of pure[3] gold. Higher [is] each step than the other in them, until one reaches the chief fortress. Fair is the host that fares on that path over crystal platforms. Many[4] hundreds and many thousands of saints fare[4] on that path, on crystal platforms and passages of pure[3] gold. There are therein lawns of bloom

---

[11] Lit., of.   [12] Nom. abs.; the subject, as a rule, following the vb.
b.—[1-1] Lit., with keeping of his truth.
[2-2] Lit., distinguished, penitential.   [3] Lit., red.
[4-4] Lit., it is a great [number] of hundreds, and it is a great [number] of thousands of saints that fares, &c. The neut. adj. (moṗ) is used as sb. (with dependent gen.).

42   Lebar brec.

[b] co top[ċib]²⁵ ceċ ċopaid co m-boltnuzud. Fil²⁶ ann pailci cen
P. 109 b. coippi ⁊ parpad biċbuan, |*poillpe²⁷ cen epdibad²⁸ ⁊ ceol cen
anad. Fil²⁶ ann dino in ní parap ceċ ploz: idon, pozap na
n-zpad ⁊ na ceol ⁊ bolud na m-blaċ. Filec andpin mop popad
⁊ mop clapp ⁊ mop ceol ceċ clappe.²⁹ Fil ann dino mop lind
pomblapca. Fil and dino mop do ppoċaib ⁊ do ċeniul ceċa³⁰
lenna pomilip ppia parpad na ploz. Fil²⁶ and dino mop do
ċoppib pína³¹. Fil ann lecca³² lozmapa; pil ann popaid
poponda[i]³³; pil²⁶ ann mop do piz[p]pocaib³⁴; pil²⁶ ann mop
m-[b]ile³⁵ m-bpoza; pil ann mop cipe³⁶ n-inznad; pil²⁶ ann mop
cec do muizib; pil²⁶ ann mop ppeaċ³⁷ ⁊ mop cec ceol nacpoiċ³⁸
cuipem³⁹ na aipneip. Fil²⁶ ann dino cec ⁊ a ceċaip ceċpaċac
piad znuip De do immpocpaiccib.⁴⁰ Cland Adaim dino o
ċopaċ⁴¹ domain⁴² co bpaċ⁴³, ni coempacip⁴⁴ uile oen poċpaicc
dib pin do paipnep.

c. Fil ann dino poppad in piz uilcċumaċcaiz pop lap na
ppimcaċpaċ. De¹ óp deppz dino doponca² pizpuide in piz op
na mupaid upapdaib³. Sopad⁴ ainzel dino, ip nepa⁵ do na
ppimdoippib. Apċanzil⁶ co n-a n-aipdpib, ip nepa⁷ do na
hainzlib: Uipcucep, ip nepa⁷ do na hapċainzlib⁸: Pocepcacep
ip nepa⁷ do Uipcucep: Ppincipacup, ip nepa⁷ do Pocepcacep:
Dominacionep, ip nepa do'n poppcemiul pil po'n pízpuide.
Fil[ec] ann dino Cponi co n-a n-dponzaid ainzel. Sloz⁹
hipuphin i cimċuaipc in¹⁰ pizpopaid¹⁰: Sapaphin (no Sepaphin)
co n-a ploz cuap, imon apdpiz peppin. Amlaid dino accac noi
n-zpaid nime, cen cnuċ, cen popmac.¹¹ Ip e imoppo a n-aipem
na ploz pin: idon, da pe pepcac ploz⁹ ceċ oen zpaid do na
zpadaib. Ocup ni pil neċ connipad na ploiz pin, aċc in piz
doppoine do nephni¹². Aca imoppo in c-apdpiz uapal uapaib¹³

---

²⁵ copċib.   ²⁶ Fail.   ²⁷ poilpi.   ²⁸ Fipdibad.   ²⁹ clappi.   ³⁰ caċ.
³¹-³¹ Findcoppaib.   ³² lecza.   ³³ Foponbai.   ³⁴ pizppocaib.   ³⁵ m-bile.
³⁶ cipi.   ³⁷ ppeċ.   ³⁸ nadpóiz.   ³⁹ cuipim.   ⁴⁰ poċpaiscaib.   ⁴¹ copucc.
⁴² domuin.   ⁴³ bpad.   ⁴⁴ coempaicip.
c.—¹ di.   ² poznid.   ³ epopdaib.   ⁴ poppaid.   ⁵ neppaim.   ⁶ apċanzeil.
⁷ neppam.   ⁸ -anzlib.   ⁹ pluaiz.   ¹⁰⁻¹⁰ ind pizpoppaid.   ¹¹ impopdac.
¹² nemphi.   ¹³⁻¹³ uapdaib uili.

* This line marks commencement of MS. column.

and they [are] ever-new with aromatic⁵ fruits of every kind⁵. There [b]
is therein felicity without weariness and satiety ever-constant; light
without waning and music without ceasing. There is therein also the
thing that satiates every host: to wit, the sound of the [heavenly]
grades and of the melodies and the perfume of the flowers. There are
therein many⁶ seats and many⁶ choirs and many⁶ melodies of every
choir. There is therein also much⁶ of liquors pleasant-tasting. There
are therein, likewise, many⁷ streams and [many] a kind of every plea-
sant-sweet liquor for the satiating of the hosts. There are therein also
many⁷ wells of wine, precious⁸ stones, golden⁸ thrones, many⁸,⁷ royal
streams, many⁸,⁶ large⁹ trees⁹, much⁸,⁶ wondrous land, many⁸,⁶ hundreds
of plains, many⁸,⁶ ranks and many⁶ hundreds of melodies that numbering
or telling attaineth not. There are therein also a hundred and four
[and] forty rewards before the face of God. Now, the children of
Adam from the beginning of the world to doom, they could not, all
of them, recount one reward of those.⁹

c. There is therein also the seat of the king all-powerful, in¹ the
centre of the chief city. Of pure² gold, in sooth, was made the regal
seat of the king, above the very high walls. The seat³ of the angels
is next to the chief doors. Archangels³ with their troops are⁴ next to
the Angels: Virtues³ are⁴ next to the Archangels; Powers³ are⁴ next
to Virtues: Principalities³ are⁴ next to Powers: Dominations³ are⁴
next to the footstool that is under the regal seat. Therein likewise
are Thrones with their throngs of angels. The host of the Cherubim
[is] around the royal seat: the Seraphim with their host [are] above,
around the high king himself. Thus, in sooth, are the nine grades of
heaven,—without jealousy, without envy. Now, this is the⁵ tale of
those hosts: to wit, twelve⁶ [and] sixty hosts in⁷ each grade of the

---

⁵⁻⁵ Lit., fruits of every fruit with perfume.
⁶ Lit., a great (number of, etc.): same idiom as in ⁴⁻⁴.
⁷ Lit., much of (ɔo, corruptly for ɔi, ɔe, used as a partitive).
⁸ *There is therein* (Ḟıl anɔ) is prefixed in the original.
⁹⁻⁹ Lit., trees of (i.e. trees as large as those that surround) a burgh.
⁹ There is an additional quatrain (ll. 521-524) in *S. R.*
c.—¹ Lit., upon.   ² Lit., red.   ³ Nom. abs. in the original.
⁴ Sing., according to native idiom, in the text.
⁵ *Their*, by prolepsis of the possessive, in the original.
⁶ Lit., two sixes.   ⁷ Lit., from (with partitive meaning).

[c] uile¹³ ⁊ n-a ṗíḡṗuiḋe ⁊ ⁊ n-a p̓ıḡṗoppuḋ.¹⁴ Iṗ e ḋıno poopḋaıḡ oṗ ın¹⁵ ṗloḡ¹⁵ p̓ın : ıḋon, ceol na ceėṗı ṗancc ṗínḋ pıċeċ ⁊ ıṗ eḋ ċanaıċ ḋo ḡṗeṗu—Sanccuṗ, Sanccuṗ, Sanccuṗ, Ḋomınuṗ Ḋeuṗ Sabaoċh. Iṗ e ḋıno poopḋaıḡ ın enlaıė n-alaınḋ pıl ṗoṗ nım; ıḋon, con canuc ceol comlan, cen eṗėṗa ⁊ con ṗaṗcaṗ ḋo coṗaḋ na n-ḋuıllepaḋ. Iṗ alaınḋ ḋıno ın¹⁶ enlaıė ṗın : ıḋon, ceċ eċċı ṗoṗ ceċ n-en¹⁷ ⁊ ceċ ceol ceċ¹⁸ eċċı¹⁸. Iṗ e ḋıno poopḋaıḡ cṗeċ na n-uan n-enḋacc ımon uan nemelnıḡċı nemloċċaċ ṗoṗ ımluaḋ ıaṗṗın ṗleıḃ; ıḋon, ceėṗaċa ⁊ ceċṗı mıle¹⁹ uan ennacc ı n-ḋıaıḋ ın¹⁵ uaın ṗın, con canaċ ṗıḋe ceol n-aḋampa ḋo ḡṗeṗ oc molaḋ ın Choımḋeḋ. Iṗ e ḋıno poopḋaıḡ claṗṗ ḋo na hoḡaıḃ cen elnıuḋ, con canuc ceol ı n-ḋıaıḋ ınn¹⁵ uaın eċṗoċċḡlaın ⁊ ṗıaċ comċoema, comluaċa ıṗın ṗleıḃ²⁰ ı n-ḋıaıḋ ınn¹⁵ uaın ⁊ anmunḋa a n-aċaṗ ṗcṗıḃėa ı n-a n-ḡnuıṗıḃ.

d. Ačaċ ımoṗṗo noı n-uıṗḋ ⁊ noı n-ḡṗaḋa ṗoṗ aınḡlıḃ. Ačḃeṗc ḋıno ın Coımḋıu ṗṗı Lucıṗeṗ¹ : "ḃıc² ṗoċ," ol ṗe, "aıṗḃṗıu³ ıle aṗċaınḡel⁴ ⁊ ċaḃaıṗ oıṗmıcıu⁵ ḋo Aḋam, ḋom' ċoımḋelḃaıḋṗea ṗen." " Nı ċıḃeṗṗa on," oṗ Lucıṗeṗ, "oıṗmıcıu⁵ ḋo Aḋam; uaıṗ am⁶ ṗıne⁷ ⁊ am uaıṗlıu olḋáṗ Aḋam ⁊ nımċaıṗḃeṗıuḃ ṗo'n ṗoṗaṗ⁸." Ačḃeṗc ın Coımḋe ṗṗıṗıum: " Nocomluaṗu ḋıno ın aıṗmıcın⁵ lımṗa, uaıṗ na ḋene ṗeıṗ Aḋaım." Ačḃeṗc ḋıno Lucıṗeṗ cṗıa uaıll ⁊ ḋıumuṗ : " ḃam⁹ ṗıḡ ṗea⁹," ol ṗe, " ṗoṗ aıṗḃṗıḃ ıle aınḡel ⁊ ḋoḡenaċ ṗoḡnam ḋam ⁊ ṗamaıḡṗeċ mo ċeḡḃaıṗ ı n-aıṗċeṗ ċuaıṗceṗċ nıme ılloċ ṗuḋomaın ⁊ nı ḃıa ṗıḡ¹⁰ aıle uaṗum." Conıḋ annṗın ṗocṗaṗcṗaḋ Lucıṗeṗ ḋe nım collın a ṗloḡ | cṗıa n-a ḋıumuṗ ⁊ ḋoṗımaṗc¹¹ ḋoċum n-ıṗıṗn¹²* cen cṗıċ, cen ṗoṗcenḋ. Ocuṗ

---

¹⁴ pıḡṗoṗṗuḋ.   ¹⁵⁻¹⁵ ın c-ṗlóḡ.   ¹⁶ ınḋ.   ¹⁷ en.   ¹⁸⁻¹⁸ caċa ḋen heıċċe.
¹⁹ mılı.   ²⁰ c-ṗleıḃ.
d.—(IV.) ¹ Lucıṗuṗ.   ² ḃıaıċ.   ³ aıṗḃṗı.   ⁴ -anḡel.   ⁵ aıṗmıcıu.   ⁶ ım.
⁷ ṗınıu.   ⁸ ṗóṗuṗ.   ⁹⁻⁹ ḃam ṗı.   ¹⁰ ṗı.   ¹¹ ḋoṗımmaṗc.   ¹² n-ıṗṗıṗn.

* Here and in **h**, the MS. contraction reads n-ıṗoṗn. Similarly, in ıṗṗıṗn (**k, l, o**).

grades. And there is no one that could know those hosts, except the [c] king who made them from nothing. Now, is the noble high-king above them all, in his regal seat and in his regal position[6]. It is He that ordered over that host the chant of the fair four score and it is this they sing continually—Holy, Holy, Holy, Lord God of Sabaoth. It is He also that ordered the beauteous flock[9] of birds[9] that is in[1] heaven; namely, that they sing a perfect song, without ceasing and that they be satiated with the fruit of the foliage. Beauteous, indeed, is that flock[9] of birds[9]: namely, one hundred wings[10] upon each bird and one hundred melodies[11] in[12] each wing.[12] It is He also ordered the flock of the innocent lambs around the undefiled, faultless Lamb, to move upon the mountain: namely, forty and four thousand innocent[13] lambs[13] behind that Lamb, so that they sing a wondrous melody continually, a-praising of the Lord. It is He, too, that ordered the choir of the virgins without defilement, so that they sing melody behind the Lamb pure-shining. And they [are] equally comely, equally swift on the mountain, behind the Lamb and the name[14] of their Father [is] written on[15] their countenances.

d. There are also nine orders and nine grades in[1] the angels. Now, said the Lord to Lucifer: "There shall be under thee," quoth He, "many troops of archangels and[2] give reverence to Adam, to my own very likeness." "I will not give, indeed," said Lucifer, "reverence to Adam; for I am senior and I am nobler than Adam and I will not place myself under the junior." Said the Lord unto him: "You shall not merit reverence with me, since you do not the will of Adam." But said Lucifer, through haughtiness and pride: "I will be king myself," quoth he, "over many troops of angels and they will make submission to me and build my dwelling in the north-east of heaven, in a deep place and there shall not be another king over me." So that then was cast Lucifer from heaven with the full tale of his

---

[6] Three quatrains (ll. 569–580) follow in *S. R.* In addition, the order of the *birds* and the *Lamb* is inverted. The treatment is likewise more diffuse. The poem concludes with eight verses (ll. 625–666) upon heaven.

[9–9] The textual word (enlait) is a collective.

[10] Lit., of wings (part. gen.). [11] Lit., of melodies (part. gen.).
[12–12] Lit., of each wing. [13–13] Part. gen. in the text.
[14] *Names* in the original. [15] Lit., in.

d.—[1] Lit., upon. [2] The conjunction has here a conditional force, "provided that."

[**d**] Atberut na scribenda[13] co fuil mile[14] bliadan o cruthugud in aingil conice a tairmtectur. Atberat araile scribenda ir tri huairi dec collet o cruthugud in aingil co a tairmtecht, ut dixit poeta:

> Letuair ir tri huaire dec,
> Ir fir ir ni himerbrec,
> O cruthugud domain dil
> Co himarbur in aingil.
>
> Uair ar medon lai cen locht,
> Indirimm co réid, rodocht,
> Re Eua rin i parrthur
> Ir Adaim ria n-imarbur.
>
> Oen uball do'n aball ain
> Dochoirmirc Dia cen dodáil;
> Rorbean Eua, bord in brec,
> Adam, rodait a certlet.—Letuair.

Dorigne[15] imorro in rig forrad rutach ar túr do duine, idon, Parthur[16] co n-a thortib ⁊ co n-a ilceolaib. Ocur dino foordaig tobur[17] na cethri rrut: idon, rrut fína ⁊ rrut olai ⁊ rrut lemnachta ⁊ rrut mela, fri fárad na noemanmand.[18] Ocur dorat ainm for cech rrut fo leit dib: idon, Firron, Geon, Tibrir, Euphaten. Firron in olai ⁊ rair rniger; [Geon in lemnacht ⁊ fo thuaid rniger;*] Tibrir in fín ⁊ riar rniger; Euphaten in mil ⁊ fo dear[19] rniger. Mur dergoir dino fil atimcell Parrthair.

e. Ir annride tra forruthad Adam ria n-denam imarbair do. Tri trath dino bui[1] corp Adaim cen anmain do thabairt ind, oc[2] fiugrad[3] erergi Crirt, co rahordaiged ainm do iarum o na cethri pedlannaib.[4] It e dino a n-anmundride: idon,

---

[13] enna. [14] mili. (VI.) [15] dorigni. [16] Parthur. [17] torur.
[18] noebanman. [19] der.

e.—[1] bai. [2] ic. [3] figrad. [4] fetglannaib.

---

* The omission of this sentence was doubtless owing to homœoteleuton—a fruitful source of lacunæ in transcripts.

hosts, through his pride and he was thrust into hell without limit, [d] without end. And the writers say that there are a thousand years from formation of the angel to his transgression. Other³ writers say it is thirteen hours and a half from formation of the angel to his transgression, as said the poet:

> Half an hour and three hours [and] ten,
> It is true and [it is] not a very great falsehood,
> From formation of the world pleasant
> To the offence of the angel.
>
> An hour beyond⁴ mid-day, without defect,
> I tell plainly, very precisely,
> That [was] the time of Eve in Paradise
> And of Adam before [they committed] offence.
>
> One apple of the apples⁵ fair,
> God commanded⁶ not to partake [thereof];
> Eve took it, foolish the decision,
> Adam, he consumed its exact half.—Half an hour.⁷

Now, the king made a pleasant place at first for man, namely, Paradise with its fruits and with its many melodies. And moreover he prepared the spring of the four streams: namely, the stream of wine and the stream of oil and the stream of new milk and the stream of honey, to satisfy the holy souls. And he placed a name upon each stream of them separately, to wit, Phisson, Gehon, Tibris and Euphrates. Phisson [is] the oil and eastward it flows; [Gehon, the new milk and northward it flows⁹;] Tibris, the wine and westward it flows; Euphrates the honey and southward it flows. A wall of pure¹⁰ gold likewise [it is] that is around Paradise.

e. It is there indeed was formed Adam before¹ his commission of offence¹. Now, three periods was the body of Adam without a soul being put in it, to typify the resurrection of Christ, until a name was arranged for him afterwards from the four stars. These are their

---

³ From this to the end of the quatrains is omitted in *S. R.* ⁴ Lit., on.
⁵ aballl is employed collectively in this place. ⁶ Lit., prohibited.
⁷ The repetition of the opening words is to show that the poem is completed.
⁸ Seven quatrains (ll. 965-992) follow in *S. R.*
⁹ Five and a-half verses (ll. 1013-1030) are inserted here in *S. R.* ¹⁰ Lit., red.
e.—¹⁻¹ Lit., before the doing of offence by him.

48   LEBAR BREC.

[e] Anatale⁵ in t-oirtep; Oirir in t-iaptep; Arctor⁶ in tuair-
cept; Mirimbria⁷ in beirsept, ut bixit [poeta]:

    Anatale,* in t-oirtep tair;
    Oirir, iaptep 'n-a agaib;
    Arctor, in tuaircept tnuag, tepcc;
    Ir Mirimbria,* in bersept.

It he inro anmanna na cethi pot bia n-bernab Adam : ibon,
Malon, Arton, Biblon, Agore. Do Malon bino a ceanb;
bo Arton a uct; bo Biblon a bru; bo Agore a corpa. Ir e
tra cet rabaicc atconnairc Adam iar tabaipt a anma inb,
ibon, Slebti Pariath. Ocur bo'n octmab arna uattarac
cleib a leti beir Adaim boronta Eua, inbur co m-[b]ab
cutruma bo hi. Ocur ir e oen pot bo talmain tar na tainic
biliu, ibon, Golgotha: ibon, pongc mebonac [MS. mebononac]
in bomain i n-Ierupalem, oc piugrab Crirt bo crocab iartain.
Ir aire bino boronta corp Adaim bo'n talmain coitcinb, uair
roperr co n-elnigritea ⁊ co m-[b]ab bo talmain gloin nemel-
nigti Parbair bognetea corp Muire iartain ⁊ co m-bab o
corp Muire nogenritea corp Crirt, iar ririnbe na Screptra
noerh ⁊ na pata ⁊ na n-uaralatrac arcena. Ir e bino
ainmm in luice in rocruibab Adam, ibon, in agro Damurgo.
Co rotairmbemnig arrein i Partur. Noi mir bino o'n uair
arroet⁸ Adam anmain co roteireb Eua ar a toeb. Ocur ir
ro'n aicneb rin bir cec baunrcal bia ril torpac orin ille. Ir
annrin bino porabib⁹ in Coimbiu in n-aiterc ra pri hAdam ⁊
Eua ar oen. "Toimlib," ol re, "torti¹⁰ Parbuir uile, cenmota
oen cranb¹¹ namá, co perabair¹²," ol re, "bet¹³ rom' rmact ra
⁊ rom' cumacta: cen crine, cen galur¹⁴ ⁊ bul buib por neam i
n-bar corraib i n-oeir¹⁵ triccaibe¹⁶." Roporrmctig¹⁷ bino Lucifer
(ibon, biabul)† rri hAdam. Dearb lair ir e Adam nobertea
innem bar a erri.

---

⁵ Anatole.   ⁶ Arcon.   ⁷ Mirrinia.   ⁸ pohet.   (VII.) ⁹ noradbe.
¹⁰ toirti.   ¹¹ cnann.   ¹² ferrabair.   ¹³ bit.   ¹⁴ galar.
¹⁵ n-aer.   ¹⁶ triccaige.   (VIII.) ¹⁷ ba ropmtccc.

* In the scansion, e of Anatale and a of Mirimbria are to be elided.
† These two words are an interlinear gloss, placed above *Lucifer*.

names: namely, Anatole ('Ἀνατολή), the East[2]; Dusis (Δύσις), the [e] West; Arctos (Ἄρκτος), the North; Mesembria[3] (Μεσημβρία), the South, as said (the poet):

> Anatole, the East, easterly;
> Dusis, the West, opposite it;
> Arctos, the North, wretched, poor;
> And Messembria, the South.

These are the names of the four sods of which was made Adam: namely, Malon, Arton, Biblon, Agore. Of Malon, to wit, his head; of Arton, his breast; of Biblon, his belly; of Agore, his feet. This is the first sight Adam saw after the putting of his soul into him, namely, the mountains of Pariath. And of the eighth upper rib of the breast of the right side of Adam was made Eve, so that she should be equal to him. And this is the one sod of earth over which did not come the deluge, namely, Golgotha: that is, the middle point of the world in Jerusalem, to tipify that[4] Christ was to be crucified[4] [thereon] afterwards. Now, it is for this [reason] the body of Adam was made of the common earth, for it was known that it would be defiled and in order that afterwards the body of Mary should be made from the pure, undefiled land of Paradise and in order that from the body of Mary should be born the body of Christ, according[5] to the truth of the holy Scripture and of the prophets and of the patriarchs besides. Howbeit, this is the name of the place in which was formed Adam, namely, in the land of Damascus. And[6] he passed therefrom into Paradise. Nine months, indeed, from the time Adam received a soul until issued Eve from his side. And it is according to that precedent is every woman of her seed pregnant from that hither. It is then, indeed, spoke the Lord this precept to Adam and Eve together. "Eat," said He, "all the fruits of Paradise, save one tree alone, that ye may know," said He, "that[7] ye are[7] under my sway and under my power. [Ye shall be] without old-age, without illness and ye[8] shall go[8] to heaven in your bodies at[9] the age of thirty[9]." Now, Lucifer

---

[2] The equivalents and the stanza are not in *S. R.*, which gives instead four quatrains (ll. 1061-1076) upon the creation of Eve.
[3] That is, the initials of the four words, Anatole, Dusis, Arctos, Mesembria, spell ADAM.   [4-4] Lit., Christ to be crucified.
[5] Lit., after.   [6] Lit., so that.   [7-7] Lit., [ye] to be.
[8-8] Lit., going for [= by] ye.   [9-9] Lit., in thirtieth age.

f. Na huile¹ anmand² notecht cpí ┐ betaid, dorrat in Coimdiu a fomamur do Adam ┐ ir e norrollamnaigend³. In tan dino notegtir⁴ rloig na rect nime dotum in apdrig, teiged⁵ dino cet anmanda for bit dotum Adaim dia anoir ┐ dia⁶ adrad ┐ dia oirriciud⁷. Ir e dino in Coimde normattad⁸ iat, co m-bitir for⁹ dreit⁹ Parrdair¹⁰ amuig fri dreit Adaim. Teged cat dib iarum dia addud¹¹, iar m-bennatud¹² do Adam. Dui dino diabul oc a tur indur nomellrad re Adam. Ir hi dino comairle fuair Luciper: idon, dul immerc na n-anmand¹³ fria¹⁴ Parbur amuig¹⁵ a n-ettair. Conid andrin fuair in natraig rettair tait. "Nir' toir imorro," or diabul fririn natraig, "dodet¹⁶* ri¹⁶ amuig¹⁵ ar t'amainre ┐ ar do tuaitli¹⁷. Ar ir mor in col," ol re, "rorar¹⁸ na n-dúl¹⁹ do airmitniugud retut ┐ ni bud mor in tin mannur²⁰ no gluaratt do tabairt fair; uair ir turca²¹ rotturmed²² tu fen oltar Adam ┐ nir' toir duit do tairbert fo'n²³ rorar²³," ol diabul fririn natraig. "Geib²⁴ mo tomairle²⁵," ol re, "┐ denamm cotat ┐ cairder²⁶ ┐ na heirg for amur Adaim ┐ tabair inad damra it'turr co n-detram, 'n-ar²⁷ n-dir, dotum²⁸ Eua ┐ erailem²⁹ forri³⁰ torad in troind³¹ aurgarti³² do tomailt, co rurerali³³ Eua for Adam iarum in tetna. Ocur ticrait iar rin dar timna a tigerna³⁴ ┐ nirbia a n-grad oc Dia dia eri ┐ tartraider a Parbur immat iat iarum." "Cia lóg³⁵ dino," ol in natir, "ardomtara³⁶ dia tind rin, idon, comaittreib duit im' turr do admilliud Eua ┐ Adaim?" "Rotbia dino," ol diabul, "idon, ar comainmniugud³⁷, ar n-dir, dogrer iar rin."

---

f.—¹ huili. ² anmanna. ³ noropdaiged. ⁴ teigtir. ⁵ do ticed. ⁶ fria. ⁷ airriciud. ⁸ normattartar. 9-9 ar d[n]eid. ¹⁰ Parduir. ¹¹ addai. ¹² -tad. ¹³ n-anmanna. ¹⁴ fri. ¹⁵ immuic. 16-16 dobit. ¹⁷ tuaitle. ¹⁸ oror. ¹⁹ n-duli. ²⁰ mandrad. ²¹ toiretu. ²² notuirtiged. 23-23 fo'nd orror. ²⁴ Gaib. ²⁵ tomarle. ²⁶ cardder. ²⁷ ar. ²⁸ adotum (the prothesis is for the metre). ²⁹ aurailem. ³⁰ fuirri. ³¹ trainn. ³² -gairti. ³³ rohepala. ³⁴ -nai. ³⁵ luag. ³⁶ nomta. ³⁷ n-anmnigud.

* The mark of aspiration is wanting in the Lithograph.

(that is, the devil) envied[10] Adam. [It was] certain to him [that] it [e] is Adam that would be taken into heaven in[11] his place[11].

f. All the animals that possessed body and life, the Lord gave them in subjection to Adam and it is he that used to govern them. Now, the time the hosts of the seven heavens used to come unto the high-king, every being in[1] the world used also to come unto Adam, to honour him and to adore him and to delight him. It is the Lord indeed that used to compel them so that they used to be in sight of Paradise, outside, in the sight of Adam. Each of them used to go afterwards to his dwelling, after paying respects to Adam. Now, was the devil a-thinking how he could deceive Adam. This, then, is the council that Lucifer found : namely, to go amidst the animals [that were] hard by Paradise, on the outside. So that then found he the serpent [suited to his intent] beyond every [other animal.] "It was not just indeed," quoth the devil to the serpent, "to have thee outside for thy subtlety and for thy cunning. For great is the wrong," quoth he, " the younger of the beings to be honoured beyond thee and it were not a great crime to inflict destruction or temptation upon him ; for sooner wast thou begotten thyself than Adam and it were not right for thee to place thyself under the junior," quoth the devil to the serpent. "Take my counsel," quoth he, "and make we covenant and friendship and go thou not to[2] wait on Adam[2] and give a place to me in thy body, that we may go, both[3] of us[3], unto Eve and enjoin upon her to eat the fruit of the forbidden tree, so that Eve may enjoin the same upon Adam afterwards. And thereby[4] shall they transgress the command of their master and God[5] will not love them[5] after that and they shall be driven from out Paradise afterwards." "What reward, now," quoth the serpent, "is there for me on account of that, namely, co-dwelling for thee in my body to destroy Eve[6] and Adam[6]?" "There shall be for thee, indeed," quoth the devil, "[this] namely, our being named together, both[7] of us[7], constantly after that."

---

[10] Lit., envied against.   [11-11] Lit., after him.
f.—[1] Lit., upon.   [2-2] Lit., upon attack of Adam (an idiomatic expression).
[3-3] Lit., in our duality.   [4] Lit., after that.
[5-5] Lit., there will not be their love with God (possessive used objectively).
[6] Gen., governed by vbl. sb. (the infinitive), in the original.
[7-7] Lit., our duality.

g. Annrin porlai¹ Lucifer i n-veilb na naṫrac ⁊ vocoiv² cu vorur³ Parvu[i]r, cor'zart in⁴ naṫir amuiz⁵ ⁊ aṫbert: "A Eua, a ben Avaim, vena mo acallam," ol ri. "Ni huain vam acallam neic," ol Eua, "ar atu⁶ oc⁷ fricailem⁸ na n-uile anmanv⁹ [n-i]nvlizṫec⁹." "Mara ṫú Eua, ir fort erailim re mo lerr vo vénam," ol in naṫir. "Tan¹⁰ natbí¹¹ Avam ínv, ir mire coimetur¹² Parvur¹³ ⁊ vozní frertul na n-uli anmann¹⁴," ol ri. "Cia leṫ¹⁵ ṫeit Avam uait," ol in naṫir, "in tan natbí¹¹ fri frertal na n-anmanv?" "Vo avrav in vuileman," ol Eua. "Avair frim, a Eua," ol in naṫir, "in maiṫ var¹⁶ m-beṫa i Parvur¹³?" "Ni cuinzim¹⁷ ní ir mo," ol Eua, "olvar a fil i Parvur, to n-veṫram i n-ar corraib¹⁸ vocum ricív. Uair cec maiṫ voronraic¹⁹ Via i Parvur¹³ to fil for ar comar, acṫ aen²⁰ crann nama. Ocur pohaiṫnev vino cen ní vo ṫorav in croinvrin²¹ vo caiṫem. Ocur pozebav frinv via caiṫmir co fuivbemir var." Aṫbert in naṫir fri Eua: "Ni mo var firr, no var n-zliccur oltar cec anmanna vorb invlizṫec arcena ⁊ ni ṫuc var tizerna fir uilc vib, acṫ fir maitura namá: ir mor var²² n-erbaiv²² ⁊ ata 'za var²³ tozaeṫav²⁴ in tan ·natleicc²⁵ vuib ní vo ṫorav in croinv ic ata firr uilc ⁊ maitura vo ṫomailṫ²⁶," ol in naṫir. "Ocur ir ar oireṫur²⁷ in croinvrin²⁸ na[tleicc] a ṫomailṫ vuib, arvaiz na raib [invb]tleṫṫ occaib²⁹ firr maitura ⁊ uilc," ol in naṫir. "Na³⁰ ba vlomav vuit,³⁰ eirz vo'n | crunn³¹ via fromav ⁊ rotbia oc'tizerna fen firr uilc ⁊ maiṫura, acṫ to tomli aen uball vo'n crunv," ol in naṫir. Aṫbert Eua frirr naṫraiz: "Civ maiṫ vo ṫomairle ⁊ vo³² invtleṫṫ,³² ni lamaim³³ vul curin³⁴ crand, ar na roeblar³⁵." Conuv ann aṫbert Eua: "Tair fen, a naṫir, curin³⁶ crand³⁶ ⁊ tuc vam in uball,³⁷ to rorannar etram ⁊ Avam, to feram in ba fír cec ni rotria ve."

---

g.—¹ roramlai. ² vovoeṫaiv (to suit the metre). ³ vorop. ⁴ inv. ⁵ immaiz. ⁶ itu. ⁷ ic. ⁸ -alim. ⁹⁻⁹ n-anmanna n-invlizṫec. ¹⁰ In tan. ¹¹ navbi. ¹² comeṫar. ¹³ -vor. ¹⁴ n-anm[ann]a. ¹⁵ leit. ¹⁶ for. ¹⁷ -zem. ¹⁸ corr. ¹⁹ vorrorrut. ²⁰ oen. ²¹ crand. ²²⁻²² for n-errbaiv. ²³ for. ²⁴ tozáer. ²⁵ navleic. ²⁶ ṫormailt. ²⁷ arrancar. ²⁸ crann. ²⁹ accaib. ³⁰⁻³⁰ Nabvat volam. ³¹ crannn. ³²⁻³² t'inctiucṫ. ³³ lamur. ³⁴ corin. ³⁵ hérvalur. ³⁶⁻³⁶ vo'n crannn. ³⁷ uvull.

g. Then cast Lucifer himself into the figure of the serpent and went to the door of Paradise and[1] the serpent called outside and said: "O Eve, O wife of Adam, address[2] me[2]," quoth it[1]. "[There] is not time for me to address any one," quoth Eve, "for I am attending all the lawless beings." "If thou art Eve, it is upon thee I enjoin to assist me," quoth the serpent. "The time Adam is not here, it is I care for Paradise and perform attendance on[4] all the beings," quoth she. "What direction goeth Adam from thee," quoth the serpent, "the time he is not in attendance on[4] the beings?" "To adoring of the Creator," quoth Eve." "Say to me, O Eve," quoth the serpent, "is [it] good, your life in Paradise?" "We ask not aught that is more," quoth Eve, "than what is in Paradise, until we shall go in our bodies unto the kingdom. For every good [that] God made in Paradise, it is at our disposal, save one tree alone. And he commanded [us], indeed, not to eat a whit of the fruit of that tree. And he assured us if we should eat, we should[5] die.[5]" Said the serpent unto Eve: "Not greater [is] your knowledge or your acuteness than [that of] every ignorant, lawless being besides and your Lord gave not knowledge of evil to ye, but knowledge of good alone: great is your deficiency, and he is deceiving[6] ye[6], when he does not allow ye to eat a whit of the fruit of the tree that has the knowledge of evil and of good," quoth the serpent. "And it is for pre-eminence of that tree that he does not allow ye to eat it, in order that ye may not understand the knowledge of good and of evil," quoth the serpent. "Do not refuse; go to the tree to try it and you shall have from your own Lord knowledge of evil and of good, provided you eat one apple of the tree," quoth the serpent. Said Eve to the serpent: "Though good thy counsel and thy intelligence, I dare not go to the tree, lest I die." So that then said Eve: "Come thyself, O serpent, to the tree and give me the apple, that I may divide between me and Adam, that we may know whether everything be true that shall be from it." So then said the serpent to Eve: "Open before me the door of Paradise, that I may give the apple

---

g.—[1] Lit., so that. [2-2] Lit., make my addressing (possessive used objectively).

[3] Lit., she; naċıp (serpent) being feminine.

[4] Lit., of. [5-5] Lit., should get death.

[6-6] Lit., at your deceiving (same idiom as in [2-2]).

LEBAR BREC.

[g] Conid ann atbert in nathir fri hEua: "Orlaic remum[38] dofur Pardu[i]s,[39] co tucar in uball[37] duit do'n crund[40]." "Cia orlaicer[41] dofur Pardu[i]s," ar Eua, "ꞇ cia éir ind, nirbia[42] fuirec fort ann, act co tuca in uball[43] dam do'n crund[40]." Atbert in nathir fri Eua: "Act co tucar in uball[37] do'n crund, dogena dib deochair iter olc ꞇ maith ꞇ dofagara[44] imach iarsin ꞇ nimtair[45] cacht na cuidrech[46]."

h. Orlaicid[1] iarum Eua in dofur rerin nathraig, co riact 'n-a[2] rit for amur in craind hergairche, co tarut in[3] uball[3] de ꞇ dorat do Eua, co[4] n-duaid[4] a leth ꞇ dorat anaill do Adam. Orund dino a tuaid[5] Eua in uball rin ꞇ pocloechla[6] a delb ꞇ a cruth ꞇ dorochair iar rin in tlacht taitnemach dui impe di; cor'gab[7] crith ꞇ fuacht ꞇ ba hingnad lee a beth[8] lomnacht[9]. Conid ann roleic guth n-aduathmar for Adam. Dodechaid dino Adam fo gairm Eua ꞇ for' ingnad lair a beth lomnacht.[10] Atbert Adam fri Eua: "Nico[11] n-roelair amal[11] atai, a n-ingnair do thlachta ꞇ cia sorden ditt?" "Noco n-ebér[12] frit[13]," ol Eua, "cu n-etha leth in[14] uaillrea[15] fil im' láim." Gabaid Adam dino a leth in[14] uaill[16] ꞇ pothomail, cu torchair a thlacht de, co m-bui tarnocht[17], feib robui Eua. Conid ann atbert Adam: "A Eua," ol re, "cia[18] rotboethaig[19] ꞇ romboethaidrea imalle frit? Ir e inti cetna," ol re, "idon, Lucifer ꞇ demit ferta coidhce fri raethaib ꞇ gallraib examlaib," ol re. Atbert Eua: "In nathir rotguid[20] dimm[21] allecud[22] i Pardur[23] ꞇ iar tidecht[24] di ind, dorat ri dam uball[16] do'n crand[25] hergarthi[26] ꞇ atbert[27] frim[28]: "A Eua," ol ri, "geib uaimm[29] in[3] uball ra[3], co raid ocut deochair maithiura la hulc. Ocur roind[30] atrut[31] ꞇ Adam," ol ri. "Rogabura[32] in uball[33] iarum ꞇ nico n-fetur

---

[38] róm. [39] -uir. [40] craunn. [41] orlac. [42] nirbia. [43] uboll.
[44] doreg. [45] manimthair. [46] cuimrech.

h.—[1] ro orlaic (pret.). [2] for a. [3-3] inn ubull. [4-4] dofuaid. (IX.) [5] duad. [6] rochlaemcli. [7] rorgab. [8] bith. [9] imnocht. [10] -nocht.
[11-11] Noco n-alaind mar. [12] n-eber. [13] rit. [14] ind. [15] ubuill re.
[16] ubuill. [17] lomnucht. [18] ti (t, by oversight, for c). [19] rotbaitig.
[20] gaid. [21] dim. [22] a ticthu. [23] -or. [24] tícthain. [25] craunn.
[26] aurgairthe. [27] atrudairt. [28] rim. [29] uaim. [30] raind. [31] etrut.
[32] -rra. [33] ubull.

to thee from the tree." "Though opened be the door of Paradise," [g] quoth Eve, "and though you come into it, there shall be no tarrying for thee therein, save until you give the apple to me from the tree." Said the serpent to Eve: "Provided I give [thee] the apple from the tree, it will make for ye distinction between evil and good, and I will go out after that, if[6] [neither] subjection nor bondage come to me.

h. Afterwards opens Eve the door for the serpent, so that it[1] went running to[2] reach[2] the tree forbidden and[3] took the apple from it and gave to Eve, so that she ate the half and gave the other to Adam. Suddenly in sooth, when ate Eve that apple, changed her figure and her shape and there fell off her after that the beauteous garb that was around her, so that she got shivering and cold and it was a wonder to her to be stark-naked. So that then sent she forth a dreadful cry towards Adam. Thereupon went Adam at the call of Eve and it was a wonder to him her being stark-naked. Said Adam unto Eve: "You will not endure [to be] as thou art, without thy raiment and who took it from thee?" "I will not say to thee," quoth Eve, "until thou shalt eat half of this apple that is in my hand." Then takes Adam the half of the apple and ate, so that his raiment fell off him[3] and he was stark-naked, as was Eve. So that then said Adam: "O Eve," quoth he, "who hath deceived thee and deceived me myself along with thee? It is the same," quoth he, "namely, Lucifer and we shall be henceforth ever [exposed] to various labours and diseases," quoth he. Said Eve: "The serpent that asked of me to allow it[5] into Paradise and, after its[6] coming[6] therein, it[1] gave me an apple from the tree forbidden and said to me : 'O Eve,' quoth it[1]: 'take from me this apple, that thou mayest have [knowledge of the] difference of good from[7] evil. And divide [it] between thyself and Adam,' quoth it. Myself took the apple afterwards and I knew not [that] harm [would] be therefrom, until I saw[8] myself to be stark-naked and I knew not evil before

---

[6] Lit., and may ... not come (the copulative = condition, "provided that").
h.—[1] Lit., she.   [2-2] Lit., upon attack (of).   [3] Lit., so that.
[5] "Her" in the original.   [6] Lit., coming for (= by) her.   [7] Lit., with.
[8] Lit., saw it [namely], myself, etc. (neut. pron. = object. of *saw*, used proleptically).

[**h**] herċoıc do beṫ de, co nur[ḟ]acca³⁴ mo beṫ⁸ lomnaċc¹⁰ ⁊ nı ḟecar olc³⁵ remırın. Ir hı ın naċır rın," ol Eua, "ronmell,³⁶ a Adaım." Conıd and aċberc ḟrı Eua: "Nı³⁷ mananacar³⁷ duıc ḟrıċ' uball³⁸ ⁊ ır reıll³⁹ dún aca ar n-dual ḟrı mor olc ferca ın can acam lomnaċċ.⁴⁰ Ocur dıno aca ní ır mera⁴¹ dún de, ıdon, rcarad⁴² cuırr ḟrı hanmaın ⁊ na cuırr do leżad ı calum⁴³ ⁊ ın anımm⁴⁴ do dul doċum ıfırn⁴⁵ cen crıċ." Doroċaır dıno dıbrıum a claċċ ındrın. Lınaır ıar rın crombaċc la cruaıże ıac, co m-ba doċraıd leo a cuırr cen fıal ımpu oc⁴⁶ a n-ımdícen.⁴⁶

i. Ir annrın dıno ba reıll¹ do ċaċ dıb daċ cuırr araıle. Conıd annrın cucrac duılle² na raılme³ for a rcáċ a ḟelı.⁴ Nı ḟrıċ dıno ı Pardur crand forra m-beċ duılle, aċc ın⁵ fıccommna.⁶ Conıd annrın ıccualad Adam żuc Mıċıl arċanżıl oc⁷ a rad ḟrı Żabrıel⁸ aınżel: "Seıncer," ol re, "corn⁹ ⁊ rcocc foccra lıb, co cluınncer fo na reċċ nımıb¹⁰ ⁊ ercıd¹¹ uıle¹² ı combaıl dar n-duıleman. Ocur ercıd uıle, a ḟlożu ⁊ a aırdrıu aınżel na reċċ nıme, co n-deċraıd mar aen P. 111 b. rıa dar n-duılemaın doċum Pardu[ı]r." | Dolluıd ın Coımdıd ċuca ıarum, co n-a morḟlóż¹³ laır, co Parcur¹⁴ ⁊ clara aınżel oc claırcecul ımme. Derıd¹⁵ dıno hıruphır oc rıżruıde ın⁵ arbrıż ı Parcur, ıc c-ermedon Parcaır, baıle ı ca crand¹⁶ beċad. Locc ruċaċ, dıno, errıde hı Parcur. Rorernad dıno ceċ rloż¹³ dıb ıarum ı n-a freıċ ⁊ ceċ żrad co n-a aınżlıb ımme. Ocur derıd¹⁵ ın rıż¹⁷ fen ı n-a rıżruıde for hıruphır.¹⁸ Ir ann dıno roloıżrec¹⁹ croınd ⁊ fıodbuıd²⁰ Parċu[ı]r²¹ co lar ċalman ar oırmıcın²² ın duıleman. Conıd annrın aċberc Dıa ḟrı muıncer nıme: "In cualu[b]arrı²³," ol re, "ın żnım doroıne²⁴ Adam, ıdon, mo ḟarużudra ⁊ cıdecc car²⁵ mo ċımnaı²⁶ ⁊ car²⁵ mo forcecul²⁷?" Ir and dıno doċoıd²⁸ Adam ⁊ Eua for rcaċ ın croınd,²⁹ for ceċed

---

³⁴ co facca. ³⁵ olcc. ³⁶ ronmıll. ³⁷⁻³⁷ nımanḟacamar. ³⁸ udoll. ³⁹ rcıl. ⁴⁰ noċc. ⁴¹ merru. ⁴² rcarċaın. ⁴³ calmaın. ⁴⁴ anmaın. ⁴⁵ n-ıffırn. ⁴⁶⁻⁴⁶ dıa n-ımdícen.

i.—¹ ḟeıl. ² duıllı. ³ ralme (corrected into fıċċ). ⁴ ḟeılc. ⁵ ınd. ⁶ fıcomna. ⁷ co. ⁸ -al. ⁹ cornn. ¹⁰ nıme. ¹¹ heırżıd. ¹² huılı. ¹³ -rluaż. ¹⁴ -dur. ¹⁵ derrıd. ¹⁶ crann. ¹⁷ rı. ¹⁸ -ḟeın. ¹⁹ -rcd. ²⁰ ınd [ḟ]ıddad. ²¹ -duır. ²² aırmıcıu. ²³ cualabarrı. ²⁴ dorıżnı. ²⁵ dar. ²⁶ -na. ²⁷ -cal. ²⁸ dodeċaıd. ²⁹ crainn.

that.⁹ It is that serpent," quoth Eve, "that deceived us, O [h] Adam." So then said he unto Eve: "It has not succeeded for thee respecting thy apple and it is clear to us our destiny is for much evil henceforth, now[10] that we are stark-naked. And, moreover, there is a thing that is worse for us from it: namely, separation of the body from the soul and the bodies to decay in earth and the soul to go unto hell without end." Then indeed fell from them their raiment. After that heaviness with wretchedness fills them, so that it was miserable to[11] them [to have] their bodies without a veil around them to[12] protect them[12].

1. It is then, indeed, manifest to each of them the colour of the body of the other. So that then took they foliage of the palm for the concealment of their nakedness. Now, there was not found in Paradise a tree upon which was foliage, except the sycamore. So that then heard Adam the voice of Michael, the Archangel, a-saying[1] to Gabriel the Angel: "Let there be sounded," quoth he, "the horn and trumpet of summoning by ye, that they be heard throughout the seven heavens and go ye all into the assembly of your Creator. And go ye all, O hosts and O troops of angels of the seven heavens, that ye may proceed together with your Creator unto Paradise." Went the Lord to them afterwards, with his great host along with him, to Paradise and the choirs of angels a-quiring around him. Then sit the Cherubim by the royal seat of the high king in Paradise, at the very centre of Paradise, the place wherein is the tree of life. A pleasant place, in sooth, this in Paradise. Ranged indeed was each host of them afterwards in its rank and each grade with its angels around it. And sits the king himself in his royal seat above the Cherubim. It is there, indeed, bent the trees and forests of Paradise to the level of the earth, for reverence of the Creator. So that then said God to the people of heaven: "Have ye heard," quoth He, "the deed Adam did, namely, to[2] affront me[2] and to transgress my commandment and my precept?" It is then, indeed, went Adam and Eve under the shade of the tree, upon fleeing before the voice of the Creator. So that there spoke

---

⁹ A quatrain (ll. 1337-1340) is inserted here in *S. R.*   [10] Lit., the time.
[11] Lit., with.   [12-12] Lit., at their protecting.
1.—[1] Lit., at its saying; the possessive, = object of vb., being employed proleptically.   [2-2] Lit., my affronting.

[1] re guċ in buileman. Conid ann atbert Adam in n-aiterc n-erċoiteċ ra, idon: "Ma roraraiger[30] do rmaċt, ir i in ben doratairiu dam rorarlaig[31] rorm,[31] idon, Eua." Atbert dia rri[32] hAdam[32]: "Uair naċ atmai[33] do ċin," ol re, "betit do ċland tria biċu a n-imperain fritt. Ocur dia[34] m-[b]ad[34] aiċrige[35] dognetea[36], dollogfaitea duit a n-defnair ⁊ dobetea irin maiċiur cetna."

k. Ir andrin dino rororconzair[1] dia for a aingliu[2]: "Cuirid[3]," ol re, "Adam a Partur[4] doċum in talman coitċind deor." Annrin dino rodlomrat aingil fri Eua ⁊ Adam a Partur amaċ, co tanic doib iarum, idon, dognai ⁊ domenma ⁊ dommai ⁊ gortai ⁊ luinde ⁊ torri ⁊ gallra hile examla. Conid ann atbert Adam fri haingliu nime: "Lecid fuireċ bicc dam," ol re, "co m-blarind[5] ní do torud ċroind[6] betad." "Ni blairfea[7] iter," ol riat, "ní do torad in ċroindrin[8] na betad, oiret[9] ber[9] do ċorr ⁊ t'animm imalle.[10] Ir andrin dino rohetercarad Adam fri Partur orin immaċ, ut dixit [poeta]:

Rig[11] roraidi,[12] erim n-glan,
Fri hEua ⁊ fri hAdam:
"Uair[13] doċuadar[14] dar mo rmaċt[15],
Nirta[16] ní do[17] deolaideċt.

"Eroid[18] i m-betaid m-boetnaig,[19]
Sen[gċ]ig,[20] rnimaig, rirfaetnaig,
Torrig,[21] truagaig,[22] cen ril[23] foirr[23],
Rorbia[24] luag dar n-imordo[i]rr[24].

"dar[25] clanna, dar[25] meic, dar[25] mna,
Fognam[26] doib ceċ aen trata,[26]
Noċurta[27] maiċ, monar n-glan[28],
Co[29] ti[29] allur dar[30] n-etan[30].

---

[30] -rugur. [31-31] forom roarlaċt. [32-32] d'Adam. [33] atamar.
[34-34] dia m-bad. [35] aiċrige. [36] dognéċ.
k.—[1] fororconzart. [2] aingleib. [3] Curid. [4] Phardur. [5] -rrind.
[6] ċrainn. [7] blarfi. [8] ċraind. [9-9] hed beit. [10] 'mole. (X.) [11] ri.
[12] roraidi. [13] omitted. [14] -dair huaim. [15] reċt. [16] nirta. [17] dom'.
[18] eirgoid. [19] m-báetnaig. [20] reingtig. [21] toirreċ. [22] tróg.
[23-23] fiala for. [24-24] fordia log far n-imardor. [25] far. [26-26] fogniat duib caċ oen laa. [27] nocorta. [28] ṅ-den. [29-29] conorti. [30-30] for hécen.

Adam this plea injurious, namely: "If I have violated thy authority, [1] it is she, the woman thou thyself gavest to me, suggested [it] to³ me, to wit, Eve." Said God unto Adam: "Since thou dost not confess thy crime," quoth He, "thy children shall be always⁴ in contention against thee. And if it were penance thou hadst done, there would be pardoned to thee what thou didst do and thou wouldst be in the same happiness."

k. It is then indeed God enjoined upon his angels: "Put," said He, "Adam from Paradise unto the common land straightway." Then therefore forced the angels Eve and Adam from Paradise forth, so that there came to them afterwards anguish and dejection and poverty and want and anger and weariness and diseases many [and] various. So that then said Adam unto the angels of heaven: "Allow respite brief to me," quoth he, "until I taste a whit of the fruit of the tree of life¹." "You shall not taste at all," said they, "a whit of the fruit of that tree of life, the while shall be² thy body and thy soul together." It is then, in sooth, was separated Adam from Paradise from that out, as said [the poet]:—

> [It is] the king who said, perfect the tale³,
> Unto Eve and unto Adam:
> "Since ye have transgressed my command,
> There is not aught [for ye] of favour.
>
> Go into life deceptive,
> Bitter, anxious, ever-toilsome,
> Wearying, wretched, without germ of rest,
> It shall be the reward of your offence.
>
> Your posterity, your sons, your wives,
> They must serve at every time,
> There is not good [to ye], perfect the work,
> Until cometh the sweat of your brows.

---

³ Lit., upon.   ⁴ Lit., through ages.

k.—¹ Here follow two quatrains (ll. 1425–1432) in *S. R.*

² Sing., agreeing with the next following subject, in the text.

³ The first, second, third and fourth of these quatrains each contain one line that has no Concord in either MS. The metre of the Poem is accordingly Irregular Debide (explained in Lecture II.).

[k]

"Imab³¹ ceċ ʒalaıp purta³¹,
Scapaḋ cuıpp ⁊ anma
Ocup³² paeċap popbıa an ḋan³²,
Oep³³ ıp³⁴ cpıne³⁵ ıp³⁶ cpıċlám.

"Fpıċoılıḋ³⁷ apláċ³⁸ ḋıabuıl,
Ceċ laċı³⁹ ıp⁴⁰ ceċ⁴⁰ blıaḋaın,
Naḋ pop[ḟ]uca⁴¹ laıp ḋıa ċıʒ,
Ḋoċum ıppıpn⁴² n-aḋuaċmaıp.

"ḃap²⁵ n-ʒnımpaḋa, ḋıa⁴³ m-ba[c]⁴³ ʒlaın,
ıap⁴⁴ cımnaıb, ıap⁴⁴ popceclaıb,
Ḋobepċep⁴⁵ nem, cloeċeċ⁴⁶ cluċ⁴⁶,
Ḋo ċaċ ıap⁴⁷ n-aıpıllıuḋ⁴⁷."

Rı pıċıḋ pannmaıp⁴⁸, nı puaıll⁴⁹,
Rı beċa blaḋmaıp, bıċbuaın,
Nıclaıċ ppı⁵⁰ ʒle ʒpaım⁵⁰ ceċ can,
Rı popaıḋ, epımm⁵¹ n-ʒle ʒlan⁵¹.—Rı popaıḋı.

1. Ḋopıḋnaċċ ḋıno Ḋıa ḋo Aḋam¹ ın calmaın coıċċınḋ pea, ıap n-ımappup ı Pappup ⁊ nı baḋ² ḋımmaċ³ pum ḋe pın, mına⁴ beċ⁴ epċpa⁵ ıap n-aımpıp ḋó. Ḃuı⁶ ḋıno Aḋam peċcmaın ıap n-a ḋıċup⁷ a Pappup⁸ cen eċaċ, cen ḋıʒ, cen bıaḋ, cen ċeċ, cen cenıḃ⁹, po¹⁰ ċoppı¹⁰ ⁊ aıċmela ḋepmaıp, co n-aıċḃep ⁊ ımaıċḃep¹¹ occu ppıa apaıle. Conıḋ anḋpın acḃepc Aḋam ppı hEua: "Ronlaaḋ¹² a Pappup⁸ cpıa ċınaḋ ımapḃoıp," ol pe, "⁊ ıp mop popp̄acpum¹³ ḋa¹⁴ ceċ maıċ ann. Uaıp pobuı Pappup¹⁵ co n-a uıle aıpmıċın pop ap comap: ıḋon, aıcce¹⁶ aılle ⁊ planċı¹⁷

P. 112 a. cen ʒalap ⁊ aıḃnep¹⁸ cen epċpaı, | ḃpúıʒe¹⁹ blaċı,¹⁹ luıḃe²⁰ ampaı, oıppıċeḋ²¹ bıċbuaın, papaḋ²² cen paeċap, beċa cen ḃpón, aıḃnep cen epḋíḃaḋ, nóıme ḋıap n-anmanḋaıḃ, compaḋ cunnaıl ppı haınʒlıu, bıċḃeċa²³ cen bap, ⁊ na huıle²⁴ Ḋó oc²⁵ áp n-aıpmıċın

---

³¹⁻³¹ ımmaḋ n-onʒalap popċá.   ³²⁻³² pnım ocup paeċap ceċ can. (This and the foregoing are the true readings.)   ³³ ḋep.   ³⁴ ocup.   ³⁵ cpını.   ³⁶ omitted.
³⁷ -alım, corrected into -alıḋ.   ³⁸ correction of aplaıʒ.   ³⁹ laıċı.   ⁴⁰⁻⁴⁰ ceċ oen.
⁴¹ popp̄uca.   ⁴² n-ıppıpn.   ⁴³⁻⁴³ ḋıa mı-[b]ac.   ⁴⁴ ıap mʾ.   ⁴⁵ -ċap.
⁴⁶⁻⁴⁶ noıċeċ cpuċ (wrong reading).   ⁴⁷⁻⁴⁷ ıap n-a ċaın aıplıuḋ (the true reading).   ⁴⁸ panmaıp.   ⁴⁹ puaıl.   ⁵⁰⁻⁵⁰ a ʒle ʒpaım.   ⁵¹⁻⁵¹ épaım n-epʒlan.
1.—(XI.) ¹ Aḋaum.   ² nıpʾḃo.   ³ ḋímḋaċ.   ⁴⁻⁴ manḃaḋ.   ⁵ aıpepa.
⁶ ḃáı.   ⁷ ċaċcop.   ⁸ -ḋop.   ⁹ ċeın.   ¹⁰⁻¹⁰ ppı coıppı.   ¹¹ ımaıċp̄éup.
¹² ponlaḋ.   ¹³ -pam.   ¹⁴ ḋo.   ¹⁵ -ḋup.   ¹⁶ oecıu.   ¹⁷ plaınce.
¹⁸ oeḃınneop.   ¹⁹⁻¹⁹ ḃpuıʒı balċaı.   ²⁰ luḃaı.   ²¹ aıppıcıuḋ.   ²² pappaḋ.
²³ -ċu.   ²⁴ ḃuıle.   ²⁵⁻²⁵ ʾco ap n-aıpmıċeın.

Much of every disease is [for ye], [k]
Separation of body and of soul,
And labour shall be the lot,
[Old] age and decrepitude and palsy[4].

Endurance of assaults of the devil,
Each day and each year,
That he carry ye not with him to his house,
Unto hell very horrible.

Your actions, if they be pure,
According to commands, according to precepts,
Heaven shall be given, renowned the fame,
To each according to merit.

The king of the kingdom spacious, not trifling;
The king of life famous, everlasting,
Not remiss [is he] for a conspicuous deed every time,
The king who said—tale bright, perfect. The king, &c.

1. Then granted God to Adam this common earth, after the offence in Paradise and [Adam] would not be displeased therewith, if there were not dissolution after a time for him. Now, was Adam [for] a week after his expulsion from Paradise without raiment, without drink, without food, without house, without fire; under very great weariness and distress, with reproach and recrimination by[1] them towards each other. So that then said Adam to Eve: "We have been cast from Paradise through guilt of offence," quoth he, "and great is what we have left of every good there. For there was Paradise with all its honour at[2] our command: namely, youth joyous and health without disease and delight without decay; meadows of bloom, herbs excellent, pleasure ever-constant, satiety without toil, life without sorrow, delight without failure; holiness for our souls, converse fitting with[3] angels, lasting life without death and the elements[4] of God reverencing[5] and honouring us.[5] And all

---

[4] Lit., trembling of hands.
1.—[1] Lit., with.   [2] Lit., upon.   [3] Lit., towards.
    [4] The reading of *Saltair na Rann*. The text has "the [things] all."
    [5-5] Lit., at our reverencing and at our honouring. The possessive, as elsewhere, is used objectively with the verbal substantive (infinitive).

[1] ⁊ oc ár n-onoir. Ocur na huile²⁶ anmand²⁷ batar for bit, i[r]rind²⁸ norobaiged²⁹. Ocur nintoircfed tene ⁊ nirbaired³⁰ urce³¹ ⁊ nirtercrad foebur³² no iarn ⁊ nirgebad galar no faet. Ni boi³³ dino innim no hi talum³⁴ dúil tírad³⁵ frind, mine tírad Lucifer³⁶. Ocur cid Lucifer³⁶ dino, ni cóemrad³⁷ ar n-aimler³⁸, cen³⁹ bamar fo fmaċt in Choimded. O rofaraig-rimar⁴⁰ dino in Coimdid, ata ceċ dúil i⁴¹ cotarrna⁴¹ frind⁴² ⁊ ni he Dia ba cintaċ frind⁴³, aċt rinne rofaraig erium ⁊ tuc rum ceċ mait dun, céin bamar fo [a] fmaċt rum." Atbert dino Eua fri hAdam: "Uair ir mire ar cintaċ ann, a Adaim," ol rí, "tarri ċucamm ⁊ imbir bár form im' ċintaib. Ar, aċt co taeċairra⁴⁴ am' ċintaib, ir moti⁴⁵ dogena Dia trocaire orutra." "Ir lor ċena roċraidrim⁴⁶ in Coimdid," ol Adam, "⁊ ni⁴⁷ din-genter⁴⁷ fíngal⁴⁸ fortra," ol re, "ar atai co truag ⁊ co taebnoċt ⁊ ni todáileb mo ḟuil fen fo ċalum," ol re. "Ar i[r] rirrandur dom' ċurr ċura, a Eua," ol re, "⁊ ni cóir dun atamur do ċabairt ar in Coimdid, no ar n-didud,⁴⁹ no ar n-dilcend,⁵⁰ co na robilrigea in Coimdiu rind do demnaib i ḟudomain irrirn ⁊ na⁵¹ robilrigea rinn⁵¹ doridire⁵² do Lucifer⁵³. Ar atam ċena i n-ar reinn ⁊ atbelam di ḟuaċt ⁊ gortai cen biad, cen etaċ." "A ḟir mait," ol Eua, "cid na cuire cuairt⁵⁴ ar⁵⁵ ceċ⁵⁶ leċ, dúr in ḟuigbiċea⁵⁷ dún ni noṁelmair."⁵⁸

m. Atraċt Adam iar rin, cor'laa cuairt¹, oc iarrud bíd noċaiṫricir. Ocur ni ḟuair biad, aċt luibe² in talman ⁊ cuit na n-anmand³ n-indligteċ. Nirbat fartai' leo eride iar m-biadaib blarta⁴ Parċu[i]r.⁵ Conid annrin atbert Adam fri Eua: "Denum⁶," ol re, "rendaic⁷ ⁊ aiṫrige⁸, co cuirmir dind

²⁶ huili. ²⁷ -nn. ²⁸ ir rind. ²⁹ norodon[aig]e[d]. ³⁰ ninbaidred.
³¹ omitted. ³² faebur. ³³ bai. ³⁴ talmain. ³⁵ noċirred.
³⁶ -fur. ³⁷ ċoemnacair. ³⁸ n-amlerr. ³⁹ cein. ⁴⁰ rardraigrem.
⁴¹⁻⁴¹ hi cotarrnai. ⁴² frim (sing.) ⁴³ rind. ⁴⁴ toċċrorra. ⁴⁵ mote.
⁴⁶ -rem. ⁴⁷⁻⁴⁷ níben (fut. 1. sg.). ⁴⁸ fingail. ⁴⁹ n-didad.
⁵⁰ lándilgen. ⁵¹⁻⁵¹ naċarndilri. ⁵² doriri. ⁵³ -fur. ⁵⁴ cuaird.
⁵⁵ for. ⁵⁶ caċ. ⁵⁷ rogebta. ⁵⁸ domelmair.
m.—¹ cuaird. ² lubai. ³ n-anman. ⁴ blaiċib. ⁵ -duir. ⁶ denam.
⁷ penn-. ⁸ aiṫeirge.

the beings that were in[2] existence, it is we that used to control [1] them. And fire would not burn us and water would not drown us and edged[6] weapon[6] or iron would not cut us off and illness or weariness would not seize us. There was not, moreover, in heaven or on[7] earth an element that would have come against us, if Lucifer had not come. And even Lucifer, indeed, he could not have caused our destruction, whilst we were under the obedience of the Lord. Since however we have offended the Lord, every element is in opposition to us and it is not God that was the[6] cause thereof to us[5], but ourselves who have offended him, although[9] he gave every good to us, whilst we were under his obedience." Then said Eve to Adam: "Since it is I that am guilty therein, O Adam," quoth she, "come you to me and inflict death upon me for[7] my crimes[10]. For if I be destroyed for[7] my crimes, the[11] more will God work mercy upon thee." "Enough[11] already have we afflicted the Lord," quoth Adam, "and murder[12] shall not be done upon thee," quoth he; "for thou art wretched[13] and stark naked[13] and I will not shed my own blood along the earth," quoth he. "For[9] true portion of my body art thou, O Eve," quoth he, "and [it is] not just for us to give fresh offence to[14] the Lord, or to destroy ourselves or to annihilate ourselves, that the Lord may not forfeit us to demons in the depth of hell and may not forfeit us again to Lucifer. For we are already in[15] punishment[15] and we are dying of cold and hunger, without food, without raiment[16]." "O good man," quoth Eve, "why dost thou not make[17] circuit on every side, to know whether there should be found for us anything we would consume?"

m. Uprose Adam after that and[1] made circuit, a-seeking food that they would eat. And he found not food, save herbs of the earth and the pittance of the lawless beings. That was not sufficient for them after the savoury foods of Paradise. So that then said Adam unto Eve: "Let us do," quoth he, "penance and contrition, that we may put

---

[6-6] Lit., edge. More likely, *edge or iron* is a hendiadys = edged iron (weapon).
[7] Lit., in.   [8-8] Lit., guilty against us.   [9] Lit., and.
[10] Another quatrain (ll. 1529-1532) is spoken by Eve in *S. R.* It is an amplification of what is given here.   [11] *It is* stands prefixed in the text.
[12] The textual word, ᚠingal, means slaying a relative.
[13] The original phrase is adverbial.   [14] Lit., on.   [15-15] Lit., in our punishment.
[16] In *S. R.* the second clause of this sentence is spoken by Eve. She adds (ll. 1557-1560) that they had food and raiment before transgression and neither one nor the other thereafter.   [17] Lit., put.   **m.**—[1] Lit., so that.

[**112**] ni di ar cintaib ⁊ di ar tairmtectur⁹," ol se. Atbert Eua dino: "Denaru mo tintorcra," ol si, "ar¹⁰ nirfetur¹¹ cindur¹² dognīter pendaic¹³ no aitrize." Atbert dino Adam: "Adrumm¹⁴ in Coimdiu ⁊ denum tuidect cen¹⁵ comlabra¹⁵ do neoc fri araile ocaind iter. Ergriu¹⁶, a Eua, i frut Tigir ⁊ regutra¹⁷ i frut Iordanen," ol se, "⁊ bi tri laa tricat i frut Tigir ⁊ biatru fett laa cetratat i frut Iordanen. Ocur ber¹⁸ lat¹⁹ licc clodi fot' toraib²⁰ ⁊ poiced in n-urce do bragait ⁊ bid [d']polt rcailte²¹ for cet²² let for uactar in t-rrota. Ocur tocaib do df²³ laim i n-airdi frirn Coimdiu ⁊ do norc frir na nemdaib ⁊ guib in Coimdiu um dilgud duit darcend t'imarbroir." Atbert Eua: "Nidat²⁴ glan²⁵ do guide Dé. Uair at elnige ar m-beoil iar tomailt in uball [ubaib, *Lith.*] hergairti." Atbert dino Adam fri Eua: "Aittem in²⁶ n-uli duile²⁶ doponta

P. 112 b. | tria glaine co²⁷ n-guidet in Coimdiu lind²⁸ im dilgud dun diar tairmtectur²⁹ ⁊ dena³⁰ amlaid rin do mod ⁊ do monar ⁊ comaill ⁊ na cumrcaig arr." Sett laa³¹ cetratat iar rin do Adam i frut Iordanen ⁊ tri laa³¹ tricat³² do Eua i frut Tigir. Ocur ticdir aingil³³ do nim o Dia cet lai³¹ do imacallaim fri hAdam ⁊ dia forcetul³⁴, co cend³⁵ noi la³⁶ n-décc³⁷. Ir ann dino roguid³⁸ Adam frut Iordanen co n-a ilmilaib co rotroirced³⁹ lair co Dia im dilgud do dia tairmtectur. Rotairir⁴⁰ tra in frut indrin ⁊ cet mil beo boi and, rotinoilrit im Adam ⁊ rogabutar⁴¹ uli, iter mil ⁊ frut, in Coimdiu ⁊ doronrat nuallguba moir fri na hulib gradaib filet imon Coimdiu, im dilgud do Adam i n-a imarbur⁴². Dorigne⁴³ tra Dia for⁴⁴ a gradaib rlandilgud tinad do tabairt do Adam ⁊ aitteb i talmain do ⁊ nem iar n-eterrcarad anma fri a torp. Ocur dorat dia tloind dia érri, attmad inti⁴⁵ ticfad dar rett De.

---

⁹ tarmtett. ¹⁰ huair. ¹¹ nat fetar. ¹² cinnar. ¹³ pennaind.
¹⁴ adnam. ¹⁵⁻¹⁵ hi comlabrae. ¹⁶ eirggriu. ¹⁷ ragra. ¹⁸ beir.
¹⁹ let. ²⁰ torraib. ²¹ rcailti. ²² cat. ²³ da. ²⁴ nidar. ²⁵ glain.
²⁶⁻²⁶ na huili duili. ²⁷⁻²⁷ cor'guidet. ²⁸ lenn. ²⁹ tarmtett. ³⁰ deni.
³¹ la. ³² tricat. ³³ aingeil. ³⁴ -tal. ³⁵ cenn. ³⁶ laa. ³⁷ h-decc.
³⁸ rogaid. ³⁹ troirced. ⁴⁰ tarraraip. ⁴¹ -datur. ⁴² imm-. ⁴³ dorigni.
⁴⁴ ar. ⁴⁵ inté.

put from us something of our crimes and of our transgression," quoth [m] he. Said Eve indeed: "Instruct² thou me²," quoth she, "for I know³ not³ how is done penance or contrition."⁴ But said Adam : "Let us adore the Lord and spend⁵ a time⁵ without conversing, one⁶ with the other of us, at all. Go thou, O Eve, into the stream of Tigris and I will go myself into the stream of Jordan," quoth he, "and be thou three days [and] thirty in the stream of Tigris and I will be myself seven days [and] forty in the stream of Jordan. And take with thee a flagstone [to put] under thy feet and let the water reach thy throat and be thy hair loosened upon every side upon the surface of the stream. And raise thy two hands on high towards the Lord and thy eyes towards the heavens and pray the Lord for forgiveness to thee on account of thy offence." Said Eve: "We are not pure [enough] to pray the Lord. For defiled are our lips after the eating of the apple forbidden." But said Adam to Eve : "Let us beseech all the elements that were made in⁷ purity, that they may pray the Lord with us for forgiveness to us for our transgression and perform like that thy measure and thy work and persevere and stir not out of it." Seven days [and] forty after that [were spent] by Adam in the stream of Jordan and three days [and] thirty by Eve in the stream of Tigris. And there used to come angels of heaven from God each day, to converse with Adam and to instruct him, to the end of nine days [and] ten. It is then, indeed, besought Adam the stream of Jordan with its many creatures, that it might fast with him to God for forgiveness to him for his transgression. Then stood the stream and every living creature that was in it, they assembled around Adam and besought they all, both⁸ creature and stream, the Lord and they made wailing great to all the grades that are around the Lord, for forgiveness to Adam in his offence. But God caused for his grades full forgiveness of his crimes to be given to Adam and a dwelling on⁹ earth to him and heaven after separation of the soul from his body. And he gave [the same] to his children after him, except whoever should transgress the law of God.

---

²⁻² Lit., do thou my instructing (possessive used objectively).

³⁻³ Lit., know it not : the infixed pronoun (r) used proleptically.

⁴ In *S. R.* another quatrain (ll. 1581-1584) is given to Eve. In it she asks for instruction, that she may not err by excess or deficiency.   ⁵ Lit., make going.

⁶ Lit., for [= by] anyone.   ⁷ Lit., through.   ⁸ Lit., between.   ⁹ Lit., in.

n. Atcuala imorro diabul in aitérc tucad do Adam o Dia ⁊ dochoid for amur Eua doridire¹ i picc aingil: dia brecad arin rruc ⁊ do locc a aithrige impe. Co nd-ebert fria: "Ir fata² atai i rruc Tigir, a Eua," ol re, "⁊ cén' mait dognē, roclaechlair³ crut," ol re. "Rotmarbair⁴ buden ⁊ tair co luat arin rruc. Ocur Dia romcuirre doc' t-airchirecht ⁊ doc' tabairt arin rruc." Tic dino Eua arin rrut⁵, co m-boí oc⁶ a tirmugud⁶ for tir ⁊ tanic iarum nell⁷ chuice, co tarmairt écc⁸ cen anmain. Ocur nir'aichin⁹ Eua co m-bad he Lucifer tírad i picht in aingil ⁊ boí¹⁰ a menma¹¹ i cunntabairt¹² moir ime. Atbert Lucifer: "A Eua," ol re, "ir mor do imratib¹³ dogní; uair ir re¹⁴ forcongra¹⁵ Dé do nim tanucra chucut. Tiagum arr," ol re, "dochum Adaim, co n-guidem Dia lib im díłgud do tabairt duib da bar cintaib." Dochuatur¹⁶ iarum co hairm i m-boí Adam, oc rrut Iordanén. Amal¹⁷ rodercc¹⁸ Adam for Eua ⁊ Lucifer,¹⁹ forgab²⁰ crít ⁊ grain re gnúir diabuil. "Mo nuar, a Eua," ol re, "rotmellurtar inti rotmell i Partur²¹. Trog rin tra, do tibecht a rrut Tigir, co tírad aingel glan o 'n Choimdid doc' tabairt arr." Amal¹⁷ itchuala²² Eua atcoran²³ Adaim, dofuit²⁴ for lartalmain, conid bec na dechaid dianbar. Conid ann atbert Adam: "A Lucifer, a diabul," ol re, "cid tai diar lenmain²⁵? Ocur fornindarbair a Partur ⁊ forcarratur ar cuirp fri ar n-anmannaib acht bec ⁊ doratair i caċt ⁊ i cuibreċ. Ocur ní rind rotgab²⁶ do flaitiur ⁊ ní rind rotcuir a n-iferm do dingnaib ricid (no ricig)*. Ní rind dino ro [f]urail fort diumur ⁊ anúmla doc' tigerna."

---

n.—¹ dorire (syncopated form, to suit the metre). ² cian. ³ rochoemclair. ⁴ rotmarmair. ⁵ t-rrut. ⁶⁻⁶ 'cotir. ⁷ nél. ⁸ héc. ⁹ ni haitgen. ¹⁰ be. ¹¹ -mai. ¹² cumt-. ¹³ -teib. ¹⁴ la. ¹⁵ fornGairi. ¹⁶ -tar. ¹⁷ mar. ¹⁸ roderr[c]e. ¹⁹ -fur. ²⁰ rongab. ²¹ -dor. ²² at-. ²³ adchoram. ²⁴ dorfuit. ²⁵ lenamuin. ²⁶ rogab.

* Over the -id of ricid is placed no (in the contraction of the Latin *vel*) ᵹ—*or g*; meaning that the true reading was perhaps ricig.

n. Howbeit, heard the devil the precept that was given to Adam by God and he went to¹ tempt Eve¹ again in guise of an angel² : to entice her from out the stream and to³ injure her in respect to her penance.³ So said he to her: "It is long art thou in the stream of Tigris, O Eve," quoth he, "and though good is what dost thou, thou hast changed [thy] shape," quoth he. "Thou hast [almost] killed thyself and come quickly from out the stream. And God [it was] that sent myself to spare thee and to bring thee from out the stream." Then comes Eve from out the stream, so that she was a-drying herself upon land and there came afterwards a swoon to her, so that she had like to die without consciousness. And Eve did not know that it was Lucifer that would come in guise of the angel and her mind was in great perplexity regarding him. Said Lucifer: "O Eve," quoth he, "many⁴ are the [vain] thoughts thou hast⁴ ; for it is by command of the God of heaven came I myself unto thee. Come we from this," quoth he, "unto Adam, that we may beg God with ye to give forgiveness to ye for your crimes." They went afterwards to the place wherein was Adam, at the stream of Jordan. When looked Adam upon Eve and Lucifer, took⁵ he trembling and abhorrence at sight of the devil. "Woe is me, O Eve," quoth he, "there hath deceived thee the one that deceived thee in Paradise. Sad [is] that in sooth, thy coming out of the stream of Tigris, until the angel pure would come from the Lord to bring thee thereout." When heard Eve the reproach of Adam, fell she down upon the very earth, so⁶ that she nearly met with sudden death⁶. So that then said Adam : "O Lucifer, O devil," quoth he, "why art thou a-following us? And thou hast expelled us from Paradise and our bodies have all but⁷ separated from our souls and thou hast given us into subjection and into bondage. And [it is] not we took thy kingdom from thee and [it is] not we put thee into hell from the heights of the [heavenly]

---

n.—¹⁻¹ Lit., upon attack of Eve.

² *S. R.* says (l. 1671), like a swan in guise of a white angel (ᴍᴀɴ ʜᴇʟᴀ ɪᴘᴘɪóᴄ ᴀṅꙅɪʟ ꙅɪʟ).   ³⁻³ Lit., to injure her penance respecting her

⁴⁻⁴ Lit., [It] is much of thoughts thou makest.

⁵ Lit., he took them ; the pronoun (ᴘ) being used proleptically.

⁶⁻⁶ Lit., so that it [is] little that she went not swift death.

⁷ Lit., except a little.

o. Atbert Lucifer: "A¹ fuapura de ulc¹," ol fe, "if tret'² daiʒinfe² fuafur. Ocuf dino indiffetfa³ duit amal⁴ foncuifed⁵ af oen do nim: idon, dia tafdad t'ainimfea o Dia dotum do tuifp ⁊ fottfutaiʒ fo tofmailef⁶ a delbi⁷ duden ⁊ dia nd-ébfad⁸ ffia tet n-dúil do aifmitnuʒudfa ⁊ dia⁹ fofpúid⁹ Dia Mitel do nim tucut, co n-datfut¹⁰ do adfad in duileman¹¹ ⁊ o faadfaif do fiʒ na n-ainʒel, fofofconʒfad fof tet n-dúil t'aifmitinfea do denam tfia bitu. Conid annfin fofpuid Dia Mitel fo na fett nimib, co tiftaif ainʒil to n-a n-dfonʒ-aib ilib do aifmitniuʒud a delbefium¹². Ocuf fofaid Mitel ffimfa tu m-bad me bud toifet fempu. | Iaf fin imoffo dode-tudfa fa¹³ deoid tof'fuidef¹⁴ i fiadnaife in duileman¹¹. Ocuf atbert¹⁵ ffind¹⁶ in fiʒ¹⁷, idon, ffia noi n-ʒfadaib nime: "Tadfaid uile uafli ⁊ oifmitin¹⁸ doim' tomdelbfea,¹⁹ idon, do Adam," ol fe. If annfin atbert Mitel: "If tóif di²⁰ tet ʒfád fil fof nim do tomdelbaidfea²¹ do adfad ⁊ do aifmitin²²." Conid atbeftfa: "Nat é Adam fofaf²³ na n-uli²⁴ dúl²⁴ ⁊ ni tóif in finnfef do aifmitniuʒud in t-fofaif ⁊ nat é in fofaf bid tóif do aifmitniuʒud in t-finnfif?" Annfin dino fofaidfet tfian muintife nime, itef²⁵ ainʒel ⁊ aftainʒeal,²⁵ to m-ba toif an utbeftfa. If annfin atbert in fiʒ ffinne: "If e in fofaf²⁶ buf²⁷ uaifle ten²⁸ beofa fof nim." "Atbeftfa," of Lucifef, "na faʒaid fen do aifmitniuʒud²⁹ Adam, té difed táit uile; uaif³⁰ bam³⁰ finiu oltáf. Romlaadfa iaf fin do nim fo tetoif tfiat' tinaidfiu, a Adaim," of Lucifef; "oif tanut i n-aʒaid toile mo tiʒefna, idon, Ifu Tfift: to foncuifedne, lín af flog, i fudomain iffifn ⁊ tufa i Pafturf³¹ d'af³² n-éfi³². Ocuf ba fóinmet do betu ann, mina bet tumfuʒud foft efti.

---

o.—¹⁻¹ 'na fuafuf d'ulcc. ² tfiat' daʒain. ³ adfiafa. ⁴ feib. ⁵ donfalad. ⁶ -liuf. ⁷ deilbi. ⁸ n-efbfad. ⁹⁻⁹ diaf'fáid. ¹⁰ tonotfut. ¹¹ dul-. ¹² deilbifeom. ¹³ dodetad. ¹⁴ to taffafaf. ¹⁵ fofdói. ¹⁶ finn. ¹⁷ fi. ¹⁸ aifmitiu. ¹⁹ tomdeilbfi. ²⁰ do. ²¹ -delbfu. ²² -tain. ²³ óffaf. ²⁴⁻²⁴ ń-dúle n-uile. ²⁵⁻²⁵ oten anʒle if aftainʒle. ²⁶ t-fofaf. ²⁷ baf. ²⁸ tein. ²⁹ -niuʒud. ³⁰⁻³⁰ huaif im. ³¹ -dof. ³²⁻³² daf af n-effiue.

kingdom⁸. [It is] not we, moreover, that enjoined upon thee haughtiness and want⁹ of humility⁹ to thy Lord."

o. Said Lucifer:¹ "What I have gotten of evil," quoth he, "it is through thy account I got [it]. And moreover, I shall tell thee how we were put together from heaven: namely, when was given thy soul by God unto thy body, and [God] formed thee in² likeness of his own form and when it was said unto every element to reverence thee and when God sent Michael from heaven to thee, so that he took thee to adore the Creator and when thou didst adore the King of the angels, it was enjoined upon each element to³ do reverence to thee³ through ages. So that then sent God Michael throughout the seven heavens, that the angels might come with their many throngs to reverence his image. And said Michael to me that it is I should be first before them. After that indeed went I at⁴ length⁴ and⁵ sat⁵ in presence of the Creator. And said unto us the king, namely, unto the nine grades of heaven: 'Give ye all [of you] eminence and respect to my likeness, namely, to Adam,' said He. It is then said Michael: 'It is just for every grade that is in⁶ Heaven to adore and to honour thy likeness.' So that said I: 'Is not Adam the junior of all the elements and [it is] not just that⁷ the senior should honour⁷ the junior and is it not the junior it were just should honour the senior?' Then, indeed, said⁸ a third of the people of Heaven, both⁹ angel and archangel, that what I spoke was just. It is then said the king to us: 'It is the junior is noblest whilst I am in⁶ heaven.'"
"Said I," quoth Lucifer, "that I would not go myself to honour Adam, though every one else should go; for I was older than he. I was cast after that from Heaven immediately¹⁰ through thy fault, O Adam," quoth Lucifer, "since I went against the will of my Lord, namely, Jesus Christ: so that we were put, the whole of our hosts, in

---

⁸ Six additional quatrains (ll. 1733–1756) are spoken by Adam in *S. R.* One couplet (ll. 1751–1752) corresponds (not very closely) to the final sentence of this section.   ⁹⁻⁹ Lit., inhumility.

o.—¹ In *S. R.* Satan proceeds to remind Adam, in seven quatrains (ll. 1757–1784), of the various evils inflicted upon himself on account of Adam.   ² Lit., under.

³⁻³ Lit., to do thy reverence (possessive used objectively).   ⁴⁻⁴ Lit., at the end.
⁵⁻⁵ Lit., so that I sat.   ⁶ Lit., upon.   ⁷⁻⁷ Lit., the senior to honour.
⁸ Plural in the original; third (cριαn) being a collective.
⁹ Lit., between.   ¹⁰ Lit., under the first hour.

[v] Ocus atberimrea ffritt³³, a Adaim," or Luciferr, "cech olc ⁊ cech imned fogéba, ir mire fogéba duit ⁊ cech olc dogén, ir fritra dogéntar, a Adaim," ol se. "Ocus uino doberra do chloind ⁊ t'iartaisc i catoaib ⁊ i n-sallraib³⁴ ⁊ tedmannaib ⁊ imnedaib mora[ib], cén co n-dicret fo talmain, triarsin n-imperain fil etrum ⁊ tu," ol se.

p. Tanic¹ dino Adam arsin rruch, iar forba na reoch la cechradach fo aiérige ⁊ rennaic n-dichra. Ocus dochoid² Luciferr uadib, co furfacaib Adam ⁊ Eua amlaid sin fo meschin ⁊ mela. batar dino in lanamain trog sin a n-oenur co cend m-bliadna, cen sarad bid no dige, acht luiberad ⁊ fér in talman do caichem, amal cech n-anmand n-indligtech archena ⁊ urce di a m-baraib do dis fair: cen teth, cen tenid, acht fo³ forcadaib³ crand⁴ ⁊ uamaib⁵ tirmaib talman, ⁊ araile.*

---

³³ fric. ³⁴ ṅ-salraib.
p.—¹ dofuarsaib (arose). ² rorāid. ³⁻³ hi forcadais. ⁴ na crann.
⁵ i n-huamaib

* In the MS., ⁊ araile is represented by ⁊c̄, the contraction for *et cetera*. Similarly, *sed* (once written in full, but in all other places represented by *s* with horizontal line overhead) is regularly put for acht (but). The Roman notation is likewise frequently employed to express the numerals.

the depth of hell and thou [wast put] in Paradise in our stead. And [o] pleasant were thy life there, if[11] thou hadst not been disturbed[11] therefrom[12]. And I say to thee, O Adam," quoth Lucifer, "every evil and every misery you shall get, it is I shall cause [it] to thee and every evil I shall do, it is against thee it shall be done, O Adam," quoth he. "And, moreover, I shall bring thy children and thy posterity into trials and into diseases and plagues and miseries great, until they go under earth, through the contention that is between me and thee," quoth he.

p. Howbeit, came Adam out of the stream, after completion of the seven days [and] forty in[1] contrition and penance earnest. And went Lucifer from them, so that left[2] he Adam and Eve in that manner in[1] misfortune and deception. Now, were that wretched wedded couple alone[3] to the end of a year, without sufficiency of food or of drink, but to consume the roots and grass of the earth, like every other lawless animal besides and water from their palms for drink therewith[4]: without house, without fire, but under the shades of the trees and [in] dry caves of the earth, and so on.[5]

[11-11] Lit., if there were not disturbance upon thee.

[12] Two additional quatrains (ll. 1865-1872) are spoken by Satan in *S. R.*

p.—[1] Lit., under.   [2] Lit., left them; the infixed pron., ɼ, being used proleptically.
[3] Lit., in oneness.   [4] Lit., upon it.

[5] The phrase *and so on* (lit., *and the rest*) refers, perhaps, to the fact that the poem in *S. R.* contains thirty-one quatrains (ll. 1897-2020) in addition. The chief contents of these are:—Birth of Cain; sending of Michael by God to teach Adam agriculture and use of animals; birth of Abel; Eve's vision of Cain drinking Abel's blood; building of house for each son by Adam; Gabriel's announcement that Cain would kill Abel and Seth be born; seventy-two sons and as many daughters born for Adam; Abel killed at the age of 200 years; Adam's children commanded by God not to kill Cain, whose forehead is marked by a protuberance which struck against a tree and killed him, in the valley of Jehoshaphat (thenceforth barren in consequence); birth of Seth in place of Abel.

INDEX VERBORUM. (I.)

[*Figures denote the pages of the Lecture; Roman letters, the sections of the Lebar Brec text,* pp. 38 *to* 71.]

a (poss. 3 sg. masc.), 24, 25, **a, b, c, d, h, i, k, l, m, o.**
a (poss. 3 sg. fem.), 27, **e, h, n.**
a(llecub, poss. 3 sg. fem.), **h.**
a (poss. 3 sg. neut.), **i, m.**
a (poss. 3 p.), 28, **c, f, h, i.**
a n- (p. poss.), **a, b, c, e, f, h, o, p.**
a (pron. infix. 3 p.), ḃapıʒne, 24.
a (prep.), 15, 24, 25, **f, k, l, n.**
a (ı, prep.), **f.**
am' (ı mo), **l.**
a n- (ı n-), **f, h, i, n, p.**
a (rel.), **g, o**; a n- (rel.), **i.**
a (voc.), 15, 16, 20, **g, h, i, l, m, n.**
abaıll, **d.**
abaıp, **g.**
ac (ıc), 25.
acallam, **g.**
aċt, **c, g, i, l, m, n, p**; aċt co, **g, l.**
aċtmaḃ, **b, m.**
acup (ocup), 20, 26, 27, 28.
Aḃam (n., d., ac.), *passim.*
Aḃaem (gen.), 25.
Aḃaım (g.), 24, 26, **b, e, f, g, n**; (ac.), **d.**
Aḃaım (voc.), **l, o.**
n-aḃampa, **c.**
abbap, 28.
aḃbuıḃ, **f.**
Aḃılon, 24.
aḃmıllıuḃ, **f.**
aḃpaḃ, **f, g, o**; poaḃpaıp ḃo, **o.**
aḃpumm, **m.**
n-aḃuaċmap, **h**; -maıp (g.), **k.**

aen, 27, **g, k.**
aeop, 25; aeo[ı]p, 24.
('n-a) aʒaıḃ, **e**; (ı n-)aʒaıḃ, **o.**
Aʒope, **e**; Aʒopıa, 25.
aıḃnep, **l.**
p'aıċın (po aıċın), **n.**
aıcneḃ, **e.**
aıle, **d, l.**
aılle, **l.**
aımlep, **l.**
n-aımpıp, **l.**
aın, **d.**
aınʒel (n.), **a, i, n**; (ac.), **o**; (g.p.), **c, d, i, o**; -ʒıl (g.), **d**; (n.p.), **k, m, o.**
aınʒlıḃ (d.p.), **d, i**; aınʒlıu (ac.p.), **k.**
aınm (name), **d, e, o**; (soul), 25.
aıp, 27.
aıpḃpıḃ (d. p.), **c, d.**
aıpḃpıu (n. p.), **d**; (voc.), **i.**
aıpċaınʒel (g.p.), **a.**
aıpcıpeċt, **n.**
aıpḃe, **a, b**; aıpḃı, **m.**
aıpḃpıʒ (n. s.), **a.**
aıpe (ap and pr. suf. 3 s. neut.), **e.**
aıpem, **c.**
n-aıpıllıuḃ, **k.**
(h)aıpm, **n.**
aıpmıtın, **d, l, o**; -nıuʒuḃ, **f, o.**
aıppoptaċ (d., ac.), **a**; (g.p.), **a.**
aıppoptaıʒ (g.s.), **a**; (n. p.), **a.**
aıptep, **d.**
aıpneıp, **b.**
n-aıtḃep, **l.**
aıtċem, **m.**

INDEX VERBORUM. (I.)

aiterc, e, i, n.
aitmela, 1.
aitrize, i, m, n, p; -zeċ, b.
aitte, 1.
aittneb, m.
alaind, c; -acn, 24.
Albain, 15.
allur, k.
am, d.
amaċ, a, b, k.
amainre, f.
amal, h, n, o, p.
amlaib, 25, a, c, m, p.
ampa, a, b; ampai, 1.
amuiz, b, g, f.
amur, f, h, n.
an (art.), k.
an (rel.), o.
anad, b.
anail, 25; anaill, h.
ananacan, h.
Anatale, e.
and (a (i) and pron. suf. 3 s. neut.), a, b, h, i, m.
andrin, b, f, k.
anım, 24; anımm, h, k.
anma, e, k, m; anmaın (ac.), e, n.
anmand (n. p.), f; 1; (g. p.), g, m, p.
anmanda (n. s.), f.
n-anmandaib, 1, m, n.
anmann (g. p.), g.
anmanna (n. s.), g.; (n. p.), e.
anmund (n. p.), e; anmunda, c.
ann, 26, a, b, c, g, h, i, k, l, n.
annribe, e.
annrin, d, e, g, i. k, l, m, o.
anoin, f.
anúmla, n.
an (poss. 1 p.), f, g, l, m, n, o.
an-m (poss. 1 p.), m.
an-n (poss. 1 p.), f, l, n.
an (prep.), 26, 28, d, e, f, g, l.

an oen, e, o.
an (conj.), d, f, g, l, m.
an (vb.), g.
Anabia, 25; -ion, 24.
Anabon, 24.
anaile, a, b, d, g, i, l, m, p.
anċaingel (ac. s.), o; (g. p.), d.
anċangil (g. s.), i; (n. p.) c.
anċena, e, g, p.
Anctor, e.
and, 24.
andriz (n.), c; (g.), f, i; (ac.), c.
anzait (g.), a.
n-anmaċ, 27.
annoet, e.
Anton, e.
ar (prep.), e.
ar (vb. rel.), 1.
arrein, e; arın, n, p.
arlaċ (g. p.), k.
arna, e.
arr (a and pron. suf. 3 sg. n.), m, v.
at (ind. pres. 3 p.), m.
ata, c, g, h, l; atai, h, l, n.
atam, h, l.
atamur, 1.
atan (g.), c.
atat, 25, d.
atbelam, 1.
atbenat, d; atbenimrea, o.
atbent, d, g, h, i, k, l, m, n, o.
atbentra, o.
atbenut, d.
atcomanc, b; -cc, a.
atconnainc, e.
atcoran, n.
atċuala, n.
atimċell, d.
atmai, i.
atraċt, m.
atrut (etın and pron. suf. 2 s.), h.
attat, a, c.

INDEX VERBORUM. (I.)

atu, g.
atuaib, h.
Aurbrocait, -tib, b.
aurgartí, f.

ba, 24, 26, g, h, i, l, o.
(co m-)ba, o.
bab, l.
(co m-)bab, n.
bae, 17, 25, 26, 28.
baile, i.
(nir)bairreb, l.
bam, d, o; bamar, l.
ban (g. p.), 27.
bannrcal, e.
bar, e, g, n.
bar-m, g.
bar-n, g, i, k.
bar, g, l.
m-baraib, p.
(bia m-)ba[t], k.
batar, l, p.
(nor)bean, d.
bec, n.
bemit, h.
ben, 26, 27, g, l.
(nor)ben, h.
beniamin, 27.
bennac, 20; bennacub, f.
beo, m; -ba, 27.
m-beoil, m.
beor, a, k.
beora, o.
ber, m; boberra, o.
(no)berta, e; bertair, b.
(bo)berter, k.
ber, k.
bet, e, f, h, i, l, o.
beta, g, k, l.
bitbeta, l.
betab (g.), i, k.
betaib, f, k.

(bo)betea, i.
betit, i.
betu (n. s.), o.
bi, g, m.
bia, d.
(nir)bia, f, g.
(nor)bia, k.
(not)bia, f, g.
biab, l, m; m-biabaib, m.
biatru, m.
biblon, e.
bicc (ac.), k.
bib (g.), m, p.
bib (vb.), b, o.
m-[b]ile, b.
bir, e.
bit, d.
bit, f, l; bitbennac, 20.
bitbuan, b, l; bitbuain (g.), k.
bitnua, b.
bitir, f.
bitu, i, o.
blabmair (g.), k.
blaeb, 26; -t, 26.
blairrea, k.
blaite, b.
blarinb, k; blarta, m.
blat (d. or ac.), a.
blat (g. p.), b.
blati, l.
bliabain, 15, k; -in, 15.
m-bliabna (g. s.), p; (n. p. bl-), 25.
bliaban (g. p.), 20, d.
m-boetraig, k.
boi, l, m, n.
(co m-)boi, n.
bolub, b.
boltnugub, b.
borb, d, g.
brarlacc, 16.
bragait (ac.), m.
brat, 24, b.

INDEX VERBORUM. (I.)

bṙéc (bṙon), 24; bṙecaḋ, n.
bṙcó, 20.
bṙeṫ, d.
bṙiʒic, 20; -ce, 9, 16.
m-bṙoʒa, b.
bṙón, 24, 1.
bṙu, 24, 25, e.
bṙúiʒe, a, 1.
bṙuinḃi, 25.
bṙunncóoṙ, 24.
buḋ, f, o,
buḋen, n, o; -ḃniḃ, 24.
bui, e, f, h, l; ṙobui, 1.
buṙ, o.

caċ, a, b, f, i, k, o; ċáiċ, f.
caċc, n, g.
cain, b.
caiṙḃeṙ, f.
ċaicem, g, p; (ṙo)ċaiṫṙicṙ, m.
caiṫmiṙ, g.
ċalleċ, 20.
ċanaic, c.
canac, c; canuc, c.
caṙcṙaiḋen, f.
caṫ, 21, 27; caṫaiḃ, o.
caṫiṙ, a; caṫṙaiʒ (ac. s.), a, b.
cé, (conj.), n, o.
ceanḋ, e.
ceċ, 20, 24, 26, a, b, c, d, e, f, g, i, k, l, m, o.
ceċa (g.), a, b; ceċ n-, a, b, c, o.
ceimen, b; ceimenḋ, a.
céin, 1.
cén (conj. temp.), 26, 1, o.
cen (prep.), b, c, d, e, g, h, k, l, m, n, p.
ċena, 1.
cenḋ, 25, m, p.
ċeniul, b.
cenmoṫa, e; cenmoṫaṫ, a.
cenn, 24.

ccol, a, b, c, d; ceolaiḃ, a.
ceṙc, 28; ċeṙcloc, d.
ceṫ (first), e.
ceṫ (num.), 15, 28, a, b, c.
ceṫaiṙ, b; -aṙ, 17.
ceṫna (the same), f, h, i.
ceṫna (num. ord.), 15, a.
(ṙo) ceṫoiṙ, o.
ceṫṙaċa, a, c.
ceṫṙaċaṫ, b, m, p.
ceṫṙi, c, d, e; -ṙoṙ, 26.
cia (pron. inter.), f, g.
cia (conj. concess.), g.
ciḋ (pelc. inter.), 1, n.
ciḋ (conj. concess.), g, l.
cin, f, i.
ċinaḋ (ac. s.), 1; (g. p.), m.
ċinaiḋ (ac.), o.
ċinḋ, f.
cinḋuṙ, m.
cinmoṫaṫ, a.
cinṫaċ, 1; cinṫaiḃ, 1, m, n.
(ṙo)claċóiaṙ, n.
claen, 26; clanḋ, b, i.
claenne, 26; clanna, k.
claiṙceṫlaiḃ, a; claiṙceṫul, i.
claṙa (p.), i.
claṙṙ, b, c.
claṙṙe, b.
clauṙenaiṙ, 9, 16.
ċlciḃ, e.
cloċi, m.
(ṙo)ċlocċla, h.
cloċtoc, k.
ċloinḋ (d.), m; (ac.), o.
cluinnṫeṙ, i.
cluṙail, 15.
clúṙenaiṙ. 15.
cluṫ, k.
co (prep.), a, b, i, m, n, p.
co m- (co n-), 26, b.
co n- (prep.), b, c, d, i, l.

INDEX VERBORUM. (I.)

co (péıb), d.
co (caebnoċc), 1.
co (cpuaᵹ), 1.
co (conj.), 25, b, d, e, g, h, i, k, l, m, n, o, p.
co n- (conj.), c, e, f, g, h, i, m, n, o.
co nb- (conj.), n, o.
coémpab, 1.
coempacıp, b.
coı, 25.
coıc, 26; -ca, 26, 27; -aec, 26.
(bo)ċoıb, g, i, n, p.
ċoıbċe, h.
Coımbe (n.), d, f; ċoımbeb (g.), c, l.
ċoımbelbaıb, d.
Coımbıb (d., ac.), i, l, m, n.
Coımbıu (n.), d, e, f, l.
coımec, b; ċoımecup, g.
coımpcepċaıp, b.
cóıp, f, l, o.
coıcċınb, e, k, l; coıcccenn, 16.
col, f.
colaınn, 26.
col[leċ] (co n-), (prep.), d.
col[lın] (co n-), d.
com (co n-, conj.), comba, h, o; combab, e, n; combıcıp, f; combuı, h; comblapınb, k.
comaıll, m.
comaınmnıuᵹub, f.
ċomaıp, a.
comaıple, f, g.
comaıccpeb, f.
comap, g, l.
comċoema, c.
combaıl, i.
ċombelb, o; aıb, o.
comla (n. s.), a; comlabaıb, b.
comlabpa, m.
comlan, c.
comleċan, a.
comluaċa, o.

compab, 1.
Conaċcu, 20.
conaıp, b.
conıcc, d.
conıb, d, f, g, h, i, k, l, m, n.
connıpab, c.
ċopcaıp, a.
copn, i.
ċopp, 25, e, k, m.
copnaıb, e, g.
ċoppa, 24, 25, e; ċopaıb, m.
ċopmaılıup, o.
cocaċ, f.
cocappna, 1.
cocnıc, 24.
Cocpaıᵹe, 17.
(po)ċpaıbpım, 1.
cpaınb (g.), h.
cpanb (n., d.), e, g, h, i; (g. p.), p.
cpann, g.
(bapo)ċpacap, 27.
ċpebem, 20.
cpebuma (g. s.), a.
cpı, f.
cpıċ, d, h.
cpıne, e, k.
Cpıpc, e, o.
cpıċ, h, n; cpıċlám, k.
ċpoċab, e.
ċpoınb (g. s.), f, g, i, k.
cpoınb (g. s., n. p.), i.
cpoıp (d.), a; -pe (g.), a.
cpop (n.), a; ċpopı (g.), a.
cpunb (d.), g; ċpunn (d.), g.
cpuċ, h, n; pocpuċab, e.
(poc)cpuċaıᵹ, o; ċpuċuᵹub, d.
cu (prep.), g.
cu n- (co n-, conj.: cu n-eċea), h.
cu m- (co n-, conj.: cu m-bab), o.
cuaıpc, l, m.
(bo)ċuabap, k; (bo)cuacup, n.
cualu[b]appı, i.

INDEX VERBORUM. (I.) 77

ċuca, i; ċucamm, l; ċucuc, n, o.
(co and pr. suf. 3 p., 1 s. and 2 s. respectively.)
cuıbṗeḋ, g, n.
ċuıce (co and pr. suf. 3 s. f.), n.
ċuınȝım, g.
(ṗoc)cuıṗ, n.
cuıṗe, l.
(ṗon)cuıṗeḋ, o; (ṗon)cuıṗeḋne, o.
cuıṗıḋ, k; cuıṗmıṗ, m.
(ṗom)cuıṗṗe, n.
cuıṗṗ (g.s.), g, h, i, o; (n.p.), h, n.
cuıc, m.
Culı-ḃṗemne, 21.
cumaḋca, e.
cumṗcaıȝ, m; cumṗcuȝuḋ, o.
cunnaıl, 1.
cunncaḃaıṗc (ac.), n.
ċuṗṗ (d., ac.), f, 1.
cuṗın (co and art.), g.
cucṗuma, a, e; cucṗumma, a.

ḋ' (ḃe, ḃı), 25.
ḋ' (ḃo, poss. 2 s.), m; (prep.) 26.
ḋa (do), n.
ḋa (num.), 26, a, c.
ḋa (prep.), 1.
Ḋaȝaṗıa, 24.
ḋaıȝın-ṗe, o.
ḃam (ḃo and pr. suf. 1 s.), 27, d, g, h, i.
ḃamṗa (ḃo and pr. suf. 1 s.), 16, f.
ḃan, b, 1.
ḃaṗ, 20, b, e, f, k, m.
ḃaṗ(ceṅḃ), m.
Ḋaṗḃóen, 15.
ḋ'aṗ n- (ḃe aṗ n-), o.
ḃaċ, i.
Ḋé (g.), 24, 25, b, 1, n; n-Ḋe, b.
ḃc (prep.), a, c, d, l, o.
ḃe (ḃe and pron. suf. 3 sg. masc.), h.
ḃe (ḃe and pron. suf. 3 sg. neut.), g, h.
ḃcac (num.), 26.

ḃeaṗḃ, e.
ḃec (num.), 25, a, d.
n-ḃécc (num.), m.
ḃeċaıḃ, n; ḃoḃeċaıḃ, h; ḃoḃeċuḃṗa, o.
ḃeċṗaıḃ, i; ḃeċṗam, f.
ḃeıċ (num.), a.
ḃeılḃ, g.
ḃeıṗ (g.), e.
ḃeıṗcenc, e.
ḃelḃ, h; ḃelḃaıḃ, ḃ.
ḃelḃe, o; ḃelḃı, (g.), o.
ḃemnaıḃ, 1.
ḃe'n (ḃe ın), 15.
ḃena, g, m.
ḃénam, e, g, o; ḃenamm, f.
ḃene, d; ḃenum, m.
ḃeoċaıṗ, g, h.
ḃeoıḃ, o.
ḃeoın, 24.
ḃeolaıḃeóc, k.
ḃeṗ, 25.
(ṗo)ḃeṗcc, n.
ḃeṗȝ, c.
ḃeṗȝoṗ, a, b; ḃeṗȝoıṗ, a, b, d.
ḃeṗmaıṗ, a, l.
ḃeṗnaḃ, e.
ḃeṗnaıṗ, i; -ncaıṗ, 16.
ḃeṗcenc, e.
ḃecıḃ, i.
Ḋéṗeḃ, 20.
Ḋeuṗ, c.
ḃı (prep.), a, e, l, m, p.
ḃı (ḃo), o.
ḃí (num.), m.
ḃı (ḃo and pron. suf. 3 sg. f.), h.
Ḋıa, 24, 25, a, d, f, i. k, l, m, n, o.
ḃıa (conj. temp.), o.
ḃıa nḃ- (conj. temp.), o.
ḃıa (conj. conditional), g.
ḃıa m-[ḃ]aḃ, i.
ḃıa (ḃe and a, poss. masc. 3 sg.), 24, m.

INDEX VERBORUM. (I.)

dia (de and a, poss. fem. 3 sg.), e, f.
dia m- (conj.), 17.
dia n- (de and rel.), e.
dia (do a), f, g, k, m, n.
Dia-Mairt, 16.
diap (do ap), m, n.
diap n- (do ap n-), 1.
diabul, e, f, n; diabuil (g.), k, n.
diaipmib, a.
dian-bap, n.
Diapmait, 15. [f, g, i.
dib (de and pron. suf. 3 p.), a, b, d,
dib (do and pron. suf. 2 p.), g.
dibpin, a, b; dibpium, h.
n-dibud, 1.
n-diópa, p.
dioped, o; -et, o.
didup, 1.
dig, 1, p; dige (g.), p.
(nop)digbann, 26.
dil, d.
n-dilcend, 1.
dilgud, m, n.
diliu, e.
(po)dilpigea, l.
dimm (di and pron. suf. 1 s.), h.
dimmat, l.
dind (di and pron. suf. 2 p.), m.
dingnaib, n.
dino, a, b, c, d, e, f, l, m, n, o, p.
n-dip, f.
Dipip, e.
ditt (di and pron. suf. 2 s.), h.
diumup, d, n.
dlegaid, 15.
n-dligteċ, b, g.
dlomad, g; -pat, k.
do (vbl. pelc.), dobenpa, o:
    dobepten, k; dobetea, i;
    doċoid, g, i, n, p; docuabap, k;
    docuatup, n; dobeċaid, h;
    dobeċubpa, o; dofuit, n;
    dollogfaitea, i; daipigne, 24;
    dopigne, a, d, m; -i, 25;
    do lott, n; dolluid, i;
    dopat, d, h, m; dorpat, f;
    dopatiup, n; dopatairiu, i;
    dotairpmirc, d; dopidnaċt, 24,1.
do (prep.), 17, a, c, d, f, h, i, k, l, m, n, p.
do (di, de), 24, 25, 26, 27, a, b, c, d, e, g, k, m, n, o.
do'n (di de) and in, art.), d, g, h.
do'n (do and in, art.), g.
do (do with pron. suf. 3 sg. masc.), 24, e, l, m.
do (poss. 2 sg.), f, g, h, i, k, m, n, o.
doċpaid, h.
(po)doċt, d.
doċum, b, d, f, g, h, i, k, n, o.
dodáil, d.
dogpai, k.
dogpepu, o.
doib (do and pr. suf. 3 p.), k.
doinib, b.
doipre, b; doiprib, a.
dom' (do mo), d, l, o.
domain (g.), a, b, d, e.
domenma, k.
dominationep, c.
Dominup, c.
dommai, k.
do'n (do in), 26.
donair (g. sg.), a, b; (n. p.), a.
donidire, l, n.
donup, a, g, h; (ac.), a; (g.pl.), a, b.
dot' (do, prep. and do, poss. 2 sg.), n.
dpeid, f.
dpongaib, c, o.
dú, 20.
duaid, h.
dual, h.
duib (do and pron. suf. 2 p.), e, g, n.
dúil, l, o.

buile, (ac. p.), m; -ı (n. p.), 25.
builemain (ac.), i; buileman, g, i, o.
buille, i; buillepab, c.
buine, 25, b, d.
buic, f, g, h, i, m, o.
bul, e, f, g, h. [1, m.
bun (bo and pron. suf. 1 p.), 15, 16,
bún (sb.), h.
búp, 1.

e (pron.), 26, a, c, e, f, h, o.
(noco n-)ebep, h.
ebepc, n.
(po)eblap, g.
ébpab, o.
ecoıp, 27.
eb (pron.), 26, c.
écc, n.
eócaıp, f.
eıpჳ, g.
cinıჳe, m; einıჳpıcca, e.
cinıub, c.
en, a, c.
n-enbacc, o.
enlaıc, c.
cnnacc, c.
eol, 27.
epcıb, i, k.
n-epóoıceépa, i.
epcpaı, c.
epópaı, l.
epbíbab, b, l.
epaılem, f; epaılım, g.
(pup)epalı, f.
Cpenn (ac.), 20.
epჳpıu, m.
epım, k; epımm, k.
c-epmebon, i.
h-eppopcaóaıb, a; eppopcaıb, b.
er (ır, ocur), 20, 26; er (ır, vb.), 27.
ép, 25; épe, 20; epı, f, o.
erbaıb, g.

erépჳı (g.), e.
eríbe, m.
eríum, l.
errı, e, m; errıbe, i.
ercı (a (arr) and pr. suf. 3 s. f.), o.
eca, h.
ecaó, l.
n-ecan (g. p.), k.
(poh)ecepcrcapab ... ppı, k.
n-ecepcrcapab ... ppı, m.
ecpam (ecep and pr. suf. 1 s.), g.
ecpócc, 24; ecpoóczlaın, c.
ecpum (ecep and pr. suf. 1 s.), o.
eccı, c.
Cua, 25, 26, d, e, f, g, h, k.
Cuppacen, d.
eχamla, k; eχamlaıb, a, h.

pa (ba), 26.
pa (po), o.
(pup)pacaıb, p.
(co pup)[ṗ]acca, h.
paჳuba, a.
paıóċı, a, b; -ċıb, a, b.
paılcı, b.
paıp (pop and pr. suf. 3 s. masc. or neut.), 27, f, p.
ṗaıpneıp, b.
pac, 24; paca (g. p.), e.
paca (adj.), n.
peıb, h.
ṗél, 15; ṗelı, i.
pen, d, f, g, i, l, o.
pep (n.s.), 24, 27; (ac.), 26; (g.p.), 27.
ṗép, p.
perabaıp, e.
ṗeram, g.
(po)perr, e.
perrın, b, c.
perca, h.
ṗecap, h.
pecup, h, m.

80 INDEX VERBORUM. (I.)

(noc)fia, g.
fiab, b.
fiabnaire, o.
fial, h.
ficcommna, i.
fici, 26; ficet, c; -ćit, 26.
fibbuib, i.
fil, a, b, c, d, g, h, o.
filet, a, b, m.
fin, d.
fína, b, d.
fínb, c.
finbruine, a.
fínʒal, 1.
fir (g. s.), 26-7; (n. p.), 27; ḟir (voc.), 1.
firu (ac. p.), 20.
fír, d, g.
firinbe, e.
ḟirinne (g.), b.
firmamint, a.
fir, g; firr, g.
ḟirron, d.
fiuʒrab, e.
flaićiur, n.
fo, a, c, d, h, i, l, o, p.
fo bear, b, d.
fo leić, b.
foruca, k.
foccna (g.), i.
foćnaicc, b.
foebur, 1.
foʒnam, 17, d, k.
foelair (fut. 2 s. of folanʒim), h.
foʒur, b.
foirr (g.), k.
(nor)follamnaiʒenb, f.
ḟolt, m.
fom' (fo mo), e.
ḟomamur, f.
fo'n (fo in), d, e, f.
fonb, a.

fon, 16, 27, a, b, c, d, e, f, g, h, i, k, m, n, o.
fonaib, b.
fonba, p.
foncenb, d; -nn, 24.
foncetlaib, k.
foncetul, i, m.
(no)fonconʒair, k.
fonconʒna, n.
(no)fonconʒnab.. fon, o.
fonfaćrum, 1.
fonm (fon and pr. suf. 3 s.), i, 1.
fonmat, c.
(no)fonmtiʒ, e.
ḟoronba, b.
fonni (fon and pr. suf. 3 s. f.), f.
fonra m- (fon and rel.), i.
font (fon and pr. suf. 2 s.), g, n, o.
fontra (fon and pr. suf. 2 s.), 1.
ḟoraiʒer, a.
ḟorcabaib, p.
fonrcemiul (d.), c.
ḟot (n. s., g. p.), e.
fot' (fo and bo), d, m.
fnertal, g.; -ul, g.
fri, a, d, e, f, g, h, i, k, l, m.
fria, b, f, l, n, o.
frim (fri and pr. suf. 1 s.), g, h.
frimra (fri and pr. suf. 1 s.), o.
frinb (fri and pr. suf. 1 p.), g, l, o.
frinne (fri and pr. suf. 1 p.), o.
fririn (fri and art.), a, b, f, g, m, o.
frir na[ib], m.
frit (fri and pron. suf. 2 s.), h.
fritʼ (fri bo), h.
frić (vb.), i.
frićailem, g.
frićmuir, a.
frićoilib, k.
fritra (fri and pr. suf. 2 s.), o.
fritt (fri and pr. suf. 2 s.), l, o.
fromab, g.

INDEX VERBORUM. (I.)

fuacc, h, 1.
fuaıp, f, m; fuapup, o.
fubomaın, d, l, o.
(nop)fuıb, o.
fuıbbemıp, g.
fuıʒbıċea, l.
fuıl (sb.), 24, 25, 1.
fuıl (ind. pres. 3 sg.), d.
fuıpeċ, g, k.
fuıppı (pop and pr. suf. 3 s. f.), a.
(bo)fuıc, n.
no[f]upaıl, n.
fuċıb (po and pr. suf. 3 p.), a.

'ʒa (oc a), g.
(nop)ʒab, n; ʒabaıb, h.
Ꙗaba, 27.
Ꙗabpıel, ı.
ʒaċ, 25.
Ꙗaʒonıa, 24.
ʒaıpm, h.
(no)ʒabucap, m.
ʒalap, 1; ʒalaıp (g. s.), k.
ʒallpa, k; ʒallpaıb, h, o.
ʒalup, e.
Ꙗapab, 24, 25.
(nopbı)ʒbann, 26.
(cop')ʒapc (co poʒapc), g.
(nıp)ʒebab, 1; ʒeıb, f, h.
ʒel, 26.
ʒell, 24.
ʒemıu, a.
ʒen, 20, 26.
(bo)ʒen, o; (bo)ʒena, g, 1.
(bo)ʒenac, d.
(no)ʒenfıċea, e.
(bo)ʒencap, o; (bın)ʒencup, 1.
Ꙗeon, d.
ʒıl (g.), a.
ʒlaen, 26; ʒlaın (d.), a; (n. p.), k.
ʒlaıne (sb.), m.
ʒlaınıbe, b; ʒlaınebaıb, b.

ʒlan, 24, k, m.
ʒle, 24, k.
ʒleʒpeım, k.
ʒlıccup, g.
ʒloın, e; ʒloıne, a.
ʒluapaċc, f.
(bo)ʒné, n.
(bopı)ʒne, a, d, m; (bopı)ʒnı, 25; (bapı)ʒne, 24.
(bo)ʒneċea, e, ı.
(bo)ʒní, g, n.
ʒnım, 24, ı.
n-ʒnımpaba, k.
(bo)ʒníċep, m.
ʒnuıp, b, n.
ʒnuıpıb, c.
ʒopcaı, k, 1.
Ꙗolʒocha, e.
ʒpab, (n., d.), b, f, ı, o.
ʒpaba (n. p.), d.
ʒpabaıb, c, m, o.
ʒpaıb (g. s., n. p.), c.
ʒpaın, n.
ʒpeʒa, 26.
ʒpeın, a.
(bo)ʒpep, c, f.
ʒpıan, 26; -nba, 24.
ʒuıb (imp.), m.
(no)ʒuıb, m.
ʒuıbem, n.
ʒuıbec, m.

hꙄbam, e, k, l, m.
haınʒlıb, c.
haınʒlıu (ac.), k, 1.
haıpm, n.
hanmaın, h.
hapċaınʒlıb, c.
haċcomaıpc (n. p.), b.
he, e, l, n.
heıpʒ, f.
hepċoıc, h.

G

82 INDEX VERBORUM. (I.)

heṅgaiṅte, h; -ċi, m; -ġaṅċi, h.
heṅpoṅtaċaib, a.
heṅcai, a.
heua, g, k.
hi (pron.), e, f, h; hi (rel.), a.
hi (prep.), a, i, l.
h[ṙ]il, 27.
hile, k.
himaṅbuṅ, d.
himeṅbṅéc, d.
himṅeb, 27.
hiṅġnab, h.
hiṅuphin, c, i.
hiṅta, k.
hiṫe, a, b.
hoġaib, c.
huain, g.
huaiṅi, d.
h[ṗ]uil, 24.
huile, f, 1; hulib, m.
hulc, h.

i (pron. 3 s. fem.), 15.
i (prep.), 26, c, e, h, i, l, m, n, o.
i n- (prep.), 20, 25, a, c, d, e, g, i, l, m, o.
i m- (i n-), k.
im(boi i n-), n.
i ṅ-(i n-), 15.
i n-aġaib, o.
i (rel.), g, i; i ṅ-(i n-), 15.
Iacoib, 27.
iaṅ, 26, e, h, k, m, p.
iaṅ m-, f, m.
iaṅ n-, k, l, m.
iaṅṅub, m.
iaṅ ṅin, a, c, f, g, h, m, o.
iaṅtaiġe, o.
iaṅtain, e.
iaṅteṅ, e.
iaṅum, e, f, h, i, k, n.
iat, b, f, h; iatṅibe, b.

ic, 17, i.
ibon, 25, a, b, d, k, l, o.
ieṅuṅalem, e.
iḟinn, d, h; iḟḟinn, k, l, o.
il (i n-), b, d.
il(ċeolaib), d.
ile, d; ilib, o.
ille, e.
im, 26, 28, a, m, n.
im' (i mo), f, h, l.
imaċ, g.
imacallaim, m.
imab, k.
imaiċbeṅ, l.
imalle, h, k.
imaṅbaiṅ (g.), e.
imaṅboiṅ (g.), k, l.
imaṅbuṅ (ac.), m; n-imaṅbuiṅ (g.), l.
imáṅim, 26.
imbiṅ, l.
imbíten, h.
ime, n; imme (imb and pr. suf. 3 s.), i.
imeċtṅaċ, a.
imluab, c.
immaċ, a, f.
immeṅc, f.
immṗoctaicċib, b.
imneba, 25; -baib, o.
imon (im in), a, c, m.
imoṅṅo, a, b, c, d, f, n, o.
impe (imb and pr. suf. 3 s. f.), h, n.
impu (imb and pr. suf. 3 p.), h.
imṅatib, n.
himṅeb, 27.
imṅeṅain, i, o.
in (art. n. s.), 26, 29, a, b, d, e, f, g, h, i, l, m, o, p.
in (art. g. s.), 16, 24, 25, 26, 27, b, c, d, e, f, g, h, i, k, l, m, o, p.
in (art. ac. s.), 25, b, c, d, f, g, h, l, m, n.
in n- (nom. s.), m; (ac. s.), e, i.

INDEX VERBORUM. (I.) 83

ın n- (ac. p.), m.
ın (conj.), l.
ın (interrog.), g, i.
ın (in which), e.
ınd (ı and pron. suf. 3 sg. masc.), h.
índ (ı and pron. suf. 3 sg. neut.), e, g.
ınad, f
(nonn)ındanbaır, n.
ı n-dıaıd, c.
ındıɼɼectɼa, o; ındıɼımm, d.
ındıu, 15, 16.
ındlıȝceḋ, g; n-ındlıȝceḋ, m, p.
ındɼaıȝıd, b.
ındɼın, h, m.
ındcleḋc, g.
ındur, e, f.
ınȝen, 26, 27.
ınȝnad, h; n-ınȝnad, b.
ınȝnaıɼ, h.
ınn (art. g. s.), c.
ınɼo, e.
ın c- (art. n. s. m.), 28, a, c, e.
ın c- (art. g. s. m.), o; (n.), m.
ıncı (he who), h, m.
ınncıb (ı and pr. suf. 3 p.), b.
loḃıɼ ȝalad, 27.
lonḋanen, m.
ıɼ (vb.), 15, 16, 25, 26, 27, a, b, c, d, e, f, g, h, i, k, l, n, o.
ıɼ (conj.), d.
ıɼın (ı and art.), 15, b, c, i.
Iɼu, o.
ıc' (ı and do, poss. 2 sg.), f.
ıc, e.
ıcóuala, n; ıccualad, i.
ıcen (adv.), k, m.
ıcen (prep.), g, m, o.
luda, 27.

la (g. p.), m, p; laa (n. p.), m.
la (prep.), h.
(con')laa (co nolaa), m.

(non)laad, 1; nolad, 27.
(nom)laadɼa, o.
Laban, 24.
laeı, a; laı, d, m.
Laȝnıu, 20; Laıȝen, 15.
láım (d. s., ac. dual), h, m.
laıɼ (la and pr. suf. 3 s. m.), e, h, i, k, m.
lamaım, g.
lan, a.
lanamaın, p.
lan, c, i; lanċalmaın, n.
lac (la and pr. suf. 2 s.), m.
lacı, k.
lebendaıb, b; lebeunn, 16.
lecaıb, b; lecca, b.
lecıd, k; (al)lecud, h.
lee (la and pr. suf. 3 s. f.), h.
(do) leȝad, h.
(nac)leıcc, g.
leıċ, d.
[lemnaḋċ], d; lemınaḋca, d.
lenṁaın, n.
lenna, b.
leo (la and pr. suf. 3 p.), h, m.
len, 26.
leɼ (le and pr. suf. 3 s. masc.), 24.
leċ, a, d, e, g, h, l, m.
leċı, e.
Leuı, 27.
lıa, 24.
lıb (la and pron. suf. 2 p.), i, n.
lıca, a; lícc, m.
lıȝdaıb, a.
lıı (hı ?), 26.
lım(ɼa) (la and pr. suf. 1 s.), d.
lín, 26, d, o; lınaıɼ, h.
lınd (sb.), b.
lınd (la and pron. suf. 1 p.), m.
loc, d; locc, i.
loḋc, d.
Loḋaın, 25.

INDEX VERBORUM. (I.)

lóg, f; bollogṗaiċea, i.
logmaiṗ, a; logmaṗa, b.
logmaṗaib, b.
(ṗo)loigṗec, i.
(nin)loiṗcṗeb, 1.
lomnaċc, h.
loṗ, 1; loiṗ, 27.
bo locc, n.
luag, k.
(co) luaċ, n.
Luciṗeṗ, d, e, f, g, 1, n, o, p.
luibe, 1, m; luibib, a.
luibeṗab, p.
luicc, c.
(bol)luib, i.
luinbe, k.

m (pron. inf. 1 s.), ṗomcinol, 9;
    ṗomboeċaibṗea, h;
    ṗomcuiṗṗe, n; ṗomlaabṗa, o;
    nimcaiṗ, g; nimcaiṗbeṗiub, d;
    aṗbomcaṗa, f.
m for n (ni m-ananacaṗ), h.
m' (mo), 20.
ma, 16, g, i.
mac, 27; -cc, 26.
maiċ, g, k, 1, n.
maiċiuṗ, i; maicuṗ (g.), g.
maiċiuṗa, h.
Malon, e.
maneṗcṗeċ, 16.
mannuṗ, f.
maṗ (aen), i.
maṗbub, 28; (ṗoc)maṗbaiṗ, n;
    (ṗo)maṗbac, 15; -bṗac, 27.
me, o.
mebon, d; mebonaċ, e.
meic, k.
Mél-bṗigce, 16.
mela, d, p.
(ṗoc)mell, n; (ṗo)mellṗab, f.
(ṗo)ṁelmaiṗ, 1.
(ṗoc)melluṗcaṗ, n.

menma, n.
ṁeṗcin, p.
meṗa, h.
mec, a.
Miċel (n., ac.), o; Miċil (g.), i.
míl, m.
mile, 27, 28, a, b, d.
mín, 26, 27.
mina, 1, o.
mine, 1.
miṗ, e.
miṗe, g. i.
Miṗimbṗia, e.
mna (p.), k; mnae (s. and d.), 26,
    27, 28.
mo (poss. l sg.), d, f, g, h, i, k, l, m, n, o.
mo (comp.), g.
mob, m.
Moel-bṗigce, 9, 15.
moiṗ (ac.), m, n.
molab, c.
monaṗ, k, m.
moṗ, 26, 27, a, b, f, h, 1, n;
    moṗa[ib], o.
moṗcaċṗaċ, b.
moṗḟlog, i.
moṗ (adj. as sb.), b.
moci, 1.
muigib, b.
muiṗ (n. p.), a.
Muiṗe,
muinceṗ, i; munceṗ, 27.
muinciṗe (g.), o.
Muman, 20.
múṗ (n. s.), a, d; (g. s.), a; (d. s.), a;
    (ac.), b; (n. dual), a; (g. p.), a.
muṗaib, a, c.

'n (i n- aphæresis of i), b, c, e, h.
n (pron. inf. 1 p.), ṗoncuiṗeb, o;
    ṗoncuiṗebne, o; ṗoṗṗinbaṗ-
    baiṗ, n; ninloiṗcṗeb, 1;
    ṗonmell, h.

INDEX VERBORUM. (I.)

na (art. g. s. f.), b, c, g, i, k.
na (art. n. p.), 25, a, b, d, f, h, l.
na (art. g. p.), 26, a, b, c, d, e, i, p.
na (art. ac. pl.), a, c.
na (conj. neg), b, d, f, g, l, m, n, o.
na (naib, d. p. of ın, art.), 20, a, c, e, i, m, o.
na m- (na n-, art. g. p.), b.
'n-aṅ (for ı n-aṅ ; aphæresis of ı), f.
na n- (art. g. p.), a, b, c, e, f, g, o.
na nn- (art. g. p.), 26.
naċ (conj. neg.), i, k.
nac (interr. neg.), o
nab, 24.
nama, e.
naṫıṅ, f, g, h.
nacleıcc, g.
naṫṗaċ (g. s.), g ; naṫṗaıʒ, f, g, h.
neam, e.
neċ, c ; neıċ (g.), g.
nell, n.
nem, k, m; nembaıb, m.
nemelnıʒṫı, c, e.
nemloċtaċ, c.
neoċ, m.
neṗhnı, c.
neṗa, c.
ní (sb.), b, g, h, k, l, m.
nı (neg.), 16, a, b, c, d, f, g, h, i, k, l, m, n, o.
nıco n-(ṗeṫuṅ), h; -(ṗoelaıṗ), h.
nı m-(ananacaṅ), h.
nım, c, d, l, m, n, o.
nıme, c, d, f, i, k, o; nımıb, i, o.
no (vbl. pcle.), nobeṅṫa, e ;
noċaıṫṗıṫıṗ, m; conuṗ-
[ṗ]acca, h; noṗṗollam-
naıʒenb, f; noṗbıʒbann, 26.
noʒenṗıṫea, e; nomellṗab, f;
noṁelmaıṗ, l; noṗoṗbaıʒeb, l;
noṗmaċṫab, f; noṫeʒċıṗ, f.
no (conj.), 24, c, f, g, l, m, p.

noco m-(luaṗu), d.
noco n-, h.
nóeb, 20.
noem, b; -maıb, b.
noemanmanb, d.
noemcaṫṗaıʒ, b.
noeṁı, e.
noı (num.), e, m, o.
noım (n. p.), b; noıme, l.
noımuaʒa (n. p.), b.
noı n- (num.), c, d.
nuallʒuba, m.
nuaṅ, n.

o (prep.), a, b, d, e, m, n, o.
o (conj. temp.), l, o.
obenn, 16.
oc, c, e, f, g, h, i, l, m, n.
ocaınb (oc and pron. suf. 1 p.), m.
occaıb (oc and pron. suf. 2 p.), g.
occu (oc and pron. suf. 3 p.), l.
oċṫmab, e.
ocuṗ (⁊), *passim*.
ocuṫ (oc and pron. suf. 2 s.), h.
oemenn, 15.
oen, 26, 28, a, b, c, d, e.
oeıṗ, e ; oeṗ, k.
oʒ, b.
oıṅ (conj.), o.
oıṅeċuṗ, g.
oıṅeṫ, k.
oıṅṗıṫeb, l; oıṅṗıṫıub, f.
oıṅmıṫıṅ, i, o ; oıṅmıṫıu, d.
oıṅṫeṅ, e.
ol, 20, d, e, g, h, i, k, l, m, n, o.
olaı (n. g.), d.
olc, g, h, o.
olbaṗ, d, g.
olṫaṗ, f, g, o.
o'n (o ın), e, n.
on, 26, d.
n-onoıṅ, l.

INDEX VERBORUM. (I.)

opunb, **h.**
op (sb.), **a, c**; óıp (g.), **20**.
op (vb.), **d, f, o.**
(po)opbaıʒ, **c, d.**
(nop)opbaıʒeb, **l.**
opucpa (aıp and pron. suf. 2 s.), **l.**
op, **c.**
opın, **b, e, k.**
opɫaıc, **g**; opɫaıcep, **g.**
opɫaıcıb, **h.**
oc' (o bo), **g.**

pop' (po pa), **h.**
paılme (g.), **i.**
Papıach, **e.**
Papbaıp (g.), **e**; -uıp (g.), **e, g, i.**
Papbup, **f, g, h, i.**
Pappbaıp (g.), **f.**
Pappċaıp (g.), **d.**
Pappċup, **d.**
Papċaıp (g.), **i**; -uıp (g.), **m.**
Papċup, **d, i, k, l, n, o**; -ċup, **e, l.**
Paċpaéċ, **20.**
peınn, **l.**
penbaıc, **m**; pennaıc, **p.**
ponʒc, **e.**
Peċaıp, **15.**
poċepċaċep, **c.**
ppımcaċpaıʒ, **a, c.**
ppımboıppıb, **a, c.**
ppımbopup, **b.**
ppímbun, **b.**
ppıncıpaċup, **c.**

ράδ, **24.**
pabapcc, **e.**
paʒaıb, **o.**
paıb (po baı), **g, h.**
pahopbaıʒeb (= po-), **e.**
popáıb, **e, k, o**; popaıbı, **k.**
popaıbpeċ, **o.**

pappmaıp (g.), **k.**
(po)pappap, **g.**
(bo)paċ, **d, h, m**; (bop)paċ, **f.**
(bo)paċaıp, **n**; (bo)paċaıpıu, **i.**
pe (Le), **b, d, i, n.**
peċċ, **m.**
peblannaıb, **e.**
peʒuċpa, **m.**
peıll, **h, i.**
peıp, **d.**
pemıpın, **h**; pempu, **o**; pemum, **g.**
pempa, **a.**
pepın, **h.**
pı, **15, k.**
pıa, **15, i.**
pıa-n, **d, e.**
pıaċċ, **b, h.**
pıóıb, **a, g, k, n**; pıóıʒ (g.), **n.**
pıċċ, **n.**
pıʒ (n.), **c, d, i, k, o**; (g.), **c**; (d.), **a, o.**
pıʒan, **26.**
pıʒboıppe, **a.**
pıʒropaıb, **c**; pıʒṙoppab, **c**; -ub, **c.**
pıʒ[p]poċaıb, **b.**
píʒṙuıbe, **c, i.**
pıʒċeċ, **a.**
pıʒċıʒ, **a**; pıʒċıʒe, **a.**
pıċ, **h.**
po (vbl. pcle.), po abpaıp, **o**;
p'aıċın, **n**; pohaıċneb, **g**;
paıb (po baı). **h**; pobopbae, **28**;
nıp'baċ (nı pobaċ), **m.**;
popbean, **d**; popben, **h**;
popbıa, **k**; poċbıa, **f, g**;
poċboeċaıʒ, **h**; pobuı, **l**;
poċaıċ, **d**; poclaeċlaıp, **n**;
poċloeċla, **h**; poclaıbpım, **l**;
pocpuċab, **e**; pocpuċaıʒ, **o**;
poċcuıp, **n**; poncuıpeb, **o**;
poncuıpebne, **o**; pomcuıppe, **n**;
pobepcc, **n**; pobılpıʒea, **l**;
poblompaċ, **k**; poeblap, **g**;

INDEX VERBORUM. (I.)

no (vbl. pcle.)—*continued*.
　nuɼeɳalı, f; ɳoheċeɳɼcanaḃ, k; nuɼꝼacaıb, p;
　noꝼaɼlaız, i; noꝼeɼɼ, e;
　noċꝼıa, g; noɼoɳconʒaıɼ, k;
　noꝼoɳconʒnaḃ, o;
　noꝼoɼnmcıʒ, e; noɼꝼuıḃ, o;
　no[ꝼ]uɳaıl, n; noɼʒaḃ, n;
　noʒaḃuɼa, h; noʒaḃucaɳ, m;
　coɳ'ʒaɳc, g; noʒeḃaḃ, g;
　noʒuıḃ, m; noċʒuıḃ, h;
　noɳnınḃaɳbaıɼ, n; naċɼoıc, b;
　noıċeḃ, m; coɳ'laa, m;
　noɼlaı, g; nolaḃ, 27;
　nonlaaḃ, 1; nomlaaḃɼa, o;
　noleıc, h; noloıʒɼec, i;
　noċmaɳbaıɼ, n;
　nomaɳbɼac, 27; -bac, 15;
　nooɳḃaıʒ, c, d;
　nahoɳḃaıʒeḃ, e; nop', h;
　noɳdıḃ, e, k, o; noɳaıḃı, k;
　noɳaıḃɼec, o; noɳannaɳ, g;
　noꝼaɳaıʒ, 1; noɼaɳaıʒeɼ, i;
　noꝼaɳaıʒɼımaɳ, 1;
　noɼeɳnaḃ, i; noɼocıc, b;
　noɼoıc, b; coɳ'ꝼuıḃeɼ, o;
　nuɼca, k; noċaıɳıɼ, m;
　noċaıɳmcemnıʒ, e; noċecc, f;
　noceıɼeḃ, e; nomcınol, 9;
　noċınoılɼıc, m; noċomaıl, h;
　noċnaɼcnaḃ, d;
　noċnoıɼceḃ, m; nuc, 26;
　noɼnuc, 25; conḃacnuc, o;
　nocuɼmeḃ, f.
no (vbl. pcle. infixed), annoec, e;
　ḃanoċnacaɳ, 27; ḃeɳnaḃ e;
　ḃeɳnaıɼ, i; ḃoɳaʒaɼa, g;
　ḃonıḃnaóc, 24, 1; ḃaɳıʒne, 24;
　ḃonıʒne, a, d, m; -nı, 25;
　ḃonımaɳc, d; ḃonoċaıɳ, h;
　ḃonoıne, i; ḃoɼɳoıne, c;
　ḃoɳoɳɼaıc, g, m;

ḃoɳoɳca, c, e, m; ꝼonuca, k;
　caɳḃaḃ, o; caɳmaıɳc, n.
no (intens.), noaɳḃa, a;
　no[ꝼ]nı[c]ʒnımı, 25; noɳıʒ, 26.
noınḃ, h.
noɼc, m.

ɼ (pron. infix. 3 s. m.), noɼʒaḃ, n;
　noɼꝼuıḃ, o; noɼlaı, g.
ɼ (pron. infix. 3 s. f.), noɼɳuc, 25.
ɼ (pron. infix. 3 s. neut.), nıɼbıa, f, g;
　noɼbıa, k; nuɼeɳalı, f;
　conuɼ[ꝼ]acca, h;
　nıɼꝼecuɼ, m; nıɼca, k;
　noċuɼca, k; nuɼca, k.
ɼ (pron. infix. 3 p.), noḃoɼbae, 28;
　nuɼꝼacaıḃ, p;
　noɼꝼollamnaıʒenḃ, f;
　noɼoɳḃaıʒeḃ, 1; ḃoɼnoıne, c.
—ɼa, 15, 16, d, e, f, h, i, m, n, o.
Sabaoth, c.
ɼaeċ, 1; ɼaeċaıb, h.
ɼaecaɼ, k, 1.
ɼaıɳ, d.
ɼamaıʒɼec, d.
ɼamaıl, a; ɼamaılceɼ, a.
ɼancc (g. p.), c.
Sanccuɼ, c.
(no)ꝼaɳaıʒ, 1; -aıʒɼımaɳ, 1.
(no)ɼaɳaıʒeɼ, i; ꝼaɳuʒuḃ, i.
Saɳaphın, c.
ɼaɼaḃ, d, l, p; ꝼaɼaɼ, b.
ɼaɼɼaḃ, b; ɼaɼcaı, m; ɼaɼcaɳ, c.
ɼcaılce, m.
ɼcaɳaḃ, k; ɼcaɳaḃ...ꝼnı, h.
(no)ɼcaɳɼacuɼ...ꝼnı, n.
ɼcaċ, i.
ɼceɳċaıɼ, b.
ɼcoloca, 16.
Scɳeɼcɳa, e.
ɼcnıḃenḃa, d.
ɼcnıḃċa, c.

INDEX VERBORUM. (I.)

ṡe (pron.), d, e, f, g, h, i, k, l, m, n, o.
—ṡe, o.
ṡe (num.), c.
—ṡea, d, h, l, o.
ṡeċ, a.
Seċna, 26.
ṡeċt, f, i, m, o, p; ṡeċt n-, a.
ṡeċtaiṙ, f.
ṡeċtmain, 1; -tmoẓaet, 26.
ṡeċut (ṡeċ and pron. suf. 2 s.), f.
ṡeinteṙ, i.
Seṅaphin, c.
ṡeṅẓ, 25.
ṅoṡeṅnab, i.
ṡeṅ[ċ]iẓ, k.
ṡeṙca, 27; ṡeṙcat, 28, c.
ṡi, a, f, g, h, i, l, m.
ṡiaṙ, d.
ṡiat, a, c, k.
—ṡibe, 15, c, e.
ṡil, 27, b, e, k.
Sil, 26.
ṡin (dem.), 25, a, b, c, e, f, g, h, k, l, m, n, p.
ṡinb, l, n; ṡinne, l.
ṡine, d; ṡiṅiu, o.
ṡinnṙeṅ, o.
t-ṡinnṙiṙ (g.), o.
ṡiṅliẓi, 25.
ṡiṙṅaṅbuṙ, l.
ṡiṙṡaeṫṅaiẓ, k.
- - ṡiu, m.
— ṡium, d, o.
ṡlaṅbilẓub, m.
ṡlanti (n. s.), l.
ṡleib, c.
ṡlebti, e.
ṡloẓ (n., ac. and d. s.), a, b, c, i; (g. p.), b, c, d, o.
ṡ́loẓ (d. s.), a.
ṡloiẓ (n. p.), b, c, f.
ṡ́loẓu (voc. p.), i.

ṙmaċt, e, i, k, l.
(no)ṙmaċtab, f.
ṙniẓeṙ, d.
ṙnimaiẓ, k.
ṅoṙoċit, b.
ṅoṙoiċ, b.
ṙoluṙ, 26.
ṙoillṙe, b.
ṙoínmeċ, o.
ṙomblaṙta, b.
ṙomiliṙ, b.
ṙoṙab, c.
ṙoṙṙab, b, c, d.
ṡoṙṙaib (g.), b.
ṙoṙaṙ, 26, d, f, o.
t-ṡoṙaiṙ (g.), o.
ṙoṙta, a; ṙoṙtaib, a.
ṙṅeat (g. p.), b; ṙṅeiṫ, a, i.
t-[ṙ]ṅeib, a.
t-ṙṅoċa (g.), m; ṙṅoċaib, b.
ṙṅuṫ, d, m, n, p.
ṙtocc, i.
—ṙu, m.
ṙuaill, k.
(coṅ')ṡuibeṙ (co ṅoṙuibeṙ), o.
ṙuibiuẓub, a.
ṙum, l.
ṙuċaċ, d, i.

t (pron. infix. 2 s.), ṅotbia, f, g; ṅotcṙuiċaiẓ, o; ṅotcuiṙ, n; ṅotẓab, n; ṅotmaṙbaiṙ, n; ṅotmell, ṅotmelluṙtaṙ, n; conbatṅuc, o.
t (pron. infix. 3 s. neut.), ṅotẓuib, h; natleitc, g.
t' (bo, poss. 2 sg.), f, k, m, o.
ta, i.
(aṅbom)taṙa, f.
(ṅuṙ)ta, k.
(noċuṙ)ta, k.
tabaiṙt, e, f, l, m, n.

INDEX VERBORUM. (I.) 89

tabraid, o.
taebnocc, l.
taetairra, l.
tai, n.
tainic, e.
tair, e, g, n.
tairbept, f.
(ro)tairir, m.
(ro)tairmoemnig, e.
tairmtect, d.
tairmtectur, d, m.
taitnemad, h; -ada, b.
talmain (d., ac.), a, e, h, l, m, o.
talman (g.), i, k, m, p.
talum (n., d., ac.), 25, l.
tan, 20, f, g, h, k.
tanac, 15, n.
tanic, k, n, p; tanuc, o.
tar (vb.), l; tar (prep.), e, i.
tarbad, o.
tarmairt, n.
tarnoct, h.
tarut (tar and pron. suf. 2 s.), h.
tear, 25.
tet, l, p.
teded, i.
(ro)tect, f.
tedmannaib, o.
tegdair, d.
teged, f; teiged, f.
teinid, 25.
(ro)teired, e.
teit, b, g.
tene, l; -nid, l, p.
terca, e.
termedon, i.
(nir)terpad, l.
ti, k.
tiagum, n.
tiber (fut.), d.
Tibrir, d.
tic, n; ticbir, m.

ticrad, m; -rait, f.
tidect, h, i, n.
(don)idnact (dorotidnact), 24, 1;
tig, k; tige, 16.
tigerna, f, g, n, o.
Tigir, m, n.
timcell, 27, a.
timduairt, o.
timna, f; -naib, k.
timnai, i.
tindorc, m.
tinfed, 25; -riud, 24.
(rom)tinol, 9; (ro)tinoilrit, m.
tir, 24, 25, n; tire, b.
tirmaid, p; -mugud, n.
tir, g.
tirad, l, n; tirtair, o.
tlact, h.
tlacta (g.), h.
tlait, k.
tnut, o.
tobur, d.
tocaib, m.
todaileb, l.
toeb, e.
togaetad, g.
toile (g.), o.
toimled, e.
toirrib, b.
(do)toirmirc, d.
toirri, b.
toiret, o.
tomailt, f, g, m.
tomli, g.
tomur, a.
torad, f, g, k.
toraid, b.
torrad, e.
torri, k, l; -rig, k.
torti, e; -tib, b, d.
torud, k.
torat, b.

TODD LECTURE SERIES, VOL. III.   H

INDEX VERBORUM. (I.)

τρια, 25, e, m.
(ρο)τραρςραδ, d.
τρατ̇, e; -τα, k.
τρεδ, 17; -δe, 27; eιδ, 27.
τ-[ρ]ρειδ, a.
τρεn[ḟ]ερ, 28.
τρετ (sb.), c.
τρετ̇' (τρο δο), o.
τρι (num.), 28, a, b, d, e, m.
τρια, d, i, l, m, o.
τρια n- (prep.), d.
τριαn, a, o.
τριαρ, b.
τριαριn n-, o.
τριατ̇' (τρια δο, poss. 2 sg.), o.
τριδα, 20, 28; -δετ, m.
τριδταιδε, e.
τροςαιρε, l.
τρος, n, p.
(ρο)τροιρςεδ, m.
τρομδαδ̇τ, h.
Τροnι, c.
τρυας, 28, e, l; -ςαις, k; -ςe, h.
τú, f, g, o.
τυαιδ́lι, f.
[τυαιδ], d.
τυαιρςερτ, d, e.
τυαρ, c.
τυδ̇, g, l.
τυςα, g; -αδ, n; -αρ, g.
τυςρατ, i.
τυιδεδτ, m.
τυιρεμ, b.
τυρ, f.
τυρ, d.
τυρα, l, o.
τυρςα, f.
(ρο)τυρμεδ, f.

υαδορ, 26.
υαδ̇ταρ, m; -αδ̇, a, e.
υαδα[ιδ], a; -ιδ (υα with pr. suf. 3 p.), p.
nοιμυασα (n. p.), b.
υαιll, d.
υαιμμ (υα and pron. suf. 1 s.), h.
υαιn (g. s.), c.
(h)υαιn, g.
υαιnε, a.
υαιρ (sb.), d, e.
υαιρ (conj.), d, e, f, g, i, l, m, n, o.
(h)υαιρε (p.), d; hυαιρι (p.), d.
υαιρlιυ, d.
υαιτ (υα and pr. suf. 2 s.), g.
υαμαιδ, p.
υαn, c.
υαραιδ (υαρ and pr. suf. 3 p.), c.
υαραlατραδ̇ (g. p.), e; υαρlι (sb.), o.
υαρυμ (υαρ and pron. suf. 1 s.), d.
υδαιll (g.), h, m; (ac.), h, m.
υδαll, d, g, h.
υδ̇τ, 25, e.
υιlς (g.), g; υιlςς (g.), g.
υιlε, b, c, e, g, i, o.
(h)υιlε, f, l.
υιleδυμαδ̇ταδ̇, a.
υιleδυμαδ̇ταις (g.), c.
υιρδ (n. p.), d.
υιρτυτερ, c.
(h)υlς, h.
υlε, 28; υlι (n. p., g. p., ac. p.), g, m, o.
(h)υlιδ, m.
υμ, m.
υραρδαιδ, c.
υρςε, 24, p; υιρςι[υ], 26.
Ulτυ, 20.

LECTURE II.

THE CODEX PALATINO-VATICANUS,

No. 830.

THE CODEX PALATINO-VATICANUS, No. 830.

SUCCESSIONS FROM BOOKS OF LEINSTER AND BALLYMOTE.

III.

AT folio 15 b, Marianus inserted the following catalogue of Irish kings who belonged to the northern half of Ireland:

hi runt ꝼlachi [ꝑinciper] hiberniae qui ex dimedia parte eiur, id ert, do Leth Chuinn [ex dimedio Connii], regerunt, o Chunn cetchatach co Ꝼland, mac Ṁail-Sechnaill.

  Conn, Apt, Copmac, annir lx.
  Corpri, mac Copmaic, annir xxx.
  Ꝼiache Mulletan, annir xxu.
  Mupedeach Tipeach, annir iiii.
  Euchu Muzmedoin, annir xxu.
  Conlae Roirr, annir iiii.
  Niall, annir xxuii.

These are the princes of Ireland of the moiety [called] the Half of Conn, that reigned from Conn of the Hundred Battles to Flann, son of Mael-Sechnaill.

  Conn [of the Hundred Battles], Art, Cormac, 60 years.
  Corpri, son of Cormac, 30 years.
  Fiache Mullethan, 25 years.
  Muredeach Tireach, 4 years.
  Euchu Mugmedoin, 25 years.
  Conlae Roiss [read Colla Uais], 4 years.
  Niall, 27 years.

Nathi [Dathi], annir lx.
Loegaere, mac Nell, annir lxui.
Aillill Molt, mac n[D]athi, annir xx.
Lugaed, mac Loegaere, annir xxiii.
Murchertach, macc Ercca, annir xx.
Tuathal Mailgarb, annir xuiii.
Diarmeat, mac Fergura, annir xx.
Fergur ⁊ Domnall, da mac Muircertaig meic Ercca, annir xxx.
Muiredach Munderg, annir xii.
Anmire, mac Sétnai, annir iiii.
Baitan, mac Muirchertaig ⁊ Echoid, mac Domnaell, meic Murchertaig, annir iiii.
Baetan, mac Murchada, annir xui.
Anmire, annir uii.
Colman bec, mac Diarmata ⁊ Aed, mac Anmerach, annir xiii.
Suibni, mac Colma[i]n moir, annir ui.

Dathi, 60 years.
Loegaere, son of Niall, 66 years.
Aillill Molt, son of Dathi, 20 years.
Lugaed, son of Loegaere, 23 years.
Murchertach, son of Erc, 20 years.
Tuathal Mailgarb, 18 years.
Diarmait, son of Fergus, 20 years.
Fergus and Domnall, two sons of Murchertach, son of Erc, 30 years.
Muiredach Muinderg [Red-neck], 12 years.
Anmire, son of Setna, 4 years.
Baitan, son of Muirchertach and Echoid, son of Domnall, son of Muirchertach [son of Erc], 4 years.
Baetan, son of Murchad, 16 years.
Anmire, 7 years.
Colman the Little, son of Diarmait and Aed, son of Anmire, 13 years.
Suibni, son of Colman the Great, 6 years.

Aeð Slane, mac Diarmata, annır ıııı.
Aeð Alaeinn, mac Domnaill, annır uıı.
Oenzur, mac Colma[ı]n, annır uıııı.
Suıbnı Menð, mac Pachtna, annır uıı.
Domnall, mac Aeða, annır xxxu.
Conall ⁊ Cellach, ða mac Maılecoba, annır xu.
blaðmecc ⁊ Dıarmaıt, ða macc Aeða Slane, annır uıııı.
Sechnarach, mac blaðmeıcc, annır u.
Cenðfaelað, mac blaðmeıcc, annır ıııı.
Fınnachta, mac Ðunchaða, annır xuııı.
Lonzrech, mac Oenzura, annır uıııı.
Conzall, mac Pepzurra, annır uıı.
Pepzal, mac Maeleðuın, annır xıı.
Pozartaz, mac Cernaız, annır ıı.
Cınaıð, mac Irzalaız, annır ıııı.
Flaıthbertach, mac Lonzrız, annır uı.
Aeð, mac Pepzael, annır x.
Domnall, mac Murchaða, annır xx.

Aed Slane, son of Diarmait, 4 years.
Aed Alaeinn, son of Domnall, 7 years.
Oengus, son of Colman, 9 years.
Suibni Mend, son of Fachtna, 7 years.
Domnall, son of Aed, 35 years.
Conall and Cellach, two sons of Mailcoba, 15 years.
Bladmecc and Diarmait, two sons of Aed Slane, 9 years.
Sechnasach, son of Bladmecc, 5 years.
Cendfaelad, son of Bladmecc, 4 years.
Finnachta, son of Dunchad, 18 years.
Longsech, son of Oengus, 9 years.
Congall, son of Fergus, 7 years.
Fergal, son of Maelduin, 12 years.
Fogurtach, son of Cernach, 2 years.
Cinaid, son of Irgalach, 4 years.
Flaithbertach, son of Longsech, 6 years.
Aed, son of Fergael, 10 years.
Domnall, son of Murchad, 20 years.

Niall, mac Feṗꝼaele, annır ҳu.
Ꝺonnchaꝺ, mac Ꝺomnael, annır ҳuııı.
Ꝉeꝺ, mac Neıl, annır ҳҳıı.

———*

Conchoḃor, mac Ꝺonnchaꝺa, annır ҳuıııı.
Niall, mac Ꝉeꝺa, annır ҳııı.
Maelrechnaell, annır ҳıı.
Ꝉeꝺ, mac Nel, annır ҳııı.
Flann, mac Moılrechnaıll.

Niall, son of Fergael, 15 years.
Donnchad, son of Domnall, 18 years.
Aed, son of Nial, 22 years.

Conchobor, son of Donnchad, 19 years.
Niall, son of Aed, 13 years.
Mael-Sechnaill, 12 years.
Aed, son of Nial, 13 years.
Flann, son of Moil-Sechnaill.

With respect to the transcription, the word Mulleċan was first written Mullachleċan. Marianus then placed a deletion-dot under each letter of lach. Eppca, of Murcheptach, mac Eppca, was originally ceppca, but a point was put over, and another under, the initial c. These and such variants as Muırcepcaıꝼ—Muırcheptaıꝼ—Murcheptaıꝼ, Murevech—Muırevach, Nell—Neıl were probably the result of oversight.

The following, however, cannot be accounted for in a similar manner. They show how early, and to what extent, phonetic forms and the consequent corruption made their appearance in the transcription of Irish MSS. Passing over the *vox nihili*, Nachı, in which the radical Ꝺ was omitted, as not being pronounced when eclipsed by n, we have evidence under his own hand that the copyist,

---

* A line is drawn here in the original.

whether he worked from memory or from an exemplar, had the accurate forms available. Yet he wrote the same words correctly or corruptly at haphazard.

Corrupt forms.	Correct forms.
(Ae.)	(Ai.)
Aeḃ.	baican.
Alaeinn.	Cinaiḃ.
baecan.	Mailganḃ.
Diaṗmaec.	Mailecoba.
Domnaell.	
Fenġael.	
Fenġaele.	
Loeġaeṗe.	
Luġaeḃ.	
Mael-Sechnaill.	
Maelḃuin.	

(*Nominative.*)

| blaḋmecc. | Copmac. |

(*Genitive.*)

Colman.	Colmain.
Domnael.	Domnaill.
Fenġael.	Fenġaele.
Mael } Sechnaill.	Mailecoba.
Moil }	Sechnaill.
Sechnaell.	

This confirms the conclusion already drawn, that, namely, the presence of such phenomena can form no linguistic basis whereon to determine the date of a composition.

Respecting the subject matter, the list was manifestly drawn up to show that since the bipartite division of Ireland, in the second century of the Christian era, between Conn of the Hundred Battles and Eogan Mor, or Mogh Nuadhat, the Half of Conn, namely, the northern moiety, supplied nearly all the over-kings. Why the compiler stopped short at Flann (*ob.* 916), it is apparently useless to suggest; especially, as Donnchad, son of Flann, reigned from A.D. 919 to A.D. 944.

There is no break to correspond with the native division of national history. Irish chroniclers divide our annals into Pre-Christian and Post-Christian: the point of discrimination being the advent of St. Patrick as missionary. The pagan portion of the Catalogue of Marianus includes from Conn to Dathi. The errors contained therein are considerable. Conlae Roiss is an unaccountable form for Colla Uais. The true sequence is: Fiacha, Colla Uais, Muridech Tirech, Coelbad, Eochu Mugmedon, Niall. This will be apparent by comparison with the poem appended from the *Book of Leinster* (L) with variants from the *Book of Ballymote* (B).

The author, Gilla Coemain (Devotee of St. Coeman; of, perhaps, Russagh, co. Westmeath), flourished in the second half of the eleventh century. The other chronological poem composed by him and already referred to* is dated A.D. 1072. One of the additional verses in L calls him son (*mac*); the B copy, grandson, or descendant (*ua*), of Gilla Samthainne—Devotee of [abbess] Samthann (*ob.* 739). He may thus have belonged to the Ui-Cairbre: a sept that inhabited the barony of Granard, co. Longford, in which the establishment of the saint in question was situated.

He gives the names, regnal years and modes of death of the over-kings who ruled Ireland from the grandson of Noah to Loegaire, the contemporary of St. Patrick. To discuss the reliability of the information thus afforded is beside the present purpose.† The piece is here given for two reasons. It presents in a convenient form the traditional knowledge of the subject. The chief object of the selection is, however, to illustrate the metrical form—Debide—in which the great bulk of native poetry has been cast. In connexion herewith, one fact is of special significance. The synopses‡ subjoined relative to *Concord* prove that, as regards one of the chief elements, B is superior to L,—fresh proof that an older MS. is not necessarily the more reliable.

The data to my knowledge appertaining to Debide are as follows:—

The authorities in MS. number five. They will be found, text and translation, appended to the present Lecture. I.–IV. are taken from the *Book of Ballymote*. I. is contained in a tract upon metric forms; II. in a treatise explanatory of the measures peculiar to the different orders of bards. III. and IV. belong to the *Book of the*

---

* Lect. I., p. 23.

† The chronology derivable from the text is annexed, for comparison with that of the Synchronistic Tracts appended to Lecture III.

‡ Notes L, M.

Ollam, or Professor of Poetry : the former, to a section treating of metres ; the latter, to a recapitulation thereof. V. is from the *Book of Leinster*. The **a** and **b** verses are respectively the eighth and ninth of fourteen quatrains descriptive of twelve chief kinds of poetry (*ard aiste in dana*). The **c** stanza occurs amongst verses illustrative of bardic technical terms.

I., in the present recension, to judge from one of the examples, was compiled in the latter half of the eleventh century. Flannacan O'Kelly, king of Bregia (the eastern portion of Meath), died, according to the *Annals of Ulster*, A.D. 1060. In the following year, his son, Flann, was slain by Garvey O'Casey, head of a rival family, who thus acquired the kingship.* This Flann was, perhaps, the person to whom the bardic exhortation in **m** was addressed.

The Tract is one of the two authorities which give details of the metres. It opens, somewhat inauspiciously, by reproducing without comment a statement calculated to render dubious the distinction between Regular and Irregular Debide. According to what is given below under Rule **3**, the **a** quatrain would seem to belong to Regular Debide. The *Clithar* mentioned therein was probably a wooded plain either near Dundalk, or in Fir-Cell (barony of Eglish, King's Co.).

The lines in **c** show the vitality of tradition, being the most ancient to be found in the five pieces. They deal with a subject that is purely pagan, and were apparently composed to deride the inefficacy of the Lobe Charm.† Of the author, the Ultonian poet, Flann, I know nothing more.

In the *Book of Ballymote*,‡ the opening line of the example in **d** is given as an instance of *Emain*, or Duplication (of the initial letter). The authorship is there ascribed to no less a personage than Cuchullain : *the doughtiest hero of the Scots*§ thus acquiring a fresh title to fame.‖

That the Composite in **e** was not merely theoretical, but brought into operation at an early period, is proved by the occurrence of the

---

* Note A.   † Note B.   ‡ P. 302 a, ll. 46–7.
§ *Fortissimus heros Scotorum*, Tigernach. O'Flaherty, as if not to be outdone, calls him *decantatissimus pugil* (Ogygia, Pars III., cap. xlvii., p. 279).
‖ Note C.

same metre in the *Tale of the Swine of Mac Dathó*, given in the *Book of Leinster*.*

The similar formation in **g** is of interest, as being that in which the "Ten poems [= 94 quatrains] of the Resurrection" appended to *Saltair na Rann* are composed. It likewise supplies the name, which has not been given in the published transcript of the *Psalter*.† In the Rules, to be mentioned hereafter, the measure is one of those included under the term *Oglachus*.

The metre of **l** is employed in a quatrain upon St. Mochta of Louth (Aug. 19), quoted in the Martyrology of Tallaght, in the *Book of Leinster*. The verse is mutilated, but another copy occurs amongst the *Lebar Brec* glosses on the *Calendar of Oengus*.‡

The versification, such as it is, of the final section (**o**) reflects more credit on the composer than the biographical and historical knowledge displayed therein.

II., if *Donnchad the Brown* (**a**) be the same as *Donnchad the Brown* of a quatrain in the *Annals of Ulster* (A.D. 929), cannot date, in its present form, beyond the second quarter of the tenth century.§

The references in the **c** stanza are explained by another entry (A.D. 840) in the same *Annals*: which likewise has a copy of the verse that fortunately preserves the true reading, *hostages*, instead of the unmeaning words of II. and III.‖

Attention may be directed to the charming description (**j**) of the blackbird in song. It will bear comparison with the two similar quatrains on the margin of the St. Gall *Priscian* (foll. 203-4), of which Nigra¶ wrote with such true feeling.

Amo figurarmi il povero monaco che, or fa più di mille anni, stava copiando il manoscritto, e, distratto un istante dal canto dei merli, contemplava dalla finestra della sua cella la verde corona di boscaglie che circondava il suo monastero nell' Ulster o nel Connaught, e, dopo avere ascoltato l'agile trillo degli uccelli, recitava queste strofe e ripigliava poi più allegro l'interrotto lavoro.

Mael-fabaill (**k**) may have been either the king of Carrigabracky,

---

* Note D. For the text, with the variants of two other MSS., see Windisch: *Irische Texte*, pp. 96 *sq*. † P. vi.

‡ Note E. § Note F. ‖ Note G.

¶ *Reliquie Celtiche: Il MS. Irlandese di San Gallo*, Torino, 1872, p. 23.

in Inishowen, co. Donegal, who died A.D. 881 ; or the king of Aidhne, a territory in Galway, co-extensive with the diocese of Kilmacduagh, who died in 891.*

III. is of equal authority with II. The example in the opening section may be taken as showing that the authorship was different. The same writer would hardly have varied in the illustration of one measure. In a poetic eulogy of king Aed, preserved in an eighth-century MS. of the Monastery of St. Paul, Carinthia, Rairiu (the hill of Reerin, co. Kildare) signifies the province of Leinster. It has probably the same meaning here ; not Rairiu = Offally, Queen's Co., as in Gilla Coemain's poem (**f** 6).

In accordance with the quatrain in **k**, the composition may date from the last quarter of the ninth century.†

The verse (**g**) ascribed to the national patroness is more in keeping than the similar attribution in Terminational Debide given in the *Tripartite Life*.‡

The connexion of St. Columba (**h**) with the Cauldron, or Charybdis, of Brecan (between Rathlin Island and the northern coast of Antrim) took place, according to the Life of St. Ciaran of Clonmacnoise,§ when the saint was returning to Iona after his final visit to Ireland, a few years before his death.

With reference to the stanza in **m**, Robartach and Suibne, sons of Maenach, died as stewards of the monastery of Slane, co. Meath, A.D. 787 and 814, respectively.‖ The quatrain in question, with its mention of *meal-sifting and door-keeping*, may accordingly embody the complaint of a lay-brother of that establishment respecting the comparative lightness of the duties assigned to the *Son of Cu-abba* by one of the above mentioned *oeconomi*.

IV. is chiefly valuable for the statements respecting the abbreviated line in Short Debide. The substitution of the opening lines as mnemonics instead of the full text of the examples is proof that the piece was transcribed, perhaps composed, with knowledge of II. and III.

V. **a, b** are intended to exemplify in themselves the formation of the measures they respectively describe. The author belonged

---

* Note II. † Note II (a). ‡ Rolls' Ed., p. 150.
§ Quoted in *Adamnan*, p. 263. ‖ Note I.

to the sept of O'Rooney, hereditary poets of Mac Gennis, king of Ulidia (cos. Antrim and Down). His death took place, according to the *Annals of Ulster*, A.D. 1079.* V. **c** supplies independent authority for Lobe Debide. Its chief importance, however, consists in the reading of the example.

The pieces, it will be seen, afford no information, except in a few instances, beyond the name and example of the metre. They were, in fact, mere memoranda for proficients. The principles of the art and the application thereof must consequently have been imparted orally. That instruction of the kind existed in active and continuous operation is sufficiently attested by the magnitude, influence and vitality of the Bardic Order.

The metric doctrine thus delivered finds a partial echo in the Rules formulated by the Franciscan, O'Mulloy, in his *Grammatica Latino-Hibernica*, published at Rome in 1677. (From that work they were transferred by O'Donovan into his *Irish Grammar*.) In the author's time, versification was still cultivated as a hereditary avocation. To judge, however, from accessible material, bardism had already in part become a lost art.

In reference to the present treatment, it has to be mentioned that the lines of the verses are written without a break in the MSS. Furthermore, the labour of discrimination is rarely relieved by punctuation, or otherwise. Not infrequently indeed it is aggravated by considerable illiteracy of transcription. To these difficulties has to be added the meagreness of the native vocabularies within reach. (For obvious reasons, the illustrative character of the examples can seldom be preserved in the translation.) Under the circumstances, no finality is claimed for the conclusions arrived at in this Lecture.

To illustrate the Rules, I set down the opening lines of Gilla Cocmain's poem :—

hEriu ard, inir ranrig,	Eriu sublime, isle of the kings,
Magen molbtac na morgnim,	Laudible scene of great deeds;
Noco n-fitir duni a diac,	Nor knows any person its state,
Co norruair hua Laimiac.	Until the grandson of Lamech found it.

---

* Note J.

1. The verse or quatrain is called *rann iomlan*, and consists in its normal form, as seen above, of four *quarters* (*cethramhna*), or lines. Each quatrain must make independent sense. Not infrequently, each distich is similarly complete. The first half-quatrain is called *the leading* (*seolad*); the last, *the closing* (*comhad*).

To this Rule, I. **i, j, n, o** form exceptions. The example of heptasyllabic *Laid Luascach* (**o**) given elsewhere in the *Book of Ballymote** has five (not six) lines in the verse.

2. Each line is made up of seven syllables. In the numeration, what is called *vowel-drowning* (*bathudh guthaighe*) is taken into account. When, namely, a word ending in a vowel is followed by a word commencing with a vowel, elision of the first takes place, when necessary for the scansion. Thus, line 3, ouni a oiaċ, is to be pronounced oun' a oiaċ, three syllables. In all other cases, they are retained, each being counted separately. Thus we have, **a** 1, hepiu apo (three syllables).

By means of this Rule we can conclude, for instance, that the B reading of **a** 1, which omits biċh, is correct. The L lection makes the line hypermetrical, ua being a dissyllable. biċh was, accordingly, a gloss that crept into the text.

Aphaeresis is likewise employed to produce the requisite number of syllables. Thus we have (**a** 4):—

'Sin Mumain oo mall ċpine.

In [S]leċt Scaipn 'pin oebaio ouino (**b** 3), the omission of ı was owing to the scribe of L reading Scaipn as a dissyllable. Ipin is correctly given in B.

To the Rule relative to heptasyllabic lines, there are the following exceptions: namely, four (opening) syllables are wanting (1) in the first line (II.-III. **b, d, h, i, l**, IV. **c, e, g**: the authority for the amount omitted is IV. **d**); (2) in the first and fourth lines (II.-III. **e**, IV. **a**, V. **c**); (3) in the second and fourth (I. **k, l**); (4) four syllables in the first line and six in the fourth (I. **b, c**, II.-III. **f**, if my arrangement be correct); (5) three in the fourth (I. **i**, according to my division).

---

* Note K.

How completely the short initial line, which is so well authenticated, had become forgotten is shown, to take a typical instance, in the first volume of the new edition of the *Annals of Ulster*.* The opening lines of a quatrain are printed thus: [The metre is Rannaidacht Bec.]

ᴀ muilınn,
Ce ꝛo mılc moꝛ ꝺı cuıꝛınn.

At foot is a note: "ᴀ muilınn. These words should be repeated, to complete the line, according to a practice frequently followed by Irish poets."

But, in the first place, repetition of the words will still leave the line a syllable short; secondly, this distich is proof in itself that the abbreviation took place in the beginning of the line. For muilınn is in *Correspondence* (Rule 5) with cuıꝛınn. The collocation accordingly is:—

ᴀ muilınn,
Ce ꝛo mılc moꝛ ꝺı cuıꝛınn.

3. In every line, two words, whereof neither is to be the article, possessive pronoun, preposition, or conjunctive, must begin with a vowel, or the same consonant. This is called *Concord* (*uaim*). Hence, line 1, we find Eꝛıu—aꝛꝺ (vocalic); l. 2, maıgen molbchach na moꝛgnım (consonantal): where na, being the article, does not hinder the *Concord*.

(*a*) In compounds, the *Concord* is formed by the initial letters:—

Coıca ıngen ıngnacac (ı—ı), **a** 2.
Immaıg Rúaıꝺ poꝺacaoín (ꝛ—ꝛ), **h** 4.
Deg mac Slánuıll, nı ꝛaeb-ꝛó (ꝛ—ꝛ), **j** 4.
Aꝛꝛın gꝛeíc uacmaıꝛ, acgaıꝛb (u—a), **b** 5.

(*b*) The verbal particles ꝺo and ꝛo (when not joined with other particles), no and negatives do not form *Concord*:—

Docep coemꝺoꝛꝛ Cınꝺmaꝛa (c—c), **p** 6.
Noco n-ṗıcıꝛ buní a ꝺıac (ꝺ—ꝺ), **a** 1.
Co ꝑocoglaꝺ Coꝛ Conaınꝺ (c—c), **b** 6.
Co noꝛꝛuaıꝛ Ua Lamíac (u—u), **a** 1.

---

* Pp. 110-11.

(c) The eclipsing letters are not employed in *Concord*:—

Nuabu Argatlám na n-eċ (a—e), **d** 6.
Arim tri n-beiċ m-bliaḋan brar (b—b), **g** 1.

From this it follows, either that *Concord* was introduced before Eclipsis; or that the eclipsing letters were rightly regarded as not radically connected with the words to which they were prefixed.

(d) Similarly, ṗ, ḟ and ṫ are not available for *Concord*:—

(ṗ) I torċair ár f[h]er ṅ-hEreno (e—e), **g** 2.
D' hErimón ir b'Eḃer ṗoltċaem (e—o), **f** 1.

(ḟ) Cóic bliaḋna bo Shetna art (e—a), **h** 6.
bliaḋain bo Shláne, bo'n laeċ (l—l), **d** 1.

(ṫ) Co n-erbailt be ṫám iartain (a—i), **a** 6.
Doċoib Neimeo éc be ṫám (e—a), **b** 2.

The quiescence of these letters was accordingly established prior to the Rule relative to *Concord*.

(e) According to the Rule, r, when followed by a vowel or consonant, requires a vowel or the same consonant to form the second alliterative. This, however, has to be modified with respect to l, n and r. Thus:

Sláno ll—rúaire (**i** 6);   Sétna—rláin (**l** 4);
Slánuill—raeb (**j** 4);   Sirlam raiʒeb rluaʒ (**m** 3);
Sirna—rlatteain (**j** 5);   rlúaʒ—raer (**q** 1);
Sírna—rríanaib (**j** 6);   rnimaiʒ—rirfaeṫraiʒ.*
Sirna—rleṫṫaib (*ib.*);

It may consequently be concluded that r forms Concord with rl, rn, rr and *vice versa*.

Concord is twofold—*Improper* and *Proper*. The *Proper*, or *true*, *Concord* (*fíruaim*) takes place when the vocalic or consonantal agreement (as defined above) is found in the two final words of the line; otherwise, it is called *Improper* (*uaim gnuise*). Hence we have,

---

* Lecture I., p. 58 **k**, *supra*.

l. 2, molbthach—morȝnim; l. 3, buni—biach, *Proper Concord*: l. 1, Epiu—aρb; l. 4, (p)uaip—ua, *Improper Concord*.

The *Improper Concord*, it is laid down, may replace the *Proper* in the first and second lines; but the *Proper* must of necessity occur in the third and fourth. With respect to Irregular Debide, however, V. **b** and the poem of Gilla Coemain show that this Rule has to be taken with some exceptions.* The test of Regular and Irregular Debide may be respectively defined, according to these, as the presence or absence of *Concord* (whether *Proper* or *Improper*) in all, or from any, of the lines of a quatrain.

It may be well to quote a few examples to show the textual value of *Concord*. In the *Annals of the Four Masters*,† O'Donovan gives the text and translation of the second line of a quatrain as follows:—

"hic at cuma in t-peirip—At Ath-Cuma-an-tseisir: i.e. the Ford of the Slaughtering of the Six. This name is now obsolete."

In Vol. I. of the *Annals of Ulster*,‡ we have:

"hic atcumai inb feirip.—The Ford of the Slaughter of the Six. Not identified."

Here the *Concord* is plainly between the a of atcumai and the e of feirip. This proves that at is the inseparable particle; not the substantive at, a ford. The meaning is consequently: "At the cutting-off of the six" (whose names follow). Besides, there is no ford at the place in question.

In the Rolls' edition of the *Tripartite*,§ the following occurs: "*Aed .. xxuii . cotorchair icath Da Fherta*—Aed [reigned] twenty-seven [years] and fell in the battle of Da Fherta." That is, the combination icath is resolved into ι cath, *in the battle*. In the poem from the *Book of Ballymote*‖ appended to Lecture IV., there is a quatrain (**q** 4) on the subject, which presents the same MS. grouping. But the *Concord* gives the true division:—

Ic Ať-ba-pepta innpuap—At very cold Ath-da-ferta.

This agrees with the *Annals of Ulster* (A.D. 819), which have the Latin equivalent:¶ iuxta Uabum-buapum-uiptutum—*near the Ford of the two (marvellous) feats.*

---

* Note L.   † Vol. I., pp. 244-5.   ‡ Ed. Hennessy, pp. 96-7.   § Pp. 320-1.
‖ P. 50 b.   ¶ Most probably, the meaning is *Ford of two tombs.*

THE CODEX PALATINO-VATICANUS, 830. 107

The conditions above laid down respecting *Concord* are verified in V. **a**, the typical example of Terminational, or Regular Debide. Herewith agree II. **a, b**, III. **b**. The *Concord* of I. **a**, 1. 2, is *Improper:* ꝼeaꞃaıb-ꝼeaꞃcan ; not b'[ꝼ]eaꞃcan-beıꞃeoıl, which was a scribal error. Hence, doubtless, the statement with which the quatrain is introduced in the text: namely, that the verse, according to some, was Irregular Debide. II. **b** is included as amended by the reading of III. **b**. III. **a** is excluded; the first distich being obscure to me, I am unable to restore the *Concord*.*

Irregular Debide may accordingly be defined as that which contains a hemistich without *Concord*. This is the criterion in V. **b**, in which the final line is thus composed. The same holds good of I. **a** (1. 2), II.-III. **c** (1. 1). From V. **b** we likewise learn that the metre was peculiar to historical poems. In illustration of this, synopses are appended, giving the references of (1) first, (2) second, (3) third and (4) fourth lines not containing *Concord*.† On verifying these, the reason, it will be seen, was that proper names, as a rule, did not accommodate themselves to the requirements of *Concord*.

4. *Termination*, or *Rinn*, is the characteristic of Debide. It signifies that the second and fourth lines of the quatrain shall respectively exceed the first and third by one syllable. The ending of the first and third is called *rinn (imrinn);* that of the second and fourth, *ardrinn (cenn-imrinn)*. Thus, in the quatrain quoted, ꞃíꞃ is the monosyllabic *rinn;* whilst moꞃꞃnım, the corresponding *ardrinn*, is dissyllabic. Likewise, bıać, the second *rinn*, is exceeded in one syllable by its *ardrinn*, Lamıać.

Compounds and words with proclitics may be employed to produce this excedence. When the *rinn* consists of two syllables, the *ardrinn* has three; when the *rinn* has three, the *ardrinn* has four. The present poem contains but three instances of a distich without *Termination:* ꞃíꞃaıb—nıꞃaıꞃ, **c** 3; ꝼınꞃaıl—ınbaıꞃ, **x** 4; ꞃíꞃ—ꝼíꞃ, **y** 5.

To this Rule are to be referred the statements in I. **e, f, g, i**. To understand them, an explanation of the technical terms employed therein becomes necessary.

Terminational Debide (*a*) is a quatrain with the first and third

---

* Very probably, it is a-ı (phacen-ımmceann). III. **a** can thus be included.
† Note M.

lines ending in monosyllables and the second and fourth in trisyllables.

Duplication of Termination (aa) is a quatrain with the first and third lines ending in dissyllables, the second and fourth in trisyllables.

Rannaidacht Mor (β), ⎫   A quatrain ⎧ Monosyllables.
Casbardne (γ),   ⎪   of hepta-   ⎪ Trisyllables.
Ae freslige (δ),   ⎬   syllabic   ⎨ Alternate Trisyllables and
                      ⎪   lines end- ⎪ Dissyllables.
Rannaidacht Bec (ε), ⎭   ing in :—   ⎩ Dissyllables.

Now, transpose a (given in I. d) : that is, replace the first and third lines by the second and fourth respectively and *vice versa*. The result (I. e) will be a Composite of γ and β.

The text heads the example γ, from the opening line being in that measure. The previous textual statement respecting the Composite of β and γ has reference to I. d, in which the first line belongs to β. I. d, in fact, by having a monosyllabic ending in the first and third, with a trisyllabic in the second and fourth lines, is one of the irregular kinds (made in imitation of the normal measures) to which the Rules give the generic title of *Oglachus*.

In the same way, transpose aa (given in I. f). The result (I. g) will have a twofold appellation : δ and a Composite of γ and ε. In the text, it has the same heading and for the same reason as I. e. It likewise comes under *Oglachus*.

The distinction with which I. g closes is this. The example there given is δ. *Separate* the lines by transposition (as described above) : the result (f) will be a Composite of ε and γ.

With reference to I. h, i, *great imrinn* signifies trisyllabic *rinn*; to correspond with which the *head imrinn*, or *ardrinn*, must (according to Rule 4) be quadrisyllabic. It is called *great*, because thereby the *ardrinn* can be duplicated : a process confined, it is stated, to the *rinn* in the other Debides. In h accordingly, paċa paſo forms the *rinn*; plaċa pinonaip, the *ardrinn*. How the latter is doubled, appears in i. Whatever metrical arrangement be adopted (that given below being merely tentative), the change, it will be seen, has transformed the original almost out of the semblance of Debide. I. i, as it stands, is a Composite of β and ε.

That the alteration is purely arbitrary seems proved by the fact that the *ardrinn* of the second distich has not been similarly treated. In fact, **h** is a good example of Regular Debide, with monosyllabic *rinn* (ꝑaꞅb-mail) and dissyllabic *ardrinn* (ꝑinbnaiꝑ-binꝣbail).

5. The final requisite is what is called *Correspondence (comharda)*. To understand this, the native classification of vowels and consonants has to be attended to.

The vowels are divided into *broad:* a, o, u, and *slender:* e, i.

The consonants are classed as follows :—

1. ꞃ.
2. c, p, т (smooth).
3. ꝣ, b, ꞇ (middle).
4. ċ, ꝑ(ṗ), ṫ (aspirates).
5. ll, m, nn, nꝣ, ꞃꝑ (strong).
6. b, ḃ, ꝣ, l, ṁ, n, ꞃ (light).

Perfect Correspondence means that in each distich the last syllable of each line shall agree with the last syllable of the other in vowels and consonants of the same class. This frequently approaches, and occasionally becomes, rhyme. Initial consonants need not be taken into account, unless when two or more (whether belonging to the last syllable, or partly thereto and partly to the penultimate) come together in (1) one, or (2) both of the syllables in question. *Correspondence* then takes place (chiefly in the finals), in (1), between the single consonant and one of the group; or, in (2), between one consonant of one group and one of the other. Thus, in ꝑíꝣ and moꝑꝣnim, the agreement between ġnim and ꝑíꝣ is perfect: consisting of the same vowel, i, with the *light* consonants ꝣ and ṁ (which, although not thus marked in the MSS., were aspirated), ꝑ and n. In the second distich, La in Lamꞅaċ is not taken into account. The vocalic consonance is identical (biaċ—mꞅaċ); the consonantal is also perfect, ḃ and ṁ (for the m in Lamꞅaċ was infected) belonging to the *light* division.

Imperfect, or *broken*, *Correspondence* (*Comharda briste*) is defined a vocalic consonance, without any regard to consonantal agreement. This species, it is added, allows one word to terminate in a vowel and the other in a consonant.

An example of this rarely-occurring *Correspondence* is found in the opening distich of **w** 5:—

    Fengur Dubbetad, cen bianblaib,
    Cen ecnad, ni oen bliadne.

But the instance is more apparent than real; for the final ᴅ of ᴅianblaib was not pronounced.

Under this Rule are to be classed the examples of which the characteristic is *Correspondence* without *Termination* (Rule 4). They fall into three classes: quatrains having *Correspondence* (1) between all the lines (II. **i**); (2) between those of each distich (I. **b**, II.–III. **e, f**—with a sub-division of monosyllabic, II.–III. **j** and dissyllabic, II.–III. **k**); (3) between the first and third, second and fourth, lines (II.–III. **g, h**).

Of these, **e, g, k** belong (not to Debide, but) to ϵ; **h** and **j** to β. II.–III. **l**, being a Composite of β and ϵ, is misnamed. With it are to be grouped I. **b**, II.–III. **f, i**. I. **c** is an imitation (*Oglachus*) of β; II.–III. **e** and V. **c** are modelled upon ϵ.

Debide, it may thus be concluded, was applied generically to a quatrain, of which the basis was a heptasyllabic line.

II.–III. **g, h** enable us to correct with certainty a scribal error which possesses a prescription of more than a thousand years, and which may be quoted as an instance of the conservatism of copyists. The MS. of St. Paul, Carinthia, contains two verses of a poem (in β), preserved in its entirety in the *Book of Leinster* and elsewhere.* The first quatrain is as follows† :—

    Ir én immo n-iaba fár,
    Ir nau toll bian t-erlinn zuar,
    Ir lertan fár, ir cnanb cnín,
    Nab béni toil inb nig tuar.

    He is a bird, around which closes a snare,
    He is a leaky ship, to which is fated destruction,
    He is an empty vessel, he is a withered tree,
    Whoso doeth not the will of the king above.

---

* For the Poem and the legend connected therewith, see *The Calendar of Oengus* (R. I. A. edition), pp. civ.–vi.

† Windisch: *Irische Texte*, p. 319.

Throughout the poem, *Concord* (Rule **3**) is subordinated to *Correspondence*. The clauses of the third line have consequently to be reversed, and the reading will thus be :—

Iſ cnanb cnín, iſ leſcaɲ ɼáɲ.
He is a withered tree, he is an empty vessel.

Some of the terms (*e.g.* Meagre Debide, I. **c**, II.–III. **m**, Distiched Debide, I. **j**, etc.) it has not been deemed necessary to deal with in detail. The explanation of them lies in the application of the general principles and will present no difficulty, when these have been mastered.

To facilitate reference, the accompanying Tables exhibit the results derived from the foregoing discussion respecting the connexion between the Rules and the MS. authorities.

They will likewise show that the fresh material amounts very closely to two fifths. When it is added that the present texts form but a small portion of the general subject, as treated in the *Book of Ballymote*, the native language will be conceded to have been rich in forms of versification. To what extent the bardic compositions, as a whole, are entitled to rank as poetry, in the present state of our knowledge it is impossible to decide.

A.—SYNOPSIS OF DEBIDE.

No.	RULE.	EXAMPLES.	EXCEPTIONS.
1.	Four-line Verses,	I. a–h, k, l, m; II.–III. a–m; V. a, b, c.	I. i, j, n, o.
2.	Heptasyllabic lines,	I. a, h, j, m–o; II.–III. a, c, g, j, k, m; V. a, b.	(1) II.–III. b, d, h, i, l, IV. c, e, g; (2) II.–III. e, IV. a, V. c; (3) I. k, l; (4) I. b, c; (5?) I. i.
3.	Concord,	[Quatrains containing Concord (whether Proper or Improper) in every heptasyllabic line :—]	[Quatrains containing at least one heptasyllabic line without Concord (whether Proper or Improper) :—]
		I. a, b, c, f, h; II. a; II.–III. b, 1, k.	I. d, c, i–o; III. a; II.–III. c–h, j, l, m; IV. b, d; V. b.
		I. a, h–l, n; II.–III. a, b, c, m; V. a, b.	I. b–g, i, m, o; II.–III. d, e, f-l; V. c.
4.	Termination,		
5.	Correspondence,	[Quatrains containing Correspondence in each distich :—]	[Quatrains containing a distich without Correspondence :—]
		I. a, b, d–g, k–o; II. a; II.–III. b, d–g, i–m; III. a; V. a, b.	I. c, h, i, j; II.–III. c, h.

THE CODEX PALATINO-VATICANUS, 830.

B.—TABLE SHOWING THE REGULARITY AND IRREGULARITY (RELATIVE TO THE RULES) OF THE ITEMS IN I. II. III. IV. V.

+ denotes Example; – denotes Exception.

Section	I. RULES.					II. RULES.					III. RULES.					IV. RULES.	V. RULES.				
	1	2	3	4	5	1	2	3	4	5	1	2	3	4	5		1	2	3	4	5
a	+	+	+	+	+	+	+	+	+	+	+	+	+	+	+	[= e II.]	+	+	+	+	+
b	+	–	–	–	+	+	–	+	+	+	+	–	+	+	+	[= m II.]	+	+	–	+	+
c	+	–	–	–	–	+	+	–	+	+	+	+	–	+	+	[= b II.]	+	–	–	–	+
d	+	+	–	+	+	+	–	–	–	+	[+]	–	[–	+	+]	[= c II.]					
e	+	+	–	–	+	+	–	–	–	+	[+]	–	[–	–	+]	[= d II.]					
f	+	+	+	+	+	+	–	–	–	+	[+]	–	–	–	[+]	[= g II.]					
g	+	+	+	–	+	+	+	–	–	+	+	+	–	–	+	[= h II.]					
h	+	+	+	+	+	+	–	–	–	+	+	–	–	–	+						
i	–	–	–	–	–	+	–	–	–	+	[+]	–	–	[–	+]						
j	–	+	–	–	+	+	+	–	–	+	+	+	–	–	+						
k	+	–	–	+	+	+	+	+	–	+	+	+	+	–	+						
l	+	–	–	+	+	+	–	–	–	+	+	–	–	–	+						
m	+	+	–	+	+	+	+	–	–	+	+	+	–	–	+						
n	–	+	–	+	+																
o	–	+	–	–	–																

C.—TABLE SHOWING THE RESPECTIVE AND COLLECTIVE TOTALS OF REGULARITY AND IRREGULARITY (RELATIVE TO THE RULES) OF I. II. III. IV. V.

+ denotes Example; – denotes Exception.

	No. of Sections.	RULES.									
		1		2		3		4		5	
		+	–	+	–	+	–	+	–	+	–
I.	15	11	4	10	5	4	11	8	7	12	3
II.	13	13	0	6	7	3	10	3	10	13	0
III.	13	13	0	6	7	3	10	4	9	13	0
IV.	7	[7	0	3	4	1	6	2	5	7	0]
V.	3	3	0	2	1	1	2	2	1	3	0
		47	4	27	24	12	39	19	32	48	3
		51		51		51		51		51	

NOTES.

A.—(a) Annals of Ulster.

A.D. m°. xx°. uiii. Sitriuc, mac mic Amlaim, ri Gall ⁊ Flannacan, hUa Ceallaiġ, ri breġ, a n-dul do Roim.

A.D. 1028. Sitriuc, grandson of Amlam, king of the Foreigners and Flannacan O'Kelly, king of Bregia, went to Rome.

(b) Annals of Ulster.

A.D. m°. lx°. Flannacan hUa Ceallaiġ, ri breġ, do ec i n-a ailitre.

A.D. 1060. Flannacan O'Kelly, king of Bregia, died in his pilgrimage.

(c) Annals of Tigernach.

[A.D. m°.lx°.i°.] Fland hUa Cellaiġ, ri breġ, do marbad do na Saitnib.

[A.D. 1061.] Flann O'Kelly, king of Bregia, was slain by the Saitni.*

Gairbret hUa Caturaiġ, ri breġ, mortuus ert [in penitentia. Ann. Ult.].

Garvey O'Casey, king of Bregia, died [in penance. *Annals of Ulster*].

B.—Lode Charm.

(a) Cormac's Glossary (*Lebar Brec*, p. 264 a).

bri ġac n-[f]accair (no, cac n-[f]occur), ut ert a m-bretaib Nemid[-ed]. Idon, briamon smet-
P. 264 b raiġe : idon, ainm | nemteorra doġniat filid [im n]eċ adatoing. Melid fmitt in duine iter a dá mer ⁊ doecci in duine im a n-béni nemterr. Fir inron, amal ar fria in duine a n-eotair ata in ball ro, ir fria duine[-i] a

Bri is every contiguity, as in [the Brehon Law Tract called] *The Laws of the [privileged] Grades.* Namely, *briamon smethraige:* to wit, the name of a charm the poets perform respecting one who has forsworn them. He [the poet] grinds the lobe of the person between his two fingers and the person respecting whom he performs the charm dies. That [comes] true [thus] : as it is externally

---

* A sept in Fingal, East Meath, the chief family of which was O'Casey.

n-eccaıp aca ın buıne ṗeo. Amal
aṗ cımme ┐ ıṗ claċı ın ball ṗo
quam alıa membṗa, ṗıc ec hıc
homo.

this member is upon the person, so in
regard to people this person is external.
[Or,] as this member is thinner and
weaker than the other members, so
[is] this man also.

(b) *Book of Leinster* (p. 187 a).

bṗıamon ṗmecṗaċ: ıbon, bṗı,
bṗıaċaṗ ┐ mon, cleṗ; ıbon, cleṗ
bṗıaċaṗba ṗın boġnícıṗ ınb ḟılıb.
Ibon, cenéle nemċıuṗa ın ṗın:
ıbon, ṗmıcc a ċluaṗı bo ġabáıl ı
n-a láım: ıbon, amal ná ḟıl cnáım
anbṗın, ıṗ amlaıb na ḟıl eneċ, no
neṗc acon cí ecnaıġeṗ ın ḟıle.

Briamon smetrach: that is, *Bri*, word,
and *Mon*, feat; namely, a verbal operation [is] that which the poets used to
perform. That is a species of charm:
namely, to catch the lobe of his ear in
his hand: to wit, as there is not bone in
that, it is thus there is not honour or
strength in the person whom the poet
satirizes.

(c) *Book of Ballymote* (p. 326 b).

bṗımon ṗmecṗaċ. beṗla na
ḟıleb ṗo: ıbon, ın ġne beıbenaċ
ıṗunb. Ibon, bṗı, ıbon, bṗıaċuṗ;
mon, ıbon, cleaṗ ┐ ṗmıc, ıbon,
cluaṗ ┐ ḟoṗṗaċ, ıbon, ṗıġı. No,
bṗı, ıbon, bṗıaċuṗ ┐ mon, ıbon,
cleaṗ ┐ ṗmecṗaċ, ıbon, ṗmıc-
ḟoṗṗaċ: ıbon, co ḟoṗṗıġıbıṗ neaċ.
Cleaṗ bṗıaċuṗba ṗın bonıbıṗ na
ḟılıb oc eġnuċ: ıbon, ṗmıc a
cluaṗı bo ġabaıl ı n-a laım:
ıbon, amal nac ḟıl cnaım ṗunb,
nı ṗaıb eneac hıcon cı eġnaıġeaṗ
ın ḟılıb [ḟıle].

Brimon smetrach. The language of
the poets [is] this: to wit, the last
species [is] here. Namely, *bri* = word;
mon = operation, and *smit* = ear, and
forrach = satirizing. Or [thus]: *bri* =
word, and *mon* = operation, and *smetrach*
(that is, *smit-forrach*) [= lobe-satirizing]: they used to satirize a person.
A verbal operation [was] that which
the poets used to perform in satirizing:
to wit, to catch the lobe of his ear in
his [the poet's] hand. That is, as there
is not bone here, there [is] not honour
for the person whom the poet satirizes.

C.—DUPLICATION.

Cmaın elı bıno, Cu-Cullaın:

Another Duplication indeed [is the
verse] Cu-Cullain [sang]:

O bo beġan, ġabuṗ ġle ┐ aṗaıle.

Since he was small, he took pasture, etc.
—*Book of Ballymote*, p. 302 a, ll. 46-7.

D.—Composite of Casbardne and Rannaidacht Mor.

Tucad turbaid cotulta	There was caused disturbance of sleep
Do Mac Datò co [a] teċ:	To the son of Datho ['Two Mutes'] with his house:
Rorbói ní no comairled,	There was a thing he used to counsel
Cen co labradar fri neċ.	Without his speaking to any one.

—*Book of Leinster*, p. 112 a.

E.—Unusual Irregular Denide.

Nir' bo boc[h]ta do Moċta	Not strait was for Mochta
Lugmaid [lirr*:	The fort of Louth:
Tri cet racart, cet† ercor,	[For] 300 priests [and] 100 bishops
araen fririr].	[Were] together with him.

—*Book of Leinster*, p. 361, marg. inf.
Lebar Brec, p. 94, gloss between ll. 5, 6.

F.—Annals of Ulster.

A.D. dcccc°.xx°.ix°. Slogad la Donnċad co Liat[h]-druim fri [Muircertaċ] mac Neill.	A.D. 929. A hosting by Donnchad to Liath-druim against [Muircertach] the son of Niall.
Abbred neċ fri Donnċad Donn, Ririn ronnċad rlaidi clann:	Let some one say to Donnchad the Brown, Unto the protector of the raiding of the clans:
Cia beit Liat-druim ar a ċinn, Ata gilla diardaind ann.	Though Liath-druim be in front of him, There is a very stubborn wight there.

---

* The parts of the text within brackets are from *Lebar Brec*; the place in the *Book of Leinster* having been illegible to the facsimilist.

† *L. B.* has an cet—*above a hundred*; to the ruin of the metre.

Colgan (*Acta SS.*, p. 734: quoted in the *Martyrology of Donegal*, p. 224) is far worse. He reads, in the first line: Nir' bo doċta muinnter Moċta—*Not straitened was the community of Mochta*—and, in the third: Tri ċed ragart um ċed n-errоc—*Three hundred priests, along with one hundred bishops*: thus making each of the lines a syllable too long.

The *L. B.* copyist altered boc[h]ta (*strait*) into boċtai (*poverty*). Mr. Stokes (*Cal. Oengus.*, p. cxxxii.) adopts and improves upon this by translating the nom. lirr "in the burgh," as if the text were illirr. Throughout the edition of the *Calendar*, he prints the short lines as though the abbreviation took place at the end, not at the beginning.

G.—Annals of Ulster.

A.D. ɔcccº.xlº. Feiɔilmiɔ, ri Muman, ɔo innriuɔ Miɔe ⁊ breg, coniɔɔeirig i Temraig. Ct in illa uice inɔreɔ Cell ⁊ beitri la Niall, mac Aeɔa:

Ir he Feiɔlimiɔ in ri,
Dianiɔ orair oen laiti,—
Citrige Connact cen cat

Ocur Miɔe ɔo mannrat.

A.D. 840. Fedilmidh, king of Munster, plundered Meath and Bregia, so that he sat down in Tara. And on that occasion [took place] the plundering of [Fir-]cell and Beithre by Niall, son of Aed:

Feidhlimidh is the king,
To whom it was the work of one day,—
[To get] the hostages of Connacht without battle
And Meath to devastate.

H.—Annals of Ulster.

(a)

A.D. ɔcccº.lxxxº.iº. Mael-fabaill, mac Loingrig, rex Cairgebracaiɔe, moritur.

A.D. 881. Mael-fabaill, son of Loingsech, king of Carraig-brachaide, dies.

(b)

A.D. ɔcccº. xcº.iº. Mael-fabuill, mac Cleirig, rig Aiɔne, mortuur ert.

A.D. 891. Mael-fabhuill, son of Cleirech, king of Aidhne, died.

I.—Annals of Ulster.

(a)

A.D. ɔccº.lxxxº.uiiº. Robartac, mac Moenaig, economur Slane ⁊ abbar Cille-Foibrig [mortuur ert].

A.D. 787. Robartach, son of Moenach, steward of Slane and abbot of Cell-Foibrigh [perhaps Kilbrew, co. Meath], died.

(b)

A.D. ɔcccº.xº.iiiiº. Suibne, mac Moenaig, economur Slane [mortuur ert].

A.D. 814. Suibne, son of Moenach, steward of Slane, died.

J.—Annals of Ulster.

A.D. mº.lxxº.ixº. Ceallac hUa Ruanaɔa, arɔ ollam Crenn, quieuit in pace.

A.D. 1079. Ceallach Ua Ruanadha, chief bardic professor of Ireland, rested in peace.

K.—Laid Luascach.

Incipit do laid Luarcaig :

O bacuip in gaet a n-dep
Fop tip Sacpan pciatan glar,
Do tparcaip conn inpi Scit,
Donean docuip Calad nit,
A brat Luimneac hatan glar.

It beginneth concerning *Laid Luascach* :

When put the wind from the south
O'er the land of the Saxons a fresh wing,
Overwhelmed a wave the Island of Sky
As it put Calad nit [under water],
. . . Luimnech grey-green.
—*Book of Ballymote*, p. 292a, l. 23 *sq.*

L.—Poem of Gilla Coemain.

(a)
Quatrains containing Improper Concord in third line:—

a 1.*	n 3.
,, 3.	o 4.
,, 4.*	r 3.
b 6.	u 6.*
d 2.	v 3.
f 4.	,, 5.
h 6.	w 1.
i 4.	y 1.
k 4.	
l 1.	
m 1.†	

* No Concord in L.
† Proper Concord in B.

(b)
Quatrains containing Improper Concord in fourth line:—

a 1.*	p 6.
,, 4.*	q 1.
b 2.	s 4.
,, 6.	t 5.
c 1.	u 5.
e 3.*	v 4.
j 3.	w 1.
k 3.	x 1.
l 4.	y 1.
m 2.*	,, 2.
p 4.	

* No Concord in L.

M.—Poem of Gilla Coemain.

(a)
Quatrains not containing Concord in first line:—

b 4.	h 3.*
c 3.	,, 4.
,, 4.	i 1.
e 1.	,, 4.
,, 5.	j 4.
f 1.	k 1.
,, 4.	,, 2.
g 5.	,, 3.

(b)
Quatrains not containing Concord in second line:—

a 5.	e 6.
c 2.*	g 2.
,, 4.	,, 4.
,, 5.	,, 6.
d 3.	h 5.
,, 4.	i 5.*
e 4.	j 1.
,, 5.	k 3.

k 4.	u 3.	l 5.	v 5.*
,, 5.	v 5.	n 6.	w 2.
l 2.	w 4.	q 6.	,, 3.
o 4.*	x 3.	s 5.	y 1.
q 3.	,, 6.*	u 1.	,, 2.
,, 5.*	y 3.	,, 3.	y 4.†‡
t 4.	,, 5.	v 1.	

* Proper Concord in B.

* Proper Concord in B.

† If the author took ⲆⲀϾⲒ [*recte*, ⲛ-ⲆⲀϾⲒ] to be the correct form of the name, this line has Proper Concord.

‡ In y 5, the Concord is ṗ[= ⲡ]ⲁⲧ-ⲛⲁⲓⲥ-ⲣⲓⲛ.

(c)		(d)	
Quatrains not containing Concord in third line :—		Quatrains not containing Concord in fourth line :—	
a 4.*	n 1.	a 2.	j 6.
b 3.	,, 2.	,, 3.	k 1.†
,, 5.	,, 4.	,, 4.*	l 3.
c 4.	r 4.†	,, 5.	,, 6.
d 1.	s 3.	c 2.	m 2.*
,, 6.	t 1.	,, 5.†	,, 5.†
e 1.	,, 4.	d 4.	,, 6.
,, 2.	,, 6.	,, 5.	n 1.
,, 5.	u 1.	e 2.	o 1.
h 4.	,, 2.	,, 3.*	,, 6.
,, 5.	,, 6.	,, 6.	p 1.‡
i 2.	w 3.	f 3.	q 4.
,, 3.†	x 2.	g 3.	t 3.†
,, 6.	,, 3.	,, 6.	,, 4.
j 4.	,, 4.	h 1.	v 5.
m 3.	y 2.	i 1.	w 2.
		,, 3.	,, 3.
		,, 4.	x 4.
		j 1.	y 4.†
		,, 5.	

* Improper Concord in B.
† Proper Concord in B.

* Improper Concord in B.
† Proper Concord in B.
‡ Proper Concord in L.

Lebar bAili in ṁota, p. 289 a.

I.

[Deibide.]

a Cia lín aiste an aiṗ[ce]ḃail? Nin. A cuiġ ḟearcat ap tri ceḋaiḃ, ar e a lín. O Deiḃiḋiḃ imorro a tinḋsceḋul. Deiḃiḋe Scailte tra ro ar tus, iar tairind:

> Uar in aḋaiġ i Moin ṁoir,
> Peasaiḋ ḋ'[ḟ]eartan*, ni ḋeireoil:
> Dorrḋan ḟorciḃ in ġaeṫ ġlan,
> Ġeisiḃ or ċailli Cliṫaisr.

b Deiḃiḋe ḃairi re coin ano ro:

> Roċuala
> In t-oḃair: eoċu ar ḋuana;
> Doḃer inḋi ir ḋuṫaiġ ḋo—
> ḃo.

c Deiḃiḋi Smot ann ro 7 Ḟlann, ḟili, ḋo Ulltaiḃ, ḋoroinḋe:

> Roġaḃ o
> Cho ḃuiḋi ḃor: norroḋe
> Dia er[i] ar a mac
> smot.

Deiḃiḋe ḟoċael acuḃaiḋ ann reo. A imallġura, niḋat neiṁni: ni ġano ḋorala ḋuit ḋ'a srsiḃeano.

d Oḃra ḃecan, ġaḃur ġleṫ
A tír caiċ, ġan ḟiarraiġiḋ:
Noco n-[ḟ]aca ḃeolu eiċ,
Amal ḃeolu in liaṫanaiġ.

---

* Over this word is a gloss: iḋon, sneaċta—*namely, snow!*

BOOK OF BALLYMOTE, p. 289 a.

I.

[DEBIDE.]

a What is the number of the kinds of Versification? Not difficult [to answer]. Five and sixty above three hundred, that is their number. Now, from the Debides [is] the beginning. Irregular Debide, indeed, is this [which is placed first], according to some:

>Cold is the night in Moin-mor [Great Bog],
>It pours rain, not trifling:
>A loud noise has the pure wind laughed,
>That shrieks over the Wood of Clithar.

b Debide *baisi re toin* [*palmae* (gen.) *ad podicem* follows] here:

>I have heard of
>The deed,—horses [to be given] for poems;
>I shall give that which is due thereto—
>   A cow.

c Lobe Debide [follows] here. And Flann, the poet, of Ulster, made it:

>He caught the ear
>With [his] yellow palms*: [but] there was
>After that upon the youth
>   A lobe.

Meagre Non-Correspondent Debide [is] here. Its enticements are not [a mere] nothing [i.e. they are considerable]: not seldom [i.e. often] chances it [to be convenient] to you to write it.

d
>Since he was small, he took pasture
>In the land of every one, without question:
>I have not seen the mouth [*lit.*, lips] of a horse,
>Like the mouth of the grey.

---

* *Literally*, yellowness of palms.

[I.] **e** Deibidi Impind ann ro. A himpod ro ⁊ ir ead parar de rin, co nac Deibidi Impind, act Cro Cumairc eter Randaidact Moir ⁊ Carbairni. Carbairdni andro:

> I tír caic, can fiarfaigid,
> O bur becan, [gabur] gleic:
> Amal beolu in liacanaig,
> Noco n-[f]aca beolu eic.

Ir e rin in Cro Cumairc.

f Ir firid caidi beicber idir Deibidi Impind ⁊ Eamain Impind. Nin. A hImpind deamnad conid coimbear a cumarc fri ceactarna da Rannaidact. Ir i reo in Eamain Impind:

> Ir imda duine daca
> Ocur cuire ir cialbraca,
> Ir imda ramcac fada
> Ig rluag dabcac Diarmada.

g Ir e ro a himpod na hEamna. Ocur fараid da airde de: idon, Ae [f]rerlíge, idon, airberc roraiglige [frerlíge] ⁊ Cro Cumairc ider Rannaidact m-bic ⁊ Carbairdni. Carbardne ro:

> Ocur cuire ir cialbraca,
> Ir imda duine daca
> Ig rluag dabcac Diarmada,
> Ir imda ramcac fada.

Aei [f]rerlígi [f]ria ha cancain i n-aen baili ⁊ Cro Cumairc fri a n-deliugud.

e Terminational Debide [is the verse just given] here. [Proceed] to invert this and what arises therefrom is that it is not [any longer] Terminational Debide, but a Composite of [*lit.*, between] Rannaidacht Mor and Casbardne. Casbardne [follows] here:

> In the land of every one, without question,
> Since he was small, he took pasture:
> Like the mouth [*lit.*, lips] of the grey,
> I have not seen the mouth of a horse.

That is the Composite.

f It is to be known what is the difference between Terminational Debide and Duplication of the [first-and-third-line] Termination. Not difficult [to tell]. From Duplication of the [first-and-third-line] Termination [arises] that its Composite is suitable to each of two Versifications. This is the Duplication of the [first-and-third-line] Termination:

> There is many a worthy person
> And troop and deadly banner,
> There is many a battle-axe lengthy
> In the warlike host of Diarmaid.

g This [which follows] is the inversion of the Duplication. And there arise two species therefrom: namely, Ae Freslige, that is, normal Ae Freslige and a Composite of [*lit.*, between] Rannaidacht Bec and Casbardne. This [is] Casbardne:

> And troop and deadly banner,
> There is many a worthy person
> In the warlike host of Diarmaid,
> There is many a battle-axe lengthy.

Ae Freslige [is applied] to pronouncing them [the lines] in the same place [as they are in the example just given]; and Composite [of Rannaidacht Bec and Casbardne], to their separation [by inversion].

Lebar bailI In Ṁota.

[I.] h Iṡ i ṡo in Ḋeiḃiḋe Imṡinḋ Ṁoiṡ :

> Ricḟac moṡainn, ṡaċa ṡaiḃ,
> Co hUa Ḟlainḋ, ḟlaċa ṡinḋnaiṡ ;
> Cṡinmainḋ cṡainḋ caṡḋ[ḟ]aic mail,
> In ḃiglaim ḃaill ḃo ḃinǵḃail.

i Iṡ aiṡe iṡ Ḋeiḃiḋe Imṡinḋ Ṁo[i]ṡ, uaiṡ iṡ ḃí ḟaṡaṡ Eaman im ceanḋimṡinḋ. Ocuṡ ni ḟaṡann ḋo Ḋeiḃiḋe ele, aċc Eamain Imṡinḋ nama. Iṡ i ṡo ḃeiṡmíṡeċc :

> Ḋo ḃinǵḃail in ḃiglaim ḃaill,
> Caṡḋ[ḟ]aiḃ cṡuaṡ, cṡinmainḋ cṡainḋ :
> Caṡḋ[ḟ]aiḃ mail co hUa Ḟlainḋ,
>   —ḟlaċa ṡinḋnaiṡ—
> Co hUa ṡinḋnaiṡ ḟlaċa Ḟlainḋ,
> Raċa ṡaiḃ, caṡċ[ḟ]aiḃ moṡainḋ.

j Ḋeiḃiḋe Scaillċe coṡṡanaċ annṡo :

> A mic Conleamna, a laiṡ ǵeaṡṡ,
> ḃean ḃo ċleamna ni coiċǵleann :
> A ċoṡṡ liaċṡoici luḃain,
> A colḃċaċ, a cenḃaċ n-ḃaim,
> A ol oṡḃlaċ ḃ'aiṡǵeclaiḃ,
> A iuċṡa maiǵṡi a Ṁumain.

k Ḋeiḃiḋe Imṡinḋ eccoiċcenn inḋṡo :

> Noċo n-ṡoṡleaċan in ḃṡuíǵ
>   Ḋoċ' ḃuaḋaiḃ,
> Ṁaine coṡṡǵiċeaṡ ṡa ḃaim
>   Ḋo ḃuanaiḃ.

h This [which follows] is the Debide of Great [first-and-third- [I.] line trisyllabic] Termination :

                                                    [of saying],
    There shall come many, felicitous the words [*lit.*, felicities
    To Ua Flaind of sovranty fair, noble ;
    Seasoned [spear-]wood heroes shall bear
    The vengeance blind to repel.

i It is for this it is [called] Debide of Great [first-and-third-line trisyllabic] Termination, because it is therefrom arises Duplication respecting the Head [second-and-fourth-line quadrisyllabic] Termination. And there arises not from any other Debide [any Duplication], except Duplication of the [first-and-third-line] Termination alone. This is an example [of the Inversion and Duplication] :

    To repel the vengence blind,   [wood :
    [Heroes] shall bear hard [*lit.*, hardness] seasoned [spear-]
    Heroes shall bear it to Ua Flaind
        —Of sovranty fair, noble—
    To Ua Flaind of sovranty fair, noble :   [bear [it].
    Felicitous words [*lit.*, felicities of saying], many shall

j Distiched Irregular Debide [follows] here :

    O son of Cu-leamna, O
    The wife of thy son-in-law
            ball
    Her heifer, her ox,
    Her great   of silver,
    Her   salmon from Munster.

k Unusual Terminational Debide [follows] here :

    Not full-wide [is] the burgh
            For thy spoils,
    Unless they are prepared by poets
            For poems.

[I.] **1** Debide Scailte ecoiccenn annro:

> Aicneað [A cneð] in mileċ roðmarb,
>   Iſ aɼarb,—
> Eceɼ ðomuinciɼ ðolam
>   Do leſſað.

m Debidi Imrind cenncrom annro:

> A mic Plannacain 1 Ceallaiɼ,
> A ɼi in ciɼi caiceððennaíɼ,
> A ɼaðail ſrenðruíníɼ, bennaiɼ,
> Or Muinɼairíɼ a cecrellaíɼ.

P. 289 b   **n** | Debidi Imrind ſorðalaċ annro:

> A mic Murċaða moir,
> Rir [? ric] na ɼeið ſið na ſiaðmoin,
> Maiðm aſ ðaſ n-ɼeincið cu ðoin,
> Ria ðaſ n-ɼaillmeiſɼið ɼrianſroill.
> Sceirðic[-ac] ðroiɼ ſneċca aſ a ſroin
> Occaið, ðaſ Eċcɼa im iaſnoin.

o Iſ aiſe na ceċcann Debiðe Imrind corranaċ, aſ na ſocomnaiċeſ co m-ðað Laið Luarcaċ. Aſ aeſin, ðoċuaðaſ na ſileð aſ a cuiɼrin, co n-ðeſſnſaðaſ corſan ſorſain, amal aca i n-aſ n-ðiaið:

> ɼeaċcuſ ðocuaið Ciſ, mac Daiſ,
> Do cɼiall ſorðuſe i n-Eðail,
> Airſceſ na cíſe carſneaſ;
> Siðlaið ſo cɼeċ iſ ſo cain
> Auɼaiſc iſ Choili ɼrecam[-ain];
> ɼor in Siċile ſſaiɼleaſ.

>   ɼinic ðo na Deðiðið.

l Unusual Irregular Debide [follows] here : [I.]

His wound [it was] that killed the warrior,
It is very bitter,—
Amongst ill folk [and] slow
It was [badly] healed.

m Heavy-headed Terminational [second-and-fourth-line trisyllabic, or quadrisyllabic] Debide [follows] here :

O son of Flannacan O'Kelly,
O king of the princely-peaked country,
O reign [*lit.*, possession] victory-leading, pre-eminent,
O noble-minded [ruler] over Mungairech.

n Terminational Excedent Debide [follows] here :

O son of Murchadh the great,
To whom [? thee] may neither wood nor hare belong,
[May] defeat [be inflicted] upon your Foreigners, down to a cow,
Along with your foreign banners of sun[-bright] satin.
May flakes of snow issue from the nostril [of each man]
With ye, [as ye retreat] over Echtga* towards evening [?].

o It is for this that Debide does not possess a Distiched Termination, that it may not be supposed that it is *Laid Luascach*. For all that, the poets came to understand it, so that they made an [excedent] final distich [*lit.*, distich of the end], as it is in the following [*lit.*, after us] :

Once went Cyrus, son of Darius,
To essay conquest in Italy,
The east of the territories subdues he ;
Places [*lit.*, pours] he under raid and under tribute
Augusta and the   Frentani ;
Greatly Sicily scourges he.

It endeth concerning the Debides.

---

* Slieve Aughty, on the confines of Clare and Galway.

(Lebar baili in mota, p. 298 a, l. 44).

II.

Do Dhebidib ro rir.

a Debide Impind ṗata ⁊ Debidi n-Impind gairet ⁊ Debidi Scailti [ṗota ⁊] gairet ⁊ Debidi baíri ṗri toin ⁊ Deibi[di] Smítaċ ⁊ Deċubaid Ṗota ⁊ Deċubaid Gairet ⁊ Deċubaid [Debide] Chenelaċ ⁊ Debeti Guilbneaċ dealtaċ ⁊ Debeti Guilbneaċ recomarcaċ ⁊ Deibeti Cumairc ⁊ Debide daċel acubaid.

Deibidi n-Impind ṗota ro rir:

P. 298 b

   Eirig ruarr, a Dhonnċaid duind,
   For Foolai ṗínd|gaill, foruill:
   Bid do ċert or ċorrlae Cuinn,
   A hUi caín corcrai Conaill.

b Debide n-Impind gairet, ut ert:

   In gaet glar,
   Luaiger innaig, ni[?ra] [er]brar,
   Atċiu ffirrnaig-nuall a frar,—
   Dodebaid to [n-ṗuaċ] dur[er-]glar.

c Debeti Scailti ṗota dono, ut ert:

   Ir e Feolimeċ in rí,
   Diar'[b]a monur aen laiċi,—
   Arorigi [aitiri] Connaċt cean ċaċ
   Ocur Míde do mannrad.

d Debeċe Scailti gairet, ut ert:

   Rorraċ ruad,
   O rartuigiċear in rluag,
   Taċig mor fear ocur eaċ
   Doċum Craibi Firt Lugaċ.

(BOOK OF BALLYMOTE, p. 298 a, l. 44).

II.

OF DEBIDES HERE BELOW.

a Long Terminational Debide and Short Terminational Debide and Irregular Debide [Long and] Short and Debide *baisi fri toin* and Lobe Debide and Long Double [Alternate-]Correspondent [Debide] and Short Double [Alternate-]Correspondent [Debide] and General [Quadruple-Correspondent] Debide and Monosyllabic [Double] Binary[-Correspondent] Debide and Dissyllabic [Double] Binary[-Correspondent] Debide and Composite Debide and Meagre Non-Correspondent Debide.

Long Terminational Debide [follows] here below:

> Arise up, O Donnchadh the Brown,
> Over Fodla fair-valorous, very noble:
> Be thy right over the portion of Conn,
> O descendant excellent, brilliant, of Conall.

b Short Terminational Debide, as is:

> The fresh wind,
> That sweeps swiftly [with great] force,
> I hear the pelting-roar of its rain-drops,—
> Fell strife of [*lit.*, with] very fresh [fury].

c Long Irregular Debide, indeed, as is:

> Fedlimidh is the king,
> To whom it was the feat of one day,—
> [To get] the hostages of Connacht without battle
> And Meath to devastate.

d Short Irregular Debide, as is:

> Rossach red,
> When reached it the host,
> Great [was] the recourse of men and horses
> Unto the branch[ing Tree] of the Grave of Lugaid.

[II.] **e** Debiðe Smítać ro:

> Ir caingin
> bet forrin lear ni[m]bai[n]ǵen,
> Ocur ǵairm neić 'n-a dorur
> Doromur [dorroinur].

f Debetí bairri fri coin ro:

> Tr[u]adan truad,
> Noco tabair do neoć luaǵ;
> Dober indi ir cumunǵ do—
> bó.

g Deaćned [Dećubaid] Fota, amal adudairt briǵita:

> ba het arǵnum do flata,
> Ma[d] dian [dron]ta do c[h]umul,
> A rí berur na breata,
> Do feart ocur do omun.

h Dećned [Dećubaid] Ǵairet, ut ert:

> Ir ard n-uall,
> Fićear in ćoiri na n-druad:
> Dirran, a ri reitear ǵre[i]n,
> Nać a cen dompala uað.

i Debetí Chenelać, dono:

> Ní étar,
> Cía rear re raitrea Etan;
> Ać roreter Eatan an,
> Noco n-rai[t]rea a henaran.

j Debetí Ǵuilbneać dealtać, ut ert:

> In t-én ǵairear irin t-fail,
> Alaínd n-ǵulban ir ǵlan ǵaír;
> Raind [Rind] bind buidi firduið n-druin,
> Carr cor cuirter ǵut in luin.

e Lobe Debide [is] this: [II.]

   It is a peril
  To be upon the fort [that is] unfortified,
  And the shout of the person in its door
    That has conquered.

f Debide *baisi fri toin* [*palmae ad podicem* is] this:

    The wretchock wretched,
  He gives not to anybody recompense;
  I shall give that which is possible to him—
     A cow.

g Long Double [Alternate-]Correspondent [Debide], as said [St.] Brigit:

  It were access to [*lit.*, of] thy kingdom,
  If fervently were done thy service,
  (O king that gives the judgments)
  Thy love and thy fear.

h Short Double [Alternate-]Correspondent [Debide], as is:

    Loud is the roar,
  That seethes the Cauldron of the druids:
  Alas, O king that makes the sun to run,
  That afar I betook me not therefrom.

i General [Quadruple-Correspondent] Debide, indeed [is as follows]:

    I know not
  What man will Etan smile upon [*lit.*, with]:
  But knows Etan the brilliant
  That she will not [always] smile alone.

j Monosyllabic [Double] Binary[-Correspondent] Debide, as is:

  The bird that calls within the sallow,
  Beauteous [his] beak and clear [his] call; [bird],
  The tip [is] charming yellow of the true-black glossy
  A trilling lay is warbled the note of the merle.

[II.] **k** Debeti Guilbneach recomarcach rir inro:

> Fiu mor do maié Mael-rabaill,
> I[n]ma[i]n rí, amra, alaind;
> Evrocc liarr [MS., barr] ro bend [buaball],
> buidi folt for finn gulbaind [gualaind].

l Debeti Cumairc ro:

> Noco [Nom-]geib fearg
> Fri cach n-immar, ac[h]t mo dealg;
> Gae [Cia] teir tre mo dernaind,
> Fearg [f]rirride ní dearrnaim.

m Debide roceil acubaid:

> Mac Conaba, noc[h]o dein
> Moda, act criatra[d] mine;
> Do'n [mac] Mhaenaig i rineall,
> Corrgat ir [ocur] doirrreoracht.

(LEBAR BAILI IN MOTA, p. 303 a, l. 28.)

III.

a Airdi bobaird annro ris: idon, Debidi n-Imrind 7 Debidi Scailti etcer fod 7 gar [7 araile].

Debidi n-Imrind fota, idon:

> Geib do p[h]ater imm imcenn,
> A triat taicid, a t-uibell:
> Ir fírdliged deit, ni fell,
> Dan mic rigfiled Ruireand.

k Dissyllabic [Double] Binary[-Correspondent] Debide [is] [II.] here below :

> Worth much of excellence is Mael-fabaill,
> Beloved king, distinguished, handsome :
> Brilliant eyes [*lit.*, brilliancy of pupils] beneath a [very
> Yellow hair upon a fair shoulder.   [haughty] head,

l Composite Debide [is] this :

> Me seizes anger
> Against every treasure, except my brooch-pin ;
> Although it goes through my palm,
> Anger against this I do not display.

m Meagre Non-Correspondent Debide :

> The son of Cu-abba, he doeth not
> Tasks, except sifting of meal ;   [favour [?],
> With [*lit.*, for] [the son] of Maenach [he was] in
> So that he asked for that [*lit.*, it] and door-keeping.

(BOOK OF BALLYMOTE, p. 303 a, l. 28.)

III.

a The species of the Bo-Bard [follow] here below : namely, Terminational Debide and Irregular Debide, both Long and Short [etc.].

Long Terminational Debide [is as follows], namely :

> Say thy *Pater*
> O chief worthy, O thou flame :
> It is true right for thee, not a mistake,
> The avocation of the son of the royal poet of Rairiu.

[III.] **b** Debidi Impind gairit dino:

> In gen [gaeċ] glar,
> [Lu]aiger anig [innaig] ra n-erbrar,
> Aríu frirnaig, n-uall cen ċar,—
> Ir dodeabaid co n-[f]uaċ ergiar.

c Debide Scailti rota:

> Ir e Fedlimid in rí,
> Diar' do monur aen aidċi,—
> Aiċrige [aitiri] Connaċt cen ċaċ
> Ocur Midi do mannrad.

d Debide Scailti gairid:

> Rorran ruad,
> O durtuigedar in rluag, ⁊ araile.

e Debide Smitaċ:

> Ir caingen
> beċ fririn [forrin] lir [MS., br], ⁊ araile.

f Debide borr fri toin:

> Truagan truad,
> Noco tabair do neoċ luad;
> Dober, ⁊ araile.

g Decubed Fota, ricut brigid dixit, idon:

> ba eċ ar[c]nam irin flaiċ,
> Mad diann dronta a ċomul,
> In rí berur breit[h] for caċ,
> A r[h]erc ocur a omun.

b Short Terminational Debide, indeed [is as follows]: [III.]

> The fresh wind,
> That sweeps swiftly with great force,
> I hear the pelting—a roar without ceasing,—
> It is fell strife of [*lit.*, with] very fresh fury.

c Long Irregular Debide:

> Fedlimidh is the king,
> To whom it was the feat of one night,—
> [To get] the hostages of Connacht without battle
> And Meath to devastate.

d Short Irregular Debide:

> Rossach red,
> When reached it the host, *etc.* [II. **d**.]

e Lobe Debide:

> It is a peril
> To be upon the fort, *etc.* [II. **e**.]

f Debide *boss fri toin* [*palmarum ad podicem*]:

> The wretchock wretched,
> He gives not to anybody recompense;
> I shall give, *etc.* [II. **f**.]

g Long Double [Alternate-]Correspondent [Debide], as [St.] Brigit said, namely:

> It were access into the kingdom,
> If fervently were done his service,
> (The king that gives judgment upon every one)
> His love and his fear.

[III.] **h** Decubed gairit, [ricut] Colum-cille [dixit] fri Coiri m-breccain:

Is ard n-ual[l]
L[u]aiges im coire na n-d[r]uad:
Dirran do'n [? a] ri reiter gréin,
Nach a cein romlara uad.

i Debide Cenelach:

Ni edar
Cia lara míbia Etan [⁊ araile].
[*Read:* Cia lara m-bia.]

j Debide Gui[l]bnech Dialta, idon:

In t-en gairer arin t-fail,
Alainn guilbnen is glan gair;
Rinn linn [binn] buide fidduib druin,
Carr cor curchair guth ind luin.

k Debide Guilbnech [Recomarcach]:

Fiu mor do maith Mael-rabaill,
Inmain ogri, ard, alaind;
Etrocht liar [MS., bar] fo beind buaball,
Buidi folt for find gualaind.

l Debide Cummurc:

Nomgeb ferg
Fri gach n-innmur, acht mo delg;
Ci[a] ter tria m[o] dernaind,
Ferg fri ruidi ni dernnuim.

m Debide roceil acubaid:

Mac Conabba, noco dene [dein]
Mod[a], acht criatrad mine,
La mac Maenaig [i rineall],
[Corrgat] ocus doirrreorach.

h Short Double [Alternate-]Correspondent [Debide], [as St.][III.] Colum-cille [said] to the Cauldron of Breccan:

> Loud is the roar
> That sweeps around the Cauldron of the druids:
> Alas for the [? O] king that makes the sun to run,
> That afar I betook me not therefrom.

i General [Quadruple-Correspondent] Debide:

> I know not
> Who [is he] with whom Etan shall be [*etc.* II. **i.**].

j Monosyllabic [Double] Binary[-Correspondent] Debide, namely:

> The bird that calls from out the sallow,
> Beauteous [his] beak and clear [his] call; [bird],
> The tip [is] charming yellow of the true-black glossy
> A trilling lay is warbled the note of the merle.

k [Dissyllabic Double] Binary[-Correspondent] Debide:

> Worth much of excellence is Mael-fabaill,
> Beloved young king, noble, handsome:
> Brilliant eyes [*lit.*, brilliancy of pupils] beneath a very
> Yellow hair upon a fair shoulder. [haughty head,

l Composite Debide:

> Me seizes anger
> Against every treasure, except my brooch-pin;
> Although it goes through my palm,
> Anger against this I do not display.

m Meagre Non-Correspondent Debide:

> The son of Cu-abba, he doeth not
> Task[s], except sifting of meal;
> With the son of Maenach [he was in favour?],
> [So that he asked for that] and door-keeping.

(Lebar baili in rhota, p. 307 b, l. 1.)

IV.

a Ata bino airbi aili ann ⁊ ir fri Duanbarone bobepar, ibon, Rannaigaċt. Atat bino fobla for Rannaigaċt, [ibon,] Cetarcubaib ⁊ Rannaigaċt Scailteċ.

Ibon:

Ir caingen
biċ fririn [forrin], ut ruppa.

. . . . . .

l. 5 **b** | Ata gne n-aill for Debibe Scailti, ibon, Rannaigaċt boceil acubaib, ibon:

Mac Conaba, ⁊ araile.

c Atat ba fobail for Rannaigaċt, ibon, Cetar[cubaib ⁊ Scailteċ]. Ocur ni fririn b-ara n-ai arberar Debibe n-Imrinn, ut ert (ibon, Debibe Imrinn Gairet irro rir):

In gaet glar [⁊ araile].

. . . . . .

l. 19 **d** | Ocur Rannaigaċt Scailteċ bino, atat ba gne fuirri: ibon, a Debibe Fota ⁊ a Debibe Gairet. Ar inunn a Debibe Gairet Cetarcubaib i tomur: ibon, ceċri [tri] claibemni ⁊ iarcomarc in caċ haei. Ocur ir felur terta be, co ba buan. Ocur noraentaigetar bono; ar ir bialt forcenbair forba gaċa cetramun i cettar n-aei. Ocur ir lantomur buaine bono in Debibe Fota. Ocur ni gnaice i forba in bialt olbar in recomarc, ut ert:

Ir e Feblimib in ri, ut ruppa.

(139)

(BOOK OF BALLYMOTE, p. 307 b, l. 1.)
IV.

a There is indeed another species and it is to Duanbardne it is referred, namely, Rannaigacht. There are also divisions in [*lit.*, upon] Rannaigacht : [to wit,] Quadruple-Correspondent [Rannaigacht] and Irregular Rannaigacht.

[Irregular Rannaigacht is] namely :

It is a peril
To be opposite the, *as above*. [II. **e**, III. **e**.]

. . . .

b There is another kind in [*lit.*, upon] Irregular Debide, namely, Meagre Non-Correspondent Rannaigacht, to wit :

The son of Cu-abba, *and so on*. [II. **m**, III. **m**.]

c There are [as said above] two divisions in Rannaigacht, namely, Quadruple[-Correspondent and Irregular]. And it is not to one of them [alone] is applied [the term] Terminational Debide, as is (namely, Short Terminational Debide [is] this below) :

The fresh wind [*etc.* II. **b**, III. **b**.].

. . . . .

d And indeed [with regard to the second division, to wit] Irregular Rannaigacht, there are two species therein [*lit.*, -on], namely, its Long Debide and its Short Debide. Its Short Quadruple-Correspondent Debide is the same [as the normal Short Terminational Debide] in scansion : that is, there are three heptasyllabics and a trisyllabic in each [of them]. And it is a quadrasyllabic that is wanting from it to be a stanza [in scansion]. And [the Long and the Short Rannaigachts] agree nevertheless [in Termination] ; for it is a monosyllable completes the ending of every quarter in each [of them]. But the Long Debide is the full measure of a stanza. And not more usual in termination [is] the monosyllable than the dissyllable, as is :

Fedlimidh is the king, *as above*. [II. **c**, III. **c**.]

[IV.]   **e** An deibide ġairet dino, iſ aiſi ní ſuba an ġairit,
aſ a binnuſ ⁊ aſ a ṙeġḋaċt la caċ, ut:

   Roſſaċ ſuaḋ; no: Ruſcaċ ſuaḋ.

f Deiſimſeċt aſ Decuḃeḋ Ḟota, ut dixit Briġita:

   ba he aſcnum iſin ḟlaiṫ.

g Deċuḃeḋ ġairit ſo:

   Iſ aſd uall, ut ſuſſa.

(Leḃar Laiġen, p. 38 a.)

V.

Cellaċ hUa Ruan[aḋa] cecinit.

a Iſ aiſti ſaṫmaſ coſ-ſind,
Iſ eiſſiu aċlam, indlim:
baġaim conid bairḋni bind,
Deḃidi alaind imſind.

b Deḃide Scailte na ſcel,
Ni híſide naḋ aṫġen;
Iſſ hi ſeo ind aiſte blaiṫ bſaſſ,
In n-ġnaṫaiġṫeſ in ſenċaſſ.

(Ib., p. 37 b.)

c Can Roġaiſ.

   Iſ caiṅġen,
biṫ ffiſin [ſoſſin] leſſ nimḋaṅġen,
Ocuſ ġaiſm neiċ 'n-a doſuſ,
   Raſomuſ [ſaſſoinuſ].

e [With respect to] the [Irregular] Short Debide, indeed, it is [IV.] for this it does not cut off the short [line], for its sweetness and for its stateliness in the opinion of every one [*lit.*, with every one], as :

Rossach red ; or : Ruscach red [*etc.* II. **d**, III. **d**.].

f An example of [*lit.*, upon] Long Double [Alternate-]Correspondent [Debide is], as said [St.] Brigit :

It were access into the kingdom [*etc.* II. **g**, III. **g**.].

g Short Double [Alternate-]Correspondent [Debide is] this :

Loud is the roar, *as above*. [II. **h**, III. **h**.]

(BOOK OF LEINSTER, p. 38 a.)

V.

CELLACH UA RÚAN[ADA] SANG.

a   It is a felicitous species with Termination,
It is a pliant poesy which I compose :
I engage that it is bardism melodious,
Beauteous Terminational Debide.

b   Irregular Debide of the Tales,   [recognise it] :
It is not this I will not recognise [i.e. I shall willingly
This is the species blooming, vigorous,
In which is practised History.

(Ib., p. 37 b.)

Very Short Correspondence.

c   It is a peril
To be upon the fort [that is] unfortified,
And the shout of the person in its door
That has conquered it.

Lebar Laigen.

[Gilla-Coemain cecinit.]

1.

P. 127 a   **a**   hEriu¹ ard, inir nappís,
Magen molbtač² na morgnim,
Noco n-ḟicir³ duni⁴ a diač
Co norpuair⁵ bič, hua⁶ lamíač⁷.

2.

Laoru ir bič, Fintan¹ ṗáčač,
Coica ingen ingnačač,
Lucc ročeczab² banba bind³,
Cečrača la⁴ ria⁵ n-dilind.

3.

Acbač Cerrair do čám¹ crait²
C[ṙ]íar, i³ Cúil Cerra⁴, a⁵ coicaic⁶:
Do'n robanuč⁷, ruačar gand⁸,
Acbač Laoru⁹ i n-Ard Laorand.

VARIANTS.—*BOOK OF BALLYMOTE* (p. 45 b).

a 1.—¹ Eriu. ² molṗčač. ³ noco n-ecir. ⁴ duine. ⁵ cinnur[ṗ]uair. ⁶ ua. ⁷ lamṗiač. 2.—¹ Findtan. ² cedgab. ³ m-bind. ⁴ no crátʜ (*or periods*), placed above in a modern hand as an alternative reading. ⁵ re. 3.—¹ no eid (*or jealousy*), given overhead in a modern hand as an alternative lection. ² cricc. ³ a. ⁴ Cerrač. ⁵ *om.* ⁶ coicaid. ⁷ du'n rabanač. ⁸ n-gand. ⁹ Laora.

---

  a ¹ *Eriu.*—Regarding the derivation of this name:

Philologi certant et adhuc sub judice lis est.

The legendary origin is given in *L.L.* [*Book of Leinster*]: Fotla, ben Mic Cečč; banba, ben Mic Cuill; hEriu, ben Mic Grene (p. 10 a)—Fotla (**c** 6) [was] the wife of Mac Cecht (**e** 5); Banba (**e** 5), the wife of Mac Cuill (**e** 5); Eriu, the wife of Mac Grene (**e** 5).

BOOK OF LEINSTER.

[GILLA-COEMAIN SANG.]

1.

a Eriu¹ sublime, isle of the kings,   [B. C.*]
Laudable scene of great deeds;
Nor knows any person its state,
Until Bith, grandson of Lamech, found it.

2.

Ladru and Bith, Fintan prophetic,
[And] fifty maidens wondrous,
[Were] the folk that first occupied Banba pleasant,   [2635]
Forty days before the Deluge.

3.

Died Cessair of a sudden plague,
West, in the Angle of Cessair², [with] her fifty [maidens]:
Of [grief for] the great destruction, fatality rare,
Died Ladru on the Height of Ladru³.

[* The regnal dates are those of the initial years.]

² *Angle of Cessair* (Cuil-Cesra).—In Connaught, according to the *Book of Leinster* (p. 4 b). O'Flaherty (*Ogygia*, Pars III., cap. i., p. 162, Londini, 1685), says it was near *Carn Ceasrach* (Mound of Cessair), in the Barony of Clare, co. Galway. O'Donovan (*F.M.* i., p. 4) states this must be wrong: "for in Eochaidh O'Flynn's poem on the early colonization of Ireland, as in the *Book of Leinster*, fol. 3, Carn-Ceasra is placed óp buill meŋnaıb, over the fruitful [River] Boyle." But the reading (p. 5, l. 13) is:

Ocon Capn, ic muıp meŋpa,   At the Carn, at the fruitful sea,
Manb Ceppaıp ı Cuıl Ceppa.   Died Cessair in the Angle of Cessair.

Herewith agrees the *Book of Ballymote* (p. 24 b, l. 9), which has ap muıp meaŋpa, on the fruitful sea.

³ *Height of Ladru* (Ard Ladrand).—Co. Wexford (O'Flaherty, *ib.*). O'Donovan (*F.M.* i., p. 3) thinks it is the place called Ardamine, "where there is a curious moat near the sea coast."

4.

[a] Atbat¹ Fintan², fat fífe³,
'Sin⁴ Mumain do mall⁵ críne⁶ :
bít i n-a fleib⁷ bí⁸ aided feirc⁸,
Marb⁹ de cumaid⁹ a oen mic.

5.

Oen¹ bliadain déc, datta¹ in blad,
Iar² n-dílind tri cet m-bliadan,
Do'n³ h-Erind galaig can³ glór,
Conarragaib Partolon⁴.

6.

Partolon¹ fuirt Gréc² glan³ grind,
Tri cet⁴ bliadan bái i⁵ n-hErind⁵,
Co n erbailt de⁶ tám iartain,
Noi mile fa hoen⁷ fectmain.

1.

b Oén¹ tricha bliadan, can² brón,
ba fás h-Eriu³ iar Partolon⁴,
Co toract Neimed⁵ anair⁵,
Dar⁶ muir co n-a mor maccaib.

4.—¹ marb. ² Finntan. ³ if fat fífi. ⁴ 'ra. ⁵ maill. ⁶ crini.
⁷ i n-a fleb. ⁸⁻⁸ luaided feirc. ⁹⁻⁹ cuaid do cumaid. On the margin, no marb (*or dead*), the reading of L., is given.

5.—¹⁻¹ aen bliadain deg, data. ² ar. ³⁻³ du'n n-Erinn galaid gan. ⁴ go nurrogab Parrtolon.

6.—¹ Parrtolon. ² Greg. ³ glain. ⁴ tricha, with no tri cet (*or three hundred*), the L. lection, on margin by modern hand. ⁵⁻⁵ a n-Erinn. ⁶ do. ⁷ fe hen.

b 1.—¹ cert. ² gan. ³ Eri. ⁴ Parrtolon. ⁵⁻⁵ Nemed anair. ⁶ tar.

---

⁴ *Fintan.*—For the legend of Fintan, see Keating's *History of Ireland*, chap. v., and O'Donovan, *F.M.* i., pp. 4, 5.

BOOK OF LEINSTER.

4.

[B.C.]

[a] Died Fintan⁴, prophet of truth,
In Munster, of slow decay:
Bith on his Mountain⁵ died a death of affection,
Died he of grief for⁶ his only son.

5.

One year⁷ [and] ten, pleasant the fame,
[And] three hundred years after the Deluge,
[Were] for valiant Eriu without renown,
Until Partholon occupied it.   [2324]

6.

Partholon of the very vigorous Grecian Land,
Thirty⁸ years was he in Eriu,
Until died he of a plague afterwards,   [2294]
[With] nine thousand in one week.

1.

b One thirty years without sorrow   [2024]
Was Eriu deserted after Partholon,
Until arrived Neimed from the East,   [1994]
Over sea with his mighty sons.

---

⁵ *His Mountain.*—That is, *Sliab Betha* (the mountain of Bith); *anglice* Slieve Beagh, on the confines of Fermanagh and Monaghan.

⁶ *For.*—Literally, *of*.

⁷ *One year*, etc.—

ba pár cpa hEpiu ian pain Fpi   Now, Eriu was deserted after that
pó cpi óec m-bliaban, no .xii. ap   for the space of 300 years, or of twelve
.ccc., quob uepiup epc.—*L.L.*, p. 6a.   above 300, which is more true.

⁸ *Thirty.*—The reading of *B.B.* [*Book of Ballymote*]. The text has *three hundred*; on which O'Flaherty observes : Proinde triginta et tercentum non adeo Hibernice praeter quantitatem absonant, quin cpíceub, ter centum, pro cpíocab, triginta, imprudenter usurpatum censendum sit (*Ogygia*, Pars III., cap. v., p. 168). But cpí óec (three hundred) and cpíóa (thirty) are readily distinguishable. The meaning is, no doubt, as stated in the poem of O'Flynn (*L.L.*, p. 6a), that the race of Partholon occupied the country for three centuries.

2.

[b] Cethri¹ meic in laich² do'n lind²,
Starn³, Fergus, Ardán⁴, Annind⁵;
Dochoid⁶ Neimed éc⁷ de thám⁷,
Fichi cét i Crich Liatá[i]n⁸.

3.

[S]lecht Stairn¹ 'rin debaid² duind,
La Febail i Cér³ Chonaind;
Marb[th]a⁴ de gallind, ni chél⁴,
Annind⁵ ocus Iarbonél⁶.

4.

Andsin¹ luid Fergus² ri a clainid,²
Co rodsir³ Cathraig Conaind⁴,
Doroéair Fergus na ferg⁵
La Morc, mac Deiled⁸ dredbeirg.

5.

Da cét bliadan, blad cech¹ druing¹,
'O'n maidm rin Cathrach Conaind,
Co tancatar² clanna Stairn³
Arrin⁴ Gréss⁴ uathmair, athgairb⁵.

2.—¹ ceithri. ²⁻² laech du'n lind. ³ Sbarnn. ⁴ Iardan. ⁵ Aind.
⁶ docuaid. ⁷⁻⁷ d'eg do tam. ⁸ Cuindatd Corcaige (*of county Cork*), on margin in modern hand.

3.—¹ Sbairn. ² irin debaid. ³ Ceir. ⁴⁻⁴ marb du'n gaillind, nocho cel. ⁵ Ainnind. ⁶ Iarmuinel.

4.—¹ iar sin. ²⁻² Feargusr le cloind. ³ no cor'bsir. ⁴ Conaing.
⁵ *om.*; co ferg given on margin in modern hand.

5.—This quatrain follows 6 in B. ¹⁻¹ du'n droing. ² tancadar.
³ Sbairn. ⁴⁻⁴ aran Greis. ⁵ agairb.

---

b. ¹ *Ardan.*—Read *Iarbonel* (*L.L.*, p. 6 a); which, being trisyllabic, could not be introduced into the line.

BOOK OF LEINSTER. 147

2. [B.C.]

[b] Four sons of the hero [were] of the party,
Starn, Fergus, Ardan¹, Annind;
Underwent Neimed death from plague, [1978]
[Along with] twenty hundred, in the district of Liathan².

3.

The destruction of Starn [took place] in the noble com-
By [the son of] Febal³ in Ces-Choraind; [bat,
Killed by a valiant host, I shall not conceal it,
[Were] Annind and Iarbonel.

4.

Then went Fergus with his children,
So that he broke down the Fortress of Conand⁴;
Fell Fergus of the heroes
By Morc, son of Deiled the red-faced.

5.

Two hundred years, general the fame, [1978]
From that destruction of the Fortress of Conand,
Until came the children of Starn⁵
From Greece dreadful, very stern.

---

² *District of Liathan.*—The Barony of Ballymore, co. Cork.
³ *Febal.*—ɴɪ ᴍᴀᴄ Ƒebuɪɴ, by the son of Febor (*L.L.*, p. 7 a).
⁴ *Conand.*—Son of Febor, or Febar, who gave his name to the *fortress*, or *tower*, of Tory Island, off the north-west coast of Donegal: ᴍᴀᴄ Ƒebaɪɴ, ᴅɪᴀ ᴛᴀ́ Ꞇoɴ Conaɪɴᴅ, ɴɪɴɪ ɴ-ᴀᴘᴀɴ Ꞇoɴ-ɪɴɪɴ Ċeᴛɴɪ ɪɴᴅɪᴜ—son of Febar, from whom is [named] the Tower of Conand, which is called Tor-Island of Cetne to-day (*L.L.*, p. 6 a).
⁵ *Starn.*—After the destruction of the Tower of Conand, Morc engaged and defeated the victors at sea. Starn escaped to Greece, where his posterity were subjected to such slavery (carrying clay in *bags*—hence Firbolg, *bagmen*—to rough mountains, so that they became flowery plains), that they fled to their original country, 230 years after the time of Nemed (*L.L.*, p. 6 b).

LEBAR LAIGEN.

6.

[b] Sé bliadna déc¹ ir da cét,
Re árim² ní himmarbréc³,
Rocait Neimed co n-a claind⁴,
Co⁵ rotoglad⁵ Tor Conaind⁶.

1.

c Coic¹ ríg rirrin muriact marr¹
Tancatar² dar² muir morglarr;
hi³ tri longrib⁴, ni fát fand⁴,
Galiuin, Firbolg, Fir Domnand.

2.

Flait Fer m-bolg, Rudraige¹ in rí,
Gabar² for Tratt² Rúdraigi¹;
I n-Inbiur³ Slaine na rrían,
Slaine re Feraib Galiuin⁴.

3.

Fir Domnand¹ co trí rígaib,
Lam der fri² h-Erinn n-íraig³;
Sengand, Genand⁴ ocur Gand,
Gabrat irRur⁵ datta⁶ Domnand.

4.

Oen¹ cóiced ic² Feraib bolg,
Coiced Fer Gaelían³ cen⁴ anord⁴,
Ocur tri cóicid in rand
Rucrat⁵ Fir datta⁶ Domnand⁶.

6.—¹ deg.   ² re n-airim.   ³ himirbreg.   ⁴ cloind.
⁵⁻⁵ no cor'toglad.   ⁶ Conaing.
c 1.—¹⁻¹ coig ri rerin muract mar.   ²⁻² tangabar tar.
³ 'n-a.   ⁴⁻⁴ loingrib co lin claind.   2.—¹ Rugraidi.   ²⁻² rogab a Tratt.
³ n-Inber.   [P. 46 a.]   ⁴ Gailiun.   3.—¹ Domnann.   ² re.
³ ringlain.   ⁴ Genann.   ⁵ a n-Irrur.   ⁶ om.   4.—¹ aen.   ² ag.
³ n-Gailiun.   ⁴⁻⁴ n-glan ord.   ⁵ gabrat.   ⁶⁻⁶ data Domnann.

⁶ *Six years*, etc.—From this distich (with *seven* for *six*), the second distich
of **b** 1 (with *since* for *until*) and the second of **b** 5, Keating (*History of Ireland*,

6.

[b] Six years[6] [and] ten and two hundred,   [B.C.]
To count, not excessive falsehood,   [1994–1778]
Spent Neimed and [*lit.*, with] his children,
Until [*Read:* By whom] was razed[7] the Tower of Conand.

1.

c   Five kings [there were] with the sea-farers excellent
That came over the great green sea;
In three fleets, not paltry the cause,
[Were the] Gailions, Firbolg, Men of Domnand.

2.

The prince of the Firbolg, Rudraige the king,
Landed he upon the Strand of Rudraige[1],
In the Estuary of [the river] Slaine[2] of the bridles,
[Landed] Slaine with the Men of Galion.

3.

The Men of Domnand with [their] three kings,
[Sailed they with] the right hand to Eriu[3] of the plains;
Sengand, Genand and Gand
Landed in famous Ros-Domnand[4].

4.

One Fifth[5] [was assigned] to the Firbolg,
A Fifth[6] [was the portion] of the Men of Galion without
And three Fifths [were] the portion   [murmuring,
The famous Men of Domnand received.

---

chap. viii.) makes a verse, to certify the interval between the advent of Nemed and that of the Firbolg!

[7] *By whom was razed.*—I suggest O ꝏ coꝪlaꝺ—*by whom* [*Nemed's children*] *was razed;* thus giving 216 years as the Nemedian period.

c. [1] *Strand of Rudraige.*—In Ulster, according to O'Flaherty (*Ogygia*, Pars III., cap. viii., p. 171).

[2] *Estuary of Slaine.*—The mouth of the Slaney, Wexford Harbour.

[3] *Right hand to Eriu.*—That is, sailed up along the western coast.

[4] *Ros-Domnand.*—The Promontory of Domnand, in the north-west of Mayo.

[5] *Fifth.*—Ulster: from Assaroe, near Ballyshannon, to Drogheda.

[6] *Fifth.*—Leinster: from Drogheda to Waterford Harbour.

150　Lebar Laigen.

5.

[c] Doratrat¹ in cethur cain
Rígi² n-hErenn² dia m-bratair;
Conid é Sláne ráer reṅg
Cét rí rogab tir³ n-hErenn³.

6.

Erdid¹ ri haidid cach fir¹,
Ra² ainm ir ra amrir²,
Co³ roinnirur dúib uile³—
Rigu⁴ Forla roltbude⁴.

1.

d bliadain do Shláne, do'n¹ laech,
Co² rodmarb² galar garbgaeth³,
Adnacht i n-Duma⁴ Sláne⁴,
Cét rí h-Erenn⁵ echbáne⁵.

2.

Oí¹ bliadain Rúdraige² ruith²,
Co³ n-erbailt irrin³ aro bruig;
Gand⁴, Genand, marb[th]a de⁴ tám,
Cethri bliadna a flaith forlán.

3.

Cóic bliadna Sengaind iar rein¹,
[No]co² torchair la Fiachraig³:
Cóic bliadna Fiachrach³ finnaid⁴,
Conidromarb⁵ ruad Rindail.

5.—¹ foranndrat. ²⁻² rige n-Erenn. ³⁻³ iath n-Erenn. 6.—¹⁻¹ eirdig re hoidid gach fir. ²⁻² re n-anmaib, re n-amrir. ³⁻³ co n-i[n]dirur daib uili. ⁴⁻⁴ riga Forla fondglaíni.
　d 1.—¹ du'n. ²⁻² gururmarb. ³ garbaeth. ⁴⁻⁴ a n-Duma Slaine. ⁵⁻⁵ Erenn echbaine. 2.—¹ da. ²⁻² Rugraidi in ruith. ³⁻³ co fuair eg iran. ⁴⁻⁴ Gann, Geanand, marb do. 3.—¹ iar rin. ² no co. ³ Fiacaig. ⁴ findaig. ⁵ conurromarb.

5.

[c] The four generous [kings] assigned
The kingship of Eriu to their brother;
So that Slane, noble, prudent, is
The first king that occupied the land of Eriu.

6.

List to the fate of each man,
To his name and to his time,
Until I tell them all to you,—
The kings of Fodla the yellow-surfaced.

1.

d A year [was reigned] by Slaine, by the hero, [1778]
Until killed him sharp disease,
Buried was he in the Mound of Slaine[1],
The first king of Eriu of the white steeds.

2.

Two [were] the years of Rudraige, the champion, [1777]
Until died he in the lofty Brugh[2];
Gand, Ganand, died they of plague,
Four years their full sovranty. [1775]

3.

Five [were] the years of Sengand after that, [1771]
Until fell he by Fiachra:
Five [were] the years of Fiachra, the warrior, [1766]
Until slew him the bright [weapon] of Rindal.

---

d. [1] *Mound of Slaine.*—"This place is still well known. It is situated in the townland of Ballyknockan, about a quarter of a mile to the south of Leighlin-Bridge, near the west bank of the River Barrow. Nothing remains of the palace but a moat, measuring 237 yards in circumference at the base, 69 feet in height from the level of the River Barrow, and 135 feet in diameter at top" (O'Donovan, *F.M.* i., pp. 14, 15).

[2] *Brugh.*—On the Boyne.

4.

[d] Sé bliadna Rinnail¹ do'n ṗainḋ¹,
Rodmarḃ² Oḋḃgen, mac Sengaind²;
Oḋḃgen³, roċaiṫ a ceṫair,
Ḋoṗoċair⁴ la Airḃeċair⁴.

5.

Eocu, mac Eirc¹, in rí² raiṫ,
Ḋec³ iḣ-bliadna a ḟlaṫiur lánmaiṫ³;
'E¹ rin [in] céṫ rí do rind⁴
Rogaeṫ⁵ ar ṫúr i n-hErinn⁵.

6.

Nuadu¹ Argaṫlám¹ na n-eċ
Rodmarḃ² balar balcbemneċ³;
Fiche⁴ bliadan a ḟlaṫiur
'Or hErinn⁵ i⁶ n-arḋmaṫiur⁷.

4.—¹⁻¹ Rindail du'n roind.   ²⁻² gur'marḃ Oiḋḃgen, mac Sengoinṅ.
³ Ḟoiḋḃgein.   ⁴⁻⁴ co n-droċair la hAirḃeḋair.   5.—¹ Erc.   ² i[n] rí.
³⁻³ remer deiḋ bliadan m-biṫmaiṫ.   ⁴⁻⁴ gu rumarḃradar i[n] rí.
⁵⁻⁵ ṫri meic Nemiḋ, maic Ḃadrai.   6.—The following two quatrains are inserted here:—

Anmand ṫri mac Nemiḋ no,—

Cerard, Luam ocur Luacro:
Siad romarḃ, ceċ ḟer do rind,

Eoċo, mac Eirc, a n-Erinn.
    Eri ard.

Brer, mac Eladain, maic Ned,
Robo ruirí co romeid;

Seċṫ bliadna do, nir' b[ḟ]oda,

Eg adbaṫ do'n ruad doda.

The names of the three sons of noble Nemid

[Were] Cesard, Luam and Luacro:
Them slew, each man with [spear-]point,

Eocho, son of Erc, in Eriu.
    Eri sublime.

Bres, son of Eladhan, son of Ned,
He was a great king with much greatness,

Seven years [were reigned] by him, it was not long,

Death died he of the dire plague.

In the second line of the first quatrain b is placed above d, to make the reading Cerard.   ¹⁻¹ Nuada Airgedlam.   ² d om.   ³ bailcbeimneċ.   ⁴ ṫriḋa.
⁵ h om.   ⁶ a.   ⁷ maiṫur.

BOOK OF LEINSTER.   153

                          4.   [B. C.]

[¶] Six years [were] the portion of Rindal,   [1761]
     Slew him [F]odbgen, son of Sengand;
     [F]odbgen, spent he four [years],   [1755]
     Fell he by Ardechar.

                          5.

Eochu, son of Erc, the fortunate king,
Ten years his full-good sovranty;   [1751]
That was the first king that by a [spear-]point³
Was slain in the beginning in Eriu.

                          6.

Nuadu Silver-Hand⁴ of the steeds,
Him slew Balar⁵ Strong-smiting;
Twenty years his sovranty   [1741]
Over Eriu in exalted goodness.

---

³ [Spear-]point.—Thus explained in a poem in *L.L.*, p. 8 a:

Co n' [f]ár Rinnal, ní boí pino	Until grew Rinnal, there was not a point
For apm eter 1 n-hCrino,	Upon a weapon at all in Eriu, [finish,
For ɣáib aɣarɣa[ib], cen óhc cain,	Upon spears rough, without perfect
Act a m-bit 1 n-a ritcrannaib.	But the whole run of them was unpointed wood. [*Lit.*, But to be in running trees.]

| Cucrat Cuat-be-Donnano bil Laiɣne leo 1 n-a lamaib: | Brought the diligent Tuath-de-Donnand [Pointed] spears with them in their hands: |
| Oib rein romarbab Eobaib, La ril Nemib nertbretaiɣ. | With these was slain Eochaid, By the seed of Nemid the severe-judging. |

⁴ *Silver-Hand.*—His hand (according to *L.L.*, p. 9 a) was cut off in the first battle of Magh Tuired (near Cong, co. Mayo). But he was not the worse, rather the better, in consequence, according to the veracious legend:

| Lám arɣait co lánlút caca láma in cac meór ┐ in cac alt bonat rair Diancect, in liaiɣ ┐ Créibne, cerb, 1 corɣnam frir. | A hand of silver with the full suppleness of each hand in every finger and in every joint Diancecht, the leech, and Creidne, the wright, assisting him, placed upon him. |

O'Flaherty's observation is perhaps worth quotation (*Ogygia*, Pars III., cap. X., p. 174): "Non ita pridem in Italia Hieronymus Capivacius vir inaudita medendi ratione præcelluit, qui labra, nares, aures hominibus, quibus deessent, adeo affabre reponebat, ut proxime miraculum ars esset (*I. H. a Pflaumern: in Bononia, pag.* 84)."

⁵ *Balar.*—For the Fomorian Balar, see O'Donovan, *F.M.* i., pp. 18 *sq.*

1.

e Bres, mac Eladan¹, mic Néit²,
Ropo³ ruiri co roméit⁴;
Secht m-bliadna do, nir' p̄ota⁵,
Éc⁶ atbat⁶ do'n ruad rota⁷.

2.

P. 127 b
Rogiallad do Lug¹, do'n laech,
Da p̄ichit bliadan barrgaét²:
Mór³ ect dorińgni⁴ Mac Cuill,—
bár hui Diancecht⁵ i Caenduruim⁶.

3.

Eochu Ollathair¹ iárma,
Cethri² p̄ichit p̄ind bliadna;
bár in Dagdai³, derg na n-drend⁴,
Do'nd erchor⁵ tarlaic Ceithnend⁵.

4.

Deich m-bliadna do'n¹ Delbaeth dil,
Co torchair do láim Chaichir².
Deich m-bliadna Fiachach findgil,
Co rormarb³ Eogan Aird⁴-inbir.

---

e 1.—This quatrain precedes d 6. ¹ Eladain. ² Ne[i]d. ³ do. ⁴ romeid. ⁵ b'[p̄]oda. ⁶⁻⁶ eg adbat. ⁷ roda. 2.—¹ The second hand placed h after Lug (Lugaid), and, to make the emendation more certain, wrote Lug(aid) overhead. ² blatcaeih. ³ truag. ⁴ dorindi. ⁵ Ua Dencecht. ⁶ a Caendruim. 3.—¹ Eochaid Ollotair. ² ceithri. ³ Dagda. ⁴ dream. ⁵⁻⁵ urcur do teilg Ceilter. 4.—¹ do. ² Fiachaig. ³ gur'marb. ⁴ ard.

e. ¹ *Bres.*—gabar brers ... rige ... co roiscad lam Nuadat. Bres took the kingship, until the hand of Nuadu was cured (*L.L.*, p. 9 a). He and Nuadu fell in the second battle of Magh Tuired (Barony of Tirerrill, co. Mayo), which was fought twenty-seven years after the first (*L.L.*, p. 9 b).

² *Was obeyed.*—Literally, *it was served to Lug* (impersonal construction: *servitum est Lugadio*).

1.   [n. c.]

e   Bres[1], son of Eladan, son of Net,
    He was arch-king with exceeding greatness;
    Seven years [were reigned] by him, it was not long,   [1721]
    Death died he of the [gory-]red wound.

2.

Lug, the hero, was obeyed[2],
Two score of very prudent years :   [1714]
A great deed did Mac Cuill,—
The death of the grandson of Diancecht at Caindruim.[3]

3.

Eochu Ollathair afterwards,
Four score fair years [reigned he];   [1674]
The death of the Dagda, sorrow of hosts,
[Took place] from the thrust Ceithnend cast[4].

4.

Ten years [were reigned] by Delbaeth devoted,   [1594]
Until fell he by hand of Caicher.
Ten [were] the years of Fiacha the very fair,   [1584]
Until slew him Eogan of Ard-inber[5].

---

[3] *Caindruim.—Pleasant ridge.*—A name for Tara.

Liacdruim ⁊ Druimcain ⁊ Múr-   Grey ridge and Pleasant ridge and
Tea ⁊ Cathir croind anmand   Mur-Tea and Cathir-chroind [were] the
Tempad i torrud.   names of Tara in the beginning (*L.L.*,
                               30 a).

[4] *Ceithnend cast.*—Ocтmoğba bo'n Dağba, co n-epbailt bo ğai cro
bia poğuin Cecleand a catt mor Moiğe Тuiniđ : Eighty years [were
reigned] by the Dagda [Eochu Ollathair], until he died of [the wound of] the
spear wound [*lit.*, spear of gore] with which Cetleand wounded him in the
[second] great battle of Magh Tuired (*B.B.*, p. 33 b, ll. 33-4).

[5] *Ard-inber.*—Called *Inber-mor* in *B.B.* (p. 33 b, ll. 38, 39). The estuary of
the Ovoca, at Arklow, co. Wicklow.

5.

[e] Noí¹ m-bliadna rícet 'malle,
Mac Cuill, mac Cect, mac Grene,
Trí meic Cermata² co n-úaill³,
Irríge³ or banba bratrúaid.

6.

Dorochair Mac Grene gel¹
I Taltin² la hAmairgen;
Mac Cuill la³ 'Eber inn³ óir;
Mac Cect do laim hEriomoin⁴.

1.

f bliadain irríge¹ mar oén²
D'h'Erimón³ ir⁴ d''Eber roltcacm;
Co torcair Eber iartain,
Do laím hErimóin³ imglain⁵.

2.

h'Erimón¹, airdairc cen¹ on,
ba leir ind hEriu² a oenor²;
Ré rect³ m-bliadan dóc⁴ do'n dor⁴,
'Ec⁵ atbat i n-Argatror⁵.

3.

A trí meic, ró¹ bliadna ar blad,
Co bár² Mumne im Maig² Cruachan.
Luigne³ ir Laigne⁴ nallanó⁴,
Romarbta i cat Airb⁵ Laorand.

5.—¹ beió. ²⁻² Cermada, co m-buaió. ³ irrígi. 6.—¹ gcal.
² Taillcin. ³⁻³ re hEber in. ⁴ h om.
f 1.—¹ irrígi. ² aen. ³ h om. ⁴ om. ⁵ indglain.
2.—¹⁻¹ Eremon, oirdirc gan. ²⁻² an Eri a aenur. ³ oct.
⁴⁻⁴ deg du'n dur. ⁵⁻⁵ eg adbat i n-Airgeodnur. 3.—¹ tri.
²⁻² ga bair Muimni a Moig. ³ Luigni. ⁴⁻⁴ Laigní na lann. ⁵ arb.

⁶ *Mac Cuill, Mac Cecht, Mac Grene.*—Thus explained in *L.L.* (p. 10 a):
Mac Cuill .i. Setor, coll a déa;   *Son of Hazel*, namely, Sethor was [his

5. [B.C.]

[e] Nine years [and] twenty together, [1574]
Mac Cuill, Mac Cecht, Mac Grene,
Three sons of Cermat with haughtiness,
[Were] in kingship over Banba ruddy-vestured.

6.

Fell Mac Grene bright
In Tailtiu⁷ by Amairgen;
Mac Cuill, by Eber of the [sweet] voice;
Mac Cecht, by hand of Erimon.

1.

f A year in kingship together [1515]
[Was spent] by Erimon and by Eber beauteous-haired;
Until fell Eber thereafter,
By hand of the very sincere Erimon.

2.

Erimon, illustrious without fault,
To him belonged Eriu by himself; [prop,
A space of ten years [and] seven [was reigned] by the [1544]
[Natural] death died he in Argatros¹.

3.

His three sons, six years [reigned they] for fame, [1527]
To the death of Mumne in Magh Cruachan²,
Luigne and Laigne of the swords,
Slain were they in the battle of Ard Ladrand³.

Mac Cecht .i. Teton, ccct a bea; first name], hazel [was] his god; *Son of*
Mac Grene .i. Ceton, grian a *the Plough*, namely, Tethor, the plough
bea. [was] his god; *Son of Sun*, namely,
Cethor, the sun [was] his god.

⁷ *Tailtiu.*—Teltown, co. Meath.

f. ¹ *Argatros.*—Silver-wood, on the Nore, parish of Rathbeagh, barony of Galmoy, co. Kilkenny (O'Donovan, *F.M.* i., p. 51).

² *Cruachain.*—Rathcroghan, near Belanagare, co. Roscommon (*id. ib.*).

³ *Ard Ladrand.*—See a 3, note 2.

4.

[**f**] [S]lecta cetri¹ meic 'Ebir²
La Iriel³, fáid, finnfennid³.
Letbliadain⁴ a flaiṫ⁵, nir' mór⁶,
Aer⁷, Orba, Ferḃna⁸, Feron⁸.

5.

Iriel¹, fáid, fiċid² gail gáiṫ³,
A beiṫ remer in rolaiṫ,
Co n-erbailt im Maig⁴ Muaḋe⁴
De⁵ galar olc⁶ oen⁶ uaire.

6.

Eṫriel¹, mac Irieoil² na n-eċ,
Cerṫ³ fiċe bliaḋan buiḋneċ⁴,
Co torċair⁵ ipRairind⁶ rúaiḋ,
Do laim Conmail claiḋeḃ⁶ ruaiḋ.

1.

g Conmael¹, mac Ebir, cen² ail,
Céṫflaiṫ³ mor banba³ amMumain;
'Arim⁴ tri n-deiċ m-bliaḋan brar,
Co torċair la Tigernmair⁵.

2.

Tigernmar, ba trén a rig,
Seċṫ¹ m-bliaḋna ar reċt n-deċib¹;
Co n-erbailt² irrin² tám tend,
I torċair ár fer n-hErend³.

4.—¹ ceatra. ² n-Ebir. ³⁻³ hIrial, faiṫ finnfeinnid. ⁴ leitbliadain.
⁵ flaitur. ⁶ lor. ⁷ Er. ⁸⁻⁸ Ferḃna, Feron. 5.—¹ Irial. ² feṫeḋ.
³ n-gaeiṫ. ⁴⁻⁴ a Muig Muaiḋi. ⁵ do. ⁶⁻⁶ uile aen. 6.—¹ Eitrial.
² Iriel. ³ om. ⁴ immbuiḋneċ. ⁵⁻⁵ co broḋair i Rorind. ⁶ cloiḋem.
g 1.—¹ Conmal. ² gan. ³⁻³ ri Erenn. ⁴ airem. ⁵ Tigernmar.
2.—¹⁻¹ reṫtmoga reṫt do bliaḋnaib. ²⁻² co n-beḃailt irin. ³ n-Erenn.

---

⁴ *Plain of Muaid.*—According to O'Donovan (*F.M.* i., p. 34), either the plain of the river Moy, which flows between the cos. Mayo and Sligo; or, more probably, the plain of Knockmoy, six miles south-east of Tuam, co. Galway.

BOOK OF LEINSTER. 159

4. [B.C.]

[f] Destroyed [were] the four sons of Eber
By Iriel, the prophet, the fair warrior.
Half-year the sovranty, it was not much, [1521]
[Of] Aer, Orba, Forgna, Foron [Feron, *L.L.* p. 15 b].

5.

Iriel, the prophet, exciter of the din of battle,
Ten [years] the period of the great hero, [1521]
Until perished he in the Plain of Muaid[4],
Of evil disease of one hour.

6.

Ethriel, son of Iriel of the steeds, [1511]
Just twenty crowded years [reigned he],
Until fell he in Rairiu[5] red,
By hand of Conmail ruddy-sword.

1.

g Conmail, son of Eber, without objection,
[Was] first prince of great Banba from Munster;
A tale of thrice ten vigorous years [reigned he], [1491]
Until fell[1] he by Tigernmas.

2.

Tigernmas, stout was his kingship,
[For] seven years above seven tens; [1461]
Until perished he in the severe plague[2], [of Eriu.
In which fell vast numbers [*lit.*, slaughter] of the men

---

[5] *Rairiu.*—"It is the place now called Raeipe mon, in the territory of Ire3an, or barony of Tinnahinch, in the Queen's Co., which was part of the ancient Ui-Failghe, or Offally" (O'Donovan, *F.M.* i., p. 38).

g. [1] *Fell.*—In the battle of Emain Macha (Navan fort, near Armagh), according to *L.L.* (p. 16 b).

[2] *Plague.*—His death is thus told in *L.L.* (*ubi sup.*) :

Co n-epbailt imMaiʒ-pleóc, Until he died in Magh-Slecht, in the
immópdáil Maiʒe-pleóc ꝛ ceopa great convention of Magh-Slecht and
cetpamtane pep ń-hEpenn 'malle three fourths of the men of Eriu along

3.

[5] Cocu étguḋaċ[1] ampa,
Cétri bliaḋna ór bros banba:
Ni ḋalb, i caṫ Tempaċ tricc[2]
Roḋmarḃ[3] Cermna, mac Eḃric.

4.

Cermna, Sobairċe, ḟeol m-ḃil,
Ḋa mac Eḃric, mic hEḃir[1]:
Ḋafiċit bliaḋan co m-ḃlaiḋ,
Cét ríġ hErenḋ[1] a Ulṫaiḃ[2].

5.

Aiḋeḋ[1] Sobairċe 'n-a ḋún,
La Eċaiġ[2] Minḋ ḋar in múir[2].
Aiḋeḋ[3] Cermna 'rin ċaṫ car,
La Cochaiġ ḟinḋ ḟaeḃurġlar.

6.

Fiċe[1] bliaḋan, blaḋ co n-áiḃ,
Flaṫiur[2] Eċaċ, mic Conmáil:
Fiaċa Labrainni[3] nallerġ[3],
Romarḃ Eċaiḋ[4] ḟaeḃurḋerġ.

3.—[1] Coḋaiḋ eḋgoṫaċ. [2] tris. [3] ġurmarḃ. 4.—[1] h *om*. [2] hUllṫaiḃ.
5.—[1] oḋa. [2-2] hCoḋaiġ Menn ṫar in mur. [3] oiḋe. 6.—[1] Fiói. [2] Flaṫur.
[3-3] Laḃrainḋe na lerġ. [4] Coḋaiḋ.

ḟrir, is aḋraḋ ċroim Ċróiċ, riġi-   with him, [whilst] in adoration of Crom
ḋail hErenn. Conna terna amlaiḋ   Cróc, the royal idol of Eriu. So that
rin aċt oen ċetrar ḟer n-hErenn   there escaped not like that but just four
arr. Unḋe Maġ-ṡleċt.   persons of the men of Eriu therefrom.
                                     Whence *Magh-Slecht* [Plain of Destruc-
                                     tions].

Magh-Slecht is a plain in the barony of Tullyhaw, co. Cavan.—O'Donovan,
F.M. i., p. 43.

[3] *Etguḋach.*—The vestured. The rationale is given in *L.L.* (p. 16 b).

Is acirḋe ḋoronta ilḃreċta i   It is by him were made many varieties
n-eṫaiġiḃ hErenn .i. oen ḋaṫ i   in the garments of Eriu: to wit, one

BOOK OF LEINSTER.

3. [B. C.]

[g] Eochu Etgudach[3] illustrious,
Four years [reigned he] over diversified Banba : [1384]
Not false, in the vigorous battle of Tara,
Him slew Cermna, son of Ebrec.

4.

Cermna, Sobairche, good the deed,
Two sons of Ebrec, son of Eber :
Two score years [reigned they] with fame, [1380]
First kings of Eriu from the Ultonians.

5.

The fate of Sobairche [took place] in his fort[4]
By Eochu Mend [who came from] over the sea[5].
The fate of Cermna [took place] in the contested battle[6],
By Eochu the fair of the green weapons.

6.

A score of years, pleasant the fame, [1340]
[Was] the sovranty of Eochu, son of Conmail :
Fiacha Labrainni of the shields,
Slew he Eochu Ruddy Weapon.

---

n-étaiġ moġab, ba baé i n-étaiġib aiteó, cṛi baéa i n-etuó moġab ⁊ oclach, ceṫṛi baéa i n-etuó óóciġeṇn, cóic baéa i n-etuó toiṛeó, ṛé baéa i n-etuó ṛiġ ⁊ ollam ⁊ ḟileb, uii. ṅ-baéa i n-etuó ṛiġ ⁊ ṛiġan. Iṛ aṛṛin ṛo[ḟ]óṛ ibiu na huli baéa i n-etuó epṛcop.

colour in the garment of slaves, two colours in the garments of peasants, three colours in the garment of slaves and warriors, four colours in the garments of young lords, five colours in the garment of chiefs, six colours in the garment of kings and ollams and poets, seven colours in the garment of kings and queens. It is from that arose [*lit.*, grew] to-day all the colours in the garment of bishops.

[4] *Fort.*—That is Dun-Sobhairche, or Dunseverick, near the Giant's Causeway, co. Antrim.

[5] *Over the sea.*—He was son of the Fomorian king (*L.L.*, p. 17 a).

[6] *Battle.*—Fought at Dun-Cermna, or the Old Head of Kinsale, co. Cork. This quatrain is given in *L.L.* (p. 17 a), with the variants Coéaiġ, muṛ and caṛṛ.

Lebar Laigen.

1.

h Fiche a cetair[1] cen caimme[2],
ba flait Fiacha Labrainne[3];
Docer ri Fene fabair
l[4] cat Slebi[5] belgadain[6].

2.

bliadain for a beic fa dó,
Fot[1] flata Ecac[1] Mumó,
Co torchair[2] in caembor cáin
Larinn[3] Oengur n-Olmucaid.

3.

Se bliadna fa[1] di, in tucaid[1]?
ba[2] rí[2] in t-Oengur Olmucaid;
Docer i Carmon[3] in clet
La hEnna n-abbol[4] n-Airctec[4].

4.

Arim[1] nói m-bliadan fa[2] trí
D' 'Enna Airgdec[3], do'n arbrí[4];
Rodmarb[5] Rotectaid, mac Main,
ImMaig Rúaid[6] rodacaoin[6].

5.

Ré cóic[1] m-bliadan co m-blaid
Rogiallad[2] do Rotectaid[3];
Dorochair[4] la Setna n-Art[5],
Irrin[6] Chruacain cetna Connact.

---

h 1.—[1] cetair.   [2] caíme.   [3] Labrainde.   [4] a.   [5] Sleibi.
[6] belgadain.   [P. 46b.]   2.—[1-1] rod flaitur Eocac.   [2] Co dorcair.
[3] larin.   3.—[1-1] fo tri, tugaid.   [2] om., probably by oversight.
[3] Carmun.   [4-4] n-abbul n-Aircneć.   4.—[1] airem.   [2] fo.   [3] arrig.
[4] airrig.   [5] gur'marb.   [6-6] Ruad, raid ní rocain.   5.—[1] da coic. Over
da (in another hand) is cuig; which would make the total 25 (5 × 5), instead of 10.
[2] dogiallad.   [3] Rotectaig.   [4] co n-drocair.   [5] Art.   [6] rin.

h. [1] *Fian.*—The native military force.
[2] *Belgada[i]n.*—Bulgaden, near Kilmallock, co. Limerick.

BOOK OF LEINSTER. 163

1. [B.C.]

h Twenty [and] four [years] without duplicity, [1320]
Was Fiache Labrainne prince;
Fell the king of the active Fian¹
In the battle of Mount Belgada[i]n².

2.

A year above ten by two [= 21], [1296]
[Was] the length of the sovranty of Eochu Mumo³,
Until fell the fair prop beauteous
By Oengus Olmuchaid.

3.

Six years by two, understand ye? [1275]
Was Oengus Olmuchaid king;
Fell in Carmon⁴ the support [of Eriu]
By mighty Enna the Silvery⁵.

4.

A tale of nine years by three [1263]
[Was reigned] by Enna the Silvery, by the arch-king;
Slew him Rothechtaid, son of Maen,
In Magh Ruad⁶ the very pleasant.

5.

A space of five years with fame [1236]
Was Rothechtaid obeyed⁷;
Fell he by Setna the Tall,
In very Cruachan of Connacht.

---

³ *Mumo.*—O ραιτερ Ⅲumu—from whom is called Munster (*L.L.*, p. 18 a).
⁴ *Carmon.*—Wexford.
⁵ *Silvery.*—Ιρ leιρ baρóητα ρϲéιτ αιρσbιde ι η-Cρσατρορ ⁊ bοραϲ bo αιρeòαιb hEρenn.—It is by him were [first] made silver shields in Argatros (Silver-Wood) and he gave them to the leaders of Eriu (*L.L.*, p. 18 b).
⁶ *Magh Ruad.*—In the battle of [Magh] Roigne, according to *L.L.* (p. 18 b). This was a plain in ancient Ossory, at the foot of a hill called Dornbuidhe (O'Donovan, *F.M.* i., p. 51).
⁷ *Obeyed.*—It was obeyed, etc. The impersonal construction.

6.

[h] Cóic bliadna do Shetna¹ Airt,
Docer² in rí rá³ ro mac:
Ní rumait⁴ in mac, mílib tor,
Día ataír a farugud⁵.

1.

i Sé bliadna déc¹ ra¹ cetair,
Flait[ur]² Fiacac fialcretaig²;
Fiaca, flait³, rocair na flóg,
Dorocair⁴ la Munemon.

2.

Munemon¹, cóic bliadna ar blaid
Fat² flata maic Cair clotoig;
Atbat³ rí Dairbre⁴ do tám,
ImMaig⁵ 'Aidne immelbán⁵.

3.

Arim¹ deic m-bliadan can¹ brón
Do mac morgarg² Munemoin²:
Docer³ Ailderg Dóit in rait³,
La hOllomain [i Temraig]⁴.

6.—¹ do'n t-Setna. ² gur'cer. ³ re. ⁴ nir'mait.
⁵ do rarαgod.
i 1.—¹⁻¹ deg 'r a. ²⁻² flatur Fiadna fialcretaig. ³ fer.
⁴ dodrocair. 2.—¹ Muinemon. ² fad. ³ docer. ⁴ Dairbri.
⁵⁻⁵ Muig Ailbi imelban. Over Ailbi, the textual reading, Aidne, is placed as a variant by a different hand. 3.—¹⁻¹ cert trica bliadan gan. ²⁻² miadglan Munemon. ³⁻³ atbat Oilderg, data in daig. ⁴ i Temraig.

⁶ *Outraged.*—Rothechtaid (*L.L.*, p. 18 b) was slain in Ratheroghan, co. Roscommon, by Setna, whilst under the protection of Fiacha, son of the slayer. The dishonour thus put upon him Fiacha avenged by killing his father. Rumait governs a farugud. The possessive, a, is employed objectively, in reference to mac (son).

6.   [B.C.]

[h] Five years [were reigned] by Setna the Tall,   [1231]
     Fell the king by his great son [Fiacha]:
     Forgave not the son, great [?] the deed,
     To his father his being outraged⁸.

1.

i Six years [and] ten by four [= 64]*   [1226]
   [Was] the sovranty of Fiacha, the generous raider;
   Fiacha, the prince, succour of the hosts,
   Fell he by Munemon.

2.

Munemon¹, five years with [*lit.*, for] fame   [Cas;[1206]
[Was] the length of the sovranty of the famed son of
Died the king of Dairbre of plague,
In Magh Aidne² the white-bordered.

3.

A tale of a decade of years without sorrow   [1201]
[Was reigned] by the very stern son of Munemon:
Fell Ailderg Dóit³ of felicity,
By Ollam [in Tara].

---

i. * The B reading, 20, is adopted in the chronology.

¹ *Munemon.*—Thus explained in *L.L.* (p. 18 b):

Ir leir rotinreantá munceba óir ro braigtib boene i n-hErinn: .i. muinmaine .i. maine ro munclaib.

It is by him were introduced [*lit.*, begun] necklets of gold about the throats of persons in Eriu: that is, [*Munemon* signifies] *neck-valuables*, to wit, valuables around the neck.

² *Magh Aidne.*—"A level district in the present county of Galway, all comprised in the diocese of Kilmacduagh" (O'Donovan, *F.M.* i., p. 45).

³ Dóit.—*Of the finger.* Ir 'n-a aimrir batar ralgc óir im bóitib—It is in his time were rings of gold on [*lit.*, around] fingers (*L.L.*, p. 18 b).

4.

P. 128 a [1] Tríca bliadan ρορ a beiċ
Co¹ éc Olloman, étριὸ¹:
Ρι na n-écep², apò a ρaτ,
Co³ n-deρnad céc ρeρρ⁴ Cempaċ.

5.

Tpen a mac, Pinnaċta¹ ράιl,
A beiċ ċucab² 'n-a beρgbáil²;
Im³ Maιg Iniρ³, bo ċám tpá,
Puaip cpád pí milip Maċa⁴.

6.

Mac b'¹ Ollomain¹, Slánoll púaiρc,
Deiċ m-bliadna, ρeċt ρορ ρóepċuaipc²:
Aτbaċ cen³ ċloemċlób³ ρορ daċ
Immedón⁴ tige Cempaċ.

1.

J Tρí¹ ρeċt ṁ-bliadna, buan in ρat¹,
Roċaiċ² Gebe² Ollgotaċ;
Co topċaiρ³ Gébe³ ingapta
La Piaċaig, mac Pinnaċta⁴.

4.—¹⁻¹ ga baiρ Ollomain, eipbig. Over Ollomain the gloss Ollam Pobla is written by the second hand. ² eigeρ. ³ le. ⁴ ρeiρ. 5.—¹ Pinaċta. ²⁻² ρa bo 'na beglaim. ³⁻³ a Moig Inaíp. ⁴ Macaa. 6.—¹⁻¹ Ollamon. ² ραeρcuaiρc. ³⁻³ gan clae[n]clab. ⁴ ρορ laeclap.

J 1.—¹⁻¹ bi bliabain bec, ρeil a ρat. ²⁻² ρob' ρι Gebí. ³⁻³ bopocaiρ Gειbí. ⁴ Pinaċta.

---

⁴ *To.*—Literally, *in.*

⁵ *Magh Inis.*—The barony of Lecale, co. Down (O'Flaherty, *Ogygia*, Pars III., cap. xxxi., p. 245).

4.   [B.C.]

[**i**] Thirty years above ten   [1191]
Until the death of Ollam, list ye,
The king of sages, high his felicity,
Instituted he the first Assembly of Tara.

5.

Powerful his son, Finnachta of liberality,
Ten [years] were assigned to[4] his distinguished portion ;   [1151]
In Magh Inis[5], of plague severe,
Found the pleasant king of [Emain] Macha[6] destruction.

6.

The son of Ollam, Slanoll generous,
Ten years [and] seven [were] in [his] noble course :   [1141]
Died he without change[7] upon [his] colour
In the centre of the palace of Tara.

1.

j Thrice seven years, lasting the felicity,   [1124]
Spent Gede Ollgothach[1] ;
Until fell Gede the very liberal
By Fiacha, son of Finnachta.

---

[6] *[Emain] Macha.*—That is, king of Ireland. The term is here used proleptically, as Emain was not then founded. See **o** 4, *infra.*

[7] *Change.*—The explanation is given in *L.L.* (p. 18 b) :

Ni ᚉeᚏ ca ᚌalaᚏ ᚏoᚁnuc, aćᚉ a   It is not known what disease took
ᚃaᚌḃáil manḃ ; ᚏeć niᚏ'ᚃae ḃaé,   him off, but he was found dead ; more-
niᚏaloḃ a ćoᚏᚏ ᚌ cucaḃ a calmain   over he changed not colour, nor decayed
lia mac, la Ailill, ḃia ᚃiᚏ, i ciṁḃ   his corpse. And he was taken from
ᚏl. ḃliaḃan.   earth by his son, Ailill, to certify it,
                                     at the end of forty years.

J. [1] *Ollgothach.*—*Excellent-voiced.*—ḃa ḃinniéiᚏ céca m-[ḃ]enḃcᚏoᚉᚉ ᚌué ᚌ amoᚏ caić ḃuine inna ᚃlaić—Sweeter than the strings of *benn*-harps was the voice and   of every person in his reign (*L.L.*, p. 18 b, 19 a).

2.

[J] Fiċi¹ bliadan, blad cen² ġerr²,
Fact³ flata Fóic for lonġerr³:
Docer fí Cera na clad
I⁴ caṫ breġa⁵ la berngal.

3.

berngal, mac Gede, in ġáeṫ¹ ġrind,
Da bliadain déc a daġlind²:
Roṫairind³ 'rin ġleicc a ġail³
Ailill⁴, mac mic d'⁵ Ollomain⁵.

4.

Ailill¹, reċṫ² m-bliadna fa dó,
Deġ mac Slánuill, ni raeb ró³;
Fúair [a] aided⁴ la Sírna,
La ríġ⁵ Tempa taebidna⁵.

5.

Temair Fáil, fúair ċaraiṫ¹ caím¹,
Dia² topaċṫ² Sirna flattcaín³:
A⁴ ṫriċaiṫ céṫ láeċ iar ló⁴,
Rorcar⁵ riġe [f]ri Ulṫo⁶.

6.

Roċaiṫ Sírna co rrianaib¹
Re ṫri reċṫaib roer² bliadnaib:
Aided³ Sirna [co] fleṫṫaib³
I n-Alind⁴ la Roṫeċṫaid⁵.

2.—¹ ṫrica. ²⁻² naċ dir. ³⁻³ rocaiṫ Fiaċaċ findilénír. ⁴ a. ⁵ breaġa.
3.—¹ ġoġ. ² deíġlind. ³⁻³ ġur'toirind 'rin ġleic a ġal. ⁴ Oilill.
⁵⁻⁵ Olloman. 4.—¹ Oilill. ² oċṫ. ³ ġo. ⁴ a oidid. ⁵⁻⁵ ri
Tempaċ taebṫirma. 5.—¹⁻¹ caraíd caín. ²⁻² o ṫopaċṫ. ³ flaṫṫcaín.
⁴⁻⁴ ġu n-a ṫri ceṫ laeċ ar lo. ⁵ durcar. ⁶ re hUllṫo. 6.—¹ rrianib.
² do faer. ³⁻³ oidid Sirna co rerc blaid. ⁴ Aillind. ⁵ Roṫeċṫaiġ.

BOOK OF LEINSTER.

2. [B.C.]

[J] A score of years, fame without ill omen, [1103]
[Was] the length of the sovranty of Fiach:
Fell the king of Cera of the excavations[2]
In the battle of Breg[3] by Berngal.

3.

Berngal, son of Gede, the champion vigorous,
Two years [and] ten [were] his good complement: [1083]
Finished in the battle his valour
Ailill, son of the son of Ollam.

4.

Ailill, seven years by two [reigned he], [1071]
Good son of Slanoll, not foolish the proceeding;
Received he [his] fate by Sirna,
By the king of fair-sided Tara.

5.

Tara of [Inis]fail, it received a dear friend,
When reached [it] the erect, comely Sirna:
[With] thirty hundred heroes after a long time,
Parted he the kingship from the Ultonians[4].

6.

Spent Sirna with restrictive laws
Thrice seven honourable years: [1057]
The fate of Sirna with slaughters
[Took place] in Alend[5] by Rothechtaid.

---

[2] *Excavations.*—The *Four Masters* state (O'Donovan, i., p. 56) that Fiacha was the first who sank wells in Ireland.

[3] *Breg.*—A plain in co. Meath.

[4] *Ultonians.*—That is, the race of Ir, son of Milesius, who occupied the northern half of Ireland.

[5] *Alend.*—The hill of Allen (Knockaulin), near Kilcullen, co. Kildare.

1.

k Rotectaid¹ potairind pot¹,
Remir² rect m-bliadan m-bitboc³;
Oc⁴ Dún Sobairce⁵, ór in t-rál,
Ra⁶ loirc in⁷ tene geláin⁷.

2.

Gabair Ellim¹ co n-giallaib
Rige² or hErind³ oen⁴ bliadain:
Dorocair⁵ Ellim⁵ co n-áib
La mac Aililla⁶ Olcáin.

3.

'Arim¹ noi m-bliadan namma²
Rogiallad mac Aililla³:
Dorocair⁴ Giallcad, gart grind,
La hArt Imlec⁵, mac Ellim⁶.

4.

Arim¹ ré² m-bliadan ra dó
D'Art iarum, ní himmargó³:
La Nuadait⁴ Fáil, rictib bla,
Dorocair⁵ Art Imleca⁶.

5.

Aided¹ Nuadat, rorerr² lib,
La brerr³, rigmac Airt Imlic⁴:
Cetri deic bliadna brige⁵
Rorect⁶ Nuadu⁶ [i] nert ríge.

---

k 1.—¹·¹ Rotectaig rata irri nod [rataippi[n] nod?]. ² nemer.
³ m-bitbog.   ⁴ og.   ⁵ Sobairci.   ⁶ do.   ⁷·⁷ tene garb gelan.
2.—¹ Elim.   ² rigi.   ³ Erinn.   ⁴ aen.   ⁵·⁵ co n-dorcair Elim.   ⁶ Oililla.
3.—¹ airem.   ² namma.   ³ Oililla.   ⁴ co n-drocair.   ⁵ Imlic.   ⁶ Elim.
4.—¹ airem.   ² noi.   ³ himargo.   ⁴ Nuadat.   ⁵ dudrocair.   ⁶ Imlecda.
5.—¹ oidid.   ² fer.   ³ brer.   ⁴ Imlig.   ⁵ m-brige.   ⁶·⁶ docait Nuadat.

1. [II. C.]

k Rothechtaid, who marked out a [carriage] road[1],
   A space of seven ever-mild years [reigned he];   [1036]
  *At Dun Sobairche, over the brine,
   Burned him the fire of lightning.

2.

Took Ellim with hostages
Kingship over Eriu one year: [1029]
Fell Ellim with distinction
By the son of Ailill Olcain.

3.

A tale of nine years only   [1028]
[Was the space] the son of Ailill was obeyed:
Fell Giallchad, strong the renown,
By Art Imlech, son of Ellim.

4.

A tale of six years by two   [1019]
[Was reigned] by Art thereafter, not excessive falsehood;
By Nuadu Fail, cause of fame,
Fell Art Imlecha.

5.

The fate of Nuadu, it is known to you,
[It was inflicted] by Bress, royal son of Art Imlech:
Four decades, years of might,   [1007]
Spent Nuadu [in] power of kingship.

---

k. [1] *Road.*—*Rot* is said in Cormac's Glossary (*sub voce*) to signify a track wide enough for a chariot. In *L.L.* (p. 19 b) it is said of Rothechtaid: Iſ leiſ aſſnéṫ caſpaṫ ceṫſi n-eċ i n-hEſinb aſ ṫúſ—It is by him was introduced the chariot of four horses in Eriu at first.

6.

[k] Nói¹ ṁ-bliadna bressi na m-bedg²,
Ra³ ro mor cressia³ a trén redg;
Aided⁴ mic Airt in⁵ airm crúaid,
Im⁶ mulluċ Cairn ċairr⁷ Chonluain⁷.

1.

1 Cetri¹ ráti rúti¹ cat
Do'nd² Eoċaid urdairc³ Arċaċ:
Doċer Eoċaid Áta-Luain
la Find, mac braṫa bratrúaid.

2.

bliadain¹, ṡeċt ṁ-bliadna¹ ro ċrí,
Fot flaṫa² Find Formáili:
Aided³ ind Fhind ċétna ċlé⁴
la Séṫna ṁ-bind⁵, mac bressi⁶.

3.

Setna airegda¹ arraid,
Dorat² crod do ċét amraib:
Ċert ḟiċi bliadan cen³ brón,
Co⁴ roriaxad⁴ la Simón.

4.

Simon bress, sé bliadna ar¹ deċt,
Rop¹² ó² in t-iarla cen³ ainreċt³:
la Duaċ Find, mac Séṫna fláin⁴,
Fuair ing⁵ óca⁵ mac Aedáin⁶.

6.—¹ noe.   ² na m-bedg   ³⁻³ ro do lor cressi.   ⁴ oidid.   ⁵ inn.
⁶ i.   ⁷⁻⁷ cair Connluain.
1 1.—¹⁻¹ ceitri ráiti ruidi.   ² du'n.   ³ oirdirc.
2.—¹⁻¹ remer ṡeċt m-bliadan.   ² flaitur.   ³ oidid.   ⁴ gle.
⁵ find.   ⁶ m-brese.   3.—¹ ind Arraid.   ² durad.
³ gan.   ⁴⁻⁴ gu ruriagad.   4.—¹ ir.   ²⁻² ba ri.   ³⁻³ gun
ainreċt.   ⁴ Sedna flan.   ⁵⁻⁵ i[n] cetna.   ⁶ Aedan.

BOOK OF LEINSTER.

6. [B.C.]

[k] Nine [were] the years of Bress of the [967]
Great was the force of his strong
The fate of the son of Art of the hard weapon,
[Took place] on the summit of winding Carn Chonluain².

1.

❙ Four quarters [of a year] of continuous battles, [958]
[Were reigned] by the illustrious Eochu Apthach¹ :
Fell Eochu of Athlone [tured.
By Finn, son of Brath [Blath, *L. L.* 196] the red ves-

2.

A year [and] seven years by three [= 22] [957]
[Was] the length of the sovranty of Find Formail :
The destruction of the same Find [it was] manifest,
[Took place] by Setna sweet [voice], son of Bress.

3.

Setna, distinguished he presided,
He gave stipend² to one hundred retainers :
Just a score of years [reigned he] without sorrow, [935]
Until he was executed by Simon.

4.

Simon the Speckled, six years completely [reigned he], [915]
He was the ruler without injustice :
By Duach the Fair, son of Setna the perfect,
Received the son of Aedan the fate of death.

---

² *Carn Chonluain.*—" Not identified " (O'Donovan, *F.M.* i., p. 61).
❙. ¹ *Apthach.*—*Destructive;* which is explained in *L.L.* (p. 19 b) :
Τám caċ mír ınna ḟlaıτ, .ı. ba ṫam béc 'ṗın bliabaın—A plague (occurred) each month in his reign, that is, twelve plagues in the year.
² *Stipend.*—Iṗṗ é τoíṗcċ ḃoṗaτ ċṗoḃ ḃ'amṗaıḃ ı n-ḣCṗınn .ı. ın n-aṗṗaḃ—It is he first gave stipend to retainers in Eriu, namely, the compensation (*L.L.*, p. 19 b).

5.

[1] Eḃ¹ ḋeiċ m̅-bliaḋan co m-blaḋail
Roċaiṫ Ḋuaċ, mac Inḋaraiḋ² :
Ḋoroċair pí Claire i caṫ
ImMáᵹe³ la Mureṫaċ⁴.

6.

Mureḋaċ, mí ꝓor bliaḋain
Robo pí co¹ poᵹiallaiḃ¹ :
Ꝓuair Muriḋaċ² ceilᵹ ṫria² ċaṫ
La hEnna, n̅-ḋerᵹ³ mac Ḋuaċ³.

1.

m Ḋa bliaḋain ḋéc¹, ꝓéil a raṫ,
Roꝓo² pí mac ḋéin Ḋuaċ :
Marb, cuinniḋ³ caṫ liꝓꝓ cuminiᵹ³,
I Sleiḃ⁴ Mirꝓ co⁴ morbuiḋniḃ.

2.

Noi¹ m̅-bliaḋna, riaᵹlom ꝓéil² bla,
Luᵹḋaċ Iarnḋonḋ³, mac 'Enna :
Ḋoroċair⁴ in ꝓurí⁴ ꝓán
Iꝓ Raiṫ⁵ Chloċair la Siꝓlam.

3.

Síꝓlam raiᵹeḋ¹, rluáᵹ Mumneċ²,
Ḋa n-oċṫ³ m̅-bliaḋna brecbuiḋneċ :
Ꝓuair a ċairbirṫ⁴ [i]rin ṫrerr⁴
La Eoċaiḋ⁵ n-airḋairc n-Uárċerr⁵.

5.—¹ re. ² Inḋarrfaiᵹ. ³ Maiᵹe. ⁴ Mureḋaċ. 6.—¹⁻¹ corroᵹiallaiḃ. ²⁻² Mureḋaċ ceilᵹ i. ³⁻³ mac n-ḋerᵹ n-Ḋhuaċ.
m 1.—¹ ḋeᵹ. ² roḃo. ³⁻³ cuinᵹiḋ i ċnír cuninniᵹ. ⁴⁻⁴ Sleb Mir la.
2.—¹ nóc. ² leir. ³ Iarḋuinḋ. ⁴⁻⁴ co n-ḋroċair in ꝓurí.
⁵ i caṫ. 3.—¹ roiᵹeḋ. ² Muimneaċ. ³ oċṫ. ⁴⁻⁴ ṫoirḃerṫ irin ṫrer.
⁵⁻⁵ hEoċaiḋ n-airḋirc n-Uairċerr.

³ *Indaraid.*—*Of the compensation,* as in note 2.
⁴ *Clair.*—The plain in which stands Duntrileague, co. Limerick.
⁵ *Mage.*—"Not identified" (O'Donovan, *F.M.* i., p. 63).
⁶ *Treacherous death.*—Literally, *treachery.*

BOOK OF LEINSTER. 175

5. [B. C.]

[1] The space of a decade of years with glories   [909]
Spent Duach, son of [Setna] Indaraid³ :
Fell the king of Clair⁴ in battle,
In Mage⁵ by Murethach.

6.

Muredach, a month over a year   [899]
Was he king with many hostages :
Received Muredach a treacherous death⁶ in battle
By Enna, the ruddy son of Duach.

1.

m   Two years [and] ten, manifest his felicity,   [897]
Was the son of energetic Duach king :
Died¹ he—let everyone remember a memorable loss—
In Sliab Miss with great multitudes.

2.

Nine years, let us arrange the manifest fame,   [885]
[Reigned] Lugdach Iarrdond, son of Enna :
Fell the great king noble
In the rath of Clochar² by Sirlam.

3.

Sirlam the Reacher³, of the hosts of Munster,
Two octaves of years varied, crowded [reigned he] :   [876]
Received he his fate in the combat
By the illustrious Eochu Uarchess.

---

m. ¹ *Died.*—Co n-epbailt be tám i Sléib-mip, co pocaibe móip imme—until he died of plague in Sliab Mis, with a great multitude along with [*lit.*, around] him (*L.L.*, p. 20 a). O'Flaherty (*Ogygia*, Pars III., cap. xxxiii., p. 249) says Sliab Mis was in Munster. (It is situated near Tralee. There is another mountain of the name in Antrim.)

² *Rath of Clochar.*—" Not identified" (O'Donovan, *F.M.* i., p. 64). In the Royal Irish Academy copy of the *Ogygia*, " C. Tyrone " has been placed on the margin (p. 249). In *L.L.* (p. 20 a) the reading is *Rath Clochrain.*

³ *Reacher.*—Ro paiceb a lám lán ɿ pé 'n-a peppom—His hand reached the floor and he standing (*L.L.*, p. 20 a).

4.

[**m**] Cocho Uáṙċeṙṙ¹, aṙḃ a ṗlaiċ²,
Seċṫ³ m̄-ḃliaḃna coic poċaeṁċaiċ¹:
Ḋoṙoċaiṙ⁴ ṙí ḃanḃa aṙ ḃlaiḃ⁵
Ri maccaiḃ calma Conġail.

5.

Coċċ¹ ocuṙ¹ Conainġ co n-ġail,
Ḋa mac Conġail ċoṙṫaḋaiġ²,
ḃáṫaṙ³ ḋa ṙoċṫ¹ iaṙla in ṙaiċ
Ṙó coic m-ḃliaḋan⁵ i comṗlaiċ⁵.

6.

Coċu¹ Ṙiḃmuine¹ na ṙeṙġġ²,
Ḋoċeṙ³ la³ Luġaiḋ láṁḋeṙġ⁴;
Seċṫ⁵ m̄-ḃliaḋna⁵ ḋo Luġaiḋ lainn⁶,
Iaṙ⁷ ṙin ṙoṙmuḋaiġ⁷ Conainġ.

1.

n Conainġ, mac Conġail, cloċ¹ ġlan,
Ní² ṙonómnaiġ ṙí ṙiam²;
Ṙiḃi ṙoċaiċ³ ṙoṙ caċ loċ³,
Co ṙomaṙḃ⁴ Aṙṫ, mac Luġḋeċ⁵.

[P. 47a.] 4.—¹ Uaiṙceṙ. ² ḃlaḃ. ³⁻³ ṙocaiṫ ceiṫṙi coic ḃliaḋna.
⁴ Ġuṙ'ṫoiṫ. ⁵ co m-ḃlaiḃ. 5.—¹ Eoċaiḃ iṙ. ² coṙcuṙaiġ.
³ ḃaḋaṙ. ⁴ neṙṫ. ⁵⁻⁵ ceṙṫḃliaḋnaiḃ comḃaiċ. 6. ¹⁻¹ Coċaiḃ
Ṙiḃmuine. ² ṙeṙġ. ³⁻³ ṙoṙmuġaiḃ. ⁴ laiṁḋeṙġ. ⁵⁻⁵ oċṫ
m-ḃliaḋna. ⁶ luinḃ. ⁷⁻⁷ no ġu ṙuṙmuġaiḃ.

n 1.—¹ cleaċ. ²⁻² noċoṙ'omnaiġ nec ṙiaam. ³⁻³ ṙoṫeċṫ
aṙ ġaċ leaċ[h]. ⁴ conuṙmaṙḃ. ⁵ Luiġḋeċ.

---

⁴ *Uarchess.*—Ḋí ḃliaḋain ḃéc illoṅġaiṙ ṙoṙ muiṙ. Iṙ aiṙe aṫḃeṙaṙ

BOOK OF LEINSTER.

4. [B.C.]

[m] Eochus Uarchess⁴, exalted his sovranty,
Seven years [by] five nobly spent he: [860]
Fell the renowned king of Banba
By the [two] brave sons of Congal.

5.

Eochu and Conang with valour,
The two sons of Congal the contentious,
They were two just rulers of felicity,
[For] the space of five years in co-sovranty. [825]

6.

Eochu Fair-neck of the heroes,
Fell he by Lugaid Red-Hand;
Seven years [were reigned] by Lugaid the generous, [820]
After that destroyed him Conang.

1.

n Conang, son of Congal, column shapely¹,
Terrified² not him a king ever;
Twenty [years] spent he [prepared] on every side, [813]
Until slew him Art, son of Lugaid.

---

uaiṙceṙ ḋe. Ḟoṙ ınnaṙba ṙoḃaí ó Sıṙláṁ—Twelve years [was he] in exile on sea. It is for this he is called Uairces [Solitary]. In [*lit.*, upon] expulsion he was by Sirlam (*L.L.*, p. 20 a).

n. ¹ *Shapely.*—Literally, *clean.*

² *Terrified.*—Iṗ aıṙe aṫḃeṙṫc ḃececlaḋ, uaıṙ ní ṫánıó ṫuaıṙ n-óṁaın no ecla ḃó ṙıaṁ—It is for this he was called Little-fearing, for there came not a time of fright or fear to him ever (*L.L.*, p. 20a). "According to the *Book of Feenagh*, he held his royal residence at Feenagh, in Magh Rein, in the present co. of Leitrim, where he built a beautiful stone fort, within which the monastery of Feenagh was afterwards erected" (O'Donovan, *F.M.* i., p. 66).

2.

[n] Art, mac Lugdec¹, laecda a glumn²,
bliadain a³ coic i Caindruim⁴ :
Doroćair⁵ Art 'rin debuid⁶
La Fiaćra⁷, mac Muredaig.

3.

Mac Airt, oen¹ bliadain déc² daić
Ailill³ Find, féta in fir[f]laić⁴ :
Doroćair⁵ i Cać Odba
La Argatmár⁶ imćolma.

4.

Roćinfet¹ a céim curad,
Eoćo², Lugaid, laeć Curać³ ;
Co cend⁴ fećt m-bliadan dar⁵ rál
Roinnarbrat Argatmár⁶.

2.—¹ Lugdeć.   ² an glumd.   ³ ar a.   ⁴ Caendruim.   ⁵ co torcair.   ⁶ 'ra deabaid.   ⁷ Fiaća. The following quatrain is inserted :—

Fiaća, mac Muredaig moir,	Fiacha, son of great Muredach,
Oćt m-bliadna im cornaib co-moil,	Eight years [were reigned] by him amidst drinking-horns,
Co fuair a m-borind a brać	Until received he in Borend his doom,
La hOilill, mac mic Lugdeć.	By Ailill, son of the son of Lugaid.

3.—¹ aen.   ² deg.   ³ Oilill.   ⁴ flaić.   ⁵ co torcair.   ⁶ hArgedmar.   4.—¹ rocinbret.   ² Eoćaid.   ³ Muman.   ⁴ cenn.   ⁵ ar.   ⁶ roindarbrat Airgetmar.

---

³ *Caindruim*.—The Concord, coic-Caindruim, shows that the reading is i Caindruim, not ic Aindruim (at Aindruim). For the locality, see e 3, note 3.

⁴ *Odba*.—A name, now obsolete, of a mound on the summit of a hill giving name to a territory in ancient Meath (O'Donovan, *F.M.* i., p. 31).

⁵ *Covenanted*.—The substance of this and the following quatrain is given more clearly in *L.L.* (p. 20 a). After stating that Ailill the Fair after nine years fell by Argatmár, Fiachra and Duach, son of Fiachra, the text proceeds :

Fecta cać eter Argatmán ⁊	A battle was fought between Argat-

2.   [H. C.]

[II] Art, son of Lugaid, heroic his descent,
A year [and] five [reigned he] in Caindruim³: [793]
Fell Art in the combat
By Fiachra, son of Muredach.

3.

The son of Art, one year [and] ten of renown,   [787]
Ailill the Fair, the true prince, spent:
Fell he in the battle of Odba⁴
By Argatmar the very brave.

4.

Covenanted⁵ his chief champions,
Eochu, Lugaid [Duach], the hero of Munster⁶;
To the end of seven years over sea
Banished they Argatmar.

Fiac[p]a Tolcnaó ı n-oénuó Talcen, connoímeó pon Anɡacmán. Peóca caċ ecunnu ı ımbneɡaıb, co concaın Fiachna Tolcnaċ 'pın caċ pın.

Tınolaıc fın Muman ıan pem ım Cċaıɡ, mac Aılılla Fınó ┐ ım Luɡaıó, mac Eċaċ Fıaómuıne ┐ ım Duaċ Laónaċ co fíl hEnımóın. Ocup ınnanbnac Anɡacmán óan muın nı nó .uıı. ın-blıaóan. Eoċo, mac Aılılla Fınó, fnıfın ne fın ınnıɡı hEnenn, co conaċc Anɡacmán óan muın ┐ co n-óenna fíó nı Duaċ Laónaċ, co concaın leo Eoċu ı n-oenuċ 'Ane.

mar and Fiachra Tolcrach in the Fair of Teltown, and it went against [lit., so that it was broken upon] Argatmar. A battle was fought between them in Bregia, and Fiachra Tolcrach fell in that battle.

Assemble the Men of Munster after that around Eocho son of Ailill the Fair and around Lugaid, son of Eochu Fiadmuine and around Duach Ladrach, with the seed of Heremon. And they banished Argatmar over sea for the space of seven years. Eocho, son of Ailill the Fair, [was] during that space in kingship of Eriu, until arrived Argatmar over sea and made peace with Duach Ladrach, so that there fell by them Eochu in the Fair of Ane.

⁶ *Munster.*—The *Ballymote* reading. The lection of the text is unintelligible to me.

5.

[n] Eocho, mac Ailella¹ Find,
Romarb² Argatmár imgrind²,
Ri³ Carmuin, Claire ir Cliach³,
I n-'Áine⁴ na n-armrciacht⁴.

6.

Arim¹ tri n-déich m-bliadan m-bán²
Rogiallad do Argatmár³;
Rorcarract⁴ ria⁴ gargblaid n-glain⁵
Duach, Ladgair ir Lugaid.

1.

o Lugaid Laideć¹ ro lín mag²,
Ocht m-bliadna a bríg for³ borrrad:
Docer⁴ craeb chumneć⁵ [in cairn]⁵
La hAed m-buidneć, mac m-Baduirn.

2.

Aed, mac Baduirnn, ór Banba
'Arim¹ tri fecht raerchalma:
Bar ríg Maige² cruaid Cétne
I³ n-Err-rúaid ra [lege na] roéchne³.

5.—¹ Oililla.   ²⁻² re fecht m-bliadan a deiglínd.   ³⁻³ marb ri Cermna ir Claire ir Cliach.   ⁴⁻⁴ Aine na n-idarrciat.   6.—¹ airem.   ² ban.
³ Airgetmar.   ⁴⁻⁴ rcarrat re.   ⁵ rregoil.   Here follows a quatrain :—

Deich m-bliadna do Duach Ladgair,	Ten years [were reigned] by Duach Ladgair,
Arin n-Erinn ardabbail;	In Eriu sublime, extensive;
Bar in mail murufg maidmig	The death of the conquering hero full active
Do laim Lugdech lanlaigig.	[Took place] by the hand of full-active Lugaid.

o 1.—¹ Laigech.   ² blad.   ³ ar.   ⁴ gur'toit.   ⁵⁻⁵ cuimneć in cairn.   2.—¹ airem.   ² Muige.   ³⁻³ aig Err-ruaid na rigegne.

---

⁷ *Carmon.*—See **h** 3, note 4.

⁶ *Clair.*—See **l** 5, note 4.

BOOK OF LEINSTER.

5. [B.C.]

[11] Eochu, son of Ailill the Fair,
Slew [him] Argatmar the very valorous,
The king of Carmon⁷, Clair⁸ and Cliu⁹,
In Ane¹⁰ of the armour shields.

6.

A tale of three decades of years fair [776]
Was service rendered to Argatmar;
Separated [him] from his strong fame pure
Duach, Ladgair and Lugaid.

1.

o Lugaid Laidech, who filled the plain¹ [with his fame],
Eight years [was] his power in defiance: [746]
Fell the remembered Branch of the Carn²
By Aed Buidnech, son of Badorn.

2.

Aed, son of Badorn, [reigned he] over Banba
A tale of three sevens noble, excellent: [738]
The death of the king of hard Magh³ Cetne,
[Happened by drowning] in Ess-ruad⁴ of the large salmon.

---

⁹ *Cliu.*—The territory of which the capital was Knockany, Co. Limerick.

¹⁰ *Ane.*—Knockany, co. Limerick.

o. ¹ *Plain.*—This may be the same as the *Clair*, or level district, mentioned in 1 5.

² *Carn.*—Perhaps the hill which stands near Duntrileague.

³ *Magh.*—Probably Magh Ene, a plain in co. Donegal, between the Erne and the Drowse. In *L.L.* (p. 20 a) Aed is said to have been king of Tir-Aeda, whence Tirhugh (land of [this] Hugh), in which Magh Ene is situated.

⁴ *Ess-ruad.*— *Red cataract :* Assaroe, on the Erne, at Ballyshannon. So called from the drowning of this *Aed ruad* (Aed the Red). bαbub ρobάbub ι n-Cρρuαιb ⁊ co τucαb α ὁoρρ ιρριn ρίb ριn. Unbe Sίb n-Άebα ⁊ Cρρ ρύαιb—Drowning drowned him in Ess-ruad and his corpse was carried into that hill [a description of which was doubtless given in the preceding part of the work which the compiler employed]. Whence the Hill of Aed and the Red Cataract (*L.L.*, p. 20 b). *Sith-Aeda* is Mullaghshee at Ballyshannon (O'Donovan, *F.M.* i., pp. 70-1).

3.

[o] Doroċair¹ Diṫorba donḋ
Rir² na cuanaib i³ Coronḋ:
Fiċe ir bliaḋain ġlan ġle,
Rí⁴ for⁵ Ḟiannaib Ḟáil-Inre⁶.

4.

Fiċe¹ ir a reċt co m-blaiḋ²
Do Chimbáeṫ, mór mac Ḟintain³;
Cimbaeṫ cáem, céṫḟlaiṫ Emna,
'Ce⁴ atbaṫ⁴ rí roThemra.

5.

Remir¹ oċt m-bliaḋan co m-blaiḋ²
Dia³ éir iaram do'n⁴ riġain,
Maċa, co⁵ m-bertaib na m-berġġ⁶,
Co⁷ rormarb⁷ Reċtaiḋ Riġderġ.

3.—¹ aḋrocair. ² leir. ³ a. ⁴ ba rí. ⁵ ar. ⁶ inḃre.
4.—¹ Fiḋi. ² iar rin. ³ Ḟintain. ⁴⁻⁴ cġ aḋbaṫ. 5.—¹ remer.
² m-bloiḋ. ³ ḋa. ⁴ ḋu'n. ⁵ ġu. ⁶ m[-b]erġ. ⁷⁻⁷ ġururmarb.

⁵ *Corond.*—A barony in the co. Sligo (O'Donovan, *F.M.* i., p. 311).

⁶ *Emain.*—"Usually latinized *Emania*, now corrupted in English to the Navan Fort (from the Irish an Caṁain), a very large rath, situated about two miles to the west of Armagh" (O'Donovan, *F.M.* i., p. 72). Fossis latis, vestigiis murorum eminentibus et ruderibus pristinum etiamnum redolet splendorem (*Ogygia*, Pars III., cap. xxxvi., p. 258). The traditional derivation is given in *L.L.* (p. 20 b, 21 a). After the death of Dithorba, Queen Macha defeated and banished his five sons into Connaught and wedded Cimbaeth. A little after, she got them into her power (the stratagem is also narrated by Keating) and, according to the text:

Norbeir i n-oen ċenġul ló iat co hUltu. Arbetatar Ulaiḋ a marbaḋ. Ni tó, ar riri, ar ir coll fírḟlata ḋamra, aċt a n-ḋoirud fo ḋoire. Ocur claiḋet rait immumra. co ror' hí bar rrimċaṫir Ulaḋ co brat. Co

She took them in one gyve with her to the Ultonians. The Ultonians said to kill them. *Not so*, said she, *for it is a prohibition of a true sovereign for me, but [what shall be done is] to enslave them in [grievous] servitude. And let them dig a fort around me, that it may*

BOOK OF LEINSTER. 183

3. [B.C.]

[O] Fell Dithorba the noble
By the multitudes in Corond⁵:
A score and a year pure, brilliant, [717]
[Was he] king over the Fenians of Inisfail.

4.

A score and seven with fame [696]
[Were reigned] by Cimbaeth, great son of Fintan;
Cimbaeth mild, [was] first prince of Emain⁶,
[Natural] death died the king of great Tara⁷.

5.

A space of eight years with fame [669]
After him afterwards [were reigned] by the queen,
Macha, with feats of heroes,
Until slew her Rechtaid Red-Arm.

ροτόραιηο ρι όόιb ιη όύη co η-α hεo (.ι. belʒ) όιρ ιmm α muιη .ι. emuιη .ι. eo muιη .ι. eo ιmm α muιη Μαċα.

be the chief city of the Ultonians to doom. So that marked she for them the fort with her circlet (namely, [its] pin) of gold [that was] around her neck. That is, Emuin, namely, circlet of neck: to wit, a circlet around the neck of Macha.

Cóιc[α] bliadan aρ .cccc. ρια ή-ʒειη Cριρτ. Ocuρ .ι. bliaban aιle aρ .cccc. o ʒειη Cρίρτ co τuρρcuρ Εmna Μαċα bo na τρι Collaιb, ιaρ m-bριρριud ċaṫa Αċαιb-leιṫbειρʒ, ι Ρεηηmαιʒ, ι τορcαιρ Ρερʒuρ Ρoʒα, mac Ρραιċαιρ Ρορτρεη, τιuʒρlαιċ Ulab ι n-Εmαιη Μαċα.

Fifty years above 400 before the Birth of Christ [that happened]. And another fifty years above 400 [elapsed] from the Birth of Christ to the destruction of Emain of [Queen] Macha by the three Collas, after gaining [lit., breaking] the battle of Achad-Leithderg, in Farney [co. Monaghan], in which fell Fergus Foga, son of Fraichar the very strong, the last prince of the Ultonians in Emain of Macha.

For the chronology, which is erroneous by more than a century in the A.M., as in the A.D., period, see Lecture III.

⁷ *Tara.*—Here employed to signify the king of all Ireland.

6.

[᛫] Rectaid, rocait ficit féig¹,
Mac Lugdec Laidig² lángéir²,
Rí Clocair ir Chind³ Maige,
Doroćair⁴ la Ugaine⁵.

1.

p Ugaine maić¹, [mor] miad¹ n-glan²,
Flaić cetri deić dagbliadan³,
Ní cian⁴, or bruinne⁵ in braga,
Romarb⁶ buille badbćaća⁶.

2.

Da bliadain Laegaire Luirc
Inrige¹ or banba brecbuic²;
Ralocrad³ in craeb cen ćol⁴
La Cobtać⁵ cael i Carmon.

3.

Cobtać¹, cóic² deić bliadna m-buán³
Roriarad in rí rorúad,
Co⁴ roloirc⁴ tene irin⁵ tig⁵,
Ic ól na⁶ fleóe ic⁷ Labraid.

6.—¹ fen.   ²⁻² Laigid, lanfeil.   ³ cind.   ⁴ co n-droćair.   ⁵ hUgaine.
p 1.—¹⁻¹ mor miad. Overhead is placed, *alia manu*, maić, with corresponding marks, to show it was to be inserted after mor.   ² n-gal.   ³ n-deigbliadan.   ⁴ dalb.   ⁵ bruinni.   ⁶⁻⁶ gur'marb builli badbćada. Here a quatrain is given:—

Badbćad, bad ri benur ćać,	Badbchadh, he was a king that wins battle,
Scainreać, congalać, coctać,	Fearful, brave, warlike,
Aenlaići co leić a lind,	One day with a half [was] his complement,
Gur'marb Loegaire or boaind.	Until slew [him] Loegaire over the Boyne.

2.—¹ inrigi.   ² blaćbuig.   ³⁻³ doloćrad.   ⁴ gen'col.   ⁵ Cortać.
3.—¹ Cortać.   ² re.   ³ m *om*.   ⁴⁻⁴ gur'loirc.   ⁵⁻⁵ ćall 'n-a ćaig.
⁶ na *om*.   ⁷ la.

⁸ *Clochar and of Cend Maige* [*head of the Plain*].—Clogher, co. Tyrone, which was anciently the *head*, or capital, of Magh Lemna, the plain occupied by the Airghialla. Hence the latter expression is employed to fill up the line.

p. ¹ [*River*] *brink of Bregha*.—In *L.L.* (p. 22 a) the place is said to be *Telach*

BOOK OF LEINSTER.

6. [B.C.]

[o] Rechtaid, spent he twenty vigilant [years], [661]
Son of Lugaid Laidech the full-vigourous,
King of Clochar and of Cend Maige⁶,
Fell he by Ugaine.

1.

p Ugaine the good, [great] pure dignity,
Prince [was he] four decades of good years, [641]
Not long [thereafter], over the [river] brink of Bregha¹,
Slew [him] a stroke of Badbchath.

2.

Two [were] the years of Laeghaire Lorc [601]
In kingship over Banba diversified, gentle;
Destroyed was the branch without fault
By Cobthach the Slender in Carmon².

3.

Cobthach, five [times] ten years lasting [599]
Was served the king very illustrious,
Until burned³ [him] fire in the house,
A-partaking of the banquet with Labraid.

---

in *choscair* (Hill of victory), in Magh Mairedu, in Bregia. The locality, according to O'Flaherty, was Kill-droichent on the estuary at Drogheda (*Ogygia*, Pars III., cap. xxxviii., p. 261). This O'Donovan (*F.M.* i., p. 75) was unable to correct. Not so, however, Dr. Reeves: who, in an admirable note (*Adamnan*, pp. 108-9), shows that *Magh Maireda* was *Moymurthy*, near Gormanstown, where the Delvin, on the *brink* of which the *Hill* probably stood, flows into the sea.

² *Carmon.*—See **h** 3, note 4.

³ *Burned.*—A different cause is assigned in *L.L.* (p. 22 a, b):

Dorodaip cpa Cobcaó Cael
bpeaʒ ı n-Dınbpıʒ ⁊ .xxx. pıʒ
ımbı, abaıʒ Notlac mór, la
Labpaıb Lonʒreó, ı n-dıʒaıl a
acap ⁊ a penacap [p. 22 b]. Un.
ıh-blıabna ⁊ .ccc. blıaban o'nb
aıbóı pın coppın aıbóe ınpoʒe-
naıp Cpırc ı m-becɦıl luba.

Now, fell Cobthach the Slender Handsome in Dinnrig [Mound of Slane, **d** 1, note 1, *supra*] and thirty kings along with [*lit.*, around] him, the eve of Great Christmas, by Labraid the Mariner, in revenge of his father and of his grandfather. Seven years and three hundred years from that night to the night in which was born Christ in Bethlehem of Iuda.

4.

[p] Labraid Loingrech¹ laech, rochait
Noi bliadna déc co² dégmait:
Labraid bérre³ corin⁴ m-blaid,
Romarb⁵ Melge⁵, mac Cobthaig.

5.

Rochait¹ Melge, maith a lí,
Secht m-bliadna déc², ba³ degrí;
Dorochair⁴, darbord cia bé⁴,
'Sin chath la⁵ Mogcorb Cláire.

6.

Mogcorb¹ a Mumain cen² meirgg²,
Mac³ mic Rectaid[e] Rigderg³,
Docer⁴ coemborr⁴ Cindmara
La Oengus⁵, hua Labrada⁵.

1.

¶ Oengus¹ Ollam, a hocht déc²,
Dorat³ rocht for⁴ rluag raer gres⁵;
Docer rí Cone⁶ cen⁷ ail
La mac Meilge⁸, mic Cobthaig.

2.

Mac Melge¹, Irireo² án,
Rémir ocht³ m-bliadan bithlán⁴:
La⁵ Fercorbb⁵, mac Mogacuirb,
Docer rí broga⁶ in brecduirnd⁶.

4.—¹ Loingreach. ² fa. ³ berrai. ⁴ gurin. ⁵⁻⁵ domarb Meilge.
5.—¹ Dochait. ² deg. ³ a. ⁴⁻⁴ nocon torcair gu bord de. ⁵ le.
6.—¹ Modcorb. ²⁻² gan méirg. ³⁻³ a hocht do Rectaig Ri[g]derg.
⁴⁻⁴ gur'thoit caembor. ⁵⁻⁵ hAengus o Labrada.
¶ 1.—¹ Aengur. ² deg. ³ rolai. ⁴ tar. ⁵ gres. ⁶ Ch.
⁷ gan. ⁸ Melge. 2.—¹ Melgi. ² Iareneo. ³ recht.
⁴ m-bithlan. ⁵⁻⁵ re Fercorb. ⁶⁻⁶ i[n] broga brecduirb.

BOOK OF LEINSTER.

4. [B.C.]

[p] Labraid the Mariner, the hero, spent he
Nine years [and] ten excellently well: [549]
Labraid of Berr with fame,
[Him] slew Melge, son of Cobthach.

5.

Spent Melge, excellent his splendour,
Seven years [and] ten, he was a good king; [530]
Fell he, haughty though he was,
In the battle by Mogcorb of Clair[4].

6.

Mogcorb from Munster, without defect,
Son of the son of Reetaid Red-Arm,
Fell the fair column of Cendmara[5]
By Oengus, grandson of Labraid.

1.

q Oengus Ollam, eight [years and] ten [reigned he], [513]
Imposed he silence upon the noble shouting host;
Fell the king of Eli[1] without offence
By the son of Meilge, son of Cobthach.

2.

The son of Meilge, Irireo noble,
A space of eight years ever-full [reigned he] : [495]
By Fercorb, son of Mogcorb,
Fell the king of Brug[2] of the speckled fist.

---

[4] *Clair.*—See l 5, note 4.
[5] *Cendmara.*—*Head of the sea;* Kenmare, co. Kerry.

q. [1] *Eli* (the *Ballymote* reading).—There were two territories so called—Ely O'Carroll in the King's County and Eliogarty (Eili-Ua-Fhogartaigh), co. Tipperary.
[2] *Brug.*—Perhaps, *Brugh-righ*, Bruree, co. Limerick.

3.

[q] bliadain ar¹ a deic d' Ḟirċorb,
Ropo² ruiṫneċ a ríẓdorbb³:
Dorobbad⁴ inn⁵ omna aro,
Arrondliẓ⁶ Conla cleṫẓarẓ⁶.

4.

A ceṫair¹ ṗa¹ ċóic cen² ċeo
Remir³ irdairc Irereo³;
'Sin⁴ Ṫemraiẓ moẓda cen mair⁴
Aṫbaṫ Conla⁵ hua⁵ Cobṫaiẓ.

5.

Cóic¹ bliadna riċeṫ ṗria² ro²
Ailella³ 'n-a ardriẓe³;
Amaṫair⁴, mac Ḟirċuirṗ⁵ cairr⁶,
'E⁷ roẓlacc in duird dreċmair⁸.

6.

Deiċ¹ m-bliadna ro ṫrí i ṫuilẓṫe²
Mac Ṗirċuirṗ³ i co[ṡ]mriẓe⁴;
Doċer la Coṫaid⁵ ṫo n-áib
Amaṫair⁶ Ḟliḋair ṗolṫṫáin.

1.

r Ṗice¹ aṫṫ ṡé bliadna ar blad¹
ba rí Eoċo² Alṫleṫan²,
Co ṫorṫair, ṫ[ṡ]íar inn-a ṫaiẓ³,
La Ḟerẓur ṗial Ḟorṫamail.

3.—¹ ṡor. ² robo. ³ rísorb. ⁴ ro ṫrarṫrad. ⁵ in.
⁶⁻⁶ ṡeib nordliẓ Connla cleaṫẓarẓ.   4.—¹⁻¹ ṫeaṫair ṡo.   ² ẓan.
³⁻³ do mac airdirc Ierereo.   ⁴ ⁴ i Ṫemraiẓ monẓmaiṫ dunmaiẓ.
⁵⁻⁵ Connlaeṫ ua.   5.—¹ re.   ²·² ṡiri.   ³⁻³ ṡe Oililla i n-airdriẓi.
⁴ Adamair.   ⁵ Ḟirṫuirb.   [P. 47b.] ⁶ ṫairr.   ⁷ ir e.
⁸ n-dreṫmair.   6.—¹ re.   ² ṫuilṫe.   ³ Ḟirṫuirb.
⁴ ṫaemriẓe.   ⁵ hCoṫaid.   ⁶ Adamair.

3.   [n.c.]

[q] A year above ten [was reigned] by Fercorb,   [487]
    Shining was his royal rule:
    Destroyed was the lofty oak,
    When Conla, the strong prop, demanded the debt³.

4.

Four by five [years] without obscuration,   [476]
[Was] the space of the illustrious [son of] Irereo;
In Tara spacious without delay
Died Conla, grandson of Cobthach.

5.

Five years [and] twenty [were] in the span   [456]
Of Ailill in his arch-kingship;
Amathair, son of Ferchorp the curled,
He [it was] that took off the hero fair-visaged.

6.

Ten years by three in   [431]
[Was] the son of Ferchorp in excellent kingship;
Fell by Eochaid with honour
Amathair Flidais the beauteous-haired.

1.

r   Twenty, except six years¹, with fame   [401]
    Was Eocho Altlethan king,
    Until fell he, west in his house,
    By Fergus Fortamail the liberal.

---

r 1.—¹⁻¹ τρι bliaḋna ḋec, ḋaτa ιn blaḋ.   ²⁻² ιn τ-Eoċaιḋ Poltletan.
³ ι n-a τιġ.

---

³ *Demanded the debt.*—Fercorb had slain Irereo, the father of Conla.

r. ¹ *Twenty, except six years.*—This periphrasis for *fourteen* is employed to make up the requisite number of syllables in the line.

2.

[r] Fergur¹, fuair óen bliadain déc,
Maith forfarad² in rogéc².
Docer, bid cumnech in³ cath,
La Oengur⁴ Turmech⁴ Temrach.

3.

Trí fichit bliadan co¹ m-blaid¹
D'Oengur² Turmech i² Temraig:
ba fním ri³ cuane Cnuic breg³,
'Ec⁴ ríg Tuage ir Talten⁴.

4.

Cóic¹ bliadna 'n-a ró currat¹,
Conall cialla² Collompach²:
Nia Segamain³ romúdaig³,
Fer⁴ feramail findchodail.

5.

Fuair Nia Segamuin¹ a recht
Or mó² 'Erind cen andrecht²:
Dorochair³ in carrbech carr³
La hEnna n-Airgdech⁴ n-amnarr⁴.

6.

Enna Airgdech¹, ardd² a blad³,
Rochaith cethri chóic bliadan⁴:
Rí banba, docer i⁵ cath
La Crimthand calma Coscrach⁶.

2.—¹ Fcargur. ²⁻² dorfarad irrogeg. ³ i. ⁴⁻⁴ hAengur Tuirbig. 3.—¹⁻¹ ar blaid. ²⁻² Aengur Tuirbig a. ³⁻³ re cuaine cnuic breag. ⁴⁻⁴ eg ri Tuaidi ir Tailten. 4.—¹⁻¹ Tarraid recht m-bliadna gan brath. ²⁻² calma Collamrach. ³⁻³ Seagamair rorcedbain. ⁴ triach. 5.—¹ Segamair. ²⁻² n-Erinn gan anrecht. ³⁻³ co torcair in carrfech car. ⁴⁻⁴ n-Airgteach

2. [B.C.]

[r] Fergus, received he one year [and] ten, [387]
Well was obeyed the excellent branch.
Fell he, remembered be the battle,
By Oengus Turmech of Tara.

3.

Three score of years with fame [376]
[Were reigned] by Oengus Turmech in Tara:
It was anguish to the multitudes of the Hill of Bregha[2],
The death of the king of Tuadh[3] and of Tailtiu[4].

4.

Five years in his span with felicity [316]
[Reigned] Conall Collomrach the judicious:
Nia Segamain destroyed [him],
A man[5] brave [and] very loyal.

5.

Received Nia Segamain seven [years in kingship] [311]
Over Eriu without injustice:
Fell the charioteer curled
By Enna the Raider the cruel.

6.

Enna the Raider, exalted his fame,
Spent he four [times] five years: [304]
The king of Banba, fell he in battle
By Crimthand brave, the conqueror.

---

n-amnar.   6.—[1] Cioneḋ.   [2] anḋ.   [3] blaḋ.   [4] bliaḋna.   [5] a.   [6] corgnaḋ.

[2] *Hill of Bregha.*—That is, the Hill of Tara.
[3] *Tuadh.*—Probably, the Tuath-Luighne, the barony of Lune, co. Meath. See v 6, notes 5, 7.
[4] *Tailtiu.*—See c 6, note 7.
[5] *A man.*—Namely, Nia Segamain.

1.

s Cetri¹ bliadna Crimthaind cairr²
'Or ind³ hErind immelglair³:
Docer⁴ ní cumraide in cairn⁴
De⁵ laim Rudraige⁶ rogairb⁶.

2.

Rudraige¹, rí Fáil co² m-blaid²,
Sect deich bliadna de³ bliadnaib:
brat ir⁴ béc⁴ do⁵ banba bind,
'Ec⁶ atbat i n-Argatglind⁶.

3.

In¹ Fintait Már¹ a Mumain mait,
A nói do'n² curad² combait;
Dorocair³, mar rofírad⁴,
Larin m-brerat m-bodíbad⁵.

4.

brerat¹ bodibat co bett¹,
Nói² m-bliadna ór hErind a nert²;
Docer³ rí Cualngne 'con trait³,
Do⁴ láim Luagne, mic Fhintait⁴.

---

s 1.—¹ ceitri. ² cair. ³⁻³ an Erinn eochanglar. ⁴⁻⁴ gur'toit craeb cubraidi in cairn. ⁵ do. ⁶⁻⁶ Rugraidi in rigairm.
2.—¹ Rugraidi. ²⁻² gu fraid. ³ do. ⁴⁻⁴ om.; ir is placed on margin. ⁵ do'n. ⁶⁻⁶ eg abbat i n-Airgetglend.
3.—¹⁻¹ Findab Mar. ²⁻² du'n curaid. ³ co n-dorcer. ⁴ dofirad. ⁵ m-bodibbad. 4.—¹⁻¹ brerral, bliadain fon a deic. ²⁻² an Fiannaib Fail ba cumgid. ³⁻³ gur'cer ri Cuaibi 'ra croid. ⁴⁻⁴ le Lug Luaigni, mac Indoid.

---

s. ¹ *Carn*.—I do not know what mound is here intended.
² *Doom and evil*.—Hendiadys for *evil doom* (to make up a heptasyllabic line).
³ [*Plague*].—bai trá Rudraige .lxx. bliadan hirrige, co n-erbailt

1.   [n. c.]

s   Four [were] the years of Crimthand the accomplished   [284]
    Over Eriu the green-bordered:
    Fell the king pleasant of the Carn¹
    By the hand of Rudraige the very stern.

2.

Rudraige, king of [Inis]fail with fame,
Seven [times] ten years of years [reigned he]:   [280]
Doom and evil² [was it] to Banba pleasant,
[Plague³] death died he in Argatglend⁴.

3.

The great Fintait from Munster good,
Nine years [were reigned] by the champion active;   [210]
Fell he, as hath been certified,
By Bressal of the Cow-plague⁵.

4.

Bressal of the Cow-plague with perfection,
Nine years over Eriu [was] his power;   [201]
Fell the king of Cualgne⁶ at the contest,
By hand of Luagne, son of Fintat.

---

do tám i n-Argatglinn—Now was Rudraige seventy years in kingship, until died he of plague in Argatglend (*L.L.*, p. 23 a).

⁴ *Argatglend.—Silver-glen.—*" This was the name of a glen in the barony of Farney, in the county of Monaghan" (O'Donovan, *F.M.* i., p. 84).

⁵ *Cow-plague.—*Tánic dít do búaib, conna térna díb acc tarb ┐ samaisc i n-Glinn-samaisce—There came murrain to kine, so that there escaped not of them except a bull and heifer in *Glend-Samaisce* (*L.L.*, p. 23 a). "Gleann Samhaisg, or Glen of the Heifer, is the name of a remarkable valley in the county of Kerry, where this tradition is still vividly remembered" (O'Donovan, *F.M.* i., p. 86).

⁶ *Cualgne.—*Cooley, a district in the north of co. Louth, well known as the scene of the *Cattle-Raid of Cualgne* (*Tain-bó Cuailgne*), in which figured Cuchullain, Tigernach's *fortissimus heros Scotorum.*

5.

[s] Lugaid¹ Luagne¹, léir² a blad,
Cen³ buadre³ tri cóic bliadna;
Dorochair⁴ hua Airt⁴ Imlig
Do glaic Congail Chláringnig⁵.

6.

Congal, cóic bliadna déc¹ dóig
Do mac Rudraige² romóir;
Larin³ Duac, bailec⁴ Dedaid⁴,
Fúair tráig⁵ ocus tromdebaid⁵.

1.

† Duac, dalta Dedaig¹, ind aig¹,
Irrige² os Temraig tolgaid³:
Nói⁴ m-bliadna d'a⁵ rmacc immac⁶,
Coromarb⁷ Fachtna Fatach.

2.

Fachtna, fich, acc a cetair¹,
Do mac Rorra irris² betaid²;
La Ecaid³ Feidlig, mac Find,
Docer in rí de⁴ ruad rind⁴.

3.

Ré¹ da bliadan déc, buan brec¹,
Rogiallad² Eoco² Feidlec;
Irin Temraig mongaic³, mait,
Fuair dig⁴ tonaid in t-arbflaic.⁴

5.—¹⁻¹ Lug Luaignec. ² ler. ³⁻³ gan buadre. ⁴⁻⁴ co n-dorcer
o hAirt. ⁵ Clairingnig. 6.—¹ dec. ² Rugraidi. ³ laran.
⁴⁻⁴ dalta Dedad. ⁵⁻⁵ gain ocus gairgdebaid.
† 1.—¹⁻¹ Deadad ind aid. ² 'n-a rí. ³ tondbain. ⁴ deic. ⁵ do.
⁶ amac. ⁷ gu rurmarb. 2.—¹ ceatair. ²⁻² righrectaid. ³ hEocaid.
¹⁻¹ du rorind. 3.—¹⁻¹ da re m-bliadan, buan i[n] brecat.

BOOK OF LEINSTER.

5. [B.C.]

[s] Lugaid Luagne, manifest his fame,
Without molestation [reigned he] thrice five years; [192]
Fell the grandson of Art Imlech
By hand of Congal Flat-face.

6.

Congal, five reputable years [and] ten [177]
[Were reigned] by the son of very great Rudraige;
By Duach, fosterling of Dedach,
Received he reverse and heavy destruction.

1.

t Duach, fosterling of Dedach, of the good fortune,
In kingship over haughty Tara [succeeded he]:
Nine years of his sway [had passed] away[1], [162]
When slew [him] Fachtna the Prophet.

2.

Fachtna, twenty [years], except four[2], [153]
[Were reigned] by the son of Ross in royal life;
By Eocho Feidlech, son of Find,
Fell the king by the red [spear-]point.

3.

The space of two years [and] ten, abiding decision, [137]
Was obeyed Eocho Feidlech;
In Tara grassy, excellent,
Received the arch-prince a drink of death[3].

2-2 ꞃoꞃiaꞃaⳄ CoċaiⳄ.   3 moꞃꞡaiꞡ.   4-4 ⰱi[ꞡ] ꞇonⳂaiꞡ i[n] ꞇꞃenꝓlaiꞇ.

t. [1] *Away.*—Literally, *out.*

[2] *Twenty [years], except four.*—Cf. ꞃ 1, note 1.

[3] *Drink of death.*—'Cc aꞇⰱaꞇ i Ꞇemꞃaiꞡ—[Natural] death died he in Tara (*L.L.*, p. 23 a).

4.

[t] Cóic¹ bliadna déc dó iar rin¹,
D'Eochaid² bite, dia² bráṫair:
Noco³ bréc in rcél³ dia claind,
Raloirc⁴ tene i⁵ Fremaind⁵.

5.

Eterrcél¹, rer rigda in raiṫ¹,
Fuair² cóic bliadna co biṫmaiṫ²;
Docer rí na rect do rind
La³ Nuadait³ Necṫ i n-Alind⁴.

6.

Aided¹ Nuadat i caṫ Chlíaċ
La Conaire² na cóemrciaṫ³:
Ní⁴ roċaiṫ⁴ aċt da ráṫe⁵
I flaiṫ⁶ hErend arodlaṫe⁶.

1.

u Aroflaiṫ Conaire for cáċ,
Secṫ n-deiċ m-bliadna¹ co deggnáṫ¹:
Dár ríg² nallaeċ 'rin bruidin²
La Inċél³ caeċ, creċdulig⁴.

4.—¹⁻¹ Fuair tri coic bliadna 'ar blaid. ²⁻² Eochaid Oirem a.
³⁻³ nír'breg in rcel e. ⁴ no gur'loirc. ⁵⁻⁵ a Fremainn.
5.—¹⁻¹ Fuair Eterrcel i roid raiṫ. ²⁻² bliadain ar coic do'n daemflaiṫ.
³⁻³ le Nuadu. ⁴ Ailind. 6.—¹ oidid. ² Conairi. ³ caemrciaṫ.
⁴⁻⁴ nocur'ċaiṫ. ⁵ raiṫi. ⁶⁻⁶ flaicur Crenn arodlaiṫi.
u 1.—¹⁻¹ m-bliadna fo biṫblaṫ. ²⁻² rí na laeċ a m-bruidin.
³ hAingcel. ⁴ creċfuilig.

⁴ *Burned.*—Siugmall roloirc i Fremaind—Siugmall burned [him] in Fremand (*L.L.*, 23 a).

⁵ *Fremand.*—"It is now called, *anglice*, Frewin and is applied to a lofty hill rising over the western shore of Loċ Uair, *anglice*, Lough Owel, in the townland of Wattstown, parish of Portlemon and county of Westmeath" (O'Donovan, *F.M.* i., p. 89).

⁶ *Alend.*—See J 6, note 5. *L.L.* (p. 23 a) adds:

Ir hí reo tra amrer inrogenair Crirt, mac Dé bí, do terrargain in ċiniuda doendai.

Now, this is the time in which was born Christ, son of the living God, to deliver the human race.

⁷ *Cliu.*—In Ui-Dróna (barony of Idrone, co. Carlow), according to *L.L.* (p. 23a).

BOOK OF LEINSTER.

4. [B. C.]

[t] Five years [and] ten [were reigned] by him after that, [125]
[Namely] by Eocho Bithe, by his brother
Not false the tale for his children,
Burned[4] him fire in Fremand[5].

5.

Eterscel, royal person of felicity,
Received he five years of constant goodness; [110]
Fell the king of equities by [spear]-point
By Nuadu Necht in Alend[6].

6.

The destruction of Nuadu [took place] in the battle of Cliu[7]
By Conaire of the beauteous shields:
Spent he not except two quarters [of a year] [105]
In sovranty of very blooming Eriu.

1.

u   The arch-prince Conaire, over everyone [ruled he]
Seven [times] ten years with excellent customs: [105]
The death of the king of heroes [took place] in the Bruden[1]
By Incel One-eye[2], the plunder-minded.

---

u. [1] *Bruden.*—In the *Togail Bruidne Da Derga*, or *Demolition of the Court of Da Derga* (a tale in *L.U.* [*Lebar na hUidri: Book of the Dun (Cow)*], an 11th cent. MS.]), we are told that the Bruden stood on both sides of the Dodder (near Dublin). King Conaire, after returning from slaying a number of the outlaws who had surrounded the Court, asked for a drink. Ní fúaratar na deogbaire dig dó irin Dothae (.i. abann) ⁊ noboí in Dothra triarin teč—The drinkbearers found not drink for him in the Dothra (namely, a river), although [lit., *and*] the Dothra ran [lit., *was*] through the house (p. 97 b, ll. 4, 5). The place is at present called Boher-na-breena (*Bothar na bruidhne*—Road of the Court).

[2] *One-eye.*—Literally, *blind.* The reason is thus given in *L.U.* (p. 84 b, ll. 21-3).

Fer anmín, mór, úatmar,   A man rough, gross, repulsive, un-
anaicnid in t-Ingcél. 'Oen fúil   natural [was] that Ingcel. One eye in
i n-a čind; letidir dampeče,   his head; larger than an oxhide,
duibitir degaid ⁊ trí maic im-   blacker than a chafer? and three pupils
leppen inte.   in it.

He is said (*ib.*, ll. 19, 20) to have been the son of Ua Chonmaic, of the Britons. Of

2.

[u] Cóic bliadna do¹ Chempaig trice²
Cen³ purig h-dedgair³, h-diangbcc,
Co¹ n-érracc⁴ Lugaid, [S]ríabńderg⁵
Ro po⁶ talcair a trenredg⁶.

3.

A ré ricec do Lugaid,
Co n-ebailc do tromcumaid.
Conċobar, bliadain a¹ band¹,
No² co torcair² la Crimtand.

4.

Crimtand¹ cdem cliarac, ročaiċ¹
Sé bliadna déc co² degmaic²,
Co³ n-ébailc aiċle a eċtra³
Mac Lugdec in laeċrecta⁴.

2.—¹ du'n. ² tric. ³⁻³ gan ruiri n-degair. ⁴⁻⁴ co n-derracc.
⁵ Sriabnderg. ⁶⁻⁶ do ruicread a rigferg. 3.—¹⁻¹ bai and.
²⁻² no go drocair. 4.—¹⁻¹ docaic Crimtann, ni breg buin.
²⁻² gan dubrun. ³⁻³ ruair [bar] a haiċli rocca. The bracketted
word, which is necessary for the meaning, is written, *alia manu*, on the margin.
⁴ lancrecta.

---

the passages of the *Togail*, respecting which Windisch (*Irische Texte*, p. viii.) observes *Wo finden sich sonst noch solche Angaben ?*, the following may be quoted: [In going to attack the Court, each man brought a stone to make a mound.]

Ar did fácaid dorigret a carnd
.i. ar ba fer carnd la diberg ⁊
dano co fintair a n-erbada oc
brudin. Caċ oen noċicrad slán
úadi, nobered a cloic arin carnd.
Co farccair imorro cloċ in loċta

For two reasons made they a mound:
namely, for it was a custom [to make]
a mound in a raid, and moreover that
they might know their losses at Bruden.
Each one that would come safe therefrom used to carry a stone from the

2. [B.C.]

[ıı] Five years for active Tara [35]
Without an arch-king befitting, perfectly prudent,
Until reached [it] Lugaid Red-stripe,
Vigorous was his strong domination.

3.

Six [and] twenty [years were reigned] by Lugaid, [30]
Until perished he of heavy grief[3].
Conchobar, a year [was] his span, [4]
Until fell he by Crimthand.

4.

Crimthand of the splendid hosts, spent he
Six years [and] ten with exceeding goodness, [3]
Until perished on the morrow of his faring[4]
The son of Lugaid the heroic.

---

no maıṗṗıcıṗ occı. Conıḃ aṗṗın
ṗoṗeṗṗacáṗ a n-eṗḃaḃa.

mound. But they left on it the stone[s] of the folk that were killed. So that from that they knew their losses.

[3] *Heavy grief.*—Topċaıṗ 'ma claıḃeḃ ṗeın ḃı ċumaıḃ a mná—fell he on his own sword for grief of his wife (*L.L.*, p. 23 a).

[4] *Expedition.*—Explained in *L.L.* (p. 23 b):

Iṗ é ḃoċoıḃ ı n-eccṗa a Ḋún
Cṗımċaınḃ ṗe Naıṗ, banṗṡḃaıʒe,
co m-ḃoı coıcċıʒıṗ ṗoṗ míṗ anḃ.
Co cuc ṗeocu ımḃa leıṗ, ımon
caṗṗac n-oṗḃa ⁊ ımon ṗıḋóıll óıṗ
⁊ ımon cecaıʒ (.ı. lenı) Cṗımċaınḃ.
Co n-eṗḃaılc ıaṗ cıaccaın ım-
muıʒ, ı cınḃ cóıcċıʒıṗ aṗ míṗ.

It is he went on a faring from the Fort of Crimthand [the site of the Bailie lighthouse, Howth], with Nair, the banshee, and he was a fortnight over a month thereon. And [*lit.*, so that] he brought valuables numerous with him, including [*lit.*, around] the golden chariot and including the chessboard of gold and including the *cetach* (that is, tunic) of Crimthand. And he died after coming to land, at the end of a fortnight above a month.

5.

[u] Lan pí Corpri Chinncaitt¹ crúain
Or in Temraig taile, tonnbúain:
Coíc bliadna a pat ar² in rainn²,
'Ec³ atbat³ atair Morainn.

6.

Mait flatiur¹ Feradaig finn,
Fict ir² a bó a dag² linn:
Ir³ bét cuimnct⁴ illeit Chuinn⁴,
'Ec⁵ uí Luigdct illiatbruim⁵.

1.

v Trí¹ bliadna ríge corpat¹
D'Crinn fo² nirt Fhiacat²;
La Fiacaig Finn, bu³ áir ferda³,
Doroċair⁴ rí roemna⁵.

2.

p. 129 b Ba¹ rí Fiacna² for Fiannaib
A rect³ bét do dag⁴ bliadnaib;
Docer im⁵ Maig bolgg barrglarr⁵
La Cllim⁶ ord, imamnarr⁶.

5.—¹ cinncaít. ²⁻² or in poinn. ³⁻³ eg abbat. 6.—¹ flatéur.
²⁻² bliadain a deig. ³ ba. ⁴⁻⁴ cuimneat re leat Cuinn. ⁵⁻⁵ eg ua
Luigcc a Liatbruim (Died the grandson, etc.).

v 1.—¹⁻¹ ba bliadain b[rige?] gan brat. ²⁻² Fa ragail Fiatat.
³⁻³ fuair fedda. ⁴ co torcair. ⁵ rotempa. 2.—¹ lan. ² Fiato.
³ ré. ⁴ deig. ⁵⁻⁵ a Muig balg barrglar. ⁶⁻⁶ hCllim n-ard n-imamnar.

---

⁵ *Morand.*—The brehon of Feradach the Fair. "This Moran had a *sid*, or chain,
called *Idh Morainn* [chain of Morann], which, when put around the neck of a

5.   [A.D.]

[u] Full king [was] Corpri of the Cat-head repulsive
     Over Tara strong, firm-founded:
     Five years [was] his felicity from his portion,   [13]
     [Natural] death died the father of Morand⁵.

6.

     Good [was] the sovranty of Feradach the Fair,
     Twenty and two his good complement: [18]
     It is a disaster to be remembered in the Half of Conn⁶,
     The death of the grandson of Lugaid in Liathdruim⁷.

1.

v   Three years of kingship with felicity   [40]
     [Were] for Eriu under the power of Fiachra;
     By Fiacha the Fair, it was manly destruction,
     Fell the king of great Tara¹.

2.

     King was Fiachna over the Fenians
     Seven [and] ten of good years;   [43]
     Fell he in Magh Bolg green-surfaced
     By Ellim the haughty, very cruel.

---

guilty person, would squeeze him to suffocation, and when put about the neck of an innocent person would expand so as to reach the earth" (O'Donovan, *F.M.* i., p. 95, from the *Lebar-Gabala* or *Book of Occupation* [of Ireland]).

⁶ *Half of Conn.* The northern moiety of Ireland, so-called (by prolepsis in this place) from Conn of the Hundred Battles (**w** 1, *infra*).

⁷ *Liathdruim.—Grey ridge*, a name for the Hill of Tara. See **c** 2, note 3.

v. ¹ *Great Tara.*—The *Ballymote* reading.

Magh Bolg.—"Now Moybolgue, a parish in the south-east of the county Cavan and extending into Meath" (O'Donovan, *F.M.* i., p. 98).

3.

[v] Arim¹ ba n-beić b'Erinb áin
Roborreić² Ellim² imláin:
Rí cruaib Cnuća³, i ćać Aićle
Fúair cruća⁴ ocur crenaićbe⁴.

4.

Cuaćal cren, cnića¹ roćećć,
Roćenb cnića² crí ćoemnerc²;
Irin crerr³, ror³ lár Line,
Romarb Mál, mac Rócribe⁴.

5.

Cećri bliabna roćećć¹ Mál,
Romarb² Feiblimib imnár³,
A nói [Feiblimib⁴], ir⁵ fír rin,
Na⁶ co n-erbailć mac Cuaćail.

6.

A¹ ré ríćeć¹ cen caćair craic,
(No: crí bliabna cen caćair craic)
Roćaić Caćair, hua² Comaic;
Doroćair³ rí Cuage⁴ ćer
La⁵ Féin Luagne nalluamćlerr⁵.

3.—¹ nemer. ²⁻² norreb nerc Elim. ³ Cnući. ⁴⁻⁴ crući ir cromaire. 4.—¹ crica. ²⁻² crica go comnerc. ³⁻³ ćać an. ⁴ Rocraibc. [P. 48 a.] 5.—¹ rocaić. ² gun'marb. ³ finnár. ⁴ Feiblimib. ⁵ *Om*. It is hypermetrical. ⁶ no. 6.—¹⁻¹ crí bliabna. The alternative reading of L. ² ua. ³ bubrocair. ⁴ Cuaibi. ⁵⁻⁵ le Conn Luaigni na luać[c]ner.

---

² *Cnucha*.—Castleknock, near Dublin.

³ *Aichil*.—The ancient name of the hill of Skreen [*Shrine* of St. Colum-cille], a little to the south-east of Tara.

⁴ *Magh Line.*—Doroćair cra Cuaćal i n-Dálaraibe, immonai in ćaća cria ćaingnaćć, bale arra m-brucca Olor 7 Olarba. Now fell Tuathal in Dalaraide [a territory comprising the greater part of co. Antrim] in the *Bog of the* [present] *battle*, through treachery, [in] the place whence spring Olor and Olarba (*L.L.*, p. 24 a).

BOOK OF LEINSTER.

3.   [A. D.]

[v] A tale of two decades [of years] for Eriu noble,   [60]
Ellim spent it completely:
The king of bleak Cnucha², in the battle of Aichil³
Received he short life and stern cutting off.

4.

Tuathal the powerful, thirty [years] obtained he,   [80]
Established he [the] thirty through excellent sway;
In the contest, in the centre of [Magh] Line⁴,
Slew [him] Mal, son of Rochraid.

5.

Four years obtained Mal [the kingship],   [110]
Slew [him] Fedlimid the very noble,
Nine [years reigned] Fedlimid, true is that,   [114]
Until perished the son of Tuathal.

6.

Six [and] twenty [years] without reproach severe   [123]
(Or: Three years without reproach severe)
Spent Cathair, descendant of Comac;
Fell the king of Tuath⁵ in the east
By the Fenians⁶ of Luagne⁷ of the pre-eminent deeds.

" The [Olor] is the Six-mile Water [flowing into Lough Neagh] and the [Olarba] is the Larne Water [flowing into the Irish Sea]. The Larne river rises by two heads in the parish of Ballynure; the Six-mile Water, in the parish of Ballycor, a little south of Shane's Hill: after a course of about 100 perches it becomes the boundary between the parish of Kilwaughter [*Caill-uachtair*—Head-wood?], as well as between the baronies of Upper Glenarm and Upper Antrim. Following the direction of a ravine, which runs down the face of the hill, it arrives at the townland of Head-wood [= *Caill-uachtair*?], near the place where the three baronies of Upper Glenarm, Upper Antrim, and Lower Belfast [meet?]. In this townland there is a spot where a branch of the Six-mile Water can be turned into the Larne river; and here is a large bog, probably the *Moin-an-chatha*, or Battle-bog, mentioned in the text, lying between the two rivers" (O'Donovan, *F.M.* i., pp. 100-1).

⁵ *Tuath*.—(The *Ballymote* reading.) See r 3, note 3.
⁶ *Fenians*.—A collective noun in the original.
⁷ *Luagne*.—The barony of Lune, co. Meath.

Lebar Laigen.

1.

W Cond, cóic bliadna ra[1] cetair
ba[2] iarla co n-airlecaib[3];
Doroċair[4] Cond[4] cláir Mide[5]
la[6] mac Máil, mic Rocride[7].

2.

Rocait[1] Conaire, a chamain,
Secht bliadna ir oen[2] bliadain;
Doroċair[3] flait Femin[3] find
Do láim Nemid, mic Srobcind[4].

3.

Art, mac Cuind, calma ro[1] glacc[1]
In banba fri ré trichat:
Romudaig[2], ciar'bo[2] cara,
Lugaid i cath Mucrama[3].

4.

Lugaid, mac Con, mic Lugdec,
Trica bliadan balc, buidnec[1]:
La Fercor, mac Commain[2] cain,
Fuair forrain[3] ir[4] fritargain.

---

w 1.—[1] fo. [2] rob'. [3] ardeċaid. [4-4] co n-dorcair Conn.
[5] ihidi. [6] le. [7] Rocraidi. 2.—[1] docait. [2] en. [3-3] co n-dorcair
ri Feimin. [4] Sraidcind. 3.—[1-1] do glac. [2-2] rormugaid, ger'rat.
[3] Mucroma. 4.—[1] blatbuidnec. [2] Comain. [3] forran. [4] i.

---

w. [1] *With contests.*—An allusion to the title *Cétcathach*, of the Hundred Battles (*lit.*, hundred-battled), bestowed upon Conn.
   [2] *Son of Mal.*—Tipraite Tirech (*L.L.*, p. 24 a).
   [3] *Son-in-law.*—He was married to Saraid, daughter of Conn.

BOOK OF LEINSTER.

1. [A. D.]

w   Conn, five years by four   [149]
Was he king with contests[1];
Fell Conn of the Plain of Meath
By the son of Mal[2], son of Rochraid.

2.

Spent Conaire, his son-in-law[3],
Seven years and one year;   [169]
Fell the prince of Femen[4] fair
By hand of Nemed, son of Stripe-Head.

3.

Art, son of Conn, excellently received he
Banba for the space of thirty [years]:   [177]
Destroyed [him], although he was his friend[5],
Lugaid in the battle of [Magh] Mucrama[6].

4.

Lugaid, son of Cu[7], son of Lugaid [Laidech],
Thirty years powerful, crowded [reigned he]:   [207]
By Ferchess, son of Comman the noble,
Received he [his] end and utter defeat.

---

[4] *Femen.*—A plain comprising Iffa and Offa East, co. Tipperary; here employed to signify the southern part of Ireland.

[5] *Friend.*—Lugaid Laidech, otherwise *Cu* (*hound*, a term of distinction amongst the ancient Irish), otherwise *Macniadh* (son of the champion), married Sadb, daughter of Conn of the Hundred Battles (who after his death became the wife of Olioll Olum), and thus his son, Lugaid, was nephew of Art, whom he slew.

[6] [*Magh*] *Mucrama.*—Prope Athenriam, octo millibus passuum Galvia dissitam . . . Turloch-airt [*recte*, Tullach-Airt, collis Arturi] in facti memoriam paludi nomen adhaesit, quae, inter Moyvoelam et Killcornan sita, in hunc usque diem eodem nomine gaudet (*Ogygia*, Pars III., cap. lxvii., pp. 327–9).

[7] *Cu.*—See note 5, *supra*.

5.

[w] Fergur¹ Dubḃetaċ, cen¹ ḋianblaiḋ,
Cen² ecnaċ ri oen² bliaḋne:
Doroċair³ gilla na n-glacc
I caṫ Chrina⁴ la Cormac.

6.

Cormac, ceṫri¹ deiċ datta²,
Roḟeiṫ³ in⁴ láeċ lamḟata⁵:
Rombáiḋ⁶ i⁶ tig Cletiṫig⁷ srúaiḋ
Cnáim inḋ⁸ iáiċ ettig innuáir.⁸

1.

x Eoċo Gunnat¹, rogiallaḋ
I² n-'Erinḋ² eḋ oen³ bliaḋain:
Romuḋaig⁴ glacc⁴ in gorra,
Lugaiḋ, mac mic Oengora⁵.

2.

'Arim¹ ré ṁ-bliaḋan ḋa² deiċ,
Rogiallaḋ Carrre³, cuinniḋ³:
'Sin⁴ Gaḃair, ciḋ⁵ truag linni⁶,
Romaḋaiḋ⁷ ruaḋ rorinni⁷.

5.—¹⁻¹ Fearguf Dedaċ co n-. ²⁻² gan egna re hen. ³ co n-brocair.
⁴ Crinḋa. 6.—¹ ceiṫri. ² data. ³ rorḟeiṫ. ⁴ i[n].
⁵ lamḟada. ⁶⁻⁶ rorbaiḋ a. ⁷ Cleitig. ⁸⁻⁸ in có citig inḋḟuair.
x 1.—¹ Gunḋaḋ. ²⁻² or Crinn. ³ aen. ⁴⁻⁴ rormugaiḋ glac. ⁵ Aen-
gura. 2.—¹ airem. ² 'r a. ³⁻³ Corrre, in cuingiḋ. The in
is interrogative. ⁴ irin. ⁵ giḋ. ⁶ linḋ. ⁷⁻⁷ rorḟarrnaig
ruaḋ ḋo'n rorinḋ.

---

⁸ *Crina*.—"Keating calls this place Crioma-Chinn Chumair, and says that it is situated at Brugh-nic-an-oig, which is the name of a place on the River Boyne, near Stackallan Bridge" (O'Donovan, *F.M.* i., p. 110). O'Flaherty (*ubi sup.*, c. lxviii., p. 332) states that it is in Bregia (a plain in East Meath), but gives no authority.

5.   [A.D.]

[w] Fergus Black-toothed, without lasting fame,
     Without reproach [reigned he] for one year: [237]
     Fell the practiser of manual feats
     In the battle of Crina[8] by Cormac.

6.

Cormac, four decades pleasant   [238]
Spent the hero long-handed:
Killed him in the house of barren Clettech[9]
The bone of the deadly[?] very cold salmon[10].

1.

x   Eocho Gunnat, obeyed was he   [278]
     In Eriu the space [of] one year:
     [Him] destroyed the hand of strength,
     Lugaid, son of the son of Oengus.

2.

A tale of six years [and] two decades   [279]
Was Carpre obeyed, remember [it]:
In Gabair[1], though pity [it is] to us,
[Him] destroyed a ruddy great [spear-]point.

---

[9] *Clettech.*—"It was situated near Stackallan Bridge, on the south side of the Boyne" (O'Donovan, p. 116).

[10] *Salmon.*—Copmac, hua Cuinb, .xl. bliaban, co n-epbailt ι τιξ Cleccιξ, ιαp lenamain cnáma bpacaιn ι n-a bpaξιc. No, ιc pιabpa popopcpac, ιαp n-a bpac bo Illaelcenb (*L.L.*, p. 24 a).

Cormac, grandson of Conn [of the Hundred Battles], forty years [reigned he], until he died in [his] palace of Clettech, in consequence of the bone of a salmon sticking in his throat. Or, it was the sprites destroyed him, after his betrayal by [the Druid] Bald-Head.

According to the legend, Cormac renounced druidism and believed in God, with the fatal result here mentioned.

x. [1] *Gabair.*—Called Gabair of Aichill "from its contiguity to Aichill, now the hill of Skreen, near Tara, in the county of Meath. Gabra, *anglice* Gowra, is now

3.

[x] Rogabratar¹ na Fotaig
bliadain or banba botaig²;
Dorotair³ Fotat Carptet³
Larin Fotaig rind Airgdet⁴.

4.

Aided¹ Fotaig¹ iar fingail
I cat Ollorba² inbaig².
Fiata³ iarrotat, feit⁴ latt⁴,
Sett⁵ ih-bliadna déc ar fidet.

5.

Fiata¹, fuair dig tonnaid² tra
I cat Duib-tommuir³ la Colla.
Cetri⁴ bliadna⁴ Colla iar cat,
Co rori[n]narb⁵ Muridat⁵.

6.

Muridat¹ Tiret, a¹ deit,
Deg mac Fiatat² cu² firbreit;
Ic³ Dabull la Mac Cruind cain
Dorotair⁴ hua⁴ Cuind todail.

3.—¹ rorgabradar. ² botaid. ³⁻³ contorcair Fotaid Carptet.
⁴ findairgdeat. 4.—¹⁻¹ oidid Fataig. ²⁻² Ollarba inmain. ³ Fiatat.
⁴⁻⁴ feg lat. ⁵ ré. 5.—¹ Fiato. ² tondaig. ³ Comair.
⁴⁻⁴ a ceitri. ⁵⁻⁵ gu rurindarb Muredat. 6.—¹⁻¹ Muredet
Tiread, tri. ²⁻² Fiatna[t] gu. ³ ig. ⁴⁻⁴ adrocair ua.

the name of a stream which rises in a bog in the townland of Prantstown, in the parish of Skreen, receives a tribute from the well of Neamhnach on Tara Hill, joins the River Skene at Dowthstown and unites with the Boyne at Ardsallagh" (O'Donovan, *F.M.* i., p. 120).

² *Fratricide.*—Of his brother, Fotach the Charioteer. They were sons of Lugaid, son of Cu (Lugaid Laidech).

³ *Ollorba.*—L.L. (p. 24 a) says in [Magh] Line, in the battle of Ollorba. See ▼ 4, note 4. He was slain, according to the legend, by Cailte, son of Ronan, foster-son of Finn, son of Cumal. Finn was son-in-law of Cormac, son of Art, son of Conn of the Hundred Battles.

3.

[x] Received the Fotachs [the kingship]
A year over Banba marshy;   [305]
Fell Fotach the Charioteer
By Fotach Fair, the Raider.

4.

The fate of Fotach [took place] after [his] fratricide[2]
In the battle very victorious of Ollorba[3].
Fiacha Iarfothach[4], attend you,
Seven years [and] ten above a score [reigned he].   [306]

5.

Fiache, received he a drink of death in sooth
In the battle of Dub-chommur[5] by Colla.
Four years [reigned] Colla after the battle,   [343]
Until expelled him[6] Muridach [Tirech].

6.

Muridach Tirech, ten [years reigned he],   [347]
Excellent son of Fiacha, with true judgment;
At Daball[7] by the son of noble Cronn
Fell the grandson of loyal Conn.

---

[4] *Fiacha Iarfothach.*—Called Fiacha Sroptini in *L.L.* (p. 24 a).

[5] *Dub-chommur.*—*Black confluence;* that is, of the Blackwater (the ancient Sele) and the Boyne, now the town of Navan. O'Donovan, *F.M.* i., pp. 35, 122.

[6] *Expelled him.*—The lithograph reading of *L.L.* (*Corrig.* to p. 129 b, l. 26) is ꞃoꞃmaꞃb (killed him). Assuming this to be an accurate reproduction of the MS., the *Ballymote* variant, ꞃuꞃınbaꞃb, shows how the error arose. Of the original ꞃonınnaꞃb, the scribe omitted the horizontal stroke (= n) over the ı and read the ın as an m.

L.L. (p. 24 a) states that Fiacha Iarfothach was slain by the three Collas and that Colla Uais reigned four years, until Muridach Tirech expelled them (co ꞃonınnaꞃb Muꞃıbać Cıꞃeć).

After the lapse of a year, they returned and were received by Muridach. Four years later, they marched against Fergus Foga, King of Emain Macha (i.e. of Ulster), slew him and burned the palace of Emain.

[7] *Daball.*—The Blackwater, which separates the counties of Tyrone and Armagh and empties into Lough Neagh.

Lebar Laigen.

1.

y Coelbad¹, bliadain, blad cen² brón,
Romarb³ Eoco Muigmedón³.
A oct⁴ d' Eocaid, ní bréc⁵ rain⁵,
Co n-deocaid⁶ [d']éc⁶ i Temraig.

2.

Tri bliadna déc, datta¹ in barr¹,
Nir' bo fota² do Chrimtand:
Fuair³ dig nimnid i n-a tig³
Ra⁴ fiair, ra⁵ hingin nemid⁵.

3.

Fich¹ bliadan for² a fect
Maroen³ do Niall ra³ nert:
Ni dalb, or Mur⁴ lét elac⁵
Romarb⁶ Eocaid aroflebac⁶.

---

y. 1.—¹ Caelblad.   ² gen.   ³⁻³ gur'marb Cocaid Muigmedon.
⁴ hoct.   ⁵⁻⁵ breg rin.   ⁶⁻⁶ n-deacaid d'eg.   2.—¹⁻¹ data in-barr.
² foda.   ³⁻³ co fuair dig neimnig 'n-a taig.   ⁴ 'g a.   ⁵⁻⁵ ag
ingin Fidaig.   3.—¹ fici.   ² ir.   ³⁻³ ro gor'rcarad Niall re.
⁴ Muir.   ⁵ alac.   ⁶⁻⁶ gur'marb Cocaid Ceindrelac.

y. ¹ *Fidach.* The *Ballymote* reading: the text is unintelligible to me. Crimthand, son of Flidach, was poisoned by his sister Mongfind (Fair-Hair), relict of Eocho Mugmedon, in order that her eldest son, Brian, might become king. (According to the *Book of Ballymote*, p. 264 a, Crimthand, being suspicious, refused to be the first to drink. Whereupon, Mongfind drank and lost her life before him.) But the crime was bootless. Niall of the Nine Hostages, son of Eocho by Carinna, obtained the succession. Of the posterity of Brian, none ascended the throne, save Turlough O'Conor and his son, Roderick, the last monarch of Ireland. See O'Donovan, *F.M.* i., pp. 125 *sq.*

² *Ictian Sea.*—"This sea is supposed to have taken its name from the Portus Iccius of Caesar, situated not far from the site of the present Boulogne. Nothing seems clearer than that this Irish monarch made incursions into Britain against

BOOK OF LEINSTER.

1.　　　　　　　　　　[A.D.]

y Coelbad, a year [reigned he], fame without sorrow,　　[357]
Slew [him] Eocho Mugmedon.
Eight [years were reigned] by Eocho, not false that,　　[358]
Until underwent he death in Tara.

2.

Three years [and] ten, pleasant the amount,　　[366]
It was not long for Crimthand:
Received he drink of poison in his house,
From his sister, from the daughter of Fidach[1].

3.

A score of years above seven　　[379]
Consecutively for Niall in his power:
Not false, over the restless Ictian Sea[2]
Slew [him] Eochaid Ardfledach.

Stilicho, whose success in repelling him and his Scots is described by Claudian. 'By him,' says the poet, speaking in the person of Britannia, 'was I protected when the Scot moved all Ierne against me and the sea foamed with his hostile oars:

> [Me quoque vicinis pereuntem gentibus, inquit,
> Munivit Stilicho,] totam cum Scotus Iernen
> Movit et infesto spumavit remige Tethys.'
> 　　　　　　[*De laudibus Stilichonis, lib.* 2.]

"From another of this poet's eulogies it appears that the fame of that Roman legion, which had guarded the frontier against the invading Scots, procured for it the distinction of being one of those summoned to the banner of Stilicho, when the Goths threatened Rome:

> Venit et extremis legio praetenta Britannis
> Quae Scoto dat frena truci, ferroque notatas
> Perlegit exanimes, Picto moriente, figuras.
> 　　　　*De bello Getico.*"

—(O'Donovan, *F.M.* i., pp. 127-8: from O'Flaherty, *Ogygia*, Pars III., cap. lxxxv., pp. 403, 396, 399.)

LEBAR LAIGEN.

4.

[y] Cetri¹ cóic bliadna 'r¹ a trí,
Rogiallad do niurt² n-[D]atí² :
I Sleib³ Elpa na n-arm n-án⁴
Roloirc⁵ in tene gelán⁵.

5.

Sé ríg déc¹, ré fichit² ríg,
Ria³ tiachtain Patraic⁴ co fír,
Daréir⁵ Slane⁵ na n-gal n-grind,
Ir é lín rogab daréir⁶ hErind⁷.
hEriu⁸.

6.

Gilla-Caemain cen gainne,
Mac Gille fac[i]r Samtainne,
Fáid di'n gar[g]gním romgial,—
Ar n-árim ardríg hErenn.

4.—¹⁻¹ ficí bliadan ir.   ²⁻² nert Daéi.   ³ Sliab.   ⁴ n-aig.
⁵⁻⁵ romard roiged gand gealan. Over romard is no, roloirc (or, *burned*),
in another hand. A quatrain is inserted:—   [A.D.]

Rocait Loegaire linmar	Spent Loegaire the plenteous	[429]
Re ceitri m-bliadan m-brig-mar :	The space of four powerful years :	
Re tiachtain Padraig na penn	Before coming of Patrick of the penances,	[432]
ba rí renutad raer Erenn. Eri ard.	He was king vigilant, noble, of Eriu. Eriu sublime.	

5.—¹ deg.   ² fichet.   ³ re.   ⁴ Padraig.   ⁵⁻⁵ o da Slaine.   ⁶ *om*.   ⁷ Erinn.
⁸ Eri ard. The following verses are added:—

Ir and rogab Padraig fort,	It is there Patrick made land
I coiced Ulad edrocht,	In the Fifth of the illustrious Ulstermen,
Gur' éretread oig Emna ard,	So that believed the youths of noble Emain,
Re rluagaib aille Erenn. Eri ard.	Before the hosts of beauteous Eriu. Eriu sublime.
Secht roind, recht fichit, rand reid,	Seven divisions, [and] seven score, partition clear,
Ocur a deic co n-deigmein,	And ten with good intent,

BOOK OF LEINSTER. 213

4.   [A.D.]

[y] Four [times] five years and three,   [406]
Was service rendered to the power of Dathi:
In the mountain of Alp³ of noble weapons
Burned [him] the fire of lightning⁴.   [429]

5.

Six kings [and] ten, six score of kings [= 136],
[Reigned] before the coming of Patrick with truth,   [432]
After Slane of the vigorous feats,
This is the complement that ruled Eriu⁵.
                                           Eriu, etc.

6.

Gilla-Caemain, without penuriousness,
Son of noble Gilla Samthainne,
Thanks for the difficult feat he has earned,—
For recital of the arch-kings of Eriu.

Ir ten a linmaine lium,	It is clear, its amount, to me,
Reim rignaiḋi ḟean n-Erenn.	The series of kings of the Men of Eriu.
Eri anḋ.	Eriu sublime.
Gilla Caema[i]n go n-glaine,	Gilla-Caemain with purity,
Ua Gilli raein Shamṫainḋe,	Grandson of noble Gilla-Shamthainde,
Rug buaiḋ o ḃannḋaiḃ co binḋ,	He carried off victory melodiously from bards
Etin Albain ir Erinn.	Both in Alba and in Eriu.
Eri anḋ.	Eriu sublime.

---

³ *Alp.*—"Dathias, ethnicorum Hiberniae regum postremus, dum in Gallia lectorum militum copiis provinciam Romanam invaderet more gentium caeterarum, queis tum praeda factum imperium, immensam illam molem frustatim diripientium, sesquicentum, ut aiunt, proeliis, victor ad Alpium radices fulmine e coelo ictus interiit. Cadaver in Hiberniam perlatum apud Cruachan [Rathcroghan, co. Roscommon], Connactiae regiam, terrae mandatum est" (*Ogygia*, Pars III., cap. lxxxvii., p. 415).

⁴ *Lightning.*—"Illum e coelo tactum vindice flamma tradunt ob violatam cujusdam eremitae S. Firmini cellam et pagum; quem regem fuisse et post abdicatum seculare dominium Deo in solitudine vacantem in turri 17 cubitos altâ ad Alpes vitam transegisse prodit Codex Lecan (*fol.* 302 b)" (*id. ib.* p. 416).

⁵ *That ruled Eriu.*—The ḃanéir of the text, being hypermetrical, is to be omitted, in accordance with the *Ballymote* reading.

INDEX VERBORUM. (II.)

[*Roman numerals and letters (thus,* **I a**) *denote the texts and sections,* pp. 120 *to* 140; *Roman letters and Arabic figures (thus,* **d** 4) *refer to the Lebar Laigen text,* pp. 142 *to* 213.]

a (art.), **I a**, **c**; **d** 4, **f** 5, **g** 2, **h** 1, **i** 4, 5, 6, **j** 5, **m** 4, **n** 2, **o** 4, **q** 1, 4, **r** 5, **s** 3, **t** 2, **u** 3, 6, **v** 2, 5, 6, **x** 6, **y** 1, 3, 4.
a (pron. infix. 3 s. m.), ɴa loıɾc, **v c**, **t** 4.
a (poss.), **I a**, **c**, **d**, **e**, **f**, **g**, **n**, **o**; **II b**, **i**; **III g**; **IV d**, **e**; **v c**; **a** 1, **b** 1, 4, 6, **c** 5, **d** 1, 5, 6, **f** 2, 4, **h** 6, **i** 4, 5, **j** 3, **k** 6, **m** 1, 3, **n** 2, 4, **o** 1, **p** 5, **q** 3, 5, **r** 1, 4, 6, **s** 5, **u** 2, 3, 4, 5, 6, **w** 2.
a n- (poss. pl.), **I g**.
a (prep.), **g** 1, 4, **p** 6.
a (prep. *from*), **I j**.
a (= ı), **I d**; **II h**; **III h**; **s** 4.
a (voc.), **I j**, **m**, **n**; **II a**, **g**, **h**; **III a**.
acɢaıɾb, **b** 5; aɢaɾb, **I l**.
aċt, **I e**, **i**; **II i**, **l**, **m**; **III l**, **m**; **r** 1, **t** 2, 6.
acubaıb, **I c**; **II a**, **m**; **III m**; -aıb, **IV b**.
abaıɢ, **I a**.
abbol, n-, **h** 3.
abnaċt, **d** 1.
abubaıɾt, **II g**.
ac, **I g**, **o**.
Aeb, **o** 1, 2.
aeı, **I g**; **IV d**; haeı; **IV d**.
aen, **I g**; **II c**; **III c**; ɴoɾaentaıɢetaɾ, **IV d**.

Aep, **f** 4.
aɢaɾb, **I l**.
aı, **IV c**.
aıcneab [a ċneb], **I l**.
Aıb, **g** 6, **k** 2, **q** 6.
Aıċle, **v** 3.
aıbcı, **III c**.
aıbeb, **g** 5, **j** 4, 6, **k** 5, 6, 1 2, **t** 6, **x** 4.
haıbıb, **c** 6.
Aıbne, **i** 2.
aıɢ, **t** 1.
aıɢeɾ [luaıɢeɾ], **III b**.
aıl, **g** 1, **q** 1.
Aılbeɴɢ, **I** 3.
aılı, **IV a**.
Aılıll, **j** 3, 4; -ella (g.), **k** 3, **n** 3, 5, **q** 5; -ılla, **k** 2.
aıll, **IV f**.
Aın, **v** 3.
aınm, **c** 6.
Aıɾ, **v** 1.
aıɾbeɴt, **I g**.
aıɾ[ce]baıl, **I a**.
Aıɾctet, **h** 3.
aıɾb, **e** 4, **f** 5.
aıɾbıɾc, **f** 2, **m** 3.
aıɾe (aɴ and pron. suf. 3 s. neut.), **I i**, **o**.
Aıɾebċaıɾ, **d** 4.
aıɾeɢba, **l** 3.

INDEX VERBORUM. (II.) 215

Aipʒbcċ, r 5, 6, x 3.
aipʒctlaib, 1 j.
aipi (ap, prep. and pron. suf. 3 s. neut.), iv e.
aipiʒbcó, h 4.
aiplcċaib, w 1.
aipm (g.), k 6.
aippcep, 1 o.
Aipc (g.), k 5, 6, n 3, s 5.
afŕbc, 1 g; -bi, iii a, iv a; -cc, 1 a, v b; -ci, v a.
(cpcn)aiċbe, v 3.
aiċlc, u 4.
aiċpíʒc (*recte*, aicipi), iii c.
aláinb, ii j, k; iii k; v a; -nn, iii j.
Alinb, j 6, t 5.
Alclecan, r 1.
amal, 1 d, e, o; ii g.
Amaċaip, q 5, 6.
amnapp, r 5.
aṁpa, ii k; g 3.
ampaib, 1 3.
anipip, c 6.
an, ii i; q 2.
an (art.), 1 a; iv e.
anb (i, prep. and pron. suf. 3 s. neut.), 1 b, c, d, e.
anbpcċc, r 5.
anbpip, b 4.
Anc, n 5.
ann (i, prep. and pron. suf. 3 s. neut.), 1 c, e, j, 1, m, n; iii a.
Anninb, b 2, 3.
anonb, c 4.
unpcċc, 1 4.
Apċaċ, 1 1.
áp, g 2.
ap (conj.), 1 o; iv d.
ap (prep.), 1 a, b, c, n, o; iv e, f; d 5, f 3, g 2, i 2, 1 4, m 4, r 1, x 4.
ap n-, 1 o, y 6.
apa n-, iv c.

apailc, iii d, e, f, i, j, k, l, m; iv b.
apb, ii h; iii h; iv g; a 1, d 2, h 4, 6, i 4, m 4, q 3, 5.
apb(bláċc), t 6; apbḟlaiċ, t 3, u 1; apb(ḟlcbaċ), y 3.
apbpíʒ, y 6; apbpiʒi, ii c.
apbb, r 6.
Apʒaċʒlinb, s 2; Apʒaclam, d 6.
Apʒacmap, n 3, 5, 6; Apʒacpop, f 2.
apim, b 6, g 1, h 2, i 3, k 3, 4, n 6, o 2, v 3, x 2, y 6.
apíu, iii b.
apm n-, y 4.
apmpciaċ, n 5.
appnobliʒ, q 3.
appaib, 1 3.
Apc, k 3, 4, n 1, 2, w 3.
ap (vb.), 1 a; iv d.
ap (prep.), 1 n; iii j; u 5.
apbcpap, iv c.
ap[c]nam, iii g; -um, iv f; apʒnum, ii g.
appip, b 5.
(nib)ac, 1 d.
aca, 1 d; iv a, b; acac, iv a, c, d.
aċaip, h 6, u 5.
Aċa-luain, 1 1.
acbaċ, a 1, e 1, f 2, i 2, o 4, q 4, s 2, u 5.
aċóiu, ii b.
aċlam, v a.
Auʒaípc, 1 o.

b (ciap'b'é = cia po ba é), p 5.
ba, ii g; iii g; f 1, g 2, h 1, 3, p 5, r 1, 3, v 2, w 1.
ba (subj.), iv d, f.
biap'[b]a (po ba), ii c.
bab, 1 o.
babbċaċa, p 1.

INDEX VERBORUM. (II.)

baduipn, o 1, 2.
baȝaim, v a.
baı, a 6, b 1.
(pom)báıb, w 6.
baıpbnı, v a.
baılı, ı g.
baıpı, ı b; ıı a; -ppı, ıı f.
balap, d 6.
balc, w 4; balcbemncć, d 6.
bán, n 6.
banba, a 2, e 5, g 1, m 4, o 2, r 6, s 2, w 3, x 3.
banb, y 3.
bap n-, ı n.
bapp, y 2.
bapp(ȝacć), e 2; bapp(ȝlapp), v 2.
bap, ııı k; bapp, ıı k [*lege* lıap, -pp: *cf.* ımlıpcn, *pupillarum*, L. U. 105 b, l. 23].
báp, e 2, 3, f 3, o 2, u 1.
bacap, m 5.
(pop po)bc, ı c.
bcan, ı j.
bccan, ı d, e.
bcćc, 1 4, s 4.
beınb, ııı k; benb, ıı k.
bclȝaban, h 1.
bennaıȝ, ı m.
bcolu, ı d, e.
boben, ı b, ıı f, ııı f; bobenap, ıv a.
benȝ, k 6, o 5.
bennȝal, j 2, 3.
benpc, p 4.
benċaıb, o 5.
benup, ıı g; ııı g.
béċ, r 6, s 2, y 6.
boċ, ıı e; ııı e.
boċaıb, t 2.
bí, a 4.
bıó, ı g.
bıb, ı 2.
bıb, ıı a.

bınb, ıı j; v a; a 2, 1 2, s 2.
bınnup, ıv e.
bıċ, a 1.
bıċ (vb.), ıv a; v c.
bıċ(boc), k 1; bıċ(lan), q 2; bıċ-(maıċ), t 5.
bla, k 4, m 2.
blab, a 5, b 5, f 3, j 2, r 1, 6, s 5, y 1; -baıb, 1 5.
blaıb, g 4, h 5, ı 2, m 4, o 4, p 4, r 3, s 2.
(bıan)blaıb, w 5.
(ȝapȝ)blaıb, n 6.
blaıċbpapp, v b.
(apb)bláċc, t 6.
blıabaın (s.), a 5, d 1, f 1, 4, h, k 2, 1 6, n 2, 3, o 3, q 3, u 3, w 2, 5, x 3, y 1.
blıabaın (dual), d 2, m 1.
blıaban (g. p.), d 2, 6, e 2, f 2, 6, g 4, 6, h 4, 5, ı 1, 3, 4, j 2, 3, k 1, 3, 4, 1 5, m 1, 3, n 6, o 5, p 1, 2, 3, q 2, r 2, 3, 6, t 3, w 4, x 2, y 3.
blıabna (g. s.), x 1.
blıabna (p.), b 6, d 2, 3, 4, 5, e 1, 3, 4, 5, f 3, g 2, 3, h 3, 6, ı 6, j 1, 4, k 5, 6, 1 2, 4, m 2, 6, o 1, p 4, 5, q 5, 6, r 1, s 1, 2, 4, 5, 6, t 1, 4, 5, u 1, 2, 4, 5, v 1, 5, 6, w 1, 2, x 4, 5, y 2, 4.
blıabnaıb, j 6, s 2, v 2.
bo, (sb.), ı b; ıı f; boın, ı n.
bo (vb.), ııı c; 1 6, w 3, y 2.
bobaıpb, ııı a.
bobíbab, s 3; bobıbaċ, s 4.
bolȝ, c 2, 4; bolȝȝ, v 2.
bop, ı c; bopp, ııı f.
boċaıȝ, x 3.
bpaȝa, p 1.
bpap, ıı b; g 1.
bpaċ, r 6, s 2; bpaċa, 1 1.
bpaċaıp, c 5, t 4.

INDEX VERBORUM. (II.)

bratruaiḋ, e 5, 1 1.
breaṫa, ii g.
brecbuic, p 2.
brec, g 3, 1 4, m 3.
brec(buiḋneċ), m 3; -c(ḋuirnḋ), q 2.
bréc, b 6, t 4, y 1.
breẓ, r 3; -ẓa, j 2.
brecain, iii h.
breiṫ, iii g; (ŕíŋ)breiṫ, x 6.
brer, e 1.
breral, s 3, 4.
brerr, k 5; -rre, 1 2; -rri, k 6.
breċ, t 3.
briẓ, o 1.
briẓiḋ, iii g; briẓica, ii g.
robrir, b 4.
briċe, t 4.
broẓ, q 2.
broiẓ, i n.
bron, b 1, i 3, 1 3, y 1.
bruḋin, u 1.
bruiẓ, d 2.
brúiẓ, i k.
bruinne, p 1.
bu, v 1.
(o)bra, i d.
buaḃaill, ii k; iii k.
buaḋaiḋ, i k.
buaḋre, s 5.
buan, j 1, p 3, t 3; (conḋ)búain, u 5.
ḟolcḃuḋe, c 6.
buiḋe, iii j; -ḋi, ii j; iii k; -ḋi, i c.
buiḋneċ, f 6, m 3, o 1, w 4.
buiḋniḃ, m 1.
buille, p 1.
bur, i e.

'c(on) (prep.), s 4.
caċ, iii g; iv d, e; c 6, m 1, n 1.
caċ n-, ii 1; caiċ (gen.), i d, e.

Chacin, e 4.
caeḋ, u 1.
cael, p 2.
caém, o 4; u 4.
(ḟolc)caem, f 1; caem(ḋor), h 2.
Caemain, y 6.
rocaemcaiṫ, m 4.
caiḋi, i f.
Ċailli, i a.
caím, j 5.
ċaimme, h 1.
cain, 1 o; ii a; c 5, j 5, k 2, w 4, x 6.
(ḟolc)ċain, q 6; Cáinḋruim, e 2, n 2.
cainẓen, iii e; iv a; -ẓin, ii e; v c.
ḋoroċain, b 4, d 4, h 5, i 1, k 2, 3, 4, 15, m 2, n 2, 3, o 3, p 5, r 5, s 3, 5, v 1, 6, w 1, 2, 5, x 3, 6.
corċain, f 1, g 1, 2, h 2, j 1, u 3.
Cairn, k 6, o 1.
ċairn (g.), s 1.
Cairrceċ, x 3.
Cair, i 2.
cairr, q 5; ċairr, k 6, s 1.
rocaiṫ, b 6, d 4, j 1, 6, 15, m 4, n 1, o 6, p 4, 5, r 6, t 6, u 4, v 6, w 2.
calma, m 4, r 6, w 3; (raen)c-, o 2.
can, i e.
can (= cen), a 5, b 1, i 3.
cancain, i g.
(roḋa)caoin, h 4.
ċara, w 3; caraiṫ, j 5.
carḋ[ŕ]aiḋ, i i; carḋ[ŕ]aiṫ, i h.
Carmon, h 3; -uin, n 5.
carrḋeċ, r 5.
Carrne, x 2.
carṫ[ŕ]aiḋ, i i.
car, g 5; carr, ii j; iii j; r 5.
carḃarḋne, i g.
carḃairḋni, i e, g; carḃairni, i e.

cat, II c; III c; f 3, g 5, h 1, j 2, 1 1,
  5, 6, n 3, p 5, q 3, r 2, 6, t 6, v 3,
  w 3, 5, x 4, 5.
Catair, v 6.
catrad, b 5; catraig, b 4.
ceactar, i f.
Ceallaig, i m.
cean (cen, prep.), II c.
ceanb-impinb, i i.
ceč, b 5.
Ceòt, e 5, 6.
cectar n-, IV d.
cebaib, I a.
céim, n 4.
Coitnenb, e 3.
cel, b 3.
celg, I 6.
cein, III h.
cen, II h; III b, c; c 4, f 2, g 1, h 1,
  i 6, j 2, 1 3, 4, p 2, 6, q 1, 4, r 5,
  s 5, u 2, v 6, w 5, y 1, 6.
cenb, n 4; cenntrom, i m.
cenbač, i j.
čenelač, II a, i; III i.
čept, II a.
ceo, q 4.
bocer, h 1, 3, 6, i 3, j 2, 1 1, m 6,
  o 1, q 1, 2, 6, r 2, 6, s 1, 4,
  t 2, 5, v 2.
Cera, j 2.
Cermata, e 5.
Cermna, g 3, 4, 5.
cert, f 6, 1 3.
Cér-Chorainb, b 3.
Cerrair, a 3; Cerrra (g.), a 3.
cet (card.), a 5, b 2, 5, 6, j 5, 1 3.
cét (ord.), c 5, d 1, g 1, 4, i 4,
  o 2, 4.
rocetgab, a 2.
cet-pelláig, I m.
cetair, d 4, h 1, i 1, q 4, t 2, w 1.
cetarcubaib, IV a, c, d.

cetna (adj.), h 5.
cótna (num.), 1 2.
cotraca, a 2; -ramun, IV d.
cetri, IV d; b 2, d 2, e 3, f 4, g 3,
  k 5, 1 1, p 1, r 6, s 1, v 5, w 6,
  x 5, y 4.
cetrur, c 5.
ci(oe), III l.
cia (pron. interr.), I a; II i; III i.
cia (conj. concess.), p 5, w 3.
cialbrata, i f, i g.
cialla, r 4.
cian, p 1.
cib (conj.), x 2.
Cimbaeč, o 4.
Chinb, o 6.
chinbčaitt, u 5; Cinbmara, p 6.
ročinret, n 4.
Cir, i o.
clab, j 2.
claibeb, f 6.
claibemin, IV d.
ólainb, b 4, t 4.
cláir, w 1.
Claire, 1 5, n 5, p 5; Clare, n 5.
clanna, b 5.
Chlárrúigrig, s 5.
cló, 1 2.
(laam)ólerr, v 6.
cleč, h 3, n 1; cletgarg, q 3.
Clettig, w 6.
Cliac, n 5; Chliač (g.), t 6.
óliamain, w 2; óleamna, i j.
cliarač, u 4.
Chločair, m 2, o 6.
Clitair, i a.
olotaig, i 2.
cnáim, w 6.
[čnebl] i l.
Cnuča, v 3.
Chnuic, r 3.
co (conj. conseq.), i e; co r-, II m.

INDEX VERBORUM. (II.) 219

co (conj. temp.), b 1, 4, 6, c 6, d 1, 3,
  e 4, f 1, 6, g 1, h 2, j 1, l 3, n 1,
  o 5, p 3, r 1, t 1.
co m- (conj.), ɪ o.
co n- (conj.), ɪ f, o; ɪv d; v a.
co n- (conj. temp.), a 1, 5, 6, d 2, 3,
  f 5, g 2, i 4, u 2, 3, 4, y 1.
co (prep.), ɪ h, i; ɪɪ b; c 3, e 1, f 3,
  g 6, i 4, j 6, l 6, m 1, n 4, p 4,
  s 4, t 5, u 1, 4, y 5.
co m- (prep.), s 2; co n-, ɪɪɪ b; b 1, 6,
  e 5, k 2, o 5, q 6, w 1.
choılı, ɪ o.
Ċoıpı, ɪɪ h; Coıpı m-, ɪɪɪ h.
coımbeap, ɪ f.
Cobtać, p 2, 3; -aıʒ, p 4, q 1, 4.
ċobaıl, x 6; (pınb)ċobaıl, r 4.
Coclbab, y 1.
coem(boꞃꞃ), p 5.
ċoem(nenc), v 4; coem(pcıaċ), t 6.
cóıo, c 1, d 3, h 5, 6, i 1, m 4, 5,
  n 2, p 3, q 4, 5, r 6, s 5, 6, t 4, 5,
  u 2, 5, w 1, y 4; coıca, a 2;
  -aıc, a 3.
coıceb (sb.), c 4; (num.), c 4.
boċoıb, b 2.
coıcʒleann, ɪ j.
col, p 2.
colbtaċ, ɪ j.
Colla, x 5.
Collompaċ, r 4.
ımcolma, n 3.
Colum-cılle, ɪɪɪ h.
complaıt, m 5.
Comaıc, v 6.
ċombaıt, s 3.
Commaın, w 4.
compıʒc, q 6.
ċomul, ɪɪɪ g.
Con (g.), w 4.
'con (= oc ın), s 4.
Conaba, ɪɪ m; ɪv b; -bba, ɪɪɪ m.

Conaınb, b 4, 5, 6; -ʒ, m 5, 6, n 1.
Conaıpc, t 6, u 1, w 2.
Conall, r 4; Conaıll, ɪɪ a.
Conċobap, u 3.
Conb, w 1.
Conʒaıl, m 4, 5, n 1, s 5; -al, s 6.
conıb, ɪ f; c 5, x 5.
Conla, q 3, 4.
Conleamna, ɪ j.
Chonluaın, k 6.
Connaċt, ɪɪ c; ɪɪɪ c; h 5.
Conmacl, g 1; -maıl, f 6, g 6.
cop, ɪɪ j; ɪɪɪ j.
cop (= co n-, prep.), v a; v 1.
copepaı, ɪɪ a.
Copmac, w 5, 6.
Coponb, o 3.
ċopplac, ɪɪ a.
Coppꞃı, u 5.
ċopp, ɪ j.
coppan, ɪ o; coppanaċ, ɪ j, o.
Corepaċ, r 6.
cortabaıʒ, m 5.
cpáb, i 5.
cpaeb, o 1, p 2; cpaıbı, ɪɪ d.
cpaınb, ɪ h, i.
cpeċ, ɪ o.
cpeċ(bulıʒ), u 1; (pıal)cpeċaıʒ, i 1.
cpıaċpa, ɪɪ m; cpıaċpab, ɪɪɪ m.
cpıó, b 2.
Cpımtaınb (g.), s 1, u 3; -anb, r 6,
  u 4, y 2.
cpınmaınb, ɪ h, i.
Chpına, w 5.
cpınc, a 4.
cpo, ɪ e, g.
cpob, l 3.
Cpuacaın, h 5; -an, f 3.
cpuaıb, k 6, o 2, u 5, v 3, w 6.
cpuap, ɪ i.
Cpuınb, x 6.
cu (= co, prep.), ɪ n, x 6

TODD LECTURE SERIES, VOL. III.   R

INDEX VERBORUM. (II.)

boċuaban, ɪ o; bocuaıb, ɪ o.
cuaıpc, i 6.
poċuala, ɪ b.
Cualʒne, s 4.
cuane, r 3; cuanaıb, o 3.
cuıʒ, ɪ a.
Cuıl, a 3.
Cuıll, e 2.
Cuınb, x 6, w 3; Cuınn, ıı a.
Chuınn, u 6.
cuınnıb, m 1, x 2.
cuıpe, ɪ f, g.
cuıpcep, ıı j.
cumaıb, a 4; (cpom)cumaıb, u 3.
cumaıpc, ɪ e, g; ıı a, l.
cumapc, ɪ e, f; cumımupc, ııı l.
cumneċ, o 1, r 2, u 6; -nıʒ, m 1.
cumpaıbe, s 1.
cumul, ıı g.
cumunʒ, ıı f.
cu n- (for co n-; cuppaċ), r 4.
cupaċ, n 4.
cupab, n 4, s 3.
cupċaıp, ııı j.

b (pron. infix. 3 s), ɪ d, 1; d 1, 4, 6, g 3, h 4.
b' (= be, bı), ɪ a, j.
b' (= bo), t 4, v 1, 3, y 1.
b' (bo, pref. pcle.), (bıann)b'popca, ııı g.
ba (num.), ɪ f, g; ɪv c, d; b 5, 6, e 2, g 4, m 1, 3, 4, p 2, t 3, 6, x 2.
ba n- (num.), v 3.
b'a (bo a), ɪ c, t 1.
babcaċ, ɪ f, g.
Dabull, x 6.
baċel, ıı a.
baʒ, u 6, v 2; baʒblıaban, p 1; baʒlınb, j 3.
Daʒba, e 3.
baı[n]ʒen, ıı e; v c.
Daıleċ, s 6.
baıll, ɪ h, i.
baım (sb. col.), ɪ j, k.
Daıp, ɪ o.
Daıpbpe, ɪ 2.
baıc, n 3.
balb, g 3, y 3.
Dalca, t 1.
ban, ııı a.
bap (prep.), ɪ n; b 1, c 1, g 5, n 4.
bapbopb ?, p 5.
bapéıp, y 5.
baċ, i 6.
baca, ɪ f, g; bacca, a 5, c 3, 4, w 6, y 2.
[D]aċı, y 4.
be (prep.), ɪ e; a 3, 4, b 2, 3, d 2, f 5, s 1, 2, t 2.
be (be and pron. suf. 3 s. masc.), ɪ p; (neut.) ɪv d.
beaċneb, ıı g; beċneb, ıı h.
bealʒ, ıı 1; belʒ, ııı 1.
bealcaċ, ıı a, j.
beamnab, ɪ f.
beappnaım, ıı l.
bebaıb, b 3; -uıb, n 2.
bebeċe, ıı d; -ċı, ıı a, c, f, i, j, k, l.
bebıŀe, ɪ i, j, k, l; ııı c, d, e; ɪv b, c, d; v b; -ŀe, ıı b, e, m.
bebıŀe, ıı a; -ŀı, ıı a.
bebıbı, ɪ m, n; ııı a, b; v a; -ŀı, ıı a.
bebıbıb, ɪ o; -ŀıb, ıı a.
béc (num.), a 5, b 6, d 5, f 2, i 1, j 3, m 1, n 3, p 4, 5, q 1, r 2, s 6, t 3, 4, u 4, v 2, x 4, y 2, 5.
beċıb, g 2.
beċubaıb, ıı a.
becubeb, ııı g, f; ɪv f; beċ-, ɪv g.
Debaıb, s 6; -aıʒ, t 1.
bebʒaıp, u 2.

INDEX VERBORUM. (II.)

ḋeġ, j 4, x 6; ḋeġ(ḃail), i 5; ḋeġ-
(ġnáṫ), u 1; ḋéġ(maiṫ), p 4, u 4;
ḋeġ(ṗí), p 5.
ḋeiḃeṫi, II a.
ḋeiḃiḋe, I a, c, h, i; IV e; -ḋe, I b;
-ḋi, I c, f; -ḋi, I e; II a.
ḋeiḃiḋiḃ, I a.
ḋeiċ (num.), e 4, f 5, g 1, i 3, 4, 5, 6,
k 5, l 5, n 6, p 1, 3, q 3, 6, s 2,
v 3, w 6, x 2, 6.
ḋeiċ ṁ-, u 1.
ḋeileḋ, b 4.
ḋéin (adj.), m 1; ḋein (vb.), II m.
ḋeineoil, I a.
ḋeirimpeċṫ, IV f; ḋeirṁipeċṫ, I i.
ḋeiṫ (ḋo, prep. and pron. suf. 2 s.), III a.
ḋeiṫḃen, I f.
Ḋelḃaeṫ, e 4.
ḋeliuġuḋ, I g.
ḋene [ḋein], III m.
ḋeoċaiḋ, y 1.
ḋenġ, e 3, g 6, 1 6, m 6, o 5.
(niġ)ḋenġ, p 6; ḋenġ(ḃail), i 5.
ḋepnaḋ, i 4; ḋepnṗaḋan, I o.
ḋepnnuim, III l.
Ḋer, c 3.
ḋi (prep.), y 6.
ḋi (ḋi and pron. suf. 3 s. fem.), i i; d 2.
(ṗa)ḋí, h 3.
ḋi(aer), I c; ḋi(aeiṗ), o 5.
ḋia (ḋo and a rel.), II c; III c.
ḋia (ḋo and a poss.), h 6, t 4.
ḋia (conj. temp.), j 5.
ḋiaċ, a 1.
ḋiaiḋ, I o.
ḋialṫ, IV d; ḋialṫa, III j.
ḋian, II g; ḋian(ḃlaiḋ), w 5; ḋian
(ġliċċ), u 2; ḋiann(ḋṗonṫa),
III g.
Ḋianċeṫṫ, e 2.
Ḋiaṗmaḋa, I f, g.
ḋiġ, ṫ 3, x 5, y 2.

ḋiġlaim, I h, i.
ḋil, e 4.
ḋiliṅḋ, a 2, 5.
ḋinġḃail, I h, i.
ḋinḋ, III b; IV a, d, e.
ḋinṗan, II h; III h.
Ḋiṫonḃa, o 3.
ḋó (num.), h 2.
ḋo (poss. 2 s.), I j, l; II a, g; III d.
ḋo (prep.), I i, k, o; II f, m; III f, h;
a 5, b 2, d 4, e 2, 3, f 1, h 4, 5, 6,
i 6, k 4, 1 1, n 6, o 4, 5, q 3, r 3,
6, s 2, 3, 6, t 2, u 2, 3, y 2, 3, 4.
ḋo (= ḋe, ḋi), I c; II a, k; III k; a 3,
4, d 5, e 1, 6, f 1, 6, s 4, 5, t 5,
u 3, v 2, w 2.
ḋo (= ḋo and pron. suf. 3 s. m.), I b;
II f; e 1, t 4.
ḋo (vbl. pcle.), ḋoḃen, I b; II f; III f;
ḋoḃeṗan, IV a; ḋoċoiḋ, b 2;
ḋoċuaiḋ, I o; ḋoċuaḋan, I o;
ḋo ḋinġḃail, I h, i; ḋoṗala, I c;
ḋomṗala, II h; ṗomlaṗa, III h;
ḋo leṗṗaḋ, I l; ḋo mannṗaḋ,
II c; III c; ḋoṗaṫ, l 3, q 1; ḋo-
ṗaṫṗaṫ, c 5; ḋoṗomuṗ [ḋo[ṗ]-
ṗoinuṗ, II e; ḋo ṫṗiall, I o.
ḋoċeil, IV b.
ḋoċum, II d.
ḋe(ḋeaḃaiḋ), III b; ḋo(ḋeḃaiḋ), II b.
ḋóiġ, s 6.
ḋoiṫ, i 3.
ḋoiṗṗṗeoṗaṫṫ, II m; III m.
ḋolam, I l.
Ḋomnanḋ, c 1, 3.
ḋo(muinṫiṗ), I l.
ḋo'n (ḋe in), e 4; (ḋo in) a 5, d 1,
h 4, o 5.
ḋo'nḋ (ḋe inḋ), 1 1.
Ḋhonnċaiḋ, II a.
ḋonḋ, o 3.
ḋonṫo, II c, i.

R 2

INDEX VERBORUM. (II.)

donoinde, ɪ c; dronta, ɪɪ g; ɪɪɪ g.
donomur [do[ḟ]roinur], ɪɪ e.
dono, ɪv d.
donndan, ɪ a.
donur, ɪɪ e; v c.
dor, f 2; dorr, p 6.
doc' (do, prep. and poss. 2 s.), ɪ k.
dreċ(deiṅġ), b 4; drec(mair), q 5.
drend, e 3.
druiṅġ, b 5.
druad, ɪɪ h; ɪɪɪ h.
druim, ɪɪ j; ɪɪɪ j.
du (for do, vbl. pcle.), durtuiġedar, ɪɪɪ d.
Duaċ, 1 4, 5, 6, m 1, n 6, s 6, t 1.
duaine, ɪv d.
duan, ɪv d; -na, ɪ b; -aid, ɪ k.
duanbairdne, ɪv a.
Dubdetaċ, w 5.
dúib, c 6.
Duib-ċommuir, x 5.
duind, ɪɪ a.
duind, b 3.
duine, ɪ f, g; duni, a 1.
duirb, q 5.
duirnd, q 2.
duit (do and pron. suf., 2 s.), ɪ c.
(creċ)duliġ, u 1.
Dumu, d 1.
dún, g 5, k 1.
durġlar, ɪɪ b.
dutaiġ, ɪ b.

e (pron.), ɪ a, e, g; ɪɪ c; ɪɪɪ c; ɪv d; c 5, 1 4, q 5, y 5.
eaċ, ɪɪ d.
ead, ɪ e.
Camain, ɪ f, i; -an, ɪ i; Cinna, o 4.
heamna (g.), ɪ g.
Catan, ɪɪ i.
ebailt, u 4.

Cben, e 6, f 1; -ir, f 4, g 1, 4.
Cbric, g 3, 4.
éc, b 2, e 1, f 2, i 4, o 4, r 3, s 2, u 5, 6, y 1; éca, 1 4.
eċ, d 6, f 6; ciċ (gen.), ɪ d, e; coċu, ɪ b.
Cċaċ, g 6, h 2; Cċaid, g 6, t 2; -aiġ, g 5.
ecbáne, d 1.
ecer, i 4; eicriu, v a.
ecoittcenn, ɪ l; ecc-, ɪ k.
ecnaċ, w 5.
(ro)ecne, o 2.
eċt, e 2.
Cċtġa, ɪ n.
eċtra, u 4.
ed, 1 5, x 1.
Cdail, ɪ o.
edar, ɪɪɪ i.
Cdne, q 1.
edroċt, ɪɪ k.
Circ, d 5.
eiriġ, ɪɪ a.
(dia)éir, o 5.
elaċ, y 3.
Claban, e 1.
ele, ɪ i.
Cllim, k 2, v 2, 3.
(ro)emna, v 1.
én, ɪɪ j; ɪɪɪ j.
henaran, ɪɪ i.
Cnna, h 3, 4, 1 6, m 2, r 6; he-, r 5.
Cocaid, 1 1, m 3, q 6, t 4, y 1, y 3; -aiġ, i 6.
Coco, m 5, n 4, 5, r 1, t 3, x 1, y 1; -cu, d 5, e 3, g 3, 1 1, m 4, 6.
Coġan, e 4.
erbailt, a 6, d 2, f 5, g 2, v 5.
er(brar), ɪɪɪ b; er(ġlar), ɪɪɪ b.
Crend, g 3, 4; hC-, t 6; hCrenn, d 1; y 6.
hCrimoin, e 6, f 1; -én, f 2.

INDEX VERBORUM. (II.)   223

Cpınꞓ, a 5, 6, ꝺ 5, 6, k 2, r 5, v 1, 3,
   x 1; hC-, s 1, 4, y 5.
Cpınn, c 5; -ıu, f 2; hCpıu, a 1,
   b 1, f 2, y 5.
éppaꞓꞓ, u 2.
ep (ꝺı a ep), ı c.
epꞓıꝺ, c 6.
épın, ꝺ 5.
Cpp-ꞃuaꝺ, o 2.
eꞓ (eꝺ), ıı g; heꞓ, ıı g.
Cꞓan, ıı ı; ııı ı.
éꞓap, ıı ı.
eꞓep, ı e, 1; ııı a.
Cꞓepꞃcel, ꞓ 5.
éꞓzuꝺaꞓ, g 3.
Cꞓꞃıel, f 6.
eꞓꞃoꞓꞓ, ııı k.
eꞓꞓız, w 6.

ꝼa(= ꝼo), h 3, 4, ı 1, j 4, k 4, q 4.
ꝼa, w 1.
ꝼaꝺaıꞃ, h 1.
(ꝼ)aca, ı ꝺ, e.
ꝼaꞓꞓna, ꞓ 1, 2.
(ꝼaeꝺuꞃ)zlaꞃ, g 5.
ꝼaıꝺ, f 4, 5.
ꝼáıl, ı 5, j 5, k 4, s 2; ꝼaıl-ınꞃe, o 3.
ꝼaıꞃꝼaızıꝺ, ı e.
ꝼaıꞃınꝺ, ı a.
ꝼaıꞓꞃea, ıı ı.
ꝼaꝺa, ı f.
ꝼálıꝺ, y 6.
ꝼanꝺ, c 1.
ꝼáꞃ, b 1.
ꝼaꞃaıꝺ, ı g; ꝼaꞃann, ı ı; -aꞃ, ı e, ı.
ꝼaꞓ, a 4, c 1.
ꝼaꞓ, ı 2, j 2; ꝼaꞓa, ı g; ıı a;
   (lam)ꝼ-, w 6.
ꝼaꞓaꞓ, a 2, ꞓ 1.
ꝼcaꞓꞓuꞃ, ı o.
ꝼeaꞃ, ıı ꝺ, ı.

ꝼeaꞃaıꝺ, ı a.
ꝼeaꞃz, ıı 1; ꝼcꞃz, ııı 1; b 4; -zz,
   m 6.
[ꝼ]eaꞃꞓan, ı a.
ꝼeꝺaıl, b 3.
ꝼeꝺlımeꞓ, ıı c; -lımıꝺ, ııı c; -mıꝺ,
   ıv ꝺ; ꝼeıꝺlımıꝺ, v 5.
ꝼéıc, j 2.
ꝼeıꝺleꞓ, ꞓ 3; -lız, ꞓ 2.
ꝼéız, o 6.
ꝼéın (ac.), v 6; ꝼene, h 1.
ꝼeıꞓ, x 4.
ꞃoꝼeıꞓ, k 5, w 6.
(noꝺoꞃ)ꝼeıꞓ, v 3.
ꝼell, ııı a.
ꝼeluꞃ, ıv ꝺ.
ꝼemın, w 2.
(ꝼınn)ꝼennıꝺ, f 4.
ꝼeꞃ (n. s.), r 4 (g. p.), c 2, 4, g 2, ꞓ 5;
   (g. p.), c 2, 4, q 2; -aıꝺ, c 2.
ꝼeꞃaꝺaız, u 6.
ꝼeꞃamaıl, r 4; ꝼeꞃꝺa, v 1.
ꝼeꞃceꞃ, w 4.
ꝼeꞃcoꞃꝺꝺ, q 2.
ꝼcꞃzuꞃ, b 1, 4, r 1, w 5.
ꝼeꞃꞃ, ı 4; ꞃoꝼeꞃꞃ, k 5.
ꝼéꞓa, n 3.
ꞃoꝼeꞓeꞃ, ıı ı.
ꝼıaꞓa, g 6, h 1, ı 1, x 4, 5; -ꞓac, e 4,
   ı 1, v 1, x 6; -ꞓaız, v 1.
ꝼıaꞓna, v 2.
ꝼıaꞓꞃa, n 2; -ꞃaꞓ, ꝺ 3; -ꞃaız, ꝺ 3.
ꝼıaꝺmoın, ı n.
ꝼıal, r 1; ꝼıalcꞃeꞓaız, ı 1.
ꝼıannaıꝺ, o 3, v 2.
ꝼıaꞃꝼaızıꝺ, ı ꝺ.
ꝼıꞓe, ꝺ 6, f 6, g 6, h 1, o 4, r 1, u 6,
   y 3; -ꞓeꞓ, e 5, q 5, u 3, v 6,
   x 4.
ꝼıꞓeaꞃ, ıı h.
ꝼıꞓı, b 2, j 2, 1 3, n 1, o 3, ꞓ 2; -ꝺıꞓ,
   a 2, e 2, 3, g 4, o 6, r 3, y 5.

INDEX VERBORUM. (II.)

fioib (vb.), f 5.
ficcib; k 4.
fiḃ, i n.
fileb, i o; fili, i c.
finb, e 3, g 5, 14, u 6, w 2, x 3.
finb(ċobail), r 4; fínb(ʒaill), ii a.
finb(ʒil), e 4; finb(ʒualainb), iii k.
finb(nain), i h, i.
Finb, 1 1, 2, n 3, t 2, v 1.
Finbmuine, m 6.
finʒail, x 4.
finn, ii k.
finnḟennib, f 4.
Finnaċta, i 5, j 1.
finnaib, d 3.
Fincan, a 2, 4; -ain, o 4.
Fincaic, s 3, 4.
fír, c 6, v 5, y 5.
fír(bliʒeb), iii a; fír(breit), x 6.
fir(buib), ii j; iii j.
Fir, c 1, 3, 4.
nofirab, s 3.
Fhirċorb, q 3; -ċuirr, q 5, 6.
fire, a 4.
firt, ii d.
firib, i f.
fir, ii k; iii k.
ḟicir, a 1.
Flaimb, i h, i; Flann, i c.
flaiṫ, iii g; iv f; c 2, d 2, f 4, g 1, h 1, m 4, t 6, w 2.
flaiṫ[iur], i 1; (anb)flaiṫ, u 1.
(com)flaiṫ, m 5; fir[ḟ]laiṫ, n 3.
Flannacain, i m.
flaṫa, i h, i; ii g; h 2, i 2, j 2, 1 2.
flaṫiur, d 5, 6, g 6, u 6.
flebe, p 3; (anb)ḟlebaċ, y 3.
Flibair, q 6.
fo, i o; ii k; iii k; 1 2, q 6, v 1.
foċael, i c; foċeil, ii m; iii m,

fob, iii a.
fobail, iv c; fobla, iv a.
Foblai, ii a.
folc, ii k; iii k; -cbube, c 6; -coaem, f 1; Folcċáin, q 6.
for, i o; ii a; iii g, k; iv a, b; c 2, h 2, i 4, 6; j 2, 1 6, n 1, q 1, u 1, v 2, 4, y 3.
forba, iv d.
forbure, i o.
forcenbair, iv d.
forbalaċ, i n.
Forʒna, f 4.
forleaċan, i k; forlán, d 2.
Formaili, 1 2.
Foron, f 4.
fornain, i o; w 4.
forrin, ii e; iii e.
Forcamail, r 1.
fornill, ii a.
foṫ, h 2, 1 2.
foṫa, ii a, c, g; iii c, g; iv d, f; e 1, y 2.
Foṫaċ, x 3; -aiʒ (g. s.), x 4; (ac. s.) x 3; (n. p.) x 3.
Foṫla, c 6.
fnar, ii b.
Fnemainb, t 4.
Fneċam[-ain], i o.
fri, i f, g; ii a, f, 1; iii f, h, 1; iv a; c 3, w 3.
[f]ri, i g; fria, q 5; frirín, iv a, c; v c.
frirnaiʒ, ii b; iii b.
friċarʒain, w 4.
fuair, a 1, i 5, j 4, 5, 14, 6, m 3, r 1, 5, s 6, t 3, 5, v 3, w 4, x 5, y 2.
fuba, iv e.
fuirri (for, prep. and pron. suf.) 3 s. fem.), iv d.

INDEX VERBORUM. (II.)

ɴoɢaḃ, ɪ c; ɴaɢaıḃ, a 2, 5, c 5, ʏ 5;
   ɢaḃaıl, ɪ m.
Ɠaḃaıɴ, x 2.
ɢaḃaıɴ, ᴋ 2; -aɴ, c 2; -uɴ, ɪ d.
ɢaḃɴaᴄ, c 3; ɴoɢaḃɴaᴄaɴ, x 3.
ɢaċa, ɪᴠ d.
ɢaċ ɴ-, ɪɪɪ l.
ɢae (cıa), ɪɪ l.
Ɠaelıaɴ, c 4.
ɢaeᴄ, ɪ a; ɪᴠ o.
(ḃaɴɴ)ɢaeᴄ, e 2; (ɢaɴḃ)ɢaeᴄ, d 1.
ɴoɢaeᴄ, d 5.
ɢaıl, f 5, j 3.
ɢaıll-meıɴɢıḃ, ɪ n.
ɢaıɴɴe, ʏ 6.
ɢaíɴ, ɪɪ j; ɪɪɪ j.
ɴoɢaıɴḃ, s 1.
ɢaıɴeaɴ, ɪɪ j; -ɴeɴ, ɪɪɪ j.
ɢaíɴeᴄ, ɪɪ a, b, d, h; ɪᴠ c, d, e; -ɴıḃ,
   ɪɪɪ d; -ɴıᴄ, ɪɪɪ b, h; ɪᴠ e, g.
ɢaıɴm, ɪɪ e; ᴠ c.
ɢaíᴄ, f 5, j 3.
ɢal ɴ- (g. p.), ʏ 5; ɢalaıɢ, a 5.
ɢalaɴ, d 1, f 5.
Ɠalıuıɴ, c 1.
ɢallıɴḃ, b 3.
ɢaɴ, ɪ d.
Ɠaɴḃ, ɪ c (pr. name), a 3, o 3, d 2.
ɢaɴḃ, d 1.
ɢaɴɢ(ḃlaıḃ), n 6; (clec)ɢaɴɢ, q 3;
   (moɴ)ɢaɴɢ, 1 3; ɢaɴɢ(ɢɴım),
   ʏ 6.
ɢaɴɴ, ɪɪɪ a.
ɢaɴᴄ, ᴋ 3.
(ıɴ)ɢaɴᴄa, j 1.
ɢeaɴɴ, ɪ j.
Ɠeḃe, j 1, 3.
ɢeıḃ, ɪ n; ɪɪ l; ɪɪɪ a; ɴoıɴɢeḃ, ɪɪɪ l.
ɢeıɴᴄıḃ, ɪ n.
(laɴ)ɢeıɴ, o 6.
ɢeıɴıḃ, ɪ a.
ɢeᴄaɴ, ʏ 4; -aɴ, ᴋ 1.

ɢeɴ [ɢaeᴄ], ɪɪɪ b.
Ɠeɴaɴḃ, c 3, d 2.
ɢeɴɴ, j 2.
ɴomɢıal, ʏ 6; ɴoɢıallaḃ, e 1, h 5,
   ᴋ 3, n 6, t 3, x 1, 2, ʏ 4.
ɢıallaıḃ, ᴋ 2; ɴoɢ-, 1 6.
Ɠıallċaḃ, ᴋ 3.
ɢılla, ᴡ 5, ʏ 6; -e, ʏ 6.
ɢlaᴄᴄ (sb.), ᴡ 5, x 1; ɴoɢlaᴄᴄ (vb.),
   q 5, ᴡ 3.
ɢlaıᴄ (sb.), s 5.
ɢlaɴ, ɪ a; ɪɪ j; ɪɪɪ j; a 6, n 1, o 3;
   ɢlaıɴ, n 6; ɪmɢ-, f 1.
ɢlaɴ, ɪɪ b; ɪɪɪ b; ɪᴠ c; ḃaɴɴɢ-, ᴠ 2;
   ɴaeḃuɴɢ-, g 5; moɴɢ-, c 1.
ɢle, o 3.
ɢleıᴄᴄ, j 3.
ɢleıᴄ, ɪ e; ɢleᴄ, ɪ d.
(ḃıaɴ)ɢlıᴄᴄ, u 2.
ɢloɴ, a 5.
ɢɴaıᴄe, ɪᴠ d.
(ḃeɢ)ɢɴáċ, u 1; ɢɴaċaıɢċeɴ, ᴠ b.
ɢɴe, ɪᴠ d; ɢɴe u-, ɪᴠ b.
ɢɴım, a 1, ʏ 6.
(hımmaɴ)ɢó, ᴋ 4.
ɢoɴɴa, x 1.
Ɠɴec, a 6; -eıc, b 5.
ɢɴéıɴ, ɪɪɪ h; -e[ı]ɴ, ɪɪ h.
Ɠɴeɴe, e 5, 6.
ɢɴıaɴ-ɴɴoıll, ɪ n.
ɢɴıɴḃ, a 6, j 3, ᴋ 3, ʏ 5;   ımɢ-,
   n 5.
ɢuılḃneaċ, ɪɪ a, j, ᴋ; ɪɪɪ j, ᴋ.
ɢuılḃneɴ, ɪɪɪ j.
ɢulḃaıɴḃ, ɪɪ ᴋ; -ḃaɴ, ɪɪ j.
Ɠunnaᴄ, x 1.
ɢuċ, ɪɪ j; ɪɪɪ j.

ha, ɪ g.
hÁeḃ, o 1.
hÁeı, ɪᴠ d.

INDEX VERBORUM. (II.)

haıbıb, c 6.
he, ıv f.
hamaıpʒen, e 6.
hapc, k 3.
heamna, ı g.
henapan, ıı i.
hcnna, h 3, 4.
hcpenb, g 2; -nn, y 6.
hcpımaın, e 6, f 1; -ón, f 1, 2.
hcpınb, a 5, 6, c 3, k 2, y 5; -nn, c 4, d 1, 5, 6.
hcpın, a 1, b 1, f 2, y 5.
heċ (heb), ıı g.
hı, v b; c 1.
hımmapbnéc, b 6.
hımmapʒo, k 4.
hımpoù, ı g.
hımpınb, ı f.
hınʒın (ac.), y 2.
hoen, a 6.
hlla, ı h, i; a 1, s 5, v 6, x 6.
hlli, ıı a; e 2.

ı (g. s.), ı m.
ı (pron. pers. 3 s. fem.), ı f, h; h 1, v b.
ı (prep.), ı a, e; ıı m; ıv d; a 3, b 2, 3, c 1, e 2, 6, f 3, g 3, h 1, 3, i 3, j 2, l 5, m 1, 5, n 2, 3, o 3, p 2, q 6, r 2, 3, 6, t 4, 6, v 3, w 3, 5, 6, x 4, 5, y 1, 4.
ı (in which), g 2.
ı (ıll- = ı n-l-), u 6.
ı m- (n assim. to m), f 3, 5, h 4, i 2, 5, 6, v 2.
ı n- (prep.), ı g, o; ıv d; v b; a 3, 4, 6, c 2, d 1, 5, 6, f 2, j 6, k 6, n 5, o 2, r 1, s 2, t 5, x 1, y 2.
ı p- (n assimilated to p), c 3, e 5, f 1, 6, m 2, p 2, t 1, 2.
ı(pın), t 3, v 4.
ıáıċ, w 6.

ıap, ı a; a 5, b 1, j 5, t 4, x 4, 5.
ıap pem, d 3; ıap pın, m 6.
ıapam, o 5; ıapma, e 3; ıapum, k 4.
ıapbonel, b 3.
ıapcomapc, ıv d.
ıappoċaċ, x 4.
ıápla, w 1.
ıapnbonb, m 2.
ıapnoın, ı n.
ıapcaın, a 5, f 1.
ıc (prep.), c 4, p 3, x 6; ıʒ, ı f, g.
ıb, ı f.
ıbcp, ı g; ıbıp, ı f.
ıbon, ı g; ııı a, g, j; ıv a, b, c, d.
ım, ı i, n; ııı a; ımm, ııı h.
ımamnapp, v 2.
ımcenn, ııı a.
ımċolma, n 3; ımʒlaın, f 1.
ımba, ı f, g.
ımʒpınb, n 5; ımláın, v 3.
ımleċ, k 3; -ċa, k 4; -lıċ, k 5; -lıʒ, s 5.
ımmaċ, t 1.
hımmapbnéc, b 6; hımmapʒo, k 4.
ımmap, ıı l [ınmap].
ımmelban, i 2; ımmelʒlaıp, s 1.
ımnap, v 5.
ımoppo, ı a.
hımpoù, ı g
ımpınb, ı e, f, h, i, k, m, n, o; ıı a; ııı a, b; v a; -pınn, ıv c.
ın (art. nom., gen., ac., masc., fem.), ı a, d, e, f, h, i, k, l, m; ıı b, c, d, h, j, o; ııı c, d, g; ıv a, c, d, f; a 5, b 2, c 2, 4, 5, d 5, e 3, f 5, g 5, h 2, 3, 6, i 3, j 3, k 1, 6, m 2, 5, n 3, o 1, p 1, 2, 3, q 5, r 2, 5, s 1, 3, t 2, 4, 5, u 4, 5, w 3, 6, x 1, y 2, 4.
(app)ın, b 5; (ıpp)ın, d 2, g 2, h 5.
ıpın, p 3, t 3.
(lapp)ın, h 2.

INDEX VERBORUM. (II.)

ın b- (art.), ɪv c; v b.
ın c- (art.nom., gen., dat., masc., neut.),
 ɪ b; ɪɪ j; ɪɪɪ j; ın c- (art.), h 3,
 k 1, 14, t 3.
ınbaıᵹ, x 4.
ınbɪp, e 4.
íncel, u 1.
ınb (art. n. s. masc.), v b; (g. s. masc.),
 ɪɪɪ j; 12, w 6; (neut.), t 1; (fem.),
 f 2; (dat. s. fem.), r 5, s 1.
ınb (ɪ and pron. suf. 3 s. neut.), ɪ k.
ınbapaıb [ınb apaıb], ɪ 5.
ınbɪ, ɪ b; ɪɪ f.
ınblɪm, v a.
ınᵹ, 1 4.
ınᵹanca, j 1.
ınᵹen, a 2; hınᵹın, y 2.
ıṅᵹnacać, a 2.
ımallᵹupa, ɪ c.
ınɪp, a 1, ɪ 5.
ınmaın, ɪɪ k; ɪɪɪ k.
ınnmup, ɪɪɪ l.
ınn (art.), ɪɪ b; e 6, q 3.
ınnaıᵹ, ɪɪ b.
ı[n]napb, x 5; ınnapbpac, n 4.
ρo ınnıpıup, c 6.
ınpe, o 3.
ınpo, ɪɪ k.
ınunn, ɪv d.
ıpaıᵹ, c 3.
ıpbaıpc, q 4.
ıpeρeo, q 2, 4.
ıpıel, f 5; ıpıcoıl, f 6.
ıp (vb.), ɪ b, e, f, g, h, i, l, o; ɪɪ c, e,
 f, h; ɪɪɪ a, c, e, h; ɪv a, d, e, g;
 v a, b, c; v 5, u 6, y 5.
ıp (abbrev. of ocup), ɪ f, g, o; ɪɪ g, j,
 k, m; ɪɪɪ b, j; a 2, b 6, f 1, 3,
 n 6, o 3, 4, 6, r 3, s 2, u 6, w 2, 4.
(ıp)ın (art.), ɪɪɪ g; ɪv f; v 4.
ıpın c-, ɪɪ j.
ıućpa, ɪ j.

lá (sb.), a 2.
la (prep.), ɪɪɪ m; ɪv e; b 3, 4, d 3, 4,
 e 6, f 4, g 1, 5, h 5, ɪ 3, j 2, 4,
 k 2, 3, 4, 5, 11, 2, 3, 4, 5, 6, m 2,
 3, 6, n 2, 3, o 1, 5, p 2, q 1, 2, 6,
 r 1, 2, 5, 6, t 2, 5, 6, u 1, 3, v 1,
 2, 6, w 1, 4, 5, x 5, 6.
bopala, ɪ c; bompala, ɪɪ h; ρom-
 lapa, ɪɪɪ h.
Labpaıb, p 3, 4; -ρaba, p 6.
Labpaınne, g 6, h 1.
Labᵹaıp, n 6.
Labpu, a 2, 3; Labpanb (g.), a 3,
 f 3.
Laeć, d 1, e 2, j 5, p 4, u 1, w 6;
 -óba, n 2; Laećpećca, u 4.
Laeᵹaıpe, p 2.
Laíć, b 1.
(ρo)Laíć, f 5.
Laıb, ɪ o.
Laıbeć, o 1; -bıᵹ, o 6.
Laíᵹne, f 3.
Laım, e 4, 6, s 1, 4, w 2; Lam, c 3.
Laınn, m 6.
Laıp, ɪ j.
Laıćı, ɪɪ c.
Lam(beρᵹ), m 6; Lam(ṗaca), w 6.
Lamíab, a 1.
Lan, u 5; Lan(comup), ɪv d;
 (bıc)lán, q 2; (ρoρ)lan, d 2.
Lanb, f 3.
Lan(ᵹeıρ), o 6; Lan(maıc), d 5.
láρ, v 4.
Lapa (La and a, rel.), ɪɪɪ i.
Lapın, s 3, 6, x 3; Laρρın, h 2.
Lacc, x 4.
Leaρ, ɪɪ e; ɪɪɪ e.
[ρ]lećc, b 3; [ρ]lcóca, f 4.
léıρ, s 5.
Leıć, u 6.
Leρᵹ, g 6.
Leρp, v c; Leρpab, ɪ 1.

INDEX VERBORUM. (II.)

lect, n 1; lectbliabain, f 4.
lí, p 5.
liata[i]n, b 2; liatanaig (gen.), i d, e; liatpuim, u 6.
liatpoici, i j.
lib (la and pr. suf. 2 p.), k 5.
lín, i a; y 5; polín, o 1.
linb, b 1, j 3, u 6.
line, v 4.
linn [binn], iii j.
linni (la and pr. suf. 1 p.), x 2.
lipp, m 1.
ló, j 5.
palocpab, p 2.
loingrec, p 4.
paloipc, k 1, p 3, t 4; poloipc, y 4.
longepp, j 2; longpib, c 1.
luab, iii f; luag, ii f.
luaiger, ii b; iii b, h [luaiber].
luagne, s 4, 5, v 6.
luam(clepp), v 6.
luapcac, i o.
lubain, i j.
lucc, a 2.
lug, e 2.
lugac, ii d; -gaib, n 4, 6, o 1, s 5, u 2, 3, w 3, 4, x 1; -gbac, m 1; -gbec, n 1, 2, o 6, u 4, 6, w 4.
luib, b 4.
luigne, f 3.
luin, ii j; iii j.
luipc, p 2.

m (pron. infix., 1 s.), nomgeb, iii 1; bompala, ii h; pomlapa, iii h.
m (pron. infix. 3 s. masc.), pombaib, w 6; (neut.), pomgial, y 6.
mac (n. d. ac.), i o; ii m; iii m; iv b; b 4, d 5, e 1, 2, 6, f 6, g 1, 3, 4, 6, i 3, 5, 6, j 1, 3, 4, k 2, 3, 5, 1 2, 4, 5, 6, m 1, 2, n 1, 2, 3, 5, o 1, 2, 6, p 6, q 1, 2, 5, 6, s 6, t 2, u 4, v 4, 5, w 1, 3, 4, x 1, 6, y 6.

mac (dual), g 4, m 5; maccaib, b 1, m 4.
maca, i 5, o 5.
ma[b], ii g; mab, iii g.
Mael-pabaill, ii k; iii k.
Mhaenaig, ii m; iii m.
mag, o 1.
Mage, 1 5.
magen, a 1.
maibm, i n; b 5; pomabaib, x 2.
Maig, f 3, 5, h 4, i 2, 5, v 2; -ge, o 2, 6.
maigpi, i j.
mail, i h, i; w 1.
Main, h 4.
maine, i k.
maip, q 4.
maic, iii k; p 1, 5, r 2, s 3, t 3, u 6. (beg)maic, p 4, u 4; (lan)maic, d 5. (pu)maic (vb.), h 6.
mál, v 4, 5.
mall, a 4.
malle (aphaeresis of i), e 5.
mannpab, ii c; iii c.
máp, s 3.
map (conj.), s 3.
mapb, a 4, m 1; pomapb, g 6, i 5, p 1, 4, t 1, v 4, 5, x 5, y 1, 3.
pobmapb, i 1; d 1, 4, 6, g 3; popmapb, e 4, o 5.
mapb[t]a, b 3, d 2; pomapbta, f 3.
mapoen, f 1, y 3.
mapp, c 1.
(apb)maciup, d 6.
mebon, i 6.
meic (n. p.), b 2, e 5, f 3, 4.
Meilge, q 1.
Melge, p 4, 5, q 2.
meingg, p 6.
(po)méic, e 1.
mi, 1 6.
miab, p 1.

INDEX VERBORUM. (II.)   229

níbia [m-bia], iii i.
mic (g.), iii a; a 4, e 1, g 4, 6, j 3,
　k 6, p 6, q 1, s 4, w 1, 2, 4, x 1;
　mic (voc.), i j, m, n.
Mibe, ii c; w 1; -ói, iii c.
mile, a 6.
milet, i 1.
milib, h 6.
milip, i 5.
minb, g 5.
mine, ii m; iii m.
Mipp, m 1.
mo (poss. 1 s.), ii 1; iii 1.
mob, iii m; -ba, ii m.
Mozconb, p 5, 6, q 2; Moza-
　cuipb, q 2.
mozba, q 4.
moin, i a.
móip (gen. ac.), i a, e, h, i, n;
　pomóip, s 6.
molbtac, a 1.
monzaic, t 3.
monup, ii c; iii c.
mop, ii d, k; iii k; a 1, b 1, e 2, f 4,
　g 1, o 4.
mopbuibnib, m 1; mopzapz, i 3;
　mopzlapp, c 1.
mopainb, i i; -nn, i h.
Mopainb, u 5.
Mopc, b 4.
Muabe, f 5.
Mucpama, w 3.
Muzmebón, y 1.
pomubaiz, w 3, x 1; pop-, m 6.
Muinzaipiz, i m.
(bo)muintip, i 1.
muip, b 1, c 1, g 5.
Mullac, k 6.
Mumain, i j; a 4, g 1, p 6, s 3;
　Mumnec, m 3.
Mumne, f 3.
Mumo, h 2.

Munemon, i 1; -oin, i 3.
Mup lct, y 3.
Mupcaba, i n.
Mupebaiz, n 2.
Mupietac, i 5, 6; Mupibac, x 5, 6.
mupiuct, c 1.

n (pron. infix. 3 s.), ponomnaiz, n 1.
'n (for in, art. by aphaeresis of i), ii m;
　iii h; s 3, y 6; (for i n-, prep.),
　v c.
na (art., g. s. fem.), i g, o; p 3 (n. pl.
　masc.), i o; x 3 (g. pl.); i f, v b;
　a 1, b 4, c 2, d 6, g 5, i 1, o 2,
　t 5, 6 (ac. pl.); ii g.
n-a (aphaeresis of i), ii e; v c; i 5,
　q 5, r 4.
na (neg.), i n, o; ii e.
na l- (n assim. to l), f 3, g 6, v 6.
na m- (n assim. to m), o 5.
na n- (art., g. p.), ii h; iii h; e 3, f 6,
　i 4, n 5, y 4, 5, w 5.
nac, i e; ii h; iii h.
naco n- (noco n-), v 5.
nab (conj. neg.), v b.
na[ib], i o.
naip, b 1.
nama, i i; namma, k 3.
Nect, t 5.
neic, ii e; v c.
Neimeb, b 1, 2, 6; Nemib (g.), w 2,
　y 2.
nemni, i c.
neoc, ii f; iii f.
nept, k 5, s 4, y 3; coemn-, v 4.
ni (neg.), i a, c, i, j; ii b, e, i, 1;
　iii a, i, 1; iv c, d, e; v b; b 6, c 1,
　g 3, h 6, j 4, n 1, p 2, t 6, y 1, 3.
Nia, r 4, 5.
Níall, y 3.
nimbanzen, v c; -bai[n]zen, ii e.

INDEX VERBORUM. (II.)

nimniḃ, y 2.
nin (= ni annṛa), ɪ a, f.
nip (for ni po), e 1, f 4, y 2.
nipc, v 1; niupc n- (d.), y 4.
no (conj.), ɪv e.
no (vbl. pcle.), noṛnoḃe, ɪ c; nom-
    ɜeḃ, ɪɪɪ l.
noco, ɪɪ f, ɪɪɪ f, m; t 4, u 3; -ċo,
    ɪɪ l, m; noco n-, ɪ d; ɪɪ i; a l;
    -ċo n., ɪ e, k.
nói (num.), a 6, e 5, h 4, k 3, 5, m 2,
    p 4, s 3, v 5; nói m-, s 4, t 1.
Nuaḋaic, k 4, t 5; -ḋac, k 5, t 6;
    -ḋu, d 6, k 5.
nuall [? n-uall], ɪɪ b.

o (sb.) ɪ c.
o (conj. temp.), ɪ d, e; ɪɪ d; ɪɪɪ d.
o (prep.), ɪ a; b 5.
oḃaip, ɪ b.
oc (prep.), k 1.
occaiḃ (oc, prep. and pr. suf. 2 pl.), ɪ n.
oċc, q 1, y 1; oċc m-, m 3, o 1, q 2.
ocuṛ (ꝫ), ɪ, ɪɪ, ɪɪɪ *passim*, v c, b 3,
    c 3, 4.
Oḋba, n 3.
Oḋḃɜen, d 4.
oen, a 4, 5, 6, b 1, c 4, f 5, k 2, n 3,
    r 2, w 2, 5, x 1; oenoṛ, f 2.
Oenɜuṛ, h 2, q 1, 3; r 2; -ɜoṛa,
    x 1.
oɜṛi, ɪɪɪ k.
óiṛ, e 6.
ol, ɪ j.
ol (vb.), p 3.
Olcain, k 2.
olḋaṛ, ɪv d.
Ollam, q 1.
Ollaċaiṛ, e 3.
Ollɜoċaċ, j 1.
Ollomain, i 3, 6, j 3; -man, i 4.

Olloṅba, x 4.
Olmucaiḃ, h 2.
omna, q 3.
ṗonomnaiɜ, n 1; omun, ɪɪ g; ɪɪɪ g.
on, f 2.
o'n (o and in, art.), b 5.
oṛḃ, v 2.
oṛḃlaċ, ɪ j.
oṛ, ɪ a, m; ɪɪ a; d 6, e 5, g 3, k 1, 2,
    p 1, 2, r 5, s 1, 4, t 1, u 5, x 3,
    y 3.

ṗoṛ (for ṗo ṗo), 1 4.
Ṗaṗċolon, a 5, 6, b 1.
ṗaċep [?], ɪɪɪ a.
Ṗacṛaic (g.), y 5.
ṗoṗo, e 1, m 1, q 3, u 2.
puiṗc, a 6.

nip' (for ni po), e 1, f 4.
ṗa (for la, prep.), ɪ k; a 6, c 1, 6, h 6,
    p 2, y 2, 3.
ṗa (= la a; prep. and poss. 3 ms.), y 2.
ṗa n- (la n-), ɪɪɪ b.
ṗa (vbl. pcle.), ḃoṗala, ɪ d.
ṗáiḃ, ɪ h, i.
ṗainḃ [ṗinḃ], ɪɪ j.
Ṛaiṗinḃ, f 6.
ṗaiċ, t 5.
Ṛaiċ, m 2.
ṗán, m 2.
ṗanḃ, c 4; ṗainḃ, u 5.
ṗanḃaiḃaċc, ɪ e; ṗann-, ɪ f; ṗan-
    naiḃ-, ɪ g; -ɜaċc, ɪv a, b, c, d.
ṗac, i 4, j 1, m 1, r 4, u 5; -maṛ,
    v a; (coṗ)ṗaċ, v 1.
ḃoṗac, 1 3, q 1; ḃoṗacṛac, c 5.
ṗaċa, ɪ h, i.
ṗáċc, t 6; -ċi, 1 1.

INDEX VERBORUM. (II.)

ρέ, f 2, h 5, m 5, q 5, r 4, t 3, w 3.
ρε (la and a, rel.), ιι i.
ρε (prep.), ɪ b, g; j 6.
ρεcοmαρc, ɪv d; -caċ, ɪɪ a, k; ɪɪɪ k.
ρeċτ (g. p.), t 5.
ρeċτ(ιαρlα), m 5.
Rcċταιb, o 5, 6.
(τρεη)ρébʒ, k 6.
ρóιl, m 1, 2.
ρειτεαρ, ιι h; -eρ, ιɪɪ h.
ρεmιρ, k 1, o 5, q 2, 4.
ρι (sb.), ɪ m; ιι c, g, h, k; ιɪɪ c, g, h, ɪv d; c 2, 5, d 1, 5, h 1, 3, 6, i 2, 4, 5, j 2, 1 5, 6, m 1, 4, n 1, o 3, p 3, 5, q 1, 2, r 1, 6, s 1, 2, 4, t 2, 5, u 5, v 1, 2, 3, 6.
ρι (for la, prep), b 4, 6, c 6, j 5, m 4, o 3, r 3, w 5.
ρια, ɪ n; a 2, y 5.
ρια (for la, prep.), n 6.
ριαʒlοm, m 2.
ριαm, n 1.
ροριαραb, p 3, r 2.
ριcραc, ɪ h.
ριʒ (g. s.), o 2, u 1 (d. s.); t 2 (ac. s.); j 4 (n. p.); c 1, g 4, y 5; (g. p.), a 1; -αιb, c 3, 6.
ριʒαιn, o 5; ριʒbα, t 5.
ριʒbεηʒ, o 5, p 6.
ριʒbοηbb, q 3.
ριʒριlεb, ιɪɪ a; ριʒηιαc, k 5.
ριʒε, e 5, f 1, j 5, k 2, 5, p 2, v 1.
(αηb)ριʒε, q 5; -ʒι, c 5.
ριnb, d 4, 5, t 2, 5; -nn, ɪɪɪ j.
ριnbαιl, d 3; ριnn-, d 4.
ριρ, ɪ n; ιι 1; ριρριn, c 1.
ρó, y 4.
ρο (vbl. pcle. prefixed), bιαρ'[b]α, ιι c; ροmbáιb, w 6; nορριbε, ɪ c; bιαρ'bο (bια ροbο), ɪɪɪ c; ρο-bριρ, b 4; ροcαεmcαιτ, m 4; ροcαιċ (under c); ροċmρεc,

n 4; ροċυαlα, ɪ b; ροnbliʒ, q 3; ροpειċ, k 5, w 6, v 3; ρο-ρεcεp, ιι i; ροριραb, s 3; ροʒαb, ɪ c; ραʒαιb (under ʒ); ροcετʒαb, a 2; ροʒαbραcυρ, x 3; ροʒαcc, d 5; ροmʒιαll, ρο-ʒιαllαb (under ʒ); ροʒlαcc, q 5; w 3; ρορι[n]ηαρb, x 5; ροιηη-αρbραc, n 4; ρο ιηηιριυρ, c 6; ροmlαρα, ιɪɪ h; ραlοċραb, p 2; ραlοιρc, ρο- (under l); ρυmαιċ (for ρομαιċ), h 6; ρομαρb, ροbmαρb, ρορmαρb (under m); ροηοmηαιʒ, n 1; ροριαραb, p 3, r 2; ρορcαρ, j 5; -ρραc, n 6; ραρομυρ (ρα[ρ]ηομυρ) v c; ρoτάιρινb, j 3, k 1; ρο-ceċτ, v 4, 5; ρoċεηb, v 4; ρορcιb, ɪ a; ρocoʒlαb, b 6; ρocomηαιcερ, ɪ o; ρυcραc, c 4; ραρcυιʒιċεαρ, ιι d.
ρο (vbl. pcle. infixed), bερηαb, i 4; bερηηραbαρ, ɪ o; bορηιʒηι, e 2; bοηοιηbε, ɪ c; (bιαηη)-bροηcα, ιɪɪ g; bοηοċαιρ (see under c); bοηοbbαb, q 3; εη-bαιlc, f 5, g 2; ċοηċαιρ (under c); bοmραlα, ιι h.
ρο (intens.), ροbαcαοιη, h 4; ροεcηε, o 2; ροʒcc, r 2; ροʒιαllαιb, 1 6; ροlαιċ, f 5; ρομαc, h 6; ρομéιc, e 1; ρορυαb, p 3; ρο-ċεmρα, o 4; ρομόιρ, s 6; ρυριʒ (for ρορηʒ), u 2; ρoεmηα, v 1; ρορινηι, x 2.
ραρομυρ [ρα[ρ]ηομυρ], v c.
ρορινηι, x 2.
ροραιʒιʒε [ρηερλιʒc], ɪ g.
Rορρα, t 2; -αċ, ιι d, ɪv e; -αη, ɪɪɪ d.
Rόċριbε, v 4, w 1.
ρoc, k 1.

ṗoca, e 1.
Roceccaıḃ, h 4, 5, j 6, k 1.
ṗuaḃ, ıı d; ııı d; d 3, e 1, t 2, x 2; ıv e; ṗuaıḃ, h 4, f 6, o 2.
(ḃpac)ṗúaıḃ, e 5, 1 1.
ṗuacap, a 3.
Ruḃpaıʒe, e 1, 2, 6.
Ruıṗenḃ, ııı a.
ṗuıṗı, e 1.
ṗuıċ, d 2; -ċneċ, q 3.
ṗuṗı, m 2; ṗuṗıʒ, u 2.
Ruṗ, c 3.
Ruṗcaċ, ıv e.

ṙ (pron. inf. 3 s.), noṙṗoḃe, ı c; no-ḃoṙṗeıċ, v 3; conoṙṗuaıṙ, a 1; noṙmaṙḃ, e 4, o 5; noṙmuḃaıʒ, m 6; ḃuṙcuıʒıḃaṙ, ııı d; ṗaṙcuıʒıċeaṙ, ıı d.
'ṙ (= ıṙ = ocuṙ), y 4.
ṙaeḃ, j 4.
ṙaeṗ, c 5, q 1, y 6; ṙaeṗ (ċalma), o 2.
ṙaıʒeḃ, m 3.
ṙaıl, ıı j; ııı j.
ṙaıṅ, y 1.
ṙál, k 1, n 4.
ṙamċaċ, ı f, g.
Samċaınne, y 6.
ṙaṗuʒuḃ, h 6.
ṙcaılce, ı a, 1; v b; -ceċ, ıv a, c, d; -llce, ı j; -lcı, ıı a, c, d; ııı a, c, d; ıv b.
ṙoṙcaṗ, j 5; -ṗṙac, n 6.
ṙceıṗḃıc, ı n.
ṙcél, v b; t 4.
(aṙm)ṙcıaċ, n 5; (coem)ṙcıaċ, t 6.
ṙcṙıḃeanḃ, ı c.
ṙé (num.), b 6, d 5, f 3, h 3, ı 1, k 4, 1 4, ṙ 1, u 3, 4, v 6, y 5.
ṙé ıṅ- (num.), x 2.

ṙeaṙc, ıı g; ṙeṗc, ııı g; ṙeıṗc, a 4.
ṙeaṙcac, ı a.
ṙeċc, 1 6, o 2, 4, ṙ 5, s 2, v 2, w 2, y 3.
ṙeċc m-, e 1, f 2, j 1, 4, k 1, 1 2, m 4, 6, n 4, p 5, x 4.
ṙeċc n-, g 2, u 1.
ṙccaıḃ, j 6.
ṙeċcmaıṅ, a 6.
Seʒamaıṅ, ṙ 4; -uıṅ, ṙ 5.
ṙeʒḃaċc, ıv e.
ṙeıṅ (pron.), d 3.
ṙenċaṙṙ (g. pl.), v b.
ṙeııʒ, c 5.
Senʒanḃ, c 3; -aınḃ, d 3, 4.
ṙeo (demon.), ı c, d, f; v b.
Sccna, h 5, 1, 2, 3, 4.
ṙıaıṅ (ac.), y 2.
ṙıḃlaıḃ, ı o.
Sıċıle, ı o.
-ṙıḃe (demon.), ıı 1; v b.
Sımón, 1 3, 4.
'ṙıṅ (aphaeresis of prep. ı), a 4, b 3, g 5, j 3, m 3, n 2, p. 5, q 4, u 1, x 2.
ṙıṅ (demon.), ı e, o; b 5, d 5, g 5, t 4, v 5.
ṙıṅeall, ıı m.
Sıṅlam, m 2, 3.
Sıṗna, j 4, 5, 6.
ṙıṙ, ıı a, k; ııı a; ıv c.
Slaıṅ, 1 4.
Slaıne, c 2; Sláne, c 5, d 1, y 5.
Slanoll, ı 6; -uıll, j 4.
ṙlaccaın, j 5.
Sleḃı, h 1; ṙleıḃ, a 4, m 1; -ḃ Elpa, y 4.
ṙleċcaıḃ, j 6.
ṙlıʒe, ı g; -ʒı, ı g.
ṙlóʒ, ı 1; ṙluaʒ, ı f, g; m 3, q 1; -ʒ, ıı d; ııı d.
ṙmaċc, t 1.
ṙmıṅcaċ, ıı a, e; ııı e.

INDEX VERBORUM. (II.)

rmoc, **i** c.
rneóca, **i** n; rnea-, **i** a.
rním, **r** 3.
ro (dem.), **i** a, c, e, g, i, j, k, l, m, n;
  ii a, e, f, l; **iii** a; **iv** c, g.
Sobaiṗċe, **g** 5, **k** 1.
roċaiṗ, **i** 1.
roóc, **q** 1.
roep (bliaḋnaiḃ), **j** 6;   roep
  (ċuaiṗc), **i** 6.
rpaiʒleaṗ, **i** o.
rpen-bpuíníʒ, **i** m.
[p̃]piaḃ ṅ-ḋepʒ, **u** 2.
rpian, **c** 2; -naiḃ, **j** 6.
Spoḃcinḃ (g.), **w** 2.
rpoin, **i** n.
Scaipn, **b** 3, 5; Scapn, **b** 1.
rúaiṗc, **i** 6.
ruapp, **ii** a.
ruiḃi, **iii** 1.

caḃaiṗ, **ii** f; **iii** f.
caiceḃ-bennaíʒ, **i** m.
caiciḃ, **iii** a.
caiʒ, **r** 1.
caiṫc, **u** 5.
caim, **b** 2.
caiṗḃipc, **m** 3.
poċaiṗinḃ, **j** 3, **k** 1.
ṫaḋċaiṗ, **u** 2.
Ṫalcen, **r** 3; -cin, **e** 6.
ṫam, **a** 3, 6, **g** 2, **i** 2, 5.
ṫancaċaṗ, **b** 5, **c** 1.
ṫaplaic, **e** 3.
ṫappneaṗ, **i** o.
ṫaċaiṗ, **v** 6.
ċaṗ, **iii** b.
ċaċíʒ, **ii** d.
poċeóc, **v** 4, 5; ceóċaṇi, **i** c.
ċeip, **ii** 1.

Ṫemaiṗ, **j** 5, **t** 1; -mpa, **j** 4; -mpaó,
  g 3, **i** 4, 6, **r** 2; -mpaiʒ, **i** 3, **r** 3,
  t 3, **u** 2, 5, **y** 1; po Ṫempa, **o** 4.
cenḃ, **g** 2; poó-, **v** 4.
cene, **k** 1, **p** 3, **t** 4, **y** 4.
ċeṗ, **ir** 1; **v** 6.
ceṗca, **iv** d.
ciaóċaiṇ, **y** 5.
c[r̃]iap, **a** 3, **r** 1.
ciʒ, **w** 6; ċiʒ, **y** 2; ciʒe (g.), **i** 6.
Ṫiʒepnmaiṗ, **g** 1; -maṗ, **g** 2.
ċinḋṗceḃul, **i** a.
cíp, **i** d, e; -pe, **i** o; -pi, **i** m.
Ṫipeó, **x** 6.
coeḃiḃna, **j** 4.
poċoʒlaḃ, **b** 6.
coin, **i** 6; **ii** a, **f**; **iii** f.
ċolʒaió, **t** 1.
poċoimnaiċeṗ, **i** o.
comuṗ, **iv** d; lanċ-, **iv** d.
conaiḃ, **t** 3; ċonn-, **x** 5.
ċonḃ (búain), **u** 5.
coṗ, **b** 6, **h** 6.
coṗaóċ, **b** 1, **j** 5.
coṗċaiṗ, **d** 3, **e** 4, **f** 1, **g** 1, 2, **h** 2,
  j 1, **r** 1.
coṗṗʒiceaṗ, **i** k.
cṗa, **i** a; **i** 5, **x** 5.
cṗaóc, **c** 2.
cṗaḃan [cṗuaḃan], **ii** f.
cṗáiʒ, **s** 6.
cṗaic, **a** 3, **s** 4, **v** 6.
cṗe, **ii** 1.
cṗen, **g** 2, **i** 5, **k** 6, **v** 4.
cṗen(aiċḃe), **v** 3; ċṗen(peḃʒ), **u** 2.
cṗeṗṗ, **m** 3.
cṗi (num.), **i** a; **a** 5, 6, **c** 1, 3, 4, **e** 5,
  f 3, **g** 1, **h** 4, **j** 1, 6, **l** 2, **n** 6, **o** 2,
  r 3, **s** 5, **v** 1, 4, 6, **y** 2, 4.
cṗia, **iii** 1.
cṗiall, **i** o.
cṗiac, **iii** a.

trica, b 1, v 4, w 4; -cait, j 5;
-ċat, w 3.
tricc, g 3, u 2.
trom(ċumaid), u 3; trom(dcbaid),
s 6.
truad, II f; III f.
truaʒ, x 2; -ʒan, III f.
truċa, v 3.
tuaʒe, r 3, v 6.
Tuaċail, v 5; -al, v 5.
tucad, i 5.
tucrat (potucrat), c 4.
tartuiʒiteart, II d.
tuiʒrin, I o.
tuilʒte, q 6.
Turmeó, r 2, 3.
tur, I a; d 5.

hUla, I h, i; a 1, p 6, s 5, v 6
x 6.
uad (o and pron. suf. 3 s. masc.), II h
III h.
uaill, e 5.
(inn)úaip, w 6.
uaip (conj.), I i.
uall, II h; III b, h; IV g.
uar, I a.
Uarcerr, m 3, 4.
uaċ, III b.
uaċmair, b 5.
ui (g.s.), u 6.
hUi (voc.), II a; (gen.), e 2.
uibell, III a.
uile, c 6.
Ulltaid, I c; Ult-, g 4.

LECTURE III.

THE CODEX PALATINO-VATICANUS,

No. 830.

THE CODEX PALATINO-VATICANUS, No. 830.

(SYNCHRONISMS FROM THE BOOK OF BALLYMOTE.)

III.

IN the present Lecture, with reference to the traditional regal series given in the foregoing, I deal with two texts from the *Book of Ballymote* which treat of the Synchronisms current in the native schools. Both Tracts are of interest, as shewing the basis on which our chroniclers constructed the system of adjusting events to foreign occurrences. It is only by the publication of the *Book of Ballymote* that students have been enabled to study these questions from a linguistic and historical point of view. In the present case, we have an instance how the issue of an original enables the work of the most conscientious workers to be revised with effect.

Discussing the first document, O'Curry* says it is stated therein that Cimbaeth, King of Ulster, began to reign in the fifth year of Alexander (B.C. 326). Reference (A **d**) will shew that Cimbaeth is said to have commenced to rule in the eighteenth year of Ptolemey, Alexander's successor (B.C. 307). O'Curry alleges, furthermore, that the interval between the death of Conor MacNessa and the accession of Cormac, son of Art, is reckoned at 206 years. The original (A **f**) has "seven years [and] fifty over two hundred." Finally, the initial year of Cormac's reign was, according to O'Curry, the eighth after the eighth Persecution. The MS. (A **g**) counts twenty years from that Persecution, the date being equated with the third of the Emperor Probus (A.D. 278).

The A-Tract, as it now stands, is made up of two independent portions. The opening section (**a**), we see from the tenor of the

---

* *Lectures on the MS. Materials*, etc., p. 520.

rest, did not originally belong to the text. The present fortuitous connexion is due to a copyist, who was led to make it by the similarity of the subject matters.

A junction of similar but more aggravated incongruity, which imposed upon Mr. Stokes, is presented by a piece contained in *Lebar Brec*.* After an introductory statement, that tract gives the initial A.D. of the Patrician mission. Next are data, chronological and other, respecting the life of St. Patrick and the year and day of his death. Then follow the respective durations of ten periods, ending with the obits of Conor, son of Donough, king of Ireland and of Artri, archbishop of Armagh. (They are mentioned together, as both, according to the Annals of Ulster, took place in one month, A.D. 833.)

Lastly, without any break in the MS. or the printed text, comes (with some verbal variants† and the omission of two items) the present A-Tract, from the martyrdom of SS. Cyprian and Cornelius (**g**); who are thus represented as having suffered between A.D. 781 and 833! Besides, as will be seen below, the chronographic method of the final portion is radically different from, as well as older than, that employed in the opening. But Mr. Stokes detected no contrariety; the tractate, according to him, was written by one author.

The part in question of A contains the respective lengths of the five divisions, or ages, of the Mundane or Pre-Incarnation period of the world. Portions of this, there is internal evidence, have been taken from the work of Bede, *De sex aetatibus saeculi*. For the description of the Sixth Age is a fairly accurate native rendering of: Sexta . . . aetas nullâ generationum vel temporum serie certa est, sed, ut aetas decrepita, ipsa totius seculi morte consummanda.

Sexta etar munbi,—ibon, in peped aip ꞇ ni ꝼuil comup bliaban popci, acc a bec man aip penopadda aꝫon domun ꞇ eꝫ in boma[i]n uile a ꝓipdenn.	*Sexta etas mundi*, namely, the sixth age and there is no measure of years thereon, but it is like a senile age of the world, and the dissolution of the whole world [will be] its end.

---

* It is transcribed and translated, to illustrate the Patrician Chronology [?], in the Rolls' *Tripartite* (pp. 550-4).

† An error of transcription, which has been continued without correction in the Rolls' edition, deserves to be noted. Palladius, it is said, was sent to Ireland in the 401st year from the Crucifixion, and Patrick came the year after, in the 302nd

The following synopses exhibit the items contained in it, together with rectifications thereof. With reference to the gross numerical errors, in the *Book of Ballymote*, it has to be observed, the Roman notation is regularly employed as a contraction for the native reckoning. The liability to mistake arising from this source is well known. In addition, the Latin transcription is, unfortunately, illiterate. Two striking instances may be quoted. In a tract on the *Ages of the World*, we are told that Regma had two sons, Saba and Dadan (Gen. x. 7; 1 Par. i. 9)—*gens moriens tali plaga*. Overhead is a gloss, signifying *a tribe on whom came a plague*.* The original thus doubly travestied is, of course: *gens in orientali plaga*, a people in an eastern region.

In the A-Tract (**h**), Palladius is stated to have been sent by Pope Celestine to preach the Gospel in Ireland in the 5602nd year from the beginning of the world. Further on, in the same section, the year following is given as the 5633rd of the Creation. The latter, it will be seen, is the true reading. It shews the ignorance or carelessness of the copyist, that within eleven lines he omitted and inserted the Roman notation for *thirty*.

FIVE AGES OF THE WORLD.

A.

Hebrew Reckoning.

	Bede (a).	Ballymote (b).
I. Adam—Deluge,	1656	1656
II. Deluge—Abraham,	292	942
III. Abraham—David,	942	942
IV. David—Captivity,	473	473
V. Captivity—A.D. 1,	589	589
	[3952]	[4602]

year from the Crucifixion. In the first date, the scribe wrote correctly *cccc.*; in the second, *ccc*. A letter more or less was, apparently, of no consequence to the copyist and the editor.

* Da mc ic Reabta . . . . .ı. Saṇa ⁊ Daḃaṁ .ı. ᵹeṇr moṇieṇr caƚı plaᵹa .ı. cıṇıub aṇ a caıṇıc plaıᵹ (P. 4 b, ll. 29-30).

B.

	Septuagint Reckoning according to Bede.	"School" Reckoning according to *Book of Ballymote.*	
	(a)	(b)	(c)
I.	2242	1659	[2242]
II.	1072	943	[942]
III.	942	942	[941]
IV.	485	475	[485]
V.	589	589	[589]
	[5330]	[4608]	[5199]

With regard to **A**, II. (*a*) shews that the textual reading of II. (*b*), aṗ noċ cecaıḃ (above nine hundred), is to be altered into aṗ ḋıḃ cecaıḃ (above two hundred). This is confirmed by the *Lebar Brec* (p. 113 a): In oeṗ canaıṗe ın ḋomaın ımoṗṗo, ḋa ḃlıaḋaın noċac ḟoṗ ḋıḃ cecaıḃ ḟıl ınce.—Now, the second age of the world, two years [and] ninety over two hundred that are in it.

Connected herewith are six verses,* in the *Debide* metre illustrated in the Second Lecture. The date of composition, according to the last quatrain, was A.D. 1126. Of these, five give the respective durations of the periods set down above, **A** (*a*), (*b*). The sixth sums them up as 3952. But the items, when totted, amount only to 3644, 308 years short. **A** (*a*) localizes the errors and renders the textual rectification a matter of certainty. The corruptions occur in the second line of the fourth verse and in the opening distich of the fifth.

In the former, the reading is:

(4)
aṗ cṗı cecaıḃ co comṗlan.

(4)
Above three hundred, completely.

For this we have to substitute:

aṗ ceıṫṗı cecaıḃ comṗlan.

Above four hundred complete.

In the latter, for:

(5)
ḃlıaḋaın ıṗ oċcmoḋa oġ
aṗ cṗı cecaıḃ, nı commoṗ.

(5)
A year [and] eighty perfect
Above three hundred, not too great.

---

* Note A.

we are to read:

Nae m-bliadna octmoda og   Nine years [and] eighty perfect
ap coic cecaib, ni commop.   Above five hundred, not too great.

In each case, the *Concord* confirms the emendation.

Similarly, in the poem of Gilla Coemain dealing with chronology, the Hebrew calculations—**A** (*a*)—are adopted. In the lines giving the years of **A** v, the reading of both copies in the *Book of Leinster* is: a noi coicac, occmodga—nine [and] fifty [and] eighty. This is not Irish. The true lection is, of course: a noi, coic cét, octmoga —nine, five hundred [and] eighty (589).

The opening entry in the *Annals of Innisfallen* (O'Conor's text) is: *Kl. Ab initio mundi vdcxxx., juxta lxx. Interpretes; secundum vero Hebraicam veritatem, ivccclxxxi. Loega[i]re, mac Neill, regnum Hiberniae tenuit.* (The Reckoning here styled the Septuagint is the Victorian = Mundane Period of 5201 years. It will be found treated at length in Lecture IV.) The Hebrew Computation thus gives A.D. 529 for Loeghaire's accession. The numerals should accordingly be *ivccclxxxi*. (4381). The emendation is rendered certain by the Victorian Numeration and by the date which follows next in the Annals: *Kl. Ab Incarnatione Domini cccxxx.* (430).

In the same Annals we find (same text):

[*Annus*] *millesimus centesimus sexagesimus ab Incarnatione Domini. Ab exordio vero mundi quinque millia et xcii.* This is also the Hebrew Computation. Read, accordingly: *vcxii*. The scribe, namely, reversed the order of *c* and *x*; thus giving 5092 for 5112.

With respect to **B**, the correct notation of I. (*b*), in accordance with **B** I. (*a*), is given in the A-Text (**b**),—da bliadain cetorcat, da cet ⁊ da mili (two years [and] forty, two hundred and two thousand [2242]). On the other hand, in IV., the difference between (*a*) and (*b*) arose from the omission of a word. For da bliadain (two years), read da bliadain deac (twelve years).

The divergencies between I. (*a*) and I. (*b*), II. (*a*) and II. (*b*) are too wide to be attributable to transcription. The source must, accordingly, be sought elsewhere. Speaking of the fifteenth year of Tiberius, Bede says, respecting the computation of Eusebius: "Juxta vero Chronica quae de utraque editione . . . composuit, anni sunt v. m., cc., xxviii." (*De sex aet. saec.*) Deducting twenty-nine (the difference between the Abrahamic years 2015 and 2044), we have 5199 as the length of the Mundane Era according to the Eusebian Chronicle.

The Chronicle (Lib. II.) has at the year 2015 of Abraham : Colliguntur omnes ab Abraham usque ad nativitatem Christi anni, duo millia quindecim. Ab Adam usque ad Christum, quinque millia ducenti, duo minus. The year following is given as the first of our Lord. Read accordingly: uno minus (**B** I. *c* + **B** II. *c* + 2015 = 5199).

At the 15th of Tiberius [Eusebian A.D. 29], the Chronicle gives: Ab Abraham et regno Nini et Semiramidis anni MMXLIV. A diluvio usque ad Abraham, anni DCCC[C]XLII.* Ab Adam usque ad diluvium MMCCXLII. That is, **B** I. *c* + **B** II. *c* + 2044 = 5228. The Passion year is the 19th of Tiberius : A.D. 33; A.M. 5232.

A statement setting forth the details of the Eusebian sum mentioned by Bede is given in the *Book of Ballymote*.† It is dated 900 from the Passion (probably = A.D. 932). The errors, including the strange substitution of the Hebrew for the Septuagint reckoning in I., I have rectified from the Chronicle of Eusebius. Here is found the correct lection of **B** II. (*b*) (942). From the text as amended the other dated periods of Note B. are obtained to correspond with A.M. 5199, as follows :—

III. Note B.	From Abraham to Moses [Exodus],		505 years.
	,, Moses [Exodus] to Building of Temple,		479 ,,
			[984]
	Deduct 40 years of David and 3 of Solomon,		[43]—[941].
[III. Abraham—David,			941]

IV. Note B.	From Solomon to Rebuilding of Temple,		512 years.
	Add 43 (as in III.),		[43] ,,
			[555]
	Deduct Captivity,		[70]—[485].
[IV. David—Captivity,			485]

---

* The omission of the fourth c is a manifest error, as appears from the Prœmium of the Second Book, § 5.

† Note B. The Eusebian sums are also employed in the first of the excerpts appended from the *Book of Ballymote*, Note C.

v. Note B. From Rebuilding of Temple to 15th year of
Tiberius, ... 548 years.
Add Captivity (as in iv.), . . [70] ,,
                                                    ―――――
                                                    [618]
Deduct age of our Lord, . . [29]—[589].
[v. Captivity—A.D. 1, . . 589]

This calculation of Eusebius is clearly what is called the "School" Reckoning in the A-Tract (**a**). It is, moreover, that which, as a rule, is intended by the native chroniclers when they give the years according to the Septuagint Computation.

The foregoing enables us to correct scribal errors in the dating based upon the length of this Mundane Era. For instance, in *Lebar Brec* (if it be not a mistake of the fac-similist) we have :—

Noı m-bliaḋna ınnoṗṗo ⁊ ẋ. ceṫ   Nine years indeed and ten hundred
aṗ u. mīle o ċpuṫuṡuḋ Aḋaım co   over five thousand [6009] from the for-
ṡen Cṗıṗt (P. 132 a).   mation of Adam to the birth of Christ.

The periphrasis (ten hundred) here given for a thousand is out of place in a calculation containing other thousands. The numerical reading, accordingly, there can be no doubt, is : noı m-bliaḋna ıẋ.ċaṫ ⁊ ceṫ aṗ u. mīle—nine years [and] ninety and a hundred over five thousand (5199).

In the *Annals of Boyle* (O'Conor's text), we read :—

Annus ab Incarnatione Domini mxlvi. ; *ab initio vero mundi* vıccxliv.

Here, likewise, the Septuagint is followed. The reading should consequently be *vıccxlv.* (1046 + 5199 = 6245).

The original A-Tract contains no ascription of authorship. The design, contents and probable age will be considered later on.

The B-Text is likewise anonymous. Prefixed, in the handwriting of Charles O'Conor of Belanagare, is the title: Leaḃaṗ Comaımṗıṗeaḋḋa Ḟlann maınıṗṫṗe ṗıoṗana—*The Book of Synchronisms of Flann of the Monastery* [of St. Buite, Monasterboice, Co. Louth] *down here.* No evidence, however, has come to light in support of this attribution.

Of the supposed author, the following notice is given in O'Conor's *Tigernach* (Rer. Hib. Script. *ii.*, 300) :—

A.D. 1056. Kl. [Jan.] ii. f., lu. x.
Fland Mainiptrach ugdan Saibel etin leigind ⁊ trencur ⁊ filigect ⁊ aincedal in uii. Kl. Decemb., xui luna uitam feliciten in Chpipto finiuit.

Kl. [Jan.] ii. feria, Luna x.
Flannus Monasterii Butensis, auctor Hibernensis, tam Prælector Theologicus quam Historicus, Poeta et Propheta, die vii. Kl. Decemb., xvi. luna, vitam feliciter in Christo finivit.

" Flann of the Monastery, an Irish author, both in literature and history and poetry and the bardic art, ended his life happily in Christ, on the 7th of the Kalends of Dec. [Nov. 25], 16th of the moon."

It is scarcely necessary to point out that *Theologian* and *Prophet* were evolved by the translator. Here, it may be observed in passing, we have another instance of the perplexity caused by alphabetical numeration. For *uii. Kal. Dec.* and *xui. luna* are incompatible. The moon's age on Nov. 25, 1056, was 13. The reading must, accordingly, be either *iiii. Kal. Dec.* (Dec. 28), *xui. luna;* or, *uii. Kal. Dec., xiii. luna.* Judging from the *Four Masters* (who say the "fourth[*] Calend," but, as usual, omit the lunation), the former was the original. The error, which is of frequent occurrence, arose from mistaking *ii.* (2) for *u.* (5), or *vice versa*.

The design and contents of the Tracts next demand attention. That the Irish possessed letters before the introduction of Christianity, may be taken as established by one fact. In substance the same as the present language, the Ogam script belongs to a stage centuries older than that to which, according to the progress of linguistic development, the most archaic of our other literary remains can be assigned. When, in addition, the vitality of tradition is taken into account, there appears nothing improbable in the transmission of the number, order and leaders of the various so-called Invasions, or Occupations. Much less, coming to later times, does it seem impossible to have preserved the remarkable story of the foundation and the names of the rulers of a kingdom established and maintained in despite of the central government.

Next came the Christian missionaries. With them or soon there-

---

[*] O'Donovan, by a manifest oversight, translates "fourteenth" (vol. ii., p. 871).

after, along with compositions of a similar kind, arrived the works of St. Jerome. Among the writings of that Father was a version of the (lost) Chronicle of Eusebius. A reflex of the natural order, whereby many events have simultaneous origin and progress, that compilation, with some defects of detail, stands in design beyond the reach of emendation. To adjust the traditional history to such a system and thereby invest national events with the certitude arising from co-ordinate and dated sequence, was too obvious to remain long unattempted by native literati.

Such was the origin of the Synchronisms. Of these, the present texts represent two recensions: one (A) dealing mainly with the chief events; the other (B), with persons and years in detail. The former, it would thus appear, was the older.

The time in which A was composed is determined by the calculations given at the close. The consulship of Ætius and Valerius shews that the years intended are A.D. 431-2. But the textual A.P. 401-2 = A.D. 431-2 = A.M. 5632-3 gives a Mundane Period = 5201 and the Passion Year A.D. 31. This reckoning cannot be reconciled with Eusebius. His Mundane Period, we have seen, is 5199 and his Passion Year A.M. 5232 = A.D. 33 (the 19th of Tiberius); giving A.P. 401-2 = A.D. 433-4 = A.M. 5632-3. Hence the Eusebian formula would be: A.P. 399-400 = A.D. 431-2 = A.M. 5630-31.

A.D. 431-2 = A.M. 5632-3 is the Victorian Computation (Lecture IV., Table VII.). The Passion Years are consequently 404-5. Hence, in accordance with Chronological Canon III. (Lect. IV.), the original A-Tract (**b-h**) can date from the end of the sixth century. That the computist did not work at first hand, is proved by the absence of Bassus and Antiochus, who are correctly given as consuls at the 404th year of the Cycle of Victorius.* Where he found Ætius and Valerius is a question of great importance. But this is not the place for its discussion.

The time of B, owing to the loss of the conclusion, cannot be fixed with similar precision. But it contains nothing inconsistent with

Coss.	Annus	B.	Kal. Jan.	Luna in Kal. Jan.	Paschæ dies	Ætas lunæ in Pasch.	Indict.
Basso et Antiocho	CDIV		f. V	III	XIII Kal. Maii	XXII	XIV
Ætio et Valerio	CDV	B.	f. VI	XIV	III Non. Apr.	XVII	XV

being compiled before the introduction of Incarnation dating into Ireland (A.D. 632-3). Against this is not to be placed the mention (**s**) of the Paschal Rule. For the false attribution respecting the *Shepherd* of Hermes may well have been known here long before that fraud imposed upon Bede.*

In each Tract, it will readily suggest itself that the numbers, whether in sum or item, were for the greater part supplied or altered to correspond with those of the Eusebian Chronicle. This is confirmed by a typical instance, namely, the final or Milesian Occupation.

[The B.C. is found by the Victorian Rule (given in the following Lecture) of subtracting the given (Eusebian) year of Abraham from 2017.]

DATES OF THE MILESIAN OCCUPATION.

[B.C.]

1. A-Text (**b**), 440 years after Exodus, ... [1071].
2. B-Text (**i**), 5th year of Mithraeus, ... [1229].
3. Note C (*i*), year of the death of Darius, son of Arsames, . . [331].
4. ,, . ,, 7th year after the death of Balthasar, . . . [544].
5. ,, ,, in the Third Age of the World, . . . [2017—1076].
6. ,, (*j*), year in which David purposed to build the Temple, [1066?].
7. Lebar Laigen Text (**f**: Lect. II., p. 156, *supra*), . . . 1569.

The discrepancies in the foregoing Table are too great to allow the existence of reliable data relative to the time of the occurrence in question. It is accordingly unnecessary to labour in harmonizing the A and B Tracts. Similarly, the numerical errors of each text can be rectified by reference to the (Eusebian) B.C. placed on the margin.

The continuation of the B Synchronisms from the end of St. Jerome's additions to the Eusebian Chronicle (A.D. 378) down to the coming of St. Patrick is explained in the extract given below† from the *Book of Ballymote*. The passage is otherwise significant, as furnishing direct proof that the advent was regarded as a national epoch. From this it may be concluded that B, owing probably to a lacuna in the exemplar, is defective at the end.

But the chief value of the Tracts taken together lies in their connexion with the *Annals of Tigernach*. To deal adequately with

---

* See note under B **s**. † Note C (*h*).

this portion of the subject, it has first to be proved that the so-called *Chronicon Scotorum** is a compendium of *Tigernach*. In the preface to the Rolls' edition, in proof that the work which the abbreviator, Mac Firbis, professed to compendiate could not have been *Tigernach*, eight entries are given to shew that he could not have copied from any existing MS. of that compiler. The underlying assumption, namely, that the extant MSS. were as meagre in the time of Mac Firbis as they are now, is purely gratuitous. Passing over this, on looking into the subject, one will be surprised to find that, of the eight items, four fall within a well-known chasm of 208 years, A.D. 767–974 inclusive; three belong to another hiatus of 14 years, A.D. 1004–1017 inclusive; whilst the eighth appertains to a year later than A.D. 1088, the date to which *Tigernach* extends. The conclusion based on these premises respecting the diversity of Mac Firbis's original and *Tigernach* is consequently without foundation.

To shew the identity of the two native compilations, I first place side by side the following portions of the *Chronicon Scotorum* and *Tigernach*, and the passages of Bede from which, with exception of the Septuagint reckoning of the Second Age, they are verbally taken :—

Chronicon Scotorum.[1]	BEDE, *De sex aetatibus seculi.*
Prima mundi aetas continet annos iuxta Ebra[e]os M., dc., lui. Iuxta vero lxx. Interpretes, ii. millia, cc., xlii., quae tota periit in diluvio, sicut infantiam mergere solet oblivio. X. generationes.	Prima est ergo mundi hujus aetas ab Adam usque ad Noe, continens annos juxta Hebraicam veritatem M., dc., lvi.; juxta lxx. Interpretes, MM., cc., xlii. Generationes juxta utramque editionem numero x. Quae universali est deleta diluvio, sicut primam cujusque hominis oblivio demergere consuevit aetatem.
[1] P. 2.	
Secunda aetas mundi incipit, quae continet annos cc., xcii., iuxta vero Ebra[e]os . . . Iuxta vero Interpretes dcccc., xl.[1]	Secunda aetas a Noe usque ad Abraham . . juxta Hebraicam veritatem complexa . . . annos cc., xcii., porro juxta lxx. Interpretes annos M., lxxii.
[1] P. 4.	
Tertia aetas incipit, quae continet annos dcccc., xlii. Et incipit a nativitate Abram.[1]	Tertia ab Abraham usque ad David, . . . annos dcccc., xlii. complectens.
[1] *Ib.*	

---

* It has been published as an original work in the Rolls' Series.

At A.M. 2444 (Hebrew B.C. 1508),* Mac Firbis complains of having a labour such as that whereon he was engaged imposed upon him. Then, having described the adventures of Milesius and his sons, up to the gaining the sovereignty of Ireland by the latter, he says: "I break off to another time" and passes (over the Fourth and Fifth Ages) to the year of St. Patrick's birth (A.D. 353 according to the chronology of the editor!).

Now, the first entry in O'Conor's *Tigernach* relates to the 18th year of Ptolemey Lagus (B.C. 307; O'Conor makes it 305). The hiatus here accordingly embraces the whole of the Fourth Age and about half of the Fifth, and therewith the respective Latin summaries.

Next we find (A.D. 1):

O'CONOR's *Tigernach* (Rer. Hib. Script., ii., p. 12).	BEDE, *De sex aetatibus seculi.*
Incipit sexta mundi aetas, ab Incarnatione Christi usque ad diem iudicii. Beda beatus breviter sequentia habet: Sexta mundi aetas nulla generatione uel serie temporum certa, sed, ut aetas decrepita, ipsa totius seculi morte consumanda.	Sexta, quae nunc agiter aetas, nulla generationum vel temporum serie certa est, sed, ut aetas decrepita, ipsa totius seculi morte consummanda.

Secondly, appended to these descriptions of the Ages are native verses, embodying for mnemonic purposes the years of the respective periods. They are composed in quatrains of hexasyllabic lines, with alliteration and assonance (*Concord*), ending in dissyllabic words, the second and fourth lines rhyming (*Correspondence*). The metre, namely, is *Rinnard:* a measure well known from being that in which the Calendar of Oengus was written.

After the First Age, the *Chronicon Scotorum* has:—

Aɼ ro man aben an [ꝑile] ꝺaoibeal nuimiꞃ na haoꞃa ꞃo:— Iꞇ ꞃe bliaꝺna caoɼaꞇ, Se ceꝺ cnuꞇ[1] ꝺo ꝑlihim, Mile móꞃ an aiꞃmím, O Aꝺam ɼo Ꝺilinn.	It is thus the Gaedelic [poet] saith the number [of years] of this Age:— There are six years [and] fifty [And] six exact hundred, as I reckon, [And] a thousand great, noble I reckon, From Adam to the Deluge.

[1] *Lege* ceꞇ.

---

* The MS. has *ii.m.cccxcxliiii*. The date immediately preceding is *ii.m.cccxc.*

After the Second Age (between the Hebrew Reckoning and that of the Septuagint) :—

Ut poeta ait :—

O Dilinn go hAbpam,
hi genaip iap pébuib,
Da bliadain baile, toact,
Noact an bib cébaib.[1]

¹ céboib, MS.

As the poet saith :—

From the Deluge to Abram,
In which he was born with blessings,
Two years strong, bountiful,
[And] ninety above two hundred.

After the Third Age :—

Ut dixit poeta :—

O'n gen pin gen gabad

Go Dauid, in plait pedil,
Cetpata do bliadnaib,
[Cetpata, da bliadain]
Naoi ceb go indemin.

As said the poet :—

From that birth [of Abram] without doubt

To David, the faithful prince,
Forty [years] of years
[*Read :* Forty-two years]
[And] nine hundred, very certainly.

The Fourth and Fifth Ages, it has been remarked, were omitted by Mac Firbis. Items belonging to the Fifth are given in O'Conor. His text contains two quatrains of the same metre as those in the *Chronicon Scotorum*. They follow Bede's description of the Sixth Age. The first gives the years of the Fifth Age, as in the *De sex aetatibus;* the second sums up those from the Creation to the Nativity.

O'Conor's *Tigernach* (Rer. Hib. Script., ii., p. 12) :—

Mad o lorcad Tempuill

Co gen Cript iap petaib,
Octmoga noi m-bliadna,
Act ip an coic cetaib.

Cind da bliadan coicat
O cput[ug]ad in[1] domuind,
Noi cet, teopa mile,

Co gein Cript iap colaind.

¹ This is hypermetrical.

If [we reckon] from burning of the Temple

To birth of Christ with blessings,
[It is] eighty-nine years,
But it is above five hundred.

At the end two years [and] fifty
From Creation of the world,
[There were] nine hundred [and] three thousand [years]
To birth of Christ according to the flesh.

The coherent sequence of the Latin passages and the metric identity of the Irish verses in the *Chronicon Scotorum* and in *Tigernach*, as set out in the foregoing, constitute apparently decisive evidence that the latter has been the source of the former.

Thanks to Mr. Gilbert, the proof is no longer of an indirect kind. The *Fac-similes of the National MSS. of Ireland* (Pt. II., Pl. xc.) contain the first page of folio 11 of the Bodleian *Tigernach* (Rawlinson, 488). I append a transcript, together with the corresponding work of Mac Firbis.* The item at A.D. 668 and isolated expressions of the *Chronicon* not given in the *Annals* shew that the original of *b* was fuller than *a*. The graphic forms and, notably, the entry at A.D. 681 prove that it was likewise the better MS.†

The A.D. numeration is supplied from the Annals of Ulster. The sole date given in the MSS. is A.M. 4658 in *a* (at A.D. 673). This, being taken from the Chronicle of Bede, is to be amended into 4649. The ten years of Justinian's reign are next to be deducted, in accordance with the chronography of the Chronicle, leaving the first of Justinian at A.M. 4639 = A.D. 687. Justinian the Younger ascended the throne in 685. Here, accordingly, the foreign chronology of Tigernach is eleven years erroneous; the native, fourteen.

The parallelism set forth in the Note will, it is submitted, be deemed conclusive. How far the abbreviator was fitted for the execution of the task entailed upon him, will furthermore appear therefrom. One glaring instance of Irish and another of Latin will here suffice. The MS. has copcpaoh ailig Fpigpeno, demolition of Ailech Frigrenn (Greenan Ely, Co. Donegal). But Mac Firbis makes the opening word into coipeacpao, a loan word from the Latin *consecratio*, consecration. To shew his knowledge of Latin, he took *abatis Iea* (abbot of Iona) to be one word, thus producing *abbatissa;* with the result of making the Columban Superior a woman!

Of the conclusions resulting from the fact that *Tigernach* and the *Chronicon Scotorum* stand in the relation of original and compendium, the following have reference to the present subject. In the first place, comparing the *Chronicon* fragments with the *Annals* (in the edition of O'Conor), we find that the native pre-Patrician portion of Tigernach was mainly based upon the Synchronisms.

---

* Note D.   † Mac Firbis, it also appears, worked from a copy of the *Annals* in which the only defect was from A.D. 723 to 830 both inclusive.

Next, with regard to the identification of the Tracts so employed, the *Chronicon* shews that one was a piece contained in the *Book of Ballymote* (pp. 17-42). It is given in the traditional form in the *Book of Leinster* (pp. 1-24). The *Chronicon* likewise exhibits Tigernach's characteristic of turning native items now and again into Latin, doubtless to harmonize with the Hieronymo-Eusebian Chronicle. The astounding perversions of meaning observable in the work of Mac Firbis it were unjust to attribute to Tigernach.

Another of the sources drawn upon, it may be concluded, was the present A-Text. In connexion herewith, great praise has been bestowed upon Tigernach, to the implied depreciation of the other native chroniclers, for the honesty of his decision respecting the credibility of the pre-Christian history of Ireland. O'Donovan writes thus on the subject:—"At what period regular annals first began to be compiled with regard to minute chronology we have no means of determining; but we may safely infer from the words of Tigernach that the ancient historical documents existing in his time were all regarded by him as uncertain before the period of Cimbaeth, the commencement of whose reign he fixes to the year before Christ 305 [O'Conor's, not Tigernach's, B.C.]. His significant words, *Omnia monumenta Scotorum usque Cimbaeth incerta erant*, inspire a feeling of confidence in this compiler which commands respect for those facts which he has transmitted to us, even when they relate to the period antecedent to the Christian era."*

But it is satisfactory to find that, after all, the credit of the decision rests not with Tigernach, but with the native school of chronologists. Tigernach, in fact, apparently did nothing more than put into Latin (as was his wont) the substance of the Irish found in the first of our texts (**d**). The words run as follows:—

Nibab ꝼeꞃꞃa ocuꞃ niḃaḃ ḃeṅḃa ꞃcela ocuꞃ ꞃenċuꞃa Ꝼheꞃ n-hEꞃeꞃn coniꝫi Cimbaet́, mac Ꝼinḃtain.	They are not known and they are not certain, the Tales and the Histories of the Men of Ireland as far as Cimbaeth, son of Finntan.

On the other hand, to obviate the suggestion that the Irish was a paraphrase of Tigernach's Latin, passing over the fact that some of the A-Tract items are not to be found in his *Annals*, the (Victorian)

---

* *Annals of Ireland*, pp. xlv.-vi.

Mundane and Passion Reckonings place beyond doubt that the Irish text was composed long before the last quarter of the eleventh century. Even if we allow Tigernach to have been acquainted with these Computations (of which however I have failed to find proof), he nowhere employs them to date by. They had, in fact, become obsolete more than a century before his time.

The passage in Tigernach which led to the statement just dealt with has given rise to an error that is somewhat redeemed by originality. Discussing a fragment bound up with the Trinity College MS. of the *Annals of Ulster*, which he (rightly, I believe) took to belong to *Tigernach*, Dr. Todd writes, in a letter published by O'Curry: " I have considered very carefully the passages of *Tigernach* to which you called my attention—*Omnia monumenta Scotorum usque Cimbaeth incerta erant*. I thought at first that there might be some emphasis in the past tense *erant;* they *were* uncertain, but are not so now. But on consideration, I believe that the writer only meant to say that the historical records relating to the period before the reign of Cimbaeth are not absolutely to be relied on. He had just before said that Liccus is said by some to have reigned, and, to apologize for the uncertain way of speaking (*regnare ab aliis fertur Liccus*), he adds the apology: *Omnia monumenta Scotorum usque Cimbaeth incerta erant.*"*

Dr. O'Conor, having given in the text *Regnare ab aliis fertur Liccus*, says in a note : " These show that there existed different histories of Ireland known to Tigernach, which envious time has carried away; for those extant are silent respecting Liccus."†

The passage discussed by Dr. Todd is given in *fac-simile* by O'Curry (BBB.). It is transliterated in the Irish character (at p. 519); but no attempt has been made to render it into English or to elucidate the obscurities. Subjoined in a note O'Curry gives the reading of the Royal Irish Academy MS. and O'Conor's text.

This Irish king Liccus had his origin in the Bodleian *Tigernach*, Rawlinson 488. The necessity of caution in following that MS. can be seen in the extract therefrom already referred to.‡ In the native items, for instance, the scribe either himself confused, or was unable

---

* *Lectures*, vol. i., pp. 518-9.
† Haec ostendunt diversas extitisse Hiberniae historias, Tigernacho notas, quas invida aetas abstulit. Quae enim extant tacent de Licco (*R. H. S.*, ii. 1).
‡ Note D.

to restore, the entry (A.D. 678) relative to the Cenel-Loairn. Equally unversed was he in Latin; as witness (A.D. 683) the incident, taken from Bede, connected with Pope Sergius. From Rawlinson 488, as O'Conor has for once rightly shewn,* was made the Trinity College transcript. In this, some of the glosses of the exemplar have been incorporated in the text.† To judge from the writing, it was copied by the Mac Firbis that executed the *Chronicon Scotorum*.

I give, in parallel columns, the readings of the original (O'Conor's edition) and of the copy :—

O'Conor, R.H.S., ii., p. 1.	MS. H. 1. 18, T.C.D.
In anno xviii° Ptolomaei initiatus est regnare in Emain Cimbaoth filius Fintain, qui regnavit annis xviii. Tunc in Temair Eachach buadhach, athair Ugaine. Regnare ab aliis fertur Liccus. Praescripsimus ollam ab Ugaine regnasse. Omnia monumenta Scotorum usque Cimbaoth incerta erant.‡	In anbo ⱈuɪɪɪ. Ptolomeɪ ꝼuɪc ɪnɪcɪacuꞃ ꞃeʒnaꝺe ɪ n-Eammoɪn Cɪombaoc, ꝼɪlɪuꞃ [Fɪncaɪn], quɪ ꞃeʒnauɪc annɪꞃ ⱈuɪɪɪ. Tunc acTemhaɪꞃ Eochaɪꝺ buaꝺać, acaɪꞃ Uʒoɪne, ꞃeʒnaꞃ[ꞃ]e ab alɪuꞃ ꝼeꞃcuꞃ. Lɪccuꞃ ꝼꞃeꞃcꞃɪꝺꞃɪmuꞃ ollɪm ab Uʒaɪne ɪmꝺeꞃaꞃꞃe. Omnɪa monumenca Scocoꞃum uꞃque Cɪmbaoc ɪnceꝺca eꞃanc.

Here again Mr. Gilbert has placed students of Irish history under lasting obligation. Turning to his *Fac-similes of National MSS.*, we find a page of the Bodleian fragment of *Tigernach*, Rawlinson 502. The entries in question are thus given :—

(*Fac-similes*, etc., Pt. I., Pl. xliii.)	(*Translation.*)
[A. ABR. 1710 ; Ante C. 307.]	[A. ABR. 1710 : B.C. 307.§]
In anno ⱈuɪɪɪ. Ptolomeɪ ꝼuɪc ɪnɪcɪacuꞃ ꞃeʒnaꝺe ɪ n-Emaɪn Cɪmbaeꝺ, ꝼɪlɪuꞃ Fɪncaɪn, quɪ ꞃeʒnauɪc ⱈⱈuɪɪɪ annɪꞃ. Tunc Eću buaꝺach, ꝺaceꞃ	In the 18th year of Ptolemey, commenced to reign in Emania Cimbaed, son of Fintan, who reigned 28 years. At that time, Echu the Victorious,

---

* See his description of the T.C.D. MS. in O'Curry (*Lectures, etc.*, pp. 524-5).

† O'Curry says that, "although on paper, [it] is the most perfect, the oldest and the most original, of those now in Ireland" [*Lectures, etc.*, p. 62). With the final part of the eulogium few will be disposed to disagree.

‡ O'Conor's textual arrangement from *Tunc* to *regnasse*, we may safely conclude from H. 1. 18, does not represent the original. For the amended text and translation, see the extract from Rawlinson 502, which follows in the text.

§ For the dates, see p. 254 *sq.*

Uзaine, in Temoria peзnar[r]e
alir pencun, liquet [licet]
pperónipримur olim Uзaine im-
penappe.

Omnia monumenta Scotorum
urque Cimbaeδ incepta epanc.

father of Ugaine, is said by others to have reigned in Tara, although we have written before that Ugaine [and not his father] ruled [then in Tara].

All the monuments of the Scoti as far as Cimbaed were uncertain.

The MS. form of *liquet* is *liqt*. The same contraction of *que* to represent *ce* is employed in the *Book of Ballymote* (p. 16 b, l. 44): Ir i peo .c. q̄ipc (ceipc)—*this is the first question.*

Early examples of *qu* for *c* are: huiusquemodi (*Book of Armagh*, fol. 6 a); qualicis mei (Ps. xv. 5; Milan *Columbanus*, fol. 37 c); torquolaribus (torcularibus: Ps. lxxxiii., title; Psalter of St. Columba enshrined in the *Cathach*, R. I. A.).

But, what appears decisive, the MS. in the Royal Irish Academy substitutes *vero* for *liquet*:

Eodem tempore initiatus est regnare in Emania (*i.e.* a n-Eamhain) Cimbaoth, mac Fiontain, qui regnavit annis xviii. Interim a Teamhair Eocha Buadhac, athair Ugaine, [regnasse] ab aliis fertur. Nos vero prescripsimus olim ab ipso Ugaine tunc ibi imperatum esse.

At the same time commenced to reign in Emania (that is, in Emain) Cimbaoth, son of Fintan, who reigned 18 years. Meanwhile, Eocha the Victorious, father of Ugaine, is said by others [to have reigned] in Tara. We, however, have written before that Ugaine himself [not his father] was then reigning there.

Omnia monumenta Scotorum usque ad Ciombaoth incerta erant.

All the monuments of the Scoti as far as Ciombaoth were uncertain.

It remains only to add, as bearing on the trustworthiness of Tigernach, that the name of Echu, father of Ugaine, does not appear in any known series of the kings of Tara, or Ireland.

The A-Tract leads to the additional inference, that Tigernach followed the synchronists in dating in detail by Eusebius. This we are in a position to establish by direct proof. Accordingly, from the internal evidence of the Bodleian and Trinity College MSS., I restore by Table VII. (a)* the textual chronology of the entries immediately connected with the above-quoted extracts from the *Annals.*

---

* Lecture IV.

ANNALS OF TIGERNACH.

(a) Rawl. B 502, fol. 6 d.

(b) H. 1. 18, T. C. D., fol. 113.

[A. ABR. 1704:]
[Ante C. 313.]
Reȝno Siriae ⁊ Alexandriae in Minori Arria connegnatum ert ⁊ primur regnauit ibi Antiȝonur annor xuiii., Ptolomei primo [reptimo] anno regnare inchoanr. hic iȝicur annur xiii.ur ert Antiȝoni ricut Ptolomei.—Connegnatum quoque ert in Macidonia [a] Ptolomeir ⁊ Seleucir ⁊ primur regnauit ibi port Alexandrum Pilippur, qui ⁊ Anideur, fratep Alaxandri,

[A. ABR. 1693:]
[Ante C. 324.]
annir uii. regnanr, primo anno¹ Ptolomei regnare incipienr.

regnare inchoanr. hic iȝicur annur xii.ur Antiȝoni ricut Ptolomei primo. Connegnatum ert quoque Macedonia Ptolomeur ⁊ Seleuorir ⁊ primur regnauit ibi port Alaxandrum Pilipur, qui ⁊ Anedeur, Alexanden andir uii. regnanr, primo anno Ptolomei regnare incipienr.

K [A. ABR. 1705 : Ante C. 312].
K [„   „   1706 :   „   „ 311].
K [„   „   1707 :   „   „ 310].
K [„   „   1708 :   „   „ 309].
K [„   „   1709 :   „   „ 308].
[K „   „   1710 :   „   „ 307.]

K. quinquier (5°, MS.).

[A. ABR. 1704:]
[B.C. 313.]
The kingdom of Syria and Alexandria and Asia Minor were reigned over at the same time, and the first to reign was Antigonus, who reigned twenty years, commencing¹ to reign in the first [seventh] year of Ptolemey. This year therefore is the 12th² of Antigonus, as of Ptolemey².—Macedonia was also simultaneously reigned over by the Ptolemies and Seleuci³, and the first to reign there after Alexander was Philip, who [was] also [called] Arideus, brother of Alexander, who
[A. ABR. 1693:]
[B.C. 324.]
reigned seven years, and commenced to reign in the first year of Ptolemey².

K [A. ABR. 1705 : B.C. 312].
K [„   „   1706 :   „   311].
K [„   „   1707 :   „   310].
K [„   „   1708 :   „   309].
K [„   „   1709 :   „   308].
[K „   „   1710 :   „   307.]

---

¹ Here commences b.   ²⁻² Read: 6th of Antigonus and 12th of Ptolemey; 13th of Antigonus, a; 12th of Antigonus [and] 1st of Ptolemey, b. The errors are doubtless scribal.   ³ *Ptolomeus et Seleuosis, b.*

256   THE CODEX PALATINO-VATICANUS, 830.

[A. ABR. 1699:]
[Ante C. 318.]

Undecimo anno priore² Aridеuр,
ғрaтер Alaxandri, qui ⁊ Pilipur,
рех Macedonium (uel Macedonum), cum рua uxoрe, Euridice,
a Macedonibur iprir, ruadente
Olimpiade, matre Alaxandri (⁊
ipra portea intеррeста ert a
Carandro), occirur ert. Port
quem режnauit in Macidonia
Cerranden (uel Carranden) annir
xix.; a quo hencoler, Alaxandri
Magni ғiliur, xiiii.o anno etатir
ruae, cum Roxa, matre рua,
intеррестur ert (ið ert, in An-
cipolitana).

Kl. xi.o anno priore Ariduir,
ғрaтер Alaxandri, qui ⁊ Pilipur,
рех Macedonum, cum рua uxoрe,
Erodice, a Macedonibur iprir,
ruadenta Olimpiade, matre Alaxandri, occirur ert. Port quem
режnauit Caranden anno xix.; a
quo herculer, Alaxandri ғiliur,
xuii. etатir ғue anno, cum Rexa,
matre рua, intеррестur ert.

[K A. ABR. 1711: Ante C. 306.]
[K ,,   ,,   1712: ,, ,,   305.]
[K ,,   ,,   1713: ,, ,,   304.]
[K ,,   ,,   1714: ,, ,,   303.]
[K ,,   ,,   1715: ,, ,,   302.]
[K ,,   ,,   1716: ,, ,,   301.]

Antiзonur, рех Arriae Mino-
nir, a Seleuco ⁊ Ptolomeo in

A[nti]зonur, рех Arriae Mino-
nir, a Seluco et Ptolomeo occi-

[A. ABR. 1699:]
[B.C. 318.]
In the previous 11th year[b], Arideus, brother of Alexander, who [was] also [called] Philip, king of the Macedonians, was slain with his wife, Euridice, by the Macedonians themselves, at the instigation of Olympias, mother of Alexander (and[5] herself was afterwards slain by Cassander[5]). After him reigned in Macedonia Cassander for nineteen years; by whom was slain (namely[5], in Ancipolis [? Pydna][5]) Hercules, son of Alexander the[6] Great[6], in the 18th year of his age, together with Roxana, his mother.

[K A. ABR. 1711 : B.C. 306.]
[K ,,   ,, 1712 :   ,, 305.]
[K ,,   ,, 1713 :   ,, 304.]
[K ,,   ,, 1714 :   ,, 303.]
[K ,,   ,, 1715 :   ,, 302.]

[K A. ABR. 1716 : B.C. 301.] Antigonus, king of Asia Minor, was slain in[6]

[5-5] interlined in *a*; om., *b*.   [6-6] om., *b*.

bello occipur ept. Popt quem   pur ept. Popt quem peznauic
peznauic Demetpiup (cui nomen   Dimetpip, qui non Poliepcibip,
Poliepcicep), piliup eiup, annip   piliup, annip χuiii.
χuiii.

[ABR. 1710:]   In anno χuiii.o³ Ptolomei [ut   In anno χuiii.o Ptolomei [ut
Ante C. 307.] supra, pp. 253-4].—   supra, pp. 253-4].—
               hoc tempope, Ƶenon Ƶoicup   hoc tempope, Ƶemon Ƶoicup ⁊
               [Stoicup] ⁊ Minandep Comicup   Minandep Comicup ⁊ Teuppap-
               ⁊ Teuppaptpip philopophi clap-   te]p pilopophi clapepunt.
               uepunt.

battle⁶ by Seleucus and Ptolemey. And after him reigned Demetrius (who⁷ was called Poliercites⁷), his son, during eighteen years.

[ABR. 1710:]   In the 18th year of Ptolemey [as above, pp. 253-4].
[B.C. 307.]
At this time, Zeno⁸, the Stoic and Menander, the comic poet and Theophrastus, the philosopher, flourished.

The foregoing items have not been printed by O'Conor. What his elucidation would have been is not open to doubt. Having quoted from the MS. Rawlinson 502 that 1000 years elapsed between the departure of the Scoti from Egypt and the 10th year of Darius, A.M. 3529, he adds: "The 10th year of Darius was 4169 of the Julian Period, B.C. 545,—the most learned chronographers agreeing herein with Petavius."* But this parade of learning is a typical instance of what is abundantly proved in his *Tigernach*, that O'Conor was unable to reduce the A.M. to the corresponding B.C. Otherwise, he would have been saved from the ludicrous error of mistaking Darius the Mede for Darius the Bastard. The year intended is the 10th of the latter, B.C. 413. The year of Petavius, it is scarce necessary to add, refers to the former.† We are consequently relieved from discussing its accuracy.

---

⁷⁻⁷ interlined, a; *who* [*was*] *not* [*called*] *Poliercides!* b.   ⁸ This is erroneous: at A. ABR. 1742 [B.C. 275], is: Zeno, Stoicus philosophus, agnoscitur.

* Fol. 4, b, Columna 1, lin. 23:

Ab egressu Scotorum de Ægypto mille anni sunt ad decimum hunc annum Darii, regis Persarum, mundi III.D.XXIX.

Decimus Darii annus fuit Periodi Julianae 4169, ante Christum 545,—consentientibus cum Petavio doctissimis chronographis (R.II.S., ii. p. xvii.).

† *De Doctrina Temporum*, Antwerpiae, 1703, Lib. XIII., tom. II., p. 307.

Similarly, I supply the chronology of the excerpts from the Academy copy given by O'Curry.

(*c*) MS., R.I.A.

[A. ABR. 1699:] [B. C. 318.]	Arideus, frater Alexander Magni, occisus est in Olympiade cxv. et anno Urbis Conditae 436 occisus est.	Arideus, brother of Alexander the Great, was slain in the [3rd year of the] 115th Olympiad and in the 436th year of the Foundation of the City was he slain.
[A. ABR. 1716:] [B. C. 301.]	Antigonus, rex Asiae Minoris, occisus est anno Romae [Conditae] 453.	Antigonus, king of Asia Minor, was slain in the year of [the Foundation of] Rome 453.
[A. ABR. 1710:] [B. C. 307.]	Eodem tempore [*etc.*, *ut sup.*, p. 254].	At the same time [*as above*, p. 254].
[A. ABR. 1718:] C. 299.]	Cessander, rex Macedoniae, obiit anno Romae [Conditae] 456.*	Cassander, king of Macedonia, died in the year of [the Foundation of] Rome 456 [-5].

To enable an independent judgment to be formed, the corresponding portion of the Hieronymo-Eusebian Chronicle is appended.†

Tigernach's "singular preference of the provincial to the national monarch as the one from whose reign to date the commencement of credible Irish history" has seriously embarrassed O'Curry.‡ He is consequently at pains to give grounds for thinking it "not unreasonable to conclude that this great annalist was surprised by the hand of death, when he had laid down but the broad outlines, the skeleton as it were, of his annals, and that the work was never finished"!§ One "great cause of surprise" is "that the Emanian dynasty is given the place of precedence."‖

Whether the "great annalist" was likely to be affected by dynastic considerations of the kind, can be estimated from the examples of his "broad outlines" set forth in Lecture IV. As regards O'Curry's difficulty, an apparently conclusive solution suggests itself. The Ulster kings, like the synchronism of the 18th of Ptolemy with the 1st of Cimbaeth and the credible limit of native history, were taken by Tigernach from the A-Tract. In this they were given as having reigned for a period approximating the duration of the Egyptian kingdom.

---

* O'Curry, *Lectures, etc.*, p. 519. † Note E.
‡ *Ubi sup.*, p. 68.   § *Ib.*, p. 70.   ‖ *Ib.*, p. 68.

Finally, with reference to the B-Text, the synchronistic arrangement from the 15th of Tiberius to the last of Valerian (**q-t**) is the basis of that adopted by Tigernach (O'Conor's edition, p. 16–39). In addition, nearly all the native items of the Tract are found, sometimes with close verbal resemblance, in the Annals. As a typical instance may be quoted the entry corresponding to that with which our compilation abruptly concludes. (The text is taken from the T.C.D. Fragment.)

ıııclxuı. Kl. en. uıı. p., l. ıx. Cat Maıġı-Mucruma u. ꝼeꞃıa ꞃıa Luġaıꝺ, mac Con, ꝺu hı toꞃcaıꞃ Aꞃt Oenꝼıꞃ, mac Cuıꞃꝺ Cetcataıġ ꞏ uıı. meıc Aılılla Auluım. Luġaıꝺ Laġa, ꞃo bı Aꞃt hı Tenloc Aıꞃt. beıꞃne bꞃıtt ımoꞃꞃo, ꞃo bı Coġan, mac Aılılla Aulaım.	[A.M.] 4166 [A.D. 214]. Jan. 1, Saturday, moon 9 [4]. The battle of Magh-Mucruma [was gained] on Thursday by Lugaid, son of Cu, a place where fell Art the Solitary, son of Conn the Hundred-Battled and 7 sons of Oilill Olom. Lugaid Lagha, he slew Art on the Hill of Art. Beinne Britt moreover, he slew Eogan, son of Oilill Olom.
Alıı aıunt Luġaıꝺ, mac Con, ꞃꞃo [ꞃoꞃt] hoc bellum ın Temoꞃıa ꞃeġnaꞃꝛe annıꝛ uıı., uel. xxx., ut alıı [aıunt].	Some say that Lugaid, son of Con, after this battle reigned in Tara 7 years, or 30, as others [say].

We have thus, through the A and B Texts, discovered the chief sources and the operative chronological system of the pre-Patrician portion of the *Annals of Tigernach.*

NOTES.

A.—*BOOK OF BALLYMOTE*, p. 10 b, l. 31.

1.	1.
Se bliaꝺna coıcat malle,	Six years [and] fifty together
Aꞃ ꞃe cetaıb, aꞃ mıle,	Over six hundred, over a thousand,
O cꞃutuġuꝺ Aꝺaım ġan on	Since the formation of Adam without defect
Coꞃ'baıꝺ ın Dılı ın ꝺoman.	Until the Deluge drowned the world.

2.

Da bliadain nocab, ni bneg,
Ap bib cecaib pa coimeb,
Ip pip, map pimim, pe pab,
O Dilinn co hAbp[a]ham.

2.

Two years [and] ninety, not false,
Over two hundred to be observed,
It is true, as I reckon, to say,
From the Deluge to Abram.

3.

Da bliadain cetpacat coin,
Ocup nae cet bo bliadnaib,
O gein Abpaham gen pic
No co popigab Dauib.

3.

Two years [and] forty fair,
And nine hundred of years,
From birth of Abraham without error?
Until David was made king.

4.

Cpi bliadna, pectmoba plan
Ap cpi cecaib co complan
[Ap ceitpi cecaib complan]
O po hoipneb Dauib na penn

Cop'haipgib Iepupalem.

4.

Three years [and] seventy perfect,
Over three hundred very fully
[*Read*: Over four hundred very full]
Since David of the hosts? was inaugurated

Until Jerusalem was plundered.

5.

bliadain ip octmoba og
[Nae m-bliadna octmoba og]
Ap cpi cecaib, ni commop,
[Ap coic cecaib ni commop]
O popba na Daipe 'le
gop'genaip Cpipc 'n-ap Coimbe.

5.

A year and eighty perfect
[*Read*: Nine years (and) eighty perfect]
Over three hundred, not excessive
[*Read*: Over five hundred, not excessive]
From the end of the Captivity hither
Until was born Christ our Lord.

6.

Cpi mili bliadan, ni bneg,
Da bliadain coicat, nae cet,
Co pogemip i puan plan,
Op' bealbab boman bpecnap.

6.

Three thousand years, not false,
Two years [and] fifty, nine hundred,
Until He was born in sound repose,
From the time when was formed the
[bright-faced world.

7.

Cet bliadan ip mili mop,
O pogein in pi poog
gupin m-bliadain pea namta,
Pice bliadan, pe bliadna.
    Se bliadna, ⁊ pl.

7.

A hundred years and a great thousand,
Since was born the king very perfect
To this year in which I am,[1]
[And] twenty years [and] six years.
    Six years, etc.

[1] Lit., which is for me.

B.—*BOOK OF BALLYMOTE*, p. 10 b., l. 9.

Ab Adam usque ad diluvium, anni mille dc.,lvi.[1] A diluvio usque ad Abraham, anni dcccc.,xlii. Ab Abraham usque ad Moisen, anni dc.[2] A Moisi usque ad Salamonem et ad primam edificationem templi, anni cccc.,lxxx.,viii.[3] A Salamone usque ad transmigrationem Babilonis,[4] quae sub Dario, rege Persarum,[5] facta est, anni[6] d.,xii. computantur.[7] Porro a Dario rege usque ad predicationem Domini nostri, Jesu Christi et usque ad x.[8] annum imperii Tiberii Imperatoris[9] explentur anni d.,xl.,viii.

Ita simul fiunt ab Adam usque ad predicationem Christi et decimum [quintum] annum Romani imperatoris, Tiberii, v milia, cc., xxviii.

A[10] passione Christi peradti [peracti] sunt anni dcccc.

[I.] Prima ergo etas mundi, ab Adam usque ad Noe.
[II.] Secunda, a Noe usque ad Abraham.
[III.] Tertia, ab Abraham usque ad David.
[IV.] Quarta, a David usque ad Danielem.
[V.] Quinta etas, usque ad Iohannem Baptistam.

Sexta, a Iohanne usque ad iudicium, in quo Dominus noster veniet iudicare vivos ac mortuos in [et] seculum per ignem. Finit.

---

[1] II.m.,cc.,xlii. Euseb., *Chronicus Canon* (ed. Scalig.), p. 55.   [2] dv., *ib.*
[3] cccc.,lxxix., *ib.*   [4] instaurationem templi, *ib.*   [5] Persarum rege, *ib.*
[6] colliguntur anni, *ib.*   [7] om., *ib.*   [8] quintum decimum, *ib.*
[9] principis Romanorum, *ib.*   [10] The remainder is the work of the tenth-century computist.

C.—(a¹) *BOOK OF BALLYMOTE*, p. 26 a, l. 23.

Da mili ⁊ uí. c., aċt bí bliaḋain ḋ'a eaṙḃaiġ ḃe, o Aḋam co hAḃṙaham.

Two thousand and six hundred, except two years wanting therefrom [2598], from Adam to Abraham. [2598-942 (Second Age) = 1656 (First Age).]

(b) *Ib.*, l. 7.

In n-aeṙ ċanaiṙḃi ḃono,—o Ḋilinḋ co hAḃṙaham; iṙ ḋa bliaḋain .ẋl. ⁊ .iẋ.c. bliaḋan a ṙaḋ ṙiḃein.

The Second Age indeed,—from the Deluge to Abraham : two years [and] forty and nine hundred years is the length of this.

---

[1] *a, b, d, e, i, k* belong to the Synchronistic Tract already mentioned (p. 251); *e, f, g, h,* to a Tract on the *Ages of the World*. The piece of which *j* forms the opening is imperfect, owing to the loss of portion of the MS.

(c) *Ib.*, p. 5 a, l. 51.

Do'n treaſ aeiſ anoſo ſiſ.

In tſeaſ aeiſ in domain,—iſ é ſeó in lin bliadan ſil intí : .i. da bliadain ceatſadat aſ naí .c.aib ; .i. o ſein Abſaim i tiſ Caldeoſum ſu ſabail ſiſi do Dauid. Sein Abſaim, dano, iſ i toſſać na haiſſ ſeo iaſ ſiſ.

Of the Third Age here below.

The Third Age of the world,—this is the complement of years that is in it: namely, two years [and] forty above nine hundred; that is, from the birth of Abram in the land of the Chaldeans until the assumption of kingship by David. The birth of Abram indeed, this is the commencement of this Age in reality.

(d) *Ib.*, p. 23 a, l. 29.

Da faſ tſa Eſiu ſſia ſe .ccc. m-bliadain, conaſtoſſaćt Paſſtolon ; no, da bliadain aſ míle. Ocuſ iſ fíſ eiſſein. Doiſ iſ .lx. bliadan da ſlan do Abſaham in tan ſoſad Paſſtolon Eſſu[-inn] ⁊ da bliadain .xla. ⁊ ix.c. o Abſaham co Dilind ſuaſ : .i., lx. aiſſi Abſaham ſſiſin .lx. [xl.] ſin, conad .c. In .c. ſin ſſiſſna .ix.c., conad míle ; ⁊ da bliadain faiſ ſin. Conad ſolluſ aſſin, conad da bliadain aſ míle o Dilind co tiactain Paſſtolo[i]n a n-Eſinn.

Now Eriu was deserted for the space of three hundred years, until reached it Parrtholon ; or, two years above a thousand. And that [latter calculation] is true. For it is sixty years were complete for Abraham [at] the time Parrtholon occupied Eriu. And two years [and] forty and nine hundred from Abraham to the Deluge upwards: to wit, sixty of the age of Abraham [added] to the that sixty [*read:* forty], so that [the sum] is a hundred. [Let] that hundred [be added] to the nine hundred, so that it is a thousand and [there are] two years above that. So it is manifest therefrom, that it is two years over a thousand from the Deluge to the coming of Parrtholon into Eriu.

Oćt m-bliadna .l. ⁊ ſe .c. ⁊ da míli o toſać domain co tainiſ Paſſtolon a n-Eſinn. Uí .c. bliadan ⁊ da mili, aćt di bliadain d'a eaſbaiſ, o Adam co hAbſaham.

Eight years [and] fifty and six hundred and two thousand from the beginning of the world until came Parrtholon into Eriu. Six hundred years and two thousand, except two years wanting from it, from Adam to Abraham.

(e) *Ib.*, p. 27 b, l. 20.

Da ḟiceat bliadan ┐ ṫe .c. o ᵹein Abraham co tiactain Neiṁið in n-Erinn : .i., in .lx. roćait Abraham co tiactain Parrtolo[i]n in n-Erinn ┐ in .l. ar .u. c.aið robai ril Parrtoloin in n-Erinn ┐ in .xxx. robai Eriu iᵹ ṫar. Conað iað rin na ða .xx. ┐ na .uí. c. bliadan o Abraham co Neimeað. Da bliadain imorro ┐ .lx. ┐ .u[i]. c. ┐ míle o Dilínð co tiaċt Neimeað a n-Eriɴɴ.

Two score years and six hundred, from the birth of Abraham to the coming of Nemed into Eriu: to wit, the sixty Abraham spent until the coming of Parrtholon into Eriu and the fifty over five hundred the seed of Parrtholon was in Eriu and the thirty that Eriu was deserted. So those are the two score and the six hundred years from Abraham to Nemed. Two years indeed and sixty and five [*read*: six] hundred and a thousand from the Deluge until came Nemed into Eriu.

(f) *Ib.*, p. 8 a, l. 41.

Do'n ceatramað aeir annreo roberta.

In ceatramað aeir ðano,—ir i reo a nuimir bliadan ḟil inte : .i., cccc.lxx.iii. bliadan. Ir and imorro roᵹaðar torać na hairi rein, o ᵹaðail riᵹi ðo Dauið (colleccað na braite ror culu, p. 66, l. 39).

Of the Fourth Age henceforth.

The Fourth Age indeed,—this is the complement of years that is in it: namely, four hundred and eighty-three [*read* 485] years. It is where the commencement of this Age is reckoned, from the assumption of kingship by David ([and it lasted] to the dissolution of the Captivity, p. 6 b, l. 39).

(g) *Ib.*, p. 6 b, l. 44.

In coiceð aeir ðano,—ir i reo a nuimir bliadan : .i., naei m-bliadna lxxx.at ar .u.c. bliadan. Ir i in aeir rea uile o rorða na Daire ðaibilonða ᵹo ᵹein Crirt.

The Fifth Age indeed,—this is its number of years: namely, nine years [and] eighty above five hundred years. This Age is entirely from the completion of the Babylonian Captivity to the Birth of Christ.

(h) *Ib.*, p. 7 b, l. 1.

Sexta etar incipit : .i., in reireað aer,—o ᵹein Crirt co ðraċ. [Ni ḟil] imorro nuimir bliadan

Sexta etas incipit : namely, the Sixth Age,—from the Birth of Christ to Doom. Now [there is not] a definite

airigti popran aeir [r]ea illeit fninbi, cia nobet [il]leit fni bia. Oin ni fil ian n-[b]iniuct rcnib- nib irin Scriptuin bail ara tirab, cia beit bo toib inbti cena inab ara fagbaitea, nuimir bliaban na n-aerab.

Act cena, borimtar a nuimir bliaban o Incollugub Crirt co creibem bo Gaebealaib. Muire- bac Muinberg, ba rig Ullab in tan boriact Pabraic Eriub 7 Laegairi, mac Neill, ba ri Tem- rab. Finbtab, mac Fraeic, for Laignib 7 Aengur, mac Nabfraic, for Mumain; Amalgaib, mac Fi- acrac, for Connacta.

Finit.

number of years in this Age as regards us, although there be as regards God. For there is not in directness of expression a place in the Scripture whence would come, though there be indeed in context a place therein whence could be found, the number of the years of the Ages.

But still there is reckoned the number of years from the Incarnation of Christ to [the reception of] Faith by the Gaidil. Muiredach Red-Neck, he was king of Ulster the time reached Patrick Eriu and Laegaire, son of Niall, he was king of Tara. Findchad, son of Fraech, [was king] over Leinster and Aengus, son of Nadfraech, over Munster; Amalgaid, son of Fiachra, over Connacht.

It endeth.

(i) *Ib.*, p. 41 a, l. 16.

Ir irin bliabain robrir Alaxan- bair mor, mac Pilir, in cat an torcair Bairiur mor, mac Air- riri, ibon, tiug[f]lait na Perr; no, i cinb .uii. m-bliaban ian marbab ballartair 7 ian togail babiloine bo Chir mor, mac Bair (gu ruleig rin in m-braib arin baire baibilonba. Or ir e Cir forfuarlaig 7 ballartair for- catt. Or ir e ballartair tiug[f]- lait na n-Gallagba 7 Cir c. rig na Perr), mab bo reir na coim- aimrirbact, ir mar rin: mab bo reir in coittinb, irin trear air in bomain tangabar meic Milib a n-Erinn.

It is in the year that Alexander the Great, son of Philip, gained [*lit.*, broke] the battle in which fell Darius the Great, son of Arsames, namely, the last ruler of the Persians; or, at the end of seven years after the slaying of Balthasar and after the destruction of Babylon by Cyrus the Great, son of Darius (so that he allowed the captives from the Babylonian Captivity. For it is Cyrus liberated and Balthasar was enslaving them. For Balthasar was the last ruler of the Chaldeans and Cyrus, first king of the Persians), if [we reckon] according to the Synchronisms, it was thus: if according to the common [reckoning], [it is] in the Third Age of the world came the sons of Miled into Eriu.

THE CODEX PALATINO-VATICANUS, 830.

(j) *Ib.*, p. 42 b., l. 1.

Incipic do placiupaib Epenn ⁊ dia n-aimpeapaib, ó pé Mac Miliḋ Eppaine co haimpip mic Phiacpaḋ, idon, Da[t]hi.

It beginneth concerning the dynasties of Eriu and of their durations [*lit.*, times], from the time of the Sons of Miled of Spain to the time of the son of Fiachra, namely, Da[t]hi.

hip ipin ceatpamaḋ aimpeap in doṁain cangaḃap Ǵaeḋil docum n-Epenn: idon, a n-aimpip Dauid, mic Ieppe [Iopeḃ, MS.], dia pocpiallaḋ cempull Solman ⁊ ix. m-bliaḋna plaicupa impepii pesip Aripiopum, Dia-ḋapdain do laiti receṁaine, .i. uii.des epca, ⁊ Calainn Mai mip ṡpene.

It is in the Fourth Age of the world came the Gaidil unto Eriu: namely, in the time of David, son of Jesse [Joseph, MS.], when was attempted the temple of Solomon, and nine years of the rule of the kingdom of the Assyrians [were passed], on Thursday of the day of the week, on the seventh [and] tenth of the moon, on the Kalend [1st] of May of the solar month.

(k) *Ib.*, p. 36 b, l. 38.

(Poem of Eochaiḋh Ua Ploind:

Eipceaḋ, aep eagnai aibind.)

Dauid, diapḃ' aimpeap ilbaḋ,

Reimpeaḋ poppeis su poslan,

Ranncap in cpic pin ceandcap,

Dia pasnic ceampull Solṁan.

Seaccmaḋ des, Dia-ḋapdaine,

Doppic peaccmaḋ peap Péne,

Ǵabpaḋ ⁊ callaind cipe,

⁊ Callaind Mai mip ṡpene.

(Poem of Eochaidh Ua Floinn, beginning with:

Listen, folk of wisdom pleasant.)

David, for whom the time was lengthened,

The space spent he very innocently,

Divided is that territory [Eriu] on this side [of the world], [Solomon.

Whilst he was making the temple of

The seventh [and] tenth [of the moon], Thursday, [Fene, Occurred the expedition of the Men of Landed they on the soil of the country, On the Kalend [1st] of May of the solar month.

D.

(a) ANNALS OF TIGERNACH.
Rawl. B 488.
Fol. 11 a.

[A.D. 665]. [Secnuṗaċ] mac blaiṫmaic ṗeznaiṗe incipit.
[A.D. 666] Kal. Moṗṗ Aililla Ḟlanneaṗṗ, mic Domnaill, mic Aeḋa, mic Ainmeṗeċ.—Maelcaiċ, mac Scanblain, ṗi Cṗuiṫne; Maelḋuin, mac Scanḃail, ṗi Cenéoil Caiṗṗṗe, obieṗac.—Eoċaiz Iaṗlaiṫe, ṗi Cṗuiṫne Miḋi; Duibinnṗaċc, mac Dunċaḋa, ṗi hUa-mbṗiuin Ai, moṗcuuṗ eṗc.—Moṗṗ Cellaiz, mic Uzaiṗe.—Caṫ Ḟeiṗcṗe iceṗ Ulcu ⁊ Cṗuiṫne, in quo cecibic Caṫuṗaċ, mac Luiṗċine.—baiṫine, ab benċaiṗ, quieuiṫ.—Ḟaelan, mac Colmain, ṗi Laizen, moṗcuuṗ eṗc.
[A.D. 667] Kal. Moṗcalicaṗ in quo quocuoṗ abaicep benċaiṗ peṗieṗunc,—beṗaċ, Cumine, Colum, [⁊] mac Aeḋa.—Caṫ Aine eceṗ Aṗaḋo ⁊ hUa-Ḟizence, ubi cecibic Eozan, mac Cṗunḋmail.—Ɀuin

(b) CHRONICON SCOTORUM.
Rolls' Ed., pp. 98-106.

[665]. [Secnuṗaċ] mac blaṫmaic ṗeznaṗo incipic.
[666] Kl. Moṗṗ Oililla Ḟlainneṗṗa, mic Domnaill, mic Aeḋa, mic Ainmiṗeċ.—Maelcaiċ, mac Scanḃail, iḋon, ṗí Cṗuiṫne; Maelḋuin, mac Scanḃail, ṗí Cinel Coiṗṗṗi, obieṗunc.—Eoċaiḋ Iaṗlaiṫe, ṗi Cṗuiṫne, moṗcuuṗ.—Duibinḋṗaċc, mac Dunċaḋa, ṗí hUa-mbṗiúin Ai, moṗicuṗ.—Moṗṗ Ceallaiz, mic Ɀuaiṗe.—bellum Ḟeṗ[c]ṗi eciṗ Ulcu ⁊ Cṗuiṫne, in quo cecibic Caṫuṗaċ, mac Luiṗcini.—baiṫini, ab benncaiṗ, quieuic.—Ḟaelan, mac Colmain, ṗi Laizen, moṗicuṗ.
[667] Kl. Moṗcalicaṗ in qua quacuoṗ abbaceṗ benncaiṗ peṗieṗunc, iḋon, beṗaċ, Cumine, Colum ⁊ Aeḋan.—Caṫ Aine eciṗ Aṗaḋu ⁊ hUa-Ḟibzeincc, ubi cecibic Eozan, mac Cṗunnmail.—

[A.D. 665.] [Sechnusach] son of Blathmac begins to reign.
[A.D. 666.] Death of Ailill Flannessa, son of Domnall, son of Aedh, son of Ainmire.—Maelcaich, son of Scannlan, king of the [Irish] Picts; Maelduin, son of Scannal, king of Cenel-Cairpre, died,—Eochaidh Iarlaithe, king of the Picts of Meath; Duibinnracht, son of Dunchad, king of the Ui-Briuin-Ai, died.—Death of Cellach, son of Cuaire[1].—The battle of Fersad between the Ultonians and [Irish] Picts, in which fell Cathasach, son of Luirchin.—Baithine, abbot of Bangor, rested.—Faelan, king of Leinster, died.

[1] Ughaire, *a*.

[A.D. 667.] The plague [took place], in which four abbots of Bangor perished: Berach, Cumine, Colum and the[1] son of Aedh[1].—The battle of Ainne between the Men of Ara and the Ui-Figenti, where fell Eogan, son of Crunnmael.—The

[1-1] Aedhan, *b*.

bṙain Ḟinḃ, mic Mailoċtṗaiġ, ibon, ṗi na n-Ḋeṗe Muman.

[A.D. 668] Kal. Nauiġatio Colmane, epircopi, cum ṗeliqui[i]ṗ ṗanctoṗum aḃ inṗolam uacc[a]e ailb[a]e, in quo ḟunḃaḃat eaclmam [sic: eccleṗiam] ⁊ nauiġatio ḟilioṗum Ġaṗtnait aḃ Iḃeṗniam cum pleḃe Sciṫ.—Ḟeaṗġuṗ, mac Muiceḃa, moṗtuuṗ eṗt.

[A.D. 669] Kal. Oḃitur Cumaine Ailbe [Albi], aḃaiteiṗ lea ⁊ Cṗitan, aḃateiṗṗ ḃenḋaiṗ ⁊ Moḋua, mic Chuiṗt ⁊ moṗṗ Mailṗotaṗataiġ, mic Suiḃne, ṗi nepotum Tuiṗtṗi.—Itaṗnan ⁊ Coṗinḃu apuḃ Pictoṗeṗ ḃeḟuincti ṗunt.—luġalatio Maileḃuin, ṗilli Maenaiġ.

[A.D. 670] Kal. Niġ[n]iṗ ḟacta eṗt occiḃ[enṗ].—Maġna eṗtolt.—luġalatio Maeleḃuin, nepotiṗ Ronain.—Moṗṗ ḃlaiṫmaic, mic

Ġuin ḃṗain Ḟinḃ, mic Mailectṗaiġ, ṗi na n-Ḋeṗi Muman.

[668] Kal. Nauiġatio Colmain, epircopi, cum ṗeliqui[i]ṗ Scotoṗum [ṗanctoṗum] aḃ inṗolam uaccae albae, in qua ḟunḃaḃat eccleṗiam : ⁊ nauiġatio ḟilioṗum Ġaṗtnait aḃ hiḃeṗniam cum pleḃe Set [Sciṫ].—Ḟeṗġuṗ, mac Muccebo, moṗitup.—Muiṗceṗtaċ Náṗ, ṗí Connaċt, iḃon, mac Ġuaiṗe, moṗitup.

[669] Kl. Oḃituṗ Cuimini Albi, abbatiṗ Iae, ⁊ Cṗitáin, abb ḃenḋouiṗ ⁊ Moḋuae, mic Cuiṗt: ⁊ moṗṗ Maeliḟotaiṗtiġ, mic Suiḃne, ṗiġ Nepotum Tuiṗtṗi.—Itupnan ⁊ Coṗmba apuḃ Pictoṗeṗ ḃeḟuncti ṗunt.

[670] Kl.

Ġuin Maeliḃuin, nepotiṗ Ronain.—Moṗṗ ḃlaiṫmaic, mic Ma-

[mortal] wounding of Branfinn, son of Maelochtaraigh, namely[2], the king of the Desies of Munster.

[2] om., b.

[A.D. 668.] The sailing of Colman, the bishop, with relics of saints to the Island of the White Cow [Inisbofin], in which he founded a church and the sailing of the Sons of Gartnat to Ireland with the people of Skye.—Fergus, son of Muicedh, died.—Muircertach[1] Nar, king of Connacht, namely, the son of Guaire, dies[1].

[1-1] om., a.

[A.D. 669.] Obit of Cumine the Fair, abbot of Iona and of Crittan, abbot of Bangor and of Mochua, son of Cust and the death of Maelfothtairtigh[1], son of Suibne, king of Ui-Tuitre.—Itharnan and Corindu[2] died amongst the Picts.—The[3] slaying of Maelduin, son of Maenach[3].

[1] Maelfotharataig, a.   [2] Cormda, b.   [3-3] om., b.

[A.D. 670.] The[1] West became black.[1]—Great[1] dearth[1].—The slaying of Maelduin, grandson of Ronan—Death of Blaithmac, son of Maelcoba and the slaying of

[1-1] om., b.

Maılcoba ⁊ ıuȝalatıo Cuanna, mıc Maılebuın, mıc Cellaıȝ.—Uenıt ȝenr̃ Ȝartnaıt ꝺe heberꞃıa.—Iuȝalatıo bꞃaın Fınꝺ, mıc Maılꝑotartaıȝ.—Morr̃ Ꝺunċaꝺa, nerotır Ronaın.

[A.D. 671] Kal. Morr̃ Orru mıc Etılbrıċ, rıȝ Saxan.—Iuȝalatıo Seaċnuꞃaıȝ, mıc blaıtmaıc, ꞃıeȝur̃ Temorıa ınıtıo hıemır :—

bá¹ rꞃıanaċ¹, ba heclorcaꝺ, A[n] teaċ a m-bıt [Seċnaꞃaċ] ; ba hımꝺa ꞃuıȝell ꞃon rlaıt Irtaıȝ a m-bıꝺ mac blaıtmaıc.

Ꝺubꝺuın, rı ȝenaır Caırrꞃı, ıuȝalauıt ıllum.—bran Fınꝺ, mac Maıloċtraıȝ, rı na n-Ꝺeırꞃe Muman, mortuur̃ ert.—Maelruba ın brıtanıam nauıȝat.

¹⁻¹ ꞃıanan, MS.

[A.D. 672] Kal. Caṫ Ꝺunȝaıle, mıc Maıletuıle, rı Ceneoıl boȝuıne. Loınȝreaċ uıctor ꞃuıt ; Ꝺunȝal cecıꝺıt.—Lorcaꝺ Aırꝺ-

elıcoba ⁊ ıuȝulatıo Cunꝺaı, mıc Cellaıȝ.

Uenıt Ȝenur̃ Ȝartnaıꝺ ꝺe hıbernıa.— Ȝuın bꞃaın Fınꝺ, mıc Maelꝑotartaıȝ. — Morr̃ Ꝺunċaꝺa, nerotır̃ Ronaın.

[671] Kl. Morr̃ Orru, ꝼılıı Etılbrıt, ꞃí Saxan.—Ȝuın Seċnuꞃaıȝ, mıc blaıtmaıc, rȝır Temorıae, ınıtıo hıemır :—

ba rꞃıanaċ, ba heċlar̃ȝaċ, An teċ ambıoꝺ Seċnaꞃaċ ; ba ımꝺa ꞃuꝺell ꞃon rlaıt Irın teċ ambıoıꝺ mac blatmaıc.

Ꝺubꝺúın, ꞃí Cınel Coırrꞃı, ıuȝulauıt ıllum.—bran Fıonn, mac Maelıoctraıȝ, mortuur̃.

Maelruba ın brıtanıam nauıȝat.

[672] Kl. bellum Ꝺunȝaıle, mıc Maeılıtuıle, ꞃí Cıneoıl boȝaıne. Loınȝreċ uıctor ꞃuıt ⁊ Ꝺunȝal cecıꝺıt.

Cuanna, son of Maelduin, son of Cellach.—The[1] Clan Gartnait came [back] from Ireland[1].—Slaying of Brannfinn, son of Mael-Fothartaigh.—Death of Dunchadh, grandson of Ronan.

[A.D. 671.] Death of Oswy, son of Ethelfrith, king of the Saxons.—Slaying of Sechnusach, son of Blaithmac, king of Tara, in the beginning of winter:

> It was full of bridles, it was full of horse-rods,
> The house in which was Sechnusach[1]:
> There were many leavings of plunder
> In the house in which was the son of Blaithmac.

Dubduin, king of Cenel-Cairpre, that slew him.—Branfinn, son of Mael[Fh]ochtraigh, king[2] of the Desies of Munster[2], died.—Maelruba sails into Britain.

¹ om., a.   ²⁻² om., b.

[A.D. 672.] The battle [in which took place the death] of Dungal, son of Maeltuile, king of Cenel-Boguine. Loingsech was victor; Dungal fell.—Burning[1]

Maċaᚁ Ciġi-ᴄelle.—Monṗ Cumuṗ-
caıġ, mıc Ronaın.—Cennṗaelaḋ,
mac blaıᴄṁaıc, ṗeġnaıṗe ıncıṗᴄ.
—Cxpulṗıo Oṗoṗᴄo ḃe ṗeġno ᚁ
comḃuṗᴄıo ḃennċaıṗ ḃṗıᴄonum.
ıııı.ḋc.lxııı.   [A.D. 673]   Kal.
Iuṗᴄ[ın]ıanuṗ¹ mınoṗ, ꝼılıuṗ Conṗ-
ᴄanᴄ[ını], annıṗ x. ṗeġnauıᴄ¹.—
Ġuın Domanġuıṗᴄ, mıc Domnuıll
ḃṗıcc, ṗı Dáılṗıaᴄa.—Nauıġaᴄıo
Ꝼaılḃe, aḃ Iea, ın Iḃeṗnıam.—
Maelṗuḃa ꝼunḋaḃıᴄ ecclerıam²
Aṗoṗcṗoṗan.—Comḃuṗᴄıo Muıġe
Luınġe.

¹⁻¹ From the Chronicle of Bede.
² MS. ecleṛıam.

[A.D. 674]   Kal.   Ġuın Conġaıl
cenḋꝼaᴄa, mıc Dunċaḋa, ṗı Ulaḋ,
o ḃec ḃoıṗċe, mac blaıᴄṁaıc.—
Ꝼeṗġuṗ, mac Loᴄaın, ṗı Ulaḋ,
[hoc] anno.—Nuḃ[e]ṗ ᴄenu[ı]ṗ ᚁ
ᴄṗemula, aḃ ṗḃecıam [ṗṗecıem]
celeṛᴄıṗ aṗcuṗ, ıııı. uıġılıa nocᴄıṗ, quınᴄa ꝼeṗıa anᴄe Ṗaṗca,
aḃ Oıṗıenᴄı ın Occıḋenᴄem ṗeṗ
ṛeṗenum celum aṗṗaṛuıᴄ. Luna
ın ṛanġenem ueṗṛa eṛᴄ.

Monṗ Cumuṗccaıġ, mıc Ronaın.
—Cenḋṗaelaḋ, mac blaᴄṁaıc, ṗeġ-
naṗe ıncıṗᴄ.

[673] Kal.

Ġuın Domanġaıṗᴄ, mıc Dom-
naıll ḃṗıcc, ṗı Dáılṛıaḋa.
Nauıġaᴄıo Ꝼaılḃe, aḃ Iae, ın
hıḃeṗnıam.—Maélṛuḃa ꝼunḋauıᴄ
ecclerıam Aṗoṗcṗoṗan.

[674] Kl. Ġuın Conġaıle cenn-
ṗoḋa, mıc Dunċaḋa, ṗı Ulaḋ;
ḃecc ḃaıṗċe ınᴄeṛꝼecıᴄ eum.

Nuḃeṗ ᴄenuıṗ ᚁ ᴄṛemula, aḃ
ṛṛecıem coeleṛᴄıṗ aṗcuṗ, ıııı.
uıġılıa nocᴄıṗ, u. ꝼeṛıa anᴄe
Ṗaṗcha, aḃ Oṛıenᴄe ın Occıḋenᴄem ṗeṗ ṛeṗenum coelum aṗṗaṛuıᴄ. Luna ın ṛanġuınem ueṛṛa
eṛᴄ.

---

of Armagh and Tehelly¹.—Death of Cumuscach, son of Ronan.—Cennfaeladh, son Blaithmac, begins to reign.—Expulsion¹ of Drost from the kingship and burning of Bangor of the Britons.
¹⁻¹ om., b.

[A.M.] 4658 [! A.D. 673.] Justinian¹ the Younger, son of Constantine, reigned ten years¹.—The [mortal] wounding of Domangart, son of Domnall Brec, king of Dalriata.—Sailing of Failbe, abbot of Iona, to Ireland.—Maelruba founded the church of Apercrossan.—Burning¹ of Magh Luinge.¹
¹⁻¹ om., b.

[A.D. 674.] [Mortal] wounding of Congal Long-head, son of Dunchadh, king of Ulidia, by¹ Bec Boirche, son of Blaithmac¹.—Fergus², son of Lotan, king of Ulidia, died this year.²—A thin and tremulous cloud in the appearance of a rainbow appeared, in the fourth watch of the night of the fifth day before Easter, from east to west, through a serene sky. The moon was changed into blood [colour].
¹⁻¹ Becc Bairche slew him, b.   ²⁻² om., b.

[A.D. 675] Kal. Cat ꝼor Cenꝺ-ꝼaelaꝺ, mac blatmaic, maic Aeꝺa Slaine, oc tiᵹ hUi Maine i n-Dail Cealtꞃu, ꞃe Finꝺacta ꝼleaꝺać. Mac n-Duncaꝺa uictoꞃ eꞃat. Finacta ꝼleᵹać ꞃeᵹnaꞃe incipit. —Moꞃꞃ Noi, mic Dainel.—Moꞃꞃ ꝼilii Panntea.

[A.D. 676] Kal. Colamban, epiꞃcopuꞃ inꞃol[a]e uacc[a]e ailb[a]e ⁊ Finaen aꞃꞃennam pauꞃant.— Coꞃcꞃaꝺ Ailiᵹ Fꞃiᵹꞃenꝺ la Finꝺacta ꝼleᵹać.—Failbe ꝺe hibeꞃnia ꞃeueꝺtuꞃ [ꞃeueꞃtituꞃ].—
11 b Conᵹal, mac Maileꝺuin ⁊ ꝼilii Scanꝺail ⁊ Uꞃtuile iuᵹalaci ꞃunt.

[A.D. 677] Kal. Stella comiteꞃ [comata] uiꞃa eꞃt luminoꞃa in menꞃe Ceptimbiꞃ et Octimbiꞃ.—Dunćaꝺ, mac Ulltain, ꞃi Oiꞃᵹiall, occiꞃuꞃ eꞃt la Maelꝺuin, mac Maeliꝼitꞃiᵹ.—Cat eteꞃ Finꝺacta ⁊ Laiᵹnećo, in loco pꞃoximo Loća ᵹabꞃa, in quo Finꝺacta uictoꞃ

[675] Kl. bellum Cinꝺꞃaelaꝺ, mic blaitmaic, mic Aoꝺa Slaine. Occiꞃuꞃ eꞃt Cennꞃaelaꝺ; Finꝺacta, mac Dunćaꝺa, uictoꞃ eꞃat. Finnacta Fleꝺać ꞃeᵹnaꞃe incipit.

[676] Kal. Columba, epiꞃcopuꞃ Inꞃolae uaccae albae ⁊ Finan, [mac] Aiꞃenꝺain quieueꞃunt.— Coiꞃeacꞃaꝺ Ailiᵹ Fꞃiᵹꞃeinn la Finnacta, mac Dunćaꝺa.—Failbe ꝺe hibeꞃnia ꞃeueꞃtituꞃ. Conᵹal, mac Maeiliꝺuin ⁊ Auꞃtaile iuᵹulati ꞃunt.

[677] Kal. Stella comitiꞃ [comata] uiꞃa eꞃt luminoꞃa in menꞃe Septembꞃiꞃ ⁊ Octobꞃiꞃ.—Dunćaꝺ, mac Ulltain, ꞃi Aiꞃᵹiall, occiꞃuꞃ eꞃt a n-Dún Foꞃᵹo la Maelꝺúin, mac Maeliꞃitꞃaiᵹ.—Cat eꝺiꞃ Finnacta ⁊ Laiᵹnećaiꝺ, in loco pꞃoximo Loća ᵹaboꞃ, in

---

[A.D. 675.] A battle was gained over[1] Cennfaeladh, son of Blaithmac, son of Aedh Slaine, at[2] Tech-Ua-Maine in Dal-Celtre by Finnachta the Festive[2]. The[3] son[3] of Dunchadh was the victor. Finnachta the Festive begins to reign.—Death[4] of Noe, son of Daniel[4.]—Death of the son of Penda.

[1] of, *b*. [2-2] Cennfaeladh was slain, *b*. [3-3] Finnachta, the son, *b*. [4-4] om., *b*.

[A.D. 676.] Columban[1], bishop of the Island of the White Cow [Inisbofin], and Finan, son[2] of Airendan[2], repose.—Destruction[3] of Ailech-Frigrend by Finnachta the[4] Festive.[4]—Failbe returns from Ireland.—Congal, son of Maelduin, and[5] the sons of Scannal[5] and Urthuile were slain.

[1] Columba, *b*. [2-2] Asrennam ! *a*. [3] consecration ! *b*.
[4-4] son of Dunchadh, *b*. [5-5] om., *b*.

[A.D. 677.] A luminous comet appeared in the month[s] of September and October.—Dunchadh, son of Ultan, king of the Oirghialla, was slain in[1] Dun-Forgo[1] by Maelduin, son of Mael-Fithrigh.—Battle between Finnachta and the Lagenians, in a place in the immediate proximity of Loch Gabra, in which Fin-

[1-1] om., *a*.

epac.—Congnerpio Cuile Maine, uibi oecioepunc ba mac Maileaó-bain. beccan Ruimean quieuic in inrola bpicania.
[A.D. 678] Kal. Mopp Colgan, mic Pailbe Plainb, pi Muman.—Pinbgaine, mac Con cen macaip, pi Muman; Oaipóill, mac hUipice, eppoc Glinbi ba laóa; Comane, eppoc; Maelbogan, eppoc Pep-nann, paupanc.—ecep¹ Pepóaip pecció genipip .i. pocai 7 bpiconer qui uicconep epanc loaipnn i Cip m.¹—Cuaimpnama, pi Oppaibi, mopcuup epc la Paelan Senóopcal.—bapp Opopco, mic Oomnaill.
—Caé i Calicpop, in quo uiccup epc Oomnoll bpeacc.
¹·¹ [Read: Inceppeccio Genipip Loaipnn i Cipínn, ibon, caé eéep Peróaip pocai 7 bpiconep, etc.]
[A.D. 679] Kal. Cfuiep Pailbe, abacip léa.—Cenbpaelab, papienp, paupaé.—Caé Caillcen pe Pinb-pneaéca concpa beicc m-boipée.
—Oopmicacio Neécain.

quo Pinnaéca uiccop epac.—Congnerpio Cuile Maine ubi cecibe-punc ba mac Maeliaóbain.—becan Rúminb quieuic in inpola bpicaniae.
[678] Kal. Mopp Colgan, mic Pailbe Plainn, pí Muman.

Oaipcill, mac Cuipecai, eppcop Glinbe ba loóa, quieuic.

Mopp Opopco, mic Oomnaill.

[679] Kl. Cfuiep Pailbe, abacippa.—Cenbpaelab, papienp, quieuic.—Caé Pinnaéca concpa bec baipce.—Oopmicacio Neccain.

nnchta was victor.—The encounter of Cuil Maine, where fell the two sons of Mael-Achdain.—Beccan Ruimen rested in the island of Britain.

[A.D. 678.] Death of Colgu, son of Failbe Flann, king of Munster.—Finnguine[1], son of "Hound-without-mother," king of Munster[1]; Dairchill, son of hUirithe[2], bishop of Glendalough[3]; Cumaine[1], bishop; Maeldogair, bishop of Ferns, repose[1].—Massacre[1] of Cenel-Loairn in Tirenn: namely, a battle between Ferchair the Tall and the Britons, who were victors[1].—Tuaimsnama[1], king of Ossory, was killed by Faelan Senchostal[1].—Death of Drost, son of Domnall.—A[1] battle in Calatross, in which was vanquished Domnall Brecc[1].

[1-1] om., b.   [2] Cuirete, b.   [3] rested, ad., b.

[A.D. 679.] Resting of Failbe, abbot[1] of Iona[1].—Cennfaeladh, the sage, reposes[2].—The battle of[3] Teltown[3] [was fought] by[4] Finnshnecta against Becc Boirche.—The falling asleep of Nechtan.

[1-1] abbess! b.   [2] rested, b.   [3-3] om., b.   [4] of, b.

[A.D. 680] Kal. Colman, abar bencaıp paurac. — Catal, mac Ragallaıʒ, morcuur erc.—ʒuın Pıanamla, mıc Maılecuıle, pı Laıʒın ⁊ roıbreaḋan bıa muınncır rеın poʒеoḃaın ar Pınaċta.—Caṫ Saxonum, ubı ccерıc [cecıbıc] Almuíne, filiur Oru. — Morr Maelroṫарcaıʒ, errıc Aırbrraċa.—bran, mac Conaıll, pı Laıʒen, anno.—Caṫ ı m-baʒna, ubı cecı[bı]c Conaıll oırʒnıʒ, pı Ceneoıl Caırрpı.—Learra ʒnauır[r]ıma ın hıbernıam, qu[a]e uocacur bolʒaċ.

[A.D. 681] Kal. Conburcıo реʒum ı n-Ðun-ceıtırn : ıbon, Ðunʒal, mac Scanbaıl, pı Cruıcneċ ⁊ Cenbraelaḃ, pı Cıannaċta ʒlınbı ʒemın, ın ınıcıo ercacır, la Maelbuın, mac Maıleriсрıʒ.

Caṫ blaı Slebe porcea, ıcer Maelbuín, mac Maılerıсрıʒ ⁊

[680] Kl. Colman, ab benncaır, quıeuıc.—ʒuın Pıanamlo, mıc Maelıcuıle, реʒır Laʒenorum. Ocur roıċreḋan bıa muıncır rerın robʒeʒuın ar Pınnaċta.— Catal, mac Roʒallaıʒ, morıcur.— Caṫ Saxonum ubı cecıbıc Almune, filiur Orru.—Morr Maelroṫарcaıʒ, еrrcoır Aırb Sraṫa.

Caṫ ı m-boḃʒnu, ubı cecıbıc Conall Oırʒnec, ıbon, pí Coırрре. —Lерра ʒnauırрıma, quae uocaсur bolʒaċ.

[681] Kl. Comburcıo реʒum a n-Ðún-cetırn, ıbon, Ðunʒal, mac Scanbáıl, рí Cruıcne ⁊ Cennraelaḃ, mac Suıbne, pí Cıannaċta ʒlınne ʒemeın, ınıcıo aercacır, lá Maelbúın, mac Maelrıcnaıʒ.— Cıár, ınʒen Ðuıbrea, quıeuıc.— Caṫ blaı Slebe porcea, ınıcıo hıemır, ın quo ıncerreccur ers

---

[A.D. 680.] Colman, abbot of Bangor, reposes[1].—Cathal[2], son of Ragallach died[2].—[Mortal] wounding of Fianamail, son of Maeltuile, king of Leinster, and a messenger of his own people slew him for Finnachta.—A battle of the Saxons, where fell Alfwine, son of Oswy.—Death of Mael-Fothartaigh, bishop of Ardsmtha.—Bran[3], son of Conall, king of Leinster, [died this] year[3].—A battle [was fought] in Bagna, where fell Conall[4] the Raider[4], king of Cenel-Cairpre.—Most severe leprosy in Ireland, which is called the Pox.

[1] rested, b. [2-2] placed after next entry, b. [3-3] om., b. [4-4] in the genitive, a.

[A.D. 681.] Burning of the Kings in Dun-Ceithirn : namely, Dungal, son of Scannal, king of the [Irish] Picts and Cennfaeladh, son[1] of Suibne[1], king of the Ciannachta of Glenn-Given, in the beginning of summer, by Maelduin, son of Mael-Fithrigh.

(a).

The battle of Blai-sliabh afterwards, between Maelduin, son of Mael-Fithrigh and Flann, son of Mael[tuile, in which was slain Maelduin, son of Mael-

(b).

The battle of Blai-sliabh afterwards, in the beginning of winter, in which was slain Maelduin, son of Mael-Fitraigh, by the Ciannachta of Glenn-

[1-1] om., a.

Fland, mac Maile, la Ciannacta Glindi Gemin.

barr Conaill cail, mic Duncad, ı Cind-tıre.—barr Sechurais, mic Airmedais ⁊ Conains, mic Consail. —Ciar, insen Duibne, quieuit.
[A.D. 682] Kal. Guin Cindraelad, mic Colsan, ri Condact ⁊ Ulca bers O Caellaise do Cinmaicne Cuile occibit eum, iar n-sabail tise rair do Conmaicne.—Duncad Muirrce, mac Maelduib, ri Conact, anno.—Cat Rata-moire Muise Line contra britoir [britoner], ubi ccerit [cecibit] Caturrac, mac Maileduin, ri Cruicne ⁊ Ulltan, mac Dicolla. —Obitur Suibne, mic Mailumae, princirir Corcaise. — Orcabe-ir[-er] beletea[-ae] runt la bruide.—Iurt[ın]ianur¹, ob culpam rerribiea[-iae] resnı slopıa rribatur[-uatur], exul ın Pontum recetıb [recebıt]¹.

Maelduin, mac Maeliptrais, la Ciannacta Glinne Geimin ⁊ la Pland Pionn, mac Maelituile.— Iusulatıo Conaill, mic Duncada, a cCinn-tıre.—Iusulatıo Sechurais, mic Airmedais, ⁊ Conains, mic Consaile.
[682] Kl. Iusulatıo Cindroalad, mic Colsan, rí Connact ⁊ Ulcu bers hUa Cailliδe di Conmaicnib Cuile occibit eum.

Cat Rata-móıre Muise Line contra britoner, ubi cecibe-runt Caturac, mac Maelduin, rí Cruicne ⁊ Ulltán, mac Dicolla.

¹⁻¹ From the Chronicle of Bede.

Fithrigh,] by the Ciannachta of Glengevin.
gevin and by Flann the Fair, son of Maeltuile.

[Violent] death of Conall the² Slender², son of Dunchadh, in Cenn-tire.—[Violent] death of Sechnusach, son of Airmedach and of Conang, son of Congal.—Ciar³, daughter of Duibre, rested³.

²⁻² om., b.   ³⁻³ misplaced after first entry, b.

[A.D. 682.] [Mortal] wounding of Cennfaeladh, son of Colgu, king of Connacht and "Red-Beard" Ua¹ Caillidhe¹ of the Conmaicni-Cuile slew him, after² a house [in which he chanced to be] was seized upon him² by³ the Conmaicni³.—Dunchad³ of Muirisc,'son of Maeldub, king of Connacht, [died this] year³.—Battle of Rathmor of Magh-Line against the Britons, where fell Cathusach, son of Maelduin, king of the [Irish] Picts, and Ulltan, son of Dichull.—Death³ of Suibne, son of Maelume, abbot of Cork³.—The³ Orkneys were laid waste by Bruide³.—Justinian³ was deprived of the regal dignity for the crime of perfidy and retired in exile to Pontus³.

¹⁻¹ O'Caellaighe, a.   ²⁻² lit., after the capture of a house upon him. Om., b.
³⁻³ om., b.

[A.D. 683] Kal. Leo¹ .iii. annis [683] Kl.
regnauit¹.—Papa¹ Sergius [Ser-
gius] in sacrario beati Petri
apostoli cappam argenteim[-am]
qu[a]e in angulo obscurissimo
diutisimo[-e] iacuerat ¬ in ea
crucem dueprir ac pretiosis
lapid[ib]ur adornatom[-am],
Domino reuelante, reperit : de
qua trassis quatuor petalir
quibur gemm[a]e inacaura [in-
clurae] erant, minea[-ae] magni-
tudinis portionem ligni salutis-
feri dominic[a]e crucis interius
repositum[-am] inspeicris[-exit];
qu[a]e ess e more [ex tempore
illo] annis omnibus in barilica
Saluatoris[-is] qu[a]e apellato
[appellata] Constantiniana, die
Exaltationis[-tionis] eius, ab
omni aculatur[orsu-] atague
asoratur[ad-] populo¹.—Duncad Dunchad Muirsce, filius Maeil-
Muirsce, mac Maelbuid, ri duid, idon, rí Connact, iugula-
Con[n]acc, iugulatur.—Feargal tur.
Aidne, mac Artgaile, ri Con[n]acc.
—Cat Corainb in quo ceci[di]t bellum Corainb in quo ceciderunt
Colgu, mac blaitmaic ¬ Fergur, runt Colcu, mac blaitmaic ¬
mac Mailbuin, ri Cenuil-Cairpre. Fergus, mac Maeilbuin, ri
¹⁻¹ From the Chronicle of Bede. Cineoil-Coirpri.

[A.D. 683.] [Pope][1] Leo reigned three years[1].—Pope[1] Sergius by revelation of the Lord found in the sacristy of the church of Blessed Peter, the Apostle, a silver casket, which had lain for a very long time in a very dark corner, and in it a cross adorned with divers precious stones. The four plates in which the gems were embedded having been removed from it, he beheld laid within a portion of wondrous size of the salutary wood of the Lord's Cross; which from that time is every year kissed and adored by all the people, in the basilica of the Saviour, which is called the Constantinian, on the day of its Exaltation [May 3][1].—Dunchadh of Muirisc, son of Maelduin, namely[2], king of Connacht, is slain.—Fergal[1] Aidhne, son of Artgal, [became ?] king of Connacht[1].—The battle of Corann, in which fell Colgu, son of Blaithmac and Fergus, son of Maelduin, king of Cenel-Cairpre.

[1-1] om., *b*. [2] om., *a*.

E.—HIERONYMO-EUSEBIAN CHRONICLE.

AN. ABR. 1693-1718 [B.C. 324-299].

R. COND.	OLYMP.	ABRAHA-MUS	ÆGYPT. Ptolemaeus Lagi	MACED. Philippus Aridaeus	ROM. Consules	
			I. PTOLEMÆUS, Lagi filius, annis xL.			
				I. PHILIPPUS ARIDÆUS annis vi.		
CDXXX.	114.1	1693	1	1	189	Macedonum duces in seditionem versi. Lydiam et Thraciam et Hellespontum Lysimachus tenuit.
		1694	2	2	190	Perdiccas adversum Ægyptios dimicat, sed obtinere non potuit.
		1695	3	3	191	
		1696	4	4	192	Menander primam fabulam cognomento Ὀργήν docens superat.
	115	1697	5	5	193	. Demetrius Phalereus habetur illustris.
		1698	6	6	194	

Appius Claudius Caecus Romae clarus habetur, qui aquam Claudiam induxit et viam Appiam stravit.

Agathocles Syracusis in Sicilia tyrannidem exercet.

Lamiacum bellum motum.

Ptolemaeus, Lagi filius, tertio regni anno, Hierosolymis et Judaea in ditionem suam dolo redactis, plurimos captivorum in Ægyptum transtulit.

Theophrastus philosophus agnoscitur, qui divinitate loquendi, ut ait Cicero, nomen accepit.

Judaeorum pontifex magnus, Onias, Jaddi filius, clarus habetur.

Romani Samnitas latrones diutissimo contra se praeliantes ad extremum servituti subiiciunt.

E.—HIERONYMO-EUSEBIAN CHRONICLE—*continued.*

AN. ABR. 1693-1718 [B.C. 324-299].

R. COND.	OLYMP.	ABRAHAMUS	ÆGYPT. Ptolemaeus Lagi	MACED. Philippus Aridaeus	ASIÆ Antigonus	ROM. Consules	
					I. ANTIGONUS annis xviii.		
		1699	7	7	1	195	Antigonus Antigoniam ad amnem Orontem condidit, quam Seleucus instauratam appellavit Antiochiam.
				II. CASSANDER annis xix.			
		1700	8	1	2	196	
	116	1701	9	2	3	197	Menedemus et Speusippus philosophi insignes habentur.
		1702	10	3	4	198	
CDXL.		1703	11	4	5	199	
		1704	12	5	6	200	

R. COND.	OLYMP.	ABRAHAMUS	ÆGYPT. Ptolemaeus Lagi	MACED. Cassander	ASIÆ Antigonus	SYRIÆ Seleucus Nicanor	ROM. Consules
						I. SELEUCUS NICANOR annis xxxii.	
	117	1705	13	6	7	1	201
		1706	14	7	8	2	202

Hinc Asiae regnum nascitur et mox Syriae: et regnat in Asia primus Antigonus.

Machabaeorum Hebraea historia hinc Graecorum supputat regnum. Verum hi duo libri inter divinas Scripturas non recipiuntur.

Regnum Syriae et Babylonis et superiorum locorum nascitur: et regnat primus Seleucus Nicanor.

Ab hoc anno Edesseni tempora computant civitatis suae.

Romani Marsos et Umbros et Pelignos superant.		1707	15	8	9	3	203
	118	1708	16	9	10	4	204
		1709	17	10	11	5	205	Lysimachia in Thracia condita civitas.
Romani colonias deducunt.		1710	18	11	12	6	206	Demetrius Phalereus, ad Ptolemaeum veniens, impetravit ut Atheniensibus democratia redderetur.
		1711	19	12	13	7	207
Cyprum Ptolemaeus invasit insulam.		1712	20	13	14	8	208
Theodorus atheus agnoscitur philosophus, qui impius vocabatur.	CDL. 119	1713	21	14	15	9	209
		1714	22	15	16	10	210
		1715	23	16	17	11	211	Seleucus Antiochiam, Laodiceam, Seleuciam, Apamiam, Edessam, Beroeam et Pellam urbes condidit: quarum Antiochiam XII. anno regni sui exstruxit.
Judaeorum pontifex maximus Simon, Oniae filius, clarus habetur, cui cognomentum Justus fuit propter sollicitiam in Deum religionem et in cives suos pronam clementiam.		1716	24	17	18	12	212
					II. DEMETRIUS annis XVII.		
	120	1717	25	18	1	13	213
[CDLV.]	[120.2]	1718	26	19	2	14	214	Seleucus Babylonem obtinuit.

III. FILII CASSANDRI, Antigonus et Alexander, annis IV.

A

[comaimsiraċta.]

(ɫebar baiɫi in mhoṫa, p. 9a.)

a Prima eċar mundi, don, in ced áir do'n doman,—ir e reo ɫin bliadan aċa indċi, idon, re bliadna coicaċ ar re ceċaib, ar miɫi, do reir Maiġiṡoreċ na n-Eabrad. Ocur, mad do reir na Sġoile, ir ċri bliadna ar rin. Secunda eċar mundi, idon, in d-ara hair,—da bliadain ceċorċaċ ar nóe ceċaib, do reir na Maiġirċreċ. Ocur, mad do reir na Scoile, ar bliadain ar rin. Ċerċia eċar mundi, idon, in ċrer air do'n doman,— idon, da bliadain ceċorċaċ ┐ nóe ceċ, do reir na Maiġirċreċ ┐ na Scole. Quarċa eċar, idon, in ceaċramad aír,—idon, ċri bliadna reċċmoġad ar ceṫri ceṫib, do réir na Maiġirċreċ. Ocur, maġ (! lege mad) do reir na Scoiɫi, ir da bliadna [deaċ] ar rin. Quinċa eċar mundi,—idon, nóe m-bliadna oċċmoġad ┐ coic ceċ, do reir in da rand. Ocur iran air [r]in robadar na hEabraide ann-a n-Đairre re re reċċmoġad bliadan. Ocur irin n-air ceċna rin do rcribad lúbích, rċair do'n bibla. Seẋċa eċar mundi,—idon, in rereḋ aír ┐ ni ḟuil ċoihur bliadan rorċi, aċċ a beċ mar air renoraċda aġon domun ┐ eġ in doma[i]n uile a ḟoirċenn rin [? lege rin] ┐ do na hairib.

---

b O Adam co Điɫind, da bliadain ceċorċaċ, da ceċ ┐ da miɫi. O Điɫind co ceċġabail Erenn, idon, da bliadain ┐ mile : idon, in ċan roġad Parċalon. Miɫi bliadan imorro roċaiċ a ril ríbein, co ċanic duinebaċ, idon, ċam ; conid de aċa Ċamlaċċ a n-Erinn. Da bliadain ar ċriċaiċ dono robai Eri ḟar iar rin, co n-daġad Neimeḋ, mac Aġnomain, do Ġreġuib Sceiċia. O Điɫind co Abraham, da bliadain ceċorċaċ ┐ nóe ceċ. O Abram, imorro, ġo ceċġabail Erenn, rerca bliadan. O Abraham co bar Iorerh i n-Eġirċ, bliadain ┐ rerca ┐ ċri ceċ. O bar Iorerh co ċoirimċeċċ Mara Roihuír, bliadain ┐

A

[SYNCHRONISMS.]

(*BOOK OF BALLYMOTE*, p. 9 a.)

a *Prima etas mundi*, the first age of the world,—namely, this is the complement of years that is in it, to wit, six years [and] fifty above six hundred, above a thousand, according to the Masters of the Hebrews. And, if it is according to the School, it is three years above that. *Secunda etas mundi*, that is, the second age,—two years [and] fifty above nine hundred, according to the Masters. And, if it is according to the School, it is a year above that. *Tercia etas mundi*, namely, the third age of the world,—to wit, two years [and] two score and nine hundred, according to the Masters and the School. *Quarta etas*, namely, the fourth age,—to wit, three years [and] seventy above four hundred, according to the Masters. And, if it is according to the School, it is two years [and ten] above that. *Quinta etas mundi* [namely, the fifth age of the world],—to wit, nine years [and] eighty [and] five hundred, according to the two sides. And [it is] in that age were the Hebrews in their captivity for the space of seventy years. And [it is] in the same age was written Judith, a history in [*lit.*, from] the Bible. *Sexta etas mundi*, namely, the sixth age and there is no measure of years upon it, but it is like a senile age in the world. And the dissolution of the whole world [will be] the end of that and [*lit.*, for] the ages.

---

b From Adam to the Deluge, two years, [and] forty, two hundred and two thousand. From the Deluge to the first occupation of Eriu, namely, two years and a thousand : that is, the time Partholon occupied [it]. A thousand years indeed spent his seed, until came the man-plague, namely, pestilence : so that from it there is [the local name] Tamlacht in Eriu. Moreover, two years above thirty was Eriu deserted after that, until occupied it Neimed, son of Agnoman, of the Greeks of Scythia. From the Deluge to Abraham, [n.c.] two years [and] forty and nine hundred. From Abraham[1], however,[1] [2017] to the first occupation of Eriu, sixty years. From Abraham to the death of Joseph[2] in Egypt, a year and sixty and three hundred. From[2] [1656] the death of Joseph to the Passage of the Red Sea[3], a year and sixty[3] [1511]

280 Lebar baili in mota.

[b] ꞃeꞃca ⁊ ceꞇ. O ꞇoiꞃimꞇecꞇ Maꞃa Romaiꞃ ᵹo ᵹabail Eꞃenn ꝺo macaiƀ Milid Eꞃbaine ceꞇoꞃca ⁊ ceꞇꞃi ceꞇ bliaꝺan. O ᵹabail Eꞃenn co ꞇoᵹail Ꞇꞃae, oꞀ m-bliaꝺna ꞃiceꞇ ⁊ ꞇꞃi ceꞇ. O ꞇoᵹail
p. 9b Ꞇꞃac co | cumꝺacꞀ Ꞇempoill Solman, coica ⁊ ceꞇ bliaꝺan. O cumꝺacꞀ in Ꞇempoill ᵹu ꝺeoꝺꝼlaꞀa Aꞃaꞃꝺa, coic ꝺec ⁊ ꝺa ceꞇ.

c Coic ꞃiᵹ ꞇꞃicaꞇ ꞃoꝺaꝺaꞃ oc Aꞃaꞃꝺaiƀ. Ceꞇoꞃca bliaꝺan aꞃ ꝺiƀ ceꞇaiƀ aꞃ mili ꞃoꝺai a ꝼlaiꞇuꞃ. O ꞃoꞃba ꝼlaꞇiuꞃa Aꞃaꞃꝺa ᵹuꞃin ceꞇ n-Aenac n-Olimp la Ꞡꞃeᵹu, ꞇꞃi bliaꝺna ceꞇoꞃcaꞇ. O'n ceꞇna Olimp ᵹu ꝺaiꞃe ꝺeic Ꞇꞃeꝺe, ꞃé bliaꝺna coicaꞇ ⁊ ceꞇ. O ꝺaiꞃe ꝺeiᵹ Ꞇꞃebe ᵹo loꞃcuꝺ in Ꞇempoill, ꞃé bliaꝺna ꞇꞃicaꞇ. Ꝺa bliaꝺain ceꞇoꞃcaꞇ aꞃ ceꞇꞃi ceꞇaiƀ ꞃoꝺai in Ꞇempoll iaꞃ n-a cumꝺacꞀ ᵹo a loꞃcaꝺ. O loꞃcuꝺ in Ꞇempaill co ꞃoꞃcenn ꝼlaꞀ[iuꞃ]a Meꝺ, ꞇꞃica bliaꝺan [ann(oꞃum), MS.]. OꞀ ꞃi ꞃoꝺalnaꞃꝺaiꞃ o Meaꝺaiƀ. Nóe m-bliaꝺna coicaꞇ aꞃ ceꞇ ꝺoiƀ. O ꞃoꞃcenꝺ ꝼlaꞀ[iuꞃ]a Meaꝺ co ꞇoꞀuꞃ aꞃ ꝺaiꞃe babilonꝺa ⁊ ᵹo haꞀnuiᵹeaꝺuᵹ in Ꞇempaill, ceꞇoꞃca bliaꝺan. O aꞀnuiꝺeaᵹuꝺ in Ꞇempoill ᵹu ꝺeiꞃeaꝺ ꝼlaꞀ[iuꞃ]a na Peꞃꞃ, ꞇꞃi ceꞇ [bliaꝺan]: iꝺon, ꝺa ꞃiᵹ ꝺec ꞃo[ꝼ]olla[m]naꞃꝺaiꞃ o Peꞃꞃaiƀ. bliaꝺain aꞃ ꞇꞃicaiꞇ aꞃ ꝺa ceꞇaiƀ ꞃoꝺai a ꝼlaiꞀiuꞃ.

d ꝼlaiꞇiuꞃ Ꞡꞃeᵹ iaꞃum [ꞃoꞃꞇ, MS.]. Iꞃ e ceꞇna ꞃiᵹ ꞃoꝺai ꝺiƀ ꞃiꝺein, iꝺon, Alaxanꝺaiꞃ, mac Pilip: ꞃé bliaꝺna a ꝼlaiꞇuꞃ. Poꞇolameuꞃ, mac Laiꞃᵹe, iaꞃum [ꞃoꞃꞇ, MS.]: ceꞇoꞃca bliaꝺan ꝺo. Iꞃin oꞀmaꝺ bliaꝺain ꝺec a ꝼlaiꞇuꞃa ꞃaein ꞃoᵹaꝺ Cim-baeꞀ, mac Ꝼinꞇain, ꞃiᵹi Eamna-Maca. O ᵹabail Eꞃenn co haimꞃiꞃ in CimbaeꞀ ꞃin, ꝺa bliaꝺain ⁊ ꝺa ceꞇ ⁊ mile. Maꝺ o ꞇoꞃꞃacꞀ ꝼlaꞇiuꞃa Ꞡꞃeᵹ, ꞇꞃi bliaꝺna ꞇꞃicaꞇ. Niꝺaꝺ ꝼeꞃꞃa ⁊ niꝺaꝺ ꝺeꞃꝺa ꞃcela ⁊ ꞃenꞇuꞃa Ꝼeꞃ n-Eꞃenn coniᵹi CimbaeꞀ, mac Ꝼinꞇain. (1) CimbaeꞀ, mac Ꝼinꞇain, ꞃeᵹnauiꞇ annoꞃ, iꝺon, a oꞀ ꝼiꞁeꝺ. (2) Eocaiꝺ Ollacaiꞃ ꞃeᵹnauiꞇ annoꞃ uiᵹinꞇi. (3) Uamancenn, mac Coꞃainꝺ, ꝼiꞁe bliaꝺan. (4) Concoꝺaꞃ Roꝺ, mac Caꞇaiꞃ, ꞃeᵹnauiꞇ ꞇꞃiᵹinꞇa annoꞃ. (5) Ꝼiaca, mac ꝻeiꝺlimꞀe, ꞃeᵹnauiꞇ annoꞃ ꞃeꝺecim. (6) ꝺaiꞃe,

and a hundred. From the Passage of the Red Sea to the occupation [b]
of Eriu by the sons of Milesius of Spain, forty and four hundred [b.c.]
years. From the occupation of Eriu to the Destruction of Troy[4], [4] [1182]
eight years [and] twenty and three hundred. From the Destruction
of Troy to the building of the Temple of Solomon[5], fifty and a hundred [5] [1033]
years. From the building of the Temple to the last prince of the
Assyrians[6], five [and] ten and two hundred. [6] [821]

c Five kings [and] thirty were for the Assyrians. Forty years
above two hundred, above a thousand was their rule. From completion of the Assyrian kingdom until the first Olympian Assembly[1] [1] [776]
by the Greeks, three years [and] forty. From the first Olympiad to
the Captivity of the Ten Tribes[2], six years, fifty and a hundred. [2] [747]
From the Captivity of the Ten Tribes to the burning of the Temple[3], [3] [591]
six years [and] thirty. Two years [and] forty above three hundred
was the Temple after its building[4] to its burning. From the burning [4] [1033]
of the Temple to the end of the kingdom of the Medes[5], thirty years. [5] [561]
Eight kings ruled of the Medes. Nine years [and] fifty above a
hundred [were reigned] by them. From the end of the kingdom of
the Medes to the return from the Babylonian Captivity[6] and to the [6] [521]
renewal of the Temple[7], forty years. From the renewal of the Temple [7] [520]
to the end of the kingdom of the Persians[8], three hundred [years] : [8] [330]
that is, two kings [and] ten ruled of the Persians. A year above
thirty, above two hundred was their rule.

d The kingdom of the Greeks afterwards. This is the first king
that was of these, namely, Alexander[1], son of Philip: six years his [1] [325*]
reign. Ptolemey[2], son of Lagus, afterwards: forty years [were [2] [285*]
reigned] by him. It is in the eighth year [and] tenth[3] of his reign [3] [307]
that Cimbaeth, son of Finntann, assumed the kingship of Emain of [*Obit.]
Macha. From the occupation of Eriu to the time of that Cimbaeth,
two years and two hundred and a thousand. If from the beginning
of the kingdom of the Greeks, three years [and] thirty. They are not
known and they are not certain, the Tales and the Histories of the
Men of Eriu as far as Cimbaeth, son of Finntan. [The kings of Ulster
were:] (1) Cimbaeth, son of Finntan, reigned eight [and] twenty
years. (2) Eochaidh Ollachair reigned twenty years. (3) Uamancenn, son of Corand, a score of years. (4) Conchobar Rod, son of
Catair, reigned thirty years. (5) Fiacha, son of Feidlimid, reigned
sixteen years. (6) Daire, son of Fuirg, a year [above] seventy.

[**d**] mac Forgo, bliadain [ar] rectmogaid. (7) Enna, mac Roetec, coic bliadna. (8) Fiac, mac Fiadcon, coic bliadna cetorcat regnauit. (9) Findcad, mac daic, ... (10) Concobar Mael, mac Fuici, da bliadain dec. (11) Cormac Loigte, ocht bliadna ricet a rige. (12) Moccai, mac Murcorad, tri bliadna. (13) Eochaid, mac Daire, coic bliadna regnauit. (14) Eochaid Salbuidi, mac Loic, trica bliadan regnauit.

e Irin octmad bliadain déc a plaitura raein dericit rex [*lege* regnum] Grecorum. Ir iad fidein robai ain bliadain ar cetri riccaid ar da cetaid. Da rig deg dofollamnartair uaidib 7 aen rigan. Ir ann rin tindrena plaitura Roman. Ir iad ridein foillrigter co dereod in beata. Gabair luil Cerrair rige. Ar eiriden cetna rogab rige Roman: coic bliadna robai i n-a plaitur.—Octarin Ugairt, ré bliadna coicat regnauit. [Tiber] Cerrair Ugairt 'n-a deadaig ridein. Ocur irin cetramad bliadain dec plaitura [Octarin] Cerair addat Eochaid Salbuidi, ri Ulad. Irin coiced bliadain deg plaitura Tiber Cerar Uguirt dotindrcain Concobar, mac Neara, follamnact a n-Eamain; qui regnauit annor, rerca bliadan. Irin octmad bliadain ficed plaitura Conchobair, mic Nearra, (Ir e ridein in b-ara bliadain cetorcat plaitura Cerair Ugairt.) rogeinair in Coimdi, idon, Iru Crirt. Iran b-ara bliadain cetorcat plaitura Conchobair acbat Cerar Ugairt, irin trer bliadain rectmogad a airi.

f Tibir Secrair, rogab in rige a n-deadaid a atar: ceitri bliadna ficed a plaitur. In deachmad bliadain plaitura Tibir Segrair acbat Conchobar, mac Nerra. In octmad bliadain iarum [port, MS.] ar Tibir, rocrochad Crirt. Sect m-bliadna coicat ar da cetaib [o bar Conchobair, mic] Nerra, go gabail rige do Chormac, mac [Airt, mic Cuind. Irin] coiceod bliadain deg plaitura Tibir Shegrair [do baitred] Crirt ocur do tindrcain proige[pt Eoin bartairt. Irin octmad] bliadain deg plaitura Tibir [Segrair do crochad Crirt.] | Irin trer bliadain deg iar crochad Crirt, dodeadaid Peadar docum Roma 7 irin coiced bliadain iarum [port, MS.] rocrochad

(7) Enna, son of Roethach, five years. (8) Fiach, son of Fiadhcu, [**d**] five years [and] forty reigned he. (9) Findchadh, son of Bac. . . . (10) Concobar the Bald, son of Futh, two years [and] ten. (11) Cormac Loighthe, eight years [and] twenty his reign. (12) Mochtai, son of Murchorn, three years. (13) Eochaidh, son of Daire, five years reigned he. (14) Eochaidh Yellow-heel, son of Loch, thirty years reigned he.

e It is in the eighth year [and] tenth of his [Eochaid's] reign failed [B.C. the kingdom[1] of the Greeks. It is these same that were [in power][1] [29] one year, above four score, above two hundred. Two kings [and] ten ruled of them and one queen. It is then [was] the beginning of the kingdom of the Romans. It is these that are revealed to the end of the world. Julius Cesar assumes[2] kingship. It is he first assumed[2] [49] kingship of the Romans: five years was he in his reign.—Octavius Augustus[3], six years [and] fifty reigned he.—[Tiberius] Cesar Augus-[3] [44] tus[4] after this one. And it is in the fourth year [and] tenth of the [A.D. 14*] rule of [Octavius] Cesar died Eochaid Yellow-heel, king of Ulster. In the fifth year [and] tenth of the rule of [Octavius] Cesar [Tiberius Cesar, MS.] Augustus, began Concobar, son of Ness, domination in Emain and he reigned sixty years. In the eighth year [and] twentieth of the rule of Concobar, son of Ness (This same is the second year [and] fortieth of the rule of Cesar Augustus.), was born the Lord, namely, Jesus Christ. In the second year [and] fortieth of the rule of Concobar died [Octavius] Cesar Augustus, in the third year [and] seventieth of his age.

f Tiberius Cesar[1], received he the kingship after his [step-]father : [1] [14] four years [and] twenty his rule. In the tenth year of the rule of Tiberius Cesar died Concobar, son of Ness. In the eighth year afterwards of [*lit*., for] Tiberius was Christ crucified. Seven years [and] fifty over two hundred [from the death of Concobar, son of Ness,] to the taking of kingship by Cormac, son [of Art, son of Conn. In the] fifth year [and] tenth of the reign of Tiberius Cesar [was] Christ [baptised] and began the preaching [of John the Baptist. In the eighth] year [and] tenth of the reign of Tiberius [Cesar was Christ crucified]. In the third year [and] tenth after the crucifixion of Christ, went Peter to Rome[1]. And in the fifth year after was Peter[1] [43]

---

* The regnal A.D. dates are those of the initial years.

[f] Feadap a Roiṁ ⁊ boċuaıḋ Pol ṗo cloıḋem, ın ppıma peppſe-
cuṫıone, ſub Nepone. Seaċṫ m-blıaḋna ıapum [popṫ, MS.] co
ṫocuıpeḋ Eoın, mıc [Ẓebeḋe, o] Oıpſpıſ aḋ baṫmoſp ınſpolum.
Ṫeopa blıaḋna ıapum [popṫ, MS.] co ṫıċṫaın co hOpſpıſ ıṫepum,
popṫ mopṫem Ḋomıḋıanı. Iſp ſpo ſpıḋeın ſpecunḋa peppſecuṫıo.
Ceıṫpı blıaḋna o ṫacuſp Ióno co haımpıp Ṫpoıanı. Iſp le ſpıḋe ın
ṫpeaſp ınzpeım. Iſp anḋpın ḋaſpınḋſpcaın hıp, ſpexṫo anno ſpezni
ſpuı. Seċṫ m-blıaḋna coıcaṫ ıaſp ſpıḋe copın ceaṫſpamaḋ n-ınzpeım, ſpub Ualepıano eṫ Ẓallıeno.

g Nae m-blıaḋna ſpıċeṫ ıaſp ſpaıḋe, ın ſpeıſpeaḋ ınzpeım, ſpub
Maxımıano. Quaṫuor annı ıaſp ſpaıḋe copın ſpeċṫmaḋ n-
ınzpeım, ſpub Ḋecıo. Oċṫ m-blıaḋna o ſpaıḋe copın n-oċṫmaḋ
n-ınzpeım, ſpub Ualıpıano eṫ Ẓallıone : ın qua Sıppıane epıſ-
copoſp eṫ Copnılıſp maſpṫıpıo coſponaṫı ſpunṫ. Fıċı blıaḋan o'n
oċṫ[maḋ] ınzpeım ſpın zo zabaıl pızı Ṫempaċ ḋo Choſpmac, ua
Cuınḋ, ıſpın ṫſpeſp blıaḋaın Pſpobı Impeſpaṫopıſp. Coıc blıaḋna
ſpıċeṫ ıaſp ſpaıḋe, ın noemaḋ ınzpeım, ſpub Ḋıoclıſpıano. Seċṫ
m-blıaḋna ḋez ıaſpum [popṫ, MS.], ṫuſpcompaz ſenaıḋ Nóece :
oċṫ n-eapcoıb ḋez aſp ṫpı ceṫaıb ıſpın ḋaıl ſpın. Ṫpıċa blıaḋan
ıaſpum [popṫ, MS.] zu baſp Ǎnḋṫonı monachı. Seċṫ m-blıaḋna
ḋez ıaſpum [popṫ, MS.] zu baſp hılapıı Pıċṫanıe. Seċṫ m-
blıaḋna ıaſp ſpaıḋeın zu hez Ǎmbſpoıſp.

h Nae m-blıaḋna ḋez ıaſpum [popṫ, MS.] zu hez naem
Maſpṫaın. Ḋa blıaḋaın ıaſp ſpaıḋe zo zabaıl eaſpcobaıḋe ḋo
Ǎuzuſpṫın, ın hıpone Ǎppſpıce. Coıc blıaḋna ſpıċeṫ ıaſpum
[popṫ, MS.] co Cıſpıne. Ḋeıċ m-blıaḋna ıaſp ſpın co hez Ǎuzuſpṫın. Iſp ı ſpın blıaḋaın ḋoſpaḋaḋ Palaḋıuſp a Papa Celeſpṫıno
ḋo pſpozeċṫ ſpoſpcela ḋo Scoṫaıb. Iſp ı ſpın ın ṫ-aenmaḋ blıaḋaın
aſp ceṫſpı ceṫaıb o ċſpoċaḋ Cſpıſpṫ. Maḋ o ṫoſpaċ ḋomaın, ımoſpſpo,
ıſp ḋa blıaḋaın [ṫſpıċaṫ] aſp ſpe ceṫaıb aſp coıc mılı. Iſp é lín
blıaḋan aſp ſpın ḋoḋeaċaıḋ Paḋſpaıc zu pſpozepṫ ḋoċum n-Eſpenn.
Eṫıuſp ⁊ Ualepıanuſp, ḋa ċonſul ıſpın blıaḋaın ſpın. Iſp ı ſpın
blıaḋaın pozaḋ xıxṫuſp abbaıne na Roma a n-ḋeaḋaız Che-
leſpṫını. Iſp ı ſpın ın ceaṫſpamaḋ blıaḋaın ḋo pıze Laezaıpe,
mıc Neıll, ı Ṫempaız. Iſp eıpıḋe ın ṫſpeſp pız ḋec poſpollam-
naſpṫaſp Eſpınn o aımpıſp na cuız pızſpa n-oıpḋeſpc ſpopoı[n]ḋ-

crucified[2] in Rome and Paul underwent[2] the sword, in the First Persecu- [f]
tion, under Nero. Seven years after, until the deportation[3] of John, [A.D.]
son [of Zebedee,] [from] Ephesus to the island of Patmos. Three [2] [67]
years after, to [his] coming to Ephesus again[4], after the death of [3] [93]
Domitian. It is under this [emperor took place] the Second [4] [96]
Persecution.[5] Four years from the return of John to the time of [5] [93]
Trajan. It is by this [emperor was caused] the Third Persecution[6]. [6] [107]
It is then he began Hir [?], in the sixth year of his reign. Seven
years [and] fifty after this, to the Fourth Persecution[7], under [7] [162]
Valerianus and Gallienus [read Aurelius and Ælius Verus].

g Nine years [and] twenty after this, [took place] the Sixth
Persecution[1], under Maximianus [Maximinus]. Four years after this [1] [235]
to the Seventh Persecution[2], under Decius. Eight years from this to [2] [250]
the Eighth Persecution[3], under Valerianus and Gallienus: in which [3] [257]
Cyprian[4], the bishop and Cornelius[5] were crowned with martyrdom. [4] [258]
A score of years from that Eighth Persecution to the taking of the [5] [252]
kingship of Tara by Cormac, grandson of Conn, in the third year[6] of [6] [278]
Probus the emperor. Five years [and] twenty after this, [took
place] the Ninth Persecution[7], under Diocletian [Aurelius]. Seven [7] [272]
years [and] ten after, the assemblage of the Synod of Nice[8]: eight [8] [325]
bishops [and] ten above three hundred in that Council. Thirty years
after, to the death of Antony[9], the monk. Seven years [and] ten [9] [359]
after, to the death of Hilary[10] of Poitiers. Seven years after this, [10] [369]
to the decease of Ambrose[11]. [11] [397]

h Nine years [and] ten after, to the decease of Saint Martin[1]. [1] [397]
Two years after this, to the reception of the episcopate[2] by Augustin, [2] [396]
in Hippo of Africa. Five years [and] twenty after, to Jerome[3]. A [3] [420]
score of years after that, to the decease[4] of Augustin. It is that year [4] [430]
was sent[5] Palladius by Pope Celestine to preach the Gospel to the [5] [431]
Scots. That is the first [read fourth] year above four hundred from
the Crucifixion of Christ. If from the beginning of the world, however, it is two years [and thirty] above six hundred, above five
thousand. This [which follows] is the complement of years above
that when went Patrick to preach unto Eriu. Etius and Valerianus
[were] the two consuls in that year[6]. That is the year in which [6] [432]
received Sixtus the abbacy of Rome after Celestine. That is the fourth
year of the kingship of Loegaire, son of Niall, in Tara. This is
the third king [and] tenth that governed Eriu from the time of the

X 2

[h]redar Erinn eterro a coic rennaib: idon, Conchobar, mac Nerra ⁊ Ailill, mac Mata ⁊ Cairpri Niafer, mac Rorra Ruaid ⁊ Eochaid, mac Lucta ⁊ Cuiri, mac Daire. In d-ara bliadain ar ceitri cetaib anorin o crochad Crist. In treas bliadain trichat imorro, ar re cetaib, ar coic mili o torac domain connigi rin.

Finit. Amen.

B

[COMAIMSIRACHTA.]
(LEBAR BAILI IN MOTA, p. 11 a.)

[*Notes at end of sections are variants of the Hieronymo-Eusebian Chronicle.*]

a Adam primus pater fuit et Eua ced bean in beatha ocus cet matair na n-uile. Cain a cet mac; is leis rocumdaiged cathair, idon, Enoch, ocus leis dorigned ar ocus buain ar tus. Abel, imorro, in mac tanairde d'Adam. Ar eirsen cet firen ocus cet mairtir ocus cet ragart ocus cet og dobai do sil Adaim. Laimiach, mac Matusalem, mic Manatelem, mic Siriat, mic Enot, mic Cain, mic Adaim, as e fear tug da mnai, idon, Ada ocus Alla. Rug Ada mac do Laimiach, idon, Iuban. Is e toisech poclecht cruit ocus organ. Ruc dino Sealla mac ele do['n] Laimiach cetna, idon, Tubalcain. Rob' eiride cet goba ocus cet ceard ocus cet saer dobai do sil Adaim. Ocus Nema, a siur siden, as i dorinoi uaim ⁊ cuma ar tus.

b Enog, mac Iafet, as e cet lintba dobi riam. Rotuirim Noi tri maccu rian n-[O]ilind. Conad uaidibrigen rosenair na da cenel rectmodad iar n-dilind. Teora meic ag Noi: idon, Sem ocus Cam ocus Iafed. Rorainb iarum Noi in doman a tri eter a triur mac: Cam i n-Affraice, Seim i n-Airria, Iafed i n-Eorair. Ocus Oliua a bean ride. Ocht meic lais, idon, Gomer ocus Magog ocus Magai ocus Iuban ocus Tubal ocus Tiras ocus Maroch ocus Maireacha. Gomer, is uad atat Gallabagbai, idon, Gallagrege. Magog, is uad Sceithegba. Ocus d'a sil ride do Gaidelaib, idon, Gaidel glas, mac Inuil, mic Feiniusa

five illustrious kings that partitioned Eriu between them into five [**h**] parts: to wit, Concobar, son of Ness and Ailill, son of Mata and Coirpri the Champion, son of Ross the Red and Eochaid, son of Lucht and Cuire, son of Daire. The second [*read*, fifth] year above four hundred [was] then from the Crucifixion of Christ. But the third year [and] thirtieth above six hundred, above five thousand from the beginning of the world to that.

It endeth. Amen.

B

[SYNCHRONISMS.]

(*BOOK OF BALLYMOTE*, p. 11 a.)

a Adam was the first father and Eve the first woman of the world and the first mother of all. Cain [was] their first son; it is by him was built a city, namely, Enoch and by him were [lit. was] done sowing and reaping at first. Abel indeed [was] the second son for Adam. It is this one [was] the first righteous and first martyr and first priest that was of the seed of Adam. Lamech, son of Mathusalem, son of Manathelem, son of Siriath, son of Enoch, son of Cain, son of Adam, he is the man that took two wives, Ada and Alla. Ada bore a son for Lamech, namely, Iuban. It is he first practised harp and organ. Sealla too bore another son for the same Lamech, namely, Tubalcain. This one was the first smith and the first artificer and the first mason that was of the seed of Adam. And Nema, his sister, it is she that did sewing and embroidery at first.

b Henoch, son of Jared, he is the first fowler that ever was. Noah begot three sons before the Deluge. So that [it is] from these were born the two tribes [and] seventy after the Deluge. Three sons had Noah: namely, Sem and Cham and Japhet. Afterwards divided Noah the earth in three between his three sons: Cham in Asia, Sem in Africa and Japhet in Europe. And Oliva [was] the wife of this [last]. Eight sons had he: namely, Gomer and Magog and Magai and Juban and Tubal and Tiras and Masoch and Maisech. Gomer, it is from him are the Galladagdae, that is, the Gallogregi. Magog, it is from him [are] the Scythians. And from his seed [were] the Gadelians, namely, Gadel the Green, son of Inul, son of Fenius

[b] Farrraiḋ, mic baata, mic Maʒoʒ, mic Iafeṫ, mic Noí, o ṫaṫ Ʒaiḃil. Maʒai, ir uaḋ aṫaiṫ Meḋa, iḋon, in flaṫur. Iricon, mac Aloínsur, mic Ibaiṫ, mic Maʒoʒ, mic Iafeḋ. Aiʒe riḋe compaiʒiḋ Franʒcaiḋ ocur Romanaiʒ, iḋon, in flaṫur, ocur Albania i n-Aria ocur breṫaín. Saxar, mac Neua, o raiṫer Saxain.

c Cam, mac Naei, ceiṫri meic lair: iḋon, Cur ocur Mearram ocur Fuṫ ocur Canḋan. Ar uaiḃiḃ riḋe Affaccaiʒ. Sem, mac Naei, coic meic lair, iḋon, Alam ocur Arur ocur Arafaxaḋ, Luíḋ ir Aram. Ealam, ir uaḋ aṫaiṫ Elamiḋa, iḋon Perra, iḋon, in flaṫur. Arur, ar uaḋ aṫaṫ Aranḋa, iḋon, in ceṫ flaiṫur in ḋomain. Arafaxaḋ, ar uaḋ aṫaṫ Callaḋa ocur Eaberḋa, iḋon, Eber, mac Saile, mic Airefaxaḋ. Iaṫṫan, mac Eber, ceiṫre meic ḋeʒ occa. Ar uaiḃiḃ rorilraḋ Iranusḃia. Sem, mac ḋo riḋe Arur; mac ḋo riḋe bel; mac ḋo riḋe Nin. Ir eriḋe coiṫ ri in ḋomain. Irin aenmaḋ bliaḋain ḋeʒ iar n-ʒen Nin, mic beil, ḃar Caim ocur Iafeḋ. Ocur in bliaḋain ḋ'a n-ḋeiri, Nín, mac beil, ḋoʒaḃail riʒe, iḋon, irin [írí MS.] aen [bliaḋain] fiċeṫ ḋo riʒe Nin, ʒéin Abraṫam. Oṫṫ [m-bliaḋna] ceṫorċaṫ ar noí ċéṫaiḃ o Aḋam ʒo ʒein Abraṫaim.—Samíraímír, ben Nín, ḋa [bliaḋain] ceṫorċaṫ. Ar le ḋoronaḋ mur ḃaiḃiloinia. Ocur ṫuccarṫair a mac fein cuiṫce ḋ'fir, iḋon, Nínsar, ocur aḃḃaṫ iar rin.

d Nínsar, iḋon, a mac ┐ a fear, ḋoʒaḃ riʒe oṫṫ [m-bliaḋna] ṫriċaḋ. Ocur irin cuiʒeḋ (no, irin iii.maḋ) bliaḋain a riʒe, ḃar Nae. Coica ar noí ċéṫaiḃ aer Naei corin reṫṫmaḋ [uii.feaḋ, MS.] bliaḋain Nínsar ṫainiʒ Parrṫalon a n-Erinn. Ocur irin ferċamaḋ bliaḋain aera Abraṫam. Arin oṫṫmaḋ bliaḋain iar ṫeṫṫ ḋo Parrṫalon, aḃḃaṫ in ceṫ fear ḋ'a muinnṫer, iḋon, Fea, mac Ṫorn, ḋi a ḋa Maʒ Feaa. Ocur in bliaḋain ḋ'a ere, ḃar Slanʒa, mic Parrṫoloin, ḋia ṫa rl . . Slanʒa. Aen bliaḋain iar rin, [ḃar] Laiʒlinni, ḋi a ṫa Loċ

Farsad, son of Baath, son of Magog, son of Japhet, son of Noah, from [**b**] whom are the Gaidil. Magai, it is from him are the Medes, namely, the kingdom. Isicon, son of Aloinius, son of Ibath, son of Magog, son of Japhet. At him unite the Franks and Romans, namely, the kingdom and Albania in Asia and the Britons. Saxas, son of Neva, [it is] from him are called the Saxons.

c Cham, son of Noah, four sons had he: namely, Cus and Mesram and Futh and Candan. It is from these [are] the Africans. Shem, son of Noah, five sons had he: namely, Elam and Assur and Arphaxad and Lud and Aram. Elam, it is from him are the Elamites, that is, Persians; namely, the kingdom. Asur, it is from him are the Assyrians, that is, the first kingdom of the world. Arphaxad, it is from him are the Chaldeans and Eberians, namely, [from] Heber, son of Sale, son of Arphaxad. Jactan, son of Heber, four sons [and] ten had he. It is from them sprang Isanudia. Sem, a son to him [was] Asur; son to this one, Belus; son to this one, Ninus. It is this one [was] first king of the world. In the eleventh year after the birth of Ninus, son of Belus, [took place] the death of Cham and Japhet. And in the year after them Ninus, son of Belus, took kingship; namely, in the one [two and-]twentieth [year] of the reign of Ninus [took place] the birth of Abraham. Eight [*read* two] years [and] forty above nine hundred from Adam [*read* Deluge] to the [B.C.] birth of Abraham.—Semiramis¹, wife of Ninus, [reigned] two [years¹ [1965*] and] forty. It is by her was built the wall of Babylon. And she took her own son to her for husband, namely, Ninias and she died after that.

d Ninias¹, namely, her son and her husband, he took kingship [for]¹ [1927] eight [years and] thirty. And in the fifth (or, in the third) year of his reign, [took place] the death of Noah. Fifty above nine hundred [was] the age of Noah, up to the seventh year of Ninias, [when] came Parthalon to Eriu. And in the sixtieth² year of the age of Abraham² [1957] [came he]. In the eighth year after the coming of Parthalon, died the first man of his people, namely, Fea, son of Torn, from whom is [named] Magh Fea. And in the year after that, [took place] the death of Slainge, son of Parthalon, from whom is [named Inber-] Slainge. One year after that, [took place the death] of Laiglinn,

---

* The regnal B.C. dates are those of the final years.

290   Lebar bailI IN uIoca.

[d]Laiglinni. Aen bliadain iar sin, domaidm Loc[a] Estra. Irin deachmad bliadain, bar Rugraide, mic Pappcoloin, a quo Loc Rudraige. Irin aenmad bliadain deg, bar Pappcoloin sor Sen Mad Elta Edair.—Arnius[1], trica bliadan ; gen Isaic, mic Abracam, i n-a re.—Arailius, cetorca [bliadan] ; bar Tara ocus Eber, mic Saile, 'n-a re.—Sersег, trica [bliadan] ; ocus bar Abracaim, ocus irin trer bliadain deg a raige.—Armimentеs[2], oct [m-bliadna] triсаt ; bar Saile, mic Airерaхаd ocus Iрmail, mic Abracaim, re [a] linD.

d.—[1] Arius.   [2] Armamithres.

P. 11 b   e beloccur, trica [bliadan][1].—balleus, coic [bliadna] coiсаt[2]. Tomaidm Loca Merca 'n-a re.—Altadus[3], coic [bliadna] triсаt[4]. —Maimincur[5], trica [bliadan]. Caimlecta muinncipe Pappcoloin 'n-a re.—Marailius[6], trica [bliadan], irin richecmad bliadain a rige tainig Nemed a n-Erinn. Irin dechmad bliadain iar tect do Nemed, domaidm Loca Cal ocus Loca Munpemair. Irin ocтmad bliadain iar sin, cat Ruis Raechan sop Gann ocus sor Seangann, da rig Pomorach. Irin b-arna bliadain deg iar sin cat sin, poclara rigrait la Nemead, idon, Rait Cindeс i n-Dail-Ibnu ocus Rait Cimacit arSeminiu.—Sераrus[7], riсе bliadan ; ocus ar e ba ri in domain ag denam na n-gnimарtad rin.—Mamiliur[8], trica bliadan. Gen Maire irin trer bliadain a rige. Irin richecmad bladain iar sin, poclaра da mag deg la Nemed i n-Erinn.—Marрarcur[9], cetorca [bliadan].—Arcaiciar[10], cetorca, 7 irin rесcmad bliadain a rige, cat bagna la Nemead, ocus irin b-ara bliadain iar sin, cat Murbuilg ocus Cnamroir re [a] linn. Sру, mac Erru, sor loinger a hEarpain co Sceicia a cinn da bliadan ocus a mac, idon, Eber Scot.

e.—[1] 35.   [2] 52.   [3] Altadas.   [4] 32.   [5] Mamylus.   [6] Manchaleus.
[7] Spherus.   [8] Mamylus.   [9] Sparethus.   [10] Ascatades.

f Nemed, mac Agnomain 7 da mile d'a muinncip, abbatadар irin trer bliadain deg rige Arcaiciar. Irin bliadain iar sin, bar Aindinn, mic Nemid, a quo Loc n-Aindinn ocus aidid

from whom is [named] Lake Laiglinni. One year after that, the [**d**] eruption of Lake Echtra. In the tenth year, [took place] the death of Rugraide, son of Parthalon, from whom [is named] Lake Rudraige. In the eleventh year, [took place] the death of Parthalon on Old [B.C.] Magh-Elta of Edar.—Arius[3], thirty years [reigned he]; the birth of[3] [1897] Isaac, son of Abraham, [took place] in his time[4].—Aralius[5], forty[4] [1917] [years]; the death of Tara and of Heber, son of Sale, [took place][5] [1857] in his time.—Xerxes[6], thirty [years]. And the death of Abraham[6] [1827] [took place][7]. And [it is] in the thirteenth [fifteenth] year of his[7] [1842] reign [it happened]. Armamithres[8], eight [years and] thirty. The[8] [1789] death of Sale, son of Arphaxad and of Ishmael, son of Abraham, [happened] in [his] time.

e Belocus[1], thirty [and five years].—Balleus[2], five [*read*, two years[1] [1754] and] fifty. The eruption of Lake Mesca [took place] in his time.—[2] [1702] Altadas[3], five [*read*, two years and] thirty.—Mamithus[4], thirty [years].[3] [1669] The plague-destruction of the people of Parthalon [happened] in his[4] [1639] time.—Manchaleus[5], thirty [years]; in the thirtieth year of his reign[5] [1609] came Nemed into Eriu. In the tenth year after the coming of Nemed, [took place] the eruption of Lake Cal and of Lake Mundremair. In the eighth year after that, [was gained] the battle of Ros-Raccain over Gann and Seangann, two kings of the Fomorians. In the twelfth year after that battle, were erected [*lit.*, dug] royal forts by Nemed, namely, the Fort of Cendech, in Dal-Idnu and the Fort of Cimaeth, in Semine.—Spherus[6], a score of years; and[6] [1589] it is he was king of the world at the doing of those deeds.— Mamylus[7], thirty years[8]. The birth of Moses [took place] in the third[7] [1559] year of his reign [*read* 17th year of Sphaerus]. In the twentieth[8] [1592] year after that, there were cleared twelve plains by Nemed in Eriu.— Sparethus[9], forty [*read* 39 years].—Ascatades[10], forty. And in the[9] [1520] seventh year of his reign [was fought] the battle of Bagain by[10] [1480] Nemed in Eriu. And in the second year after that, [took place] the battle of Murbolg and the battle of Cnamros in [his] time. Sru, son of Esru, [went] upon an expedition from Spain to Scythia to the end of two years and his son, namely, Eber Scot.

f Nemed, son of Agnoman and two thousand of his people, they died in the thirteenth[1] year of the reign of Ascatades. In the year[1] [1509] after[2] that, [occurred] the death of Aindenn, son of Nemed, from[2] [1506] whom [is named] Lake Aindinn. And the death of Starn [took

Lebar baili in Mota.

[**f**] Sdairn i Copanb. Irin ceatramad bliadain iar m-bar Nemid, togail Túir Conaing la ril Nemid, co na terna act trica trenfer. Eber Scot a rige Sceitia. Irin d-ara bliadain iar togail Túir Conaing, bar beotaig.—Amenter¹, coic [bliadna] cetorcat. Irin d-ara bliadain a rige, bar Ebir Scuit. Irin coiced bliadain iar rin, bar Agnamain irin Sceitia. Fir-bolg co n-a coic rigaib docum Erenn, irin rectmad bliadain ficet rige Amenter. Irin d-ara bliadain iar rin, bar Slainge, mic Dela, cet ri Erenn. Da bliadain iar rin, bar Rudraige, mic Deala, irin druig. Ceitri bliadna, in tan abbat Gann ocur Genann ocur Gaidel arna Gaedlaigib. Ocur irin octmad [bliadain] iar rin, bar Seangaind.

f.—¹ Amyntes.

g belocur, coic [bliadna] ficed, ocur a ingen, idon, Ahora¹ ocur Araimiraimir² a da hainm. Ocur in bliadain arer rige do gabail do, bar Fiaca Ceinnfindain. Ocur irin rectmad bliadain a rige, bar Rinnail. Ocur ir 'n-a aimrir bar Seangaind. Eocaid, mac Erc, dedflactur Fear-mbolg. Irin t-rectmad bliadain deg rige belocur abbat Eocaid. Ocur Tuata de Danand do tect a n-Erinn ocur cet cat Muige Tuired ocur brer do gabail rige n-Erenn. Ocur irin rectmad bliadain iar rin, Nuada Airgeadlam do gabail rige ocur brer do dicur.—Poiliporir³, trica [bliadan], ocur ir i n-a octmad bliadain ficed, cat Muige Tuired eter Tuataib de Danand ocur Fomoraib, a dorcair Nuada. Ocur Lug dogabail rige ocur bar brere, mic Eladan, a Carn Ua-Neid.

g.—¹ Atossa. ² Semiramis. ³ Baleparesq.

h Lamprider, da [bliadain] tricat, ocur irin octmad bliadain a rige, bar Cearmada, mic in Dagda. Ocur irin coiced bliadain deg iar rin, bar Cairbri, filed, do gae Grene ocur bar Eadaine ocur bar Cein, atar Loga. Ceitri bliadna iar rin, bar Alloid ocur Danoinne.—Sorrairrer¹, den [bliadain] ficet², ocur irin trer bliadain a rige, bar Loga Lampada la Mac Cuill. Ocur Eocaid Ollatar, idon, in Dagda, do gabail rigte.

place] in Corann. In the fourth[3] year after the death of Nemed, [f] [took place] the destruction of the Tower of Conang by the posterity, [n.c. 1502] of Nemed, so that there escaped not but thirty brave men. Eber Scot [was then] in the kingship of Scythia. In the second[4] year after[4] [1500] the destruction of the Tower of Conang, [happened] the death of Beothach.—Amyntes[5], five [years and] forty. In the second[6] year of [1435] his reign [took place] the death of Eber Scot. In the fifth[7] year after[7] [1479] that, [took place] the death of Agnaman in Scythia. Fir-Bolg with [1474] their five kings [came] unto Eriu, in the seventh [and] twentieth[8,8] [1454] year of the reign of Amyntes. In the second year after that, [took place] the death of Slainge, son of Dela, first king of Eriu. Two years after that, [occurred] the death of Rudraige, son of Dela, in the Brugh. Four years [of his reign were spent], the time died Gann and Genann and Gaidel of the Gaidil. And in the eighth year after that, [took place] the death of Seangann.

g Belocus[1], five [years and] twenty and his daughter, namely,[1] [1410] Atossa and Asaimiramis her two names. And the year after kingship being taken by him, [took place] the death of Fiacha White-head. And in the seventh year of his reign, [took place] the death of Rinnal. And it is in his time [happened] the death of Seangann. Eochaid, son of Erc, [was] the last prince of the Fir-Bolg. In the seventh [and] tenth year of the reign of Belocus died Eochaid. And the Tuatha de Danann came into Eriu and the first battle of Magh Tuired [was fought] and Bres took the kingship of Eriu. And in the seventh year after that, Nuada Silver-Hand took the kingship and Bres was expelled.—Balepares[2], thirty [years]. And it is in[2] [1380] his eighth year [and] twentieth [was fought] the [second] battle of Magh Tuired, between the Tuatha de Danann and the Fomorians, wherein fell Nuada. And Lug took the kingship and the death of Bres, son of Eladu, [took place] in the Carn of the Ui-Neid.

h Lamprides[1] two [years] and thirty. And in the eighth year[1] [1348] of his reign [took place] the death of Cearmad, son of the Dagda. And in the fifth year [and] tenth after that, [took place] the death of Cairbre, the poet, by the spear of [Mac] Grene and the death of Edain and the death of Cian, father of Lug. Four years after that, [took place] the death of Allod and of Danoinn.—Sosares[2], one [year[2] [1328] and] twenty [read, twenty]. And in the third year of his reign [took place] the death of Lug Long-Hand by Mac Cuill. And Eocho

[h] Deich m-bliadna iar sin, in tan adbatadar in t-aes dana, idon, Credne, cerd ocus Goibnend, goba ocus Diancecht liaid. Ocus do cam adbatadar. Sé bliadna iar sin, bar Aeda, mic in Dagda ocus Cridín bel-cainte ocus lorcad Neid a n-Oilech.—Lampairer³, ocht [m-bliadna] sichat⁴ do airrige, in tan adbath Manandan a cath Cuillinn. Secht m-bliadna iar sin, in tan adbath Mfoir brileith.—Siaminear⁵, coic [bliadna] cethorchat, ocus coic bliadna do airrige, in tan adbath Aengur, mac in Dagda. Da bliadain deg iar sin, in tan tangadar Gaidil go hErrain a cethri longaib: idon, Brath, mac Deotha, diar'bo mac Breogan. Tri bliadna deg iar sin, in tan adbath in Dagda ocus Delbaeth do rigad. Dech m-bliadna iar sin, bar Delbaeth ocus Fiaco do rigad.—Surrardur⁶, nói [m-bliadna] richet⁷, ocus coic bliadna

P. 12 a do a rige, in tan adbath Fiaca, | mac Dealbaeith. In bliadain iar sin rogabrat clainne Cermada rige n-Erenn.

h.—¹ Sosarces.   ² 20.   ³ Lampares.   ⁴ 30.
    ⁵ Panyas.   ⁶ Sosarmus.   ⁷ 19.

i Metaralmur¹, ocht [m-bliadna] richet². Tri bliadna do a rige, in tan tanic It, mac Breogain, a n-Erinn ocus adbath. Ocus coic bliadna do a rige, in tan tangadar mic Miled a n-Erinn, Dia-sardain, ocus cath Tailten eter macaib Milid ocus Tuata de Danand. Eremon ocus Eber, idon, bliadain. Eremon iar sin ocus Muimne ocus Luigne ocus Laigne.—Tutaner³, da bliadain sichat⁴; ocus ir re [a] linn dogab Iarnual, Faith, rige n-Erenn ocus Eithrial, mac Ireil ocus Conmael, mac Ebir.—Flaithiur⁵, sicha [bliadan]⁶; ocus Tigernmur, mac Follaig, re [a] linn.—Darrellur⁷, cethorcha [bliadan]. Ocus 're re lin Dauid, ocus re [a] lind torach na ceathraime aere. Ocus Tigernmur, ba ri Erenn annsin.—Lasaler⁸, noi [m-bliadna] sichat⁹. Ocus ir re [a] linn bar Tigernmair ocus tri ceathraime fear n-Erenn. Ocus Eocho Edgothach du gabail rige.—Lairtenter¹⁰, coic [bliadna] cethorcha. Ocus rannta Erenn eter Cearmna ocus Sobairce ocus adbath Cearmna iar sin.—Peri-

Ollathar, namely, the Dagda, took the kingship. Ten years after that, [**h**] [was] the time died the folk of handicraft, to wit, Credne, the wright and Goibnenn, the smith and Diancecht, the leech. And of plague died they. Six years after that, [took place] the death of Aed, son of the Dagda and [the death] of Crithin of the satirical mouth and the burning of Niad in Ailech.—Lampares[3], eight [years and] thirty[3] [were spent] by him in kingship, the time died Manannan, in the battle of Cuillenn [*read*, Lampares reigned thirty years]. Seven years after that, the time died Midir of Bri-liath.—Panyas[4], five [years and][4] forty. And five [were spent] by him in kingship, the time died Aengus, son of the Dagda. Two years [and] ten after that, the time came the Gaidil to Spain in four ships: namely, Brath, son of Deoth, whose son was [*lit.*, for whom was son] Breogan. Three years [and] ten after that, the time died the Dagda and Delbaeth was made king. Ten years after that, [took place] the death of Delbaeth and Fiacha was made king.—Sosarmus[5], nine [years and] twenty[5] [*read*, ten]. And five years [were spent] by him in kingship, the time died Fiacha, son of Delbaeth. The year after that, assumed the children of Cermad the kingship of Eriu.

1 Mithreus[1], eight [*read*, seven years and] twenty. Three years[1] [were spent] by him in kingship, the time came Ith, son of Breogan, into Eriu and died. And five years [were spent] by him in kingship, the time came the sons of Miled into Eriu, on Thursday and [was fought] the battle of Tailltiu, between the sons of Miled and the Tuatha de Danann. Eremon and Eber, namely, [reigned] a year [jointly]. Eremon [reigned] after that and Muimne and Luigne and Laigne.—Tautamus[2], two [years and] thirty [*read*, thirty-one]. And[2] it is in [his] time took Irual, the prophet, kingship of Eriu and Eithrial, son of Irial and Conmael, son of Eber.—Teuteus[3], thirty[3] [*read*, forty years]. And Tigernmus, son of Follach, [was] in [his] time [—Thinaeus[4], thirty years.].—Dercylus[5], forty [years]. And it[4] is he [was] in the time of David and in [his] time [was] the beginning[5] of the Fourth Age. And Tigernmus, he was king of Eriu then.—[6] Eupales[6], nine [*read*, eight years and] thirty. And it is in [his] time [took place] the death of Tigernmas and of three fourths of the men of Eriu. And Eocho the Vestured took the kingship.—Laosthenes[7], five [7] [years and] forty. And the Divisions of Eriu [took place] between Cearmna and Sobairce [in his time]. And Cearmna died after that.—

[B.C.]
[1298]
[1253]
[1234]
[1207]
[1176]
[1136]
[1106]
[1066]
[1028]
[983]

[**i**] Dioidir¹¹, trica [bliadan] ocus a err aen bliadna dugab rige ocus dugab Eocaid Faeburderg, mac Conmail, ocus irin coiced bliadain a rige, tomaidm Loca Erne. Da bliadain deg iar sin, tomaidm Loca Ce ocus Loca Gabair. Tri bliadna iar sin, bar Ecdec, mic Conmail. In bliadain iar sin, rogab Fiaca Labrainne rige n-Erenn.

i.—¹ Mithreus. ² 27. ³ Tautamus. ⁴ 31. ⁵ Teutaeus. ⁶ 40. Here follows Thinaeus, with 30 regnal years. ⁷ Dercylus. ⁸ Eupales. ⁹ 38. ¹⁰ Laosthenes. ¹¹ Peritiades.

j Ofratolur¹, rice [bliadan]. Ocus irin reired bliadain deg a rige, in tan adbat Fiaca Labrainne ocus in bliadan d'a er dogab Eocaid Mumo rige.—Ofratener², rect [m-bliadna] rerdat³ do a rige, in tan adbat Eocaid Mumo. Ocus in bliadain iar sin rogab Aengur Olmuccaid rige n-Erenn ocus adbat Aengur iar sin, irin t-reiread bliadain deg ar ficid a rige Ofratener. Irin bliadain iar sin rogab Enda Airgneach rige n-Erenn.—Acrartaber⁴, cetorca [bliadan]⁵. Ocus ré bliadna deg do a raige, in tan adbat Enda Airgneach. Ocus in bliadain iar sin, rogab Roteactaig rige n-Erenn ocus adbat Roteactaid ⁊ rogab Sedna airdrige n-Erenn.—Tomur Concoler⁶, do'n Greig, idon, Sardanapallur⁶, rice [bliadan]: deodflait Ararda. Ocus irin rectmad bliadain a rige, rogab Fiaca Finrcoited rige n-Erenn. Adbat Fiaca iar sin.

j.—¹ Ophrataeus. ² Ophratanes [ph = f]. ³ 50. ⁴ Acrazapes. ⁵ 42. ⁶⁻⁶ Tuonos Concolerus, qui vocatur Graece Sardanapallus. [36 Assyrian kings in Eusebius = B-Text, plus Thinaeus.]

k Aarbatur¹, idon, cet ri Mead, ceitri [bliadna] ficet². Ocus tri bliadna do a rige, in tan adbat Muineathon ocus Oilledergoid, mac Muineamoin, do gabaib [*lege* gabail] rige. Ocus ceitri bliadna deg do Arbatur a rige, in tan rogab Ollam Fodla rige n-Erenn.—Sogaraner³, trica [bliadan]. Ocus coic bliadna deg do a rige, in tan adbat Ollam Fodla. Ocus in bliadain iar sin, rogab Finacta, mac Ollaim Fodla, rige n-Erenn.—Maidiur⁴, cetorca [bliadan]. Ocus ré bliadna do a rige, in tan rogab Slanoll, mac Ollaim Fodla, rige n-Erenn. Sect bliadna deg iar sin, in tan rogab Gede Ollgotach rige n-Erenn.—Cairdirir⁵, tri [bliadna] deg. Ocus bliadain do a rige, in tan rogab Fiaca, mac Finacta, rige n-Erenn.—Dioner⁶, da [bliadain] coicat⁷. Ocus coic bliadna

Peritiades[8], thirty [years]. And at the age of one year took he the [i] kingship. And Eochaid Ruddy-Weapon, son of Conmael [took the kingship in his time]. And in the fifth year of his reign [occurred] the eruption of Loch Erne. Two years [and] ten after that, [occurred] the eruption of Loch Ce and of Loch Gabair. Three years after that, [took place] the death of Echaid, son of Cumael. The year after that, took Fiacha Labrainne the kingship of Eriu. [B.C. 953]

 j Ophrataeus[1], a score [of years]. And in the sixth year [and][1] tenth of his reign [was he] the time died Fiacha Labrainne and the year after it took Eochaidh Mumo kingship.—Ophratenes[2], seven[2] [years and] sixty [were spent] by him in kingship [*Read:* Ophratanes reigned fifty years.], the time died Eochaidh Mumo. And the year after that, took Aengus Olmuccaid kingship of Eriu. And died Aengus after that, in the sixth year [and] tenth above twenty in the reign of Ophratenes. In the year after that, took Enda the Silvery the kingship of Eriu.—Acrazapes,[3] forty [*read:* 42 years]. And six[3] years [and] ten [were spent] by him in kingship, the time died Enda the Silvery. And the year after that, took Rotectech the kingship of Eriu. And Rotectaid died and Sedna took the arch-kingship of Eriu.—Thonos Concolerus[4], namely, in [*lit.* from] the Greek, Sardanapallus, a score [of years]: the last Assyrian prince. And in the seventh year of his reign, took Fiacha Finscoitech the kingship of Eriu. Died Fiacha after that. [933] [883] [841] [821]

 k Arbaces, namely, the first king of the Medes, four [years and] twenty. And three years [were spent] by him in kingship, the time died Munemon and Oilledergoid, son of Munemon, took the kingship. And four years [and] ten [were spent] by Arbaces in kingship, the time took Ollam Fodla kingship of Eriu.—Sosarmus, thirty [years]. And five years [and] ten [were spent] by him in kingship, the time died Ollam Fodla. And the year after that, took Finachta, son of Ollam Fodla, the kingship of Eriu.—Mamycus, forty [years]. And six years [were spent] by him in kingship, the time took Slanoll, son of Ollam Fodla, the kingship of Eriu. Seven years [and] ten after that, the time took Gede the Great-voiced the kingship of Eriu. —Cardaces, three [years and] ten. And a year [was spent] by him in kingship, the time took Fiacha, son of Finachta, the kingship of Eriu.—Dejoces[1], two [*read:* four years and] fifty. And five years[1] [655]

[k] do a ṙıġe, ın ċan ṗoġab beaṗnġal, mac Ǧede, ṙıġe, ocuṗ ḟıċe bliadan do a ṙıġe, ın ċan ṗoġab Oılıll, mac Slanoıll, ṙıġe n-Eṙenn, ocuṗ coıc [bliaḋna] ṫṙıċaċ do a ṙıġe, ın ċan ṗoġab Sıṗna Saeġlaċ ṙıġe n-Eṙenn. Coıc bliaḋna deġ ıaṗ ṙın, caċ Mona-Ṫṗoġaıde, a doṗċaıṗ ḟıṗ Eṙenn ocuṗ Ḟomoṗaıċ.

k.—¹ Arbaces. ² 28. ³ Sosarmus. ⁴ Mamycus: he precedes Sosarmus. ⁵ Cardaces. ⁶ Dejoces. ⁷ 54.

l Ḟṗaoṗṫeṗ¹, ceıṫṗı bliaḋna ḟıċeṫ. Ocuṗ ceṫṗı bliaḋna do a ṙıġe, ın ċan ṗoġab Ṙoṫeċṫaıd ṙıġe n-Eṙenn. Ocuṗ ıṗın ṗeċṫmaḋ bliaḋaın ıaṗ ṙın ṗoġab Eılım, mac Ṙoṫeċṫaıd, ṙıġe ocuṗ ṗoġab ıaṗ ṙın Ġıallċaḋ, mac Oılella, ocuṗ ṗoġab ıaṗ ṙın Aṙṫ Imleaċ, mac Eılım.—Cıṗaṗṙeṗṙeṗ², da [bliaḋaın] ṫṙıċaċ. Ocuṗ ıṗın ḋeċmaḋ bliaḋaın a ṙıġe, ṗoġab Nabcodon Ḟınḋṗaıl ṙıġe n-Eṙenn. Iṗ 'n-a aımṙıṗ doċuaıd Nabcodon[oṙoṗ] a m-baıbılóın ocuṗ ıṗ 'n-a ṙe ṗoloıṗceḋ ṫeamṗall Solman.—Aṗḋaıġeṗ³, ṗeċṫ [m-bliaḋna] ḟıċeṫ⁴. Ocuṗ complaṫuṗ do ocuṗ do Nabġadon[oṙoṗ].—Cıṗ⁵, mac Ḋaıṗ, ceḋ ṙıġ Ṗeṗṙ. Ocuṗ ıṗ leıṗ aḋṗoċaıṗ Ḟalladaṗ, ıdon, ṙıġ do Ġenncallaġdu ocuṗ ṗuġaṗdaṗ m-bṗoıd a baıbıloın. Ocuṗ Nuaḋa Ḟınḋṗaıl, ba ṙı Eṙenn anḋṗın.—Campaıṗeṗ⁶, mac Cıṗ, ṙe ṗaıṫea Nabġadonaṙṙoṗ⁶, oċṫ [m-bliaḋna]. Ocuṗ bṙeaṙ-ṙıġ, mac Aıṗṫ Imlıc, ṙıġ ı n-a ṙe.—Ḋaṙıuṗ, mac⁷ Ioṙṫaṗṙeṗ⁷, ṙé [bliaḋna] ṫṙıċaċ⁸. Ocuṗ Eoċaıḋ Oṗṫaċ, do ḟıl Luıġḋeċ, mıc Iṫa, mıc bṗeoġaın, ı n-a ṙe. | Ocuṗ Ḟınd, mac bṙaṫa, ocuṗ Seḋna ınd Aṙṙaıd, deıċ m-bliaḋna a complaṫuṗ do.—Seṗxeṗ⁹, mac Ḋaıṗ⁹, ḟıċe [bliaḋan]. Ocuṗ baṗ Seḋna ınd Aṙaıd ı n-a ṙe. Ocuṗ Sımon bṙeaċ ṙe [a] lınd. Ocuṗ Ḋuaċ, mac Seḋna, du ġabaıl ṙıġe.

l.—¹ Phraortes [ph = f]. ² Cyaxares. ³ Astyages. ⁴ 38. ⁵ 30 years are assigned to him. ⁶⁻⁶ Cambysen aiunt ab Hebræis secundum Nabuchodonosor vocari: sub quo historia Judith, quæ Holophernem interfecit, scribitur. ⁷⁻⁷ filius Hystaspis. ⁸ 36. ⁹⁻⁹ Xerxes [filius] Darii.

m Aṙṫapaneṗ¹, ṙeċṫ mí.—Aṙṫaṗṙexeṗ² Lonġemanuṗ², ıdon, lamṗada, ceṫoṙċa. Ocuṗ ıṙ 'n-a aımṙıṗ aḋbaċ Ḋuaċ, mac Seḋna, ocuṗ ṙemıṗ coıc ṙıġ do ṙıġaıb Eṙenn ṙoċaıṫ Aṙṫaṗ-ṙeṗxeṗ: ıdon, Muıṙeaḋaċ bolġṙaċ ocuṗ Enḋa Ḋeṗġ, mac Ḋuaċ Ḟınd, ocuṗ Luġaıḋ Iaṙdonan, mac Seḋna ocuṗ Sıṙlam, mac Ḟınd, ocuṗ Eoċaıḋ Uaıṙċeaṗ. Ocuṗ ıṙ 'n-a ṙe ṗoġab Eoċaıḋ Ḟıaḋmuıne ocuṗ Conaınġ beaġeġlaċ ṙıġe n-Eṙenn.—

BOOK OF BALLYMOTE. 299

[were spent] by him in kingship, the time took Berngal, son of Gede, [**k**] kingship. And twenty years by him in kingship, the time took Oilill, son of Slanoll, the kingship of Eriu. And five [years and] thirty by him in kingship, the time took Sirna Long-lived [*read*, the Reacher] the kingship of Eriu. Five years [and] ten after that, [was fought] the battle of Moin Trogaide, wherein fell the men of Eriu and the Fomorians. [B.C.]

l Phraortes[1], four years [and] twenty. And four years [were [1] [631] spent] by him in kingship, the time took Rotechtaid the kingship of Eriu. And in the seventh year after that, took Eilim, son of Rotechtad, the kingship. And there took [it] after that Giallchad, son of Oilill. And there took [it] after that Art Imlech, son of Eilim.—Cyaxares[3], two [years and] thirty. And in the tenth year [3] [599] of his kingship, took Nuada Findfail the kingship of Eriu. It is in his time went Nebuchodonosor into Babylon and it is in his period was burned the Temple of Solomon.—Astyages[4], seven [*read:* 8 years and] [4] [561] twenty [*read:* 30.] And synchronous reigning [was] by him and by Nebuchodonosor.—Cyrus[5], son of Darius [reigned 30 years], [he was] [5] [531] the first king of the Persians. And it was by him fell Balthasar[6], [6] [560] namely, king of the Chaldeans and he took spoil from Babylon. And Nuada Findfail, he was king of Eriu then.—Cambyses[7], son of Cyrus, [7] [523] who was called Nebuchodonosor [the Second], eight [years]. And Breasrig, son of Art Imlech, [was] king in his time.—Darius[8], son of [8] [486] Hystaspes, six [years and] thirty. And Eochaidh Opthach, of the seed of Lugaid, son of Ith, son of Breogan, [was] in his time. And Finn, son of Brath and Sedna of the Recompense, ten years were [they] in synchronous reigning with him.—Xerxes[9], son of Darius, a [9] [465] score [of years: *read* 21 years]. And the death of Sedna of the Recompense [took place] in his time. And Simon the Speckled [was] in [his] time. And Duach, son of Sedna, took the kingship.

m Artabanus[1], seven months.—Artaxerxes Longimanus[2], that is, [1] [465] Long-Hand, forty [years]. And it is in his time died Duach, son [2] [425] of Sedna. And the time of five kings of the kings of Eriu spent Artaxerxes: to wit, Muredach Bolgrach and Enna the Red, son of Duach the Fair and Lugaid Iardonan, son of Sedna and Sirlam, son of Finn and Eochaidh Uairches. And it is in his time took Eochaid Fair[?]-Neck and Conaing Little-Fearing the kingship of Eriu.—

[m]Seppep³, ba mí. Ocup Eoċaıb ocup Conaıng ı n-a pe.—Seg-
benup⁴, pecc mí. Ocup Eoċaıb ocup Conaıng [ı n-a pe].—
Daıpıup Nocup, noı [m-blıabna] beg. Ocup pemíp cpı pıg bo
pıgaıb Epenn pocaıc: ıbon, Lugaıb, mac Eċbeċ Uaıpcep ocup
Conaıng begeglaċ ocup Apc Imleaċ, mac Luıgbeċ. Ocup ıp
'n-a pe pogab pıge Pıaċa, mac Muıpebaıg.—Apcappepxep⁵,
ıbon, Memnon⁵, ceċopċa [blıaban]. Ocup Oılıll Pınb, mac Aıpc,
ı n-a pe, ocup Eoċaıb, mac Oılella Pınb ocup Aıpgebmaıp bo
gabaıl pıge ı n-a pe pop.—Apcapxexpep Ocup⁶, peċc [m-blı-
abna] cpıċaċ⁷. Ocup ıp 'n-a aımpıp abbaċ Aıpgebmaıp ocup
Duaċ Lagpaċ ocup Lugaıb Laıgeċ. Ocup Aeb Ruab, mac
babuípnn, bu gabaıl pıge.

m.—¹ Artabanus. ²⁻² Artaxerxes Longimanus. ³ Xerxes.
⁴ Sogdianus. ⁵⁻⁵ Artaxerxes ... Mnemon. ⁶ Artaxerxes, qui et Ochus. ⁷ 26.

n Peppep Oċe¹, ceċpı [blıabna]. Ocup ıp 'n-a aımpıp abbaċ
Aeb Ruab.—Daıpıup² mop, mac Appamín², ıbon, pıg beıgınab
Pepp, oċc³ m-blıabna ocup abpoċaıp la hAlaxancaıp, mac Pılıp,
ıbon, ceċ pı gpeg. Ocup Dıċopba, mac Dímaín, ı n-a pe.—
Alexancaıp, ıbon, ceċ pıg gpeg, coıċ⁴ blıabna. Ocup Cımbaeċ,
mac Pınncaın, ı n-a pe.—Colamenp⁵, mac Laıpge⁵, ceċopċa
[blıaban]. Ocup Maċa Mon[g]puab ı n-[a] pe.—Ocup
Reċcaıb Rıgbepg ocup Ugaıne mop ı n-a pe pop.—Colamenp
Plobealbup⁶, oċc [m-blıabna] cpıċaċ. Ocup ıp 'n-a aımpıp
abbaċ Ugaıne mop. Ocup Laegaıpe Lopc pe [a] lınn. Ocup
Cobċaċ Caelbpeg ocup Labpaıb Loıngpeċ bu gabaıl pıge ı n-a
pe.—Colamenp Ebepgıcep⁷, peċc [m-blıabna] pıċeċ⁸. Ocup ıp
'n-a aımpıp abbaċ Labpaıb Loıngpeċ. Ocup Mogcopb pe [a] lınn.
Ocup Aengup Oılıll ı n-a pe. Ocup Iapaınbgleo bu gabaıl pıge.—
Colamenp Pılıpocup⁹, oċc [m-blıabna] beg¹⁰. Ocup Peapcopb ı
n-a pe. Ocup Connla Cupaıb-celupg pe [a] lın. Ocup Conċobap Rob, mac Caċaıp, a pıge n-Ulab pe [a] línb pop.

n.—¹ Arses Ochi [filius]. ²⁻² Darius Arsami [filius]. ³ 6. ⁴ 6.
⁵⁻⁵ Ptolemæus, Lagi filius. ⁶ Philadelphus. ⁷ Evergetes. ⁸ 26.
⁹ Philopater. ¹⁰ 17.

o Pocolomeup¹ Epıpanep², pılıup Ebılıpocup, cpı [blıabna]
pıċeċ³. Ocup Oılıll, mac Conlla, pe [a] lınb. Ocup Abamap
Polccaın ocup Eoċaıb Polcleabup bu gabaıl pıge [ı n-a pe].—

Xerxes³, two months. And Eochaid and Conaing were in his time.—[**m**]
Sogdianus⁴, seven months. And Eochaid and Conaing [were in his ₃[B.C. 425]
time].—Darius Nothus⁵, nine [years and] ten. And the time of ⁴[425]
three kings of the kings of Eriu spent he : to wit, Lugaid, son of ⁵[406]
Eochaid Uairches and Conaing Little-Fearing and Art Imlech, son of
Lugaid. And it is in his time took Fiacha, son of Muredach, the
kingship.—Artaxerxes⁶, that is, Mnemon, forty [years]. And Oilill⁶ [366]
the Fair, son of Art, [was] in his time. And Eochaid, son of Oilill
the Fair and Airgedmair took the kingship in his time also.—
Artaxerxes Ochus⁷, seven [*read:* six years and] thirty [*read:* twenty]. ⁷ [340]
And it is in his time died Airgedmair and Duach Lagrach and Lugaid
Laigech. And Aed the Red, son of Badornn, took the kingship.

n Arses Ochi¹, four [*read:* three years]. And it is in his time died¹ [337]
Aed the Red.—Darius the Great², son of Arsames, namely, the last king² [331]
of the Persians, eight [*read:* six] years and fell he by Alexander, son
of Philip, that is, the first king of the Greeks. And Dithorba, son of
Diman, [was] in his time.—Alexander³ [son of Philip], first king of the ³ [325]
Greeks, five years. And Cimbaeth, son of Finntan, [was] in his time.—
Ptolemey⁴, son of Lagus, forty [years]. And Macha Red-Hair, in ⁴ [285]
[his] time [was she]. And Rechtaid Red-arm and Ugaine the
Great [were] in his time also.—Ptolemey Philadelphus⁵, eight years ⁵ [247]
[and] thirty. And it is in his time died Ugaine the Great. And
Laegaire Lorc [was] in [his] time. And Cobthach Caelbreg and
Labraid Loingsech took the kingship in his time.—Ptolemey Ever-
getes⁶, seven [*read:* six years and] twenty. And it is in his time died⁶ [221]
Labraid Loingsech. And Mog-Corb [was] in [his] time. And Aengus
Oilill [was] in his time. And Iarainngleo took the kingship.—
Ptolemey Philopater⁷, eight [*read:* seven years and] ten. And Fer-⁷ [204]
corb [was] in his time. And Connla Curaid-celurg [was] in [his]
time. And Concobar Rod, son of Cathair, [was] in the kingship of
Ulster in [his] time also.

o Ptolemey Epiphanes¹, son of Philopater, three [*read:* four years ¹ [180]
and] twenty. And Oilill, son of Conla, [was] in [his] time. And
Adamar Fair-hair and Eochaidh Flowing-hair took the kingship [in

302   Lebar baili in mota.

[o] Tolamenr¹ Pilametur⁵, cois [bliadna] trícat. Ocur Ferzur Poltleabur ı n-a re. Ocur Aenzur Turbeać du zabail rıze. Ocur Fiaċa, mac Feıdlız, arrıze n-Ulad.—Tolamenr⁴ Eberzıter⁶, noı [m-bliadna] rıċet. Aenzur Turmeaċ ı n-a re. Ocur Conall Collamrað ocur Nıa Sezamaın ocur Enda Aırzneċ du zabail rıze.—Tolamenr⁷ Firo⁷, reċt [m-bliadna] dez. Crımtann Corcaraċ ı n-a re, ocur Ruzraıde do zabail rıze.—Tolamenr⁸ Alaxa[n]der⁸, deıċ [m-bliadna]. Ocur Ruzraıde ı n-a re. Ocur Etınd Admaır ocur dreral dodıbad ocur Luzaıd Luaızne du zabail rıze. Ocur Fıac, mac Fıadcon, arrıze n-Ulad.—Tolomenr Fırcon, oċt [m-bliadna]. Ocur Conzal Claırınzneaċ ı n-a re.—Tolomenr Dıonırıur⁹, trıċa [bliadan]. Ocur Conzal Claırınzneaċ ı n-a re. Ocur Duaċ, dalta Dezaıd, ocur Fındcad, mac baıs, a rıze n-Ulad. Ocur Conċodar Mael, mac Fuıċe ocur Cormac, mac Laıtız, ı n-a re ror. Ocur ır 'n-a aımrır tuzad ı[n] caċ Catarda, ocur Cormac, mac Laıtız, a rıze n-Ulad az tabaırt ın caċa Catarda. Ocur Moċta, mac Murcorad, re [a] lınd.—Cleoratra, ıdon, ın rızan, ocur ır ı deozrlaıċ Grez, da bliadaın dı. Faċtna Faċaċ ı n-a re.

o.—¹ Ptolemœus.   ² Epiphanes.   ³ 24.   ⁴ Ptolemœus.
⁵ Philometor.   ⁶ Evergetes [Secundus].   ⁷–⁷ Ptolemœus Phuscon, idemque Soter.
⁸–⁸ Ptolemœus, qui et Alexander.   ⁹ Dionysus.

p luıl Seraır, ıdon, cet rı Roman, cois [bliadna]. Ocur Eoċaıd Feıdleaċ ı n-a re, ocur 'n-a aımrır addat. Ocur Eoċaıd, mac Daıre, a rıze n-Ulad a comrlaċur frı hluıl. Ocur Eoċaıd Aırem du zabail rıze, ocur Eoċaıd Sulbuıde, mac Loc, trı bliadna a comrlaċur frı Eoċaıd Oıream.—Octarın luzuır, ró [bliadna] coısat. Ocur da bliadaın do a rıze,
P. 13a ın tan rozad Ferzar, mac Lete, rıze n-Ulad. | Ocur ır 'n-a re addaċ Eoċaıd Oıream. Ocur Eterrcel, cois bliadna 'n-a re. Ocur Nuada Neċt, da raıċe. Ocur ırın coısed bliadaın dez do rıze Oċtarín dozad Conaıre mor rıze n-Erenn ocur dozadartar Conċodar rıze n-Ulad. A n-aen bliadaın, ınar rın, do rızad Conċodar ocur Conaıre. Ocur ırın bliadaın cetna

his time].—Ptolemey Philomotor[2], five [years and] thirty. And [o] Fergus Flowing-hair [was] in his time. And Aengus Turbech took[2] the kingship. And Fiacha, son of Feidlech [was] in the kingship of Ulster [in his time].—Ptolemey Evergetes[3] [the Second], nine [years and] twenty. Aengus Turmech [was] in his time. And Conall Collamrach and Nia Segamain and Enda the Raider took the kingship [in his time].—Ptolemey Phuscon[4], seven [years and] ten. Crimthann the Conqueror [was] in his time. And Rudraige took the kingship [in his time].—Ptolemey Alexander[5], ten [years]. And Rudraige [was] in his time. And Etind [son] of Admar and Bresal of the Cow-Plague and Lugaid of the Spear took the kingship. And Fiac, son of Fiadcu, [was] in the kingship of Ulster [in his time].—Ptolemey Phuscon[6] [reigned again] eight [years]. And Congal Clairingnech [was] in his time.—Ptolemey Dionysus[7], thirty [years]. And Congal Clairingnech [was] in his time. And Duach, foster-son of Degad and Findead, son of Bac, [were] in the kingship of Ulster [in his time]. And Concobar the Bald, son of Fuith and Cormac, son of Laitech, [were] in his time also. And it is in his time was fought [*lit.* given] the Civil battle [of Pharsalia][8] and Cormac, son of Laitech, was in the kingship of Ulster at the fighting [*lit.* giving] of the Civil battle. And Mochta, son of Murcoru, [was] in his time.— Cleopatra, namely, the queen and it is she [was] last ruler of the Greeks, two years [were reigned] by her [when Julius Cæsar became Dictator][8]. Fachtna the Prophetic [was] in her time.

[B.C. 145]

[116]

[99]

[89]

[81]

[7] [51]

[8] [49]

[8] [49]

p Julius Cesar[1], namely, the first king of the Romans, five years. And Eochaid the Hospitable [was] in his time and in his time died he. And Eochaidh Airem, son of Daire, [was] in the kingship of Ulster in synchronous rule with Julius. And Eochaid Airem took the kingship and Eochaid Yellow-eye [*recte*, -heel], son of Loc, [was] three years in synchronous rule with Eochaid Airem.—Octavius Augustus[2], six [years and] fifty. And two years [were spent] by him in kingship, the time took Fergus, son of Leith, the kingship of Ulster. And it is in his time died Eochaid Airem. And Eterscel [was] five years in his time and Nuada Necht, two quarters [of a year]. And in the fifth year [and] tenth of the reign of Octavius took Conaire the Great the kingship of Eriu and took Concobar the kingship of Ulster. In one year, according to that, were Concobar and Conaire made kings. And in the same year was Eriu divided between the

[1] [44]

[A.D.]
[2] [*ob.* 14]

Lebar baili in móta.

[p] do randad Eriu eter na coizeadacaib, idon, Conćobar, mac Neara, ocur Cairpri Níafear ⁊ Tizearndać Teddandać ⁊ Dedad, mac Sin ocur Oilill, mac Madac. Ocur in bliadain areir na ronda rin ruzad Cuculaind. Ocur irin reired bliadain dez do rize Oćtarín Azurd, ceatra bliadna dez iarran roind rin na coizedṁad, ruzad Muire: idon, irin ceatramad bliadain dez do rize Conaire ocur Concobair rozenair Muire; idon, tri [bliadna] dez ba rlan do Choínculaind andrin. Ocur irin ceatramad bliadain iar n-zein Muire, rluaizeḋ Tana bo Cuailzne. Ar follur ar rin zurub' taerca Tain na [Tozail na] brurṫṅí; ordoiz ir andran oćtmad bliadain dez do rize Conaire rluaizeḋ Tana bo Cuailzne.

q Seċt m-bliadna dez ba rlan do Coinculaind andrin: idon, ira[n] d-ara bliadain dez ar ricit do rize Oćtarin Iuzurd, in rluaizeḋ cetna. Oćt m-bliadna iar rluaizeḋ Tana bo Cuailzne rozenair Crírt ocur ba rlan ba bliadain dez do Muire annrin. Ocur cetorċa bliadan ba rlan d'Oćtarin i n-a rize annrin. Ocur irin reired bliadain fićet do rize Conaire ocur Concobair ocur ba bliadain iar n-zein Crírt ceardo Cuculaind. Ocur reċt bliadna fićet raezul Chonculaind co rin. Oćtarin Azurd, coic [bliadna] dez do a rize iar n-Zein.—Tiber Sexair, reċt [m-bliadna] fićet¹. Ocur reċt bliadna dez do a rize in tan doceraḋ Crírt. Tri [bliadna] triċat do Crírt a colaind, o zein co ceraḋ. Ocur irin [ir i in, MS.] bliadain arer cerḋa Crírt bar Concobair: idon, irin oćtmad bliadain dez Tibir ocur irin rerćadmad bliadain do a rize Conaire addać Concobar. Ocur aderaid araile ar irin m-bliadain [ir i in bliadain, MS.] iar ceraḋ Crírt bar Muire. Coic bliadna do Tibir a rize iar m-bar Concobair. Zlairní, mac Concobair, noi [m-bliadna] a rize n-Ulad. Ocur irin coiced bliadain a rize bar Tibir.

q.—¹ 23.

r Zair Cailliculа, reċt [m-bliadna]¹. Ocur ir 'n-a aimrir ced rcribeann in t-[ṡ]oircela la Maċa. Ocur Conaire a

five [Provincials]: namely, Concobar, son of Ness and Cairpre the [p]
Champion and Tigernnach Tedbannach and Dedad, son of Sin and
Oilill, son of Madu. And in the year after that division, was born
Cuculainn. And in the sixth year [and] tenth of the reign of
Octavius Augustus, four years [and] ten after that division of the
five [Provincials], was born Mary: namely, in the fourth year [and]
tenth of the reign of Conaire and of Concobar was born Mary; that
is, three [years and] ten were complete for Cuculainn then. And in
the fourth year after the birth of Mary, [took place] the Hosting of
the Cattle-foray of Cuailgne. It is manifest therefrom that earlier
was the Cattle-foray than [the Destruction] of the Palace [of Da
Derga]; for it is in the eighth year [and] tenth of the reign of
Conaire [took place] the Hosting of the Cattle-foray of Cuailgne.

q Seven years [and] ten were complete for Cuculainn then:
namely, in the second year [and] tenth above the twentieth of the
reign of Octavius Augustus [took place] the same Hosting. Eight
years after the Hosting of the Cattle-foray of Cuailgne, was born
Christ and there were complete two years [and] ten for Mary then.
And forty years were complete for Octavius in his reign then. And
in the sixth year [and] twentieth of the reign of Conaire and
Concobar and two years after the birth of Christ, failed Cuculainn.
And seven years [and] twenty the age of Cuculainn to that. Octavius
Augustus, five [years and] ten [were spent] by him in kingship after [A.D.]
the Nativity.—Tiberius Cesar[1], seven [years and] twenty. And seven[1] [14*]
years [and] ten [were spent] by him in kingship, the time suffered
Christ. Three [years and] thirty [were spent] by Christ in the body,
from Birth to Passion. And in the year after the Passion of Christ
[took place] the death of Concobar: that is, in the eighth year [and]
tenth of Tiberius and in the sixtieth year of the kingship of Conaire
died Concobar. And others say it is in the year after the Passion of
Christ [took place] the death of Mary. Five years [were spent] by
Tiberius in kingship after the death of Concobar. Glaisni, son of
Concobar, nine years [was he] in the kingship of Ulster. And in
the fifth year of his reign [took place] the death of Tiberius.

r Caius Caligula[1], seven [years]. And it is in his time [took[1] [37]
place] the first writing of the Gospel by Matthew. And Conaire

---

* A.D. regnal dates are those of the initial years.

[r] compige fpip.—Clauoiup, cpi [bliaona] oeg. Ocup ipin cper bliaoain a pige togail bpuioni Oaberg pop Conaipe mop, mac eceppceoil [eceripceoil, MS.]. Ocup Ipial Ʒlunmap, mac Conaill Cepnaig, a pige n-Ulao ag Togail bpuioni. Ocup coic bliaona ou Tempaig gan pig iap Togail bpuioni. Lugaig Spiaonepg ou gabail pige n-epenn ocup Ipial Ʒlunmap a pige n-Ulao annpin.—Neapo Sexap, pect [m-bliaona]² oeg. Ocup ip 'n-a aimpip bap Muipe Magoalen. Ocup ip 'n-a aimpip tomaiom Lino-muine cap Liac-muine, ioon, Loc n-Cacac, ocup tomaiom Loca Rib, mic Muipeoa, cap Mag n-Aippen. Ocup Ipial Ʒlunmap, mac Conaill, a pige n-Ulao anopin ocup Lugaig Spiaonepg a pige n-epenn. Ocup ip 'n-a aimpip po cpocao Peoap ocup po oiceannao Pol ocup poiloipceo Roim.—Ʒallua³ ocup Pipon, ioon, a oalta, loca ocup becilliup³, cpi leicbliaona ooib.—Ueppepianup, noi [m-bliaona]. Ocup ipin coiceo bliaoain a pige [6c] Luigec Spiaonepg. Ocup Concobap Abpaopuao oo gabail pige i n-a pe; ocup Cpimcann Nianap oo gabail pige. Ocup in bliaoain apeip pige oo gabail oo, oo cpocao Anopiap appoal.—Cicup, oa bliaoain oo. Ocup Cpimcann Nianap i n-a pe.

r.—¹ 3 years and 10 months. ² 13. ³⁻³ Galba, 7 months; Otho, 3 months; Vitellius, 8 months.

s Oomicianup, coic [bliaona] oeg. Ocup bap Ipeil Ʒlunmaip in bliaoain ougab pige. Ocup Piaca Pinoamnap ou gabail pige, ioon, mac Ipiail. Ocup ip 'n-a aimpip aooac Cpimcann Nianap. Ocup Caipbpi Cinocaio i n-a pe. Ocup Peapaoac Pinopeccnac, pect bliaona a complacup fpip. Ocup Mopan, mac Main, i n-a pe. Ocup oa bliaoain apeip pige ou gabail oo Peraoac, oomapbao Tomap Appoal.—Neap[u]u, ioon, bliaoain. Ocup ip 'n-a aimpip popcpib Eoin in Sopcela, ioon, ipin pectmao bliaoain a pige Peapaoaig Pinopectnaig.—Tpoianup, noi [m-bliaona] oeg. Ocup ipin cper bliaoain a pige aooac Eoin, ocup ipin cper bliaoain oeg oo pige Peraoaig [Pino]pectnaig. Clemenp Papa oo batuo i n-a pe. Ocup Piacac Pinn a pige n-Ulao pop. Ocup ip 'n-a aimpip aooac Peraoac Pinn[pectnac]. Ocup Piacac Pinn, mac Oaige, ou gabail pige n-epenn i n-a

[was] in synchronous rule with him.—Claudius,[2] three years [and] [r] ten. And in the third year of his reign, [took place] the Destruction of the Palace of Da Derga against Conaire the Great, son of Eterscool. And Irial the Kneed, son of Conall Cernach, [he was] in the kingship of Ulster at the Destruction of the Palace [of Da Derga]. And five years for Tara without a king, after the Destruction of the Palace [of Da Derga]. Lugaid Red-Stripe took the kingship of Eriu and Irial the Kneed [was] in the kingship of Ulster then.—Nero Cesar,[3] seven [years and] ten. And it is in his time [took place] the death of Mary Magdalen. And it is in his time [happened] the eruption of the Pool of the Hedge over the Grey [Plain] of the Hedge, namely, Loch Neagh and the eruption of the Lake of Rib, son of Muired, over Magh-Airfen. And Irial the Kneed, son of Conall [Cernach, was] in the kingship of Ulster then and Lugaid Red-Stripe in the kingship of Eriu. And it is in his time was Peter crucified and Paul beheaded and Rome burned.—Galba and Piso,[3] namely, his fosterling, Otho[5] and Vitellius[5], three half-years [were reigned] by them.—Vespasian[5], nine [years]. And in the fifth year of his reign, [took place the death] of Lugaid Red-Stripe. And Concobar Red-Eyebrow took the kingship in his time and Crimthann Nianair took the kingship. And the year after kingship was assumed by him, was crucified Andrew, the Apostle.—Titus[6], two years [were reigned] by him. And Crimthann Nianar [was] in his time.

[A.D.] 2 [41]

[3] [54]

[5] [68]
[5] [69]

[6] [79]

s Domitian[1], five [years and] ten. And the death of Irial the Kneed [took place in] the year he took the kingship. And Fiacha Findamnas took the kingship, namely, the son of Irial. And it is in his time died Crimthann Nianar. And Cairbre Cat-Head [was] in his time. And Feradach Finnfechtnach [was] seven years in synchronous rule with him. And Moran, son of Man, [was] in his time. And two years after the taking of kingship by Feradach was slain Thomas, the Apostle.—Nerva[2], one year. And it is in his time wrote John the Gospel, namely, in the seventh year of the reign of Feradach Finnfechtnach. Trajan[3], nine years [and] ten. And in the third year of his reign, died John and in the third year [and] tenth of the reign of Feradach [Finn]fechtnach. Pope Clement was drowned[4] in his time. And Fiatach the Fair [was] in the kingship of Ulster also. And it is in his time died Feradach Finn[fechtnach]. And Fiatach the Fair, son of Daig, took the kingship of Eriu in his

[1] [81]

[2] [96]

[3] [98]

[4] [100]

[s]pe. Ocur Piatat Pinb|alaċ bo ʒabail piʒe n-Epenn pop.—
Abpianup, ibon, bliabain ap piċit. Ocur ir 'n-a aimpip
aċnuʒub lapuralem, ocur bap Piaċaiʒ Pinnalaiʒ la hElím,
mac Connpaċ, ocur Elím bo ʒabail piʒe. Ocur ir 'n-a pe
boʒab Tuatal Teaċtmap piʒe n-Epenn.—Antoniup, ba [bli-
abain] piċet a compiʒe bo Tuatal. Ocur ir 'n-a pe tuʒab
piaʒail na Carc ʒurna Cpirtaiʒib ocur potaibbeb in bopoma.
Ocur Mal, mac Rocpaibe, i n-a pe.

t Mapcur Anntoni[n]ur noi [m-bliabna] beʒ. Ocur Peiblímíb
Reċtmap i n-a pe. Ocur Caċaip Mop i n-a pe. Ocur Conn
Cebcataċ bu ʒabail piʒe.—Antoni[n]ur Commabur, tri [bli-
abna] beʒ. Ocur irin coiceb bliabain a piʒe tuʒab cat Muiʒe
Lena, ait abpoċaip Moʒ Nuabab. Da bliabain iappin cat pin
Muiʒe Lena, atorcaip Conn Cebcataċ a Tuait Ampoip la
Tibpaibe Tipeaċ, la piʒ Ulab. Conaipe, mac Moʒa Lama,
i n-a pe. Ocur Apt Aenpep bu ʒabail piʒe.—Pertinax[1]
Se[ne]x, peċt mi[1].—Seuerur Portinax[2], oċt [m-bliabna] beʒ
a complatur ppi hApt Aʒaman, mac Piatat Pinn, a piʒe
n-Ulab.—Auipilianur, peċt [m-bliabna]. Ocur cat Cinb-
Abpab pia maccaib Conaipe, mic Moʒa, ibon, na tri Caipppi. Ocur pop Luʒaib, mac Con, ait abpoċaip Nemib, mac
Spaibcinn, la Caipppi Riʒpoba, ocur, bo pear abpai[le], la
hEoʒan, mac Oilella. Cat Muiʒe Mucpuma Dia-bapbain pia
Luʒaib, mac Con, [ait] abpoċaip Apt, mac Cuínb ocur peċt
meic Oilella Oluim. Luʒaib Laʒa, pobiċ Apt a Tuplaċ Aipt.
benne bpit, pobiċ Eoʒan, mac Oilella. Luʒaib, mac Con,
bu ʒabail piʒi.

t.—[1-1] Ælius Pertinax, 6 months.   [2] Severus, 19 years.

---

* Sub hujus [Pii I] episcopatu frater ipsius, Hermes, librum scripsit, in quo
mandatum continetur, quod ei praecepit angelus Domini, cum veniret ad eum in
habitu Pastoris, ut sanctum Pascha die dominico celebraretur (*Liber Damasi pon-
tificalis* [*spurius*]).

Licet nos idem Pascha praedicta [Dominica] die celebremus, quia tamen quidam

time. And Fiatach Findalach took the kingship of Eriu also.—[s]
Adrian[5], a year above twenty. And it is in his time [was] the [A.D. 117][s] renewal of Jerusalem and the death of Fiachach Findalach by Elim, son of Connra and Elim took the kingship. And it is in his time assumed Tuathal the Acceptable kingship of Eriu.—Antoninus[6],[6] [138] two [years and] twenty in cotemporary sovereignty with Tuathal. And it is in his time was brought the Rule of the Easter to the Christians* and was exacted the Boromean Tribute. And Mal, son of Rocraide, [was] in his time.

†Marcus Antoninus[1], nine [years and] ten. And Fedlimid the[1] [161] Law-giver [was] in his time. And Cathair the Great [was] in his time. And Conn the Hundred-Battled took the kingship.— Antoninus [*read* Aelius Aurelius] Commodus[2], three [years and] ten.[2] [180] And in the fifth year of his reign was fought [*lit.* given] the battle of Magh Lena, a place where fell Mog Nuadad. Two years after that battle of Magh Lena, fell Conn the Hundred-Battled in Tuaith-Amrois by Tibraide Tirech, [namely] by the king of Ulster. Conaire, son of Mogh Lama, [was] in his time. And Art the Solitary [*lit.* Sole Man] took the kingship.—Pertinax Senex[3], seven months.—Severus[3] [193] Pertinax[3], eight [years and] ten, in cotemporary sovereignty with Art Aganan, son of Fiatach the Fair, in the kingship of Ulster.— Aurelian[4], seven years. And the battle of Cenn-Abrad [was gained][4] [211] by the sons of Conaire, son of Mog, namely, the three Cairpris. And [it was gained] over Lugaid, son of Cu,—a place where fell Nemid, son of Stripe-Head, by Cairpre Long-Arm, or [*and*, MS.], according to others, by Eogan, son of Oilill. The battle of Magh Mucruma [was gained] on Thursday, by Lugaid, son of Cu, [a place] where fell Art, son of Conn and seven sons of Oilill Olum. Lugaid Laga, slew he Art on the Hill of Art. Benne Brit, slew he Eogan, son of Oilill. Lugaid, son of Cu, took the kingship.

---

inde dubitarunt, ad corroborandas animas eorum eidem Hermae angelus Domini in habitu Pastoris apparuit et praecepit ei, ut Pascha die Dominica ab omnibus celebraretur (*Epistola* [*spuria*] *Pii I ad Justum episcopum*).

Hermes scripsit librum qui dicitur *Pastor*, in quo praeceptum angeli continet, ut Pascha die dominico celebraretur (Beda, *Chronicon*, sub Antonino Pio, A.D. 139–61).

1.

u Nin, mac bel, roga na riz,
Oirderc a blad, 'r a buain briz,
A zezli ba blodaib ber,
Cet ri in domain co biler.

2.

Fici ocur bliadain bladaiz
Do Nin a zein Abrataim:
Linn ar mebar zan merblad,
'N a lebair 'z a landerbad.

3.

Tri ficit bliadan brezda
Dhair Abrataim oirezda
Nertib adbroflioz ra bloid
Az tect Parrtaloin rortzloin.

4.

En bliadain cert re comol
Suil duzab rort Partalon:
Dofuair znai ir bectoail zo m-blad,
Az terrbail noi ba nertmar.

5.

Nínsar, mac Nin, nía zo nert,
'N-a rearcd bliadain bitcert,
Fuair arzart beara ir badba
Mac Searа co rean banba.

1.

v Partalon, Nínsar nert nia,
Diar brizmar zo m-buain recad;
Ni ba raeibriazail u a rlat,
Re haen bliadain adbatrat.

1.

u   Ninus, son of Belus, choice of the kings,
Illustrious his fame and his firm strength,
His branching splendour with different good customs,
The first king of the world legitimately.

2.

Twenty famous [years] and a year
[Were ruled] by Ninus at the birth of Abraham :
A complement that is certain, without deceptive fame,
In its length being full-certified.

3.

Three score of years diversified
[Were passed] of the age of Abraham eminent

At the coming of Parthalon

4.

One year exact was in completion
Before a port received Parthalon
Found he
In managing a ship was he powerful.

5.

Ninias, son of Ninus, a champion with power,
In his sixth year ever—just
Received he
The son of Ser with old Banba.

1.

v   Parthalon, Ninias powerful hero—
A vigorous pair with abiding guilt;
It was not a deceptive rule [that arose] from their destruc-
In one year died they.   [tion,—

2.

[v]   O bar Partaloin primda,
O bair Abraim oillmilla,
A lug gan luibi mar caruid
Coic coic ur ar octmodaid.

3.

O bar Abraim ruair onoir
Go r' claided clann Partaloin,
Ni dott blad, ir blad nac breg,
A rett, octmoda, ir aen.

4.

Maminitur ra mor ag,
'N-a rig Arada imrlan;
Gac oirett robai ir betta
Fai ag toitett in taimletta.

5.

Da bliadain, tri beit demin,
O'n tam go tett triat Nemid;
Ir labra nat lomar cor,
banba rolam ag Finntan.

1.

w   Marailiur, ro bo mor blad,
Ag tett do Nemid nertmur:
Arum glan, gat tir o tarba,
'N-a ri addal Arada.

2.

Nai m-bliadna ocur tet gan coll,
O teatt Nemid na niamglond—
ba plag 'r ba dit daet dambal—
Co tam trit laetda O-Liatan.

2.

[v] From the death of Parthalon the leader,
 [And] from the death of Abraham very distinguished,
 [Eriu] lay without herbage ? like
 Five [by] five full years above eighty.

3.

From the death of Abraham who got honour,
Until were smitten the posterity of Parthalon,
Not narrow the fame, it is fame that is not falsehood;
Seven, eighty [years] and one.

4.

Mamithus with [*lit.* under] great felicity,
He was the absolute Assyrian king;
Every preeminence and goodly deed was
With him at the coming of the plague-destruction.

5.

Two years, thrice ten certain,
From the Plague to the coming of the hero Nemed;
It is a saying that endures not disturbance,—
Banba [was] deserted at [the coming of] Fintann.

1.

w Manchaleus, whose fame was great,
 At the coming of Nemed the powerful,
 Clear the narration, each land profited,
 He was the mighty Assyrian king [*lit.* in his king].

2.

Nine years and a hundred without deceit,
From the coming of Nemed of the heroic actions—
It was a plague and it was a destruction—
To the plague of the heroic districts of Ui-Liathian.

3.

[w] Argatriar, plait peidil,
Ag toideċt taim triaiṫ Nemid;
Docuir gaċ conair fo cloind,
Ir ag togail Túir Condáing.

4.

Coica ir da bliadain co m-blaid,
O taimleċt Nemid nertmair:
Ni cor airmi re rogra
Gu r'gab Slaine ren Fhodla.

5.

Amenter, ba maiṫ a mor,
Ag toideċt Fer m-bolg m-bladmor:
Dabai gan airdrig adbail,
'N-a airdrig or Arardaib.

1.

x Triċa 'r a ceaṫair 'nar'clod,
Flaṫur [na] Fer m-bolg m-bladmor:
Luċt na curaide, ir beċt in bann,
Ag teċt Tuaṫa de Danann.

2.

Ag teċt Tuaṫa de Danann
Go banba d'a buantadall,
Belocur, ba trom tarba,
Or rann rodglar Ararda.

3.

Noċa, oċt bliadna, gan bron
Remear Tuaṫa Danann, dreaċ mor;
Ni breg, aċt ir beċt a faḋ,
Ir cet co cert ir coicad.

3.

[w] Ascatades, persevering prince,
[Reigned] at the coming of the plague of the chief Nemed;
Who placed every path under [the sway of his] posterity,
And [reigned he] at the destruction of the Tower of Conang.

4.

Fifty and two years with fame,
From the Plague-destruction of Nemed powerful—
It is not obliquity of computing to proclaim [it]—
Until Slaine occupied ancient Fodla.

5.

Amyntes, good was his greatness,
At the coming of the Fir-Bolg of great fame,
Was he without vast power
The arch-king [*lit.* in his arch-king] over the Assyrians.

1.

x Thirty and four [years], in which was heard
The rule of [the] Fir-Bolg of great fame :
The folk of the coracles, eventful is the destruction,
At the coming of the Tuatha de Danann.

2.

At the coming of the Tuatha de Danann
To Banba to permanently occupy it [*lit.* for its permanent occupation],
Belocus, it was a weighty advantage,
[Reigned] over the green-swarded Assyrian slope.

3.

Ninety, eight years without sorrow,
[Was] the space of the Tuatha de Danann, great the prospect:
Not false, but eventful is its duration,
It is a hundred exactly and fifty.

4.

[x] Metarailiur ba lur aṗd aḃ,
     Aʒ teċt mac Mileḋ m-bitnʒarḃ:
P. 14 a |Oʒla ruil ba ḃreʒḋa,
     Ḋo ril Aruir oireʒḋa.

5.

Seċt cet tri bliaḋna blaḋaiʒ,
Fice o primteċt Partalain,
Ʒan ʒabail re floʒart fleaʒ,
Ʒu ʒabail mor mac Mileḋ.

6.

Cuiʒ riʒa, fiċe, fir ʒar,
O Metarailiur aʒamar—
Ḋream nar' caineaḋ re truar liḃ—
Re n-aiream ruar co raen Nin.

           Nin, mac.

4.

[x] Metarailius, distinguished the felicity,
     [Reigned he] at the coming of the sons ever-fierce of Miled:

Of the distinguished Assyrian seed.

5.

Seven hundred, [and] three years famous
[And] twenty from the first coming of Parthalon,
Without occupation by a speared host [was Eriu]
Until the great occupation of the sons of Miled.

6.

Five kings [and] twenty, knowledge brief,
From Metarailius of great felicity—
Folk that for fierceness are not lamented by ye—
[Are] to be counted up to noble Ninus.
                    Ninus, son, etc.

INDEX VERBORUM. (III.)

[*Roman capitals* (A, B) *respectively denote the* A *and* B *Texts,* pp. 278 *to* 316; *Roman letters and Arabic figures* (*thus,* d, u 4) *refer to the sections and verses.*]

a (an, art.), A a, e; B v 3, x 1.
a (pr. infix. 3 s. fem.), (conb)a(ʒab), A b.
a (poss. 3 s. masc.), A b, c, d, e, f; B a, b, d, e, f, g, h, j, l, m, n, o, p, q, r, s, t, u 1, 2, 5, v 1, 4, w 5, x 3.
a (poss. 3 s. fem.), A a; B c, d, g, v 2, x 2.
a (poss. 3 pl.), A a c; B a.
a (prep.), B e, l, u 2.
a (rel.), B d.
a (1 and rel.), B k.
a (ɪ), A e, f, h; B b, e, f, g, h, i, j, k, l, n, o, p, q, r, s, t.
a m- (ɪ m-), B l.
a n- (ɪ n-), A b, e, f, h; B d, e, g, h, i, p.
a nb- (poss. 3 p.), B c.
Aaṙbacuṙ, B k.
abbaıne, A h.
Abel, B a.
Abṙabṙuab, B v.
Abṙam, A b; -aim (g.), B v 2, 3; -aham, A b.
Abṙaċam, B c, d; -aim (g.), B c, d, u 2, 3.
Aċṙaṙcaḃeṙ, B j.
aċc, A a; B f, x 3.
ab, B x 4.
Aba, B a.
Abam, A b; B c; -aim (g.), B a.

Abamaṅ, B o.
abbaıl, B w 5; -al, B w 1.
abbaċ, A e; B c, d, f, g, h, i, j, k, m, n, p, q, s; acb-, A e, f.
abbaċabaṅ, B f, h; -cṙac, B v 1.
abeṅaib, B q.
abbṙoḟloıʒ, B u 3.
Abmaıṅ, B d.
abṅaılı, B t.
Abṙıanuṙ, B s.
Aeḃ, B m, n; -ḃa (g.), B h.
aen (num.), A e; B c, d, i, p, v 1, 3; -mab, A h; B c, d.
aenaċ, A c.
Aenʒuṙ, B h, j, n, o.
aeṙ, B d; -ṙa (g.), B d; -ṙe (g.), B i.
aeṙ-bana, B h.
Aḟṙaıcc, B b; -aıʒ, B c.
aʒ (sb.), B v 4.
aʒ (prep.), A a; B b, e, o, r, u 3, 4, v 4, w 1, 3, 5, x 1, 4.
aʒa(maṅ), B a, b.
Aʒnamaıṅ (g.), B f; Aʒno-, A b; B f.
Ahoṙa, B g.
aıbıb, B f.
aıʒe (aʒ, ac and pr. suf. 3 s. masc.), B b.
Aılıll, A h.
aımṙıṅ, A d, h; B g, l, m, n, o, p, r, s.
aıṅ, A e.

INDEX VERBORUM. (III.) 319

Aindinn, B f.
hainm, B g.
airbriġ, ʜ w 5.
airbriġ, ʙ w 5; -ġe, ʙ j.
aiream, ʙ x 6.
Airepaxab, ʙ d.
Airem, ʙ p.
n-Airpen, ʙ r,
Airġeablam, ʙ g.
Airġedmair, ʙ m.
Airġneaċ, ʙ j; -eċ, ʙ o.
airmi (g.), ʙ w 4.
Airt (g.), ʙ l, m, t.
air, ᴀ a; ʙ u 3; -ri (g.), ᴀ e; -raib, ᴀ a.
Airria, ʙ b.
ait, ʜ t.
Alam, ʙ c.
Alaxandair, ᴀ d; -der, ʙ o; -tair, ʙ, n.
Albania, ʙ b.
Alla, ʙ a.
Alloid, ʙ h.
Aloínfur, ʙ b.
Altdur, ʙ e.
Ambroir (g), ᴀ g.
Amenter, ʙ f, w 5.
an (art. ac.), ᴀ a, c.
Andpar, ʙ r.
andran (i and art.), ʙ p.
andrin, ᴀ f, h; ʙ l, p, q, r.
ann (i and pr. suf. 3 s. neut.), ʙ i.
annrin, ʙ i, q, r.
Antoniur, ʜ s.
Antoninur Commadur, ʙ t.
aprbal, ʙ r, s.
ar (sb.), ʙ a.
ar (prep.), ᴀ a, c, e, f, g, h; ʙ a, c, d, j, q, s, v 2.
ar- (i n-), ɴ h, o.
ar(eir), ʜ p; ar(rin) ᴀ a, h.
ara (ala), ᴀ a, e, h; ʙ e, f, q.

Araraxab, ʙ c.
araid, ʙ l.
araile (-li), ʙ q.
Arailiur, ʙ d.
Aram, ʜ c.
Arbatur, ʙ k.
ard, ʙ x 4.
arer, ʙ g.
arġant, ʙ u 5.
Armimenter, ʙ d.
arna (ala), ʙ e.
Arniur, ʙ d.
arrad, ʙ l.
Arramin, ʙ n.
Art, ʜ l, m, t.
Artaraner, ʙ m.
Artarrexer, ʙ m; -erxer, ʙ m.
arum, ʙ w 1.
ar (vb.), ᴀ a, e; ʙ a, b, c, e, p, q, u 2.
ar (prep.), ᴀ c; ʙ p.
Araimiraimir, ʙ g.
Aranda, ᴀ b, c; ʙ c, j, v 4, w 1, x 2; -daib, ᴀ c; ʙ w 5.
Arcaitiar, ʙ e, f.
Ardaiġer, ʙ l.
Arġatriar, ʙ w 3.
Aria, ʙ b.
arin (irin), ʙ d.
arna (arnaib: a and art. d. p.), ʙ f.
Arur, ʙ c; Ariur, ʙ x 4.
ata, ᴀ a, b; ataic, ʙ b, c; -at, ʙ b, c.
atar (g.), ᴀ f; ʙ h.
atnuġud ʙ s; (h)atnuiġeabuġ, ᴀ c; -ġud, ᴀ c.

b' (ba), ʙ a, p.
ba, ʙ e, i, 1, p, q, u 1, 4, v 1, w 2, 5, x 2, 4.
baata, ʙ b.
babiloin, ʙ l; baibiloinia, ʙ c.

babba, ʙ u 5.
babuiṗnn (g.), ʙ m.
baḋna, ʙ e.
(ḋo)baı, ʙ a; (ḋa)baı, ʙ w 5; (ṗo)baı,
    ᴀ b, c, d, e; ʙ v 4; (ṗo)baḋaṗ,
    ᴀ a, c.
baıc (g.), ᴀ d; ʙ o.
balleuṗ, ʙ e.
banba, ʙ v 5, x 2.
bann, ʙ x 1.
baṗ, ᴀ b, g; ʙ c, d, f, g, h, i, l, q,
    r, s, v 2, 3; baıṗ (?), ʙ y 2.
baṫuḋ, ʙ s.
beaḋeḋlaḋ, ʙ m; beḋ-, ʙ m.
bean, ʙ a, b; ben, ʙ c.
beaṗa, ʙ u 5.
beaṗnḋal, ʙ k.
beaṫa, ᴀ e; ʙ a.
beċṫ, ʙ x 1, 3; -ṫa, ʙ v 4; beċṫ-
    ḋaıl, ʙ u 4.
beıl, ʙ c; bel, ʙ u 1.
bel-caınṫe, ʙ h.
belocuṗ, ʙ g, x 2; -ccuṗ, ʙ e.
benne, ʙ t.
beoṫaıḋ, ʙ f.
beṗ, ʙ u 1.
beṫ, ᴀ a.
beṫılluṗ, ʙ r.
(ḋo)bı, ʙ b.
bıbla, ᴀ a.
(ṗo)bıṫ, ʙ t.
bıṫ(ceṅṫ), ʙ u 5; bıṫnḋaṗb, ʙ x 4.
blaḋ, ʙ u 1, 4, v 3, w 1, 5, x 1;
    blaıḋ (d.), ʙ w 4.
blaḋaıḋ, ʙ u 2, x 5; meṅblaḋ, ʙ u 2.
blıaḋaın (n.), ᴀ a, b, c, d, e, f, h;
    ʙ g, h, i, k, p, s, u 2, 4; (d.), ᴀ d,
    e, f, g; ʙ c, d, e, f, g, h, j, l, p,
    q, r, s, t, u 5; (ac.), ʙ v 1; (dual),
    ʙ f, h, i, o, p, q, v 5, w 4.
blıaḋan (g. p.), ᴀ a, b, c, d, e, h;
    ʙ d, e, q, u 3.

blıaḋna (g. s.), ʙ i; (n. p.), ᴀ a, b, c,
    d, e, f, g, h; ʙ f, h, i, j, k, l, n,
    p, r, s, w 2, x 3, 5.
bloıḋ, ʙ u 3; -aıb, ʙ u 1.
bo (vb.), ʙ h, w 1.
boḋıbaḋ, ʙ o.
bolḋnaḋ, ʙ m.
boṗoma, ʙ s.
bṗaṫ, ʙ h; -ṫa, (g.), ʙ l.
bṗeaḋ, ʙ l.
bṗeaṗṗıḋ, ʙ l.
bṗeḋ, ʙ v 3, x 3; -ḋba, ʙ u 3, x 4.
bṗeoḋan, ʙ h; -aın, (g.), ʙ i, l.
bṗeṗ, ʙ g; -ṗe, (g.), ʙ g.
bṗeṗal, ʜ o.
bṗeṫaın, ʙ b.
bṗıḋ, ʙ u 1; -ḋmaṗ, ʙ v 1.
bṗıleıṫ, ʙ h.
bṗıṫ, ʙ t.
bṗoıḋ, ʙ l.
bṗon, ʙ x 3.
bṗuıḋnı (g.), ʙ p, r.
bṗúıḋ, ʙ f.
buaın, ʙ a, v 1, u 1; -aṅ(ṫaball),
    ʙ x 2.

Caelbṗeḋ, ʙ n
Caıllıcula, ʙ r.
Caım (g.), ʙ c.
Caın, ʙ a.
(ṅaṗ')caıṅeaḋ, ʙ x 6.
aḋṅoṫaıṗ, ʙ l, n, t; ḋoṗṫaıṗ, ʙ g, k.
Caıṗbṗı, ʙ h, s.
Caıṗḋıṗıṗ, ʙ k.
Caıṗṗṗı, ʙ p, t.
ṗoṫaıṫ, ᴀ b; ʙ m.
Cal, ʙ e.
Callaḋa, ʙ c.
Cam, ʙ b, c.
Campaıṗeṗ, ʙ l.
Canḋan, ʜ c.

INDEX VERBORUM. (III.)

Cann Ua-Neıb, B g.
capuıb, B v 2.
carc, B s.
caċ, B e, g, h, i, k, o, t; -ċa (g.), B o.
cataıp, A d.
Caṫapba, B o.
caṫaıp, B a, t.
Caṫaıp (g.), B n.
Ce, B i.
ceapb, n a.
Ceapmaba (g.), B h.
Ceapmna, B i.
ceaṫaıp, B x 1.
ceaṫpa (num.), B p.
ceaṫpaıme (g. s.; n. p.), B i.
ceaṫpamab, A a, c, f, h; B f, p.
ceb (ord.), B a, l, r.
Cebcaṫaċ, B t.
Cóın, B h.
Ceınnfınbaın, B g.
ceıc (ord.), B c.
ceıṫpe, B c; -pı, B c, f, h, k, 1.
cenel, B b.
Cepmaba (g.), B h.
cepb, n h.
cepc, B u 4, x 3; biṫc-, B u 5.
cepab, B q; cepba (g.), B q; bocepab, B q.
Cerraın, A e.
ceċ (card.), A b, c, d; B b, w 2, x 3, 5; (ord.) A a, b, c, e, f, h; B a, c, d, f, g, k, n, p, u 1; -aıb, A a, c, e, f, g, h; B d.
ceċna (ord.), A c, d, e; (same) A a; B a, p, q.
ceṫopċa, A b; B, d, e, i, j, k, m, n, q; -óaċ, A c, d, e; B c, f, h, i.
ceṫpı, B l, n.
Cımaeıṫ, B e.
Cımbaeṫ, A d; B n.
Cınbeċ, B e.
Cınbċaıb, B s.
cınn, B e.
Cıp, B l.
Cıpappenrep, B l.
Cıpıne, A h.
claıbeb, B v 3.
Claıpınġneaċ, B o.
clann, B v 3; claınne (p.), B h.
poclapa, B e.
Claubıup, B r.
pocleċt, B a.
Clemenr, B s.
(nap')clob, B x 1.
cloıbem, A f.
Cleopatpa, B o.
cloınb, B w 3.
Cnampoıp, B e.
co (conj.), A b; B f; co n-, A b; B b.
co (prep.), A b, c, d, e, f, h; B q, u 1, 5, w 2, x 6; co m-, B w 4; co n-, B f.
co(cept), B x 3.
Cobṫaċ, B n.
coıc, A a, b, c, d, e, g, h; B c, e, f, g, h, i, k, m, n, o, p, q, r, s; v 2; -ca, A c, e; B d, w 4; -cab, B x 3; -caıc, A a; -caṫ, A b, c; B e, k, p; -ceb, A e, f; B f, h, i, p, q, r, t.
coıġeabaċaıb, B p.
coıġebṁab (g. p.), B p.
Coımbı, A e.
Choınculaınb (d.), B p, q.
Coıppı, A h.
colaınb, B q.
coll, B w 2.
Collampaċ, B o.
complaṫup. B l, p, s.
comol, B u 4.
compaıġıb, n b.
compıġe (d.), B r, s.

Con (g.), B t; Conn, B t.
Conaing (g.), B f, m, w 3.
conaiɼ, B w 3.
Conaiɼe, B p, q, r.
Conall, B o; -aill (g.), B r,
Concobaɼ, A d, f, h; B n, o, p, q, r; -aiɼ (g.), A e; B q.
Chonculainb (g.), B q.
Congal, B o.
conib, A b.
conigi, A d; conn-, A h.
Conmael, B i; -mail (g.), B i.
Connla, B o; Connla Cuɼaibceluɼg, B n.
Connɼać (g.), B s.
coɼ, B v 5, w 4.
Coɼanb, B f; -ainb (g.), A d.
Coɼmac, A d; B o; -aic (g.), A g, h.
Coɼcaɼać, B o.
coɼɼn (co and art.), A f, g; B d.
Cɼeone, B h.
cɼiać, B v 5.
cɼić, B w 2.
Cɼimtann, B o, r, s.
Cɼiɼt, A e, f, h; B q; -taigib, B s.
Cɼićin, B h.
cɼoćab, A f, h; (bo)c-, B r; (ɼo)c-, A f; B r.
cɼuic, B a.
(bo)óuaib, A f; B l,
Cuculainb, B p, q.
cuice (co and pr. suf. 3 s. fem.), B c.
cuig, A h; B x 6; -geb, B d.
Cuillinn, B h.
Cuinb (g.), A g; B t.
bocuiɼ, B w 3.
Cuiɼi, A h.
cuma, B a.
cumbac, A b, c; (ɼo)cumbaigeb, B a.
cuɼaibe, B x 1.
Cuɼ, B c.

b' (be, bi), B b, c, d, f, j, u 3, x 2.
b' (bo), B a, c, q.
ba (ta), B d.
ba (num.), A a, b, c, d, e, f, h; B a, b, c, e, f, g, h, i, k, l, m, o, p, q, r, s, t, v 5, w 4, 5.
(ɼi)bab (tat), A d.
baeó, B w 2.
Bagba, B h.
Baige (g.) B s.
bail, A g.
Bail-lbɼu, B e.
Baiɼ, B l.
Baiɼe, A c, d, h; B p; -ɼɼe, A a.
Baiɼiuɼ, B m, n.
balta, B o, r.
bambal, B w 2.
Banoinne, B h.
Baɼiuɼ, B l.
Baɼɼelluɼ, B i.
Bauib, B i.
be (be and pr. suf. 3 s. masc. or neut.), A b.
(bo)beaćaib, A f, h.
beabaib, A f; -aig, A e, h.
bec (num.), A c, d, e, f, g, h.
beó m-, B h.
Nbece, A g.
beómab, B e, l; -maib, A d, f; beać-, B d.
Bebab, B p.
bebflactuɼ, B g.
beg (card.), B c, d, e, f, g, h, i, j, k, m, n, o, p, q, r, s, t.
Begaib, B o.
beić, A b, h; B o, v 5; -ig, A c.
beió m-, B h, l.
beiginać, B n.
beiɼeab, A c, e.
Belbaet, B h; -eit (g.), B h.
bemin, B v 5.
benam, B e.

INDEX VERBORUM. (III.)

beobꝉlaċa, ᴀ b; beoȝꝉlaiṫ, ʙ o.
Deoṫa, ʜ h.
beꝑba, ᴀ d; (lan)beꝑbab, ʙ u 2.
Deꝑȝ, b, m.
bi (prep.), ʙ d.
bi (bo and pr. suf. 3 s. fem.) ɪɪ o.
bia (bo and rel.), ʙ h.
Dia-baꝑbaín, ʙ i, t.
Dianceċṫ, ʙ h.
biaꝑ, ʙ v 1.
bib (card.), ᴀ o.
bib (bi and pr. suf. 3 pl.), ᴀ d.
(ꝑo)biceannab, ʙ r.
bicuꝑ, ʙ g.
bileꝑ, ɴ u 1.
bilinb, ʙ b; -nn, ᴀ b.
Dimáin (g.), ʙ n.
Dioneꝑ, ɴ k.
Dioniꝑiuꝑ, ʙ o.
bino, ʙ a.
biṫ, ʙ u 2.
Diṫoꝑba, ʙ n.
bo (prep.), ᴀ a, h; ʙ a, b, d, e, k, q, s, u 2, ᴡ 1, ᴢ 4.
bo (bo and pr. suf. 3 s. masc.), ʙ c, g, h, i, j, k, l, p, q, r.
bo (be, bi), ᴀ a, b, h; ʙ a, c, h, l, m, p, q, s.
babai (vbl. pcle.), ʙ ᴡ 5; bobai, ʙ a; bo baṫub, ʙ s; bobi, ʙ b; boceꝑab, ʙ q; bocꝑoċab, ʙ r; boċuaib, ᴀ f; ʙ l; bocuiꝑ, ʙ ᴡ 3; bobeaċaib, ᴀ f, h; bo bicuꝑ, ʙ g; boꝑollamnaꝑṫaiꝑ, ᴀ e; boꝑuaiꝑ, ʙ u 4; baȝab, ᴀ b; boȝab, ʙ d, i, j, s; boȝabail, ɴ c, g, h, m, o, p, r, s; boȝabaꝑṫaiꝑ, ʙ p; bomaꝑbab, ɴ s; bo ꝑanbab, ʙ p; bo ꝑiȝab, ʙ h, p; boꝑonab, ʙ c; bo ꝑcꝑibab, ᴀ a; bo ṫeċṫ, ʙ g; bo ṫinbꝑcain, ᴀ e.

boċṫ, ʙ v 3.
boċum, ᴀ f, h; ʙ f.
boib, (bo and pr. suf. 3 p.), ʙ r.
bomaibm, ɴ d, e.
boman, ᴀ a; ʙ b; -ain (g.), ᴀ h; ʙ c, e, u 1; -un, ᴀ a.
Domiṫianuꝑ, ʙ s.
bo'n (be in), ʙ j.
bꝑeaċ, ʙ ᴢ 3.
bꝑeam, ʙ ᴢ 6.
bu (bo, prep.), ʙ r.
bu (bo, vbl. pcle.), buȝab, ɴ i, s; bu ȝabail, ʙ i, l, m, n, o, p, r, s, t, u 4.
Duaċ, ʙ l, m, o.
buinebaċ, ᴀ b.

e (pr. pers. 3 s. masc.), ᴀ a, d, h; ʙ a, b, c, e, i.
Eabeꝑba, ʙ c; -bꝑab, ᴀ a; Ebꝑaibe, ᴀ a.
n-Eaḋaḋ, ɴ r.
Eabáine, ɴ h.
Ealam, ʙ c; -miba, ʙ c.
eaꝑcoib, ᴀ g; -cobaibe (g.), ᴀ h.
Ebeꝑ, ʙ c, d, e, f, i; -iꝑ (g.), ʙ f, i.
Ebeꝑȝiṫeꝑ, ʙ n, o.
Ebiliꝑoṫuꝑ, ɴ o.
Ecbeċ (g.), ʙ i, m.
Eċṫꝑa, ɴ d.
Ebaiꝑ, ʙ d.
Eḋȝoṫaċ, ʙ i.
eȝ, ᴀ a, g, h.
Eilim, ɴ 1.
aꝑ(eiꝑ), ʙ p, r, s.
eiꝑibe, ᴀ h; ʙ a; -ben, ᴀ e; eiꝑꝑen, ʙ a; eꝑiben, ᴀ e.
Eiṫꝑial, ʙ i.
Elaḋan, ɴ g.
ele, ʙ a.
hElim, ʙ s.

INDEX VERBORUM. (III.)

Elta, B d.
en, B u 4.
Emain, A e; Eamna (g.), A d.
Enba, B j, m, o, u 4; Enna, A d.
Enoch, B a; -oṡ, B b.
Enoċ, B a.
Eoċaıb, A d, e, h; B g, h, i, j, l, m, o, p; Eoċo, B i; -ċu, A d.
Eoṡan, B t.
Eoín, A e; B s.
Eonaıp, B b.
Epıpanep, B o.
Epeamon, B i.
Epc, B g.
Epı, A b; Epıu, B p; -penn (g.), A d, h; B f, h, i, k, l, m, r; (d.), A b; (ac.), A h; -pınn (d.), B d, e, g, i.
Epne, B i.
ep, B j; (ap)ep, B q; epe, B d.
Eppaın, B e, h; Epbaıne (g.), A b.
Eppu, B e.
epp (aıp), B i.
eċep (prep.), B b, g, i, p; eċappo, A h.
Eċeppcel, B p; -ceoıl (g.), B r.
Eċınb, B o.

pa (prep.), B u 3; v 4.
Paċċna, B o.
pab, B x 3.
Paebunbepṡ, B i.
paı (pa and pr. suf. 3 s. masc.), B v 4.
paıċ, B i.
Pallabap, B l.
(po)palnapbaıp, A c.
pann, B x 2.
Panppaıb (g.), B b.
páp, A b.
Paċaċ, B o.
Pea, B d; Peaa, B d.
peap, B a, d, i; Peapcopb, B n.

Peap-mbolṡ (g. p.), B g; Pep-, B w 5, x l.
Peapabaċ, B s; -aıṡ (g.), B s.
peıbıl, B w 3.
Peıbleaċ, B p; -lıṡ (g.), B o.
Peıblímíb, B t; -blımċe (g.), A d.
Peın, B c.
Peınıupa (g.), B b.
pep (g. p.), A d.
Pepabaċ, B s; -baıṡ (g.), B s.
Pepṡo (g.), A d.
Pepṡup, B o, p.
peppa, A d.
Pıaċ, A d; B o; -ċa, A d; B g, h, i, j, k, m, o, s; -ċaıṡ (g.), B s; -co, B h.
Pıaċcon (g.), A d; B d.
Pıabmuıne, B m.
Pıaċaċ, B s.
pıċe, A d; B e, j, k, l, x 5, 6; -ċeb, A d, e, g, h; B g; -ċeċ, A b, f; B c, f, h, i, k, l, n, o, q, s; -ċċaıb, A e; -ċeċmab, B e.
pıċı, B u l; -ċıb, B j; -ċıċ, B q, s, u 3.
Pıleb (g.), B h.
Pınaċċa, B k.
Pınb, B l m; -bamnap, B s; -bċab, A d; B o; -bpaıl, B l.
Pınbpeċċnaċ, B s; -aıṡ (g.), B s.
Pınbalaċ, B s; -nalaıṡ (g.), B s.
Pınn, B s; Pınbċaın (g.), A d; -nċan, B v 5; -nċaın, B n.
Pınpcoıċeċ, B j.
Pıp (d.), B c; (p.) B k; -bolṡ, B f.
Pıpen, B a.
Pıpo, B o.
Pıp, B x 6.
Pıpcon, B o.
Plaıċ, B w 3; Plaċa (g.), A b, c, d; -ċıup, A c, d, e, f; -ċıupa (g.), A d, e, f; -ċup, B c, i.

INDEX VERBORUM. (III.)

beóḋplaiṫ, ʙ j.
plaṫuṗ, ʙ b, c, ᴍ 1.
po, ᴀ f; ʙ w 3.
poḃ(ʒlaṗ), ʙ ᴍ 2.
Pobla, ʜ w 4.
poʒna, ʙ w 4.
poillṗiʒċep, ᴀ e.
poinċenn, ᴀ a; pop-, ᴀ c; -nḃ, ᴀ c.
polam, ɴ v 5.
Pollaiʒ, ʙ i.
pollamnaċṫ, ᴀ e; -aṗḃaip, ᴀ c; -apṫaip, ᴀ e; -ṫap, ᴀ h.
pollup, ɴ p.
Polṫcain ʙ o; -ṫleaḃup, ʙ o.
Pomopaḋ, ʙ e; -aic, ʙ k; -aiḃ, ʙ g.
pop, ʙ d, e, r; popṫi (pop and pr. suf. 3 s. f.), ᴀ a.
popḃa, ᴀ c.
pop, ʙ m, n, o, s.
Ppanʒcaiḃ, ʙ b.
Ppaopṫep, ʙ l.
ppi, ɴ p.
ppip (ppi and pr. suf. 3 s. masc.), ʙ r, s.
puaip, ʜ u 5, ᴠ 3; (ḃo)f-, ʙ u 4.
puil (vb.), ᴀ a.
Puṫ, ʙ c; Puiṫe, ʙ o; -ṫi, ᴀ d.

'ʒ (aʒ), ʙ u 2.
ʒab, ᴀ b, d, e, h; ʙ b, d, i, j, l, m, p, s, u 4, w 4; -baıl, ᴀ b, d, g, h; ɴ c, g, h, i, j, k, l, m, n, o, r, s, t, ᴍ 5; -baip, ᴀ e; -bapṫap, ɴ p; -bpaṫ, ʙ h.
Ʒaḃaip, ɴ i.
ʒaḋ, ʙ v 4, w 3.
ʒae, ʙ h.
Ʒaeḃláiʒiḃ, ʙ f.
Ʒaiḃel, ʙ b, f; -il, ʙ b, h.
Ʒaiuṗ, ʙ r.
Ʒallaḃaʒḃai, ʙ b; -llaʒpeʒe, ʙ b.
Ʒallua, ɴ r.

ʒan (cen), ʙ r, u 2, w 2, 5, ᴍ 3, 5.
Ʒann, ʙ e, f.
ʒap, ʙ ᴍ 6.
(biṫn)ʒaṗḃ, ʙ ᴍ 4.
ʒeʒli, ʙ u 1.
Ʒeḃe, ɴ k.
ʒen (sb.), ɴ c, d, e; ʒein, ʙ c, p, q, u 2.
(po)ʒemaıp, ᴀ e; (po)ʒen-, ɴ p; -ap, ʙ b.
Ʒenann, ʙ f.
Ʒenncallaʒbu, ʙ l.
Ʒialloaḃ, ʙ l.
Ʒlaipni, ʙ q.
ʒlan, ʙ w 1.
ʒlap, ʙ h; (poḃ)ʒlap, ʙ ᴍ 2.
(popṫ)ʒloin, ʙ u 3.
Ʒlunmap, ʙ r; -maip (g.), ʙ s.
ʒnai, ʙ u 4.
bopiʒneḃ, ʙ a; bopinḃi, ʙ a.
ʒnimapṫaḃ, ʙ e.
ʒo (co, prep.), ᴀ c; ʙ c, h, u 5, ᴠ 3, ᴍ 2.
ʒo m- (co m-, prep.), ɴ u 4, ᴠ 1.
ʒoba, ʙ a, h.
Ʒoibnenḃ, ʙ h.
Ʒomep, ɴ b.
Ʒpeʒ, ʙ n, o; -eiʒ, ʙ j; -ʒu, ᴀ c; -ʒuiḃ, ᴀ b.
ʒpene, ʙ h.
ʒu (co, prep.), ᴀ b, c, g, h; ʙ ᴍ 5; (conj.), ᴀ b; ɴ p, w 4.
ʒupin (ʒo(co) and art. s.), ᴀ c.
ʒupna (ʒo(co) and art. p.), ʙ s.

hAbpaham, ᴀ b.
haen, ɴ v 1.
hainm, ʙ g.
haip, ᴀ a; -iḃ, ᴀ a.
hAlaxanṫaip, ʙ n.
haṫnuiʒeaḃuʒ, ᴀ a.

INDEX VERBORUM. (III.)

hebpaιbe, A a.
heʒ, A g, h.
helim, B s.
hIp, A f.
hluιl, B p.
heoʒan, B t.
heppaın, B h, e.

ı (prep.), A h ; B f ; ı n-, B b, d, e, g,
 l, n, o, p, q, s, t.
ı (pr. pers. 3 s. fem.), A h ; B a, o.
ιaccan, B c.
ιab (pr. pers. 3 p.), A e.
ιapeb, B b, c.
ιap, A f, g ; B c, d, e, f, g, h, i, j, k,
 l, q, r ; ιap m-, B f, q ; ιap n-,
 A c ; B c, p, q.
ιappan (ιap and fem. art.), B p ; -pιn
 (ιap and art.), A b, h ; B e, t.
ιapum, A d, f, g, h ; B b.
ιapaιnbʒleo, B n.
ιapbonan, B m.
ιapec, B b.
ιapual, B i.
ιapupalem, B s.
lbaιc, B b.
ιbon, A a, b, c, d, h ; B a, b, c, d, e,
 g, h, i, j, k, l, m, n, p, q, r, s.
lmleaċ, B l, m ; -lιċ (g.), B l.
ιmoppo, A b, h ; B a.
ιmplan, B v 4.
ιn (art. n. s. m. and f.), A a, c, e, f, g, h ;
 B a, b, c, d, f, g, h, i, j, k, l, o,
 p, q, s, x 1 ; (g. s.), A a, b, c, d,
 e ; B a, c, e, h, o, u l, v 4 ; (d. s.),
 A a, c, g ; (ac. s.) A a, b, c, f, g ;
 B b ; (g. dual f.) A a.
ιnb (art. g. s.), B l ; ιn b-, A a, e, h ;
 B e, f ; ιn c-, A h ; B h, r.
ιnbcι (ι and pr. suf. 3 s. f.), A a.
ιnʒen, B g.

ιnʒpeιm, A g, h.
lnuιl, B b.
lono (eoιn), A f.
lopep, A b.
loċa, B r.
lopcappep, B l.
hIp, A f.
lpιal, B r ; -ιaιl (g.), B s ; lpeιl (g.),
 B i, s.
ıp (vb.), A a, d, e, f, h ; B a, b, c, g, i,
 l, m, n, o, p, r, s, v 3, 5, x 1, 3.
ıp (ocup), B c, u 4, 5, v 3, 4, w 3, 4,
 x 3.
lpaιc (g.), B d.
ıpan (ι and art.), A a ; -[n]b, B q.
lpanuιbιa, B c.
lpιcon, B b.
ıpιn (ι and art.), B c, d, e, f, g, h, i, j,
 l, p, q, r, s, t.
ıpιnb (ι and art.), B e, f.
ıpιn c-, B g, j.
lċ, B i ; lċa (g.), B l.
luban, B a, b.
lubιch, A a.
luʒupb, B p, q.
luιl, A e ; B p.

la (prep.), A a, h ; B e, f, h, n, r, s, t.
labpa, B v 5.
labpaιb, B n.
labpaιnne, B i, j.
laeċba, B w 2.
laeʒaιpe, A h ; B n.
laʒa, B t.
laʒpaċ, B m.
laιʒeċ, B m.
laιʒne, B i.
laιpʒe, A d ; B n.
laιp, B b, c.
laιcιʒ, B o.
laιmιaċ, B a.

INDEX VERBORUM. (III.) 327

Lampada, B h, m.
Lampaiper, B h.
Lamppiber, B h.
lan(denbad), B u 2.
Lapaler, B i.
Lauircencer, B i.
le (prep.), A f; B c.
lebain, B u 2.
leir, B a, 1.
leicbliadna, B r.
Lena, B t.
Lece, B p.
liaid, B h.
Liacmuine, B r.
lib, B x 6.
lín, A a, h; linb, B d, i, l, n, o.
Lindmuine, B r.
linn, B e, i, n, u 2.
lincda, B b.
loċ, B d, f, p, r; -ċa, B e, i, r.
Loga (g.), B h.
Loiċ (g.), A d.
Loigte, A d.
loinger, B e.
Loingreċ, B n.
(no)loirced, B l; (noi)l-, B r.
loman, B v 5.
longaib, B h.
Longemanur, B m.
Lopc, B n.
lorcad, A c; B h; -ud, A c.
Luaigne, B d.
luċc, B x 1.
Lucta (g.), A h.
lug, B v 2.
Lug, B g; -gaid, B m, o, t; -gaig, B r.
luibi (a.), B v 2.
Luid, B c.
Luigdec, B l, m; -geċ (g.), B r.
Luigne, B i.
lur (? lair), B x 4...

mac (nom.), A b, d, e, f; B a, b, c, d,
  e, f, g, h, i, k, l, m, n, o, p, r, s,
  t, u l, 5; (ac.), A d; B r; (g. p.),
  x 4, 5.
Maċa, A d; B n.
macaib (d. p.), A b; B i; maccu
  (ac. p.), B b.
Mac Cuill, B h.
mad (mag), B d.
mad (conj.), A a, d, h; mag, A a.
Madae, B p.
Mael, A d; B o.
mag, B d, r.
Magai, B b.
Magog, B b.
Maidiur, B k.
maigerdneċ (g.p.), A a; -treċ, A a.
Maimincur, B e.
Maín (g.) B s.
maipcip, B a.
Maíre, B e.
maic, B w 5.
Mal, B s.
Maireach, B b.
Mamiliur, B e.
Maminicur, B v 4.
Manandan, B h.
Manacalem, B a.
(aga)man, B x 6.
man (conj.), A a; B p, v 2.
mana (g.), A b.
(do)manbad, B s.
Mancur Ancopinur, B t.
Mancain (g.), A h.
Marailiur, B e, w 1.
Maroch, B b.
Marpapcur, B e.
Maċa, A h; B r.
macain, B a.
Macuralem, B a.
Mead, A c; B k; -da, B b; Medaib,
  A c.

INDEX VERBORUM. (III.)

Meaṙnam, ʙ c.
mebaṅ, ʙ u 2.
meic (n. p.), ʙ b, c, t.
Memnon, ʙ m.
meṅblaḋ, ʙ u 2.
Meṙca, ʙ e.
Metaṅailiuṙ, ʙ x 4, 6; -alniuṙ, ɴ i.
mí, ʙ m.
mic (g.), ᴀ e, h; ʙ a, b, c, d, f, g,
   h, i, l, r; mic (p.), ʙ i.
Miḋiṅ, ʙ h.
mile, ᴀ b, c, d, h; ɴ f; -li, ᴀ a, b.
Mileḋ, ʙ i, x 4, 5; -iḋ, ᴀ b; ʙ i.
mnai (dual), ʙ a.
Moċċa, ʙ o; -ai, ᴀ d.
Moɀcoṅḋ, ʙ n; -ɀ Nuaḋaḋ, ʙ t.
Mona-Cṙoɀaiḋe, ʙ k.
Monɀṙuaḋ, ʙ n.
moṅ, ʙ n, p, r, t, ᴠ 4, w 1, 5, x 3, 5.
Moṅan, ᴅ s.
Mucṙuma, ʙ t.
Muiɀc (g.), ʙ g, t.
Muimne, ᴅ i.
Muincamoin (g.), ʙ k.
muinḋciṅ (d.), b f; -nnceṅ, ʙ d;
   -nnciṅe (g.), ʙ e.
Muiṙc, ʙ p; Muiṙe Maɀḋalen,
   ᴜ r.
Muiṙeḋa (g.), ʙ r.
Muiṙcaḋeaċ, ʙ m; -eḋaiɀ (g.), ʙ m.
Mumo, ʙ j.
Munḋṙemaiṅ, ʙ e.
muṅ, ʙ c.
Muṅbulɀ, ʙ e.
Muṙċoṅaḋ, (g.), ᴀ d; ʙ o.

'n (in, art.), ᴀ a, c, g.
'n- (i n-), ᴀ e; ʙ d, e, g, 1, m, n, o, p,
   r, s, u 2, 5, ᴠ 4, 5, w 1, 5.
na (art. g. s. fem.), ᴀ a; ʙ i, p, s;
   (n. p.), ʙ b; (g. p.) ᴀ a; ᴜ a, e,

ṅ, u 1, w 2, x 1; na n- (g. p.),
   ʙ e; na[iḃ], ʙ ᴘ, s.
na (conj. compar.), ʙ p; (neg.), ʙ f,
   x 1, 6.
Naḃcoḋonoṙoṅ, ʙ l; Naḃɀaḋonaṙ-
   ṙoṅ, ʙ l; -noṙoṅ, ʙ l.
naċ (neg.), ᴅ ᴠ 3, 5.
Nae, ᴅ d; Naei, ᴅ c, d.
naem, ᴀ h.
nai m- (num.), ʙ w 2.
Neaṅo, ʙ r.
Neaṅ[u]u, ʙ s.
Neaṙa (g.), ᴀ e; ʙ p; -ṙṙa, ᴀ e, f.
Nḋece, ᴀ g.
Neċċ, ʙ p.
Neiḋ (g.), ʙ h.
Neill (g.), ᴀ h.
Neimeḋ, ᴀ b.
Nema, ʙ a.
Nemeaḋ, ʙ e; -eḋ, ʙ e, f; -iḋ (n.), ʙ t;
   (g.), ʙ f, ᴠ 5, w 2, 3, 4; (d.), w 1.
neṅc, ʙ u 5, ᴠ 1; -ciḃ, u 3; -cmaṅ,
   ʙ u 4, w 1; -cmaiṅ (g.), ᴅ w 4.
Neua, ʙ b.
ni (neg.), ᴀ a d; ʙ ᴠ 1, 3, w 4, x 3.
nia, bu 5, ᴠ 1; Nianaṅ, ʙ o; -aṙeṅ,
   ᴀ h; -aṙeaṅ, ʙ p; -anaṅ, ʙ r, s.
niamɀlonḋ, ʙ u 2.
Nin, ʙ c, u 1, 2, 5, x 6.
Niniaṙ, ʙ c, d, u 5, ᴠ 1.
no (conj.), ʙ d.
noċa, (num.), ʙ x 3.
noe (num.), ᴀ a, c, d; -emaḋ, ᴀ g.
noi (sb.), ʙ u 4; (pr. n.), ʙ b; (num.),
   ᴅ c, d, h, i, m, o, q, r, s, t.
Nuaḋa, ʙ g, 1, p.

o (prep.), ᴀ b, c, d, f, g, h; ᴅ c, q,
   ᴠ 2, 3, 5, w 2, 4, x 5, 6; (o?\
   ᴅ w 1; (o and rel.), ʙ b.
O-Liatan, ʙ w 2.
oc (prep.), ᴀ c

INDEX VERBORUM. (III.) 329

occa (oc and pr. suf. 3 s. masc.), в c.
oċc, ᴀ d, ɢ; ʙ b, c, d, h, i, 1, o, ᴛ 3;
 -ᴄmab, ᴀ d, e, ɢ; ʙ d, e, f, ɢ, h,
 p, q; -ᴄmoba, ʙ ᴠ 3; -baib, ʙ
 ᴠ 2; oċcm-, ʙ n, q.
Occapin, ᴀ e; ʙ p, q.
ocup, *passim.*
oen, ʙ h.
Oppacenep, ʙ j; -ᴄolup, ʙ j.
oɢ, ʙ a.
oɢla (?), ʙ ᴛ 4.
Oileó, ʙ h.
Oillebeꞃɢoib, ʙ k.
Oilill, ʙ k, m, n, o, p; -lella (g.),
 ʙ 1, m, t.
oilmilla, ʙ ᴠ 2.
oiꞃbeꞃc, ʙ u 1; oiꞃꞃ-, ᴀ h.
Oiꞃeam, ʙ p.
oiꞃeċc, ʙ ᴠ 4.
oiꞃeɢba, ʙ u 3, ᴛ 4.
Olimp, ᴀ c.
Oliua, ʙ b.
Ollaċaiꞃ, ᴀ d.
Ollam Fobla, ʙ k; Olaim Fobla,
 ʙ k.
(ꞃo[f])olla[m]ꞃaꞃbaiꞃ, ᴀ c.
Ollaċaꞃ, ʙ h.
Ollɢoċaċ, ʙ k.
Olmuccaib, ʙ j.
Oluim (g.), ʙ t.
onoiꞃ, ʙ ᴠ 3.
Oꞃċaċ, ʙ 1.
oꞃboiɢ (aꞃbaiɢ), ʙ p.
oꞃɢaiꞃ, ʙ a.
oꞃ, ʙ ᴡ 5, ᴛ 2.
Oꞃpiꞃ, ᴀ f.

Pabꞃaic, ᴀ h.
Paꞃcalon, ʙ u 4, ᴠ 1; Paꞃꞃ-, ʙ d;
 Paꞃꞃċalon, ᴀ b; -loin (g.),
 ʙ u 3; Paꞃꞃċo-, ʙ d, e; Paꞃ-
 ċal-, ʙ ᴠ, 2, 3, ᴛ 5.

peċab, ʙ ᴠ 1.
Peabaꞃ, ᴀ f; Pebaꞃ, ʙ r.
Peꞃibioibiꞃ, ʙ i.
Peꞃꞃ, ᴀ c; ʙ 1, n; -ꞃꞃa, ʙ c; -ꞃaib,
 ᴀ c; -ꞃeꞃ Oċe, ʙ n.
Piamineaꞃ, ʙ h.
Pilamecuꞃ, ʙ o.
Pilip, ᴀ d; ʙ n; -poċuꞃ, ʙ n.
Piꞃon, ʙ r.
ꞃlaɢ, ʙ ᴡ 2.
Plobealbuꞃ, ʙ n.
Poiliꞃoiꞃuꞃ, ʙ ɢ.
Pol, ᴀ f; ʙ r.
poꞃc, ʙ u 4; poꞃc(ɢloin), ʙ u 3.
Poċolameuꞃ, ᴀ d; -omeuꞃ, ʙ o.
pꞃiṁba, ʙ ᴠ 2; -mċeċc, ʙ ᴛ 5.
Pꞃobi, ᴀ ɢ.
pꞃoɢeċc, ᴀ f, h.

ꞃ' (ꞃo, vbl. pcle.), ʙ ᴠ 3.
Raeca[i]ꞃ, ʙ e.
ꞃaiɢe (ꞃiɢe, g.), ʙ d, j.
ꞃainb (g. dual), ᴀ a; (ꞃo)ꞃainb, ʙ b.
ꞃaic, ʙ e; -ċe, ʙ p.
ꞃaicea, ʙ 1; -ceꞃ, ʙ b.
(bo)ꞃanbab, ʙ p; -nnca, ʙ i.
ꞃe (sb.), ᴀ a; ʙ d, e, 1, m, n, o, p, r,
 s, t.
ꞃe (prep.), ʙ d, e, i, 1, n, o, u 4, ᴠ 1,
 ᴡ 4, ᴛ 5, 6; ꞃe (le), ᴀ a; ꞃe n-
 (le n-), ʙ ᴛ 6.
ꞃe (le and rel.), ʙ 1.
(bo) ꞃeaꞃ, ʙ t; (bo) ꞃeiꞃ, ᴀ a.
ꞃemeaꞃ, ʙ ᴛ 3; -miꞃ, ʙ m.
Reċcaib, ʙ n; -cmaꞃ, ʙ t.
ꞃennaib (ꞃann-), ᴀ h.
ꞃi (sb.), ᴀ c; ʙ c, e, f, i, k, 1, n, p,
 u 1, ᴡ 1.
ꞃia (la), ʙ t; ꞃia n-, ʙ b.
ꞃiaɢail, ʙ s; (ꞃaeib)ꞃiaɢail, ʙ ᴠ 1.
ꞃiam, ʙ b.
Rib, ʙ r.

ṅiġ (n. s.), A d, h ; B l, n ; (d.), B v 4 ;
(ac.), B r ; (dual), B e ; (n. p.),
A c, e ; (g. p.), B m, u 1 ; -aib,
B f, m.
ṅiġaḋ, B h, p ; -ġan, B o.
ṅiġa (n. p.), B x 6 ; -ġe (g.), B c, d, e,
f, g, h, i, j, k, l, n, o, p, r, s, t ;
(d.), A h ; B c, f, h, i, k, l, n, o,
p, q, r, s ; (ac.), A e, f ; B d, g,
h, j, k, l, m, p, r, s ; ṅiġṅaiṫ,
B e ; -ġi (g.), A g ; (ac.), A d.
ṅiġan, A e ; -ġṅa (g. p.), A h.
Riġḋeṅġ, B n ; -ġṙoḋa, B t.
Rinnail, B g.
ṅo (vbl. pcle.), ṅoḃ', B a ;
  ṅoḃai, A b, c, d, e ; B v 4 ;
  ṅoḃaḋaṅ, A a, c ; ṅoḃiṫ, B t ;
  ḃiaṅ'ḃo, B h ; ṅoḃo, B w 1 ;
  naṅ'caineaḋ, B x 6 ; ṅoċaiṫ, B m ;
  ġoṅ'claiḋeḋ, B v 3 ;
  ṅoclaṅa, B e ; ṅocleṫṫ, B a ;
  naṅ'cloḃ, B x 1 ;
  ṅocṅoċaḋ, A f ; B r ;
  ṅocumḃaiġeḋ, B a ;
  ṅoḃiceannaḋ, B r ;
  ṅoṗalnaṅḃaiṅ, A c ;
  ṅo[ṗ]olla[m]naṅḃaiṅ, A c :
  ṅoġaḋ, A b, d, e, h ; B i, j, k, l,
  m, p ; ġuṅ'ġaḋ, B w 4 ;
  ṅoġaḃṅaṫ, B h ; ṅoġeinaiṅ, A e ;
  ṅoġenaiṅ, B p ; -aṅ, B b ;
  ṅoloiṅceḋ, B l ; ṅoil-, B r ;
  ṅoṅainḃ, B b ; ṅoṅoi[n]ḃṅeṫ-
  ṫaṅ, A h ; ṅoṅcṅiḃ, B s ;
  ṅoṅilṅaḋ, B c ; ṅoṫaiḃḃeḋ, B s ;
  ṅuc, B a ; ṅuġ, B a ; ṅuġaḋ, B p ;
  -aṅḃaṅ, B l ; ṅoṫuiṅim, B b.
ṅo (vbl. pcle. infixed), aḋṅoċaiṅ, B l,
  n, t ; ḃoṅċaiṅ, B g, k ; ḃoṅiġneḋ,
  B a ; ḃoṅinḃi, B a ; ḃoṅ[oṫ]inḃ-
  ṅcaiṅ, A f ; ḃoṅaḃaḋ, A h ;
  ḃoṅonaḋ, B c.

Rocṅaiḃe, B s.
Roḃ, A d ; B n.
ṅoġa, B u 1.
Roím, B r ; Roṁa, A h ; Roman,
  A e, B p ; -naiġ, B b.
ṅoinḃ, B p ; ṅonḃa (ṅanḃa), B p ;
  (ṅo)ṅoi[n]ḃṅeṫaṅ, A h.
Roṅṅa (g.), A h.
Roṫeṫṫaiḃ (g.), B l ; -eaṫṫaiḃ, B j ;
  -aiġ, B j.
ṅu (ṅo, vbl. pcle.), ġuṅuḃ', B p.
ṅuaḋ, B m, n ; ṅuaiḃ (g.), A h.
Ruḃṅaiġe, B f.
Ruġṅaiḃe, B d, o.
Ruiṅ (g.), B e.

'ṙ (iṙ, vb.), B i.
'ṙ (iṙ = ocuṙ), B u 1, w 2, x 1.
ṙaeġul, B q ; -ġlaṫ, B k.
ṙaeiḃ(ṅiaġail), B v 1.
ṙaein (ṙen, demons.), A d, e.
ṙaeṅ, B a, x 6.
ṙaġaṅṫ, B a.
-ṙaiḃe, A g, h ; -ḃein, A g.
Saile, B c, d.
ṙalḃuiḃi, A d, e.
Samṅṅaímíṙ, B c.
Saṅḃaṅaṅalluṙ, ıı j.
Saxain, B b ; -xaṙ, B b.
Sceiṫia, A b ; B e, f ; -ṫeġḃa, B b.
ṙcela, A d.
Scoṫ, B e, f ; Scuiṫ (g.), B f ;
  Scoṫaiḃ, A h.
(ṅo)ṙcṅiḃ, B s ; (ḃo)ṙcṅiḃaḋ, A a ;
  ṙcṅiḃeann, B r.
Sḃaiṙṅ, B f.
ṙé (num.), A a, c, d, e, h ; B h, i, j, k,
  l, p.
Sealla, B a.
ṙean, B u 5.
Seanġann, B e ; -ġainḃ (g.), B f, g.

INDEX VERBORUM. (III.)

Seapa, B u 5.
ſeaɼeḃ, B u 5.
Secɼaiɲ, A f; Seᵹɼ-, A f.
ɼeċc, A f, g; B j, k, l, m, n, o, q, r,
   s, t, v 3, x 5; ɼeċc m-, B h, q.
ɼeċcmaḋ, A g; B d, e, f, g, j, l, s;
   -moḋaḋ, B q; -moᵹaḋ, A a, d, e.
Seḋna, B j, l, m.
Seɼeaɲuɼ, B e.
Seᵹamaiɲ, B o.
Seᵹḃenuɼ, B m.
Séim, B b; Sem, B b, c.
ɼeiɼeaḋ, B j; -ɼeḃ, B j, p, q.
Semiɲiu, B e.
ɼen, B d, w 4.
-ɼen, B a.
ɼenaiḋ, A g.
ɼencuɼɼa, A d.
ɼenoɲaċḃa, A a.
-ɼeo, A a.
Seɲɼeɼ, B m; -ɲxeɼ, B d, l.
Seɼaiɲ, B p; Sexaiɲ, B r; -xaɲ, B r.
ɼeɼcaḋ, A b, e; -ḃmaḋ, B q; -camaḋ,
   B d; -ċac, B j.
ɼeiɼeaḋ, A g; ɼeɼeḃ, A a.
ɼᵹoile (g.), A a.
-ɼiḃe, A f; B a, b, c; -ḋem, A b, d,
   e, f; -ḃen, A e; B a; -ᵹen, B b.
ɼil, A b; B a, b, f, l, x 4; (ɲo)ɼilɼaḋ,
   B c.
Simon, B l.
ɼin, A a, e, g, h; B c, d, e, f, g, h, i,
   j, k, l, p, q; (pr. n.) B p.
Siɲiaċ, B a.
Siɲlam, B m.
Siɲna, B k.
Slaine, B w 4.
Slainᵹe, B f; Slanᵹa, B d.
ɼlan, B p, q.
Slanoll, B k; -oill (g.), B k.
ɼlac, B v l.
ɼleaᵹ, B x 5.

ɼloᵹaɲc, B x 5.
ɼluaiᵹeḋ, B p, q.
Soḃaiɲce, B i.
Soᵹaɼaneɼ, B k.
[ɼ]oiɼcela, B r; ɼoɼ-, A h; B s.
Solman, A b; B l.
Soɼɼaiɲɼeɼ, B h.
Sɲaiḃcinn (g.), B t; -ḃnḋeɲᵹ, B r.
Sɲu, B e.
ɼuaɼ, B x 6.
Suɼɼaɲḃuɼ, B h.
ɼuil, B u 4; x 4(?).
Sulḃuſḋe, B p.

ca, B d.
caḃaiɲc, B o.
caċuɼ, A f.
(buan)caḃall, B x 2.
cueɼca, B p.
ɲocaiḃḃeḋ, B s.
Caillcen, B i.
cam, A b; -mlaċc, A b.
caim (g.), B w 3; -mleċc, B w 4;
   -mleċca, B e, v 4.
Cain, B p.
cainiᵹ, B d, e,
cam, B h, v 5, w 2.
can, A b; B f, h, i, j, k, l, p, q.
canaiɼḃe, B a.
Cana-ḃo-Cuailᵹne, B p, q.
canic, A b; B i; canᵹaḃaɲ, B h, i.
caɼ, B r.
Caɼa, B d.
caɼba, B w l, x 2.
cac, B b.
ceaċc, B w 2; ceċc, B d, e, u 3, v 5,
   w 1, x 1, 2, 4.
Ceaċcmaɼ, B s.
ceaɼḃo, B q.
ceamɼall, B l.
Ceḃḃaɲḃaċ, B p.
cempoill (g.), A b, c.

INDEX VERBORUM. (III.)

Tempaiʒ, A h; B r.
ceopa, B b.
cepcompaʒ, A g.
cepna, B f.
cepṗbail, B u 4.
Ṫiber, B q; -ir, A f; B q.
ciċcain, A f.
Ṫiʒeapnḃaċ, B p.
Ṫiʒepnmair, B i; -mur, B i.
cinḋrcna, A e; (ḃo)cinḃrcain, A e, f;
    ḃor[oċ]inḃrcain, A f.
cir, B w 1.
Ṫipar, B b.
Ṫicur, B r.
coċur, A c; cocuireḃ, A h.
coʒail, A b; B f, r, w 3.
coiḃeċc, B w 3, 5; -iceċc, B v 4.
coirimceċc, A b.
coireċ, B a.
Ṫolamenr, B n, o.
comaiḃm, B e, i, r.
Ṫomar, B s.
comur, A a.
Ṫomur Concolep, B j.
Ṫopn, B d.
coraċ, A h; B i; corraċ, A d.
Ṫrae, A b.
crebe, A c.
crenpep (g. p.), B f.
crer (ord.), A a, f, g, h; B d, e, f, h,
    r, s; -rmaḃ (in.maḃ, MS.), B d.
cri (card.), A a, b, c, d, g; B b, h, i,
    k, m, o, p, q, r, t, u 3, v 5.

criċa, A c, d, g; B d, e, f, g, i, k, o,
    x 1; -ċaḃ, B d; -ċac, A c; B e,
    h, i, k, l, m, n, o, q; -ċec, A b.
criaiċ (g.), B w 3.
criur, B b.
Ṫroianur, B s.
crom, B x 2.
Ṫuḃal, B b; -lcain, B a.
Ṫuaċa-ḃe-Ḋananḃ, B g, i, x 1, 2, 3;
    Ṫuacaiḃ-, B g.
Ṫuaċal, B s.
puc (po ċuc), B a; cuccarcair, B c.
cuʒ, B a; puʒ (r[oċ]uʒ), B a; cu-
    ʒaḃ, B o, s; puʒarḃar, B l.
Ṫupḃeaċ, B o.
Ṫúir, B f, w 3.
Ṫúireḃ, B g.
Ṫuplaċ, B t.
Ṫupmeaċ, B o.
cur, B a; (po)cuirim, B b.
Ṫucaner, B i.

u (o, prep.), B v 1.
uaḃ, B b, c; uaiḃiḃ, A e; B b c.
uaim (sb.), B a.
Uairċear, B m; -cer, B m.
Uerperianur, B r.
Uʒaine, B n.
Uʒairc, A e: Uʒurḃ, B p, q; -uirc,
    A e.
uile, B a.
Ulaḃ, A e; B n, o; -ḃ, B, p, q, r, s.
ur, B v 2.

LECTURE IV.

THE CODEX PALATINO-VATICANUS,

No. 830.

THE CODEX PALATINO-VATICANUS, NO. 830.

No. IV.—(SUCCESSIONS FROM THE *BOOK OF BALLYMOTE.*)

III.

IN the post-Patrician portion of the regnal list given by Marianus, the following errors occur :—

(1) Muridach Munderg was king of Ulster, not king of Ireland. Moreover, he was contemporary of St. Patrick, so that he is here placed one hundred years too late.

(2) The Baitan who succeeded Baitan and Eochaid was not the son of Murchad, but of Nainnid. He was first cousin of St. Columba; Nainnid and Fedlimid, St. Columba's father, having been sons of Fergus, son of Conall Gulban (eponymous head of the Cenel-Conaill), son of Niall of the Nine Hostages.

(3) Baitan was succeeded (not by Ainmire, who was his predecessor, but) by Aed, the son of Ainmire.

(4) "Colman the Little, son of Diarmait and Aed, son of Anmire, 13 years." This is an unaccountable double error. Colman was king (not of Ireland, but) of the Southern Ui-Neill, and was slain by the Aed in question at the battle of Ballaghanea, Co. Cavan, in the second year of the reign of the latter. The joint-kings were Colman's eldest brother, Aed Slane and Colman Rimid, son of Baitan, son of Muircertach, king of Ireland.

(5) "Suibni, son of Colman the Great, six years.

Aed Slane, son of Diarmait, four years."

Here again we find the slayer and the slain made joint monarchs.

These two items seem to prove that Marianus was unacquainted with Adamnan's Life of St. Columba. Therein we have a prophecy "concerning the son of King Dermait, who was named Aid Slane in the Scotic tongue." Notwithstanding the prophetic warning of the saint, Aed assassinated his nephew, Suibne, with the result that, in the words of the biographer, thereafter he enjoyed the sovereignty but four years and three months.* He began to reign A.D. 598 and was slain by the son of his victim, A.D. 604.

(6) Aed Allan was succeeded (A.D. 612) by Mailcoba, not by Oengus, son of Colman the Great.

(7) Maelcoba, on the assassination of his brother, Suibne, became king of Uisnech, that is, of the western branch of the Southern Ui-Neill. He was killed A.D. 615 by Suibne Menn, king of Ireland.

(8) This Suibne was son of Fiachna, not of Fachtna.

(9) Finally, Fogartach was grandson, not son, of Cernach Sotal (the Proud).

In illustration of the post-Patrician list, I subjoin two pieces from the *Book of Ballymote*. The first is in prose. It gives the name, descent, regnal years and manner of death of each king from Loeghaire (*sl.* A.D. 462) to Turlough O'Conor (*ob.* A.D. 1156). It was composed during the reign of Roderic, son of Turlough, namely, between 1156 and 1198. Its chief linguistic interest consists in eight quatrains. Of these, six are found in Tigernach. They are also given in the *Chronicon Scotorum* and the *Annals of the Four Masters*.

The present text, though far from faultless, is one of many similar evidences of the unfitness of Mac Firbis and the O'Clerys to deal with documents written in the ancient language.

The first quatrain (**a**) is composed in the metre called *Rannaidacht mor*, that is, in heptasyllabic lines, each line ending with a monosyllabic word (Lecture II., p. 108).

Line 2 Mac Firbis† gives as ꝼoꞃ ꞇaoḃ Caiꞃi ᵹlaiꞃi i ꞇíꞃ, which is hypermetrical and meaningless.

In line 3, he reads aḋꞃeᵹaiḃ, which is equally void of sense. The true form is aḋꞃaᵹaiḃ = aḋ-ꞃo-a-ᵹaiḃ, *which he invoked*, a = infixed pron., pl. 3.

The second quatrain (**b**) is in the *Debide* metre, which has been already dealt with.

In the first line, the *Four Masters* (according to O'Donovan's

---

* Note A.   † *Chronicon Scotorum*,—Rolls' edition, p. 26.

text),* read ꞃeaꞃꞃaciꞃ ("was fought," according to the editor). Here we have a word of three syllables, though the metre requires a monosyllable.

The third verse (**b**) is metrically identical with the first.

In the second line (judging from Hennessy and O'Donovan) the *Chronicon*† and the *Annals*‡ read ıma luaıḃꞃea instead of ımaluaıḃ-ꞃea. Both editors accordingly translate, *Around whom (many storms) shall move.* But the verb is ımluaıḃım, with the infixed pronoun a, having bean (woman) as antecedent. Hence the expression means: *who shall excite (many storms).*

The next line runs in MacFirbis aꞃan ꞃeꞃ loıꞃꞃıḃeꞃ. Passing over the neuter article with the masc. ꞃeꞃ, the line is one syllable short and does not end in a monosyllable.

The fourth stanza (**c**) is in the same metre as the second. I have not found it elsewhere. The locative ıḃuꞃ has to be read ı ḃuꞃ to produce the requisite monosyllable.

The fifth (**d**) belongs to *Rannaidacht mor gairit* or *short Rannaidacht mor*, so called because the initial line is (four syllables) shorter than the others. In the first line, in accordance with what has been laid down in Lecture II. (Rule **2**, pp. 103-4), we have to read Iꞃ a m-ḃuaċ. The O'Clerys, according to the printed text,§ read the quatrain as two lines. Moreover, they give ꞃꞃı ḃꞃuaċ, a reading which makes the line a syllable short.

The third line MacFirbis reads‖ acꞃoḃ coꞃuꞃ cꞃéıċ ("[Accounts] report, though abhorrent," according to the translator), which, besides being unmetrical, means nothing. The *Four Masters* (*loc. cit.*) are somewhat better: acꞃec ꞃeela, cıa ꞃa ꞃeıċ. Cıa ꞃa ꞃeıċ (*although depressing*) O'Donovan renders by "who, in weariness"! The original is preserved intact in the Ballymote text given below.

The sixth quatrain (**d**) is in *Rannaidacht beg (small)*, which, it has been shewn (Lecture II., p. 108), differs from *Rannaidacht mor* in that each line terminates in a dissyllable.

The first line Mac Firbis¶ reads Níoꞃ ḃu aıꞃmıꞃc ın aıꞃle. The *Four Masters*** give Nı ḃa haıꞃmıꞃc ınḃ aıꞃle ("It was not a

---

* *Four Masters*, vol. i., pp. 150-1.   † P. 42.   ‡ P. 172.
§ *Four Masters*, vol. i., p. 220.   ‖ *Chronicon Scotorum*, p. 64.
¶ *Ubi sup.*, p. 68.   ** P. 226.

wise counsel," O'Donovan; followed in substance by Hennessy). But the reading of the *Book of Ballymote*, enepc a capple, is manifestly the original: *Not weak* (was) *what befell*: capple = бo-aιpρο-le (laι), with the relative a (*what*).

The seventh (**e**) quatrain is the *Debide* (a) explained above (p. 107–8). The variants in the *Chronicon* and *Four Masters* are not of importance.

The eighth (**i**) is likewise in *Debide*. In the first quarter, the *Termination* is formed by bρɪρ; ρo and бu (бo) (the latter of which was inserted to make up the requisite number of syllables) not being taken into account.

It has to be added, that, in seven of the foregoing instances, the editors have given text and translation as if neither the one nor the other presented any difficulty.

The second piece is a poem appended to the prose tract, to certify the subjects already dealt with. It is composed in Irregular Debide. The original portion closes (**s** 5) with the death of Maelsechlainn (A.D. 1122). Of the additional verses, one (**w** 6) professes to have been composed in 1143. (As the preceding quatrain apparently refers to the same year, 6242 of the text is to be amended into 6342 = Mundane Period of 5199.) The date of another (**s** 6) is denoted by mention of the invasion of (King) Henry. The eulogy of Tigernan O'Rourke (**x** 2) is noteworthy, in contrast with the dark colours in which the prince of Breifny is depicted in the Irish Annals.

Of the author, Gilla-Modubda (*Devotee of my* [*St.*] *Dubad*), nothing seems to be known beyond what is told at the close of the prose tract. From one of the quatrains (**r** 1) it may be inferred that he belonged to Meath. (The verses in praise of Devenish and Ardbraccan (**x** 5, 6) are amongst the additions.)

Concerning the saint whose name he bore, native authorities, as far as I know, mention neither the family nor the church. In the *List of Priests* of the early Irish Church (*Book of Leinster*, p. 366 c), Dubad is found. From the Martyrology of Tallaght (*ib.* p. 358 g) we learn that his feast fell on April 15: *xvii. Kal.* [*Maii*], *Dubta*.* From

---

* Syncopated genitive (= *Dubata*) of *Dubat*, a variant of *Dubad*. O'Clery (*Mart. of Donegal*, Ap. 15) gives *Dubhda* as the nominative; not knowing that in calendars the names of the saints commemorated were in the genitive.

the present text it may perhaps be concluded that St. Dubad was venerated in Meath.

The chief chronological value of the Ballymote Successions is the undesigned corroboration supplied thereby to A.D. 432, as the date of St. Patrick's coming to Ireland as missionary. Laeghaire, we are informed (**a**), reigned thirty years after that event. These regnal years belong to a portion of the *Annals of Ulster* that is accurately dated. The following afford confirmation of the Ballymote number:—

A.D. 454. The Assembly of Tara was held by Laeghaire.

A.D. 461. Laeghaire lived seven years and seven months and seven days after the Assembly of Tara.

A.D. 462. Death of Laeghaire, etc.

Against A.D. 432 as the initial year of the Patrician mission, two arguments brought forward by Dr. Todd have been adopted by Mr. Stokes in his edition of the *Tripartite*.

The first is from a tract in the *Book of Lecan*, as follows:— ɪɪɪ. bliaḋna aɼ ꜰl. o ṫaɴιc Paṫɼaιc ι n-Eɼιnn co caṫ Oċa—three years above forty since Patrick came into Ireland to the battle of Ocha. 'The battle of Ocha, according to the *Annals of Ulster*, was fought A.D. 483, and therefore, counting forty-three years back, A.D. 439 or 440 would be the date of Patrick's coming' (p. cxxv.).

Here Dr. Todd and Mr. Stokes, who copied him, failed to discover that the chronology of the Ulster Annals is correct in this place. The year, accordingly, is A.D. 482. But an error far more serious has to be laid to their charge. Both accepted the passage from which the calculation is taken as reliable. Mr. Stokes, who worked at second-hand, goes farther. He declares (p. cxxiv.) the whole tract to be "more historical in character" than another in the same MS., which makes Lugaid, who became king of Ireland A.D. 482, the reigning monarch when St. Patrick arrived. Now, the "more historical" passage says that *during that time* (the forty-three years in question) there was but *one king over Leinster, namely, Bressal Belach* (aen ɼιġ ꜰoɼ Laιġnιḃ, ιḋon, bɼeɼɼal belaċ).

But, unfortunately for the compiler and those who put their trust in him, King Bressal was some time dead before "A.D. 439 or 440."

The authority of the *Annals of Ulster* will not be impugned in the present instance.

A.D. 435. *Mors Bressail, regis Laighen.*	Death of Bressal, King of Leinster.
A.D. 436. *Vel, hic mors Bresail.*	Or, here [is to be placed] the death of Bresal.
(*Vel, hoc anno Bressal mortuus est, secundum alios.*)	(Or, this year Bresal died, according to others.)

Amongst "the others" are the *Annals of Innisfallen*, which give the obit at A.D. 436* (not A.D. 437, which is O'Conor's marginal date).

The next is from the poem of Gilla Coemain. He "counts 162 years from the advent of St. Patrick to the death of Gregory the Great, which took place on March 12, A.D. 604. Therefore, the advent of St. Patrick, according to Gilla Coemain, must be dated A.D. 442".† But, in the first place, Gilla Coemain, as has been shewn in Lecture I. (p. 23), does not place Gregory's death "on March 12, A.D. 604." Secondly, Gilla Coemain, according to the figures adopted in the Rolls' translation, counts 522 years from the Nativity "till Patrick came." That is, he places the saint's arrival fifty-nine years later than A.D. 463, the year "probably in or about which," according to Mr. Stokes' Patrician Chronology, his death took place!

Examination of the original, if I mistake not, will lead to a different result. The figures for the period from the Nativity to the coming of St. Patrick as given by Mr. Stokes are the following :‡—

(*a*)	47	(*g*)	45
(*b*)	32	(*h*)	5
(*c*)	157	(*i*)	34
(*d*)	32	(*j*)	49
(*e*)	37	(*k*)	27
(*f*)	57		
	[362	+	160 = 522.]

---

* P. 352, *infra*.   † *Tripartite Life*, p. cxxv.   ‡ *Ibid.*, pp. 535-7.

The *b* line reads:—

α δό τριὁατ o ḟein ıllε.   Two [and] thirty [years] from that hither.

Another reading is preserved in the Bodleian copy:—

α όο ḟıċετ o ɼ[h]eın [ıl]lc.   Two [and] twenty [years] from that hither.

This gives *b* 22.

The *i* line runs:—

'S α ceċαıɼ [τριὁατ], δeɼb lıb.   And four [years and thirty], certain to you.

Τριὁατ is the Bodleian lection. Here the *Concord* proves that the word missing from the *Book of Leinster* was coicατ (c - c)—fifty. This leaves *i* 54.

We have thus: (522 - 10) + 20 = 532. Gilla Coemain consequently fixes the advent of St. Patrick as missionary at A.D. 532, when, according to Mr. Stokes, the saint was about sixty-nine years dead! One calculation may pair off with the other.

With respect to the subject-matter, seeing that the obituary years are not severally reckoned from a general epoch, either in the prose tract or in the poem of Gilla Modubda, the question presents itself: How were the dates adjusted? This leads us to consider the chronology adopted in native A.D. historical documents.

Not finding the A.D. number prefixed to each year, O'Conor (*Rer. Hib. Script.*, *ii. xx.*) concluded that the Christian era was not employed in the native Annals. Tigernach, he adds, very rarely adjusts native events thereto, deeming the year sufficiently specified by the addition of the week-day number to *Kal. Ian.* This is an application of what O'Flaherty says (*ib.*, p. 34 from *Ogygia*, p. 39):—

[*Hiberni veteres*] *cujusque anni quo quidquam memoriae prodiderunt, Kalendas Ian. hebdomadis feriâ in quam incidirent, nullâ aliâ adhibitâ ærâ, signabant, hoc modo: Kl. Ian. feria 4, Connus Centimachus Rex, 20 Octobr., feria 3, occidit. . . . Aetatem Lunae etiam nonnunquam addebant et illius anni numerum decennovenalis cycli.*

Elsewhere (p. 145), O'Flaherty gives the year as A.D. 212, D.L. F.D. The entry professes to be taken from Tigernach. But the reading in the Trinity College Fragment of Tigernach (dealt with farther on, p. 354 *sq.*) is:—

[Ɑ.ⲘȢ] ⁊ⲛⲟⲭⲝⲝⲩⲛ. Κl. Ⲉⲛ. ⲩⲓ. ⲣ., l. ⲭⲩⲛⲓ. Conn Ceocacaó occiꝛ- ꝛuꝛ eꝛc ceꝛcⲓⲁ ꝑoꝑⲓⲁ hⲓ Ɫⲩⲁⲓɫ Ɑ⳽ⲛbꝛoⲓꝛ, no ⲓ n-lꝛꝛⲩꝛ Ɒo⳽ⲛⲛⲁⲛⲛ, ⲩɫ ⲁⲗⲓⲓ ⲁⲓⲩⲛɫ.

[A.M.] 4137 [A.D. 185]. Kalends of Jan. on 6th feria, moon 18[13]. Conn of the Hundred Battles was slain on Tuesday in Tuath-Ambrois, or in Irros-Domnann, as others say.

This date agrees very closely with the B-Tract of Lecture III., which equates (t) the year with the seventh of Commodus (A.D. 186). The ferial is accurate. The error in the lunar notation will be pointed out hereafter. *Tuesday* probably signifies the first Tuesday of January.

With reference to O'Conor, his competence to discuss domestic chronology can be estimated from the statement he makes, that Tigernach was acquainted with the Dominical Letters. For, if so, it remains unaccountable why that annalist never once employed them, but gave the ferial numbers. The truth is, in the known range of native Annals, Dominical Letters, whether of verbal or alphabetical sequence, are nowhere to be found.

Now, to test the vaunted value of consecutive A.D. dating, here is the recently issued volume I. of the *Annals of Ulster*. It has every year marked with the A.D. numeration as found in the two MSS. And what is the result? Why, through more than five hundred years, every date is wrong! Nor is this all. The origin of the error has baffled every inquirer from O'Flaherty to Hennessy.

Seeing then that notation, whether A.M or A.D., was employed only at wide intervals, how, the question consequently arises, was the sequence of the intervening years determined? Certainly, looking through the pages of O'Conor's *Tigernach* and *Annals of Innisfallen* and contemplating the barren results of his "supreme labour and incredible diligence" (p. xxi.), one would be led to conclude that to co-ordinate and date the blank *Kl.* and undated entries were to essay the impossible. Such was the judgment of Mr. Hennessy, and his decision seems to have been accepted as final.

"The loose method," he writes, "followed by the older annalists of simply indicating the succession of years by the repetition of the sign *Kl.*, or *K.*, for *Kalends*, to which they sometimes added the ferial, or day of the week on which the 1st of January occurred, together with their habitual practice of omitting to paginate their MSS., has led to innumerable errors in the chronology of Irish history. These errors might in some measure be corrected by the help of the ferial, if we possessed the original MSS. But these criteria have been so corrupted in the course of successive transcriptions of the earlier chroniclers by ignorant scribes, who did not understand their value, that they are comparatively useless in determining the correct chronology, unless when combined with other criteria. Even in the copies of *Tighernach* at present available, the order of the ferine is so confused and irregular that any attempt to bring it into harmony with the succession of *Kals.*, or years, would prove a fruitless undertaking."*

Naturally, therefore, he adopts the facile system introduced by O'Conor. "The marginal dates represent the actual (*sic*) enumeration of the *Kals.*, or years, contained in the chronicle."† Nay, such value does he attach thereto, that in one place (p. 337) he puts 1131 on the margin, because "the actual (*sic*) reckoning of the *Kals.* gives" that year, despite the fact of the ferial number and the epact and the A.D. reckoning being, all three, supplied in the text! No doubt, the moon's age is wrong; but the error (xui. for xiii.), which is easily rectified, does not affect the date (A.D. 1135).

Now, one would fain believe that our countrymen, whom St. Columbanus, in his Letter to Pope Gregory, extols as *most sage cyclic computists*, were not without method in their chronology likewise. Such, it is a relief to find, was the case.

The Irish A.D. Annals in the present recension were dated in detail by the ferial and Decemnovennal lunar incidence of Jan. 1. Hence the formula (for instance): *Kal. Jan. vi. feriâ, ix. lunâ* (or with variations of collocation or regimen to the same effect). The native equivalent was: Kal. enaıp pop aıne ⁊ nomaɒ uaċaɒ (epcaı) puıppı—the Kalend [1st] of January [fell] upon Friday and the ninth day [of the moon fell] thereon. Uaċaɒ is a neuter *a*-stem (gen. uaċaıɒ), *singularity (of number)* and was used idiomatically, with or without epcaı (of the moon), to signify the lunar day. When the year was blank, the signature, as a rule, became indifferently *Kal. Jan.*, *Kal.*, *Kl.*, or simply *K*.

---

* *Chronicon Scotorum*, Rolls' Ed., p. xlvi.-vii.   † *Ib.*, p. xlvii.

The ferial numbers were *feria i.* [Dominical Letter A] = Sunday; *feria ii.* [Dominical Letter G] = Monday; and so on, to *feria vii.* [Dominical Letter B] = Saturday.

Ferial Number,	.	i.,	ii.,	iii.,	iv.,	v.,	vi.,	vii.
Dominical Letter,	.	A,	G,	F,	E,	D,	C,	B.
Week-day,	.	S.,	M.,	T.,	W.,	Th.,	F.,	Sat.

In 365-day years, each year would commence on the week-day next after that on which the preceding year began. The ferial incidence of Jan. 1 would accordingly be identical every eighth year: forming a hebdomadal cycle. The seven-day sequence is, however, interrupted every fourth year by the addition of the Bissextile. The cycle thus becomes one of 28 (7 × 4). Commencing, for convenience sake, with A.D. 1, this cycle is as follows. (The Dominical Letters are annexed.)

I.

FERIAL SOLAR CYCLE.

No.	F.N.	D.L.		No.	F.N.	D.L.	
1	vii.	B		15	iii.	F	
2	i.	A		16	iiii.	ED	Bis.
3	ii.	G		17	vi.	C	
4	iii.	FE	Bis.	18	vii.	B	
5	v.	D		19	i.	A	
6	vi.	C		20	ii.	GF	Bis.
7	vii.	B		21	iiii.	E	
8	i.	AG	Bis.	22	v.	D	
9	iii.	F		23	vi.	C	
10	iiii.	E		24	vii.	BA	Bis.
11	v.	D		25	ii.	G	
12	vi.	CB	Bis.	26	iii.	F	
13	i.	A		27	iiii.	E	
14	ii.	G		28	v.	DC	Bis.

(1) Accordingly, to find the ferial number of an A.D. year, divide the given year by 28: the Roman numeral opposite the remainder is

the ferial required. If nothing remains, the Roman numeral corresponding to 28 is the ferial.

(2) The chief use of this Cycle is in connexion with determining the ferial of a given day of the month. For this purpose, to the annual number of the day add the ferial, as in Table I. (plus 1, when the day falls after Feb. 24 in a leap-year). Divide by 7. The remainder will be the requisite ferial. The computation of the day is easily made by the following Table.

II.

DIURNAL ANNUAL NUMERATION.

	a	*b*	*c*
1 Jan. in Kal.	1, in Non.	5, in Id.	13 :
2 Feb. ,, ,,	32, ,, ,,	36, ,, ,,	44 ;
3 Mar. ,, ,,	60, ,, ,,	66, ,, ,,	74 ;
4 Apr. ,, ,,	91, ,, ,,	95, ,, ,,	103 ;
5 Mai. ,, ,,	121, ,, ,,	127, ,, ,,	135 ;
6 Jun. ,, ,,	152, ,, ,,	156, ,, ,,	164 ;
7 Jul. ,, ,,	182, ,, ,,	188, ,, ,,	196 ;
8 Aug. ,, ,,	213, ,, ,,	217, ,, ,,	225 ;
9 Sep. ,, ,,	244, ,, ,,	248, ,, ,,	256 ;
10 Oct. ,, ,,	274, ,, ,,	280, ,, ,,	288 ;
11 Nov. ,, ,,	305, ,, ,,	309, ,, ,,	317 ;
12 Dec. ,, ,,	335, ,, ,,	339, ,, ,,	347 ;
Jan. ,, ,,	366.*		

---

* Thus arranged (without *a*, *b*, *c* ; 1, 2, etc.) in the Tract *De argumentis lunae*, amongst the *Dubia et spuria* appended to the works of Bede. It is contained in Chap. xxii., *De temporum ratione*, which is devoted to the illustration of Rules 1 I., 2 II. The basis of the pseudo-Anatolian Cycle is a computation according to these Rules (*Jan. in Kl. una dies, luna* I., *etc.*), including the last day of each month (*In prid. Kl. Febr.* xxxi. *dies, luna prima, etc.*). As the "holy man Anatolius" (*De temp. rat. xxxv.*) imposed upon Bede, calling the method (*c. xxii.*) a *vetus argumentum majorum auctoritate contraditum*, it may be inferred, was in reference to the forgery.

In the *Lebar Brec* Calendar of Oengus, the following items are given at the respective places on the margin :

    a 2, 4 (MS. [lxx]xxi.), 5, 6, 8 (MS. ccxui.), 9 (MS. ccxluii.).

    b 1, 2 (MS. xxiii.), 5, 6, 7, 8, 12.

    c 1, 2, 5, 6, 12.

The omission of the rest was owing to the scribe.

When the given day falls on the Kalends, Nones, or Ides, subtract 1; when it falls before them, subtract the number whereby it is designated (e.g. III. Kal., III. Non., III. Id.).

An example relative to each column will illustrate the application of this Table. According to the *Annals of Ulster*, Armagh was burned A.D. 1020, on the 3rd of the Kalends of June, the 2nd feria. *Jun. in Kal. 152.* Deduct 3 and add 7* (6 by Table I. and 1 for the bissextile). Divide by 7. The remainder is 2 = Monday.

Artri, Archbishop of Armagh, died A.D. 1020, on the 3rd of the Nones of June, the 6th feria (*ib.*). *Jun. in Non. 156.* Deduct 3 and add 7 (as in the previous date). Divide by 7. The remainder is 6 = Friday.

A.D. 878, the moon was eclipsed on the Ides of October, the 4th feria (*ib.*). *Oct. in Id. 288.* Deduct 1 and add 4 (as in Table I.). Divide by 7. The remainder is 4 = Wednesday.

The quadruple recurrence of each ferial, combined with the liability of alphabetical numeration to mistranscription,† detracts from the chronographic value of Table I.

Not so, however, with the Epacts. Forming a cycle of nineteen and differing considerably one from the other, they constitute a criterion sufficiently comprehensive and not very liable to be rendered worthless by scribal corruption.

The following table exhibits the Alexandrine (A.) and Roman (R.) Epacts, together with the Golden Numbers and such technical terms as occur in the (greatly over-rated) *Paschal Epistle* of Cummian,‡ the work *De mirabilibus Sacrae Scripturae*§ (both of the seventh century) and the native Annals.

With reference to the Epact, the common lunar year of 354 days is eleven days shorter than the common solar year of 365. Hence, if both years commence concurrently, the twelfth day of the second lunar year will coincide with the first of the second solar year. The eleven *added* days are called Epacts (ἐπάκται ἡμέραι). The Alexandrines, according to the computists, began the Lunar (Paschal) year on March 23. The Epacts they reckoned by anticipation from March

---

* Or nothing, as the divisor is 7.
† Cf. : Facilis certe librarii in tanto earumdem feriarum recursu lapsus fuerit. Bucherius, *De Doct. Temp.*, p. 119.   ‡ Note B *a*.   § Note E.

THE CODEX PALATINO-VATICANUS, 830. 347

22, which day was in consequence designated *Sedes Epactarum* in the Calendar. Their first Epact was 30,* the long lunar month, (= 0). In the Julian Calendar, the initial Epact was counted from Jan. 1 next preceding. This is 9.† With 30 (= 0) and 9 as the respective bases, the Epacts are found by adding 11 for each year and subtracting 30 (the full lunar month), when the sum exceeds that number. The exception occurs in the nineteenth year. There, on account of the *Saltus Lunae* or *Moon's Leap*,‡ 12 (instead of 11) is added; thus giving 30 (= 0) [(18 + 12) − 30] or 9 [(27 + 12) − 30], as the Epact of the twentieth year, that is, the first of the second Cycle. Common years (C.) contain twelve lunar months; Embolismal (E.), in addition, have a full month of Epactal days *thrown in* (μῆν ἐμβόλιμος). In Table III., the R. Embolisms are marked in accordance with the Julian Calendar. The 1st, 3rd, 4th, 5th and 7th are mentioned on the margin of the *Lebar Brec* Calendar of Oengus.

The division into Ogdoad and Hendecad is explained in the *Epistle to Bonifacius and Bonus*, the second prefixed to the Dionysian Cycles. This exposition of Dionysius forms the basis of the Chapter (*xlvi.*) *De Ogdoade et Hendecade* in Bede's work *De temporum ratione*. It has to be added that, seventy years before Dionysius wrote, the terms were employed (in total disregard of the meaning) to divide the years of a Cycle of **84** into alternate eights and elevens.§ A document containing them may accordingly date from before A.D. 526.

---

* I.e., moon 18 of Mar. 22 of a supposed previous (nineteenth) year (new m. Mar. 5, Table IV. xix.) + 11 + the *Saltus*. This Bede (*ubi sup.*) calls *de octava decima in nullam facere saltum*.

† That is, the year began, ex hypothesi, on Dec. 24 of the previous (nineteenth) year, according to the Calendar.

The Egyptian Decemnovennal Cycle commenced on the preceding August 28. Whence Jan. 1 next following = m. 9 (R. E.); Mar. 22 = m. 30, i.e. 0 (A. E.).

‡ See Bede, *De temp. rat. xlii.* (*De Saltu Lunae*).

§ In the Carthaginian Paschal Table of A.D. 455 (Krusch, *ubi sup.* p. 184). For instance, 449 is marked as the first of the Ogdoad. It is the fifth of the Hendecad (G. N. xiii.). 457 is given as the first of the Hendecad. It is the second of the Ogdoad (G. N. ii.). The compiler of the Table apparently copied the arrangement of the Cycles of Theophilus or St. Cyril. This was likewise erroneous. According to the original, or Metonic, Cycle, 449 would be the seventh of the Ogdoad; 457, the seventh of the Hendecad.

III.
DECEMNOVENNAL CYCLE.

EPACTS.

		A.	R.	GOLDEN NUMBER.*	
Ogdoad ('Ογδοάς)	1	xxx(o). c.	ix. c.	I.	
	2	xi. c.	xx. E.	II.	1st Embolism.
	3	xxii. E.	i. c.	III.	
	4	iii. c.	xii. c.	IV.	
	5	xiv. c.	xxiii. E.	V.	2nd Embolism.
	6	xxv. E.	iv. c.	VI.	
	7	vi. c.	xv. c.	VII.	
	8	xvii. E.	xxvi. E.	VIII.	3rd Embolism.
Hendecad ('Ενδεκάς)	1	xxviii. c.	vii. c.	IX.	
	2	ix. c.	xviii. c.	X.	
	3	xx. E.	xxix. E.	XI.	4th Embolism.
	4	i. c.	x. c.	XII.	
	5	xii. c.	xxi. E.	XIII.	5th Embolism.
	6	xxiii. E.	ii. c.	XIV.	
	7	iv. c.	xiii. c.	XV.	
	8	xv. c.	xxiv. E.	XVI.	6th Embolism.
	9	xxvi. E.	v. c.	XVII.	
	10	vii. c.	xvi. c.	XVIII.	
	11	xviii. E.	xxvii. E.	XIX.	7th Embolism.

(1) As the Golden Number II. corresponded to A.D. 1, to find the G. N., divide the A.D. year + 1 by 19. The remainder is the G. N. If nothing remains, the G. N. is 19.

(2) To find the age of the moon on a given day of the month, to the diurnal annual number of the day (found by Table II.) add the R. Epact (as in Table III.) and divide by 59 (i.e. a *full month*—mensis

---

* Thus named from being rubricated in the Calendar. A fine example is the (so called) Missal of Mary, Queen of Scots, in the Royal Irish Academy, in which the illumination is executed in gold.

THE CODEX PALATINO-VATICANUS, 830. 319

plenus—of 30 + a *hollow month*—mensis cavus—of 29 days).* The remainder, if under 30, is the requisite lunation; if over 30, subtract that number and the remainder is the lunation.

For instance, in the year of St. Patrick's death (A.D. 493), according to *Lebar Brec*, the Epact was 27 and the 16th of the Kalends of April fell on Wednesday, moon 13.† *Apr. in Kal. 91* (Table II.). Subtract 16, add the Epact 27 and divide by 59. 43 remain. Deducting 30, we obtain the lunation 13.

This Rule, however, suffers exceptions, owing to the Embolisms. Thus, the *Annals of Ulster* state the moon was eclipsed, A.D. 878, on the Ides of October, Wednesday, moon 14; the sun, on the 4th of the Kalends of Nov., Wednesday, moon 28.‡ The ferial criteria, Tables I. and II. show, are accurate. Applying the Lunar Rule, we have: *Oct. in Id. 288*. Deduct 1, add 23 (found by Table III., Rule 1) and divide by 59. The remainder is 15. Similarly: *Nov. in Kal. 305*. Deduct 4, add 23 and divide by 59. The remainder is 29. The computistic error arises from the embolismal day of the Golden Number v. This is inserted at Oct. 1, making the new moon fall on Oct. 2.

I have accordingly compiled the following Table, which sets forth the novi-lunar incidence of the Decemnovennal Cycle. The solar day of the new moon being ascertained thereby, the lunation of the given day can be readily computed. For instance, A.D. 878 has the Golden Number v. (Table III., Rule 1). Reference to Table IV. will show that a new moon of v. fell on Oct. 2. The 14th of that moon consequently fell on Oct. 15; the 28th, on Oct. 29. This proves the accuracy of the *Ulster* computations.

---

* As a rule, the odd months (Jan., March, &c.) were *full;* the even (Feb., April, &c.), *hollow*.

† See the text, p. 388, *infra*. ‡ The text is given, p. 379, *infra*.

IV.

DECEMNOVENNAL NOVI-LUNAR INCIDENCE.

G.N.	R.E.	Jan.	Feb.	Mar.	Apr.	Mai.	Jun.	Jul.	Aug.	Sep.	Oct.	Nov.	Dec.
I.	ix.	23	21	23	21	21	19	19	17	16	15	14	13
II.	xx.	12	10	12	10	10	8	8	6	5	4	3	2
III.	i.	1, 31	—	1, 31	29	29	27	27	25	24	23	22	21
IV.	xii.	20	18	20	18	18	16	16	14	13	12	11	10
V.	xxiii.	9	7	9	7	7	5	5	3	2	2, 31	30	29
VI.	iv.	28	26	28	26	26	24	24	22	21	20	19	18
VII.	xv.	17	15	17	15	15	13	13	11	10	9	8	7
VIII.	xxvi.	6	4	6	5	4	3	2	1, 30	29	28	27	26
IX.	vii.	25	23	25	23	23	21	21	19	18	17	16	15
X.	xviii.	14	12	14	12	12	10	10	8	7	6	5	4
XI.	xxix.	3	2	3	2	1, 31	29	29	27	26	25	24	23
XII.	x.	22	20	22	20	20	18	18	16	15	14	13	12
XIII.	xxi.	11	9	11	9	9	7	7	5	4	3	2	1, 31
XIV.	ii.	30	28	30	28	28	26	26	24	23	22	21	20
XV.	xiii.	19	17	19	17	17	15	15	13	12	11	10	9
XVI.	xxiv.	8	6	8	6	6	4	4	2	1	1, 30	29	28
XVII.	v.	27	25	27	25	25	23	23	21	20	19	18	17
XVIII.	xvi.	16	14	16	14	14	12	12	10	9	8	7	6
XIX.	xxvii.	5	3	5	4	3	2	1, 31	29	28	27	25	24

Being cyclic, the ferial and epact, it is obvious, could be of no utility, except in connexion with a fixed date, whether initial or other.* A typical example will prove this.

---

* In cyclo nullus annus natura, sed positione, primus est. Bucherius, *De Doct. Temp.* p. 146.

THE CODEX PALATINO-VATICANUS, 830.   351

In a MS. of Priscian preserved at Leyden, the following, written perhaps by the scribe of the work, appears (folio 7b) :—

Dubthach hos versus scripsit tempore parvo ;
Indulge, lector, quae male scripta vides.
Tertio Idus Apriles—   tribus digitis ;
Tertio anno decennovenalis cicli—tribus instrumentis ;
Tertio die ante Pascha—   penna, membrano ;
Tertia decima luna incipiente — atramento ;
Tertia hora post meridiem—   Trinitate auxiliatrice.

In Table IV., the Golden Number III., denoting the third year of the Cycle of Nineteen, is placed opposite March 31. The Paschal new moon was accordingly on that day (the 14th of the Mar. 1 moon occurring before the Paschal Term, Mar. 21), and the 14th lunation fell on April 13. Hence the earliest Easter of III. was F, that is, April 14. "The third day" (Ap. 11) is thus reckoned exclusive of Sunday. It was, in fact, Holy Thursday.

But, how futile was all the precision! Within the probable period of the transcription of the MS., the Easter of III. F occurred three times at intervals of 95 years,—A.D. 743, 838, 933.

We have next to shew the value of the ferial and epact when employed with a definite year. In the Carlsruhe Codex of Bede, well known as one of the MSS. on which the *Grammatica Celtica* was based, a second hand placed on the margin (folio 17a) of the *Computus Annalis*, or Calendar, opposite . . . d. b. v. Kl. [*Sep.*] :

bár Muirchaṫo, maic Maile-   Death of Murchad, son of Maelduin
ḋúin, hi Cluain-maccu-Noir, á   [king of Cenel-Eogain], in Clonmacnoise,
imba Chiaṗain, x. anno.   from out the bed of [St.] Ciaran, in the
                                   tenth year [of the Cycle of Nineteen].

The *tenth* is obviously reckoned from a dated *first* year. Hence, as the native Annals state that Maelduin was deposed* A.D. 823, it is easy to suggest that 832 is the year intended. But, as the Carlsruhe MS. does not give the date of deposition, the conjecture is untenable.

On the second preceding folio, the same hand made a marginal entry :

[*A.D.*] DCCCXVII. *Aed, rex Hiberniae, moritur.*†

---

* Strange to say, his death is not given.
† The *Annals of Ulster* give the obit of Aed at A.D. 819.

817 (Table III., Rule 1) is the initial year of the Cycle of Nineteen (Golden Number I.). The *tenth* therefrom is 826 (Golden Number x.; Dominical Letter G). D (without a point (.) before or after) and B are the respective lunar and ferial letters of August 28. The meaning, accordingly, is that Murchad died on Tuesday, August 28, moon 21 (new moon, August 8, Table IV.), A.D. 826.

To illustrate the use of ferial and epact in application to native annalistic dating, take, for example, the initial Solar Cycle of the *Annals of Innisfallen*, from where the ferial notation of Jan. 1 commences in O'Conor's edition.* O'Conor tacitly admits his inability to restore the chronology from the textual data.

The opening year, "Septuagint" (Victorian) A.M. 5630, Hebrew, 4481 [= *iii. f., x. l.*, A.D. 429] and the second [*iv. f., xxi. l.*], A.D. 430, have been already given.† From the latter the text gives four *Kl.* up to *Kl. i. f.*, which O'Conor counts A.D. 434. But the true date, the ferial shows, is A.D. 433. The explanation is: a duplicate entry of St. Patrick's advent was given under A.D. 432. Its heading, *Kl.*, should accordingly not be reckoned separately. This is placed beyond doubt by the remainder of that Decemnovennal Cycle and the whole of the next. The reconstruction, it will be observed, tallies exactly with the scanty portions of the ferial and epact preserved in the transcription.

        Kl. [Jan.] i. f., [xxiv. l., A.D. ccccxxxiii.] Conversio Scotorum in fidem Christianam.

        Kl. [Jan. ii. f., v. l., A.D. ccccxxxiv.] Prima preda Saxonum ab Hibernia.

        Kl. [Jan.] iii. f., [xvi. l., A.D. ccccxxxv.] Orosius et Cirillus in doctrina floruerunt.—Nix magna.

[Bis.] Kl. [Jan. iv. f., xxvii. l., A.D. ccccxxxvi.] Mors Bressail Brice [of Bressal the Speckled].

[Initium Cycli xix.alis.] Kl. [Jan. vi. f.,] ix. l. [A.D. ccccxxxvii.] Initium Circul- magni. [Beginning of the great Cycle (of St.Cyril).]

        Kl. [Jan. vii. f.,] xx. l. [A.D. ccccxxxviii.]

---

* *R. H. S. ii. Annal. Innisf.*, 1–3.   † Lecture III., p. 241, *supra*.

Kl. [Jan.] i. f. [i. l., A.D. ccccxxxix.] Secundinus et Auxiliarius et Iserninus mittuntur in auxilium Patricii: nec tamen tenuerunt apostolatum, nisi Patricius solus.

[Bis.] Kl. [Jan.] ii. f., xii. l. [A.D. ccccxl.] Quies Augustini sapientis. Mors Mane, meic Neill [son of Niall] . . . et [quies Xisti] xliii. epis[copi Romanae Ecclesiae].

Kl. [Jan. iv. f., xxiii. l., A.D. ccccxli.] Probatio sancti Patricii in fide Catholica.

Kl. [Jan. v. f.,] iv. l. [A.D. ccccxlii.] Stella crinita apparuit.

Kl. [Jan. vi. f., xv. l., A.D. ccccxliii.] Patricius in Christi doctrina floruit.

[Bis.] Kl. [Jan. vii. f., xxvi. l., A.D. ccccxliv.] Eclipsis solis in nona hora.

Kl. [Jan. ii. f., vii. l., A.D. ccccxlv.] Tethosius [regnare incipit], qui regnavit an. xxvi. Nathi [*lege* Dathi], mac Fiachrach [son of Fiachra].

Kl. [Jan. iii. f., xviii. l., A.D. ccccxlvi.]

Kl. [Jan. iv. f., xxix. l., A.D. ccccxlvii.] Cath Maige Femin eter Munechu ocus Laigniu [Battle of Magh-Femin, between the Momonians and Lagenians], in quo cecidit Mac Carthinn, meic Coelbath, qui jecit genus Laig.

[Bis.] Kl. [Jan. v. f., x. l., A.D. ccccxlviii.] Quies Secundini sancti.

Kl. [Jan. vii. f., xxi. l., A.D. ccccxlix.]

Kl. [Jan. i. f., ii. l., A.D. cccel.]

Kl. [Jan. ii. f., xiii. l., A.D. cccli.] Calcedones Senodus congregatur.

[Bis.] Kl. [Jan. iii. f., xxiv. l., A.D. ccclii.]

Kl. [Jan. v. f., v. l., A.D. cccliii.] Marciani mors, qui regnavit imperator an. vii. Leo regnavit et corpus Johannis [Baptistae] repertum est.

[Kl. Jan. vi. f., xvi. l., A.D. cccliv.]

Kl. [Jan. vii. f.,] xxvi[i]. l. [A.D. ccclv.] Pascha in viii. Kal. Maii.

[Initium Cycli xix.alis.] Kl. [Jan. i. f., ix. l., A.D. ccclvi.] Fairdbe [?] Laing [? Laigen. Destruction ? of the Lagenians]. Hic alii dicunt nativitatem sanctae Brigitae.

The blanks observable in the luni-solar notation are evidently owing to scribal remissness.

Equally striking are the results obtained in connexion with the *Tigernach* Fragment in Trinity College.* The MS. begins with the Hebrew A.M. 4033, and ends with 4522 = 490 years. But for almost three-fourths it is a skeleton. The entries that (preceded, as a rule, by the dated year and, with one exception, by the ferial and epact) occur at intervals, breaking the array of vacant *Kl.*, amount only to 125. On the other hand, "the actual reckoning of the Kals." gives but 360, instead of 365, blank years. How are the lacunae to be localized and supplied? Dr. Todd, who worked on the Fragment (O'Curry, *MS. Materials*, p. 581), can only say, "it is possible there may be some error in the transcription of the *Kl.*"

As the basis for the solution of this and kindred questions, I tabulate the luni-solar criteria of the initial cyclic years as given in the MS. (The opening entry is acephalous, but the omission can be supplied with certainty by comparison with what follows in the text.)

---

* It consists of three vellum folios bound up with the *Annals of Ulster* (II. 1. 8).

V.

TIGERNACH FRAGMENT.—LUNI-SOLAR CRITERIA OF INITIAL CYCLIC YEARS.

						[A.M.	A.D.]
	1.	[Kl. En.	ii. f.,	l. ix.,	4033.	81.]
[Bis.]	2.	,, ,,	iiii. f.,	l. ix.,	4052.	[100.]
	3.	,, ,,	vii. f.,	l. ix.,	4071.	[119.]
	4.	,, ,,	iii. f.,	l. ix.,	4090.	[138.]
	5.	,, ,,	vi. f.,	l. ix.,	4109.	[157.]
[Bis.]	6.	,, ,,	i. f.,	l. ix.,	4128.	[176.]
	7.	[,, ,,	iiii. f.,	l. ix.,	4147.	195.]
	8.	,, ,,	vii. f.,	l. ix.,	4166.	[214.]
	9.	,, ,,	iii. f.,	l. ix.,	4185.	[233.]
[Bis.]	10.	,, ,,	vi. f.,	l. ix.,	4204.	[252.]
	11.	,, ,,	i. f.,	l. ix.,	4223.	[281.]
	12.	,, ,,	iiii. f.,	l. ix.,	4242.	[290.]
	13.	,, ,,	vii. f.,	l. ix.,	4261.	[309.]
[Bis.]	14.	,, ,,	ii. f.,	l. ix.,	4280.	[328.]
	15.	,, ,,	v. f.,	l. ix.,	4299.	[347.]
	16.	,, ,,	i. f.,	l. ix.,	[4318.	366.]
	17.	,, ,,	iiii. f.,	l. ix.,	4337.	[385.]
[Bis.]	18.	,, ,,	vi. f.,	l. ix.,	4356.	[404.]
	19.	,, ,,	ii. f.,	l. ix.,	4375.	[423.]
	20.	,, ,,	v. f.,	l. ix.,	4394.	[442.]
	21.	,, ,,	i. f.,	l. ix.,	4413.	[461.]
[Bis.]	22.	,, ,,	iii. f.,	l. ix.,	4432.	[480.]
	23.	,, ,,	vi. f.,	l. ix.,	4451.	[499.]
	24.	,, ,,	ii. f.,	l. ix.,	4470.	[518.]
	25.	,, ,,	v. f.,	l. ix.,	4489.	[537.]
[Bis.]	26.	,, ,,	vii. f.,	l. ix.,	4508.	[556.]

[Ends at [iiii. f., l. xiii. = (textual) G. N. 15, A.M.] 4522 (A.D. 570).]

Next, we obtain the amount of the epacts omitted, as follows:—

8 in the 1st,* 8th and 9th cycles respectively.	[24]
9 in the 10th cycle.	[9]
11 in the 2nd cycle.	[11]
13 in the 13th and 26th cycles respectively.	[26]
14 in the 3rd, 5th, 6th, 15th, 16th and 20th cycles respectively.	[84]
15 in the 11th, 17th and 21st cycles respectively.	[45]
16 in the 14th, 18th, 19th, 23rd and 24th cycles respectively.	[80]
17 in the 4th, 7th, 12th and 22nd cycles respectively.	[68]
18 in the 25th cycle.	[18]
	[365]

In all, 365.

To shew with what certainty the omissions can be supplied, I append the respective numbers and places of those occurring in the two opening cycles:—

1st Cycle,	5 epacts are omitted between	l. x[x.]	and	l. xxv[i].
,,	,,	3	,,	,,	,,	,,	l. ii.	,, l. xvi.
2nd	,,	2	,,	,,	,,	,,	l. xx.	,, l. xxiii.
,,	,,	2	,,	,,	,,	,,	l. xxiii.	,, l. xxvi.
,,	,,	2	,,	,,	,,	,,	l. xxvi.	,, l. xxix.
,,	,,	2	,,	,,	,,	,,	l. xxix.	,, l. ii.
,,	,,	2	,,	,,	,,	,,	l. xiii.	,, l. xvi.
,,	,,	1	,,	,,	,,	,,	l. xvi.	,, l. ix. [of 3rd cycle].

Thirdly, the five missing *Kl.*, or years, can accordingly be localized. Three are wanting, along with the ferials and epacts, in the 4th cycle, between *l. xxiv.* and *l. ix.* They are, consequently [A.M.] 4106-7-8 [A.D. 154-5-6]. The year of *l. xxiv.* is IIIIciiii[*i*]. Then follows the entry; after which is IIIIcix, *vel* IIIIcx. *Kl. En. vi. f., l. ix.* The true lection, therefore, is [A.M.] 4109 [A.D. 157] (cycle 5, *supra*).

---

[1] The first epact of this cycle is not included, as it was contained on the previous (missing) folio.

The text (*a*) and restoration (*b*) relative to the fourth *Kl.* are as follows:

(*a*)	(*b*)
iiiiclxvi.	iiiiclxvi. [A.D. 214] Kl. En. vii. f., l.ix.
Kl. En. vii. f., l.xx.	iiiiclxvii. [A.D. 215] Kl. En. i. f., l.xx.

That the absence of the *Kl.* in the first line of (*a*) does not denote the omission of a year, is proved by Table V., No. 8, and by the fact that [A.M.] 4173 has the epact *xxvi.*

The fifth *Kl.* was omitted, together with the ferial and epact, in the 15th cycle; *l. xv.* is dated [A.M.] 4305 [A.D. 353]; *l. vii.*, [A.M.] 4307 [A.D. 355]. The year passed over was 4306 [A.D. 354], *l. xxvi.*

It remains to examine the accuracy of the ferial and lunar incidence presented by the Table. The first, as can be verified by Table I., Rule 1, is in every instance correct.

By Rule 1, Table III., we shall find that A.D. 81 has the Golden Number vi. = Epact 4 (not i. = Epact 9). The same holds good of the other 25 years in Table V. Similarly, 570, the concluding year, has the Epact 9 (Golden Number i.); not Epact 13 (Golden Number xv. of the preceding cycle), as given above. In a word, every lunar reckoning in the Fragment is five years wrong! Moreover, the uniformity leaves no room to doubt that in each instance the alteration was effected designedly.

Anomalies still greater are exhibited in the textual collocation of the entries relative to the dates. As a typical instance, I select the period from the birth to the captivity of St. Patrick. The purport of the following arrangement is explained by the headings. With regard to the contents, the years in β, except those printed in italics, have foreign items. Of the four here reproduced (taken from St. Jerome's continuation of the Eusebian Chronicle), the first and last show that the number of years marked is correct. The displacement of the second and third can scarcely have originated with a compiler acquainted with the source. The correct dates are given within brackets. (It is unnecessary to observe that they do not agree with the respective MS. ferials.) In γ, the years, with three exceptions, are left blank. Four have been omitted.

VI.—RECENSIONS OF *TIGERNACH*.

α	β	γ	δ
TIGERNACH.	TIGERNACH.	TIGERNACH.	Chronology in accordance with the obit of St. Patrick in γ* and the ferial sequence of β, γ.
(T.C.D. Fragment.)	(O'Conor, *R. H. S.* ii. 70-3.)	(Chron. Scot., p. 14.)	
[A.M. A.D.] 4356 [404] Kl. En. vi. f., l. ix. [Table V., No. 18.]	[A.D.] [340] K. v[i]. Constantinus a ducibus Constantis, fratris sui, in bello occisus est. Patricius nunc natus est.		A.D. 370, Kl. Jan. vi. f., l. xviii.
		Kl. Enair vi. Patritius natus est in hoc anno.	371, ,, ,, vii. f., l. xxix. Patritius natus est in hoc anno.
	[339] K. vii. f. Constans, Arianus effectus, Catholicos toto orbe persequitur.	*Kl. Enair vii.*	
		[Kl i.]	Bis. 372, ,, ,, i. f., l. x.
4357 [405] ,, ,, i. f., l. xx. Patritius secundum quosdam nunc natus est: sed falsum est.	K. i.	*Kl. iii.*	373, ,, ,, iii. f., l. xxi.
	K. iii.	*Kl. iv.*	374, ,, ,, iv. f., l. lii.
	K. vi.	*Kl. v.*	375, ,, ,, v. f., l. xiii.
	K. vi.	*Kl. vi.*	Bis. 376, ,, ,, vi. f., l. xxiv.
	K. vi.	*Kl. i.*	377, ,, ,, i f., l. v.
	K. i.	*Kl. ii.*	378, ,, ,, ii. f., l. xvi.
	K. ii.	*Kl. iii*	379, ,, ,, iii. f., l. xxvii.
	K. iii.	*Kl. iiii.*	Bis. 380, ,, ,, iv. f., l. ix.
	K. iiii.	[Kl. vi.]	381, ,, ,, vi. f., l. xx.
	K. vi.		

382,	,,	vii. f., l. l.	
383,	,,	i. f., l. xii	
384,	,,	ii. f., l. xxiii.	Bis.
385,	,,	iv. f., l. iv.	

[Kl. vii.] [356] K. vii. Reliquiae Timothei Apostoli Constantinopoli[m] invectae sunt.

[Kl. i.] K. i.
[Kl. ii.] K. ii.

Kl. v. Muridhach Tirech [same as α].

K. iv. Muiredhach Tirech [same as α, with the variant *Cruind Badhraidhe* for *Cruind*].

4386 [434] ,, ii. f., l. x. Muiredech Tirech do marbadh la Caelbadh, mac Cruind, la righ n-Uladh, oc Purt-righ uas Dabul. [M. T. was slain by C., son of Cronn, [i. e.] by the King of Ulster, at Portrigh over the Dabal [river Blackwater, between cos. Armagh and Tyrone.]

4393 [441] ,, iiii. f., l. xxvii. Coelbad, mac Cruind, regnavit anno uno. Eochu Mughmedhoin, mac Muiredhaigh Tirigh, rosmarb. [C., son of Cronn, reigned one year. E. M., son of Muiredach Tirech, slew him.]

*Kl. iii. [ui], Pacpicius apchiepircopur et Apoptolup hibepnenrium, anno aetatir ruae centerimo .xxii., xui. Kl. Apuilir, quieuit, ut vicitup:

O genaip Cpiort, aipem aic,
Cetpe ced pon caom nocaic,
Teopa bliadna beoet iap rin,
Go bar Padpaig pfiofi appal.

[A.D. 493] Jan. 1, Tuesday [Friday], Patrick, archbishop and apostle of the Irish, rested in the 122nd year of his age, on the 16th of the Kalends of April [March 17], as is said:

Since was born Christ, reckoning joyful,
Four hundred above fair ninety,
Three years eventful after that,
To the death of Patrick, chief apostle.

VI.—RECENSIONS OF *TIGERNACH*—continued.

α TIGERNACH. (T.C.D. Fragment.)	β TIGERNACH. (O'Conor, R. H. S. ii. 70-3.)	γ TIGERNACH. (Chron. Scot., p. 14.)	δ Chronology in accordance with the obit of St. Patrick in γ and the ferial sequence of β, γ.
[A.M. A.D.] 4394 [442] ,, ,, v. f., l. ix. Eochu Mughmedhoin, mac Muiredaigh Tirigh, regnavit [MS. illegible], ut alii aiunt. [E. M., son of M. T., reigned [8 years], as others say. [Table V., No. 20.]	[A.D.] K. v. Eochaidh M., m. M. T., regnavit annis viii. ['Then follows an item with a quatrain relative to the sons of E. M.] Patritius captivus in Hiberniam ductus est.	Kl. v. Eochaidh Muighmedhon, mac Muiredhaigh, Tirigh, regnavit annis octo. Patritius captivus est in Hiberniam ductus.	A.D. 386, ,, ,, v. f., l. xv.
4395 [443] ,, ,, vi. f., l. xx. Patritius captivus in Hiberniam ductus est: sed hoc falsum est.	[357] K. vi. Constantinopoli, ingrossio ossarum Andreae Apostoli et Lucae Evangelistae. [A] Constantinopolitanis miro furore suscepta sunt.* [The next folio is lost.]	Kl. vi.	387, ,, ,, vi. f., l. xxvi. Patritius captivus in Hiberniam ductus est.
4396 [444] ,, ,, f., l. i. Constantio Romam [scil. novam, i. e. Constantinopolim] ingresso, ossa Andreae Apostoli et Lucae Evangelistae n Constantinopolitanis miro favore suscepta sunt.			

* To shew the standard of the Rolls' *Tripartite*, β is given (p. 572) as "helping to fix the date [*sic*] of Patrick's birth [and] captivity," (p. cxxvii.). The assistance afforded, by comparison with "O'Conor's inaccurate edition," (p. cxxviii.), consists in the addition of no date and the omission of eight ferials (K. i.–K. iii.) Had the latter been given, we might have known whether K. vi., K. vi. were misreadings of O'Conor, or of the MS. An English version is added, from which one learns that *Constantinopoli* signifies *to* and *into* Constantinople. Sic itur ad astra.

This Table proves, assuming a, β and γ to be his work, that Tigernach carried out two 'emendations' of the Vulgar Era: one (a), making the chronology (in round numbers) three solar cycles in arrear; the other (β), one solar cycle in advance. The Table likewise shews that he reproduced (β, γ) the number and ferials of the years from the birth to the captivity of St. Patrick; thereby unwittingly preserving wherewithal (δ) to detect the alterations. In view of the foregoing, Tigernach can scarcely be regarded as the most trustworthy of the native annalists.

Reverting now to the opening part of the *Annals of Innisfallen* given above, two dissimilar elements are discernible. In the first place, the years are marked in unbroken continuity by the luni-solar incidence of Jan. 1 (A). Secondly, the entries annexed constitute a sequence that is not similarly integral (B). Given the initial year, specified by date or otherwise, A becomes perfect in meaning. Apart from the fragmentary character, B, by itself (witness the failure of O'Conor to settle the Innisfallen Chronology) is devoid of material significance. The original was consequently A. But the contents and the cyclic form (to pass over the absence of consecutive dating) prove that the primary purpose was not chronographic. The ferial and epact were, in fact, the requisite criteria from which by computistic methods the incidence of Easter and of the other moveable feasts of the current year was determined. We have thus revealed the fundamental datum in reference to the native A.D. Annals.

The Paschal Cycle was the basis of the Irish Chronicle.

The relation of A to the other Paschal Computations and the conclusions resulting therefrom relative to the native Annals demand separate treatment.

The dating employed in connexion with the Paschal Tables used in Ireland next claims attention. Of the methods whereby this was effected, reckoning from an epoch is the only one that falls within the scope of the present inquiry. The Mundane Eras found in the Cycles and Tables of **84** are not to be met with, as far as I know, in Irish documents, annalistic or other. Whether the Passion year of **84** (A.D. 29) existed in the Table introduced by St. Patrick, the data accessible to me are not sufficient to decide. The reckonings of the kind in the *Book of Armagh*, for instance, are altogether unreliable. (The initial year can, nevertheless, be determined with certainty.*)

The celebration of Easter on the sixteenth of the moon mentioned in the *Catalogue*† as followed by some of the Third Order of Irish Saints, it may be concluded, was derived from the Great Cycle of Victorius of Aquitaine. According to this, it was brought into use in Ireland during the last decade of the sixth century.

That it was known here before that time, we learn from St. Columbanus. Writing to Pope Gregory, he says that by his masters, most sage computists of cycles, Victorius, so far from being received, was deemed worthy rather of derision than of authority.‡ This is conclusive as regards the community of Bangor up to the saint's departure (about A.D. 590) for the Continent. But it is not at variance with what is stated in the *Catalogue*.

In the Prologue,§ the Mundane Reckonings profess to be taken from the Hieronymo-Eusebian Chronicle and the Chronicle of Prosper. They are as follows:—

A. From Creation to Deluge, ... 2242.
B. ,, Deluge to Abraham, ... 942.
C. ,, Abraham to (*a*) Valens VI. and Valentinian II.
        COSS. [A.D. 378], . . . 2395.
[D. ,, Creation to Passion, . . . 5229.]∥

---

* The Table of St. Cyril comes next in time. The opening year (A.D. 437) is marked in the *Annals of Innisfallen* (p. 352, *supra*). But, even though employed in Ireland (which is very improbable), as the years were those of Diocletian, it could not well form the basis of a Chronicle.   † Note C.

‡ Scias namque nostris magistris et Hibernicis antiquis, philosophis et sapientissimis componendi calculi computariis, Victorium non fuisse receptum, sed magis risu vel venia dignum quam auctoritate.   § Note D *a*.

∥ The passage (Note D *b*) containing this item, for the reasons given hereafter (*infra*, p. 366-7), may be considered spurious; but the calculation is verified by the criteria of the initial year of the Victorian Paschal Cycle:—

Consules.	An.	B.	Feria Kal. Jan.	Æt. lunæ in Kal. Jan.	Paschæ dies.	Æt. lunæ in Pasch.	Indic.
CRUCIFIXIO CHRI. Coss. duobus Geminis. Ruffino et Rubellio.	I	B.	feria v	XIX	v Kal. Apr.	XVI	I

We have thus:—

VII.
VICTORIAN CHRONOLOGY.

$C - a = 2017$: Victorian Abrahamic Period (a).
$A + B + a = 5201$:   ,,   Mundane   ,,   (β).
$D - \beta = $ A.D. 28 :   ,,   Passion   Year (γ).

(a) Applying a to the Eusebian Chronicle, we obtain the Rule employed in the Third Lecture: to find the B.C., subtract the Abrahamic year from 2015 + 2. The result will be found to coincide with that obtainable by the Olympiad Reckoning (B.C. 776)* and the Reckoning from the Foundation of Rome (B.C. 753)†.

(β) Similarly, deducting β from 5630, the initial Mundane year of the *Annals of Innisfallen*, we have A.D. 429. This, taken in connexion with two entries in these Annals—Victorius scripsit Ciclum Paschae.—Finis Cicli Victorii—, shews that the opening portion was based upon the Cycle of the Aquitanian.

The β Reckoning occurs twice in the *Annals of Boyle*.‡

(1) Ab Adam usque ad Cormac fluxerunt anni VICX. [$- \beta = $ A.D. 909].

In the Innisfallen Annals, the year in which Cormac (Mac Culennain, bishop-king of Cashel) was slain is marked *vi. f.*, *xxiv. l.* These are the criteria of A.D. 908. But a native quatrain there quoted gives 909. The entry, it is thus seen, belongs to the latter year, *i. f., v. l.*, A.D. 909.

(2) Annus ab Incarnatione Domini MXLVI. (*recte*, – III.) : ab initio vero mundi VICCXLIV. (6244–1043 = β).§ The *vi.* of the text was consequently a scribal error for *iii*.

From the *Annals of Innisfallen*, or some similar source, the β Computation passed into the A-Text of Lecture III. (thence copied into the *Lebar Brec*|| Tract), which assigns the advent of St. Patrick as missionary to A.M. 5633 [$- \beta = $ A.D. 432].

---

* Ideler : *Handbuch der math. u. tech. Chronol.*, Berlin, 1825. I. 376.
† *Ib.*, II. 154.   ‡ O'Conor : *Rer. Hib. Script., ii. Ann. Buell.*, p. 12.
§ O'Conor, *ubi sup.*, p. 18. || See Lect. III. p. 238, *supra*.

(γ) With reference to γ, therefrom, in the first place, is derived the Rule employed in the First Lecture (*supra*, p. 11): to equate the Victorian Passion Year with the A.D., add 27 to the former.

Secondly, Victorius, according to the Prologue,* intended to commence with A.M. 1, and give the Paschal data of each year, according to the Solar Cycle of 28 and (a modification of) the lunar portion of the Cycle of **84**. But, as an immense work of the kind demanded ample leisure, one Great Cycle (A.D. 28–559) was executed to meet the present need.† The Easter solar and lunar criteria of A.M. 1 and A.M. 5658 (A.D. 457) are set forth, to prove that both were respectively found by the same methods. In accordance therewith, in reference to the solar incidence (with which alone we are at present concerned), the former year has the Dominical Letters AG; the latter, F. We can thus reconstruct the original Solar Cycle of Victorius. (To facilitate reference, the Vulgar Cycle is annexed.)

VIII.

VICTORIAN AND VULGAR SOLAR CYCLES.

D.L.	Vict.	Vulg.		L.D.	Vict.	Vulg.	
AG	1.	17.	Bis.	D	15.	3.	
F	2.	18.		C	16.	4.	
E	3.	19.		BA	17.	5.	Bis.
D	4.	20.		G	18.	6.	
CB	5.	21.	Bis.	F	19.	7.	
A	6.	22.		E	20.	8.	
G	7.	23.		DC	21.	9.	Bis.
F	8.	24.		B	22.	10.	
ED	9.	25.	Bis.	A	23.	11.	
C	10.	26.		G	24.	12.	
B	11.	27.		FE	25.	13.	Bis.
A	12.	28.	Bis.	D	26.	14.	
GF	13.	1.		C	27.	15.	
E	14.	2.		B	28.	16.	

* Note D *c*. † Note C *d*.

THE CODEX PALATINO-VATICANUS, 830.   365

To test the Victorian Solar Cycle:—

A.M. 5202 ÷ 28 leaves 22, B (A.D. 1).
A.M. 5229 ÷ 28   ,,   21, DC (A.D. 28).

(1) Accordingly, the Victorian Rule for finding the A.M. Dominical Letter can be thus formulated: Divide the given year by 28: the tabular letter opposite the remainder in the Victorian Column, Table VIII., is the Dominical. If nothing remains, the letter corresponding to 28 is the Dominical.

(2) Similarly, the Victorian Rule for finding the A.D. Dominical Letter is: To the given A.D. year add 21 and proceed as in (1).*

(3) Finally, to find the Dominical Letter of a Victorian Cyclic, i. e. Passion, year: To the given year add 20 and proceed as in (1).

Connected with the foregoing and other calculations of the Prologue is a reckoning† made in Ireland in the middle of the seventh century. To the identity of his Latin name with that of the great bishop of Hippo we owe the publication, if not the preservation, of the work, *De mirabilibus Sacrae Scripturae*, of the Irish Augustinus.‡ To explain the miracle recorded in Joshua x. 12–13, of the sun and moon standing still, the writer lays down that the natural course was not thereby disturbed, as both the luminaries rested simultaneously. As proof, he gives in brief digest the cyclic recurrence from the Creation to the year of his writing: to shew that the sun and moon are always in agreement at the end of every term of 532 years.

In the A.M. period, the initial and final cyclic years are identified, internal evidence proves, by reference to the Chronicle of Eusebius. Hence, the last year of Cycle I., the first of Cycle V., and the first and last years of Cycles II., III., IV. are not specified by any events.

In the A.D. period, the tenth Cycle ended, we are informed, in the ninety-second year after the Passion, in the consulship of Aviola and Pansa (A.D. 119, according to γ). The eleventh began in the following year, in the consulship of Paternus and Torquatus (A.D. 120, in accordance with γ). Dr. Reeves quotes the Chronicle of Cassiodorus to justify the assigning of these consuls to the years in question,

---

* The Vulgar Rule is: Add 9 and proceed as in the Victorian (but in the Vulgar Column).   † Note E.
‡ See the Paper of Dr. Reeves, *Proceedings*, R. I. A., vol. vii., p. 514. The bibliography is given (p. 515) with characteristic fulness and accuracy.

instead of to A.D. 122, 123, respectively. But the writer went no farther a-field than the (partly erroneous) consular column of the Victorian Cycle, where they are so placed.*

The final year of the eleventh Cycle (A.D. 651, according to γ) is identified by the death of Mainchine (of Mendrohid, King's County), amongst other sages. In the third year of the twelfth Cycle the work was written.

A difficulty affecting all these dates arises from the fact that the obits of Mainchine and two other abbots are given in the *Annals of Ulster* at A.D. 652.† The discrepancy is explained by two calculations set forth in the Prologue of Victorius.‡

(*a*) The date of the Passover is fixed as follows. (The lunar notation it is unnecessary to deal with in this place.) In A.M. 3689 [DC Bis], March 24 fell on Thursday. A.M. 3690 began on the following day, Friday, March 25; which was the Passover. This is introductory to a reckoning of more importance.

(*b*) In A.M. 5228 [A.D. 28 DC Bis.], March 25 fell on Thursday. Adding the intercalary day, A.M. 5229 [A.D. 29 B] commenced on Friday, March 25. In this way, Holy Thursday fell in A.D. 28, on March 25; Good Friday and Easter Sunday, in A.D. 29, on March 25 and 27, respectively. This is based upon a Mundane Period of 5200. The Passion and Resurrection were thereby assigned to the traditional date, namely, A.D. 29.

But, in the first place, the Julian year, which was that followed by Victorius, began with Jan. 1, not March 25. Moreover, the diurnal progression from C to B, introduced in (*a*) and (*b*) as taking effect in March, did not come into operation until the following New Year's Day. In other words, you cannot have two intercalary days within one year.

---

*
Aviola et Pansa	XCII		Sabbato	IV *Saltus lunæ.*	XV Kal. Maii	XXI	II
Paterno et Torquato	XCIII	B.	Domin.	XVI	Kal. Aprilis	XVII	III

† Note F.   ‡ Note D *b*.

Finally, applying Table VIII., Rule 1, to (*a*), we obtain 3689 ÷ 28 = 21 DC = Wednesday (not Thursday), March 24. The following day was consequently Thursday (not Friday), March 25. In reference to (*b*), we get 5228 ÷ 28 = 20 E = Tuesday (not Thursday), March 25 : 5229 ÷ 28 = 21 DC = Friday, March 26 (not 25) ; Sunday, March 28 (not 27). Now, 5229, according to Table VII., is the Passion Year of Victorius, A.D. 28 (not 29).

The two calculations in question are consequently interpolations.* They were obviously suggested by what is stated relative to the dates of the Passover and Passion in the previous passage of the Prologue.

The text of the foregoing is that of Petavius.† On the other hand, Bucherius,‡ who does not deal with (*a*), reads *VIII. VII. V.*, instead of *VIII. VIII. VI., Kalendas Apriles* in (*b*). But this, if the original, proves that the interpolator either was unable to fit the added day into the computation, or passed it over, in order to bring his Easter incidence (March 28) into conformity with the Victorian, as given on the following folio.§

If the pseudo-Victorian Computation imposed upon the author of the *De mirabilibus sacrae Scripturae*, the fraud, it has to be borne in mind, was by comparison the work of a practised hand. The pseudo-Anatolius assigned but two Bissextiles to a Cycle of nineteen

---

* Jaffe's proofs, which, according to Mommsen (*Zeitz. Ostertafel v. J.* 447 : *Abh. der. K. A. der W. zu Berlin*, 1862, p. 564), demonstrate that the whole Prologue is a forgery, I have not seen. Mommsen himself rejects one of Jaffe's main suggestions, and, more significant still, would allow that the Prologue is partly genuine. The fact is, any argument involving the conclusion that a Cycle of nineteen Epacts was issued to supersede a Cycle of thirty Epacts without a line of explanation prefixed carries its own refutation.

† *De Doctrina Temporum*, Vol. II. p. 505.   ‡ *De Doctrina Temporum*, p. 9.

§ After the above was written, I found a copy of Bucherius in the National Library. This, I had the satisfaction to discover, has a special value in reference to the present question. On the margin of the Prologue are placed MS. readings which, as appears by comparison with the Petavian text, were taken from the Codex Sirmondi employed by Petavius and Bucherius. (These variants fully confirm the laxity of the latter in reproducing his exemplar.)

Two of them, now that the MS. is lost (Krusch, *ubi sup.*, pp. 84, 210–1), are of importance. *VII. (Kalendas Apriles)* and *V. (Kalendas Apriles)* were made *VIII.* and *VI.* by the addition of *I., alia manu*, overhead. The bissextile was thereby rightly taken into account, March 25 counted twice and Easter assigned to March 27. This proves that the interpolator, whether ignorantly or designedly, left out an integral item of his own reckoning. *Sed quis in scriptis spuriis exactitudinem praestabit ?*

years! Yet, a forgery of the kind, one of the clumsiest upon record, passed current for more than twelve hundred years,—with Columbanus, Cummian and Bede; Bucherius, Petavius and John Albert Fabricius!

These two passages of the Prologue and the entry in the *Annals of Ulster* prove that the calculation of the *De mirabilibus* was based upon A.M. 5201 = A.D. 1. The A.D. dates are accordingly 120, 121; 652 (obit of Mainchine), 653, 655.*

The Pseudo-Victorian Reckoning is also found in the *Annals of Boyle*:

In hoc anno beatus Gregorius quievit: scilicet, in DCVto anno Dominicae Incarnationis, ut Beda dicit in Historia sua . . . Anni ab initio mundi VDCCCV. (A.M. 5805 − 605 = 5200).†

It is likewise employed in the Carlsruhe Codex of Bede:

[A.D.] *Dccc.*   [=] *vi. m. ab initio mundi.* (fol. 15 a).
[,,] *Dcccxxxvi.* [=] *vi. m. xxxvi.* (ib.).
[,,] *Dcccxxxvii.* [=] *vi. m. xxxvii.* (ib.).
[,,] *Dcccxlviii.* [=] *vi. m. xlviii.* (fol. 15 b).

The earliest authenticated mention, to my knowledge, of the Cycles of Dionysius in native documents is contained in the Paschal Letter of Cummian, written in, or soon after, A.D. 632.‡ With them, as we have seen in Lecture I. (p. 10), came the consecutive reckoning by the years of the Incarnation. The protracted and embittered struggle connected with the introduction of the Alexandrine Paschal system is one that might be retold with advantage. Here it will suffice to say that in Ireland, as elsewhere, the principle of the Dionysian Cycles and the A.D. Era gradually predominated.

---

* Appended (Note G) will be found the passage in which the reckoning is dealt with by Petavius in the *Doctrina Temporum*. They are amongst the proofs of the author's imperfect acquaintance with Paschal Cycles and the Chronology connected therewith.   † O'Conor, *ubi sup. Ann. Buell.*, p. 5.

‡ The delegates deputed by the Synod of Magh-Lene to visit Rome attended the celebration of Easter in St. Peter's on a day (March 24) which differed by a month from the Irish date (April 21). (This was the 82nd year of the Cycle of **84**, Golden No. XXVII., F; Victorian G.N. XV.; Dionysian, V., A.D. 631.) They reached Ireland the following year. The ill-disguised tone of defiance leaves little room to doubt that the Epistle was composed immediately after their return.

THE CODEX PALATINO-VATICANUS, 830.

Finally, it has to be observed that the Mundane Period = 3952, employed in connexion with other reckonings in Tigernach and elsewhere, is given as his own (*nostra supputatio*) by Bede in the *Chronicle*.*

The data set forth in the preceding Lecture and in the present enable us to formulate the following Canons relative to the Chronology of the Annals and other native documents.

IRISH CHRONOLOGICAL CANONS.

I. A Passion reckoning reducible to A.D. by the addition of 28 can date from before A.D. 500.

II. (*a*) An A.M. reckoning reducible to A.D. by subtracting 5199 and (*b*) a Passion reckoning reducible to A.D. by the addition of 32 can date from before A.D. 500.

III. An A.M. reckoning reducible to A.D. by subtracting (*a*) 5201 [or (*b*) 5200],† and a Passion reckoning reducible to A.D. by adding (*c*) 27 [or (*d*) 28, employed with (*b*)],† can date from A.D. 598.

IV. An A.D. reckoning can date from A.D. 632-3.

V. An A.M. reckoning reducible to A. D. by subtracting 3952 cannot date from before A.D. 725, the year in which the Chronicle of Bede was composed.

(Other reckonings are to be met with in the Annals. But these, whether A.M. or A.D., are the result of a so-called emendation, and consequently of comparatively recent date.)

When two or more are employed, the most recent calculation, it is scarcely necessary to observe, determines the time of the document in which they are contained.

In accordance with III. (*a*), the *Annals of Innisfallen* are the most ancient body of Chronicles we possess.

IV. fixes the earliest date of the (*Tigernach*) quatrain,‡ which gives A.D. 493 as the year of St. Patrick's death. In like manner, it specifies the (*Lebar Brec*) notation of the Decemnovennal criteria appertaining to the year in question.§

Having thus traced the origin and chronographic data of the Annals, it remains to observe that a broad distinction has to be drawn between the

---

* Ad A.M. 3981, A.D. 29. † That is, on the assumption that the pseudo-Victorian Calculation was not of Irish origin. ‡ Table VI., p. 359, *supra*.
§ P. 388, *infra*.

annual register of events and historical tracts, such as those appended to the present and former Lectures. The latter, whether in prose or verse, were intended for committal to memory. They could not therefore be burthened by strings of dates. Accordingly, they start from some well-known event, the place of which they fix by the A.M. or A.D., placed sometimes at the commencement and sometimes at the end. He must be a poor computist who could not thereby easily calculate the time of every item.

Similarly, Lives of the Saints, being composed for devotional reading, contain no precise annual notation. But, as was to be expected, much historical reference is found. Herein Adamnan's *Life of St. Columba* contrasts favourably with Bede's *Life of St. Cuthbert*. Such allusions were easy of verification by those for whose edification the works were composed.

In the same way, marginal entries like that in the Marianus Codex (*supra*, p. 15) and colophons of MSS., containing allusions to local persons and events, as a rule present no difficulty in determining the precise years.

Finally, with respect to inscriptions on reliquaries and kindred objects, in which the time is fixed by mention of kings or abbots, the intention was to place upon record the names of those concerned in the donation or manufacture. The dates could be ascertained by reference to the respective regal series or monastic registers.

The foregoing, taken in connexion with the fact that in some instances the entries themselves contain either the day of the week, or the age of the moon, or both,* will enable us to estimate the irreparable injury that would have resulted to our early chronology from the *Annals of the Four Masters*, had the original materials not been preserved. The lack of knowledge betrayed by the contrast between the A.D. date which they prefix and the internal evidence of the text would be incredible in the absence of irrefragable proof.

First, with regard to the ferial number.

---

* One example of the kind is found in the Anglo-Saxon Chronicle (Cod. Domit.), A.D. 809. The sun, it is said, was eclipsed on Monday, July 16th, the 29th of the moon. This is correct. New Year's Day (Table I., Rule 1) was Monday and the July moon began (Table IV.) on June 18 (Golden Number XII.).

(1) A.D. 714. Faelcu, they say, was appointed abbot of Iona "on the 4th Kalend of September, Saturday precisely." In that year, August 29 fell on Wednesday. The date was 716.

(2) A.D. 777. The battle of Kildare was fought on the "6th of the Kalends of September, on Tuesday." Here the reckoning is five years wrong. In 777, August 27 was Wednesday. Correct, accordingly, to 782.

(3) A.D. 778. Armagh and Mayo were burned on "the night of Saturday precisely, on the 4th None of August." This year, August 2 was on Sunday. The burning happened in 783.

(4) A.D. 860. Mael-Sechlaim, King of Ireland, died "the thirtieth of November, on Tuesday precisely." November 30 fell on Saturday in 860. The obit took place in 862. The reading in the *Annals of Ulster* is, accordingly, to be changed from *iii. feria* into *ii. feria*, namely Monday.

(5) A.D. 917. Niall, King of Ireland, was slain in the battle of Dublin "on the 17th of October." Then quatrains are quoted in which Wednesday is given as the day of the battle. It is further stated that in the same year Easter fell on April 25, and Low Sunday fell in Summer. October 17 in 917 was, however, Friday. The Easter incidence shews that the year was 919. The true reading is given in the *Annals of Ulster*,—17th of the Kalends of October. September 15 fell on Wednesday in 919.

(6) A.D. 924. The battle of Cluain na Cruimther [*meadow of the priests*] was fought "the 28th of December, Thursday precisely." December 28 was on Tuesday in 924. The year was 926.

(7) A.D. 1013. The battle of Clontarf was fought "on the Friday before Easter precisely." Here are the criteria that lay to hand in the *Annals of Ulster*:—*Kl. Jan. vi. f., l. xxvi.*, A.D. *mxiiii. Hic est annus octavus circuli decin[n]ovinalis et hic est cccc. et lxxxii. annus ab adventu Sancti Patricii ad babtizandos Scotos.* Ḟeil Ġriġoir ria n-Inic ocur mincaire ı Sampaḋ ırın bliaḋain ri [the feast of Gregory (March 12 fell) before the Beginning (first Sunday) of Lent and little Easter (Low Sunday), in Summer this year]—*quod non auditum est ab antiquis temporibus.*

Nay more, the space dated A.D. 1013 is left vacant in the *Ulster* MS., so certain was it that the battle took place on Good Friday, April 23, 1014. But, as if to remove any palliation, the "advent of St.

Patrick" is given at 432 by the Four Masters themselves. It never occurred to them, perhaps, to add 582 thereto. The year, it is scarcely necessary to observe, was the same as 919 in the incidence of the moveable feasts.

Next, with reference to the age of the moon. This notation they have omitted in all instances except two. How far they could avail of such assistance, they leave no doubt. At A.D. 917 [correctly, 919], having said that Easter was on April 25 and Low Sunday in Summer, they add: "Dia cóicc mbliaöna peṛccac aṛ cṛi céö cecmonʒ ṛin—*that day 365 years that happens.*" Let us apply this rule, which says that the Paschal incidence is regulated by the solar year. Going back, we arrive at A.D. 552. In that year, Easter fell on March 31. Going forward, we come to A.D. 1282. In this year, Easter was March 29. Applying it to the true year (919), we get 554 and 1284. The respective Easters fell upon April 9 and April 5.

Non ragionam di lor, ma guarda e passa.

The first lunar notation they reproduce is at A.D. 1086. It is contained in a quatrain fixing the day of Turlough O'Brien's obit.

Aiöce Maiṛc hi ṛṛiö lö lul,	The night of Tuesday, on the day before the Ides of July,
Ria ṛéil Iacoiṛ co nʒlan ṛún,	Before the feast of James of pure mind,
Iaṛ nöó ṛiöec acöać,	After two-and-twenty (years ?) died
An caiṛö ṛí cenn Coiṛṛöealöaċ.	The strong arch-king Toirdelbach.

This passed muster with O'Conor and O'Donovan, perhaps because in the preceding prose the regnal years are given as 22. It escaped themselves and the *Masters* that the third line is a syllable short, and that the eve of the feast of St. James fell on the 13th, not the 14th, of July. But fortunately the original, which O'Clery and his followers had under their hands, is still extant in the *Annals of Ulster*. The two faulty lines run thus:—

1 ṛeil Iacoiṛ co n-ʒlan ṛuin,	On the feast of James of pure mind,
1 nomaö* ṛiöec aööać, ṛl.	On the 29th, died, etc.

In A.D. 1086, New Year's Day fell on Thursday, and the Golden Number was IV. Consequently, July 14 fell upon Tuesday, and it

---

* MS. ıx.

was the 29th of the moon, which began (Table IV.) June 16 and ended July 15.

The other lunar notation will be considered farther on.

The result is that for more than five centuries (A.D. 494–1019) every item in these so-called Annals is erroneously dated! Nevertheless, the mischief still wrought by them is strikingly illustrated by the fact that the dates of the battle of Ballyshannon* and of the death of King Niall, together with ten others equally erroneous, are quoted on one page (539) of the Rolls' edition of the *Tripartite* from the *Annals of the Four Masters*.

Apart however from the falsification of the text, allowance has to be made for O'Clery and his assistants, in view of the work of the same kind produced by those who professed to deal with the subject since their time.

O'Flaherty plumes himself on having fixed the date of the Milesian Occupation. First, he quotes the verse of O'Flynn given above,† to prove that the 7th of the moon fell on Thursday, May 1. This, he adds, agrees with 3698 of the Julian Period, which was the 12th of the Decemnovennal Cycle.‡ It requires no great computistic skill to test this. The Epact of XII. is 10. The Lunar Rule (Table III. 2 : $(121 - 1 + 10) \div 59$) accordingly leaves 12 (not 7) as the lunation of May 1. But, what is more important, the original reading is 17 (not 7); which shews that the year intended by the native versifier was the 7th (not the 12th) of the Decemnovennal Cycle (Epact 15). On this foundation the Chronology of the *Ogygia* is constructed!

The following, from his edition of the *Annals of Innisfallen*, will sufficiently set forth O'Conor's acquaintance with the Epacts :—

   A.D. 1058 [1041, O'C.], *aileuath*, i.ma lunae.
   A.D. 1172, *aile huath*, prima lunae.
   A.D. 1001 [983, O'C.], *aile huath*, ii.am lunae.
   A.D. 1096 [1079, O'C.], *eale auth*, ultima lunae.
   A.D. 1115 [1098, O'C.], *aileuath*, ultima lunae.

The reading is *aile uathad*, and the expression means the *2nd of the moon* (Epact 2). These five years (Table III., Rule 1) have the Golden Number XIV.

---

* See p. 374–5, *infra*.   † Lect. III., Note C *k*, p. 265, *supra*.   ‡ Note F.

374   THE CODEX PALATINO-VATICANUS, 830.

A text in *Tigernach* displays another notable result of what he calls his "incredible diligence."

A.D. 1066. *l. i. Retla mongac ingnad adbal do faiscin isin aer diamairt iar mincaise hic pt. Kl. mai co iiixx. fuire.* (*R. H. S. ii. p. 306.*)

Kl. l. i. Stella crinita mirabiliter ingens apparuit in aere die martis parvi Paschae (i. e. *die Martis post Dominicam in Albis*) *a Kalendis Maiis ad xxiii. lunae.*

In a note he quotes from the Anglo-Saxon chronicle : *" Hoc anno apparuit cometa xiv. Kal. Maii.*

Here we have error upon error. *Hic pt* (which, of course, means nothing) should be *hi sept*, as even the Four Masters could have taught him. Their reading is: hı ρeċt Calaınn Ɯaı—on the 7th of the Kalends of May. *Co* does not signify *ad*, but *cum*, in this place. May 1 fell on Monday, not on Tuesday, and Low Sunday on April 23, not April 29, in 1066. The text requires but one other emendation : *iii.xx.* should be *vi.xx.* (Perhaps it is a misprint.)

The meaning now presents no difficulty: *Jan.* 1 [*fell on Sunday*] 1*st of the moon. A hairy star, a wondrous marvel, was seen in the sky, the Tuesday after Little Easter* [*Low Sunday*], *on the 7th of the Kalends of May* [*Ap.* 25], 23*rd of the moon* [*lit., with the 23rd thereon*].

The Golden Number being III., the Paschal moon (Table IV.) began on March 31. One may thus, without "incredible diligence," calculate that the 26th lunation fell on the 25th of the solar month next ensuing.

With regard to the Anglo-Saxon Chronicle, there is nothing that can be tortured into the comet appearing on April 18. It states that Easter in 1066 was "*xvi. Kal. Maii*" (April 16). Then it describes the comet : saying, amongst other things, that the star first appeared on the Eve of *Letania Major*, that is, *viii. Kal. Maii* (April 24). *Litania Major* was St. Mark's Day.

Another instance of O'Conor's knowledge will be mentioned hereafter.

A date of which the day of the week and the day of the month are given is so easily determined, that it is strange how O'Donovan failed to notice the error in the account of the battle of Ballyshannon, Co. Kildare, quoted by him (A.D. 733, *F. M., i.* 332, note *o*) from the *Annals of Ulster*, "at the year 737." Therein we have *xiii. Septembris, die vi. ferie.* He ought to have known that these Annals employ the Roman method of reckoning the days of the month. Besides, he had the true reading, "on the 14th day of the Kallends of September [Aug. 19]," in the entry of the *Annals of Clonmacnoise* which he there gives.

No doubt, it may be said that Sep. 13 fell on Friday in 737. But, "the reader," according to O'Donovan (Vol. I., p. xlviii.), "is to bear in mind that the Annals of Ulster are antedated by one year up to 1014, and that . . . he should add one year to the respective dates." Now, in 738, Sep. 13 fell on Wednesday.

The *Ulster* reading in the new edition (Vol. I., p. 194) is: *xiiii. Septimbris die, vi. feriá;* that of O'Conor's *Tigernach* (*R.H.S.*, *ii*. 242): *xvii. Kl. Sept. die .i. Mairt* [*namely, Tuesday*]. The mutual corrections give: *xiiii. Kal. Sep., iii. feriá.* Aug. 19 fell on Tuesday in 878. Nevertheless, the editor of the *Annals of Ulster* (p. 195) gives "the 14th day of September, the sixth day of the week." He found nothing that required emendation. The Four Masters have placed the battle under 733!

With reference to the Epact, O'Donovan makes no correction of the statement of the Four Masters, that the Paschal incidence is tho same every 365th year.

Elsewhere (A.D. 493, *F. M.*, p. 157, note z), he quotes from *Lebar Bree* that St. Patrick died "in the 120th year of his age, that is, the 27th [*recte*, 26th] of the solar cycle," etc. But the original (p. 220 a) of the explanatory clause is: ı m-bliadaın un. xx. pop Kalaınd Enaıp—*in the year of the 27th (lunar day) on January* 1. Here, there is no mention of the Solar Cycle. A.D. 493, as stated correctly in the text, had the Epact 27 (= 19th year of the Decemnovennal Cycle).

(The passage will be found given in full below (p. 388), amongst the corrections of the *Tripartite Life of St. Patrick*.)

In a quatrain quoted by the Four Masters, A.D. 1099 is described :

        Im [ın] bliadaın coıccıde uaċa[ı]d,
        I[n] cper bliadaın paıp ıap [puıp' ap] puc, pl.

This O'Conor (*Rer. Hib. Script.* iii. 675) renders : " In the year of terrible wars, count the third year, after fear seized," etc.*

That is, coıccıde = *wars;* uaċad = *terrible!*

---

* *In anno bellorum terribilium, tertium annum numera, postquam terror corripuit, &c.*

O'Donovan is perhaps more original:

" From the year in which cook-houses were few,
The third was that in which, etc."

That is coicctbe = cookhouses (*coquinae*); uatab = *few !*

Let both divide the crown.

The commonplace original means simply:

The year of the fifth epact,
The third year [after a bissextile was] thereon, in sequence, etc.

A.D. 1099 had the Epact v. (Golden Number XVII.) and was the third year after the leap-year, 1096. For the second line, compare the notation in the *Annals of Innisfallen*: III. bl. puip [pop] bip. ┐ ın III. bl. [xx.] ap c. ap m. ab Incapnacione—3rd year after the bissextile, and the 1123rd year from the Incarnation.

Dr. Reeves is justly severe upon O'Conor's editorial shortcomings. Yet, in his edition of *Adamnan* (*Additional Notes* D O), he adopts O'Conor's *Innisfallen* dates. In the following, no excuse can be pleaded for reckoning "in opposition," to use the words of Dr. Reeves, "to the author's own notation":—

Reeves.	Text.	Reeves.	Text.
A.D. 781,	795.	A.D. 911,	927.
,, 840,	854.	,, 968,	986.
,, 866,	880.	,, 1009,	1026.
,, 877,	891.	,, 1094,	1111.

In his *Lectures on the MS. Materials of Irish History* (p. 425), O'Curry writes: "The number of the Epact for the year 1096 was 23, so that a cycle of the Epact terminated that year. And he generously gives the reason: "For," he says (p. 430), "if we add the annual increase of eleven days to twenty-three, it would make it thirty-four, thus passing into a new cycle of the Epact for the next year 1097, whose Epact would accordingly be four."

But Table III., Rule 1 $((1096 + 1) \div 19)$, gives the Golden Number XIV. = Epact 2 for 1096. Consequently, the Epact for 1097 was 13.

After this, it is superfluous to deal seriously with the following (*ib.* p. 61):—" Tigernach appears to have been familiar with some of the modes of correcting the Calendar. He mentions the Lunar Cycle, and uses the Dominical Letter with the Kalends of the several years; but he makes no direct mention of the Solar Cycle or Golden Number."

How Tigernach "corrected" the Calendar has been already shewn. The remaining statements, except perhaps that respecting the Golden Number, are taken from O'Conor; "no direct mention" being the equivalent of *non semel memoratum!**

In the Letter describing the *Tigernach* Fragment (O'Curry, *MS. Mat.*, p. 518-9), Dr. Todd gives the "Lunar Epact" of A.D. 34 as 15. That is, apparently, he subtracted 19 from 34. But the Epact is 24 = Golden Number xvi. (Table III., Rule 1).

At A.M. 4079 (A.D. 127) he reads *luna iii.* Reference to the Table (V.) of the initial cyclic years (3rd cycle) will shew that the reading should be *luna vii.*, which is the MS. lection. The true Epact is 2 = Golden Number xiv. (Table III., Rule 1).

The death of Tuathal Teachtmar he gives at A.M. 4104. The Tigernach Epact being *xxiiii.*, the year (Table V., 4th cycle) is 4105 (A.D. 153). The correct Epact is 20.

"The reign of Feidhlimid is given in the following year." Here, however, occurs the hiatus of three *Kl.*, i.e. 4106-7-8, which has been mentioned above. The death is dated "4109 or 4110."

An error that seems unaccountable remains to be mentioned. Two of the commonplaces of Irish are that *ria* (*re*) signifies *before* and *iar*, *after*. In his *Wars of the Gaidhill and Gaill* (p. 15), Dr. Todd so renders the words. Twice, moreover (pp. lxix., 22), he adduces reasons for concluding that *iar* (after) of the text is to be read *re* (before). Yet, dealing with the above-quoted *Ulster* criteria of 1014,† he gives (p. xxvi.) "the correct translation" of *Feil Grigoir ria n-Init* as "The feast of St. Gregory [12th March] fell after Shrovetide"! This, apparently, because, according to him (*ib.*), "Shrove Tuesday . . . was the 9th March."

The meaning of *Init* will be demonstrated farther on.

In dealing with the *Chronicon Scotorum*, Hennessy, as we have seen, adopts O'Conor's system of chronology. In the A.D. portion of

---

* Cyclum Solarem a Tigernacho non semel memoratum invenio. Perspexit nempe . . . septem dies cujusvis hebdomadae exprimi in Calendario per septem literas *a*, *b*, *c*, *d*, *e*, *f* et *g* . . . Cyclum Lunarem pariter . . . saepius memorat. *R. H. S.* ii. xxi.-ii. † P. 371 (7), *supra*.

the compendium, there are but two epacts retained : *x.* at 1132 and *xvi.* at 1135. In a note on the latter year, the editor is good enough to inform us that *the third feria* means Tuesday. It escaped him, however, that *xvi.* was an error for *xiii.*

The *Annals of Loch Cé* were issued under the same editorship. The notation of the Vulgar Solar Cycle is given from 1194 to 1197, the former year being marked as the 19th of the Cycle. This precious result was obtained by adding 1 (instead of 9) and dividing by 28. The reckoning is consequently eight years slow. To test it, 1194, the text correctly says, began on Saturday. But the 19th of the Vulgar Solar Cycle (reference to Table VIII. will shew) begins on Wednesday. 1194 was, accordingly, the 27th of the Cycle.

The solar notation recommences at 1231, and goes on to 1412. Here another rule is applied, with the opposite result. 1231 is given as the 19th year. The computist, namely, adds 20 and divides by 28, thus making the years eleven in advance. To put it to proof, the leap-years of the Vulgar Solar Cycle are the 1st, 5th and every fourth year thereout. Being bissextile, therefore, 1232, for instance, cannot be the 20th. It is, in fact, the 9th.

The editorial rectification of the foregoing consists of bald incidental correction (at A.D. 1309*) of the 1194, 1231 errors and remarking that, though the soli-cyclic notation was blundered throughout, as the chronology was not affected thereby, correction was deemed unnecessary.

With reference to the lunar notation, it commences in the same Annals at the initial year, A.D. 1014; the epact of which is rightly set down as *xxvi.* Whereupon, a note says: "But read 28th (although the *Annals of Ulster* have 26th)." The same epact belongs to 1204 (Golden Number VIII.). The editor, notwithstanding, gives the epact *xviii.*, noting that the MS. reads *xxviii.* ! A.D. 1215 (*l. xxvii.*) is said to have been the last of the Cycle of Nineteen and a *contrary year :* "meaning," the editor says, "opposed to the bissextile year." It signifies, however, that it was *contrary* to the other years of the cycle, in the addition of 12, instead of 11, to form the epact of the year following.

---

* The statement (*ib.* i. 544) that 1309 belonged to the 48th [not 47th] Solar Cycle is manifestly a slip of the pen.

Up to 1234 the epacts are correctly copied. But, in ignorance of the *Saltus Lunae*, the epact of 1235 is given as *viii.* instead of *ix.* The result is, that thenceforward to 1412, where the notation ceases, all the epacts are wrong. The following is the synopsis :—

1235,	. l. viii.	1349,	. l. iv.*
1254,	. l. vii.	1368,	. l. iii.
1273,	. l. vi.	1387,	. l. ii.
1292,	. l. v.	1406,	.˙ l. i.
1311,	. l. iv.	1412,	. l. vii. (*recte*, xv.)
1330,	. l. iii.		

In the foregoing, the editor saw nothing that demanded correction. In the *Annals of Ulster*, Vol. I., also edited by Hennessy, at A.D. 645 (= 646) we have *l.* 8, *alias* 9. The double reckoning is continued up to A.D. 653 (= 654). Again, at 665 (= 666) we find *l.* 8, and the following year *l.* 20. But no correction is appended : nor, here or elsewhere, is the lunation availed of to rectify the dating.

A.D. 877 (= 878), a lunar eclipse is said to have occurred on October 15, the 14th of the moon. In a note, we learn that the Oxford MS. reads *4th of the moon*. The latter was accepted by O'Donovan (F. M., p. xlix.). Perhaps for that reason, it is left undecided here, although the entry states that the 28th of the moon happened that day fortnight.

Eclipsis lunae Idibus Octobris, xiiii. lunae, quasi tertia uigilia iiii. feriae, solisque diffectus iiii. Kal. Nou., lunae xxuiii., quarri un. hora diei iiii. feriae, lunae xxuiii. : sols xu. diebus intersueuientibus.	An eclipse of the moon [took place] on the Ides [15th] of October, 14th of the moon, about the 3rd watch [12–3 a.m.] of Wednesday ; and an eclipse of sun, on the 4th of the Calends of November [Oct. 29] about the 7th hour [1 p.m.] of Wednesday, 28th of the moon : 15 solar days [inclusive] intervening.

(Dominical Letter, E ; Golden Number, v.)

---

* 1341 is l. *vii*. It ought to be *iv*., in sequence to *xxiii*. of 1340. (The true epact is *x*.) 1342 is l. *xvii*., in accordance with which the notation proceeds to the end. It should be *xv*., following 1340, and *xviii*. to accord with 1342.

A.D. 1023, a lunar eclipse is stated in the same Annals to have happened on the 14th of the moon, Thursday, January 10. A solar eclipse, it is added, took place on the 27th of the same moon, Thursday, January 24th. But apparently because O'Donovan (*loc. cit.*) received "27th," it is accepted as correct by Hennessy.

Kal. Ian. iii. p., l. u., a.b. m.xx.iii. Epcпаι ерсаι і хііі. ерсаι Єnаιп, і ііі. Io Єnаιп, Ɖια-ƀапƀаιn ; ерсηаι зneιne аυcem і xxuii[i]. inƀ ерсаι ceƀnаι, Ɖια-ƀапƀаιn, cιnn coecτιžер, і nоι Kl.	Jan. 1. Tuesday, Epact v., A.D. 1123. An eclipse of the moon [took place] on the 14th of the Jan. moon, on the 4th of the Ides [10th] of Jan., Thursday; an eclipse of the sun likewise [took place] on the 27th [*recte*, 28th] of the same moon, Thursday, at the end of a fortnight, on the 9th of the Kalends [of Feb., Jan. 24.]

(Dominical Letter, F; Golden Number, XVII.)

The *Lebar Brec* copy of the Calendar of Oengus is copiously glossed. Readers of the Academy edition will learn with surprise that the solar and lunar data given by the editor, Mr. Stokes, bear no proportion to the amount contained in the original.

With regard to the solar year, the MS. exhibits the number, order, names and length of the Hebrew, Egyptian, Grecian (Macedonian) and Roman months; also hexameters descriptive of the Zodiac, the initial days of the Signs; the Solstices, Equinoxes, Dominical Letters, portions of Table II., etc. Of all these numerous items, the following almost make up the total published by the editor.

(1) The Egyptian and Grecian vernal equinox is given at March 20 ! (p. lxiv.). Had Mr. Stokes mastered the data supplied by the MS., he would have been saved from this elementary error. In the MS. (p. 84), the gloss stands on the left margin, between March 20 and March 21. To which it belongs, is shewn in a native quatrain (not copied by Mr. Stokes) at foot of p. 102 :

hi ρéil ƀenιƀecτ co m-ƀριз, Ɖuoƀecιm Calanƀ Apnιl, Sιn ρeιl ƀoпιme, ní зó, Comрíп ιcep аιƀóe ιр lo.	On the feast of Benedict with vigour, The 12th of the Kalends of April [Mar. 21], That [is] a feast that you compute, not false, Equally long, both night and day.

In the Calendar of Oengus, St. Benedict is commemorated at March 21. Herewith agrees the Calendar in Bede's works:

Xii. Kal. [Apr.]   Benedicti abbatis. Aequinoctium secundum Orientales.

(2) June 21. "Sol[s]titium secundum grecos et egiptios" (p. cvi.). In the MS., this is rightly placed opposite June 20. Compare the marginal entry on a line with Dec. 21 (not given by Mr. Stokes): *Solstitium secundum Grecos.* See likewise the two quatrains that precede the native stanza just quoted:

In la oc ḟiniub, ṛuaiṗc in moḋ.	The day a-lengthening, excellent the
Ocuṛ aḃaiṡ oc ṛeṅṡaḋ,	And the night a-shortening, [method,
O ḟeil Tomaiṛ taebnaiṛ tain	From the feast of Thomas ...
Co ḟéil Ḟaelain amlaḃaiṛ.	To the feast of Faelan, the mute.
Aḃaiṡ oc ṛiniub, ní ṡó,	The night a-lengthening, not false,
Ocuṛ ṛeṅṡ foṛ ceċ ṛiṗlo,	And shortening upon each long day,
O ḟéil Ḟaelain, feṡ anunḋ,	From the feast of Faelan, look across,
Co ḟeil Tomaiṛ itenum.	To the feast of Thomas again.

In the Calendar of Oengus, the feasts of Faelan and Thomas are June 20 and Dec. 21, respectively. Compare the Bede Calendar:

Xii. Kal. [Jul.]   Solstitium secundum Orientem.

Xii. Kal. [Jan.]   Nativitas sancti Thomae. Solstitium hyemale.

(This equinox and the solstices are to be carefully distinguished from the Roman.)

(3) *Sol in Taurum intrat* is given (p. cxx.) at July 19. But *Sol in Taurum* is found at April 17 (p. 86 of the MS.).

Under which king, Bezonian?

Read *Sol in Leonem intrat*, and place it at July 18. The emendation is rendered certain by the Zodiacal hexameter heading August (not given by Mr. Stokes) and by the Bede Calendar:

Augustum mensem Leo fervidus igne perurit.

Xv. Kal. [Maii]   Sol in Taurum.

Xv. Kal. [Aug.]   Sol in Leonem.

(4) At August 23, we have (p. cxxxii.): "*Finis anni Egiptiorum residuos u. dies epogomenas* [*epigenomenas?*] *vocant vel intercalares.*"

(5) At August 28 (p. cxxxiii.): "*Hic incipit primus* [*mensis*] *anni secundum Egiptios nomine Toth, computantes suos menses ad cursum solis.*"

The suggested Greek emendation will excite a smile; a change of one letter giving the true reading, ἐπαγόμεναs (ἡμέραs)—*added* (*days*). Besides, here you have but *four* of such days. The glossarist, however, knew his subject better. In the MS., the second item is correctly placed opposite August 29.

With this may be compared the note (apparently taken from Bede, *De temp. rat. xi.*) in the central portion of a *rota*, or circular diagram, in the Reichenau MS. cxcii. (fol. 237),* setting forth the days of the Roman months that respectively corresponded with the first days of the Egyptian: *Dehinc* [*x. Kal. Sep.*] *reverteris ad iiii. Kl. Septimbris, talique ratione conplerentur* [? *complebuntur*] *dies ccclx. xii. mensium Aegyptiorum: u. dies residuos epagamenas* [ἐπαγόμεναs], *vel interkalares, sive additos, vocaverunt.*

(6) But for droll emendation, No. 4 must probably yield the palm to No. 6. A left-hand marginal gloss (p. 89) states, amongst other things, that St. Kevin of Glendalough had two brothers. Their sister was Aibind. The latter part stands thus in the MS.:

    Aibind soror
    clui eorum
    B N(ONAE)

B is the regular letter, signifying that when Jan. 1 falls on Sunday (or Saturday in a leap-year), June 5 is Monday. 156 is the annual number of June 5 (Table II. 6 *b*). To Mr. Stokes, however, *clui* is the diminutive *-cula!* He reads *sororcula* in the text (p. xcviii.) and gives "MS. soror clui" underneath!

With reference to the lunar year, the glossarist mentions the Decemnovennal Cycle, the Hendecad and five Embolisms; also when the new moons began, and the length of the days and nights respectively at such times. He likewise gives criteria for determining Easter and other moveable feasts.

---

* Report on Rymer's *Foedera.*—Ad. to Ap. A. and its Suppl., Plate 1.

Of the glosses in question, Mr. Stokes copies but six; five not free from error, and some with glaring misconception.

(1) February 23. "*Bisextus hic oritur in Saltu lune celerius a[s]cendit quam putatur in bisex vero tardius a[s]cendit quam putatur. bisex namque retardat saltus vero celerat*" (p. liv.). *Sudet qui legat* is the motto of the editor of the *Calendar*.

The note, naturally, belongs to February 24, and is to be amended: *Bi[s]sextus hic oritur. In Saltu, luna celerius accenditur quam [com]putatur; in Bi[s]sex[to] vero, tardius accenditur quam [com]putatur. Bi[s]sextus namque, etc.* The meaning is this. In the (normal) Computation, the epact of the first year of the cycle would be *viii*. The Saltus, however, *accelerates* the December new moon of the last (19th) year (by making it fall on Nov. 25, instead of Nov. 26, Table IV.), so that the Jan. moon begins Dec. 24 and has the epact *ix*. on Jan. 1.*

In the Bissextile year, on the contrary, if the March moon began, as according to the (normal) Reckoning it ought, on the completion of the February moon, it would, by reason of the added day, have 31 instead of 30 days, and the Paschal incidence would be thereby disturbed. To obviate this, the March new moon is reckoned as *retarded* by a day, and the February moon counted 30 instead of 29 days.

(2) "*Luna . . . accendit*" (p. liv.). Read *Luna . . . accenditur*.

(3) March 6. "*Novisimus dies forsambi primesci inite*—the last day whereon is the first moon of Shrovetide" (p. lxii.).

To shew the meaning of *Init*, I transcribe from the *Lebar Brec* copy of the *Calendar of Oengus* some computistic data which Mr. Stokes has not reproduced.

---

* Overlooking this technical Rule, Ideler (II. 196) fell into an error, the effect of which unaccountably escaped his notice. Reckoning consecutively by 30 and 29 from Oct. 27, he assigned new moon to Nov. 26 and Dec. 25. The result is that the epact of the first year of the Cycle becomes 8, not 9!

Of the authorities indicated (193), Clavius (*Rom. Cal. restituti explicatio*, 108) accurately places XIX. at Nov. 25 and Dec. 24; Wolf (*Elementa Matheseos*, IV. 127, Geneva, 1740) is partly right and partly wrong: Nov. 25 XIX.; Dec. 25 XIX.

THE CODEX PALATINO-VATICANUS, 830.

[*Lebar Brec*, p. 90, marg. inf.]

Aile uatad erci Mártai, in Dómnac ir nerrom, ir e Domnac Inite.

Tper .xx. in érci rin, in Dómnac ir nerrom, [ir e] Init corgair.

Xi. erci April, in Dardaín ir nerrom, ir e Dardaín caplait.

Ocur xiiii. in érci rin, in Dómnac ir nerrom, ir e Dómnac Cárc.

Xxi. dino in érci rin, in Dómnac ir nerrom, ir e Dómnac Mincarc.

Ocur xxiiii. erci Mái, in Dardaín ir nerrom, ir e Dardaín Fner-gabala.

Cetnumad uatad erci Iúin, in Dómnac ir nerrom, ir e Dómnac Cengoigiri.

Xxu. erci Iúin, in Dómnac ir nerrom, ir e Domnac Init[e] corgair Sampaid.

Xuii.mad erci Iuil, in Domnac ir nerrom, ir e Dómnac Samcárc in rin.

[Translation.]

The second day of the moon of March, the Sunday that is next, [that is] the Sunday of the Beginning [of Lent].

The twenty-third of that moon, the Sunday that is next, [that is] the Beginning of the [stricter] Fast.

The eleventh of the moon of April, the Thursday that is next, that is the Thursday of the Capitilavium* [Holy Thursday].

And the fourteenth of that moon, the Sunday that is next, that is the Sunday of Easter.

Moreover, the twenty-first of that moon, the Sunday that is next, that is the Sunday of Little Easter [Low Sunday].

And the twenty-fourth of the moon of May, the Thursday that is next, that is the Thursday of Ascension.

The fourth day of the moon of June, the Sunday that is next, that is the Sunday of Pentecost.

The twenty-fifth of the moon of June, the Sunday that is next, that is the Sunday of the Beginning of the [stricter] Fast of Summer.

The seventeenth of the moon of July, the Sunday that is next, that is the Sunday of Summer-Easter.

---

* Caplat .i. nomen do cendló cárc .i. quari Capitolamium : cend-díunac .i. iarrin ní bérrtair cac and 7 negtair a cend oc airicill a cormata irin cáirc. *Cormac's Glossary* (*Lebar Brec*, p. 265 a).

Caplat, namely, a name for the headday of Easter: that is, as it were *Capitolavium—head-washing*. For the reason that everyone is tonsured then and his head is washed for reception of his unction on Easter [Holy Saturday].

According to the authorities quoted by Ducange, the *Capitilavium* took place on Palm Sunday. For instance, St. Isidore : De Palmarum die. Vulgus ideo eum diem *Capitilavium* vocant, quia tunc moris est lavandi capita infantium qui ungendi sunt, ne forte observatione quadragesimae sordidati ad unctionem accederent (*De Offic. Divin.* I. xxviii.).

To illustrate the foregoing, let us take a typical instance, given in one of the glosses we are dealing with,—Golden No. VIII., Dominical Letter C = (the latest) Easter, April 25.

(The moon, it has to be premised, is regularly designated from the month in which it ends. But here, in consequence of the Embolism of the eighth Decemnovennal year being inserted at March 7, it is named from the month in which it begins.)

IX.

PASCHAL COMPUTUS OF VIII. C.

G.N.	Moon.	Month.		D.L.	Festival.
[VIII]	[1]	[March	6]	B	
	2	[,,	7]	C	
	[9]	,,	14	C	Beginning [First Sunday] of Lent.
	23	[,,	28]	C	
	[30]	April	4	C	Beginning of [stricter] Lent [Mid-Lent Sunday].
[VIII]	11	[,,	15]	G	
	14	[,,	18]	C	[Latest Paschal Term.]
	[18]	,,	22	G	Thursday of Capitilavium [Holy Thursday].
	21	[,,	25]	C	Easter Sunday.
	[28]	May	2	C	Little Easter [Low Sunday].
[VIII]	24	[,,	27]	G	
[VIII]	[1]	June	3	G	Ascension Thursday.
	4	[,,	6]	C	
	[11]	,,	13	C	Pentecost Sunday.
					[Beginning of Summer Lent.]
	25	[,,	27]	C	
[VIII]	[3]	July	4	C	Beginning of [stricter] Summer Lent
	17	[,,	18]	C	
	[24]	,,	25	C	Summer Easter Sunday.

The text and Table prove that Lent consisted of three-week moieties ; *Init* (= initium) and *Init Chorgais* signifying by synecdoche the first and last half respectively. A similar distinction is found in the Calendar inserted amongst the works of Bede.

    xvi. B viii. Id. [Feb.]
      D vi. ,, ,, Initii principium.
      D Id. [Mart.] Finis Initii, post dies triginta quinque.

Here Lent is computed by xvi D = (the earliest) Easter, March 22. The division differs from the Irish, in making the proportion 5 : 1 ; thereby limiting the more austere portion to Holy Week. The Stricter Fast and the Summer Lent (both of which are well established) do not call for discussion in this place.

The gloss in question is consequently to be translated :

[*March* 6.] *Last day on which is the new moon of the Beginning of Lent*].

In other words, the Golden Number VIII. stands opposite March 6 in the Calendar. (ꝑꞃim eꞃci, like *prima lunae* and *first of the moon*, is an elliptical expression for ꝑꞃim uaċaꝺ eꞃci—*first day of the moon*.)

(4) The corresponding day is thus given in this edition : "April 6, *Novisimus dies forsambi primesci chasc*—the latest day whereon is the first moon of Easter" (p. lxxiii.). This gives 31 days to the April moon ! Besides, no Paschal new moon falls on April 6. Herewith the *Lebar Brec* glossarist apparently disagrees. In the MS., on account of the space occupied by the preceding gloss, the sentence stands opposite the 6th ; but it is obviously misplaced. It means : April 5 is the last day on which is the first of an Easter moon. The Golden Number VIII. is placed (Table IV.) opposite that day in the Calendar.

Connected herewith is a gloss on May 5 which is noteworthy : "*laithe mis greni na cétfresgabala*—the day of the solar month of the first Resurrection" (p. lxxxiv.). Here is what the bookish theorick leads to,—Easter Sunday on the 5th of May! There is not an Irish-speaking child who could not have taught the editor that ꝼꞃeꞃꝺabal means the Ascension, and eꞃꞃeiꞃꞃe the Resurrection. The Calendar of Oengus, it is very remarkable, gives the one on the 27th of March ; the other, on the 5th of May.

(5) March 21. "*Dies Epactarum*" (p. lxiv.). On the left margin, this item is written under March 21. But on the right, it correctly stands opposite March 22., Compare p. 347, *supra* and :—

Xi. Kal. [Apr.] Sedes epactarum [*Cal. Bed.*].

(6) April 25. "*Escop mor mac caille, etc. . . . Ni thic sén co cenn u. bliadan xxx. ar cccc.*—Great bishop Mac Caille, etc. . . . He comes not till the end of 435 years" (p. lxxvi). This is perhaps the crowning achievement of Mr. Stokes,—taking a bishop for the Great Paschal

THE CODEX PALATINO-VATICANUS, 830. 387

Cycle! Reference to the facsimile and some elementary acquaintance with the subject will produce the true reading: *uiii. Kl.* [*Maii*]. *Novis*[*s*]*imus dies Pasc*[*h*]*a*[*e*]. Nı chıc pén co cenn .u. [*recte*, .ıı.] blıaḃan. *xxx*. ap cccc[c.]—[*April*] 25, *last day of Easter* [on which Easter falls]. *That comes not until the end of* 532 *years.* Mr. Stokes failed because the glossarist placed *novisimus dies pasca* under *uiii. Kl.* (April 25), and the remainder under *uii. Kl.* (April 26). The first clause Mr. Stokes omitted; the second he referred to Mac-Caille, although it precedes the gloss relative to that bishop.

The emendations are certain; the same calculation being employed elsewhere: *II. Id.* [*Mar.*] *Novissimus dies forsambi Init.* Nı chıc pén co cenḃ *xxx*. blıaḃan ıı. ap cccc., ıap nocaḃ choıp— [*March*] 14. *Last day on which is the Beginning* [*of Lent*]. *That comes not until the end of* 532 *years, according to the normal notation.* This refers to the same Decemnovennal year as the previous gloss. When Easter, as has been set forth in Table IX., falls on April 25, the first Sunday of Lent is March 14. The 'glossarist rightly added " according to the normal notation:" that is, $28 \times 19 = 532$. For the same Paschal incidence occurs in years that are not a Great Cycle apart: as, for instance, 672, 919 and 1014.

Here again a modicum of knowledge is requisite to reconstruct the gloss. For the first sentence stands a line-space above *ii. Id.*, with *forsambi Init* a-top of *novissimus dies*. The second is written underneath *ii. Id.*, and is partly interlinear. It is scarce necessary to add that the gloss has not been transcribed by the editor of the Calendar.

In the *Tripartite Life* (p. 531), following O'Conor, Mr. Stokes says that " the new moon fell in December, 1071, on the 25th December, and that therefore there were seven days thence to January 1, 1072." But that would make the epact of 1072 *viii.*, instead of *vii.* New moon, a glance at Table IV. will shew, does not occur on Christmas Day in the Cycle of Nineteen. The year in question (Golden No. VIII.) has new moon on December 26, thus giving *vii.* as the epact of 1072.

The luni-solar criteria of the year (A.D. 493) and day of St.

Patrick's death are transcribed, translated and annotated as follows (*ib.* pp. 552-3):

Roforbanastar, tra, Patraic arith mbuada isin fichatmad bliadain for cét a áisse .i. im bliadain uii. xx. for* Kalaind Enair for áine ocus cet bliadain for bisexa : hi† xui. immorro Kalne Apreil nabliadne sin for cetain ocus xiii. furri.	Now, Patrick completed his victorious course in the 120th year of his age, that is, in the 27th year,* the Calends of January (falling) on a Friday and the first year after the bis[s]extile : the 16th, moreover, of the Calends of April [March 17] of that year was on a Wednesday, and the 13th (of the lunar month) was thereon.†
* This seems superfluous. † Read *in* (the) ?	* " Of the Solar Cycle," Petrie. † Petrie says that, according to Sir W. R. Hamilton, all these astronomical definitions agree with the year 493, except 27 for the Solar Cycle, which, to agree with the Calends of January on Friday, should be 26.

In the foregoing, for " in the 27th year, the Calends of January," read : " in the year of the 27th [lunation] on the Calends of Jan. [which fell] on Friday." So far, therefore, from being superfluous, *for* (upon) is integral to the idiom.

Again, from *cet* to *hi* is to be read : *cet bliadain for bisexa hi*—the first year after a bissextile [year was] it [lit., *she ; bliadain* (year) being feminine]. In other words, instead of the article, as Mr. Stokes suggests, *hi* is a personal pronoun. It occurs a little before in the same text (*Tripartite*, p. 550) : *Ba hi tra bliadain, etc.*—Now this was the year, etc.

The Dominical Letter was C; Golden Number, xix. (Epact 27). New moon (Table IV.) fell on the 5th ; the 13th of the moon, on the 17th of March.

It is not surprising, therefore, that Mr. Stokes gives the following calculations without any attempt at correction, or reduction to the A.D. year (*ib.* p. 499) : " *Viginti tres cicli decennovenales ab Incarnatione Domini usque ad adventum Patricii in Hiberniam, et ipsi efficiunt numero quadringentos triginta octo. Et ab adventu Patricii usque ad ciclum decennovenalem in quo sumus viginti duo cicli sunt : id est, quadringenti viginti unus sunt, duo anni in Ogdoade usque in hunc annum in quo sumus.*" That is, $23 \times 19 = 438$ and $(22 \times 19) + 2 = 421$! *Mirus calculandi preceptor!* But it may be safely concluded that "Harleian 3859, fol. 176 b," from which the passage professes to be taken, has *ccccxxxvii.* (437) instead of *ccccxxxviii.* (438), and either *ccccxx.* (420) in place of *ccccxxi.* (421), or *iii* (3) for *ii* (2). For 45 Cycles of Nineteen = A.D. 855. This was the first year of the Ogdoad (Golden No. I.). Consequently, if *two* years of the Ogdoad had elapsed, the computation was made in 857; if *three*, in 858.

The foregoing corrigenda, which are not exhaustive, will suffice to shew that the attempts hitherto made to deal with native dating have been irrespective of the principles upon which it was based.

As regards the present essay, the treatment, I am fully conscious, owing in part to the deplorable lack of reliable material, is not as ample as the importance of the subject demands. Under the circumstances, nothing more is claimed than to have indicated the direction and method of research and some of the main conclusions resulting thereby. No difficulty has been consciously evaded; whilst, to enable the student to judge for himself, the original authorities have been cited or referred to throughout. For the rest, *ex primis ista peragro loca:* I have had no pioneer in the domain of Irish Chronology.

NOTES.

A.—ADAMNANI *VITA COLUMBAE.*

De Prophetia beati viri de filio Dermiti regis, qui Aidus Slane *linguâ nominatus est Scoticâ.*

Alio in tempore, cum vir beatus in Scotia per aliquot demoraretur dies, ad supradictum Aidum ad se venientem sic prophetice locutus ait: *Praecavere debes, fili, ne tibi a Deo totius Hiberniae regni praerogativam monarchiae praedestinatam, parricidali faciente peccato, amittas. Nam si quandoque illud commiseris, non toto patris regno, sed eius aliqua parte in gente tua brevi frueris tempore.* Quae verba sancti sic sunt expleta secundum eius vaticinationem. Nam post Suibneum, filium Columbani, dolo ab eo interfectum non plus, ut fertur, quam quatuor annis et tribus mensibus regni concessa potitus est parte.—*Lib.* I. *cap.* 14.

B.—CUMMIANI *EPISTOLA PASCHALIS.*

(*a*)

Postremo ad cyclorum computationem diversorum, quid unaquaeque lingua de cursu solis et lunae sentiret, conversus totus, licet diverse alium in die, alium in luna; alium in mense, alium in bissexto, alium in epacta, alium in augmento lunari (quod vos *Saltum* dicitis), inveni cyclos contra hunc, quem vos tenetis, esse contrarios : primum[-o], illum quem Sanctus Patricius, papa noster, tulit et facit,* in quo luna a xiv. usque in xxi.† regulariter et aequinoctium a xii. Kal. Ap. [!] observatur; secundo, Anatolium (quem vos extollitis quidem), [qui dicit] ad veram Paschae rationem numquam pervenire eos qui cyclum lxxxiv. annorum observant;‡ tertio, Theophilum; quarto, Dionysium; quinto, Cyrillum; sexto, Morinum; septimo, Augustinum; octavo, Victorium; nono, Pachomium monachum, Aegypti coenobiorum fundatorem, cui ab angelo ratio Paschae dictata est; decimo, ccc. x. et viii. episcoporum decennovennalem cyclum (qui Graece *Enneacedeciterida*§ dicitur), in quo Kalendas Januarii [?] lunaeque eiusdem diei [?] et initia primi mensis ipsiusque xiv. lunae recto iure ac si quodam clarissimo tramite, ignorantiae relictis tenebris, studiosis quibusque cunctis temporibus sunt adnotatae, quibus paschalis solemnitas probabiliter inveniri potest.

Hunc [hos ?] inveni valde huic, cuius auctorem, locum, tempus, incertum habemus, esse contrarium [-os ?] in Kalendis, in Bissexto, in Epacta, in xiv. luna, in primo mense, in Aequinoctio.

(*b*)

Deinde [ob dissensionem in Synodo Campi-Lene] visum est senioribus nostris, iuxta mandatum ut, si diversitas oborta fuerit inter causam et causam, et variaret iudicium inter lepram et non lepram, irent ad locum quem elegit Dominus : ut, si causae fuerint maiores, iuxta decretum synodicum ad caput urbium sint referendae, misimus quos novimus sapientes et humiles esse, velut natos ad matrem. Et prosperum iter in voluntate Dei habentes et ad Romam urbem aliqui ex eis venientes, tertio anno ad nos usque pervenerunt. Et sic omnia viderunt sicut audierunt; sed et valde certiora, utpote visa quam audita, invenerunt. Et in uno hospitio cum Graeco et Hebraeo, Scytha et Egyptiaco in ecclesia Sancti Petri simul in Pascha, in quo mense disiuncti sumus, fuerunt. Et ante sancta sic testati sunt nobis,

---

* Fecit. † *Sic ; lege* xx.
‡ Alii xxv., alii xxx., nonnulli lxxxiiii. annorum circulum computantes, numquam ad veram Paschae computandi rationem pervenerunt.—*Liber* [*spurius*] *Anatolii de Ratione Paschali.*
§ *Lege* ἐννεακαιδεκαετηρίς. Cf. :
  Hinc cyclus Graeco ἔνεα καὶ δέκα θερίδα dictis[-us]
  Quod denis currat mensibus atque novem ;
  Qui nostro sermone *decemnovennalis* habetur,
   Per quem paschalis annua Luna redit.
       Ephemeris (inter Bedae Opera).

Sed Alexandrinae urbis archiepiscopi beatus Athanasius, qui etiam ipse Nicaeno Concilio, tunc sancti Alexandri pontificis diaconus et in omnibus adiutor, interfuit, et deinceps venerabilis Theophilus et Cyrillus ab hac Synodi veneranda constitutione minime desciverunt. Imo potius eumdem decemnovennalem ciclum, qui Enneacaidecaeterida [!] Graeco vocabulo nuncupatur, sollicite retinentes Paschalem cursum nullis diversitatibus violasse monstrantur.

    Epistola (*I*.) *Dionysii de ratione Paschae* (*ad Petronium*).

dicentes: *Per totum orbem terrarum hoc Pascha, ut scimus, celebratur.* Et nos in reliquiis sanctorum martyrum et scripturis quas attulerunt probavimus inesse virtutem Dei. Vidimus oculis nostris puellam caecam omnino ad has reliquias oculos aperientem et paralyticum ambulantem et multa demonia eiecta.

C.—CATALOGUS SANCTORUM HIBERNIAE SECUNDUM DIVERSA TEMPORA.

Primus Ordo [A.D. 432–544].

Unum Pascha quartâ decima lunâ post equinoctium vernale celebrabant. . . . Hic Ordo Sanctorum per quaterna duravit regna: hoc est, pro tempore Laeogarii et Ail[ill]a Muilt et Lugada, filio[-ii] Laeogarii et Tuathail.

Secundus Ordo [A.D. 544–598].

Unum Pascha quartâ decimâ luna post equinoctium [celebrabant] . . . Hic Ordo per quaterna adhuc regna duravit : hoc est, ab extremis Tuathail et per totum Diarmata regis regnum et duorum Muradaig nepotum et Aedo, filii Oinmerech.

Tertius Ordo [A.D. 598–665].

Diversam solemnitatem Paschalem [habebant]. Alii enim Resurrectionem decimâ quartâ lunâ, alii* decimâ sextâ,* cum duris intentionibus celebrabant. Hi per quaterna regna vixerunt : hoc est, Aeda Allain [*recte*, Aeda Slaine], qui tribus annis pro cogitatione mala† tantum regnavit et Domnail et filiorum Mailcoba et [filiorum] Aeda Slaine permixta tempora et usque ad mortalitatem illam magnam perduraverunt.

Ussher: *Brit. Eccl. Antiq.*, Wks. vi. 477–9.

D.—PROLOGUS VICTORII.

(*a*)

Recensitis igitur fidelibus historiis veterum, beati scilicet Eusebii Caesariensis Palestinae civitatis episcopi, viri imprimis eruditissimi atque doctissimi, Chronicis Prologoque ac perinde his quae a sanctae memoriae Hieronymo his de Chronicis sunt adjecta presbytero, per quem in Latinum quoque probantur translata sermonem : hisque etiam quae a sancto et venerabili viro Prospero usque ad consulatum Valentiniani Augusti VIII et Anthemii constat fuisse suppleta, reperi a mundi principio usque ad Diluvium IICCXLII annos : item a Diluvio usque ad Nativitatem Abrahae annos DCCCCXLII. . . .

Porro ab Abraham usque in sextum Valentis Consulatum et Valentiniani secundum, IICCCXCV ac deinde ab Ausonio Olybrioque Coss., qui sequuntur, ad VIII Valentiniani Augusti consulatum et Anthimi [-emii] VIII et LXX. Et simul omnes a mundi

---

- The text is : vel decimâ sextâ ; with a variant : alii decimâ tertiâ celebrabant. The *xiii.* is a manifest scribal error for *xvi.*

† This refers to the slaying of his nephew, Suibne, mentioned in Note A.

origine usque ad Constantinum et Rufum Coss. praesentes VDCLVIII anni referuntur. Quibus ob veritatem certius indagandam bissextos etiam copulavi, quo manifestius appareret utrum sibi vel bissextorum ratio tam Kal. Jan. quam VIII Kal. Apr., qui [quo] mundo[-us] traditur institutus, continuata disputatione [disposi-] concinneret.

Quibus undique per versis[-us] congruentibus, restabat inquiri si lunae dinumeratio, quae die quarta existentis mundi, i.e. V Kal. Apr., plena, hoc est XIV, jubente Creatore, in inchoatione noctis exorta est, pari lege transactis praesentibusque temporibus consonaret quam tot a saeculis computatam et Kal. Jan. III feria, l. XX, et VIII Kal. Apr., II feria, XIV luna, Constantino et Rufo Coss., perseveranti oratione [ratione] pervenisse computatum est juxta Aegyptiacam disciplinam, qua evidentissime deprehensum est quod XIX annorum porrecta curriculis in semetipsa super iisdem vestigiis se revolvens annum quem XX inchoat hunc eadem metiatur et primum.

Cum itaque nihil resedisset ambigui, diebus, lunis atque bissextis inde a constitutione mundana in nostram usque progeniem mirabili decursione concordibus, necessarium fuit, propter quam maxime huic inquisitioni secundum venerationis tuae mandatum mea desudabat intentio, ut instituta Paschalia perscrutarer, vel illius temporis quo praeceptione divina per Moysen a filiis Israel agnus est immolatus in Aegypto, vel illius praecipue quo pro redemptione nostra atque salute ille verus Agnus, cuius figura praecesserat, *Pascha nostrum immolatus est Christus.*

(b)

[*Loca interpolata.*]

[Rursusque omnibus annis, temporibus, diebus ac luna maxime, quae juxta Hebraeos menses facit, rite decursis a mundi principio, secundum praedictae Historiae [Eusebii] fidem, usque in diem quo filii Israel Paschale mysterium coelesti initiavere mandato et ab Aegyptiaca clade agni occisione salvati sunt, bissextorum pariter necessitate decursa, quantum fida supputatio investigavit, anni IIIDCLXXXIX, V feria, IX Kal. Apr., luna XIII incipiente jam vespere, docentur impleti. Cujus sequenti die, tertio millesimo scilicet anno ac sexcentesimo nonagesimo, precedente [procedente] mense primo, VI feria, VIII Kal. Apr., luna XIV, noctis initio Hebraeos claruit agni sacrificium peregisse. Pascha quippe, sicut omnimoda traditione cognoscitur, anni principio, non in fine, celebratur.

Passum autem Dominum nostrum Jesum Christum peractis VCCXXVIII annis ab ortu mundi eadem Chronicorum relatione monstratur. Quod gestum inchoante XXVIII [XXIX] anno non potest dubitari: siquidem VIII Kal. Apr., primo mense, luna XIV vespere praecedente, sicut ab initio creaturae quarta die facta est, coepisse doceatur; adjunctisque bissextis ad summam VCCXXVIII annorum, sequenti XXIX anno, V feria, docet se traditione praeventum. Primo vero azymorum die, Dominus noster Jesus Christus coenans cum discipulis suis, postquam sui Corporis et Sanguinis sacramenta patefecit, ad montem Oliveti, sicut Evangelia sancta testantur, progressus ibique detentus est a Judaeis, tradente discipulo: deinceps VI feria subsequente, id est VIII Kal. Apr., crucifixus est et sepultus: tertia die, hoc est VI Kal. Apr., Dominico, surrexit a mortuis.]

(c)

Quapropter, omnibus fixo limite consonis, necessarium erat propter Paschalis observantiae rationem, dies et lunares annos a mundi ipsius describi principio, quo possit rerum cursus evidenter cognosci. Sed, quia immensum opus majoris otii est, ne diutius praecepta differrem, breviarium ejus interim explicavi.

(d)

Quod tamen ex ipsius plenitudinis ordinatione descendat, ex tempore Dominicae Passionis diebus Kal. Jan. et nominibus Consulum a duobus Geminis, Rufo scilicet et Rubellio, usque ad consulatum Constantini et Rufi diligenti annotatione collectis per cccc et xxx annos cum lunis atque temporibus, ac deinceps sine consulibus per annos centum et duos futuros, ut DXXXII annis omnis summa constaret, patefacere curavi. Quae summa ita cunctarum quibus excepta est series regularum sua revolutione complectitur, ut eodem tramite et in id, unde orta est, revocetur et ad finem pristinum de novo circumacta perveniat.

E.—DE MIRABILIBUS SACRAE SCRIPTURAE.

Ut enim hoc manifestis probationibus pateat, cyclorum etiam ab initio conditi orbis recursus in se breviter digeremus, quos semper post quingentos triginta duos annos, sole ut in principio et luna per omnia convenientibus, nullis subvenientibus impedimentis, in id, unde ceperant, redire ostendemus. Quinto namque cyclo a mundi principio, anno centesimo quarto decimo, generale totius mundi diluvium sub Noe venit, qui post diluvium quadringentesimo decimo octavo anno defecit: et inde alius incipiens, id est, sextus, in octavo aetatis Abrahae anno finitur. Et nono ejus anno, septimus incipiens, trigesimo quinto anno egressionis filiorum Israel de Egypto, quinquennio ante mortem Moysi, concluditur. Post quem octavus, in quo est illud signum in sole et luna factum, trigesimo sexto anno egressionis Israel de Egypto incipiens, in trigesimum primum annum Asae, regis Juda, incidit. Cujus trigesimo secundo anno, nonus exordium capiens, in quo et aliud signum in sole, Ezechiae regis tempore, de quo paulo post dicemus, factum legitur, centesimo octavo anno post templi restaurationem, quae sub Dario facta est, sui cursus spatium consummavit: donec decimus inde oriens, nonagesimo secundo anno post passionem Salvatoris, Alia et Sparsa [*lege* Aviola e Pansa] consulibus, peractis cursibus consummatur. Post quem undecimus a consulatu Paterni et Torquati ad nostra usque tempora decurrens, extremo anno Hiberniensium moriente Manichaeo inter octeros sapientes, peragitur. Et duodecimus nunc tertium annum agens ad futurorum scientiam se praestans, a nobis qualem finem sit habiturus ignoratur.

Quorum unusquisque uniformi statu, peractis quingentis triginta duobus annis, in semetipsum, id est, in sequentis initium, revolvitur: completis videlicet in unoquoque solaribus octovicenis nonodecies, et in lunaribus decemnovenalibus vicies octies circulis. Post quos et in lunari supputatione per communes duodecim et embolismos septem, per ogdoadem et hendecadem et incrementum lunare (quod computatores *Saltum* nominant) et [in] solari per quadrantes et bissextos diligenter dinumeratos : demum duobus luminaribus totidem dies habentibus et per cursus sui omnes lineas concordi ratione convenientibus, veluti primus conditi orbis annus innovatur.

Dum ergo hi circulorum totales recursus in se congrue et post illos cyclos, quibus in sole et luna morae vel reditus signa[-um], quomodo sub Jesu vel Ezechia factum legitur, apparuisse describitur, sine ulla varietate redeunt ; manifeste intelligitur, quod non mora illa aut reversio aliquid in luminarium et temporum assueto cursu praepeditum vel insolitum reliquerunt ; sed quasi per diem omnem in occasus sui, ut supra dixi, limitem currunt, postquam illius solito longioris diei spatium peregerunt. Per quod videtur quod nihil ad sequentis noctis longitudinem temporis illa dies longa contulerit, cujus princeps pariter in die cum sole diei praeposito luna requievit.—*Lib. ii. Cap. iv.*

F.—ANNALS OF ULSTER.

bip. Kal. Ian. 1. p., l. xu. Ⱥ.ⱺ. ⱺcli°. [-11°].

Obitur Seꜟeni, ab[b]atip Iae, ib ept, pili Piaɔnae ⁊ quiep Aiblozo, mic Camain, abbatip Cluana mac Noip ⁊ ɔopmitatio Ⰿancheni, abbatip Ⰿenoɔpoɔit.

Bis. Kalends of January on Monday, 15th of the moon, A.D. 652.

Obit of Segene, abbot of Iona, that is, son of Fiachna, and repose of Aedlog, son of Cuman, abbot of Clonmacnoise and sleep of Manchene, abbot of Mendrochit.

G.—PETAVIUS: *DE TEMPORUM RATIONE.*

Quam in sententiam [summam ab orbe condito ad Christum natum esse, ex mente Eusebii, annorum DCXCIX] illustris est locus apud Auctorem operis librorum *De Mirabilibus Sacrae Scripturae,* quod inter S. Augustini opera cusum est. Nam, Lib. ii. Cap. iv, anni mundi per Victorini Cyclos putantur ; quos ad aetatem suam scriptor ille duodenos praeteriisse significat. Quippe ab rerum primordio ad Diluvium Cyclos absolutos quatuor numerat, cum anno 114 de quinto : qui sunt anni 2240 [2242]. Hunc vero ultimum terminat anno post Diluvium 418. Sextus Cyclus desinit in annum octavum aetatis Abraami. Ita fient ab orbe condito ad Abraamum [annum octavum Abraami] anni 3192 ; a Diluvio, 1052 [950]. Septimus Cyclus desinit in annum ab exitu Israelitarum 35. Octavus, in annum Asa 31. Nonus, in annum ab instauratione Templi, 108. Decimus, in annum 92 post Passionem Christi, Alia et Sparsa Coss., quibus successerunt Paternus et Torquatus, quorum consulatus anno primo Cycli undecimi dedit exordium. Hunc autem desinit Auctor ille in morte Manichaei Hibernensis, unius e sapientibus. Duodecimi porro Cycli anno tertio ista scribebat.

Paternus et Torquatus Coss. a Cassiodoro et ante a Victorino Aquitano in Fastis manuscriptis ponuntur anno U. C. 876 ; quos Fasti Capitolini et Onuphrius vocant Paetinum et Apronianum. Congruunt iidem in annum Christi CXXIII. At anno superiore in Fastis omnibus leguntur Coss. Aviola et Pansa. Sed in membranis

Victorini *Aulia et Parsa*. Quare Auctor *De mirabilibus* vitiosum codicem Victorini nactus erat.

Qui cum anno tertio duodecimi Cycli Victorini, vel Dionysii [!], scriberet, is erat annus mundi 5855, a Passione 627. Si igitur de annis mundi 5855 detrahas annos 627, reliquus est annus mundi 5228, quo passus est Christus. Inde porro detractis 30, restat annus 5198, vel 5199, quo natus est Christus ex veteri putatione, quam Martyrologium Romanum sequitur. Christum autem anno tricesimo passum esse, fuit multorum opinio.—*Lib. ix. Cap. ii., pp. 2, 3.*

II.—EXTRACT FROM O'FLAHERTY'S *OGYGIA*.

Nostri veteres in anteriora calculando Scotici appulsus tempus a majoribus eo ipso tempore, ut credibile est, consignatum, ita anni Romani rationibus et hebdomadum systemati aptarunt, ut memoriae proditum reliquerint Scotos ad Hiberniae littora applicuisse Kal. Maii, die Jovis et aetatis lunae septimo, nullâ habitâ ratione Salomonis regni, aut aerae mundanae; ut in Hibernico poemate de diversis Hiberniae expugnatoribus (quod incipit Eirceaḋ aep eaṡna aiḃinn) ita cecinit Achaius O Floinn, author perquam vetustus:

> Seaċtmaḋ ḋeurṡ ḋia ḋaṗḋaine:
> Ro fṗiċ feaċtmaḋ ḟeane:
> Ṡaḃṗaḋ Itallaincipi:
> 1 Calon Mai a mirṡne.

Septima Luna, Jovi Sacra Lux, Maineque Kalendae
Appulsus annum Symbola certa notant.

Anno quidem periodi Julianae 3698, qui est, juxta Scaligerum, Salomonis regnantis quintus et mundi 2934, Cyclo Solis 2, Lunae 12, litera feriali E, Kal. Maiae concurrebant cum Septimo Lunae die et quintâ hebdomadis feriâ. Nec toto Salomonis regno, imo nec toto saeculo ab David patris ortu ad Salomonis obitum, ea connexio diei mensis, hebdomadis ac Lunaris aetatis accidere potuit, nisi solo hoc ipso anno; uti cuivis calculos retro supputandi perito etiam hodie quasi digito monstrare integrum est.

—Pars II., pp. 83-4.

Lebar bailí in iiiota.

(P. 48 b)

a Laegaire, mac Neill, trigenta annis regnum hiberni[a]e port aduentum Patricii tenuit.

Ard-Maċa fundata ert.

Secundinur (idon, Seċnall) et renex Patriciur in pace dormierunt.

Fuair Laeġaire iarom bar ig Ġreallaiġ Daḃil, for taeb Cairre, immMaiġ Liḟe, eter na da ċnoc, idon, Eriu ocur Alba a n-anmann. A raċa doat fri Laiġniu naċ iarfad in doroime forro, iar n-a gabail doib for creiċ occo. Co tart rom grein ocur erca friu na raigfed forro ni bad ririu. Romarbrat iarum grian ocur erca annrin eireom, ar forarai iaċ. Sicut poeta ait:

> Atbaċ Loegaire, mac Neill,
> For taeb Cairre, glar a tir,
> Dili Dé adroegaid rat,
> Tucrat dal bair forrin riġ.

Ailill Molt, mac n[-D]aċi, fiċe bliadan, co torċair a caċ Oċa, la Luġaid, mac Laeġaire ocur la Muircertaċ, mac Erca ocur la Ferġur Cerrbel, mac Conaill Cremtainde ocur la Fiacraiġ Lonn, mac Coelbad, riġ Dál-Araide.

b Unde dixit bec, mac De:

> Mor ċaċ Oċa ferra i tír,
> Immorulta caċa ili:
> For Oilill Molt, mac n[-D]aċi,
> Meabair la Dal n-Araidi.

Luġaid, mac Laeġaire, mic Neill, coic bliadna fiċet, cotorcair a n-Aċad-Phorċa, iar n-a bein o forċa ċeindtiġe do nim i n-a cenn, iar n-diultad do roiṁ Padraic.

Muirceartaċ, mac Erca, idon Muircertaċ, mac Muredaiġ,

BOOK OF BALLYMOTE.

(P. 48 b). [A.D.*]

a Laegaire, son of Niall, held the kingdom of Ireland for thirty [462] years after the advent of Patrick.
Armagh was founded. [444]
Secundinus[1] (that is, Sechnall) and Old Patrick[2] slept in peace. [1] [447]
Laeghaire received death[3] afterwards at Grellach-Daphil, on the [2] [457]
side of Caiss, in the Plain of Liphe, between the two hills, namely, [3] [462]
Eriu and Alba [were] their names. He gave his guarantees to the Lagenians that he would not seek the Cattle-Tribute from them, after he had been made prisoner by them, when he was raiding amongst them. So that he gave sun and moon [as guarantees] to them that he would not seek [it] from them any longer. Afterwards sun and moon killed him for that, for he dishonoured them. As the poet saith:

> Died Loeghaire, son of Niall,
> On the side of Caiss, green the land,
> Elements of God, which he invoked as guarantee,
> Gave fate of death to the king.

Ailill Molt, son of Dathi, [reigned] twenty years, until he fell in [482] the battle of Ocha, by Lugaidh, son of Laeghaire and by Muircertach, son of Erc and by Fergus Wry-mouth, son of Conall Crimthainn and by Fiachrach the Spirited, son of Coelbad, king of Dal-Araidhe.

b Wherefore said Bec Mac De:

> The great battle of Ocha was fought in the country,
> There were fought [therein] many battles:
> Upon Oilill Molt, son of Dathi,
> Defeat is inflicted by Dal-Araidhe.

Lugaidh, son of Laegaire, son of Niall, [reigned] five [and] twenty [507] years, until he fell in Achad-Farcha, after being struck by a fiery bolt from heaven in his head, after his refusal [to believe] in Patrick.
Muircertach, son of Erc, namely, Muircertach, son of Muiredach, [534]

---

* The regnal A.D. dates are those of the final years.

Lebar baili in mota.

[b] mic Eogain, mic Neill Noi-giallaig, ceithri bliadna ríchet, corp'baideadh a telcoma ṗína aidci Saṁna, immullad Cletig or doind. Unde dictum est a rancto Cairnech:

Irom oṁan ar in bean, (Idon, Sin, ingen Shige, ro-
lmaluaidrea ilar rin   [marb he.)
Ar pior loircpichep i ten,
For toeb Cletig baitṗer pín.

c Is día oidi pochet in pili for an rann ro ele:

Oidid Muircertaig na mod,
Guin ir batud ir lorcud:
Eg adbatadar i bur
A meic, Domnall ir Forgur.

Tuatal Maelgarb, mac Cormaic cae[i]ċ, mic Cairpre, mic Neill Nae-giallaig, aen bliadain deg, co torċair la Mael-morda, mac Airgedan, hui mic hI; qui et ipse ptacím occirrur ert. Unde dicitur Ett Maeil-morra.

Diarmaid, mac Fergura Cerrbeoil, mic Conaill Cremtaind, míc Neill Nae-giallaig, bliadain ar pichit, co torċair la hAeg dub, mac Suibne, ri Dal-Araide, irRaith-big, imMaig-Líne.

Domnall ocur Forgur, da mac Muircertaig, mic Mure-daig, mic Eogain, mic Neill Nae-giallaig, tri bliadna. D'eg atbatadar.

Baedan, mac Muircertaig ocur Eochaid, mac Domnaill, mic Muircertaig, mic Muredaig, tri bliadna, co torċair la Cronan, mac Tigernaig, ri Ciannaċt Glindi-Geiṁin.

Ainmire, mac Sedna, mic Fergura Cendfoda, mic Conaill Gulban, mic Neill Nae-giallaig, tri bliadna, co torċair la Fergur, mac Neillini.

d Baedan, mac Nindeada, mic Fergura Cendfoda, bliadain, co torċair a n-imairg la da Cumaine, idon Cumaine, mac Colmain big ocur Cumaine Librene, mac Illadain, mic Cerbaill.

son of Eogan, son of Niall of the Nine Hostages, [reigned] four [and] [**b**] twenty years, until he was drowned in a vat of wine, November Night, on the summit of Cletech over the Boyne. Wherefore was said by Saint Cairnech :

> I have fear respecting the woman, (To wit, Sin, daughter
> Who will excite many storms   [of Sigh, who
> Against a man who shall be burned in fire, [killed him.)
> [Whom] on side of Cletech wine shall drown.

c It is of his fate sang the poet also this other stave :

> The fate of Muircertach of the resources,
> [Was mortal] wounding and drowning and burning :
> [Natural] death died afterwards
> His sons, Domnall and Fergus.

[A.D.]
Tuathal Bald-rough, son of Cormac Blind[-eye], son of Coirpre, [544] son of Niall of the Nine Hostages, [reigned] one year [and] ten, until he fell by Mael-mordha, son of Airgedan, descendant of Mac I; who himself was immediately slain. Whence is [proverbially] said : "The Feat of Mael-morra."

Diarmaid, son of Fergus Wry-mouth, son of Conall Cremthann, son [565] of Niall of the Nine Hostages, [reigned] a year over twenty, until he fell by Aedh the Black, son of Suibhne, king of Dal-Araidhe, in the Little Rath, in Magh-Line.

Domnall and Fergus, two sons of Muircertach, son of Muiredach, [567] son of Eogan, son of Niall of the Nine Hostages, [reigned] three years. Of [natural] death died they.

Baedan, son of Muircertach and Eochadh, son of Domnall, son of [572] Muircertach, son of Muiredach, [reigned] three years, until they fell by Cronan, son of Tigernach, king of the Ciannachta of Glenn-Geimhin.

Ainmire, son of Sedna, son of Fergus Long-head, son of Conall [575] Gulban, son of Niall of the Nine Hostages, [reigned] three years, until he fell by Fergus, son of Neillin.

d Baedan, son of Ninneadh, son of Fergus Long-head, [reigned] [*st.* 585] a year, until he fell in an encounter by two Cumaines, namely, Cumaine, son of Colman the Little and Cumaine Librenc, son of Illadhan, son of Cerball.

[d] Aeḋ, mac Ainmireḋ, mic Seḋna, trí bliaḋna rícet, co torċair la Dranḋu, mac Eaċaċ, i caṫ Ḋuin-ḃolḋ. Ocur ir do'n caṫ rin ḋoċan in fili ro:

[Ir] a m-buaḋ
Fearair in tonn frirín m-bruaḋ:
Aḋfet rcéla, ceru rciṫ,
Aeḋ, mac Ainmireḋ, do ḋiṫ.

Aeḋ Slaine (Aoḋ Ḋurtan, comḋalta Conaill Ḋutḃinḋ 7 baetġal bile rormarḋ), mac Ḋiarmaḋa, mic Feaḋura Cearrḃeoil, mic Conaill Crematainḋ, mic Neill Nae-ḋiallaiḋ, ocur Colman Rimiḋ, mac baeḋa[i]n Briḋiḋ, mic Muircertaiḋ, mic Muireḋaiḋ, mic Eoḋain, mic Neill Nae-ḋiallaiḋ, reċt bliaḋna, co torċratar la Conall n-Ḋhuṫḃinḋ, mac Suiḃne. Ḋia n-eaḃraḋ:

Niar'ḋo enert a tarrle
Do na hoḋaiḃ a Ċhuirḃe,—
Conall, roḃí Aeḋ Slaine;
Aeḋ Slaine, roḃi Suiḃne.

e Ḋoroċair, ḋino, Colman Rimhe la Loḋan Ḋilmana. Ut ḋictum ert:

P. 49a
Ceḋu riḋi, cetḋu reċt,
Ceḋu nert for riḋraḋa;
Eniḋ Colman Rimiḋ rí,
Romḃi Loḋan Ḋilmana.

Aeḋ Uairioḋnaċ, mac Ḋomnaill, mic Muircertaiḋ, mic Muireḋaiḋ, oct m-ḃliaḋna, co n-erḃailt.

Maelcoba, Clereaċ, mac Aeḋa, mic Ainmireḋ, trí bliaḋna, co torċair i caṫ Sleḃe Belḋaḋain Ṫoḋa, la Suiḃne Menn.

Suiḃne Meanḋ, mac Fiacraċ, mic Feraḋaiḋ, mic Eoḋain, trí bliaḋna ḋeḋ, co torċair la Conḋal Caeċ, mac Scannla[i]n.

Ḋomnall, mac Aeḋa, mic Ainmireḋ, triċa ḃliaḋan, ocur ḋ'eḋ aḋḃat.

Aed, son of Ainmire, son of Sedna, [reigned] three years [and] [**d**] twenty, until he fell by Brandub, son of Eochu, in the battle of [A.D. 598] Dun-Bolg. And it is of that battle sang the poet this [verse]:

> [It is] in Buach
> Strikes the wave against the brink:
> Tidings tell, though it is tribulation,
> That Aedh, son of Ainmire, has perished [*lit.* to perish].

Aed of Slaine (Aed Gustan, foster-brother of Conall Sweet-voice [604] and Baethgal Bile that killed him), son of Diarmaid, son of Fergus Wry-mouth, son of Conall Cremthainn, son of Niall of the Nine Hostages and Colman Rimidh, son of Baedan Brighidh, son of Muircertach, son of Muiredach, son of Eogan, son of Niall of the Nine Hostages, [reigned] seven years, until they fell by Conall Sweet-voice, son of Suibne. Of which was said:

> It was not weak what happened
> To the youths from Tuirbe,—
> Conall, slew he Aed of Slaine,
> Aedh of Slaine, slew he Suibne.

e Howbeit, Colman Rimidh fell by Logan Dilmana. As hath been said:

> Natheless kingship, natheless right,
> Natheless sway over kings,
> Nought [is] Colman Rimidh, the king,
> Him slew Logan Dilmana.

Aedh Uairidhnach, son of Domnall, son of Muircertach, son of [612] Muiredach, [reigned] eight years, until he died [a natural death].

Maelcoba, the Cleric, son of Aedh, son of Ainmire, [reigned] three [615] years, until he fell in the battle of the Mountain of Belgadan-Togha by Suibne Menn.

Suibne Menn, son of Fiachra, son of Feradhach, son of Eogan, [628] [reigned] three years [and] ten, until he fell by Congal Blind[-eye], son of Scannlan.

Domnall, son of Aedh, son of Ainmire, [reigned] thirty [! thir- [642] teen] years and of [natural] death died he.

[e]   Ceallaċ ocuṗ Conall, ḋa mac Maelcoḃa Clepiċ, mic Aeḋa, mic Ainmiṗeċ, cuiġ bliaḋna ḋeġ ḋoiḃ. D'eġ aḃḃat Cellaċ iṗin ḃṗuġ-mic-inn-o[i]ġ. Ḋoṗocaiṗ Conall Cael la Ḋiaṗmaiḋ, mac Aeḋa Slaine.

Blaṫmac ocuṗ Ḋiaṗmaiḋ, ḋa mac Aeḋa Slaine, mic Ḋiaṗmaḋa, ḋ'ec aḃḃaṫaḋaṗ,—ḋo'n ḃuiḋi Connaill.

f Seaċnaṗaċ, mac Blaṫmic, mic Aeḋa Slaine, ṗeċt m-bliaḋna, co toṗċaiṗ la Ḋu[ḃ]ḋuin, ṗi Coṗṗṗi.

Cenḋṗaelaċ, mac Blaṫmic, mic Aeḋa Slaine, ceiṫṗi bliaḋna, co toṗċaiṗ la Ḟinaċta Ḟleaḋaċ i cat Ailċealtṗa.

Ḟinaċta Ḟleġaċ, mac Ḋunċaḋa, mic Aeḋa Slaine, ṗiċe bliaḋan, co toṗċaiṗ la h-Aeġ, mac n-Ḋluṫaiġ, i n-Ġṗallaiġ Ḋollaiṫ.

Loinġṗeaċ Laṁṗoḋa, mac Aenġuṗa, mic Ḋomnaill, mic Aeḋa, oċt m-bliaḋna, co toṗċaiṗ la Cellaċ Laċa-Cimi, mac Raġallaiġ, hi cat Ċoṗainḋ.

Conġal Cinḋmaġaiṗ, mac Ḟeṗġuṗa Ḟanaḋ, mic Ḋomnaill, mic Aeḋa, nae m-bliaḋna, co toṗċaiṗ ḋo ḃiġ aen uaiṗe.

Ḟeaṗġal, mac Maelaḋuin, mic Maeliṗiṫṗi, mic Aeḋa Uaiṗiḋnaiġ, mic Ḋomnaill Ilċealġaiġ, mic Muiṗceṗtaiġ, mic Muṗeḋaiġ, ṗeċt m-bliaḋna ḋeġ, co toṗċaiṗ la Muṗċaḋ, mac Ḃṗoin, hi cat Almaine.

Ḟaġaṗtaċ, mac Neill, mic Ceṗnaiġ Soṫail, mic Ḋiaṗmaḋa, mic Aeḋa Slaine, bliaḋain, co toṗċaiṗ i cat Cinḋḋelġa, la Cinaiṫ, mac Iṗġalaiġ.

g Cinaeṫ, mac Iṗġalaiġ, mic Conainġ, mic Conġaile, mic Aeḋa Slaine, ceiṫṗi bliaḋna, co toṗċaiṗ i cat Ḋṗoma Cṗocain (no Coṗcain), la Ḟlaiṫḃeṗtaċ, maċ Loinġṗiġ.

Ḟlaiṫḃeṗtaċ, mac Loinġṗiġ Laṁṗoḋa, ṗeċt m-bliaḋna, co n-eṗḃailt a n-Aṗḋ-Mhaċa ḋia ṗuil.

Aeḋ Allan, mac Ḟeṗġail, mic Maelaḋuin, nae bliaḋna, co toṗċaiṗ [i cat] Seṗeġ Maiġe, eteṗ ḋa Ṫeḃṫa, iḋon, a Cenanḋuṗ, la Ḋomnall, mac Muṗċaḋa.

Ḋomnall, mac Muṗċaḋa, mic Ḋiaṗmaḋa, mic Aiṗmeḋaiġ caiċ, mic Conaill Ġuṫḃinḋ, mic Suiḃne, mic Colmain moiṗ,

Ceallach[1] and Conall[2], two sons of Maelcoba, the Cleric, son of [e] Aedh, son of Ainmire, five years [and] ten [were reigned] by them. [A.D. 658] Of [natural] death died Cellach in Brugh-mic-in-oig. Conall the[2] [654] Slender fell by Diarmaid, son of Aedh of Slaine.

Blathmac and Diarmaid, two sons of Aedh of Slaine, son of [665] Diarmaid, of [natural] death they died,—of the Yellow Plague.

f Seachnasach, son of Blathmacc, son of Aedh of Slaine, [reigned] [671] seven years, until he fell by Dubduin, king of Coirpre.

Cendfaelach, son of Blathmac, son of Aedh of Slaine, [reigned] [675] four years, until he fell by Finachta the Festive in the battle of Ailchealtair.

Finachta the Festive, son of Dunchadh, son of Aedh of Slaine, [695] [reigned] twenty years, until he fell by Aedh, son of Dluthach, in Grellach-Dollaith.

Loingsech Long-hand, son of Aengus, son of Domnall, son of [703] Aedh, [reigned] eight years, until he fell by Cellach of Loch Cime, son of Ragallach, in the battle of Corann.

Congal of Cennmagair, son of Fergus of Fanad, son of Domnall, [710] son of Aedh, [reigned] nine years, until he perished of a fit of one hour.

Feargal, son of Maelduin, son of Maelfithri, son of Aedh Uairidh- [722] nach, son of Domnall of the many wiles, son of Muircertach, son of Muiredach, [reigned] seven years [and] ten, until he fell by Murchadh, son of Bron, in the battle of Almain.

Fogartach, son of Niall, son of Cernach the Proud, son of Diar- [724] maid, son of Aedh of Slaine, [reigned] a year, until he fell in the battle of Cenndelga, by Cinaeth, son of Irgalach.

g Cinaeth, son of Irgalach, son of Conang, son of Congal, son of [728] Aedh of Slaine, [reigned] four years, until he fell in the battle of Druim-Crocain (or, -Corcain), by Flaithbertach, son of Loingsech.

Flaithbertach, son of Loingsech Long-hand, [reigned] seven years, [734] until he died in Armagh of hæmorrhage [*lit.*, of his blood]. [*ob.*765]

Aedh Allan, son of Fergal, son of Maelduin, [reigned] nine years, [743] until he fell [in the battle] of Seredh-Magh, between the two Tebhthas, namely, in Kells, by Domnall, son of Murchadh.

Domnall, son of Murchadh, son of Airmedach Blind[-eye], son of [763] Conall Sweet-voice, son of Suibne, son of Colman the Great, son of

[g] mic Diarmada, mic Fergura Cerrbeoil, rice bliadan, co n-erbailt.

Niall Frarrac, mac Fergaili, rect m-bliadna, co n-erbailt i n-hI Colum Cille. Tri frarra le [a] gein, idon, frar airgid gil (idon, for [Fh]otain móir), ocur frar cruitnecta (idon, for [Fh]otain m-big), ocur frar fola (idon, for Glendlaigen). Inde dicitur Niall Frarrac.

Donncad, mac Domnaill, mic Murcada, rect m-bliadna ricet, co torcair i cat Droma-Rig la hAed Ua Neill.

Aed Oirdnide, mac Neill Frarraig, rect m-bliadna ricet, co torcair ic At-da-Fherta, la Mael-Canaig.

Concobur, mac Doncada, ceitri bliadna deg, co n-erbailt.

h Niall Cailli, mac Aeda Oirnide, ceitri bliadna deg, cor'baided a Callaind.

Mael-Sedlainn, mac Maelruanaig, mic Doncada, mic Domnaill, mic Murcada, re bliadna deg, co n-erbailt.

Aed Findliat, mac Neill Cailli, rect m-bliadna deg, co n-erbailt ig Druim-inarclaind.

Flann, mac Mael-Sedlainn, mic Maelruanaig, oct m-bliadna tricat, co torcair.

Niall Glundub, mac Aeda Findleit, tri bliadna, co torcair i cat Ata-cliat la Gallaib.

Doncad, mac Flaind, mic Mael-Shedlainn, mic Maelruanaig, m'c Donbcada, mic Domnaill, rice bliadan, co n-e[r]bailt.

P. 49 b Congalac, mac Maelmitig, mic Flannaga[i]n, mic Cellaig, mic Congalaig, mic Conaing Cuirrig, mic Amalgada, mic Congalaig, mic Conaing, mic Congail, mic Aeda Slaine, deic m-bliadna, co torcair la Gallaib Ata-cliat og Taig Giugrand.

Domnall, mac Muircertaig, mic Neill Glunduib, cuig bliadna ricet, co n-erbailt a n-Ard-Maca.

Mael-Sedlainn, mac Domnaill, mic Donncada, mic Flainn, mic Mael-Sedlainn, mic Maelruanaig, tri bliadna deg.

BOOK OF BALLYMOTE. 405

Diarmaid, son of Fergus Wry-mouth, [reigned] twenty years, until [g]
he died [a natural death]. [A.D.]

Niall the Showery, son of Fergal, [reigned] seven years, until he [769]
died in I[ona] of Colum-cille. Three showers [fell] at his birth: to wit,
a shower of pure [*lit.*, white] silver (namely, upon Great Fothan) and
a shower of wheat (namely, upon Little Fothan) and a shower of blood
(namely, upon Glenn-Laigen). Hence is said *Niall the Showery.*

Donnchad, son of Domnall, son of Murchadh, [reigned] seven [797]
years [and] twenty, until he fell in the battle of Druim-Righ by
Aedh Ua Neill.

Aedh Oirdnide, son of Niall the Showery, [reigned] seven years [819]
[and] twenty, until he fell at Ath-da-fherta by Mael-Canaigh.

Concobur, son of Donnchad, [reigned] four years [and] ten, until [833]
he died [a natural death].

h Niall Cailli, son of Aedh Oirdnide, [reigned] four years [and] [846]
ten, until he was drowned in the Callan.

Mael-Sechlainn, son of Maelruanaigh, son of Donchadh, son of [863]
Domnall, [reigned] six years [and] ten, until he died [a natural
death].

Aedh Fair-gray, son of Niall Cailli, [reigned] seven years [and] [879]
ten, until he died [a natural death] in Druim-inasclainn.

Flann, son of Mael-Sechlainn, son of Maelruanaigh, [reigned] [916]
eight years [and] thirty, until he fell [in battle].

Niall Black-knee, son of Aedh Fair-gray, [reigned] three years, [919]
until he fell in the battle of Dublin by the Foreigners.

Donnchad, son of Flann, son of Mael-Sechlainn, son of Mael- [944]
ruanaigh, son of Donnchad, son of Domnall, [reigned] twenty years,
until he died [a natural death].

Congalach, son of Maelmithigh, son of Flannagan, son of Cellach, [956]
son of Conang Cuirrech, son of Amalgadh, son of Congalach, son of
Conang, son of Congal, son of Aedh of Slaine, [reigned] ten years,
until he fell by the Foreigners of Dublin at Tech-Giughrann.

Domnall, son of Muircertach, son of Niall Black-knee, [reigned] [980]
five years [and] twenty, until he died [a natural death] in Armagh.

Mael-Sechlainn, son of Domnall, son of Donnchad, son of Flann, [1003]
son of Mael-Sechlainn, son of Maelruanaigh, [reigned] three years
[and] ten [*recte*, twenty, until he was dethroned by Brian Boruma].

Lebar baili in mota.

i brian boroṁa, mac Ceinbetiġ, mic Lorcain, mic Laċtna, mic Cuirc, mic Anluain, ba bliaḋain beġ, co torċair illaiġniḃ, la Ġallaiḃ Aṫa-cliaṫ i ġ[-C]luain-tarḃ.

Mael-Seclainn iterum irriġi Erenn nae m-bliaḋna, co n-erbailt i Cro-inir Loċa hAinbinḃi, iar m-buaiḋ aiṫriġi. Romeabaḋar cuiġ caṫa riċet reime, iḋon, riċe caṫ for Ġaeḋelaiḃ ocur a cuiġ for Ġallaiḃ: iḋon, caṫ Eḋair ocur caṫ Imḋain, caṫ Ruir, caṫ Raṫin, caṫ Luaċra, caṫ Lirluġeċ, caṫ Mortain, caṫ Muincille, caṫ Mulla, caṫ Finḃi, caṫ Forurorna, caṫ Feabṫa, caṫ Febḋa, caṫ Droma-Emna, caṫ Raṫa-Carman, caṫ Main, caṫ Maiġe-Manḋaċt, caṫ Ḋomnaiġ, caṫ Ḋuma, caṫ imMaiġ-cuma, caṫ Ṫemra. Ḋa caṫ Aṫa-cliaṫ. Mor maḋan [*lege* maiḋm] Aṫa-buiḋe. Ir biḃrin roċan in renċaiḋ:

> Cu[i]ġ caṫa Ġall roḋurḃrir,
> Ḋar lem, ni heċtra ainrir;
> Liṗi, leir aḋbaṫ a bu;
> Riċe caṫ for Ġaeḋealu.

j Ir e rin ri beḋenaċ Erenn. Ar, cia armit fairenḋ eter riġaiḃ Erenn ḋreim, ni raġaiḃ hErinn amal oen rainḋ bia eireoṁ, cen coiceḋ no a ḋo 'n-a ectmair. Ocur arai boberar irreim riġraiḋi cib ri co frerraḃra, minibe irreim riġraiḋi na riġ co frearaḃra. Maḋ bo Leṫ Moġo, imorro, ber, ni heḃarṫar ri Erenn frir co raiḃ Leṫ Moġa uili ocur Ṫemair co n-a tuaṫaiḃ ocur in b-ara coiceḋ bo Leṫ Cuinḋ occa.

Complaiṫur for Erinn fri re ba bliaḋan.

Ṫoirrḋelḃaċ, mac Ṫaiḋġ, mic brian boroma, ba bliaḋain beġ, ri co frerraḃra.

Ṫorrḋelḃaċ, mac Ruaiḋri na raiḋi buiḋi, mic Aeḋa in ġa bernaiġ, mic Ṫaiḋġ in eiċ ġil, mic Caṫail, mic Concoḃuir, mic Ṫaiḋġ, mic Caṫail, mic Concoḃuir, mic Ṫaiḋġ moir, mic

1 Brian Boromha, son of Ceinnetech, son of Lorcan, son of Lachtna, [A.D. 1014] son of Corc, son of Anluan, [reigned] two years [and] ten, until he fell in Leinster by the Foreigners of Dublin, in Clontarf.

Mael-Sechlainn again in the kingship of Ireland [for] nine years, [1022] until he died in Cro-inis of Loch Ainninn, after victory of Penance. There were won five battles [and] twenty by him upon the Gaidhil and five upon Foreigners: to wit, the battle of Edar and the battle of Imdan, the battle of Ros, the battle of Rathen, the battle of Luachair, the battle of Lis-lugech, the battle of Mortan, the battle of Muincille, the battle of Mulla, the battle of Findi, the battle of Fordruim, the battle of Feabait, the battle of Febaid, the battle of Druim-Emna, the battle of Rath-Carman, the battle of Man, the battle of Magh-Mandacht, the battle of Domnach, the battle of Dum, the battle in Magh-Cuma, the battle of Tara, the two battles of Dublin, the great rout of Yellow Ford. It is of those sang the historian:

> Five battles against Foreigners broke he them,
> Seems to me, it is not an achievement unknown:
> Liphe, by him perished its sway;
> Twenty battles [broke he] over the Gaedhil.

J It is he [that was] last king of Ireland. For, although some reckon others amongst the kings of Ireland, they did not possess Ireland as a whole after him, without a province or two being left out. And, nevertheless, there is mentioned in the roll of kings even a "king with opposition." [But this should not be] unless in the roll of "kings with opposition." Now, if [the king] be from the Half of Mogh, *king of Ireland* is not applied to him, until he has the whole Half of Mogh and Tara with its territories and the second Fifth of the Half of Conn.

Joint sovereignty over Ireland for the space of two years.

Toirrdelbach, son of Tadhg, son of Brian Boroma, [reigned] two [1086] years [and] ten, "a king with opposition."

Toirrdelbach, son of Ruaidhri of the Yellow Hound, son of Aedh [1156] of the Gapped Spear, son of Tadhg of the White Steed, son of Cathal, son of Concobur, son of Tadhg, son of Cathal, son of Concobur, son of Tadhg the Great, son of Muirges, son of Tomaltach, son of Murgail,

[j] Muirgerra, mic Tomaltaig, mic Muirgaili, mic Indrectaig, mic Muiredaig Muilletain, o tat Sil Muiredaig, fiche bliadan do irrigi n-Erenn ⁊ ceathracha bliadan irrigi Connact.

Ruaidri, mac Torrdelbaig moir, mic Ruaidri na raidi buidi, mic Aeda in ga bernaig.

Ir do flaithuraib na rig rin ocur dia n-aidegaib rocan in fili in duanra deir-creidmig, idon, Gilla Modubda. Ocur dall clairinech eiride. Ocur nir'chan go, na claen-renchair riam.

1.

k Eri og, inir na naem,
Commad riagail rocaem,
Rogabrat géinde garba,
Gan reilgi, gan rotarba.

2.

Trica ri 'r a beith fo beich,
Ocur reirer gu rairbrech,
Re creidim, gan creidim cruaid,
Rogabrat Erinn armruaid.

3.

A rimad, co n-gal ir chat,
Na n-deigrig croda, corcrach,
Doread gaire gaile,
O Slaini go Laegaire.

4.

O Laegaire laecda n-gluind
Co Mael—erianzalach—Sechlainn,
Rogabrat banba na m-brad
Oct ri chalma ceathrachat.

BOOK OF BALLYMOTE. 409

son of Indrectach, son of Muiredach Broad-head, from whom are the [J]
Sil-Muiredaigh, twenty years [were spent] by him in the kingship of
Ireland and forty years in the kingship of Connacht. [A.D.]
Ruaidhri, son of Toirrdelbach the Great, son of Ruaidhri of the [1198]
Yellow Hound, son of Aedh of the Gapped Spear [reigns at present].

It is of the reigns of those kings [who reigned] and of their
deaths sang the poet, namely, Gilla Modubhda, this post-Faith poem.
And blind [and] flat-faced [was] this person. And he sang not false
or misleading history ever.

1.

k Ireland pure, isle of Saints,
Very distinguished preserver of rule,
Rough gentiles occupied [it],
Without reverence, without much advantage.

2.

Thirty kings and ten by ten [130],
And six, according to correct judgment,
Before the Faith, without Faith austere,
Possessed they bright-landed Ireland.

3.

The [*lit.* their] recital, with feat and battle,
Of the good kings courageous, victorious,
Causes the joy of valour,
From Slaine [*supra*, p. 150 d] to Loeghaire.

4.

From Laeghaire of heroic vigour [462]
To Mael-Sechlainn notably valorous, [1022]
There possessed Banba of the spoils
Eight noble kings [and] forty.

5.

P. 50a [**k**]   Ceatpap, coic coic, do pigaib,
Dočuadap a n-dpočbilaib:
Nae pi bec ppi gaine n-gapt,
Puapadap eg pe hadapt.

6.

Tuipmeam peimip gač pig peig,
A ainm 'p a oibib agbeil;
Map adbepaid buidni ap beipt
Mapaid im' cuimni compeipt.

1.

1   Ceipt tpiča bliadan bloide,
A lanpeimip Loegaipe;
Puaip bap o'n gpein gleitig gpind,
Tpe bpečip tpein i[n] Tailgind.

2.

Rocač Oilill Molt o'n Muaid
Piče bliadan po bitbuaid;
Ropmugaig tpe glonn n-gaile
Lugaid lonn, mac Laegaipe.

3.

Lugaid, coic bliadna pa cuig,
I n-Ačad-[Fh]apča puaip upčoid:
Gup'lopc papča teneđ tenn
Plait na neimeđ 'p na naemčell.

4.

Mupčeptac, pa calma a cet,
Re ceitpi m-bliadan pičet:
A Cleiteč caid, a dil De,
Robaid pin, poloipc tene.

5.

[k] Four [and] five [by] five kings,
They went into ill fates : [fewness—
Nine kings [and] ten—pre-eminence in [*lit.* respecting]
Found death on the pillow.

6.

Recount we the duration of each king generous,
His name and his notable death ;
As many tell our account,
It lives in my memory equally strong.

1.

I Just thirty blooming years, [A.D.]
[Was] his full duration, Loegaire's ; [462]
Death received he from the brilliant piercing sun, [Patrick].
Through the powerful word of the Shaved-Head [St.

2.

Spent Oilill Molt from the Muaidh [482]
Twenty years in constant victory ;
Him destroyed through fierceness of valour
Lugaidh the vehement, son of Laeghaire.

3.

Lugaidh, five years by five [reigned he], [507]
In Achadh-Farcha received he [mortal] injury :
So that a powerful bolt of fire burned
The chief of the shrines and of the holy churches.

4.

Muircertach, courageous was his disposition, [534]
A space of four years [and] twenty [reigned he] :
In Cleitech pleasant, by dispensation of God,
Wine drowned, fire burned [him].

5.

[1] Tuatal Maelgarb, tren a trer,
Tri bliadna dec gan dimer:
Mael-morda, forgeodain d'a gaib,—
Flait rogab Temair tondbain.

6.

Diarmaid, da deic ir bliadain,
Mac Cerbaill, co caempiagail:
Aed dub darm rocoirc, rocraid,
Romarb, roloirc, roluabaid.

1.

m bliadain, da bliadain, adclor,
Do deg Domnall ir d' Forgur:
Marb ri na tiri catang,
Da mac mine Muircertaig.

2.

Eocaid ir baedan brige,
Da bliadain a m-blatrige;
Rurbi gan diadact in bam,
Ri rogab 'Ciannact, Cronan.

3.

Ainmire, mac Sedna raer,
Tri bliadna a flatur lancaem:
Go derb, mar do derbur dib,
Romarb Fergur, mac Nellin.

4.

Aen bliadain baedan gan bed,
Mac Nindeda na naemtet:
Rorrarraig forlond co n-aib,
A comlond cruaid da Cumain.

5.

[1] Tuathal Bald-rough, strong his sway,   [A.D.] [544]
Three years [and] ten [reigned he] without contempt:
Mael-mordha [mortally] wounded him with his spears,—
The chief that ruled fair-foundationed Tara.

6.

Diarmaid, two tens and a year [reigned he]   [565]
Son of Wry-mouth, with fair rule:
Aedh the Black checked, embittered,
Killed [and] burned [him] . . .

1.

m   A year, two years, it hath been heard,   [567]
[Were reigned] by good Domnall and by Fergus:
Dead [by natural death were] the peaceable kings of the
The two sons mild of Muircertach.   [territories,

2.

Eochaidh and Baedan Brige,   [572]
Two years [were they] in flourishing kingship:
Slew them without ruth ..
The king that possessed Ciannachta, Cronan.

3.

Ainmire, noble son of Sedna,   [575]
Three years [was] his sovranty full-fair:
Certainly, as I have certified to ye,
Slew [him] Fergus, son of Nellin.

4.

One year [reigned] Baedan without evil,   [sl. 585]
Son of Ninnedh of the holy designs:
Defeat overtook him with [good] reasons,
In the severe combat of the two Cumaines.

5.

[m] D'Aeḋ, mac Ainmíreċ, romḃeaḋ
Tri bliaḋna fira fiċet:
I caṫ bealaiġ Duín-bolġ buain
Aḃḃaṫ a orḃ re haenuair.

6.

Aeḋ Slaine is Colman Rímíḋ,
Tri bliaḋna do'n dis diris:
Fuair Colman na creċ a ġuin
'Mon teċ, iġ Loġan Ḋilmain.

1.

n Loṫ Aeḋa Slaine, ba raeḋ,
La Conall n-Ġuṫbind n-ġlecaeṁ:
Fínġal moċ nir'ḃenta de,
Ar Loċ feġḋa Seimḃiġe.

2.

Aeḋ Uairiḋnaċ i n-a ṫiġ,
Mac Domnaill, mic Muirċertaiġ:
Ri na reċtraċ co riaġail,
Aḃḃaṫ iar reċt raerbliaḋnaiḃ.

3.

Tri bliaḋna, bliaḋain nama,
Roċaiṫ Mael-croḋa-coḃa:
Rocraid ġle re Ua Cuind 'rin ċaṫ
Ar lar Sleḃe-truiṁ-Toġaḋ.

4.

Tri bliaḋna dec Suibni fenġ
I n-arḋflaṫur na hErenn:
Rororbaḋ in ġaeṫ ġan ġai
La Conġal caeċ i m-Ḃrenlas.

5.

[A.D.]

[m]   To Aedh, son of Ainmire, were assigned   [598]
      Three [and] twenty righteous years :
      In the battle of the Pass of firm Dun-bolg
      Perished his dignity in one hour.

6.

Aedh of Slaine and Colman Rimidh,   [604]
Three years for the twain just :
Colman of the forays got his [mortal] wound
Near the [i.e. his] house from Logan Dilmana.

1.

n   The [mortal] injury of Aedh of Slaine, it was treacherous,
      By Conall Sweet-voice, the bright-fair [inflicted] :
      Early fratricide was not done thereby,
      On stately Lake Seimdige.

2.

Aedh Uairidhnach, in his house,   [612]
Son of Domnall, son of Muircertach,
The king of just securities [and] of [*lit.*, with] rule,
Died he after seven noble years.

3.

Three years [and] a year only,   [615]
Spent Maelcobha the courageous :   [battle,
Vanished [his] renown by the descendant of Conn in the
On the centre of sombre Mount Togadh.

4.

Three years [and] ten [reigned] Suibne the Slender   [628]
In arch-sovranty of Ireland :
Consummated was the wise one without a dart
By Congal Blind[-eye] in Brenlai.

5.

[n] Deich m-bliadna Domnaill na n-dat,
Gu n-gleo n-gaibtech i n[-dag?]rat:
A rect iar red cruaid a cli,
Co fuair eg in n-aithrigi.

6.

Gabrat meic Maelcoba cruaid
Sé bliadna dec fa degbuaid:
Conall cael ir Cellach car,
ba cromhbaing caem a compagur.

1.

o Cellach, d'eg, duaber olc ann,
Darurfarraig fucht abann:
dar Cona[i]ll cetna na celg
La Diarmaid dedla, n-dredderg.

2.

Diarmaid, mac Aeda na n-dam,
'S a bratair, Blathmac bithnar,
Ocht m-bliadna or banba cu m-bloid,
Gu rurmarba do'n mortlaith.

3.

Mac Blathmich, Sechnarach ruairc,
Bliadain 'r a coic do caemcuairt:
Dubduin Dun-Cairpri cuireach,
Rug run airgne in t-ard ruireach.

4.

[MS. illegible.]
Cuid Cindfaelaid, mic Crunnmael,
Crad Cindfaelaid in fmachta
Do faemad la Finnachta.

5.

[n] Ten [were] the years of Domnall of the . . .   [642]
With dangerous contention in [good] luck :
Seven [years] on a hard way [was] his destiny [?]
Until received he death in pilgrimage.

6.

The sons of Maelcoba severe took [the kingship]
Six years [and] ten with prosperous sway :
Conall the Slender and Cellach the Ringletted,
A coincidence fair was their relationship.

1.

o Cellach, died he, wretched ill [was] therein,   [658]
When a sudden fit seized him :
The death of Conall of the wiles [was inflicted]   [654]
By Diarmaid brave, bright-visaged.

2.

Diarmaid, son of Aedh of the retinues,   [665]
And his brother, Blathmac the ever noble,
Eight years [reigned they] over Banba with renown,
Until they were killed by the Mortality.

3.

The son of Blathmac, Sechnasach the excellent,   [671]
A year and five [were spent by him] in fair circuit :
Dubduin the hostful of Dun-Cairpri [slew him],
Designed destruction took [off] the arch ruler.

4.

[Four years, they were]   [675]
The portion of Cennfaelad, son of Crunnmael :
The ruin of Cennfaelad of the sway
Was inflicted by Finnachta.

5.

[o] Finḋaċta Fleaḃaċ, in oil,
Seċt m-bliaḋna or cornaiḃ comoil,
Ɣur'porḃaḋ rael na [morrleḋ?]
La hAeḋ ir la Conɣalaċ.

6.

Oċt m-bliaḋna co m-briɣ n-ɣorra
Loinɣriɣ moir, mic Aenɣura,
Ɣur'ṫoit 'n-a crobainɣ 'ran caṫ,
A troiḋ Corainḃ, la Cellaċ.

1.

p   Conɣal Cinḋmaɣair, maiṫ main,
     Oċt m-bliaḋna or banba blaṫċaim:
     Ɣan caṫ, ɣan craḋ ar in maiɣ,
P. 50 b   Aṫbaṫ ḋo ṫaṁ tromɣalair.

2.

Deiċ m-bliaḋna ɣan blaḋ meabla,
Tarraiɣ Ferɣal rlaiṫemna:
bar riɣ, raraḋblaḋ roiṁe,
I caṫ aḋbul Almaine.

3.

Aen bliaḋain Fhaɣartaċ rlaiṫ,
Ɣur'ṁarḃ Cinaeṫ caemḃaiṫ:
Flaiṫberṫaċ ilaiḃ ṗiaḋnaċ,
Romarḃ Cinaeṫ tribliaḋnaċ.

4.

Nae m-bliaḋna cruaiḋi, coimriɣ,
Flaiṫberṫaċ, mac laeċ Loinɣriɣ:
bar ḋo'n ɣarɣ raṫa riaṁaċ,
A n-Arḋ-Maċa morṗiaḋnaċ.

5.

[o] Finnachta the Festive, of the liquor,   [A.D.] [695]
Seven years [reigned he] over drinking-horns,
Until was ended the generous of [the great feasts]
By Aedh and by Congalach.

6.

Eight years with force of valour   [703]
[Were those] of Loingsech the Great, son of Aengus,
Until fell he destroyed in the battle,
In the conflict of Corann, by Cellach.

1.

p   Congal of Cennmagair, good the treasure,   [710]
Eight years [reigned he] over Banba fair-famed:
Without battle, without destruction, on the plain,
Died he of illness of heavy disease.

2.

Ten years without deceptive fame   [722]
Continued Ferghal the princely:
Death of a king, as was died before [him],
[Died he] in the mighty battle of Almain.

3.

One year [reigned] Fogartach, the chief,   [724]
Until killed [him] Cinaeth of the fair complexion:
Flaithbertach of many bands,
Slew he the three-yeared [king] Cinaeth.   [728]

4.

Nine years strict, peaceable,   [734]
[Reigned] Flaithbertach, heroic son of Loingsech:
Death [came to him] from the severe . . .
In Armagh of the great hosts.

5.

[p] 'S e pata piamać d'a puil,
bap Plaitbeptaiჳ, mic Loinჳriჳ :
A pual dudpeჳ ip a pí,
De tainiჳ a tiuჳlaiti.

6.

Aed Allan, nae bliadna in mep,
Co dopcaip ap Maჳ Shepeд,
Ⴣup'toit i comlonn cata,
La Domnall, mac Mupcada.

1.

q Domnall, mac Mupcada, iaptain,
Da nae m-bliadna ip bliadain,
'N-a betaiд, ჳan бeд, ჳan col,
Co n-decaiд eჳ 'n-a aenup.

2.

Niall Fpappać, mac pind Peჳail,
Sett m-bliadna ჳan baetepnail :
Abbat ჳan lott pup lite,
Ap dott d'l d'a ailitpe.

3.

Donnćad ჳan doipći n-bata,
Mac Domnaill, mic Mupcada,
Iap tpi nae bliadnaiд abbat,
Ri ჳu piaჳail ip cu popat.

4.

Aed Opnidi du'n peim pait,
Sett bliadna picet ba pipmait:
Fpit pat a [p]letta pe luaჳ
Ic At-da-pepta innpuap.

BOOK OF BALLYMOTE. 421

5.

[p] It is . . . from his blood [A.D.]
[Was] the death of Flaithbertach, son of Loingsech : [ob. 765]
His urine flowed [continuously] and his . .
From it came his last day.

6.

Aed Allan, nine years [was] the [allotted] span, [743]
Until fell he on Magh-Seredh,
Until fell he in conflict of battle,
By Domnall, son of Murchadh.

1.

q Domnall, son of Murchadh, afterwards, [763]
Twice nine years and a year [reigned he]
Alive [as king] without injury, without crime,
Until died he when he was alone.

2.

Niall the Showery, fair son of Fergal, [769]
Seven years [reigned he] without foolish deed :
He died without fault upon [his] renown,
After going to I[ona] on his pilgrimage.

3.

Donnchadh without obscurity of colour, [797]
Son of Domnall, son of Murchadh,
After thrice nine years died he,
A king of rule and of very good luck.

4.

Aedh Oirnidi of the prosperous course, [819]
Seven [and] twenty years was he truly good :
Found he the cause of his destruction justly
At very bleak "Ford of two Graves."

5.

[q] Aireṁ ceitri bliaḋan ḋeg,
Do Conċobur ba caeṁ geg:
Aḋbaṫ, iar m-borrfaḋ ḋ'a clainn,
Mac do Ḋonnċaḋ, mac Domnaill.

6.

Tri bliaḋna deg immaille
Rofaemaḋ Niall caem Caille:
O'n Challainn calma furcraiḋ,
Fuair tallaind anma ardaiġ.

1.

r   Mael-Seclainn, re bliaḋna dec,
Mac Maelruanaiġ na riġreḋ:
Aḋbaṫ tall a Miḋe Muaiḋ
Flaiṫ ar ḟine 'r ar find sluaġ.

2.

Aeḋ Findliaṫ, feindiġ, oiliġ,
A ré dec re n-ḋian oiḋiḋ,
bar riġ na faḋuan gan rind
A n-Ḋruim aḋḟuair indarclaind.

3.

Nae bliaḋna triċat ba tren
Flann Foḋla gan eterlen:
Marb i Taillṫin tall do ṫaṁ,
Eter cairdib Clainn Colma[i]n.

4.

Niall Ġlunduḃ, mac Aeḋa in oil,
Tri bliaḋna do Neill nertmoir,
I n-Aṫ-cliaṫ luiḋ fo lamnaiḃ,
Liaċ a guin do Ġlargallaiḃ.

5.

[q]   A reckoning of four years [and] ten,   [A.D.]
     For Concobar it was a fair division :   [833]
     Died, after exaltation for his family,
     The son of Donnchadh, son of Domnall.

6.

Three years [and] ten consecutively   [846]
Was Niall Caille the fair received [as king] :
By the powerful Callan was he destroyed,
Received he the deprivation of his lofty soul.

1.

r   Mael-Sechlainn, six years [and] ten [reigned he],   [863]
    Son of Maelruanaigh of the royal ways :
    Died he yonder in Mide of the Muaidh,
    The chief of our sept and of our fair hosts.

2.

Aedh Fair-gray, warlike, noble,   [879]
Six [years and] ten [reigned he] before [his] swift death,
The death of the king [happened] without a spear[-wound],
In very bleak Druim-inasclainn.

3.

Nine years [and] thirty was powerful   [916]
Flann Fodla without an interval :
Died he in Telltown yonder of disease,
Amongst friends of the Clann-Colmain.

4.

Niall Black-knee, son of Aedh of the liquor,   [919]
Three years [were reigned] by Niall of great power,
In Dublin he went under . . .   [Green Foreigners.
The evil of his [mortal] wounding [was inflicted] by

5.

[r] Glorda glor Donncada duind,
A hocht ficet d'u fir Cuind:
Rorbean bed re Cruacain cain
Ar n-eg i[n] Thuacail Tectmair.

6.

Tri bliadna dec buidnec, breg,
Congalac, cenn mac Miled,
dar ri inallaig, airgnig,
Re Gallaib, re garg-Laignib.

1.

Gabur Domnall U Neill nert
[Re] re recc bliadan ficet:
Mard fer faca na fregra,
A n-Ard-Maca moregna.

2.

Mael-Sedlainn, flemna na fleg,
bili banba, barr Gaedel,
Re brian do riaraig a racc,
Re ceicri bliadan ficet.

3.

Fiucad fairgi, tuili tricc,
brian breo or banba bladbricc,
Gan ciamair, gan bed, gan brac,
Da bliadain deg a degrac.

4.

Danmairg Aca-cliac na cland,
Dibergaig laecraid Locland,
Cian o dogarbrac gala,
Romarbrac brian boroma.

5.

[r] Famous the fame of Donnchadh the Brown, [944]
Eight [and] twenty [were reigned] by the true descendant
Fatality attached to fair Cruachan, of Conn :
On the death of the [second] Tuathal the Acceptable.

6.

Three years [and] ten, crowded, varied, [956]
[Reigned] Congalach, head of the sons of Milesius :
The death of the king, very noble, victorious,
[Befell] by the Foreigners [and] by fierce Lagenians.

1.

Domnall Ua Neill receives power [980]
For the space of seven years [and] twenty :
Died the man who founded [learned] responses,
In Armagh of great wisdom.

2.

Mael-Sechlainn of the smooth spears, [1003]
Prop of Banba, crown of the Gaidhil,
Before Brian was obeyed his right,
For the space of four [and] twenty years.

3.

Seething of the sea, of the nimble wave, [1014]
[Was] Brian, flame o'er Banba various-famed,
Without sadness, without fatality, without [ill] doom,
Two years [and] ten was his good felicity.

4.

The Danes of Ath-cliath of the clans,
The plundering crew of Lochlann,
Long since obtained they power,
Slew they Brian of the Cattle-tribute.

5.

[s] Mael-Sechlainn t-[ṡ]iar i n-a ṫiġ,
Aḋaltraċ uallaċ Uirniġ,
Nae n-ġairġ bliaḋna ḋeir ḃriain binḋ
Rob' airḋiarla ar Erinn.
                              Eri.

6.

Areir Mael-Sheċlainn rona,
Mic Domnaill, mic Donċaḋa,
Dorcar raerḃriġ re caċ clainn,
No ġor'ġaḃ Enri Erinn.
                              Eri.

1.

t Nir'ġaḃrat clanna, aċt clann Neill,
Erinn iar creiḋem ċeimreiḋ,
Anoċt ni ċelim cu cian,
Aċt Oilill Molt ir mor ḃrian.

2.

Diar do ṡil Loeġaire luinḋ;
Aen ḋu ṡil Cairrri in comluinḋ;
Fer a Mumain, Tuaṫal tailc;
Ir fer a Cruaċain Connaċt.

3.

Se ri ḋeġ a hEoġan oll;
Ir a ḋeiċ a ḋeġ Conall;
Nonḃar ṡine ḃhreġ o'n m-ḃoin;
Seċt flaite Miḋe in miḋoil.

4.

Oilill Molt, mac Daṫi, ṫall,
A cert Conḋaċt na comlanḋ;
P. 51a ḃrian ġurun cuċt cuimneċ coir,
A huċt Muimneċ in miḋoil.

BOOK OF BALLYMOTE.   427

                    5.   [A.D.]
[s]   Mael-Sechlainn, west in his house,   [1022]
      Adulterer [i. e. usurper] haughty of Uisnech,
      Nine vigorous years after pleasant Brian
      Was he arch-ruler over Ireland.
                        Ireland, etc.

                    6.

      After Mael-Sechlainn the prosperous,
      Son of Domnall, son of Donchadh,
      Parted noble power with each clan,
      Until Henry occupied Ireland.   [1171]
                        Ireland, etc.

                    1.

t   Received not the clans, except the clan of Niall,
      Ireland [as a whole] after the smooth-progressing Faith,
      To-night conceal I not [it] for long,
      Save Oilill Molt and great Brian.

                    2.

      [And] twain of the seed of Loeghaire the vigorous ;
      One of the seed of Cairpre of equable vigour ;
      A man from Munster, Tuathal of stubborness ;
      And a man from Cruachan of Connacht.

                    3.

      Six kings [and] ten [were] from [Cenel-]Eoga[i]n noble ;
      And ten from excellent [Cenel-]Cona[i]ll ;
      Nine of the territories of Bregha from the Boyne ;
      Seven princes of Meath the mead-quaffing.

                    4.

      Oilill Molt, son of Dathi, beyond,
      From the centre of Connacht of the battles ;
      Brian of the model memorable, just,
      From the bosom of Munster the mead-quaffing.

5.

[t] Laeȝaire, mac Neill, ȝu neiṁ,
Ir a mac, Luȝaiḋ laiḋir,
Tuaṫal ḋo Sil Cairppri, ua Chuinḋ,
Ruȝ ruaṫar airȝni Umaill.

6.

Ri Erenn a Miḋi amaċ:
Diarmaiḋ, Domnall, ḋa Donnċaḋ,
Fland a Cremċaill 'r a caḋail,
Da Mael-Seċlainn, Concobur.

1.

u Aeḋ, blaṫmaċ, Seċnaraċ renȝ,
Diarmaiḋ, Foȝartaċ Femenḋ,
Cenrael aiḋ, Finaċta tra,
Cinaeṫ, Conȝalaċ Cnoḋḃa,
Na n-ȝnimraḋ trebaċ, tarba,—
Riȝra[i]ḋ breȝaċ breac-banba.

2.

Riȝraiḋ Cenel-Conaill cruaiḋ,
Roȝaḃrat banba m-braṫruaiḋ:
Ainmire, Aeḋ, baeḋan barr,
Maelcoḃa, Cellaċ, Conall,
Domnall, ḋa coimreḋ i caṫ,
Conȝal, Loinȝreċ, Fhlaiṫbertaċ.

3.

Da Ḋhomnall, tri Neill, ni nár,
Aeḋ ro ceiṫir, ir Colman,
Suiḃne, Eoċaiḋ, baeḋan baiṫ,
Forȝur, Ferȝal tabertaċ,
Muircertaċ, muirleomain luinḋ,
Riȝra[i]ḋ Eoȝa[i]n or Erinn.
                                    Eri.

5.

[t] Loeghaire, son of Niall, with bitterness,
And his son, Lugaid the strong,
Tuathal of the seed of Cairpre, descendant of Conn,
Took forcible possession of Umall.

6.

The kings of Ireland from out Meath [were]
Diarmaid, Domnall, two Donnchads,
Flann from Cremchaill and his fame,
Two Mael-Sechlainns, Concobur.

1.

u   Aedh, Blathmach, Sechnasach slender,
Diarmaid, Fogartach of Femenn,
Cenfaeladh, Finachta eke,
Cinaeth, Congalach of Cnodbha,
Of actions prudent, useful,
[These were] the different kings of diversified Banba.

2.

The kings of Cenel-Conaill the stern,
That received Banba the ruddy-vestured [were]:
Ainmire, Aedh, Baedan eminent,
Maelcoba, Cellach, Conall,
Domnall, who was aidful in battle,
Congal, Loingsech, Flaithbertach.

3.

Two Domnalls, three Nialls, noble thing,
Aedh by four and Colman,
Suibne, Eochadh, Baedan the weak,
Fergus, Fergal the liberal,
Muircertach, sea-lion of vigour,
[Were] the kings of [Cenel-]Eoga[i]n o'er Ireland.
                                    Ireland, etc.

4.

[u] Se bliaḋna ocṫmoġḋa oll
Ocuſ cuiġ ceṫ, ġan impoll,
Ġan beḋ, ḋo'n riġraiḋ ſe linḋ,
Co heġ Mael-ṫripġloin-tSheċloinḋ.

5.

Ḋa bliaḋain iar ſin, feċṫ ḃeiċ,
O eġ Mael-tSheċloinḋ ṫ-ḟuaiċniġ—
Niſ'ḃ'orḋ ḋebinḋ ḋia ḋine—
Ḋu'n Eſinn ġan aiſḋriġe.
                           Eſi.

1.

v   Co n-erraċṫ Ḋomnall Ḋaiſe,
Moſ ḃſian ḃanḃa ḃlaḋaiḋe;
'S a[n] flaiṫri cuimneċ na creċ,
Maiċní Muimneċ Muirċerṫaċ.

2.

Muirċerṫaċ Luimniġ na lonġ,
Ḋomnall Oiliġ na n-aſḋġlonn,
Fiċe iſ cuiġ lomlaiċi linḋ
A com[ſ]laiċi oſ Eſinn.
                           Eſi.

3.

Muirċerṫaċ Muman, rorṁarḃ
Ġaluſ anaiċniġ, aġarḃ;
Ḋo ḋiṫ Ḋomnaill ḋo ċaṁ ċenn,
Friṫ ḋoġraind ḋail ḋeġ Eſenn.
                           Eſi.

4.

Morfeiſer, ceṫraċa ċaiḋ
Ḋo clan[n]aiḃ Neill co nerṫḃaiġ:
Rolamſaṫ ġaċ ḋine in ḋream,
Roġaḃſaṫ riġe n-Eſenn.
                           Eſi.

BOOK OF BALLYMOTE. 431

4.

[u] Six noble years [and] eighty
And five hundred, without error, [time,
Without deception, [were reigned] by the kings in the [A.D.]
To the death of ever-sincere Mael-Sechlainn. [1022]

5.

Two years after that [and] seven tens,
From the death of Mael-Sechlainn prosperous—
It was not a precipitate order for its fate—
[Were spent] by Ireland without an arch-king.

Ireland, etc.

1.

v Until Domnall of Daire attained [the kingship],
The great Brian of Banba famous;
And the princely-king of the forays memorable,
The worthy Momonian, Muircertach.

2.

Muircertach of Limerick of the ships,
Domnall of Oilech of the high achievements,
Five [and] twenty [years] of fretful space
[Was] their co-sovranty over Ireland.

Ireland, etc.

3.

Muircertach of Munster, him killed [1119]
Disease unprecedented, very severe;
From the death of Domnall of illness intense, [land.
Anguish was found in [*lit.*, of] the assembly of good Ire- [1121]

Ireland, etc.

4.

Seven and forty just [kings reigned]
Of the septs of Niall with powerful victory:
Experienced every fate the folk
That assumed the kingship of Ireland.

Ireland, etc.

5.

[v] Seiṡer, nae ḟiċit, ḟir ḃaiṅ,
Coṁaireṁ na riġ raċmar,
Uile re remmenn riġe,
Or Erinn i n-airḃriġe.

     Eri.

6.

Ma raṡaḃrat riġ ṡu raċ
A cuiṡeḋ aṁra Ulaḋ,
Ni cleiṫ robennrea na ḟer,
Aċṫ a remri naċ ṙíṁṫer.

1.

w   ḃaeḋan, Ḟiaċa ḟinḋ, ḟeiḋm n-ṡle,
Ocur Eoċaiḋ Iarlaiṫe,
Luċṫ lanṡriḃ ṡan ḃunaiḋ m-ḃinḋ
Airmíḋ Ulaiḋ or Erinn.

     Eri.

2.

Noċor'ṡaḃ ri, ṫ-[ṙ]iar na ṫ-[ṙ]a[i]r,
Do ṫuaṫaiḃ ána Oirṡiall,
A n-ṡlonḋa, roṡluair ṡan ṡreím,
Aċṫ Colla hUair, or Erinn.

     Eri.

3.

O re Chaṫair moir muiṡmíṡ,
U Cormic re ċomaiḋem,
Ar a ṫír maiṡneaċ ṡan menṡ
Noċur'ṡaḃ Laiṡneċ lan Erenn.

     Eri.

4.

Ṡe airmiḋ Muimniṡ mine
Ḟeiḋlimiḋ i n-airḃriṡe,
Im'ḋuain ni laḃraim a línḋ,
Uair ni ḟaṡḃaim a n-Erinn.

     Eri.

5.

[v] Six [and] nine score [186], true for me,
 [Is] the full tale of the fortunate kings,
 The whole period of the series of kings,
 Over Ireland in arch-kingship.
Ireland, etc.

6.

If kings assumed the kingship with felicity
From the distinguished province of the Ulidians,
Not covertly . . .
But their periods are not reckoned.

1.

w Baedan, Fiacha the Fair, deed conspicuous,
 And Eochaidh Iarlaithe,
 [Are] the folk full-vigorous that, without clear proof,
 The Ulidians reckon over Ireland.
Ireland, etc.

2.

There assumed not [kingship] a king, west or east,
Of the noble tribes of Oirghialla,
Their valour, went it without [taking] hold,
Except Colla Uais, over Ireland.
Ireland, etc.

3.

From the time of Cathar the Great, the conquering,
Grandson of Cormac to be commemorated,
From the country plainful, without blemish,
A Leinsterman assumed not the whole of Ireland.
Ireland, etc.

4.

Although reckon the Munstermen mild
Feidlimidh in [the] arch-kingship,
I mention not in my lay his space,
For I find [it] not in [the royal series of] Ireland.
Ireland, etc.

5.

[w] Se mili bliaḋan, ní breġ,
A do, ceṫraċa ar da cet,
O denaṁ na n-dul, dar lem,
Ġur' reġaḋ run ri Erenn.
            Eri.

6.

Ceaṫraċa ar ċet, tri bliaḋna,
Ir mili, ġe mor rfaġla,
O ġein De buain, buidniġ, breġ,
Co duain tuirbiġ na trenfer.

1.

x   Ata Torrdelbaċ, tuir tren,
Mac Ruaiḋri na renn roġer,
Iġ nert[aḋ] na tuili tenn,
Iġ teċtaḋ uili Erenn.
            Eri.

2.

Tiġernan, tiġerna caiṫ,
O Ruairc, ri normar, nemtlaiṫ;
Ollċu ruair co tairrteaċ tenn,
Onċu uar, airġneaċ Erenn.
            Eri.

3.

I n-aimrir amlaiḋ, eatraiġ,
Imaletar ri sreċaiġ,
Mo duan dodelbur, dar leam,
Ġan dealġnur d'uairliḋ Erenn.

4.

Fuaradar eġ ar caċ alt,
Flaiṫe Fobla 'n-a m-beoḋaċt:
Ġan ġleo, ġu m-briġ m-blaiḋe,
Ar beo ri na riġraiḋe.

BOOK OF BALLYMOTE.   435

[w]
5.
Six thousand years, not false,   [A. M.]
Two [and] forty above two [*recte*, three] hundred,   [6342]
From formation of the elements, seems to me,
Until was seen the end of the kings of Ireland.
                                Ireland, etc.

6.
Forty above one hundred [and] three years,   [A.D.]
And a thousand, though great the calculation,   [1143]
From the Birth of God lasting, hostful, beauteous,
To the modest poem of the stout heroes.

1.
x   [Now] is Toirrdelbach, tower strong,   [1156]
Son of Ruaidhri of the very sharp [spear-]points,
Dominating the strong floods [of opposition],
Possessing the whole of Ireland.
                                Ireland, etc.

2.
Tigernan, blameless lord,   [1172]
O'Ruairc, king reputable, not weak,
Evils received he excessively, severely,
The leopard proud, plundering of Ireland.
                                Ireland, etc.

3.
In a time unpropitious, late,
Which foraying kings are spending,
My poem composed I, seems to me,
Without injustice to the nobles of Ireland.

4.
Received they death in every shape,
The chiefs of Fodla in their vigour :
Without dispute, with glorious power,
He is living, the King of the kings.

5.

[x] Daṁ-inir, Debrad, ir tír
Ar gaċ n-olc, ar gaċ n-anṗir;
Ir i roim inir na renn
Ocur oiginir Erenn.
           Eri.

6.

Ard-m-breaca[i]n, mo baili blaiċ,
And romaidiġ Crirt caemcaid:
Cadur, na ceilid, i cell,
Arur einiġ na hErenn.
           Eri.

7.

Do Ġilla-Modubda dron,
Co darba Dia gaċ dilgad:
Failid do'n gairgri romgell,
Ar n-airem airdriġ Erenn.
      Eri oġ, inir na naem.

5.

[x] Daim-inis, [by] God's doom, is the territory
[Opposed] to every ill, to every untruth :
It is the foremost isle of the . . .
And the perfect isle of Ireland.
     Ireland, etc.

6.

Ard-Brecain, my stead of fame,
There is Christ pure, holy, gloried in :
Dignity, conceal [it] not, [is] in [its] church,
Abode of the hospitality of Ireland.
     Ireland, etc.

7.

To Gilla-Modubda the brilliant,
May God grant every forgiveness :
Thanks from the powerful King earned he,
For recital of the arch-kings of Ireland.
   Ireland pure, isle of the Saints, etc.

(438)

INDEX VERBORUM. (IV.)

(*Letters refer to the textual sections ; figures to the numbered quatrains in* **k** *to* **x**.)

a (art.), i, j, k, 1 1, m 4, n 5, o 3, p 5, r 2, 5, t 3, w 3, 5.
a (poss. 3 s. m.), a, b, c, d, i, j, 1 5, m 3, 4, 5, n 2, o 2, 6, q 1, 2, 4, r 4, s 1, t 5.
a (poss. pl.), a, k 3, n 6, v 2, 6 ; a n-, w 2.
a (rel. αταnnle), d.
a (prep.), 1 4, t 2, 3, 4, 6, v 6.
a (i), a, b, d, g, h, 1 4, m 2, o 6, p 4, r 1, 2, s 1.
a m- (i m-), d.
abann, o 1.
Αὀab, b, 1 3.
aὀc, t 1, v 6, w 2.
abalcpaċ, s 5.
abant, k 5.
abbaċ, e, i, m 5, n 2, q 2, 3, 5, r 1 ; -ċaban, e.
abbenaib, k 6.
abbul, p 2.
abclor, m 1.
abreċ, d.
abfuair, r 2.
abroeʒaib, a.
aʒ, k 6.
aʒanb, v 3,
Αeb, e, g, h, 1 6, m 5, 6, n 2, o 5, p 6, q 4, r 2, u 1, 2 ; -ba (g.), e, f, g, h, j, n 1, o 2, r 4.
Αeʒ, c, d ; Αoʒ, d.
aen, c, f, m 4, 5, p 3, t 2.

Αenʒupa (g.), f, o 6.
aib, m 4.
aibċi, b.
aibeʒaib, j.
Αilcealcna, f.
aili, b.
Αilill Molc, a.
ailiċne, q 2.
aimrin, x 3.
Αinbinbi, i.
ainfir, i.
ainm, k 6.
Αinmine, c, m 3, u 2 ; -eċ (g.), d, e, m 5.
ainb(ianla), s 5; -(niʒ), x 7; -(niʒe), u 5, v 5, w 4.
aineam, q 5 ; -eṁ, x 7.
Αinʒeban (g.), c.
ainʒib (g.),
ainʒne, o 3; -ni, t 5; -neaċ, x 2; -niʒ, r 6.
ainmib, w 1.
aiċniʒi (g.), i, n 5.
Αlba, a.
allaiʒ, r 6.
Αllan, g ; -ain (g.), p. 6.
Αlmaine (g.), f, p 2.
alc, x 4.
amaċ, t 6.
amal, j.
Αmalʒaba, h.
amlaib, x 3.

INDEX VERBORUM. (IV.)

ampa, v 6.
ana, w 2.
anaıċnıġ, v 3.
anḃ (a(ı) and pers. pr. 3 s.), x 6 ; ann,
    o 1.
anpıp, x 5.
ɼlonḃa, w 2.
Anluaın, i.
anma (g.), q 6.
anmann, a.
anoċc, t 1.
annpın, a.
aoıḃıḋ, k 6.
áp, x 2.
ap (poss. 1 pl.), b, r 1.
ap (against), b, x 5.
ap (pro), x 7.
ap (upon), c, n 1, 3, p 1, 6, q 2, s 5,
    w 5, 6.
ap n- (prep.), s 5.
ap(eıp), s 6.
ap (conj.), a, j.
apa (ala), j.
apaı, j.
apḃ, o 3.
apḃaıġ, q 6.
Apḃmḃpeaca[ı]n, x 6.
apḃpɫacup, n 4.
apḃ(ɼlonn), v 2.
Apḃ-Maċa, a, g, h, p 4.
apmıc, j.
apmpuaıḃ, k 2.
apup, x 6.
ap (vb.), x 4.
ap (a and per. pr. 3 s.), w 3, x 4.
aċ, r 4 ; aċa (g.), h, i, s 4.
aċa, x 1.
aċbaċ, a, p 1 ; -ċabap, c.

b' (bo), s 5, u 5.
ba (vb.), n 1, 6, q 5, r 3.

baḋ, a.
baeḃan, c, d, m 2, 4, u 2, 3,
    w 1.
baeċepnaıl, q 1.
baeċɼal, d.
baıbeaḋ, b ; -eḃ, h.
baıċpep, b ; pobaıḃ, 1 4 ;
    baḃuḃ, c.
(nepċ)baıġ, v 4.
baılı, x 6.
banba, k 4, o 2, p 1, s 2, 3, u 1, 2,
    v 1.
bapp, s 2, u 2.
bap, a, 1 1, o 1, p 2, 4, 5, r 2, 6 ;
    baıp (g.), a.
be (vb.), j.
bealaıɼ, m 5.
bean, b.
popbean, r 5.
bec, b.
beḋ, m 4, q 1, r 5, s 3, u 4.
beıl, k 6.
beım, b.
beıpċ, k 6.
belɼaḃaın, e.
beo, x 4.
beoḋaċċ, x 4.
ḃobepap, j.
bepnaıɼ, j.
bep (vb.), j.
beċaıḃ, q 1.
bı, d, e, m 2.
bıɼ, c, d, f, g.
bıle, d ; bılı, s 2.
bınḃ, s 5, w 1.
bıċbuaıḃ, 1 2 ; bıċnap, o 2.
blaḃ, p 2 ; -ḃḃpıcc, s 3.
blaḃaıḃe, v 1 ; blaıḃe, x 4.
blaıċ, x 6.
blaċmac, e, o 2, u 1 ; -mıó (g.), f,
    o 3.
blaċcaın, p 1 ; -ċpıɼe, m 2.

INDEX VERBORUM. (IV.)

bliaḋain (n.), c, f, 1 6, m 1, 4, n 3, p 3, q 1; (du.) i, j, m 1, 2, s 3, u 4; -ḋna (n. p.), b, c, d, e, f, g, h, i, 1 3, m 3, 5, 6, n 3, 4, 5, 6, o 2, 6, p 1, 2, 6, q 1, 6, r 1, 3, 6, s 5, u 4, w 6; -ḋan (g. du.), j: (g. p.), a, d, g, i, 1 1, 2, 4, m 1, 2, n 2, o 3, 5, q 1, 3, 4, 5, r 1, 2, s 2, 3, u 5, w 5.
bloiḋ, o 2; -ḋe, 1 1.
bo (vb.), d.
boin, t 3; -nḋ, b.
bolg, d, m 5.
bonnfaḋ, q 5.
bonoime, a; -oṁa, i, j, s 4.
braḋ, k 4.
braċ, s 3.
braṫruaiḋ, u 2.
brataiṗ, o 2.
breac, u 1.
breg, r 6, w 5; -gaċ, u 1.
bhreig, t 3.
brenlaí, n 4.
breo, s 3.
breṫiṗ, 1 1.
brian, i, s 2, 3, 4, t 4, v 1; -aiṁ (g.), j, s 5.
brig, o 6, x 4; -ge, m 2; raerbriġ, s 6.
brigiḋ, d.
roḋurbrir, i.
broiṅ, f.
bruaċ, d.
bruġ, e.
bu (vb.), i.
buaċ, d.
buaiḋ, i, n 6.
buain, m 5, w 6.
buiḋi, e, i, j.
buiḋneċ, r 6; -ni, k 6; -nig, w 6.
bunaiḋ, w 1.
(i)ḋur, c.

cac, s 6, x 4.
caḋail, t 6.
caḋur, x 6.
Caeċ, c, e, n 4.
cael, e, n 6.
caem, k 1, m 3, n 1, 6, q 6; -mcaiḋ, x 6; -mcuairt, o 3; -mḋaiċ, p 2; -mgeg, q 5; -mriagail, 1 6.
caiḋ, 1 4, v 4; caiċ, x 2.
Caille, q 6; -lli, h.
ċain, p 1, r 5.
ḋoṗċaiṗ, p 6; ḋoṗoċaiṗ, e; ṫoṗcaiṗ, e, f, g, h, i.
cainḋiḃ, r 3.
Cairppre, c; -pri, o 3, t 2, 5; Corpri, f.
Caire, a.
ṗocaiċ, 1 2, n 3.
Challain, q 6; Callanḋ, h.
calma, k 4, 1 4, q 6.
ḋocan, d; ṗocan, i, j; niṗ'can, j.
Canman (g.), i.
caċ, a, b, d, e, f, g, h, i, k 3, m 5, n 3, o 6, p 1, 2, q 4, r 4, s 4; caċa, i, p 6; -ċaig, m 1.
Caċail (g.), j.
Chataiṗ, w 3.
caṫran, k 5.
Ceallaċ, e, n 6; Cellaig (g.), h.
ceaṫnaċa, w 6.
ceḋu, e; ceċḋu, e.
ceiliḋ, x 6.
ceimpeiḋ, t 1.
ceinṫ, 1 1.
ceiṫri, b, f, g, h, 1 4, q 5, s 2.
celim, t 1.
cell, 1 3, x 6.
Cellaċ, o 1, 6, u 2.
cen, j.
Cenanḋur, g.
Cenḋfaelaċ, f; Cenfaelaiḋ, u 1.
Cenḋḃoḋa, c, d.

Cenel, u 2.
cenn, b, r 6.
Cenbaill, d, 1 6; Cennbel, a; -eoil, c, d, g.
Cennaiʒ (g.), f.
ccṗu, d.
cec (sb.), 1 4, m 4.
cec (card.), u 4, w 5, 6.
cecaiṗ, u 3.
cecna (same), o 1.
cia, j.
ciamaiṗ, s 4.
cian, s 4, t 1.
Ciannaċc, c, m 2.
cib, j.
Cimi, f.
Cinaeċ, g, p 3, u 1; -aiċ, f.
Cinbbelʒa, f.
Cinbeciʒ, i.
Cinbmaʒaiṗ, f, p 1.
claen, j.
clainn, q 5, r 3, s 6, t 1; clanb, s 4; clanna, t 1; -nnaib, v 4.
clairineċ, j.
Cleiceb, 1 4; -eciʒ, b.
clepeċ, e; -ṗiċ (g.), e.
cli, n 5.
abcloṗ, m 1.
cnoca, a.
Cnobba, u 1.
co (prep.), a, b, c, d, e, f, g, h, i, j, 1 6, k 4, n 2, 5, p 6, u 4, 6, v 4, 6.
co (conj.), a, x 7.
co m- (co, prep.), o 6.
co n- (conj.), o 5, q 1, v 1.
co n- (prep.), j, m 4.
Coelbab, a.
coic (card.), b, e, h, i, k 5, 1 3, o 3: -ceb, j; -iʒeb, j.
coimpeċ, u 2; -piʒ, p. 4.
coiṗ, t 4.
pocoiṗc, 1 6.

col, q 1.
Colla hUaiṗ, w 2.
Colman, d, e, m 6, r 3, u 3; ·ain, d.
Colum-cille, g.
comaiṗeam, v 5.
comballca, d.
compaʒuṗ, n 6.
com[ṗ]laiċi, v 2; -iuṗ, j.
comlanb, t 4; comlonb, m 4; -nn, p 6; -luinb (g.), t 2.
commab, k, i.
comneṗc, k 6.
comoil, o 5.
Conainʒ (g.), g, h.
Conall, e, n 1, 6, t 3, o 1, u 2; -aill, a, c, d, e, u 2.
Concobaṗ, g, t 6; -aiṗ, j, q 5.
Conbaċc, t 4; Conn-, j, t 2.
Conʒail (g.), h; -le (g.), g.
Conʒal, k 3, n 4, p 1, u 2; -ll, f.
Conʒalaċ, h, o 5, r 6, u 1; -aiʒ (g.), h.
Coṗmic (g.), c, w 3.
Coṗain (g.), g; Choṗainb, f, o 6.
coṗcṗaċ, k 3.
cṗab, o 4, p 1.
pocṗaib, 1 6; ṗuṗc-, q. 6.
cṗeċ, m 6; -ċaiʒ, x 3; cṗeic, a.
cṗeibeaṁ, k 2; -bem, t 1; -bim, k 2; -bmiʒ (ac.), j.
Cṗemcaill, t 6.
Cṗimċainb, d; -nbe, a; -ain, c.
Cṗiṗc, t 6.
cṗobainʒ, o 6; cṗomb-, n 6.
cṗoba, k 3, n 3.
Cṗo-iniṗ, i.
Cṗonan, c, m 2.
Cṗocain (g.), g.
Cṗuaċain, r 5, t 2.
cṗuaib, k 2, m 4, n 5, 6, u 2; -bi, p 4.
cṗuiċneċca, g.

INDEX VERBORUM. (IV.)

Cpunnmael, o 4.
cu (co, prep.), o 2, q 3, t 1.
do cuadap, k 5.
(caem)cuaipc, o 3.
cucc, t 4.
cuid, o 4.
cuiz, u 4, v 2; -zed, v 6.
Cuind (g.), j, n 3, t 5.
cuimnec, t 4, v 1; -mni, k 6.
Cuipc, i.
Cuipeac, o 3.
Cuippiz (g.), h.
cumain, m 4.
Cumaine, d.

d (de, di), j, m 4, 5.
d (do, prep.), q 2, 5, x 3, 7.
da (card.), a, c, d, e, g, i, j, k 4, 1 6, m 1, 2, q 1, 4, s 3, t 6, u 2, 5, v 4, w 5.
dail, v 3.
Daim-inip, x 5.
Daipe, v 1.
Dalapaide, a, c; -di, b.
dall, j.
dam, o 2, v 5.
Danmaipz, s 4.
Dapil, a.
dap (vb.), w 5, x 3.
dap (prep.), i.
dapda, x 7.
dapm, 1 6.
dac, n 5; daca (g.), q 3.
Naci [*recte*] Daci, a, b, t 4.
De (g.), a, b, 14, w 6.
de (de and pr. suf. 3 s.), n 1, p 5.
pombead, m 5.
Debpad, x 5.
debuid (g.), u 5.
decaid, q 1.
debenac, j.

dedla, o 1.
dez, m 1, o 3, t 3, v 3; -zbuaid, n 6; -zpac, s 3; -zpiz, k 3.
deic (card.), h, k 1, n 5, p 2, u 5.
dodelbup, x 3.
denam, w 5; denca, n 1.
depd, m 3; do depdup, m 3.
(dpcc)depz, o 1.
di (prep.), d, g. j.
Dia, x 7.
diadacc, m 2.
dian, r 2.
Diapmaid, c, e, o 1, 2, t 6; -ada (g.), d, e, f, g, 1 6, u 1.
diap, t 2.
did (do and pr. suf. 2 p.), m 3.
did (di and pr. suf. 3 p.), i.
didepzaiz, s 4.
dil, 14, o 5; -li, a; dpocdilaid, k 5.
dilzad, x 7.
Dilmain, m 6; -mana, e.
dimep, 1 5.
dine, u 5, v 4.
dino, e.
dipiz, m 6.
dip, m 6.
dic (sb.), v 3; (vb.), d.
diulcad, b.
Dlucaiz (g.), f.
do (card.), j, w 5.
do (prep.), d, m 1, 6, p 4, q 5, r 4, x 7.
do (de, di), b, d, e, j, k 5, o 2, 3, r 3, t 2, 5.
do (do and pr. suf. 3 s. m.), b, j.
do (vbl. pcle.), dodepap, j; podupdpip, i; docan, d; docuadap, k 5; dodepdup, m 3; dodic, d; d'ec, e; d'ez, e; dudpez, p 5; dopaemad, o 4; dapuppappaiz, o 1; dapuil, p 5; dazaid, 1 5; dozapdpac, s 4;

INDEX VERBORUM. (IV.)

ꝺopac, a; ꝺopıapaıᵹ, s 2;
ꝺopcan, s 5; ꝺo pcan, s 6;
ꝺopeaꝺ, k 3.
ꝺoćc, q 2.
ꝺoıꝺ (ꝺo and pr. suf. 3 p.), a, e.
ꝺoıpćı, q 3.
Ꝺomnaıᵹ (g.), i.
Ꝺomınall, o, e, g, h, m 1, q 1, s 1, t 6, u 2, 3, v 1, 2; -aıll (g.), c, e, f, g, h, n 2, q 5, s 6, v 3.
Ꝺonćaꝺ, h, t 6; -nnćaꝺ, g, q 3; -ćaıꝺ, q 5.
Ꝺonćaꝺa, g, h, s 6; Ꝺonnc-, r 5; Ꝺunć-, f.
ꝺpeam, v 4; ꝺpeım, j.
ꝺpec(ꝺenᵹ), o 1.
ꝺuꝺneᵹ, p 5.
ꝺpon, x 7.
ꝺpuım, h, r 2; ꝺpoma (g.), g, i.
ꝺu (ꝺe), t 2; (ꝺo), q 4, u 5.
ꝺuaꝺen, o 1.
ꝺuan, j, r 2, x 3; -aın, w 4, 6.
ꝺuꝺ, c, 1 6.
Ꝺuꝺꝺuın, f, o 3.
(mo)Ꝺuꝺꝺa, x 7.
ꝺul (g. p.), w 5.
Ꝺuma (g.), i.
ꝺun, o 3; Ꝺuın (g.), m 5; ꝺuınꝺ (g.), r 5.

e (pron.), p 5.
Ꝗacać (g.), d.
eacpaıᵹ, x 3.
heꝺapćan, j.
ecmaıp, j.
ećc, c.
hećcpa, i.
Ꝗꝺaıp (g.), i.
eᵹ, c, e, k 5, n 5, q 1, r 5, u 4, 5, x 4.
(mop)eᵹna (g.), s 1.
eıć (g.), j.
eınıᵹ (g.), x 6.

(ap)eıp, s 6; (ꝺıa)eıp[p]eom, j.
eıpıꝺe, j; eıpeom, a.
Ꝗmna (g.), i.
enepc, d.
eníᵹ, e.
Ꝗnpı, s 6.
Ꝗocaꝺ, m 2, u 1; Ꝗoću, c.
Ꝗoᵹan, t 3, u 3; -aın (g.), b, c, d, e.
epꝺaılc, g, h, i.
Ꝗpca (g.), a, b.
Cpenn, i, j, k 2, n 4, s 6, t 1, 2, u 3, 5, v 2, 3, 4, 5, w 1, 2, 3, 4, 5, x 1, 2, 3, 5, 6, 7.
Ꝗpı, k 1, w 1, x 1, 2, 5, 6, 7; Ꝗpınn, s 5; Ꝗpıu, a.
Ꝗpıanᵹalac, k 4.
(ꝺaeć)epnaıl, q 1.
eppaćc, v 1.
epca, a.
epın, j.
ecep, a, g, j, r 3.
eceplen, r 3.

pa (ꝺa), 1 4.
pa, 1 3, n 6; po, k, 1 2, r 4.
pael, o 5.
ꝺopaemaꝺ, o 4; pop-, q 6.
Faᵹapcać, f, p 3, u 1.
paᵹꝺaım, w 4.
(com)paᵹup, n 6.
paılıꝺ, x 7.
paıpenꝺ, j.
paınᵹı, s 3.
Fanaıꝺ (g.), f.
Fapća, 1 3; Phopća, b.
ꝺapuppappaıᵹ, o 1; popfapp-, m 4.
pać, q 4; paća, p 4, 5.
Feapᵹal, f; Fenᵹ-, p 2, u 3; Fenᵹaıll (g.), g, q 2; -aılı (g.), g.
Feꝺꝺa (g.), i; Feꝺća (g.), i.

INDEX VERBORUM. (IV.)

feʒaḋ, w 5.
Ƒeıḋlımıḋ, w 4.
ƒeıḋm, w 1.
ƒeınḃıʒ, r 2.
Ƒemenḋ, u 1.
ƒeṗ, t 2, v 6; ƒıuṗ, b.
Ƒeṗaḋaıʒ (g.), e.
ƒeṗaıſ, d; ƒeṗṗa, b.
Ƒeṗʒuṗ, a, m 3, u 3; Ƒeṗṗʒ-, a;
 ƒeṗʒuṗa (g.), c, d. f, g.
ƒeṗṗaca, s 1.
ḟeṗca, g, q 4.
Ƒıaċa, w 1; Ƒıacṗaċ (g.), e; -aıʒ, a.
ƒıaḋṅaċ, p 3, 4, 5.
ƒıamaċ, p 4.
ƒıce, a, b, c, d, f, g, h, i, j, 1 1, m 5,
 4, v 2, 5; -ec, c, 14, s 1, 2.
ƒılı, j.
ƒín, b, 1 4; ḟína (g.), b.
Ƒınaċca, f, u 1; Ƒınḋa-, o 4, 5.
ƒıncaaḋ, s 3.
ƒınḋ, q 2, r 1, w 1; -ḋlıaċ, h, r 2;
 -ḋleıċ (g.), h.
Ƒınḋı, i.
ƒıne, r 1, t 3.
Ƒınʒal, n 1.
ƒıṗ (adj.), v 5; ƒıṗa, m 5; ƒıṗmaıċ,
 q 4.
ƒlaıċ, 1 3, 5, p 3, r 1; -ċe, t 3, x 4;
 -cemna, p 2.
ƒlaıċṗı, v 1; com[ḟ]laıċı, v 2;
 lom[ḟ]laıċı, v 2.
Ƒlaıċḃeṗṫaċ, g, p 3, 4, u 2; -aıʒ
 (g.), p 5.
ƒlaıċıuṗ, j; -ṗaıḃ, j; -ċuṗ m 3,
 n 4.
Ƒlanḋ, t 6; -nn, h, r 3; -aınḋ, (g.),
 h; -nn (g.), h.
Ƒlannaʒan, h.
ƒleaḋaċ, o 5; ƒleʒ-, f.
Ƒoḋla, r 3, x 4.
ƒola (g.), g.

ƒoṗ, a, b, e, g, i, j, m 4; ƒoṗṗo, a;
 ƒoṗṗın, a.
ƒoṗḃaḋ, o 5; ƒoṗ-, n 4.
Ƒoṗḋṗoma, i.
Ƒoṗʒuṗ, c, m 1.
ƒṗaṗ, g; ƒṗaṗṗa, g; -ṗṗaċ, g;
 -aıʒ (g.), g.
ƒṗeʒṅa, s 1.
ƒṗeṗṗaḃṅa, j.
ƒṗı, a, j; ƒṗıṗ, j; ƒṗıṗın m-, d;
 ƒṗıu, a.
ƒṗıċ (vb.), q 4, v 3.
ƒuaıṗ, a, 1 1, 3, m 6, n 5, x 2;
 ƒuaṗaḋaṗ, k 5, x 4.
(aḋ)ƒuaıṗ, r 2; (ınn)ḟuaṗ, q 4.
ƒual, p 5.
ƒuċċ, o 1.
ƒuıl, p 5.
ƒuıl (vb.), g.
ƒuṗ, q 2.

ʒa (sb.), j; ʒaı, n 4.
ṅoʒaḃ, 1 5, m 2, s 6; ṅocoṗʒaḃ,
 w 2; ṅocuṗ-, w 3; ʒaḃṗac, n 6,
 t 1; ṅoʒaḃṗac, k 1, 2, 4, u 2;
 ṅaʒ-, v 6; ḋoʒaṗḃṗac, s 4;
 ḋaʒaıḃ, 1 5; ṅaʒaıḃ, j; ʒaḃaıl,
 a; ʒaḃuṗ, s 1.
ʒaċ (caċ), k 6, v 4, x 5, 7.
Ʒaeḃel, s 2; -laıḃ, i; -ealu, i.
ʒaeċ, n 4.
ʒaıḃċeċ, n 5.
ʒaıle, k 3, 1 2.
ʒaıne, k 5.
ʒaıṗe, k 3.
ʒala, s 4.
Ʒall, i; Ʒallu, h; -aıḃ, i, v 4, 6.
ʒan(ceṅ), k 1, 2, 1 5, m 2, 4, n 4,
 p 1, 2, q 1, 2, 3, r 2, 3, s 3, u 4,
 5, w 1, 2, 3, x 3.
ʒaṗḋ, v 3; ʒaṗḃa, k 1.

INDEX VERBORUM. (IV.)

ᵹaṅᵹ, p 4, r 6, s 5; ᵹaiṅᵹ, x 7.
ᵹaṅc, k 5.
ᵹe (ce), w 4, 5.
ᵹeᵹ, q 5.
ᵹeimin, c,
ᵹein, g, w 6.
ᵹeince, k 1.
ɲomᵹell, x 7.
ɲoᵹeoḋain, 1 5.
(ɲo)ᵹeɲ, x 1.
ᵹiallaiᵹ, b, c, d.
Ᵹ[-C]luain-caɲḃ, i.
ᵹil (g.), g, j.
ᵹilla, j, x 7.
Ᵹiuᵹɲanḃ, h.
ᵹlaɲ, a, r 4.
ᵹle, n 3, w 1; ᵹle(caem), n 1.
ᵹleicíᵹ, 1 1.
ᵹlenḃ, g; Ᵹliṅḃi (g.), c.
ᵹleo, n 5, x 4.
ᵹloin, u 4.
ᵹlonn, 1 2, v 1; ᵹlonḃa, w 2.
ᵹloɲ, r 5; -ɲḃa, r 5.
ɲoᵹluaiɲ, w 2.
ᵹluinḃ, k 4; ᵹlun(ḋuḃ), h; (-uiḃ), h.
ᵹó, j.
ᵹo (co, conj.), k 3, m 3.
ᵹoɲ (co ɲo), s 6.
ᵹnimɲaḃ, u 1.
Ᵹneallaiᵹ, a.
ᵹɲian, a; ᵹɲein, a, 1, 2, w 2.
ᵹɲiḃ, w 1.
ᵹɲinḃ, 1 1.
ᵹu (co, prep.), k 2, q 3, v 3, 6.
ᵹu -m (co m-), x 4.
ᵹu n- (co -n), n 5; ᵹuɲun, t 4.
ᵹuin, c, m 6.
Ᵹulḃan, c.
ᵹuɲ (co ɲo), 1 3, o 2, 5, p 3, 6, w 5.
Ᵹuɲcan, c.
ᵹucḃinḃ, d, n 1.

haḋaɲc, k 5.
hᴀeḋ, g, o 5; hᴀeᵹ, c.
haen, m 5.
hᴀinḃinḃi, i.
hebaɲcaɲ, j.
heccɲa, i.
heᵹ, u 4.
hΘoᵹan, t 3.
hΘɲenn, j, n 4, x 6.
hi, f.
hl, c, g.
hoċc, v 5.
hoᵹaiḃ, d.
hu, c.
huċc, t 4.
hUaiɲ, w 2.

hl (patronymic), c.
], q 2; hl, g.
ı (pron.), x 5.
ı (prep.), b, c, d, e, f, g, i, k 6, m 5, p 2, 6, q 4, r 3, 4, u 1, v 5, w 4, x 3, 6; iɲin, e.
ıl (ı and n assim. to l foll.), i.
ı m-, a, b, c, i, w 4.
ı n-, b, 1 3, n 2, 5, s 5.
ı ɲ- (ı and n assim. to ɲ foll.), c, i, j.
ıaɲɲaiḃ, a.
ıaɲlaice, w 1.
ıaɲ, i, n 2, 4, 5, q 3, 5, t 1; ıaɲ n-, a, b; ıaɲɲin, u 5.
ıaɲom, a; -ɲum, a.
ıaɲcain, q 1.
ıac (pr. pers. 3 p.), a.
ıḃon, a, b, d, g, i, j.
ıᵹ, a, h, m 6, x 1.
ılaiḃ, p 3; ılaɲ, b.
ılċealᵹaiᵹ (g.), f.
ıllaḃaim, d.
ım, b.
ı(maiᵹ), d.

INDEX VERBORUM. (IV.)

ımaleċep, x 3.
Imbaın (g.), i.
ımluaıŏpea, b.
ımmıaılle, q 6.
ımoppo, j.
ımpoll, u 4.
ın (art.), a, b, i, j, n 3, 4, 5, o 4, 5,
   p 6, r 4, t 2, 3, 4, v 4; ın b-, j;
   ın c-, o 3; ınn, e.
ınapclaınb, h, r 2.
ın allaıg, r 6.
ınbaın, m 2.
Inbpeccaıg (g.), j.
ınır, k 1, x 5, 7; (Cpo)ı-, i.
ınnḟuap, q 4.
Ipgalaıg (g.), f, g.
ıp (vb.), d, i, j, x 5; ıpom (ıp and pr.
   suf. 1 s.), b.
ıp (ocup), c, k 3, 1 6, m 1, 2, 6, n 6,
   o 5, p 5, q 1, 3, t 1, 2, 3, 5, u 3,
   v 2, w 6, x 5.

la (prep.), a, b, c, d, e, f, g, i, n 1, 4,
   o 1, 4, 5, p 6.
labpaım, w 4.
laca (loċa), f; loċ, n 1; loċa, i.
Laċċna, i.
laeú, p 4; -ċba, k 4; -cpaıb, s 4.
Laegaıpe, a, b, k 3, 4, 1 1, t 2, 5.
laıbıp, t 5.
Laıgen, g; -gneċ, w 3; -gnıb, r 6;
   -gnıu, a.
Lampoba, f, g.
polampac, v 4.
lan, w 3; lancaem, m 3; langpıb,
   w 1; lanpeımıp, 1 1.
lannaıb, r 4.
le (la, prep.). g; lem (la and pr. suf.
   1 s.) i, w 5; leam (id.), x 3; leıp
   (la and pr. suf. 3 s. m.), i.
[p]leċċa, q 4.

leomaın, u 3.
leċ, j; leıċ, v 6.
lıaċ, r 4.
Libpene, d.
Lıṗe, a; -ṗı, i.
lınb, v 2, w 4; (pe) lınb, u 4.
Lıne, c.
Lıpluǧeċ, i.
lıċe, q 2.
Loċlanb, s 4.
loċċ, q 2; luċċ.
Logan, e, m 6.
Loımǧreċ, f, u 2; -rıǧ, g, o 6,
   p 5.
loırcpıċep, b; gup'loıpc, 1 3; po-
   loıpc, 1 4, 6; lopcub, c.
lom[ḟ]laıcı, v 2.
long, v 2.
lonn, a, 1 2; luınb (g.), t 2, u 3;
   coınlanb, t 4; coınlaınb, t 2.
Lopcaın, i.
loċ, n 1.
poluabaıb, 1 6.
Luaċpa, i.
Lugab, t 5; -gaıb, a, b, 1 2, 3.
luıb, r 4.
Luımnıǧ, v 2.

m (pron. infix. 1 s.), x 7.
mon (ım an), m 6.
mac, a, b, c, d, e, f, g, h, i, j, 1 2, 6,
   m 3, 4, n 2, o 2, 3, p 4, 6, q 1, 3, 5,
   r 1, 4, s 6, t 4, 5, x 1; mac (d.),
   m 5; mac (dual), c, m 1; meıc
   (n. p.), c, n 6; mıc (g. s.), b, c, d,
   e, f, g, h, i, n 2, o 4, 6, p 5, q
   3, 5.
mab, j.
maban (*lege* maıbm), i.
maǧ, p 6; mıaıǧ, a, c, i.
poṁaıbıǧ, x 6.

INDEX VERBORUM. (IV.) 447

Maeil-monna, c; Maelabuin, f, g; -lipitpi, f.
Mael-Canaig, g; -Coba, e, n 3, 6, u 2; -ganb, c, 15; -mitig, h; -Monba, c, 15; -Ruanaig, h, r 1; -Seclainb, h; -nn, h, i, k 4, r 1, s 2, 5, 6, t 6; -t Shecloinb, u 4, 5.
Maige-Manbact, i.
maigneċ, w 3.
mait, p 1; pinm-, q 4.
maitni, v 1.
man (conj.), k 6, m 3, v 6.
manaib, k 6.
manb, m 1, v 3, s 1; nomanb, 1 6; nomm-, d; normanb, v 3; nomanbrat, a.
meabar, b; nomeababan, i.
meabla, p 2.
men, p 6.
meng, w 3.
Menn, e.
Mibe, r 1, t 3; -bi, t 6.
miboil, t 3, 4.
mili, w 5, 6.
Mileb, r 6.
mine (adj.), m 1; w 4.
minibe, j.
mo (poss. 1 s.), t 3, 6, x 7.
moċ, n 1.
moḃ, c.
Moga, j; Moġo, j.
Molt, a, 1 2, t 1, 4.
mon, b, i, p 4, t 1, v 1, w 6; moin, g, j, o 6, r 4, w 3; monegna, s 1; monfeiren, v 4.
Montain, i.
montlait, o 2.
Muaib, 1 2, r 1.
muigmig, w 3.
Muilletain, j.
Muincille, i.

muin, u 3.
Muincentaċ, a, 1 4, u 3, v 1, 2; -aig, c, d, e, m 1, n 2.
Muinebaig, b, c, d, e, j.
Mulla, i.
mullaċ, b.
Mumain, t 2; -an, v 3; -mneċ, t 4;
Muimneċ, v 1; -nig, w 4.
Munċaḃ, f; -ḃa, g, h, p 6, q 1, 3.
Mungaili, j.
Mungerra, j.

n (i n-), j, o 6, q 1.
na (art. g. s. f.), m 1, n 4; (g. p.), k 1, 13, n 2, o 1, r 1, 2, s 3, t 4, v 1, 2, 6, w 6, x 1, 5.
na m- (art. g. p.), k 4, x 4; na n-, k 3, o 2, u 1, v 2, w 5.
na (neg.), j, w 2, x 6.
naċ (conj. neg.), a, v 6.
nae (card.), f, g, i, k 5, p 4, 6, q 1, 3, r 3, s 5, v 5.
nama, n 3.
nán, u 3.
Neilline, c; Nellin, m 3.
neim, t 5.
nemtlait, x 2.
nent, e, s 1, x 1.
ni (neg.), a, d, j, n 1, t 1, u 3, 5, v 6, w 4, 5.
Niall, g, h, q 2, 6, r 4; Neill, a, b, c, d, f, g, h, r 4, s 1, t, 1, 5, v 4, u 3.
nim, b.
Ninbeaḃa, d, m 4.
no (conj.), j; (conj. temp.), s 6.
noċo, w 2; nocu, w 3.
Noigiallaig, b, c, d.
nonban, t 3.
norman, x 2.

INDEX VERBORUM. (IV.)

o (sb.), x 2.
o (prep.), b, k 3, 4, l 1, q 6, t 3, x 2.
o (o and rel.), j, s 4, w 3, 6.
Oóa, a, b.
occa (oc and pr. suf. 3 p.), j ; occo (id.), a.
oċṫ, e, f, h, k 4, o 2, 6, p 1, r 5 ; oċṫmoʒḋa, u 4.
ocuɼ (*passim*).
oʒ, k 1, x 7 ; oiʒiniɼ, x 5.
oibiḋ, c, r 2.
(in)oil, r 4 ; miḋoil, t 3.
oiliʒ, r 2.
Oilill, b, 1 2, t 1, 4, v 2.
Oinʒiall, w 2.
Oinnḋniḃe, g ; Opniḃe, h ; -ḃi, q 4.
oic, o 1, x 5 ; ollóu, x 2.
oll, t 3, u 4.
oman, b.
onḋ, m 5, u 5.
oɼ, b, o 2, 5, p 1, s 3, v 2, 5, w 1, 2, x 2.
Oċain, g.

Paḋɼaic, b.

ɼa (intens.), ɼaḋuan, r 2.
ɼaċṫ, s 2.
Raʒallaiʒ, f.
ɼainḋ, j.
Raiṫ, c.
ḋoɼac, a.
ɼaċ, n 4 ; ɼaċa, a ; ɼoɼaċ, q 3 ; ɼaċman, v 5.
Raċa, i.
Raċin, i.
ɼe (sb.), j, 1 4, s 1, 2, v 5, w 3.
ɼe (prep.), k 2, r 2.
ɼe (le), m 5, n 3, q 4, r 5, 6, u 4, w 3.

ɼeċṫ, e ; ɼeċṫɼaċ, n 2.
ɼeiʒ, k 6.
ɼeim, j, q 4.
ɼeime, i.
ɼeimiɼ, k 6 ; 1 1 ; ɼemɼi, v 6.
ɼeimmen, v 5.
ɼenn, x 1, 5.
ɼí, p 5.
ɼi (n. s.), c, e, j, m 2, n 2, q 3, w 2, x 2, 4 ; (g.), r 6 ; (ac.), c, f ; (n. p.), k 4, 5, m 1, t 3, 6, x 3 ; (g. p.), k 2, w 5 ; ḟlaiṫɼi, v 1 ; ʒaiɼʒɼi, x 7 ; ɼiʒ (g. s.), k 6, p 2, r 2 ; (d. or ac.), a ; (ac.), a ; ɼiʒ, (n. p.), v 6 ; ɼiʒ (g. p.), j, k 3, v 5 ; aiɼḋɼiʒ, x 7 ; ɼiʒaiḋ, j, k 5 ; ɼiʒɼeḋ, r 1 ; ɼiʒe, v 4, 5 ; (aiɼḋ)ɼiʒe, u 5, v 5, w 4 ; (ḃlaṫ)-ɼiʒe, m 2 ; ɼiʒi, e, i, j ; ɼiʒɼaḋ, u 1 ; -aiḋ, u 2, 3, 4 ; -aḋa, e ; ɼiʒɼaiḃe, x 4 ; -aiḃi, j.
ɼiaʒail, k 1, 1 6, n 2, q 3 ; ɼiaʒla, w 6.
ɼiam (adv.), j.
ḋoɼiaɼaiʒ, s 2.
ɼímṫeɼ, v 6.
ɼinḋ, r 2.
Rime, e.
Rimiḋ, d, e, m, 6.
ɼo (intens.) ɼocaem, k 1 ; ɼoʒeɼ, x 1 ; ɼoɼaċ, q 3 ; ɼoċaɼḃa, k 1.
ɼo (vbl. pcle.), ɼoḃ', s 5 ; niɼḃ', u 5 ; ɼoḃaiḋ, 1 4 ; coɼ' ḃaiḋeaḋ, b ; -eḋ, h ; ɼoɼḃean, r 5 ; ɼoḃennɼea, v 6 ; ɼoḃi, d ; ɼomḃi, e ; ɼuɼḃi, m 2.
niaɼ'ḃo, d ; ɼoḋuɼḃɼiɼ, i ; ɼocaiṫ, 1 2, n 3.
ɼocan, i, j ; niɼ'can, j.
ɼocoiɼc, 1 6.
ɼocɼaiḋ, 1 6 ; ɼuɼc-, q 6 ;
ɼomḃeaḋ, m 5 ; ɼoɼaemaḋ, q 6 ;

INDEX VERBORUM. (IV.) 449

ɴoꞅꝼaɴɴaɪᵹ, m 4;
ᵹuɴ'ꝼeᵹaᵭ, w 5;
ɴoꝼoɴᵭaᵭ, n 4;
ᵹuɴ'ꝼoɴᵭaᵭ, o 5;
ɴoᵹaᵭ, 1 5; ɴaᵹaɪᵭ, j;
ɴocoɴᵹaᵭ, w 2;
ɴoᵭuɴᵹaᵭ, w 3; ᵹoɴ'ᵹaᵭ, s 6;
ɴoᵹaᵭꞃac, k 1, 2, 4.
ɴɪɴ'ᵹaᵭꞃac, t 1; ɴomᵹell, x 7;
ɴoꞃᵹeoᵭaɪɴ, 1 5;
ɴoᵹluaɪꞃ, w 2;
ɴolamꞃac, v 4; ᵹuɴ'loɪꞃc, 1 3;
ɴoloɪꞃc, 1 4, 6; ɴoluaᵭaɪᵭ, 1 6;
ɴoṁaɪᵭɪᵹ, x 6; ɴomaɴᵭ, b, 1 6;
ᵹuɴ'maɴᵭ, ᴘ 3; ɴomm-, d;
ɴuꞃmaɴᵭa, o 2; ɴoꞃmaɴᵭ, v 3;
ɴomaɴᵭꞃac, a, s 4, 5;
ɴomeaᵭaᵭaɴ, i;
ɴoꞃmuᵹaɪᵹ, 1 2;
ɴaɴaᵭlaᵭ, ᴘ 2; ɴoꞃaɪɴɪᵹ, a;
ᵹuɴ'coɪc, ᴘ 6.
ɴo (vbl. pcle. infixed), aᵭɴoeᵹaɪᵭ, a;
ᵭoɴᴄaɪɴ, ᴘ 6; ᵭoɴoᴄaɪɴ, e;
coɴᴄaɪɴ, a, b, c, d, e, f, g, h 1;
coɴᴄꞃacaɴ, d; ᵭaɴuꞃꝼaɴ-
ɴaɪᵹ, o 1.
ɴoɪm (prep.), b; ɴoɪṁe, ᴘ 2.
ɴoɪmɪɴɪꞃ, x 5
ɴuaɪᵭ, u 2.
Ruaɪᵭɴɪ, j.
Ruaɪꞃc, x 1.
ɴuacaɴ, t 5.
ɴuɪꞃeaᴄ, o 3.
Ruɪꞃ, i.
ɴuɴ, o 3, w 5.

ꞃ (pron. inf.), ɴoꞃᵭeaɴ, ꞃ 5; ɴuꞃᵭɪ,
m 2; ɴoᵭuꞃᵭɴɪꞃ, i; ᵭaɴuꞃꝼaɴ-
ɴaɪᵹ, o 1; ɴoꞃꝼaɴɴaɪᵹ, m 4;
ɴoꞃᵹeoᵭaɪɴ, 1 5; ɴoꞃmaɴᵭ,
v 3; ɴuꞃmaɴᵭa, o 2.

ꞃ (ɪꞃ, vb.), ᴘ 5.
ꞃ (ɪꞃ = ocuꞃ), k 2, 6, n 3, o 2, 3, 6,
ꞃ 1, t 6.
-ꞃa, j, v 1.
ꞃaeᵭ, n 1.
ꞃaeɴ, m 3, n 2; -ꞃᵭꞃɪᵹ, s 6; ꞃaɪɴ-
ᵭꞃeᴄ, k 2.
ꞃaɪᵭɪ, j.
ꞃaɪᵹꞃeᵭ, a.
ɴoꞃaɪɴɪᵹ, a.
Samna, b.
Scaɴɴlaɴ, e.
ᵭo ꞃcaɴ, s 6.
ꞃcela, d.
ꞃcɪᴄ, d.
ꞃé (card.), n 6, ꞃ 1, 2, t 3, u 4, w 5;
ꞃeɪꞃeɴ, k 2, v 5; moɴꞃ-, v 4.
Seaᴄɴaꞃaᴄ, f; Seᴄ-, o 3, u 1.
Seᴄɴall, a.
ꞃeᴄc, d, f, g, n 2, 5, o 5, q 2, 4, s 1,
u 5.
ꞃeᵭ, n 5; (ɴɪᵹ)ꞃ-, ꞃ 1.
Seᵭɴa, c, d, m 3.
ꞃeᵹᵭa, n 1.
Semᵭɪᵹe, n 1.
ꞃeɴcaɪᵭ, i; ꞃeɴᴄaɪꞃ, j.
ꞃeɴᵹ, n 4, u 1.
-ꞃeom, a, j.
Sheɴeᵭ, ᴘ 6; Seɴeᵹ-maɪᵹe, f.
-ꞃɪᵭe, a.
Sɪl, j, t 2, 5.
-ꞃɪɴᵭ, d; -ꞃɪɴ, a, i, j, u 5.
ꞃɪɴ (sb.), b.
ꞃɪɴ(ᵹloɪɴ), u 4; ꞃɪɴɪu, a.
Slaɪɴe, d, e, f, g, k 3, m 6, n 1.
Sleᵭe, e, n 3.
[ꞃ]leᴄca, q 4.
ꞃleᵹ, s 2.
ꞃlemɴa, s 2.
ꞃluaᵹ, ꞃ 1.
ꞃmaᴄca, o 4.
ꞃo, d; ꞃom, a.

rona, s 6.
rotail, f.
ruaicnig, u 5.
ruairc, o 3.
Suibne, c, d, e, g, n 4, u 4.

tabertac, u 3.
taeb, a; toeb, b.
Taibg, j.
Tailginb, 1 1.
Tailltin, r 3.
tainig, p 5.
t-[r]a[i]n, w 2.
tairpteac, x 2.
tailc, t 2.
tall, r 1, 3, t 4.
tallainb, q 6.
tam, p 1, r 3, v 3.
Tarb, i.
tarba, u 1; (ro)tarba, k 1.
tarraig, p 2.
tart, a.
Teactmair, r 5.
Thebta, g.
tec, m 6; tig, n 2, s 5; Taig, h.
tectab, x 1.
telcoma, b.
Temair, j, 1 5; -mra, i.
tenn, 1 3, v 3, x 1, 2.
ten, b; tene, 1 3, 4; teinbtige, b.
t-[r]iar, s 5, w 2.
tigerna, x 2.
Tigernan, x 2.
tir, a, b, w 3, x 5; tiri (g. p.), m 1.
tiuglaiti, p. 5.
(nem)tlait, x 2.
Toga, e; -ab, n 3.
Toirrbelbac, j; Torr-, x 1.
toit, o 6.

Tomaltaig, j.
tonb(bain), 1 5; tonn, d.
torcair, a, b, c, d, e, f, g, h, i; -cratar, d.
tra, u 1.
tre (prep.), 1 1, 2.
trebac, u 1.
tren, 1 1; r 3; x 1; trenrer, w 6; trenn, 1 5.
tri (card.), c, d, e, h, 1 5, m 3, 5, 6, n 3, 4, q 3, 6, r 4, 6, u 3, w 6; trer, 1 5; triar, w 3.
tribliabnac, p 3.
trica, e, k 2, 1 1, r 3.
tricc, s 3.
troib, o 6.
trom(galair), p 1; truim (g.), n 3.
tuatairb, j, w 2.
tucrat, a.
tuili, s 3, x 1.
tuir, x 1.
Thuirbe, d.
tuirmeam, k 6.
tuirbig, w 6.

u, s 1, w 3; hu, c; ua, g, n 3.
uallac, s 5.
uair, m 5; uaire (g.), f.
uair (conj.), w 4.
Uairibnac, e, n 2; -aig, f.
hUair, w 2.
uairlib, x 3.
uar, x 2.
huct, t 4.
uile, v 5; -li, j, x 1.
Uirnig, s 5.
Ulab, v 6; -aib, w 1; Ulta, b.
Umaill (g.), t 5.

THE END.

IRISH MANUSCRIPTS—FACSIMILES.

[*Editions limited to 200 copies.*]

THE accurate study and critical investigation of the ancient literary and historic monuments of Ireland have hitherto been impeded by the absence of fac-similes of the oldest and most important Irish Manuscripts.

With a view of supplying this acknowledged want, and of placing beyond risk of destruction the contents of Manuscripts, the Academy has undertaken the publication of carefully collated lithographic or photo-lithographic copies of the oldest Irish texts still extant.

In folio, on toned paper.—Price £3 3s.

LEABHAR NA H-UIDHRI : a collection of pieces in prose and verse, in the Irish language, transcribed about A. D. 1100; the oldest volume now known entirely in the Irish language, and one of the chief surviving native literary monuments—not ecclesiastical—of ancient Ireland; now for the first time published, from the original in the Library of the Royal Irish Academy, with account of the manuscript, description of its contents, index, and fac-similes in colours.

In Imperial folio, on toned paper.—Price £4 4s. ; or £2 2s. per Part. Parts I. and II. ; or in One Vol., half calf.

LEABHAR BREAC—the "Speckled Book"—otherwise styled "The Great Book of Dun Doighre": a collection of pieces in Irish and Latin, transcribed towards the close of the fourteenth century; "the oldest and best Irish MS. relating to Church History now preserved."—(*G. Petrie.*) Now first published, from the original MS. in the Academy's Library.

In Imperial folio, on toned paper, with a Photograph of a page of the Original.—Price £6 6s.

THE BOOK OF LEINSTER, sometime called The Book of "GLENDALOUGH": a collection of pieces in the Irish Language, compiled in part about the middle of the twelfth century. From the original MS. in Trinity College, Dublin, with introduction, analysis of contents, and index, by ROBERT ATKINSON, M. A., LL.D., Professor of Sanskrit and Comparative Grammar in the University of Dublin, Secretary of Council, Royal Irish Academy.

The Book of Leinster is one of the most important of the fragments of Irish literature that have come down to us. In addition to copies of the native prose historic accounts of the Táin Bó Cualnge, the Bórama, &c., it contains a large fragment of an early prose translation of the Historia de Excidio Troiae of Dares Phrygius; a great number of the poems and prose introductions of the *Dindsenchas* or legendary account of the origin of the names of places in Ireland ; very many historic poems, in which the legendary and traditional accounts of the early history of the country are preserved; Irish genealogies and hagiologies; and a great number of interesting stories, illustrative of the manners and customs, the modes of thought, and the state of culture, &c., of the people of Ireland just about the period of the Anglo-Norman Invasion.

In Imperial folio, reproduced by Photo-lithography.—Price £5 5s.

THE BOOK OF BALLYMOTE: a collection of pieces in the Irish Language, dating from the end of the fourteenth century; now published in **Photo-lithography** from the original Manuscript in the Library of the Royal Irish Academy. With Introduction, Analysis of Contents, and Index, by ROBERT ATKINSON, M.A., LL.D., Professor of Sanskrit and Comparative Philology in the University of Dublin; Secretary of Council, Royal Irish Academy.

The Book of Ballymote contains numerous articles of interest to the Scholar and to the Antiquary. The original portion consists of—Genealogical Lists; Histories and Legends; a fragment of the Brehon Laws; a copy of the *Dindsenchas;* Treatises on Grammatical Topics, &c. The other portion contains translations from Latin originals: the Destruction of Troy, the Wandering of Ulysses, the Story of the Æneid, and the Life of Alexander the Great.

THE IRISH MANUSCRIPT SERIES.

Volume I., octavo.—Part 1.—Containing: (1) Contents of The Book of Fermoy; (2) The Irish MS. in Rennes; (3) Mac Firbis on some Bishops of Ireland; (4) Tain Bo Fraich; (5) Tochmarc Bec-Fola, &c. Price 5s.

Volume I., quarto.—Part 1.—WHITLEY STOKES, LL.D.: On the Felire of Œngus. Price 14s.

Volume II., octavo.—Part 1.—ROBERT ATKINSON, M.A., LL.D.: Ɔpí bıop-ṡaoıʇe an báıʇ ["The Three Shafts of Death"] of Rev. Geoffrey Keating. The Irish Text, edited with Glossary and Appendix. Price 3s. 6d.

THE TODD LECTURE SERIES.

Volume I., octavo.—Part 1.—W. M. HENNESSY: Mesca Ulad.

Volume II., octavo.—ROBERT ATKINSON, M.A., LL.D.: The Passions and Homilies from Leabhar Breac. With an Introductory Lecture on Irish Lexicography. (Pages 1 to 958.)

Volume III., octavo.—B. MACCARTHY, D.D.: The Codex Palatino-Vaticanus, No. 830. Texts, Translations and Indices. (Pages 1 to 450.)

www.ingramcontent.com/pod-product-compliance
Lightning Source LLC
Chambersburg PA
CBHW032006300426
44117CB00008B/921